Independent Women

_____ Multimethodology

Multimethodology

The Theory and Practice of Combining Management Science Methodologies

Edited by

John Mingers
Warwick Business School

and

Anthony Gill
Phrontis Ltd

JOHN WILEY & SONS
Chichester · New York · Weinheim · Brisbane · Singapore · Toronto

Other Wiley Editorial Offices

John Wiley & Sons, Inc., 605 Third Avenue,
New York, NY 10158-0012, USA

VCH Verlagsgesellschaft mbH,
Pappelallee 3, D-69469 Weinheim, Germany

Jacaranda Wiley Ltd, 33 Park Road, Milton,
Queensland 4064, Australia

John Wiley & Sons (Asia) Pte Ltd, 2 Clementi Loop #02-01,
Jin Xing Distripark, Singapore 129809

John Wiley & Sons (Canada) Ltd, 22 Worcester Road,
Rexdale, Ontario M9W 1LI, Canada

Library of Congress Cataloging-in-Publication Data

Multimethodology : the theory and practice of combining management
    science methodologies / edited by John Mingers and Anthony Gill.
        p. cm.
    Includes bibliographical references and index.
    ISBN 0-471-97490-0 (cloth)
    1. Management science.   2. Operations research.   I. Mingers,
John.   II. Gill, Anthony.
T56.25. M85   1997
658.5—dc21   97–9288
                                                     CIP

British Library Cataloguing in Publication Data
A catalogue record for this book is available from the British Library

ISBN 0-471-97490-0

Typeset in 10/12pt Times by Dorwyn Ltd, Rowlands Castle, Hants.
Printed and bound in Great Britain by Bookcraft (Bath) Ltd, Midsomer Norton, Somerset
This book is printed on acid-free paper responsibly manufactured from sustainable forestation,
for which at least two trees are planted for each one used for paper production.

Contents

List of Contributors   vii

Foreword   xiii
Professor Jonathan Rosenhead

Preface   xv

1 Multi-paradigm Multimethodology   1
  John Mingers

Part 1—Practice of Multimethodology

  Commentary   23

2 Mixing Methods in Practice: a Transformation-Competence
  Perspective   29
  Richard Ormerod

3 Analysing Litigation and Negotiation: Using a Combined
  Methodology   59
  Peter Bennett, Fran Ackermann, Colin Eden and Terry Williams

4 One Size Doesn't Fit All: Reflections on Using Systems
  Techniques in an Operational Setting   89
  Jeremy Bentham

5 Using Models in Sequence: a Case Study of a Post-acquisition
  Intervention   105
  Allenna Leonard

6 Status and Tendencies of Management Research: a Systems
  Oriented Perspective   127
  Markus Schwaninger

7 Managing a Virtual Organization 153
  Anthony Gill

Part 2—Cognitive Aspects of Multimethodology

Commentary 187

8 Becoming Multimethodology Literate: an Assessment of the
  Cognitive Difficulties of Working Across Paradigms 189
  John Brocklesby

9 Multimethodologies—the Knowledge Perspective 217
  David J. Skyrme

Part 3—Theory of Multimethodology

Commentary 243

10 Mixing Methods: Developing Systemic Intervention 249
   Gerald Midgley

11 From Metatheory to "Multimethodology" 291
   Robert Flood and Norma Romm

12 Multimethodology and Critical Theory: an Intersection of Interests? 323
   Martin Spaul

13 Pluralism in Systems Thinking and Practice 347
   Mike C. Jackson

14 Critiquing Multimethodology as Metamethodology: Working
   Towards Pragmatic Pluralism 379
   Leroy White and Ann Taket

15 Towards Critical Pluralism 407
   John Mingers

Index 441

List of Contributors

Dr John Mingers is a Senior Lecturer in Operational Research and Systems at Warwick Business School, University of Warwick. He has published widely in a number of fields relating to OR and Systems, particularly within the areas of methodology, information, and autopoiesis. He has written a book, *Self-Producing Systems: Implications and Applications of Autopoiesis* (Plenum), and an edited book, *Information Systems: An Emerging Discipline?* (with Frank Stowell, McGraw Hill). He is a recent member of the Council of the OR Society and is currently Chair of the UK Systems Society. Further information at URL: http://www.wbs.warwick.ac.uk

Anthony Gill is a co-founder of the management consultancy Phrontis Ltd which actively applies multimethodology in its work. He has worked in a consulting capacity for the last nine years exploiting the potential of the management sciences and especially Beer's Viable System Model. Prior to this he spent some 17 years in multinational organizations in various line management positions. He is currently a part-time research student at Warwick Business School. Further information at URL: http://www.phrontis.com/

Dr Fran Ackerman is a Senior Lecturer in Management Science, Strathclyde University. Building on her PhD research, she has continued to explore how group decision support (predominantly using computers) can be developed to aid groups working on messy, complex, often strategic problems. To further this research she has worked (in a consultancy capacity) with a wide range of both public and private organizations and has published in the fields of information systems, strategy development and operational research.

Dr Peter Bennett is Reader in Management Science at Strathclyde University, currently working on secondment in the Department of Health's Economics and OR Division. His academic background includes degrees in Physics and Philosophy of Science before moving to OR. He has a particular interest in conflict analysis, and has used various "soft OR" methods with clients in industry, government and academia.

Jeremy Bentham is currently the manager of corporate strategy analysis for Shell International. After reading physics at the University of Oxford and the California Institute of Technology, he joined the Amsterdam research laboratory of Shell in 1980. In the late 1980s he was involved in reviewing global IT strategy for the refining and marketing businesses, and then went as a Sloan Fellow to the Massachusetts Institute of Technology's Sloan School of Management. Following this, he managed the production control and appraisal department at a medium-sized refinery, and was then appointed manager of the scheduling and economics team at the large Shell refinery near Rotterdam, with responsibility for coordinating and optimizing ongoing production and trading operations. Recently he has been particularly involved with change-management issues in the organizations within which he has been active.

John Brocklesby is a senior lecturer in organization theory in the Management Group at Victoria University of Wellington, New Zealand. Previously he was employed in Personnel and Industrial Relations at the British Steel Corporation, and has lectured at Coventry University and the University of Huddersfield. He has degrees from Coventry University and the London School of Economics. He has published over 60 academic papers and monographs. Recent publications have appeared in the *International Journal of Strategic Management*, the *Journal of Organisational Change Management*, the *Journal of the Operational Research Society*, the *International Journal of Manpower*, the *Australian Journal of Management, Systems Research*, and *Systems Practice*.

Dr Colin Eden is Professor of Management Science in the Strathclyde Business School. Although he started life as an OR practitioner building mathematical programming models he has become known for his work on problem structuring and the use of management science models in strategic management. He has published four books and over 100 papers and is about to release a book on strategic change. He is a consultant to several multinationals as well as being involved with community groups and not-for-profit organizations.

Dr Robert Flood is the Sir Q.W. Lee Professor of Management Sciences, Head of the Department of Management Systems and Sciences, and is Director of the Centre for Systems Studies, University of Hull. He is a Doctor of Science (Econ.). He is an active international consultant and has worked in this capacity in Australia, Bahrain, Hong Kong, Malaysia, Singapore, UAE, and the UK. He has also worked in management for NOP, Paramount Pictures, and Berkshire Area Health Authority. He has written several books including, for practitioners, *Solving Problem Solving* and *Beyond TQM* (both

Wiley); and, primarily for an academic audience, *Critical Systems Thinking: Current Research and Practice* (edited with Norma Romm, Wiley), *Diversity Management: Triple Loop Learning* (with Norma Romm, Wiley), *Creative Problem Solving* (with Michael Jackson, Wiley), *Critical Systems Thinking: Directed Readings* (edited with Michael Jackson, Wiley), and *Dealing with Complexity* (with Ewart Carson). He has written many articles and book chapters, and is the editor of *Systems Practice*.

Michael Jackson is Professor of Management Systems at the University of Lincolnshire and Humberside. After studying Politics, Philosophy and Economics at Oxford University, he spent four years in the civil service before returning to academic life at Lancaster, Warwick and Hull Universities, being appointed a full professor at Hull in 1989. Professor Jackson has authored two books, *Creative Problem Solving* (with Robert Flood, Wiley) and *Systems Methodology for the Management Sciences* (Plenum), edited six others, is editor of the journal *Systems Research*, has published over 70 articles in other learned journals, and contributed chapters to several books. He has held managerial positions as Head of Department, Director of Research and Chair of the UK Systems Society, and is currently Dean of the Lincoln School of Management and Vice-President of the International Federation of Systems Research. He has also undertaken many consultancy engagements with outside organizations, both profit and non-profit.

Dr Allenna Leonard is a partner with Professor Stafford Beer in The Complementary Set, Director of Team Syntegrity, and a Research Fellow at Liverpool John Moores University.

Dr Gerald Midgley is Deputy Director of the Centre for Systems Studies, University of Hull. His main research interest is in critical systems thinking—especially the theory and practice of making boundary judgements and mixing methods during interventions. He has also been involved in numerous projects developing and applying systems methods in community settings. Altogether, he has over 80 publications aimed at both academics and practitioners, and is the author of the forthcoming book *Beyond Disciplinary Science*, to be published by Plenum.

Richard Ormerod is Professor of Operational Research and Systems at Warwick Business School, Warwick University. After a career in engineering, operational research, corporate strategy and management consultancy, Richard entered academia in 1991. He teaches on postgraduate courses, directs executive short courses and supervises research students. He continues to advise many companies in a consultancy capacity including Sainsbury's, PowerGen and RTZ. His research interests include the design and implementation of change processes in general, and the development of information systems and management strategies in particular.

Dr Norma Romm is a Senior Research Fellow at the Centre for Systems Studies, University of Hull. Prior to this, she was Associate Professor of Sociology and then Dean of Faculty of Social Sciences, University of Swaziland. She has written *Methodologies of Positivism and Marxism* (Macmillan), *People's Education in Theoretical Perspective* (with V. McKay, Longman), and *Diversity Management* (with R. Flood, Wiley). She has also co-edited two books – *Social Theory* (Heinemann) and *Critical Systems Thinking* (Plenum)—and published many articles. Her current research interests concern alternative epistemological orientations and their implications for the practice of research.

Dr David Skyrme runs his own consulting company that specializes in the networking of information and knowledge for innovation. His clients include multinational companies, public sector organizations and the European Commission (DG XIII). After gaining a first class honours degree at Oxford University, he entered the computer industry where he spent 25 years gaining experience in a wide range of management and systems situations. Most of this was with Digital Equipment Corporation (DEC), where he held management posts in product management, marketing, strategic planning and management research. He is also an Affiliate of the Oxford Institute of Information Management at Templeton College, Oxford, and a senior research fellow of the Institute of Innovation, Creativity and Capital at the University of Austin, Texas.

Dr Martin Spaul studied philosophy at Cambridge, completing a PhD on the impact of artificial intelligence on the philosophy of language when the world was still young enough to believe that AI was a promising research programme. After a period working in the aerospace industry specifying and designing real time systems he moved to Anglia Polytechnic University, gradually migrating from software engineering to IS. His current research interests are in critical theory and the political effects of new communication technologies.

Dr Markus Schwaninger is Professor of Management at the University of St Gallen, Switzerland; according to Forbes, the No. 1 Business School in the German-speaking countries. Professor Schwaninger has lectured at universities in Austria, Brazil, Canada, England, Germany, Hong Kong, Switzerland, and the USA. His research is focused on management cybernetics and systems thinking in management, applied to corporate strategy, integrative management, organization design, management systems, organizational transformation and learning. He assumes selected consulting mandates on a regular basis. His books have been published by Campus, Frankfurt/New York, and Wiley, Chichester.

Anne Taket's academic background is in Mathematics and Operational Research. Her main area of work has been in health services research. This has included studies of a wide variety of issues in health policy, health services planning and health services evaluation, both in the UK and overseas. Her main research interests are: the theory, practice and ethics of operational research; the development of locally based primary health care services; the evaluation of health services; the role of the voluntary sector in health service provision; and the use of action research in health service settings. Common themes underlying research in all these areas are with issues of appropriateness, accessibility and equity, and with the development of participatory methods for use in health policy making and priority setting, in needs assessment and in service evaluation. Her current position is as Professor of Primary Health Care in the Faculty of Health and Social Science at South Bank University. She currently manages a major programme of activities linked to research in community and primary care (funded by North and South Thames Regions) and a multicentre study to evaluate skill-mix schemes in diagnostic imaging centres. She acts regularly as a consultant and adviser to the World Health Organization, ODA and the British Council.

Leroy White has over ten years' experience in Operational Research in both the UK and in the developing countries. He is currently a Principal Lecturer in Primary and Community Care Research at South Bank University. He has over 30 publications. His research interests include community operational research, operational research in developing countries, philosophy of Operational Research, multi-agency collaboration, and participatory methods for group decision making.

Dr Terry Williams is currently Director of Postgraduate Studies at the Department of Management Science, Strathclyde University. After a first in Mathematics at Oxford and an MSc and PhD in OR at Birmingham, he taught OR for three years at Strathclyde, then spent nine years consulting with YARD Ltd (now BAeSema) in OR, simulation and particularly Project Risk Management (PRM), acting as risk manager for some major projects. In 1992 he rejoined academia to teach OR, and research and consult in PRM.

Foreword

Once upon a time, a book on combining methods for handling problems would have been unthinkable. In that fairytale world of, say, the mid-1980s the strength of the orthodox view in the community concerned with analytic assistance to organisational decision making precluded such a notion. Certainly it was accepted that there were different *techniques*. But insofar as these were viewed in relation to each other, they were seen as special cases of one overarching analytic project. This concerned itself with identifying the consequences of alternative actions in well-defined problem situations, and with identifying the best solution when, as was thought normal, clear organisational objectives were also available.

The fairytale ended. The limited scope for such an approach became evident, and gradually alternative ways of providing analytic assistance emerged to greater prominence. Problem-structuring methods, embracing both subjective information and group process, have been added to the repertoire. It is the end of that previous rationalist reductionist hegemony which has cleared the space for the discussion in the present volume.

The difference between a technique and a methodology is that the former consists of a set of prescribed procedures which lead to an end point without the need for reflective intervention; whereas the latter embeds a set of techniques and tools within a larger process involving judgement and, commonly, social interaction among participants in the process. One consequence of this is that no two enactments of a given methodology are likely to follow the same analytic path. Another is that, since those offering analytic assistance will contribute both to judgement and to social interaction, the course of any analytic intervention cannot be free of practitioner "contamination". However, there is another consequence of particular relevance to the topic of this book. This is that the social processes which shape and select the analytic contributions offer wider opportunities for choice than just those prescribed by a methodology's original designer.

Mediated as they are by intervening social interactions, the need for precise transmission of the outputs of one phase of analysis as inputs to the succeeding phase is removed. Instead the outputs of the former are fed to a social process whose purpose is to reshape a shared understanding; this in turn may motivate a revised view of what form of analysis could usefully be employed next. Indeed the analytic intervention may be designed from the outset to have a trajectory composed of elements of more than one methodology in a specified sequence. In either case it is the social interface between different phases of analytic work which enables this uncoupling and recoupling to take place.

Arguments have been advanced that such *ad hoc* combinations will often be illegitimate—the basic assumptions of the different methodologies being pillaged, it has been claimed, are incompatible. This issue is addressed at length in the main body of this volume, so I will not attempt here to anticipate that discussion. However, it is quite evident that the question has already been substantially resolved in practice: in a high proportion of reported applications of problem-structuring methods, practitioners are mixing and matching with some abandon. The task for theoreticians concerned with the real, rather than some purely imaginary world, therefore, is to comment on and guide such methodological choices, rather than to denounce them as heretical.

Integration of methodologies is not restricted to the "soft" domain; it also takes place across the boundary between "hard" and "soft" methods. However, it has both a higher prevalence and a greater significance for problem-structuring methods. Their development and progress has already passed through a number of phases. The first phase was evangelical, as their begetters and supporters simultaneously assaulted prevailing orthodoxy and promoted their alternative. This was followed by dissemination, as a larger core of people confident enough to use the methods was built up, and consolidation, as the methods began to find their way into organisational practice and educational syllabuses. The new concern with combination of methods builds on this platform. But it also marks a breakpoint—the definitive escape of these methodologies from their inventors. The understandable initial tendency of new recruits was for cookbook repetition of recipes described by the master chef; now we can anticipate more creative cooking, responsive to the ingredients of the particular situation.

Combination of methodologies does not mean that "anything goes". But thinking about it does mean that we can explore more freely what does "go", when, and why. And practising it opens up a broader scope for handling problematic situations requiring the effective linkage of judgement and analysis.

JONATHAN ROSENHEAD

Preface

In 1994 the editors both attended the International Systems Dynamics Conference in Stirling, Scotland, although at the time we did not know each other. When we did meet, some months later, we discussed the conference and found that we had both noticed the same thing. In a surprising number of papers describing applications of systems dynamics the authors had used some other approach or methodology as well. Most commonly soft systems methodology (SSM) or cognitive mapping. This was not the first example of practitioners combining methodologies in their interventions. Mingers and Taylor (1992) had undertaken a survey of the use of SSM in practice and one of the surprising results was the wide range of methods that had been combined with SSM. There were also already reports of the practical combination of different methodologies in the literature (Bennett, 1985; Eden, 1990; Taket, 1993; Ormerod, 1995).

It seemed to us that here was a case of practice taking the lead over theory, for there was very little written theoretically about combining methodologies, particularly from different paradigms (hard, soft, critical), within a single intervention. Most of the philosophical and theoretical work, developed at the Centre for Systems Studies, Hull, by Mike Jackson and Bob Flood (Flood and Jackson, 1991; Jackson, 1991), concerned the *selection* of an appropriate methodology for a particular intervention, rather than the *combination* of *parts* of methodologies together (Total Systems Intervention (TSI) did allow the possibility of dominant and subsidiary methodologies being used but did not provide much guidance in doing this). We termed this latter idea *multi-methodology* as a way of distinguishing it from the *complementarism* of Flood and Jackson, and decided that it was an approach that held rich promise for the more effective use of systems and operational research (OR) approaches. This book was conceived as a way of bringing together those who might be involved or interested, exploring a variety of approaches, and their problems, theoretically and philosophically, and showing through real examples that it was effective in practice.

In editing the book we have tried not to reinforce some traditional dualisms. First, that between theory and practice. The authors writing about practical projects have been encouraged to reflect about the theoretical conditions and consequences of their work, while those primarily engaged with theory have tried to bear in mind the practical implications of their work. Some authors, such as White and Taket, have written chapters that combine both theory and practice. Second, that between systems and OR. Practical problems in the real world do not split themselves up along disciplinary boundaries, and neither should we in seeking to deal with them. We have therefore deliberately sought a range of contributors from both areas, as well as those who, like us, do not draw a distinction between the two. Third, that between academics and practitioners. Many of the contributors are themselves both academics and practitioners, but in terms of the readership we have tried to make the book accessible to all. However, believing in the old adage "there's nothing so practical as a good theory" we have not watered down or popularized the theory sections but given them due weight. We recognize that some practitioners may find that the costs of some chapters outweigh the benefits but believe that the case study chapters will be worthwhile in their own right.

We would like to thank all the authors for the time and trouble they have taken to make this book what it is.

JOHN MINGERS
TONY GILL
1997

REFERENCES

Bennett, P. (1985). On linking approaches to decision-aiding: issues and prospects. *Journal of the Operational Research Society*, **36**(8), 659–670.

Eden, C. (1990). Mixing methods: introduction. In C. Eden and T. Radford (eds) *Tackling Strategic Problems*. Sage, London, p. 91.

Flood, R. and Jackson, M. (1991). *Creative Problem Solving: Total Systems Intervention*. Wiley, London.

Jackson, M. (1991). *Systems Methodology for the Management Sciences*. Plenum Press, New York.

Mingers, J. and Taylor, S. (1992). The use of Soft Systems Methodology in practice. *Journal of the Operational Research Society*, **43**(4), 321–332.

Ormerod, R. (1995). Putting soft OR methods to work: information systems strategy development at Sainsbury's. *Journal of the Operational Research Society*, **46**(3), 277–293.

Taket, A. (1993). Mixing and matching: developing and evaluating innovatory health promotion projects. *OR Insight 6*, **4**(18–23).

Chapter 1

Multi-paradigm Multimethodology

JOHN MINGERS

INTRODUCTION

This book concerns the use of *methodologies* in organizational problem solving and intervention. Such methodologies have mainly been developed within the domains of operational research (OR), systems thinking, and information systems (IS) (although there are differences in the premises and areas of application of these subjects from a methodological viewpoint they can be treated together as "Management Science"). The term methodology means a structured set of guidelines for activities to undertake to improve the effectiveness of an intervention. A good example of a methodology is soft systems methodology (SSM) developed by Peter Checkland (Checkland and Scholes, 1990) at Lancaster. Other examples are Eden's (1994) cognitive mapping and SODA; Beer's (Espejo and Harnden, 1989) Viable System Model (VSM); systems dynamics; and OR with its various techniques such as mathematical programming (the distinctions between paradigm, methodology, method, and technique are defined in Chapter 15). Such methodologies are based, implicitly or explicitly, on particular philosophical assumptions concerning the nature of the organizational world and the appropriateness of various forms of action. These sets of assumptions form a particular view of the world that is sometimes called a *paradigm*. Typically reference is made to three different paradigms that can be crudely characterized as *hard* (positivist), treating the organizational world as objective, essentially the same as the natural world;

Multimethodology: The Theory and Practice of Combining Management Science Methodologies.
Edited by John Mingers and Anthony Gill.
© 1997 John Wiley & Sons Ltd.

soft (interpretivist), treating human organizations as fundamentally different, based on subjective meaning and interpretation; and *critical*, accepting the place of both hard and soft but emphasizing the oppressing and inequitable nature of social systems. These paradigms, and the methodologies that embody them, are often said to be *incommensurable* because their underlying assumptions are believed to be irreconcilable.

More specifically, this book is about the idea of *multi*methodology. That is, combining together more than one methodology (in whole or part) within a particular intervention. Thus it is not the name of a single methodology, or even of a *specific* way of combining methodologies together. Rather it refers to the whole area of utilizing a plurality of methodologies or techniques within the practice of taking action in problematic situations. As Mingers and Brocklesby (1996) show, there are a whole range of logical possibilities depending on factors such as: whether the methodologies are mixed in the same intervention or across different interventions; whether they come from different paradigms; or whether parts of (rather than whole) methodologies may be combined. Some of these possibilities are conceptually and practically straightforward, for example using different methodologies from the same paradigm in separate interventions. Others pose difficult problems, for example mixing parts of methodologies (sometimes referred to as "partitioning" (Midgley, 1989a, 1990)) from different paradigms, within the same intervention. Some options have been extensively explored, for example choosing between methodologies for an intervention via the system of systems methodologies (Jackson and Keys, 1984; Jackson, 1989, 1990), or managing the diversity of methodologies within an intervention (Flood and Jackson, 1991; Flood, 1995); others, particularly the case of multi-paradigm partitioning mentioned above, have not been. Multimethodology can be seen as a particular form of *methodological pluralism.*

The purpose of this book is to explore the possibilities of multimethodology, particularly in its multi-paradigm form, but the first thing that we should note is that Management Science is not alone in currently considering this problem of methodological pluralism. Indeed, it turns out that it is a relatively late starter, for other disciplines such as philosophy, social theory, and organizational studies have already started the debate. The first section of this chapter surveys these pluralist debates within other disciplines to see what can be learnt from them. The second section provides a brief history of methodology management within Management Science. This turns out to be largely a history of *critical systems thinking* (CST) because this is where most of the work has been carried out. The third section aims to show, however, that multimethodology is not identical with the critical systems perspective or, even more narrowly, with the particular version of CST called total systems intervention (TSI). It does this by exploring the range of logical possibilities and showing that critical systems/TSI do not exhaust them. The final two sections of the chapter present arguments as to why multimethodology is desirable, and the extent to which it is actually feasible, particularly the multi-paradigm version espoused by the editors.

GENERAL HISTORY OF PLURALISM

Since the beginning of the twentieth century the enormous success of natural science led to its methods (generally denoted as *positivism*: a belief in univer-sal laws, empirical verification through induction, and observer- and value-freedom) being seen as the most reliable way of generating knowledge, not just in the natural sciences but in the social sciences as well. However, chinks in positivism's armour were apparent within physics itself, with the unavoid-able appearance of the observer in Heisenberg's "uncertainty principle". The body blows were provided by philosophers such as Hanson (1958), Kuhn (1970), and Popper (1972) who, in various ways, demonstrated fatal flaws in the cornerstones of induction, and theory- and observer-independent obser-vation. Although this did not have a significant effect on the practice of natural science, it did on social science where it legitimated the rise of various schools of interpretivism such as phenomenology, ethnomethodology, and hermeneutics. During the 1970s and early 1980s similar situations emerged in organizational studies, and in OR/systems with the development of soft OR and soft systems methodology (SSM).

Each discipline came to be characterized by a small set of competing and supposedly incommensurable paradigms based around splits between hard, soft and critical approaches. Practical work within the disciplines, whether it be social research or organizational intervention, was expected to occur within a single paradigm, and individual researchers had to ally themselves with one paradigm or another. Burrell and Morgan's (1979) *Sociological Paradigms and Organisational Analysis* epitomized this situation with its em-phasis on the separateness of its four paradigms and the development of theory and research in isolation. However, this artificial situation could not endure as researchers and practitioners found that no one paradigm could capture the richness of real-world situations. In all the disciplines, the accept-ance of paradigm isolation and incommensurability began to break down and, in the last decade, the debate has turned to various forms of pluralism, in both methodological and philosophical terms.

In philosophy the debate has centred around *perspectivism* and *meth-odological pluralism*. Roth's (1987) book *Meaning and Method in the Social Sciences: A Case for Methodological Pluralism* sparked considerable dis-cussion (Fuller, 1990; Rouse, 1991), and a special issue of *Monist* was devoted to the subject (Ford, 1990). In social and education research, methodological pluralism grew up in practice probably before theory, based around the idea of *triangulation* originally proposed by Denzin (1970). It would now seem to be the established norm (Bulmer, 1984; Bryman, 1992). In organizational studies there has been an active debate about incommensurability, particularly with regard to Burrell and Morgan's work (Gioia and Pitre, 1990; Hassard, 1991; Lee, 1991; Jackson and Carter, 1993; Willmott, 1993); while in OR/systems, critical systems thinking and TSI have held centre stage, in recent years, in terms of orchestrating the use of different methodologies. It is to the latter that we now turn.

HISTORY OF PLURALISM IN MANAGEMENT SCIENCE

It is in some ways ironic that the idea of utilizing knowledge from a variety of disciplines was a central tenet of the early days of OR (Mingers, 1992). From the beginning, practical problems were seen not to fit into neat disciplinary boundaries, and as OR became established in organizations, interdisciplinary teams, to include mathematicians, psychologists, sociologists and so on, were the order of the day. However, over the years the interdisciplinary teams were broken up, new recruits into OR tended to come from mathematical and science backgrounds, and academically OR became increasingly focused into mathematical models and algorithms. OR (and systems from its roots in engineering) was locked into a hard, technical shell. It was not until the early 1980s that this situation was challenged by the arrival of "soft" methodologies such as SSM and SODA. Soon, the pendulum swung the other way with a plethora of new soft and critical approaches, and the problem became one of methodology choice. How should a practitioner know which approach to use and when? It was against this background that critical systems thinking (CST) developed, in part as an approach to managing the diversity of methodologies.

Critical systems thinking, or critical management science, became established as a coherent domain during the 1980s. There were sporadic contributions of a critical or Marxist nature during the 1970s (see Mingers (1992) and Jackson (1991a: 138) for details); Mingers (1980) explicitly brought in the critical theory of Jürgen Habermas, comparing it with soft systems methodology; and Ulrich developed, during the late 1970s, his major synthesis of Churchman and Habermas although this was not published until 1983. However, the largest contribution has come from the work of Jackson and Flood. Jackson (1985) was probably the first to clearly articulate the need for critical methodologies, as opposed to those stemming from hard and soft traditions, basing his claims on Habermas's (1978) version of critical social theory:

> It is argued therefore that Habermas' suggested approach is more appropriate for a certain class of social system than hard or soft systems methodologies . . .

> These social systems are characterised by inequalities of power and resources among the participants and by conflict and contradiction. (Jackson, 1985: 149)

At about the same time, Jackson and Keys (1984) developed the first meta-theoretical framework—the system of systems methodologies (SOSM). This was a typology classifying the different assumptions made by methodologies. There were two dimensions, one of complexity (from simple to complex) and one concerning the relations between participants (unitary, pluralist, and coercive) that mapped the hard, soft and critical perspectives. Alternative approaches could now be:

> presented as being appropriate to the different types of situation in which management scientists are required to act. Each approach will be useful in certain defined areas and should only be used in appropriate circumstances. (Jackson, 1991b: 199)

Jackson (1987) also identified pluralism as the desired way forward for systems thinking although tended in later work to use the term "complementarism". Up to this point critical systems was seen as an adjunct to hard and soft, based on Habermas's knowledge-constitutive interest in enlightenment and emancipation. However, a shift in thinking occurred that led to a distinction being drawn between "critical systems thinking" and "emancipatory systems thinking" (Jackson, 1991b: 184). The latter still concerned methodologies for coercive social situations, but critical systems thinking was seen as a wider approach to management science as a whole that was based on five "commitments"—critical awareness, social awareness, methodological complementarism, theoretical complementarism, and human emancipation (Jackson, 1991b).

The next development was that this framework was augmented by a methodology (or rather meta-methodology) to assist in the choice of appropriate methodology(ies) in particular situations—total systems intervention (TSI) (Flood and Jackson, 1991; Flood, 1995). In its latest guise Flood describes it as:

> The problem solving system TSI has been developed to provide managers with a practical and useful systems-based approach to problem solving. It offers procedures to integrate all methods for problem-solving in a process which ensures that they are employed to tackle only the issues they are best suited to. (Flood, 1995: 393)

While still based on a critical systems philosophy, and still having the achievement of human freedom as a basic principle, TSI mainly orients itself to the domains of consultancy and management (Flood, 1995: 393)—*A Potent Force for Effective Management*, as the book's subtitle proclaims. In fact, in the most recent characterization (Flood, 1996) the name has been changed to local systemic intervention (LSI) based on a postmodernist dislike of totalizing discourses.

Given that the critical systems approach and TSI are forms of multi-methodology (Mingers and Brocklesby, 1996), and that they are well developed both theoretically and practically, is there any need to pursue other possible types of multimethodology? I would argue that the answer is yes because TSI represents only one possible example of multimethodology as the next section will show.

TYPES OF MULTIMETHODOLOGY

The essence of multimethodology is to utilize more than one methodology, or part thereof, possibly from different paradigms, within a single intervention. There are several ways in which such combinations can occur, each having different problems and possibilities. Table 1.1 provides some examples that can be seen either as a set of logical possibilities, or as the preferred *modus operandi* of particular agents.

The first dimension is simply whether more than one methodology is used or not. If not, then there is clearly no possibility of multimethodology—possibility A, *methodological isolationism*. The next two dimensions specify whether the methodologies used come from the same or from different paradigms, and whether or not they are used within the same intervention. Where the methodologies are all from within the same paradigm there is little philosophical difficulty, it is just a question of the most effective way of fitting the methodologies or techniques together. When they come from different paradigms, however, the situation is much more complex. Similarly, using several methodologies in different interventions is conceptually much simpler than combining them in one.

The final two dimensions focus on whether whole methodologies are used or parts are taken out and combined (methodological partitioning), and, in the latter case, whether a single methodology is given overall control or whether the parts are linked to form a multimethodology particular to that situation. The last columns name the different possibilities and give literature references where known.

Table 1.1 covers the main combinations of these dimensions although some less interesting ones are omitted for simplicity, for example using parts of methodologies in different interventions. Each possibility will now be briefly characterized. Possibility B, *paradigmatic isolationism*, is where several methodologies may be used by an agent but all from the same paradigm and not in the same intervention. For example, SSM may be considered most appropriate for one situation, and strategic choice for another. Possibility C, *methodology combination*, is where several complete methodologies, from the same

Table 1.1 Different possibilities for combining methodologies

	One/more methodologies	One/more paradigms	Same/different intervention	Whole/part methodology	Imperialist or mixed	Example	Name	Literature (*Theoretical* Case Study)
A	One	One	–	–	–	SSM only	Methodological isolationism	Checkland and Scholes (1990)
B	More	ditto	Different	Whole	–	SSM | Strat. choice	Paradigmatic isolationism	Ormerod (1995, 1996a)
C	ditto	ditto	Same	Whole	–	Simulation + queueing theory	Methodology combination	Mingers and Taylor (1992)
D	ditto	ditto	Same	Part	Imperialist	Cognitive mapping in SSM	Methodology enhancement	Ormerod (1994, 1996b), Holt (1993), Taket (1993), *Bennett (1985, 1990)*
E	ditto	ditto	Same	Part	Mixed	Cog. map. + root definition	Single paradigm multimethodology	
F	ditto	More	Different	Whole	–	Simulation | SSM	Methodology selection	*Jackson and Keys (1984), Jackson (1987, 1989, 1990)*
G	ditto	ditto	Same	Whole	–	VSM + interactive planning	Whole methodology management	*Flood and Jackson (1991)*, Flood (1995)*, Ulrich (1991)*
H	ditto	ditto	Same	Part	Imperialist	JSD in SSM	Methodology enhancement	Savage and Mingers (1996)
I	ditto	ditto	Same	Part	Mixed	Cognitive map + systems dynamics	Multi-paradigm multimethodology	Eden (1994), Lehaney and Paul et al (1994), Hocking and Lee (1994), *Midgley (1989a, 1989b, 1990, 1992), Flood (1995)*, Mingers and Brocklesby (1996)*

In the Example column + means combined in the same intervention, | means used in separate interventions.
* These textbooks have both theory and case studies.

paradigm, may be combined within the same intervention, for example using both queueing theory and simulation, or SSM and SODA. Possibilities D, *methodology enhancement*, and E, *single-paradigm multimethodology*, are where parts of a methodology are split off and combined. In D, one main methodology is enhanced with part of another, for example using cognitive mapping within SSM. In E, parts of several are combined to create a new multimethodology, for example using cognitive mapping together with root definitions/conceptual models. The literature contains a number of such examples.

Possibilities F to I repeat B to E but with the complication that the methodologies involved may be from different paradigms. F is essentially the situation assumed by Jackson and Keys' system of systems methodologies (SOSM), that is that methodologies from different paradigms make particular assumptions about the contexts within which they will be used so that a methodology is most appropriate for a context matching its assumptions. This implies that, generally, only one methodology will be used in a particular intervention (there has been some debate about the proper interpretation of the SOSM and certainly the originators themselves differ on the matter. (See Mingers and Brocklesby (1996) for references to the debate and Chapter 13 for the most recent exposition of Jackson's view.) G is similar to Flood and Jackson's total systems intervention (TSI) in which different methodologies may be used within the same intervention to deal with different issues (there is debate about the interpretation of TSI, and it is still changing and developing, but certainly in the first book on the subject no mention is made of partitioning methodologies and combining parts together. (For recent developments see Flood (1995) and Flood and Romm (1995a, b) as well as Chapters 10 and 11 in this book.) H is a multi-paradigm version of methodology enhancement, for example taking SSM as the main methodology and using some parts of a hard methodology within it such as VSM, or Jackson System Design. The main problem is the legitimacy of transferring a technique developed within one paradigm to another. Finally, the most complex situation, I, is one in which parts of methodologies from different paradigms are brought together to construct an *ad hoc* multimethodology suitable for a particular problematic situation. An example would be combining cognitive mapping with developing a systems dynamics model.

DESIRABILITY OF MULTI-PARADIGM INTERVENTION AND RESEARCH

This section puts forward arguments as to why multimethodology (sometimes called "methodological pluralism", or "multi-paradigm intervention and research") is desirable. Landry and Banville (1992), within the context of IS, have put forward strong arguments in favour of pluralism in general, but it should be noted that the term "methodological pluralism" may be conceptualized in a number of different ways.

(i) *Loose pluralism*, holds that a discipline as a whole should support and encourage a variety of paradigms and methods within it, but does not specify how or when they should be used.
(ii) *Complementarism* (as advocated by Jackson (1991b)), where different paradigms are viewed as internally consistent, and based on different assumptions about their context of use, such that each paradigm would be seen as more or less appropriate for a particular research situation.
(iii) *Strong pluralism*, as advocated in this chapter, which argues that most if not all intervention situations would be dealt with more effectively with a blend of methodologies from different paradigms.

Three main arguments in favour of strong pluralism (multimethodology) are put forward. First, that real-world problem situations are inevitably highly complex and multidimensional. Different paradigms each focus attention on different aspects of the situation and so multimethodology is necessary to deal effectively with the full richness of the real world. Second, that an intervention is not usually a single, discrete event but is a process that typically proceeds through a number of phases. These phases pose different tasks and problems for the agent. However, methodologies tend to be more useful in relation to some phases than others, so the prospect of combining them has immediate appeal. Even where methodologies do perform similar functions, combining a range of approaches may well yield a better result. Third, further consideration of the philosophical and theoretical aspects of multimethodology is timely since many people are already combining methodologies in practice as the practical case studies in this book show.

The Multidimensional World

Adopting a particular paradigm is like viewing the world through a particular instrument such as a telescope, an X-ray machine, or an electron microscope. Each reveals certain aspects but is completely blind to others. Although they may be pointing at the same place, each instrument produces a totally different, and seemingly incompatible, representation. Thus, in adopting only one paradigm one is inevitably gaining only a limited view of a particular intervention or research situation, for example attending only to that which may be measured or quantified, or only to individuals' subjective meanings and thus ignoring the wider social context. This argument is a strong one in support of multi-paradigm research suggesting that it is always wise to utilize a variety of approaches.

A framework developed from Habermas (1984: 75–101, 1987) is shown in Figure 1.1. It suggests that it is useful to distinguish our relations to, and interactions with, three worlds—the material world, the social world, and the personal world. A similar position was advocated some years ago by Linstone (1984) who suggested three "perspectives", technological (T), organizational (O), and personal (P). However, these were all interpreted from within a positivist or functionalist perspective rather than from the multi-paradigm perspective underlying this book. Midgley (1992) also utilizes, in a different way, Habermas's framework. This framework also draws on ideas from Searle (1996) who distinguishes between the objective, the institutional, and the subjective worlds.

Each domain has different modes of existence and different means of accessibility. The material world is outside and independent of human beings. It existed before us and would exist whether or not we did. We can shape it through our actions, but are subject to its constraints. Epistemologically, our relationship to this world is one of external *observation* rather than participation (as with social activities) or experience (as with our personal mental states). But such observations are always theory- and subject-dependent. We

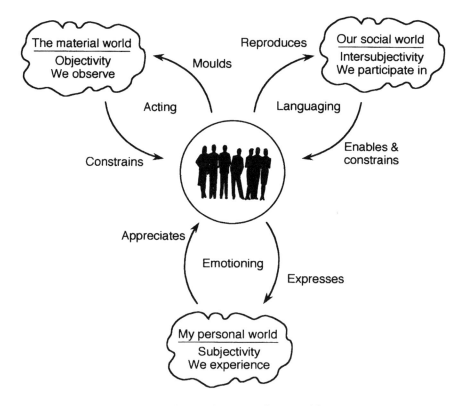

Figure 1.1   A framework based on Habermas's three worlds

can characterize this world as *objective* in the sense that it exists independent of the observer, although clearly our observations and descriptions of it are not. It is the totality of all things that are or could be *true*.

From this material world, through processes of evolution, linguistically endowed humans have developed, capable of communication and self-reflection. This had led to the social and personal worlds. The personal world is the world of our own individual thoughts, emotions, feelings, experiences and beliefs. We do not observe it externally as we would a table or a mountain; rather we *experience* it. This world is *subjective* in that it is generated by, and only accessible to, the individual subject. We can aim to express our subjectivity to others and, in turn, appreciate theirs. It is the totality of experiences to which an individual has privileged access.

Finally there is the social world that we (as members of particular social systems) share and *participate in*. Our epistemological relation to it is one of *intersubjectivity* since it is, on the one hand, a human construction and yet, on the other, it goes beyond and pre-exists any particular individual. It consists of a complex multi-layering of language, meaning, social practices, rules and resources that both enables and constrains our actions, and is reproduced through them. One of its primary dimensions is that of power (Mingers, 1992). It is the totality of normatively valid interpersonal norms and relationships (this trilogy of worlds is related to, but distinct from, Popper's three worlds, see Habermas (1984: 75–80)).

Thus, any real-world situation into which we are intervening or researching will be a complex interaction of substantively different elements. There will be aspects that are relatively hard and observer-independent, particularly material and physical processes, that we can observe and model. There will be aspects that are socially constituted, dependent on particular cultures, social practices, languages, and power structures, that we must come to share and participate in. Finally, there will be aspects that are individual such as beliefs, values, fears, and emotions that we must try to express and understand.

Intervention and Research as a Process

The second argument is that intervention and research is not a discrete event but a process that has phases or, rather, different types of activities, that will predominate at different times. Particular methodologies and techniques are more useful for some functions than others and so a combination of approaches may be necessary to provide a comprehensive outcome. To help do this in practice some categorization of the phases of an intervention would be useful, against which could be mapped various methodologies' strengths.

An SSM analysis of the general process of research and intervention led to the following activities:

- *Appreciation* of the situation as experienced by the researchers involved and expressed by actors in the situation.
- *Analysis* of the underlying structure/constraints generating the situation as experienced.
- *Assessment* of the ways in which the situation could be other than it is; of the extent to which the constraints could be altered.
- *Action* to bring about appropriate changes.

At the beginning of an intervention, especially for an agent from outside the situation, the primary concern is to gain as rich an appreciation of the situation as possible. Note that this cannot be an "observer-independent" view of the situation "as it really is". It will be conditioned by the researcher's previous experience and his/her access to the situation. The next activity is to begin to analyse why the situation is as it appears. To understand the history that has generated it, and the particular structure of relations and constraints that maintain it. Next, in cases where change to the situation is sought, consideration must be given to ways in which the situation could be changed. This means focusing attention away from how things are, and considering the extent to which the structures and constraints can be changed within the general limitations of the intervention. Finally, action must be undertaken that will effectively bring about agreed changes. We should emphasize immediately that these activities are not seen as discrete stages that are enacted one by one. Rather, they are aspects of the intervention that need to be considered throughout, although their relative importance will differ as the project progresses. This is illustrated in Figure 1.2.

It is clear that the wide variety of methodologies and techniques available do not all perform equally well at all these activities. To give some brief examples: collecting data, carrying out questionnaires and surveys, developing rich pictures and cognitive maps, and employing the 12 critical systems heuristics questions all contribute to finding out about the different aspects of a particular

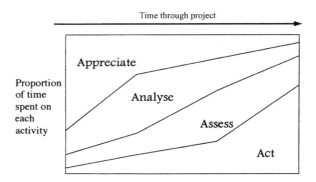

Figure 1.2 Phases of an intervention

situation. Whereas building simulation or mathematical models, constructing root definitions and conceptual models, using role-playing and gaming, or undertaking participant observation help to understand *why* the situation is as it is, and to evaluate other possibilities. A framework that helps to map the strengths and weaknesses of different methodologies will be presented in Chapter 15.

FEASIBILITY OF MULTI-PARADIGM RESEARCH

Having put forward arguments for the desirability of multi-paradigm methodology we must also recognize the inherent problems, and assess its overall feasibility. We should remember that we are concerned particularly with linking research methods together across different research paradigms. Three different levels of problems can be identified:

(i) *Philosophical*—particularly the issue of paradigm incommensurability.
(ii) *Cultural*—the extent to which organizational and academic cultures militate against multi-paradigm work.
(iii) *Psychological*—the problems of an individual agent moving easily from one paradigm to another.

Each of these is a major research area in its own right and in this chapter all we shall do is to outline the main debates and provide at least *prima facie* evidence that the problems are not insurmountable. More detailed arguments will be found in Mingers and Brocklesby (1996).

Philosophical Feasibility—Paradigm Incommensurability

The paradigm incommensurability thesis asserts that because paradigms differ in terms of the fundamental assumptions that they bring to organizational inquiry, researchers must choose the rules under which they do research from among the alternatives on offer. They must then commit themselves to a single paradigm, although sequential movement over time is permissible. Multi-paradigm research is proscribed for a number of reasons, the most notable of which is the supposed irreconcilable objectivist/subjectivist ontological and epistemological dichotomies that exist between the empirical-analytic and interpretive paradigms respectively. However, as Burrell and Morgan (1979) and Astley and van der Ven (1983) have shown, there are other related dichotomies such as structure versus agency, determinism versus voluntarism, causation versus meaning, and object versus subject. The opposing positions in each dichotomy represent alternative competing "truths" about the world, and, as such, they resist reconciliation or synthesis.

In recent years, however, several arguments have been put forward within philosophy, social theory, and organization studies against a strong view of paradigm incommensurability. First, it is argued that the characterization of paradigms as separate and mutually exclusive domains may have been overstated (Gioia and Pitre, 1990; Weaver and Gioia, 1994). Although the central prototypical characteristics are incommensurable, paradigms are permeable at the edges, in their so-called "transition zones". It is possible, these authors argue, to "construct bridges" across paradigm boundaries that are ostensibly impenetrable. Moreover, the distinctions between different paradigms are themselves fuzzy and highly questionable (Smaling, 1994). Second, it is not necessary to accept that research methods are wholly internal to a single paradigm (Smaling, 1994; Mingers and Brocklesby, 1996). Rather, it is quite possible to disconnect a particular method from its normal paradigm and use it, consciously and critically, within another setting. For example, the use of quantitative data need not imply the acceptance of a positivist, objectivist epistemology. Rather, such data can (and arguably should) be interpreted in the light of relevant social meanings, and their production as a social construction.

Third, it is claimed that the whole idea of paradigm incommensurability based upon the objective/subjective duality is fundamentally flawed (Orlikowski and Robey, 1991; Weaver and Gioia, 1994). Giddens' structuration theory (Bhaskar's (1989, 1994) "critical realism" could also be employed to similar effect) can be used to demonstrate that it is not possible to separate out objective and subjective dimensions. Reality, according to structuration theory, emerges out of the dialectic interplay of forces of structure and meaning—structural regularities are created out of subjective meanings, and through socialization processes, structures then "act back" upon individual meanings. Finally, generalizing the previous argument, different paradigms provide us with different perspectives or insights into a reality that is forever more complex than our theories can capture (Booth, 1979; Guba, 1990; Smaling, 1994; Mingers and Brocklesby, 1996). It is therefore quite wrong to wholly accept the postulates of any one paradigm.

Although the paradigm incommensurability issue has to be taken seriously in debates about methodology, there are grounds for believing that cross-paradigm research is philosophically feasible. What is required is an underpinning philosophical framework that can encompass the different paradigms,[1] and guidance on appropriate ways to mix different research methods.

Cultural Feasibility—Paradigm Subcultures

The question here is whether the existing cultural constitution of the management science community—the extent to which it is split into paradigm

---

[1] Such a framework should not be seen as somehow meta-paradigmatic, making no assumptions of its own. Rather it will be a new paradigm, subsuming existing ones, and with its own commitments (Mingers and Brocklesby, 1996).

subcultures—will facilitate or act as a barrier against the widespread adoption of multimethodology as a strategy. Obviously this depends upon the size of the "cultural gap" between where we are now, and where—in relation to multi-paradigm research—we would like to be. This issue has been discussed in some detail elsewhere (Brocklesby, 1994, 1995; Brocklesby and Cummings, 1995).

Certainly research within information systems (which is, arguably, very similar to Management Science in general) (Harvey and Myers, 1995; Banville and Landry, 1989; Orlikowski and Baroudi, 1991; Landry and Banville, 1992; Galliers, 1994; Myers, 1994; Walsham, 1995) does show that it has a fragmented character with general dominance, particularly in the US, of a positivist subculture. Although we know of no specific research, it would seem that few of our colleagues are trained across two or more paradigms or work in groups where the sorts of multi-paradigm research we have described are widely practised. Most have hard science or strongly technological backgrounds although some have moved into IS from social science. Only a small number appear to have shifted their allegiances from hard systems to soft systems and thereby develop competencies that span two major paradigms. The majority align themselves with either the hard or the soft paradigm. Within these broad paradigm groupings individuals often specialize in a single research approach, and in a specific type of situation. Arguably, practitioners are more methodologically eclectic than academics.

Individuals' methodological preferences are not randomly distributed, but often they are reinforced by institutional, physical, and geographic boundaries in which communities of like-minded people tend to congregate. These communities, perhaps as small as two in number and of which there may be several within a particular institutional grouping, may be thought of as subcultures for two reasons. First because the shared beliefs and preferences of their members are often unique to the group itself, and not always shared by the wider community. Second because the beliefs operate tacitly—they are powerful "taken-for-granted" forces that are rarely questioned or subject to debate.

If we accept that these are not particularly bold generalizations, the prospects for those wishing to develop a dominant culture sustaining multi-paradigm research do not look that bright. Culture research shows that pre-existing cultures can be remarkably resistant to change. In some business organizations "new" cultures can be manufactured over relatively short periods of time simply by bringing in new people who possess the sorts of characteristics that are valued and dispensing with those who do not. But generally this is not the case in the academic and scientific communities where most OR academics are employed. Here cultures tend to develop slowly over time in particular physical and historical settings, and cultural behaviours—including people's beliefs, values, methodological preferences and accumulated expertise—tend to emerge out of the day-to-day interactions of people going about their daily business rather than as a response to some "grand plan", even if the logic of the plan is compelling to its creators.

This does not mean that the institutionally entrenched single-paradigm, even single-method subcultures that pervade OR are inviolable. Cultures do change, albeit often slowly and in response to specific conditions and events. Perhaps the most basic condition that might trigger the sort of transformation we are talking about would be an unexpected failure in traditional ways of working combined with a consciousness of the limitations of one's preferred paradigm and knowledge of what other options might be available. Then, of course, there is the question of capability. Changes would have to be made in the curriculum to develop a better awareness of the range of ontological and epistemological options that are available, and to broaden knowledge and research skills. Changes would need to be made in the criteria required to recruit staff. These changes present a number of challenges, but they do not represent insurmountable obstacles.

Psychological Feasibility—Cognitive Barriers

The next potential difficulty in multimethodology concerns the cognitive feasibility of moving from one paradigm to another. Spanning a wide range of disciplines, there is now an extensive literature that has explored the extant links between personality traits, cognitions and research preferences, and the production of knowledge. A major issue raised in this literature is the question of whether entrenched cognitive predilections may be altered to facilitate multi-paradigm research. As this question forms the basis of John Brocklesby's chapter in this book, it will not be pursued here.

CONCLUSIONS

The purpose of this introductory chapter has been to set the scene for the rest of the book. It has made clear that the theme of the book—multimethodology—is about developing ways of mixing together or integrating a range of methodologies or techniques, from different paradigms, in the course of a particular intervention. It has shown how this forms a logical development both in terms of the history of critical systems thinking, and the wider context of other disciplines such as social theory and organizational studies that are grappling with similar problems of methodological pluralism.

Arguments have been put forward as to why this is a desirable development in terms of improving the effectiveness of OR/systems; and the potential problems of philosophical and cultural feasibility have been addressed, if not entirely solved. This leaves the stage open for the collaborating authors to put forward their own contributions to this complex problem in order to stimulate interest and debate. Some will be recounting and reflecting upon their own practical experiences in multimethodology, while others will be exploring the theoretical and philosophical problems of such an enterprise. The authors will differ among themselves, and no consensus will be arrived at for the subject is still at a very exploratory stage. Indeed no such consensus may even be possible. But the following chapters provide both a stimulating intellectual challenge and much of practical value to those who descend into the "swampy lowland [of] messy, confusing problems [that] defy technical solution" (Schon, 1987).

REFERENCES

Astley, W. and van der Ven, A. (1983). Central perspectives and debates in organisation theory. *Administrative Science Quarterly*, **28**(2), 245.
Banville, C. and Landry, M. (1989). Can the field of MIS be disciplined? *Communications of the ACM*, **32**(1), 48.
Bennett, P. (1985). On linking approaches to decision-aiding: issues and prospects. *Journal of the Operational Research Society*, **36**(8), 659.
Bennett, P. (1990). Mixing methods: combining conflict analysis, SODA, and strategic choice. In C. Eden and J. Radford (eds) *Tackling Strategic Problems: The Role of Group Decision Support*. Sage, London.
Bhaskar, R. (1989). *Reclaiming Reality*. Verso, London.
Bhaskar, R. (1994). *Plato Etc.* Verso, London.
Booth, W. (1979). *Critical Understanding: The Powers and Limits of Pluralism*. University of Chicago Press, Chicago.
Brocklesby, J. (1994). Let the jury decide: assessing the cultural feasibility of total systems intervention. *Systems Practice*, **7**(1), 75–86.
Brocklesby, J. (1995). Intervening in the cultural constitution of systems— methodological complementarism and other visions for systems science. *Journal of the Operational Research Society*, **46**(11), 1285–1298.
Brocklesby, J. and Cummings, S. (1995). Combining hard, soft and critical methodologies in systems research: the cultural constraints. *Systems Research*, **12**(1).
Bryman, A. (1992). *Quantity and Quality in Social Research*. Routledge, London.
Bulmer, M. (1984). *Sociological Research Methods: an Introduction* (2nd edn). Macmillan, London.
Burrell, G. and Morgan, G. (1979). *Sociological Paradigms and Organisational Analysis*. Heinemann, London.
Checkland, P. and Scholes, J. (1990). *Soft Systems Methodology in Action*. Wiley, Chichester.
Denzin, N. (1970). *The Research Act in Sociology: A Theoretical Introduction to Sociological Methods*. Butterworths, London.
Eden, C. (1994). Cognitive mapping and problem structuring for systems dynamics model building. *Working Paper 94/6, Department of Management Science*, Strathclyde University.
Espejo, R. and Harnden, R. (1989). *The Viable Systems Model*. Wiley, Chichester.
Flood, F. (1995). *Solving Problem Solving*. Wiley, Chichester.
Flood, R. (1996). Total systems intervention: local systems intervention. *Centre for Systems Studies Research Memorandum 13*, University of Hull.

Flood, R and Jackson, M. (1991). *Creative Problem Solving.* Wiley, London.

Flood, R. and Romm, N. (1995a). Diversity management: theory in action. *Systems Practice*, **8**(4), 469.

Flood, R. and Romm, N. (1995b). Enhancing the process of methodology choice in total systems intervention (TSI) and improving chances of tackling coercion. *Systems Practice*, **8**(4), 377.

Ford, J. (1990). Systematic pluralism: introduction to an issue. *Monist*, 331.

Fuller, S. (1990). Why epistemology just might be(come) sociology. *Philosophy of the Social Sciences*, **20**(1), 99.

Galliers (1994). Relevance and rigour in information systems research: some personal reflections on issues facing the information systems research community. *IFIP Transactions A—Computer Science and Technology*, **54**, 93.

Gioia, D. and Pitre, E. (1990). Multiparadigm perspectives on theory building. *Academy of Management Review*, **15**(4), 584.

Guba, E. (1990). The alternative paradigm dialog. In E. Guba (ed.) *The Paradigm Dialog.* Sage Publications, California.

Habermas, J. (1978). *Knowledge and Human Interests* (2nd edn). Heinemann, London.

Habermas, J. (1984). *The Theory of Communicative Action Vol. 1: Reason and the Rationalization of Society.* Heinemann, London.

Habermas, J. (1987). *The Theory of Communicative Action Vol. 2: Lifeworld and System: A Critique of Functionalist Reason.* Polity Press, Oxford.

Hanson, N. (1958). *Patterns of Scientific Discovery.* Cambridge University Press, Cambridge.

Harvey, L. and Myers, M. (1995). Scholarship and practice: the contribution of ethnographic research methods to bridging the gap. *Information Technology and People*, **8**(3), 13.

Hassard, J. (1991). Multiple paradigms and organizational analysis: A case study. *Organization Studies*, **12**(2), 275.

Hocking, A. and Lee, P. (1994). Systems thinking and business process redesign: a case for combining techniques. *International Systems Dynamics Conference*, Stirling University.

Holt, J. et al (1993). No waffle in Darlington. *OR Newsletter*, **January**, 8.

Jackson, M. (1985). Social systems theory and practice: the need for a critical approach. *International Journal of General Systems*, **10**, 135.

Jackson, M. (1987). Present positions and future prospects in management science. *Omega*, **15**(6), 455–466.

Jackson, M. (1989). Which systems methodology when? Initial results from a research program. In R. Flood, M. Jackson, and P. Keys (eds) *Systems Prospects: The Next Ten Years of Systems Research.* Plenum, New York.

Jackson, M. (1990). Beyond a system of systems methodologies. *Journal of the Operational Research Society*, **41**, 657.

Jackson, M. (1991a). The origins and nature of critical systems thinking. *Systems Practice*, **4**(2), 131.

Jackson, M. (1991b). *Systems Methodology for the Management Sciences.* Plenum Press, New York.

Jackson, M. and Keys, P. (1984). Towards a system of system methodologies. *Journal of the Operational Research Society*, **35**, 473.

Jackson, N. and Carter, P. (1993). "Paradigm wars": a response to Hugh Willmott. *Organizational Studies*, **14**(5), 721.

Keys, P. et al (1988). A methodology for methodology choice. *Systems Research*, **5**(1), 65.

Kuhn, T. (1970). *The Structure of Scientific Revolutions.* Chicago University Press, Chicago.

Landry, M. and Banville, C. (1992). A disciplined methodological pluralism for MIS research. *Accounting, Management & Information Technology*, **2**(2), 77.

Lee, A. (1991). Integrating positivist and interpretivist approaches to organizational research. *Organization Science*, **2**, 342.

Lehaney, B. and Paul, R. et al (1994). Developing sufficient conditions for an activity cycle diagram from the necessary conditions in a conceptual model. *Systemist*, **16**(4), 261.

Linstone, H. (1984). *Multiple Perspectives for Decision Making: Bridging the Gap Between Analysis and Action*. Elsevier North Holland, New York.

Midgley, G. (1989a). Critical systems: the theory and practice of partitioning methodologies. *33rd Annual Meeting of the ISSS*, Edinburgh, Scotland.

Midgley, G. (1989b). Critical systems and the problem of pluralism. *Cybernetics and Systems*, **20**, 219.

Midgley, G. (1990). Creative methodology design. *Systemist*, **12**, 108.

Midgley, G. (1992). Pluralism and the legitimation of systems science. *Systems Practice*, **5**(2), 147.

Mingers, J. (1980). Towards an appropriate social theory for applied systems thinking: critical theory and soft systems methodology. *Journal of Applied Systems Analysis*, **7**, 41–49.

Mingers, J. (1992). Recent developments in Critical Management Science. *Journal of the Operational Research Society*, **43**(1), 1.

Mingers, J. and Brocklesby, J. (1996). Multimethodology: towards a framework for critical pluralism. *Systemist*, **18**(3), 101–132.

Mingers, J. and Taylor, S. (1992). The use of Soft Systems Methodology in practice. *Journal of the Operational Research Society*, **43**(4), 321.

Myers, D. (1994). Dialectical hermeneutics: a theoretical framework for the implementation of information systems. *Information Systems Journal*, **5**, 51.

Orlikowski, W. and Baroudi, J. (1991). Studying information technology in organizations: research approaches and assumptions. *Information Systems Research*, **2**(1), 1.

Orlikowski, W. and Robey, D. (1991). Information technology and the structuring of organizations. *Information Systems Research*, **2**(2), 143.

Ormerod, R. (1994). Putting soft OR methods to work: information systems strategy development at Palabora. *Warwick Business School Research Papers*, **128**.

Ormerod, R. (1995). Putting soft OR methods to work: information systems strategy development at Sainsbury's. *Journal of the Operational Research Society*, **46**(3), 277.

Ormerod, R. (1996a). Information systems strategy development at Sainsbury's Supermarkets using Soft OR. *Interfaces*, **26**(1), 102.

Ormerod, R. (1996b). Putting soft OR methods to work: information systems strategy development at Richards Bay. *Journal of the Operational Research Society*, **47**(9), 1083.

Popper, K. (1972). *Objective Knowledge: An Evolutionary Approach*. Oxford University Press, London.

Roth, P. (1987). *Meaning and Method in the Social Sciences: A Case for Methodological Pluralism*. Cornell University Press, Cornell.

Rouse, J. (1991). Indeterminacy, empirical evidence, and methodological pluralism. *Synthese*, **86**, 443.

Savage, A. and Mingers, J. (1996). A framework for linking Soft Systems Methodology (SSM) and Jackson Systems Development (JSD). *Information Systems Journal*, **6**, 109–129.

Schon, D. (1987). *Educating the Reflective Practitioner: Toward a New Design for Teaching and Learning in the Professions*. Jossey-Bass, San Francisco.

Searle, J. (1996). *The Construction of Social Reality*. Penguin, London.

Smaling, A. (1994). The pragmatic dimension: paradigmatic and pragmatic aspects of choosing a qualitative or quantitative method. *Quality and Quantity*, **28**, 233.

Taket, A. (1993). Mixing and matching: developing and evaluating innovatory health promotion projects. *OR Insight*, **6**(4), 18–23.

Ulrich, W. (1983). *Critical Heuristics of Social Planning: A New Approach to Practical Philosophy*. Wiley, Chichester.

Ulrich, W. (1991). Systems thinking, systems practice, and practical philosophy: a program of research. In R. Flood and M. Jackson (eds) *Critical Systems Thinking: Directed Readings*. Wiley, Chichester.

Walsham, G. (1995). The emergence of interpretivism in IS research. *Information Systems Research*, **6**(4), 376.

Weaver, G. and Gioia, D. (1994). Paradigms lost: incommensurability vs structurationist inquiry. *Organizational Studies*, **15**(4), 565–590.

Willmott, H. (1993). Breaking the paradigm mentality. *Organizational Studies*, **15**(5), 681.

Part 1
Practice of Multimethodology

Commentary

As we approach the millennium, there is a greater acceptance of the turbulence facing organizations. This turbulence is brought on by numerous factors: increasing global competition; rapidly changing technologies, especially Information Technology (IT); some degree of political stability in the dominant countries of the world leading to greater openness, communication and cross-border trade; a shift in the global economic centre from the USA to somewhere in the triangle bounded by North America, the European Community and the Asia–Pacific countries led by Japan.

Through the innovative use of IT, networks are now challenging conventional business models especially with regard to organizational structure. A combination of strategic alliances and outsourcing is leading to the notion of virtual organizations such as virtual banks and virtual airlines. With good global logistic systems, manufacturing locations no longer need to be close to their markets; and behind many well-known branded products lie extremely sophisticated supply chains crossing many organizational boundaries.

How do managers compete in such an environment? Strategy formulation is going through an interesting evolution. In the early 1980s, the dominant strategy paradigm was about ensuring a fit between the organization (and its capabilities) and the market place. Underpinning this tenet was the belief that there was some form of predictability about the future. Then came the incrementalists led by Mintzberg and Quinn who saw strategy as a stream of abandoned and adopted actions over time in line with a desired strategic direction. Because of only partial knowledge and the unpredictable nature of the environment managers could at best react to events when their tactics proved to be misdirected. There was increasingly a recognition that the world is a much more complex place. In fact, Hamel and Prahalad captured the crux of the problem very succinctly in their *Harvard Business Review* article (May–June, 1989) entitled "Strategic intent":

Multimethodology: The Theory and Practice of Combining Management Science Methodologies.
Edited by John Mingers and Anthony Gill.
© 1997 John Wiley & Sons Ltd.

> It is not very comforting to think that the essence of Western strategic thought can be reduced to eight rules for excellence, seven S's, five competitive forces, four product life-cycles, three generic strategies, and innumerable two-by-two matrices.

The authors argued that: "To revitalize corporate performance, we need a whole new model of strategy." Core competence and strategic stretch form part of this new model.

We believe that complexity and chaos theory is emerging as a key element of this new strategic model to support an understanding of organizational dynamics and a shifting business paradigm. As part of this trend, Peter Senge's book *The Fifth Discipline* has had an impact in the strategy arena. The idea of systems thinking and the need to share mental models is now accepted within many organizations. In their search to develop a better understanding of all types of organizational problems, people at all levels in organizations are seeking tools to facilitate problem solving in the widest sense. Practitioners (academics, internal and external consultants, front-line employees) of Operational Research and Systems (ORS) have a finite time frame to make these disciplines accepted within organizations. The price to be paid will be a combination of presenting the ideas in accessible language and a certain amount of pragmatism as people go up the learning curve in embracing ORS tools, methods and methodologies.

The six chapters in Part 1—Practice of Multimethodology—offer a wide combination of ORS approaches under the banner of Multimethodology (MM). Readers will find that each of the authors will guide them through their experience of applying MM. While some prior knowledge of the specific ORS approach will facilitate the readers' understanding, those unfamiliar with the approach can develop an appreciation of the benefits of using the various approaches and will be pointed to definitive references should they wish to find out more about a specific approach.

After reading several chapters, readers will note a few key words being repeated:

- **Model.** Most ORS approaches are likely to have a model as an output. This model—often a graphical representation with words—is a reflection of the "reality" perceived by the practitioner. The model, especially where shared, is designed to facilitate understanding. Some models, system dynamics in particular, will permit **simulation** if data are available.
- **Complexity.** Managing complexity is a key factor for managers in all types of organizations. However, this requires a good understanding of the interconnectivity of the critical issues facing the organization. System dynamics is good at capturing dynamic complexity while the Viable System Model is good at capturing detailed complexity. Cognitive Mapping and Interactive

Management will facilitate the structuring of complex mental models at an individual and group level.

- **Competence.** Competence in applying ORS approaches is an area of concern. Expertise is far from widespread and there is often a steep learning curve involved. Ultimately, the only way to gain confidence and experience is by applying the techniques preferably with access to a guide or mentor in the early stages. Apart from the relevant specialist ORS skills there is also the need to acquire advanced social skills to work interactively with groups of people and effectively lead interventions.
- **Choice.** In applying MM, choice of suitable combinations of approaches will often present a challenge. However, in many instances this choice will be governed by pragmatism using techniques that you know and feel comfortable with.
- **Changing paradigms.** Getting people to move from their comfort zones and see the world differently is a key factor in managing change. Some of the chapters demonstrate how ORS approaches have been used to shift paradigms once the ORS language has been shared with participants.
- **Learning.** Learning is regarded as a fundamental trait of successful, adaptive organizations. Many ORS approaches will facilitate learning.
- **Knowledge.** Most ORS approaches (particularly the softer ones) will help to share not only explicit knowledge but also tacit knowledge (see Chapter 9 by David Skyrme). It is tacit knowledge that is now recognized as fundamental in cooperative work.

These are among the stimulating issues that are discussed or implied in the chapters that follow.

Richard Ormerod presents seven mini case studies of applying MM. What is particularly useful for the reader is his reflections on each of the cases. Over time it is also interesting to see the shift from hard (biased towards operational—often numerical/mathematical—problems where people are not a significant issue in resolving the problem) to soft (the relationships between people and their respective viewpoints are significant in resolving the problem) ORS approaches. Throughout, Richard is seeking explanations which lead to understanding which leads to improvement in the problem situation. Look out for his comments on imperfect objectivity, intervention transformation and intervention competence. Richard advocates an "eclectic view mixing methods and parts of methods at will".

Peter Bennett, Fran Ackermann, Colin Eden and **Terry Williams** offer a Case Study of Combined Methodology. This study combines cognitive mapping, conflict analysis and systems dynamics through which the authors were required to develop a "requisite model sufficient for the purpose of making a credible case" in a court of law. Of great interest is how the modelling process itself was used to improve both the cognitive map and the system dynamics model in an iterative way. As the authors point out "cycling between different types of model can bring benefits unattainable by a staged process which fails to recognize continuous interaction between the models. One is left with the assumption that without using MM either model on its own would not have stood up to intense scrutiny. The work represented in this chapter reflects one of a number of projects which have involved constructing models which have been developed jointly with lawyers involved in litigation.

Jeremy Bentham a practising operational manager sums up his position in the title "One size doesn't fit all". As part of a change management intervention, Jeremy and his team have combined systems dynamics, statistical process control and soft systems methodology. Developing a shared vocabulary for systems thinking techniques to be used as a catalyst for behavioural change was fundamental to the success of the project. For Shell "a common vocabulary for strategic learning to support decisions on business direction and major investments on long-lived assets under conditions of often considerable uncertainty" has existed for some years due to the generation of scenario planning by Pierre Wack which was followed by Arie de Geus's promotion of mental models and organizational learning.

Allenna Leonard has combined Kelly's Repertory Grid, the Critical Path method from project planning and management with Beer's Viable System Model to deal with a "messy" intervention. Opportunism gone wrong is often the result of ill-considered propositions. This is where the insights from an external consultant can help to clarify the alternatives facing organizations. There is a good elaboration of Kelly's Repertory Grid which should prove useful to those unfamiliar with it. Allenna has made use of multiple models to reflect on possible outcomes and has given a detailed account of how much of the work/analysis was carried out.

Markus Schwaninger gives an update of what is happening in the German-speaking countries in "Status and Tendencies of Management Research: A Systems Oriented Perspective". Some time is spent reflecting on the role of both first- and second-order cybernetics and in applying the concepts during work carried out in a German chemical company. This is followed by a review of the research and teaching framework known as the "St Gallen Management Concept" and the Cybernetics Systems Methodology for dealing with complex issues in organizations. During the RITTS project, soft systems methodology (SSM) was used to build a qualitative model while system dynamics modelling was used for the quantitative model. In contrast to Bennett et al whose qualitative and quantitative models were used iteratively to reconfirm/reconstruct each other over time, Schwaninger notes: "There are also conflicts, deficits of communication and maybe even incommensurability between certain 'schools' of the systems movement. Generally, a deep gap still yawns between 'quantitative' and 'qualitative' approaches." To conclude the chapter, Schwaninger rates the systems-oriented perspective research tasks of synthesis, languaging (systems-oriented language that managers can understand) and the raising of philosophical questions as high priorities.

Anthony Gill describes some of the partially funded UK Department of Trade and Industry research work into Computer Supported Co-operative Work that he was involved in. The intent is to combine the use of the Beer's Viable System Model (VSM) with Warfield's Interactive Management as a way of understanding complexity at the local level within an area of a major UK high street bank. The notion of "managing a virtual organization" is used to highlight how a management team at the lowest level of structural recursion within the VSM needs to manage their interdependent operational units in order to achieve viability and best serve the customer base they have in common. The bank's own organizational structure necessitates this management action so that they meet their performance targets by overcoming the deficiencies of the structure. In response to some of the difficulties concerning organization structure and business process re-engineering, Tony demonstrates a way of braiding business process with organizational processes. This combines the use of the VSM with deployment flow charting. To further build a rich picture of some of the problems facing this virtual organization a "problematique" was derived using Interactive Management.

After reading these chapters, it is hoped that ORS practitioners and neophytes will be encouraged to be both creative in their application of MM and pragmatic about the desired results. A positive response to the question "has it helped the problem situation in an effective and efficient way" is what is required. If one is always working in one's comfort zone no learning is likely to happen. A key to learning is to have a period for post-intervention reflection so the process of intervention may be enhanced in the future.

Little has been said of the software supporting the intervention process either for individual analysis or group facilitation. Without the software ORS practitioners will be overwhelmed by variety. System dynamics relies on packages such as *Powersim*, *iThink* and *Vensim* for both modelling and simulation. Cognitive mapping relies on *Graphics COPE*; strategic choice relies on *STRAD*. Interactive Management needs software to support the interpretative structural modelling process. No doubt there are many other commercially available software packages to support ORS modelling, not to mention the use of spreadsheets and statistical packages.

In working with people the ORS practitioner has a number of roles that may be adopted: the *expert* (industry or ORS) role; a *process* (coach or guide—but no content expertise) role; a *resource* to the team/project. A clear role is more likely to ensure a successful intervention. It is interesting to note Richard Ormerod's changing roles over time. Additionally, in order to get the ideas of ORS across to a wider group of people there is a conscious need to ensure some form of "technology transfer" in language that the participants can readily understand. It is left to committed individuals to get ORS thinking higher up in management's priorities; in fact, into the manager's tool kit. As will be seen in these following chapters, MM can be applied both in a strategic context and in an operational way. This must be of relevance to managers.

Mixing Methods in Practice: a Transformation-Competence Perspective

RICHARD ORMEROD

INTRODUCTION

In this chapter a series of seven practical cases are described and discussed. They cover a range of contexts and illustrate how combinations of methods were chosen to meet different client objectives. The cases are not chosen as exemplars but for their variety. They are used as a vehicle for reflecting on the choices made and debating the issues that need to be addressed at the beginning of a consultancy (internal or external) intervention. The cases illustrate mixing hard methodologies, mixing soft methodologies and mixing hard and soft methodologies together. Two sections are devoted to each case. The first section describes the case and the second comments on it. The title of each case includes some key words in brackets to characterise the case on three dimensions:

- *consultancy mode* to indicate whether the intervention was conducted as an internal, external or academic consultant
- *intervention paradigm* that characterises the approach taken (several labels are used including hard and soft OR) and
- the nature of the *consultancy activity* (again several labels are used including decision support and facilitation)

Multimethodology: The Theory and Practice of Combining Management Science Methodologies.
Edited by John Mingers and Anthony Gill.
© 1997 John Wiley & Sons Ltd.

The cases are described in chronological order. Through the comments on the cases a number of themes are developed. It is concluded that the relationship between hard and soft approaches can be best understood using the analogy of putty, clay and plastic; that the impossible pursuit of objectivity can be rescued by accepting imperfect objectivity as a desirable aim; that the design of intervention processes can be understood and guided by considering the transformation required, the transformation potential of different approaches and the competence of the different parties involved; and that there seems to be no practical difficulty in mixing paradigms in an intervention.

The cases are all based on personal experience, my role as consultant being central. The prominence I give to the part that I played, my skills and abilities may seem overly self-centred and self-indulgent. However, it is my intention to engage in reflection on experience and particularly to highlight the importance of competence in the design of interventions; to stay within the normal conventions of modesty and impersonal scientific discourse would be both constraining and artificial. You will perhaps find what follows easier to take if you remember to qualify all my references to having abilities, skills and competences with the prefix limited, rudimentary or developing. Competence is largely the result of experience; I am claiming no more than to have experienced a number of interventions in a variety of contexts. To explain the basis for my (limited, rudimentary, developing) competence I will first indulge in a little personal history.

PERSONAL BACKGROUND

I began practising OR when I joined the Operational Research Executive of the National Coal Board in 1973, having obtained an MSc in Management Science and Operational Research at Warwick University. At that time the MSc course consisted of a mixture of management and OR courses, and a summer project; there was no attempt to teach practice as such. On joining ORE I went on an induction course (to better understand the NCB) and an underground training course (an introduction to the nature of underground mining including safety). I had up to this point been designing and overseeing the construction of bridges as a civil engineer (four years) and managing factories (one year) having taken a degree in Civil Engineering. Nothing had directly prepared me for the interventions I was about to undertake except for the MSc project (on stock control in an electrical manufacturing company). Nevertheless I was confident in my analytical ability, I had gained some survival skills (on construction sites) and had joined the country's premier OR group. I was ready to tackle anything!

Over the next 20 years I moved jobs several times. Throughout, whether employed as a research scientist (five years), strategist (nine years), management consultant (four years) or academic (five years), I have considered myself to be an OR practitioner. The approach that I learnt through experience in those early days has stuck with me. It has apparently been useful or I would have abandoned it by now. But until recently I couldn't even begin to say what this approach was. Even today I find the articulation of practice difficult. At no time was I particularly surprised by this state of affairs, after all I had successfully practised engineering without ever worrying about what it was to be an engineer, nor articulating the nature of the engineering approach.

A LANGUAGE OF REPRESENTATION

Either as engineer or OR practitioner, I do not recall referring to hypotheses, nor reflecting on the nature of the scientific approach. I sought explanation. Explanation led to understanding. Understanding led to improvement. As an engineer I had experienced in practice the exploitation of the relationship between calculation (models) and reality. I was used to designing a structure (involving an enormous amount of calculation) to take loads: the accuracy of the calculations was tested by the construction of the structure and its use. I was used to backing my ability to predict the behaviour of inanimate material objects by calculation. My safety and that of others depended on the accuracy of the calculations and the reasonableness of assuming that they were relevant to the physical world. My engineering models had predictive power on which I relied. I have elsewhere (Ormerod, 1996a) entered the debate about the nature of OR, science, technology and consulting. It is not my purpose to continue that debate here, though the reflection on my practical experience that follows is relevant to it. Since entering academia I have come to value the language of organisational intervention of Boothroyd (1978), the language of purposeful human activity systems of Checkland (1981), and the language of combining methods of Bennett (1985). I will use this language without further explanation. However, the three additional concepts that I wish to pursue in the discussion that follows are *imperfect objectivity*, *intervention transformation*, and *intervention competence*.

Methods are generally chosen when an intervention is being planned. The term planning implies scheduling resources, in this case people. Activities need to be defined, sequenced and allocated to people to be carried out within the practical constraints of time and place. The choice of activities, the sequencing, the allocation are essentially a design process and the word design better captures the spirit of what is to be achieved than the word planning. Design involves generating ideas (creatively), making choices (effectively and ethically), and making sure that the product of the design fulfils the desired function (efficacy). The desired function can be defined in terms of a required transformation of inputs into outputs, this I refer to as the required intervention transformation. The inputs can be thought of in terms of intervention competence, the competence of the consultant (conducting the intervention), the competence of the participants. The methods available can be thought to have transformational potential that can be deployed by the participants. The design activity, which may be revisited during the intervention, thus proposes activities based on an understanding of transformation, competency and the practical constraints of context (Ormerod, 1996b).

Case A: Salvage of Powered Supports in North Yorkshire Area of the National Coal Board (internal consultancy—traditional OR—exploration)

My first project as an OR practitioner in 1973 was to investigate the use of powered supports (expensive capital items) in North Yorkshire, one of the 12 production Areas of the National Coal Board (NCB). The Chief Mining Engineer in the Area had agreed that I should conduct an investigation into powered support provisioning on the basis that a lot of money was involved and that OR investigations had proved successful elsewhere. In London a central OR team was conducting a national research programme into the provisioning of coal-face machinery including powered supports. A number of other production Areas had investigated, and still were, investigating the subject. I therefore had available plenty of reports to read and other OR researchers to question.

Readily available national statistics showed North Yorkshire to have an unusually low percentage utilisation of powered supports. I set out to find an explanation for this by arranging to go and see managers in the Area. I talked to the Area managers directly responsible for mechanisation, to the Area-based pit planners, to the Area statisticians, the Area plant pool managers and the Area strata control engineers. I also visited a pit and talked to the manager, the undermanagers, the surveyor and some of the overmen (foremen). Each meeting threw up data, opinions and suggestions of who else to talk to. Important meetings were written up. As time went on I built up some understanding of the issues and a formidable collection of data. I also formulated a stochastic model of the powered support life cycle (see Figure 2.1) to help me understand how various factors were interrelated.

One major factor in the decline of utilisation appeared to be the decrease in the average life of a face (the underground production unit on which powered supports are used). I needed to establish that this had indeed been the case. The data were readily available as a printout of the face data bank maintained by the Area Statistics Department. However, the estimation of face life required some care. The problem faced and the method used were sufficiently interesting to be presented at an application and research conference of the Royal Statistical Society (Howard and Ormerod, 1977). The estimates demonstrated that face life had indeed fallen by 50% in recent years.

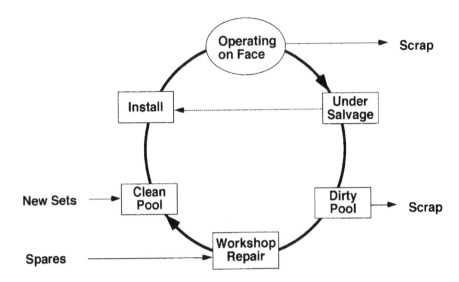

Figure 2.1 The powered support provisioning cycle

My enquiries unearthed something of a mystery, the solution of which was to be central to my investigation. A lot of the downtime of the powered supports was accounted for by time spent waiting to be salvaged (removal to the surface for deployment or repair) after a face was finished. Everyone agreed that salvage was not a long job and was most easily carried out immediately the face was finished. Why therefore was it taking so long in practice? I needed to understand the motivational factors involved. The pursuit of this question led me first to the planners (was the salvage in the plans?), then to pits and then underground at several pits (why were the plans not implemented?). I looked at the way different pits deployed the miners to different tasks on a shift by shift basis. This involved observing the senior overman (general foreman) deploying miners at the beginning of a shift. I needed to understand why the salvage of powered supports was not given priority.

The key to understanding the priority given to different tasks underground lay in the uncertainty faced by managers. If a face finished and the development work for the next face was not complete, then production would be lost. As costs were fixed in the short term, production shortfalls translated into higher costs. I could get a measure of this uncertainty by comparing planned end dates of faces with actuals over a large number of faces. I established statistically that the uncertainty was large and the further the plans looked ahead the larger it grew. Using this measured uncertainty and an estimate of the loss of production that would result if new face development was not completed by the time a production face finished (as a result of geological problems), I was able to analyse the decision and show that the low priority given to salvage was entirely rational as far as the management of the pit was concerned.

If giving a low priority to salvage makes sense at the pit, could savings be made by taking a wider, Area view? The answer to this question was yes, and to demonstrate the options I built a multi-server queueing model to explore different possible organisations. Area salvage teams seemed to offer one way of reducing costs and increasing efficiency. I discovered that another NCB Area, North Derbyshire, already used Area salvage teams so I interviewed those involved to see how well it worked and to get better estimates of the parameters for the model. Visiting North Derbyshire gave me a strong sense of what was practical. I felt I had developed some sensible proposals based on a good understanding of the mining activities and the way they were organised in North Yorkshire. I was confident that the proposals that I was suggesting were practical and would yield a set of benefits that I had quantified using organisational models based on queueing theory.

Comments on Case A

The investigation was conducted without a plan, without a declared process to follow and with methods introduced as the investigation proceeded. This seemed entirely natural. The situation was understood through direct observation (of plans, of the deployment of miners by the senior overmen, of the underground operations), through listening to others (fellow OR scientists, Area and pit management), through the collection and analysis of data (face life, planning uncertainty, organisational options), and through modelling (stochastic life cycle model, statistical estimation, multi-server queueing model). In listening to others, some statements would be given the status of data (for example, "Area policy is . . ."), some treated as ideas or opinions, others perceived as reflecting self-interest. By conducting many interviews, recording meetings, writing reports and presenting the results to client and colleagues, I felt I better understood the distinction between firm fact, speculation and opinion. I took it as my responsibility to establish the facts where this was possible and suggest a decision logic to the best of my ability. I was thus happy to mix objective and subjective data, and always sought to underpin or triangulate the more suspect subjective views. Because I was organisationally outside the Area (part of a centralised internal consultancy service) my views were considered by the client to be unbiased and objective but not necessarily right.

The idea that one can be scientifically objective, free of prejudice and bias, is clearly wrong. Just as the concept of bounded rationality gives a better description of organisational decision making in practice than simply rationality, I suggest the term *imperfect objectivity* better describes my attempts to be objective. The use of the term imperfect does not mean that I accept that the approach was fatally flawed or wrong headed (as others might argue). I am simply accepting that perfect objectivity is not obtainable. Nevertheless, I believe an objective stance has value.

The methods that I used were those of traditional OR (statistical estimation, stochastic processes, decision analysis, queueing). I had succeeded in transforming disparate data, an unobserved situation and opinion into a series of statements and conclusions which had implications for the conduct of the Area's operations (the *intervention transformation*). The (still developing) *intervention competences* that I brought to bear were:

- a theoretical understanding of some classical OR methods (and the confidence to apply them)
- tacit ability to discuss management issues with engineers (as a fellow engineer)
- an ability to put together a logical line of argument (or so I believed)
- a propensity to try to maintain an objective stance

I entirely lacked the ability to plan and design the process of intervention and had no concept of involving others (colleagues or clients) in the investigation except as sources of information and ideas. The methods were chosen on a pragmatic, instrumental basis. They were chosen from my tool bag of OR techniques to help me better understand the data and hence the situation. Many of the most important elements of the intervention were not chosen at all; these were tacit, unarticulated, taken-for-granted skills. They form the basis for action, a matrix, in which the formal methods are deployed; putty in which lumps of clay were embedded.

Each application of a formal technique within the project followed a process of application which is well described by the classic description of the process of OR, namely, formulating the problem, gathering the data, constructing the model, testing the model, implementing the conclusions. These classic OR methods were embedded in an overall investigatory process. The process in this case fits very well the exploratory approach described by Pidd and Woolley (1980) on the basis of their investigation of four OR groups. They describe the problem-structuring activities of OR practitioners thus:

> It appeared that problem-structuring can be viewed as a process of exploration as the analyst strives to comprehend the full complexity of the issues and considers carefully how to manage this complexity. Most analysts seem to see themselves as following some sort of qualitative or analytical approach in their OR. Their problem-structuring becomes an attempt to map such an approach onto the complexity of the issues under consideration. However, the behaviour of the analysts in so doing cannot neatly be divided into self-contained phases of work. As the project(s) proceed, so new information is thrown up and other issues appear.

Embedding the clay of formal classical processes within the putty of the exploratory approach appears to be a natural strategy for the analyst trained in the techniques of OR when faced with a real-world problem. As Pidd and Woolley (1980) put it:

> In their problem structuring, OR workers seem to be concerned with both the tangible (i.e. relatively objective) and socially defined (i.e. subjective) aspects. The analyst appears to be (in some sense) assessing the importance of the various factors impinging of the problems of interest . . . the questions may involve "facts" or be concerned with people and organisational politics. Providing answers to these questions can involve data analysis, controlled experimentation, observation, discussion, etc. . . . and may be sometimes rigorous and at other times, less so.

It is clear from my description that I felt I was very much at the centre of the assignment, and saw it as my task to listen to explanation, to gather data, to develop understanding, to build models, to draw conclusions and make recommendations. Further, it was my task to determine the conduct of the intervention, determine which avenues to pursue and choose the methods. Others might comment and advise but the assignment was my responsibility. In retrospect I recognise that these feelings overemphasise the importance of the individual analyst and underestimate the importance of negotiation. What I would have perceived as the gathering of data to help me make up my mind as to which direction to take, I now recognise as a negotiation about the nature and scope of the problem. The negotiation was a crucial part of the putty. The stance of objectivity provided the basis on which to resolve clashes between different viewpoints. If in doubt I would make observations, seek data or model the dilemma to resolve the issue to my satisfaction. My task was then to present and persuade the decision makers (including the client) that I had indeed resolved the issue to their satisfaction.

Traditional OR methods were thus chosen to support the resolution of dilemmas encountered during the exploration approach, an approach that was implicitly people centred. The embedding of these lumps of clay in the putty did not give rise to issues of commensurability because they were integral to the argument being developed and were conducted according to rules (imperfect objectivity) that were generally (not universally) valued by members of the organisation. In working for the North Yorkshire Area, I was clear that it was my task to further the interests of the Area. I could have been confronted with clashes in interest between the Area and my own group (the Operational Research Executive) or my perception of the interests of the NCB as a whole. In practice, it seemed to be in everyone's interest that I help the Area with the issue in hand to the best of my ability (competence).

One outcome of the assignment was that I now believed I had a considerably better understanding of the management and operations of the North

Yorkshire Area. I also had a better idea of how to plan and implement future interventions (my intervention competence had been improved).

Case B: Strategic Modelling for British Coal (internal consultancy—mature OR—decision support modelling)

I moved down from the Yorkshire coalfields to London in 1975 to work on strategic modelling. My interest in strategic modelling continued when I moved into the Central Planning Unit of the National Coal Board (the NCB, later British Coal) in 1978 and I became the sponsor of the OR strategic modelling team. In all I was involved in strategic modelling for over 10 years (Ormerod and McLeod, 1983). Over that period we had a team of four to five OR scientists continuously building, validating and updating models of the capacity of the Board to supply coal and the energy market in which we operated (Figure 2.2).

Some of the models that we worked on over the 10-year period included:

- the UK energy model (what . . . if simulation)
- investment in energy and technology model (linear programming)
- the NCB national planning model (data aggregation and DCF calculations)
- the supply and demand matching model (linear programming)
- the world coal model (linear programming)
- coal reserve evaluation model (statistical modelling)
- coal mining productivity model (statistical modelling)
- North Sea oil and gas depletion model (what . . . if simulation)

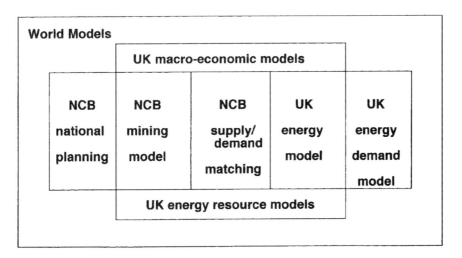

Figure 2.2 The British Coal strategic model

Some models were built and then, after a time, were abandoned. Others continued throughout the period. Pre-eminent in the latter category was the UK energy model which already existed when I joined the strategic modelling section and was still in use when I left British Coal some 10 years later. This was what I have previously referred to as mature OR (Ormerod, 1983). The UK energy model combined a framework for tracking transactions in the UK energy economy with sub-models of behaviour such as (i) consumer energy demand based on income and price elasticities, (ii) penetration rates of new technologies, and (iii) the CEGB's merit operation of generating capacity.

The models were used to inform Board decisions (for instance, investment in coal mining capacity), to prepare submissions to government (for instance, the annual submission of the medium-term development plan) and to support the Board's responses to external questioning (for instance, evidence to the inquiry into the UK's first PWR nuclear reactor, Sizewell B). More generally the models were used to try to understand better issues such as the impact of the OPEC oil price hike on the demand for coal or whether investment in mining machinery was having the desired effect on productivity.

The OR methods used included statistical regression, analysis of variance, what . . . if modelling, scenario development, decision analysis and linear programming. Much of the data used were readily available either from published government and company statistics or from our statistics gathered in the coalfields. Interviewing played little or no part in the modelling but the relationship between the Central Planning Unit (CPU) was very important, as was the general debate about UK energy policy in which the NCB was embedded. Viewpoints of powerful actors (e.g. Board members) were mediated through the views of the CPU. The models were central to our activities: they were the focus of the OR research, the vehicle for communication with the CPU, the repository for the statistical data and intelligence gathered and they provided continuity as team membership changed.

Comments on Case B

Whereas in Case A the outcome of the project was the recommendations, the knowledge and models being by-products, in this case the knowledge gained and captured in the models for further use was the important outcome, the immediate recommendations being less important. The operational research involved was a very pure form of modelling. The modellers were shielded from the political decision-making process and could concern themselves with trying to produce objective models of aspects of the business and its competitive environment. Models could be produced that fitted past behaviour quite well and it was assumed that they would give some guidance to future outcomes given that certain assumptions held true. The uncertainty associated with these assumptions were greater than the expected modelling imperfections. How fast would the economy grow? What would future oil prices be? How quickly would energy saving technologies (for instance, loft insulation) penetrate? Would the government sanction more nuclear stations? Will more natural gas be discovered? Would the miners' new incentive scheme work? What will the miners be paid in five years' time? Would the Chairman of the Board strike a deal with the miners on closures?

Although these questions could not be answered by the models, we needed to explore them and the consequences of different outcomes. What do we expect to happen on average? What would a worst-case scenario look like? What would happen if such and such an investment (for instance, a programme of nuclear power stations) were to be agreed? To address such questions one had to be interested in the politics of the day as well as the underlying economics. Who had what interests? Who lined up with whom? What is the relationship between Saudi Arabia and the United States? Will Sweden import South African coal? Would a miners' strike lead to a general strike? Will the Department of Energy support nuclear power whatever the economic case? Will the Department of Environment continue to tolerate opencast coal? Will Germany continue to subsidise its coal industry? Will the government agree to the EEC Directive on acid rain and will the CEGB invest in scrubbers or turn to imported low sulphur coal? Who will win the next election? Could the government countenance a strike? How many mine closures are in marginal constituencies? What is the new energy minister trying to do?

Thus the OR researchers in this case are, on the one hand, engaged in abstraction, careful analysis, validation and inference. On the other hand, they have to be sensitive to the undercurrents, conflicts and uncertainties of the world of politics and power. Despite the obvious importance, even centrality, of powerful actors, organisational interests, national and international politics, the role of the OR team in this instance is to concentrate on the quality of the objective "facts" to be included in the models. Pidd and Woolley's exploration approach does not fit this type of OR well. The process was much closer to a classical modelling approach but with one important difference; the models are built for continued use and improvement. Projects continue from year to year. The research programme is more important than the individual project.

At the beginning of a particular project within the overall programme, the model could be described and specified. There was no single problem to be solved and seldom a particular decision to be taken; a model needed to be designed and built for the insight it would generate and the support it would give to the activities of the CPU and more widely the complex of issues faced by the Board. Today we would probably describe the models as decision support systems (DSS) or executive information systems (EIS). The language of systems development can be used to describe our activities; we created prototypes, developed the models, and then implemented, operated and enhanced them.

As in Case A some operational research putty (to manage the relationship with the CPU) is required but here the clay is massive and dominant within the OR projects. The CPU, on the other hand, were in the putty business, working with other departments, Board members, government departments, international organisations, competitors and customers to understand the business environment, develop strategic options and advocate the Board's interests in various fora. Some mixing of methods would occur within the activities of the OR team (for instance, using regression to determine parameters for inclusion in a linear programming model). The issue of how to mix the methods lay within the CPU. The members of the CPU had to decide the role that the models could play in supporting their arguments and submissions. Argumentation of policy issues is a refined art in governmental and quasi-governmental circles. Political interests dominate, but the rules of the game are such that each case is argued in terms of existing policy positions, logic and factual evidence. Facts are contestable and have a habit of backfiring. They are therefore dangerous in an argument and are used sparingly. In the political arena putty abounds. Formal methods (hard) are accommodated by careful deployment within the putty and by general agreement that facts do matter and can be established given scrutiny of method and challenge of interpretation: in other words, if a critical view of facts is taken. Although disputes about facts often hit the headlines, in practice many facts are accepted by all the parties concerned in a debate.

The competences required in the strategic modelling section included technical modelling, appreciation of the economic and political environment, the ability to make the models relevant to the decision-making process and the ability to shape an ongoing research programme supported by the client.

From Cases A and B it is apparent that hard OR methods (for the methods and techniques I have been talking about are hard) require a good deal of soft embedding in their organisational context, whether this is part of the OR action programme or part of the client's action programme. My conjecture is that this is always the case.

Case C: An Information Systems Strategy (ISS) for National Grid (external consultancy—hard systems—process support)

The third case takes place some years later when I was employed as a consultant in the PA Consulting Group. My interest at this time was in the development of information technology strategies. Until it was privatised the Central Electricity Generating Board (CEGB) was responsible for the generation and transmission of electricity in England and Wales. In 1988 it had been decided that the CEGB would be split into three companies, two engaged in electricity generation; the third, National Grid, was to be responsible for electricity transmission. National Grid would be owned by the 12 Regional Electricity Companies responsible for local electricity distribution, who would also be privatised. Late in 1988 the CEGB set up three teams to develop systems strategies for the three proposed new privatised electricity companies resulting from the break-up of the CEGB. The National Grid team consisted of three analysts from the CEGB's IT department and myself, an external consultant. At that stage a White Paper had been published, the future directors of the company had been identified but not appointed and no staff had been allocated to the company. For existing functions the team could look at the grid management and operational functions within the CEGB. The nature of new activities needed to be established. The team followed a traditional route (interviews, analysis, report, discussions led by the analysts) despite the far from clear shape, form and style of the new enterprise.

The team had agreed terms of reference, defined responsibilities and a set time to develop the strategy. The strategy was urgently required to meet the privatisation timetable. Several development teams needed to be set away as the strategy developed. In particular, the settlement system was required to enable the proposed new trading arrangements to operate. A methodology was agreed and a plan drawn up by the members of the team. My role was to advise on the approach to be taken and to participate in the team activities. Interviews were preplanned, written up, reviewed, and analysed. All issues raised were recorded, clustered and classified. Information about functions and entities was captured in business and data models.

The analysis fell into three broad phases: business analysis, design of systems architecture and bases of data, and implementation planning. In the business analysis the objectives were formulated, a SWOT analysis was carried out, and issues raised by the interviewees were analysed and addressed. In the design phase two models were developed. The first, the functional decomposition model (sometimes called an activity decomposition diagram or a hierarchical business model or an enterprise model) was derived through discussion and agreement with senior executives. It provided a comprehensive description of all the anticipated activities of the new company. It was subjective in nature but was treated as objective by the participants and emphasis was placed on its independence of any particular organisational form. The second model was an entity-relationship model which was partly derived from an existing CEGB-wide model and partly by considering what data would be required by the decisions embedded in the functional model. The main analytical tool was an entity-usage matrix showing the input and use of data by system. The matrix was sorted to derive an information systems architecture showing data flows, subject databases and systems and a dependency diagram to guide implementation planning. Descriptions and examples of the types of models and analysis used can be found in Ward, Griffiths and Whitmore (1990).

An important aspect of the study was the first-cut definition of the new company's mission and a debate about the desired management style. The mission was subsequently reworked and published as part of an internal document "The National Grid Company 'A Blueprint for the Future' " (NGC, 1981). The debate about management style formed an appendix to the systems strategy. The loosening of central control envisaged implied the strategy needed to embrace the possibility that operational units carrying out similar functions may choose to adopt a diversity of controls, procedures and data. Thus flexibility, allowing multiple viewpoints, was built into the approach from the beginning. The softer issues of culture and control were central to the development of the IS strategy.

Comments on Case C

At first sight the case illustrates the straightforward application of hard systems methods (functional models, entity models, entity-usage matrix analysis) and classical strategy techniques (SWOT and issue analysis, mission writing), albeit on an urgent and important issue. However, it didn't feel like that. Much of the time was spent on trying to understand and reconcile the different viewpoints of the interviewees. This was not a static affair. The directors were continuously engaged in rounds of discussions with advisers, government officials and with each other. Their views were being formed as the discussions progressed. We could be told very little that was not liable to change by the next meeting. How would the new electricity pool work? What would the rules be? How would it be administered? Who would be responsible for long-term capacity planning in the privatised industry? What would the new management culture be? How would the company be organised?

There was little by way of hard data to gather. Subjective views of powerful actors were more important than any objective viewpoint that we might wish to lay claim to. Tempers were short. The stakes were high. There were thus two strands of interrelated activity, the political activity of seeking views, discussing policies and formulating objectives and the technical activity of analysing the requirements for information. Together these activities led to a systems architecture and build sequence. This distinction is similar to that drawn by Breure and Hickling (1990) between sociopolitical work and technical work in projects.

Important practical features of this case are (i) the use of a team, (ii) the urgency, and (iii) the clear deliverable specified. These three features distinguish this case from Case A which was an investigation carried out by an individual and with an undefined outcome at the outset, and Case B which involved the steady build-up of researched knowledge in an ongoing programme. Neither Case A nor Case B were required urgently. If Case A can be characterised as exploration by a lone analyst and Case B as decision support modelling by a research team, how can the intervention in this case be described?

For an answer to this question I have to examine my role carefully. My task was to help the strategy team meet their objective. Their objective was to transform the views of the future National Grid directors, data about the existing functions and systems within the CEGB, and their own knowledge and understanding, into an implementable information systems strategy to support the new company. The competences I brought to the team were (i) an understanding of business strategy and its formulation, (ii) experience in the application of hard systems approaches (particularly information systems planning), and (iii) experience in designing the process to develop an information systems strategy. It is apparent that this is not the normal list of OR competences. However, considered more generally, strategy formulation, hard systems methods and intervention processes are all subjects that are today taught on the MSc in Operational Research and Management Science in my own institution, Warwick University. One interpretation of my role is that of a participant bringing additional competence to the team.

At the heart of the project there was the problem of matching the dynamic, subjective and fuzzy process of defining the new company with the requirement to derive a sharp-edged systems strategy. Hard systems approaches are driven by clear statements of organisational objectives, functions and strategies. In this case these were lacking. Our approach was to develop a draft mission statement and functional model of the business based on interviews with the prospective directors. These were then updated on the basis of further criticism, discussion and changed positions. The results of this process were used to develop systems architectures, build sequences and the like, even though we knew the ground would shift sooner rather than later. The hard systems approach was therefore embedded in the softer analysis of issues and strategies. The artifacts of clay had to be embedded in foundations of putty. The teams that were subsequently set away to develop the systems had to continue to grapple with the same dilemma, sometimes with disastrous effects. My role was to design the process to address the central problem of mixing the hard and soft aspects of the project.

Therefore the answer to the question I posed earlier is that this case can either be characterised as participation in an interdisciplinary team or as the provision of process support.

Case D: ISS Development at Sainsbury's Supermarkets (external consultancy—soft—process design and facilitation)

In 1989 I was engaged as a consultant by Sainsbury's, a major UK chain of food and grocery stores employing some 70,000 people, to help them conduct an IS strategy development exercise. The background, process and facilitating issues that will be summarised here are more fully described in Ormerod (1995a). Sainsbury's were at that time considered by many in the field to be leaders in the application of IT in their sector. To maintain their position they wanted a process that would engage senior managers in a creative process supported by a facilitator. The inputs to the transformation would be the senior managers' knowledge of (i) the business strategy and processes, (ii) the current systems, and (iii) the technology potential. The output required was a strategy which was owned by committed managers responsible for implementing it. My role was to design the process to deliver the required output and to facilitate it. My competence lay in my ability to understand how to design a process to marshal the energy and intelligence of the managers. This included choosing which methods to use, coaching the participants in the use of the methods and facilitating the set pieces.

I decided to design the approach in the spirit of Ackoff's (1979a, b) interactive planning, the idea being to invent a desirable future and seek feasible ways of bringing it about. As the approach lacked detailed support for the process, I sought suitable methods to use. To guide the search and ultimate choice of methods I drew up some criteria:

(a) does the method support an organisational learning process
(b) does the method allow management to state and develop their interpretation of the company and its environment
(c) does the method encourage the active participation of management to give commitment to and ownership of the strategy
(d) does the method encourage the accommodation of diverging interests between groups and
(e) does the method recognise that organisations are complex, open and adaptive systems

Using these criteria I chose, from the methods that I knew about, the following three methods:

● cognitive mapping (Eden, Jones and Sims, 1983) to capture the elements of the strategy as perceived by the board
● soft systems methodology (Checkland, 1981) to provide a framework for enquiry for the senior managers and
● strategic choice (Friend and Hickling, 1987) to shape and evaluate the options

Each method was used to support a different part of the process. They were integrated in the sense that they all formed part of one process, engaging the same group of participants, with the results from one stage feeding forward and informing the next. They were not integrated in the theoretical sense;

each stood on its own. However, they were chosen because of their ability to engage relevant actors in a participative approach consistent with Ackoff's views of strategy as vision-creating, creative, and fun. The methods share interpretive epistemology and ontology. Each has an articulated process associated with its theories and models. Three methods were chosen rather than one because I felt that each offered a different transformation potential which could be best deployed at different stages of the process. Cognitive mapping could help open up a debate about the purpose and direction of the company. Soft systems methodology (SSM) could support an investigation of the organisation and its use of information, and strategic choice could support convergence on a strategy.

Cognitive mapping was used at an early stage to elicit the Board's articulation of the way the business worked and the current strategy. This was used to inform the task force (16 senior and highly regarded managers drawn from all the functions of the business) and to provide a common point of departure for their discussion of future directions. The technique of producing the maps was quickly learnt and used to identify key areas for further examination for systems opportunities.

SSM was used in the next stage to provide a simple framework for understanding and analysing the business to derive systems ideas. After a day's training, teams of four conducted their own enquiries in chosen areas of the business with only occasional support when requested. Some difficulties were encountered by the participants in getting used to the method and some of the finer points were inevitably lost on the way. However, the method did stimulate thought and discussion, providing a framework without constraining ideas.

After six weeks of field investigation the task force reported back to the steering committee, consisting of the joint managing directors and one Board member. One of the unexpected benefits of giving the responsibility for the conduct of the investigation to senior managers was that they could call on resources in a way that analysts would have felt unable. For instance, one manager concerned about customer service arranged for a survey of out-of-stock items at a particular time of day across an area containing 60 or so stores. Although this was labour intensive, he could authorise this work as director of the area concerned.

The strategic choice method was used to structure the evaluation of the systems suggestions resulting from the SSM investigation. The analysis needed to go beyond the SSM check for systemic desirability and cultural feasibility. A comprehensive evaluation of the costs, benefits and risks was required. In the event an evaluation framework was developed that was more quantitative (harder) than that envisaged in the strategic choice method.

From beginning to end the strategy development took nine months with the Board agreeing the strategy in November 1989.

Comments on Case D

In the cases up to now I have deliberately emphasised the importance of the softer aspects of the intervention, the putty, even though hard systems approaches and traditional OR methods were being applied. Case D illustrates the mixing of soft OR methods which formalise some of these soft aspects. The methods are designed to help groups (generally small groups) negotiate the problem structure and possibly seek ways to improve the situation. My account of the earlier cases described the way that hard systems and traditional OR approaches are necessarily embedded in the soft putty of the social world. The careful formalisation of the soft methods in soft OR gives guidance and support in difficult, messy circumstances such as I had encountered in the privatisation of the electricity industry described in Case C. But it was at Sainsbury's that I first decided to run with the soft methods.

The issue of mixing the soft methods arises because in this case I felt that no one method (that I was familiar with) could support the required transformation. I therefore used three methods in series under a fourth umbrella approach (see Figure 2.3). Once putty is formalised it loses some of its malleability, it becomes plastic. Incommensurability of the different methods is a potential issue. Given that the soft methods are based on similar principles (such as the importance of recognising that an intervention is a social act in a social situation involving many actors or stakeholders who have different viewpoints), there is no reason to suppose that they won't mix well in practice. This contention is supported by the experience of the Sainsbury's case.

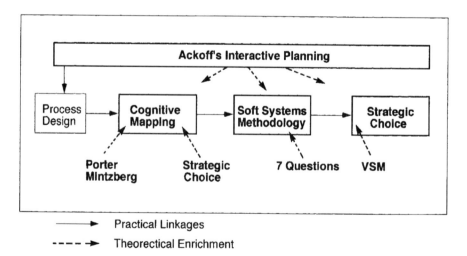

Figure 2.3 Linkages between models for Sainsbury's information systems strategy development

It might be assumed that as each soft method contained a formalised process, there would be no need for the putty. However, in my experience this is not the case. The soft methods still require the deployment of tacit skills to make them work. The new roles required are those of facilitator and coach. However, many of the more traditional skills are also required, such as political awareness, ability to empathise, clarity of thought and presentation, interviewing technique and an ability to judge whether the issues need to be widened or narrowed down at any particular point. Awareness of and sensitivity to these issues are required for both traditional, hard approaches and soft OR. It has been convenient for the advocates of soft OR to caricature traditional OR as hell bent on optimising an abstract mathematical formulation against a single objective however ill-defined, messy or complex the issue. This may be characteristic of some OR but none of the examples above fit the stereotype.

One issue that does come to the fore when several soft approaches are used in the same project is the question of process design. Used on its own SSM has its own process, as does cognitive mapping (in the form of strategic option development and analysis) and strategic choice. For each method the order in which the steps are carried out may be flexible but the design of the process is guided by the formalised method and is relatively unproblematic. With two or more methods there are questions of sequence, coverage, interface and integration. The choice of which methods to use also has to be made. With hard methods the choice is often a response to the issue faced: it is usually not difficult to decide whether queueing or linear programming or statistical analysis is more appropriate. In contrast it is seldom clear whether SSM or cognitive mapping would be more effective in a particular instance. Designing a process to contain more than one soft method, while at the same time choosing which methods to use, does involve some difficult choices. One of the factors that will affect the choice of methods is the competence of both the consultant and the participants to deploy the method. Selection from a wide choice of approaches may be desirable but most consultants will prefer to use familiar methods.

Although the Sainsbury's case is mainly of interest because of its use of several soft approaches, the evaluation method was in fact hard. Each system was analysed in terms of its costs and benefits. This arose because Sainsbury's wanted to develop a more quantitative approach to the evaluation of potential investments in systems. In contrast, the previous systems strategy had proceeded without evaluation. Gaining agreement on the likely cost and benefits of systems, as yet undefined, proved very difficult. A soft approach was used to achieve the quantification in the sense that the numbers were decided by debate between participants in many large meetings. The strategy was a five-year strategy. Five years later I returned to the scene to find out if the estimates on which the decision were taken had been a reasonable guide

(Ormerod, 1996b). If inflation is borne in mind, although estimates for individual systems were not very accurate, the results on average were remarkably good. All the systems still indicated a positive return. A hard approach had been successfully embedded in a soft approach (strategic choice).

Case E: Customer Service Strategy at Severn Trent Water (academic consultancy—soft OR—catalytic)

In 1993 Severn Trent Water, some five years after privatisation, was developing its customer service strategy. A number of task forces were working on different aspects of customer service, coordinated by a dedicated project team. The results were starting to come in from the task forces and I was asked to advise on how the findings might be pulled together. I was contracted for five consulting days to carry out the task. Time was short and as it happened I only received the one-page briefing letter on the morning of the first meeting. The letter gave a list of what they wanted to achieve. It included, *inter alia*, ambitious targets for customer service, cost reduction and introduction of a team-based approach. Each objective seemed a huge task in its own right. Taken together, the challenge seemed overwhelming. As I met with the team that morning to discuss the aims of the strategy it occurred to me that it would help the discussion to capture what they were telling me in a cognitive map. Using the process of mapping we were able to explore the interrelationships between the different objectives. The interrelatedness suggested that several birds could be killed with one stone. For instance, cost reduction could be tackled on a team basis, addressing two goals at once. Proceeding this way the problem seemed to become more manageable. We agreed to meet again in a few days' time.

At the next meeting the team said that they were having difficulty in defining the processes of the business in relation to customer service. To explore this issue, I helped them construct a root definition of the business and develop a conceptual model. We then constructed root definitions for each concept in the model and produced lower level conceptual models. This was not particularly easy as it raised many of the thorny issues they had been struggling with in the first place. Nevertheless by the time I left they had learnt the basics of the SSM approach. By our next meeting the team had produced many conceptual models and were getting to grips with their problem.

At the third meeting, we got to the heart of the issue at hand. The reports coming back from the task forces outlined options across many dimensions which involved major changes in responsibilities and organisational structure. Any one of the changes would provoke a major debate at board level and the prospects of obtaining agreement before the launch date (which had already been determined and the arrangements made) were not at all good. There was a danger that the project would run into real trouble. I was struggling to understand the number of decisions to be made and the way they were dependent on each other. I decided therefore to engage the team in the strategic choice approach. We followed the approach, starting by shaping the problem. It proved relatively easy to decide to separate out a tight knot of decisions about operational tasks and to set aside for the moment the more contentious structural questions which were in any case only loosely linked to the other issues and to each other. We continued to design options and develop an evaluation scheme. It was when the team considered uncertainties and drew up a commitment package that we obtained some real clarity. Using the commitment package concept from the strategic choice method, the team realised that they could design a strategy that could be launched that would include a mixture of decisions taken, exploratory activities that would be set in motion and decisions that would be taken at some specified time in the future. This was a real breakthrough. They could see how they could meet the deadline with a strategy which they felt sure could be agreed by the Board in time for the launch.

At the next meeting the team explained how they had taken the thinking forward. The commitment package had been expanded to a critical path network showing all the activities that would be included in the strategy and how they would be brought together at decision points at set dates in the future. They now drafted their report. I read and commented on the draft. There was nothing more for me to do. The intervention had taken only three and a half of the five consulting days allotted.

Comments on Case E

The case describes a rapid intervention, using cognitive mapping, soft systems methodology and strategic choice in quick succession. The analysis was completed by using a critical path network to map out the future decision process. We see here soft methods being used as tried and trusted friends without any design of the intervention, nor any attempt to integrate the different methods. In this sense the case is similar to Case A. The intervention can be described as exploratory with methods (in this case soft, plastic methods) being deployed in order to address particular issues when it seemed appropriate. However, I prefer the label catalytic to reflect the minimal nature of my involvement.

We can learn something about the relative merits of the methods used in this case. When should each of the methods be deployed? It is no coincidence that the same methods were used in the same order at Sainsbury's in Case D. Of course, by this time the use of the three soft methods was within my competence, so it is no surprise that they should reappear. However, they appear without prior design *in the same order*. Cognitive mapping is suited to the early stages of an intervention when the requirement is to capture the dimensions of an issue that are in people's minds. SSM is particularly useful in the middle of a project to define the system that is being examined for discussion and debate. Strategic choice is particularly powerful at the end of a project to shape and support the decision process. This suggests that the stage at which a method is useful is one way of classifying methods. This is particularly useful if the methods are to be mixed. The methods are useful at different stages because of their transformational potential. Thus the classification by the stage of the project is a simple way to characterise the transformational potential of a method.

The case also illustrates the way that soft methods can precede a hard method. It seems natural to start an intervention with the soft methods which are particularly helpful in structuring problems. Once properly defined and understood it may be appropriate to follow with hard methods which are good at working out the logical consequence of (usually quantitative) assumptions and deriving quantitative estimates of impacts. In systems development such an approach has been labelled "grafting" as opposed to "embedding" (Miles, 1988, 1992). As Mingers (1992) points out there are good reasons for preferring embedding, such that soft attributes of involving people and promoting learning are retained in the later stages of the project. In this case the hard method (critical path analysis) was grafted onto the end of the soft analysis, whereas at Sainsbury's (Case D) the quantified cost–benefit analysis was clearly embedded in an otherwise soft intervention.

Case F: Business Improvement Project at PowerGen (academic consultancy—soft and hard—process design and facilitation)

The Business Improvement Project (BIP) at PowerGen's UK Electricity Division was originally conceived as an exercise in both benchmarking and systems strategy development. The synergy between the two being that both benchmarking and systems strategy development start with an analysis of the business and its processes. In early 1994 I was engaged to design and facilitate the BIP project. It quickly became apparent that there was little point in benchmarking and supporting with IT, processes which were inappropriate. Far better to redesign the processes first. As business process redesign (BPR) or business process re-engineering starts with an analysis of the business and its processes, we concluded that the project should embrace benchmarking, information systems strategy development and BPR. If that were not enough, it soon became clear that the business wanted to reduce their costs to improve business efficiency, thus an element of downsizing was involved.

From the point of view of mixing methods the interest in the case lies in the process analysis. The project itself was designed as a soft, participative project, using task forces and a steering committee. For each task force the process was the same. At an initial foundation workshop on the Monday morning the project was introduced, the current state of the business was discussed and some systems concepts were introduced. For instance, processes were introduced as systems which could be defined and analysed as subsystems in a recursive fashion. The task force then spent the rest of the week interviewing and identifying the business processes. On the next Monday the task force reconvened to learn about process analysis, BPR and benchmarking. They then spent the rest of the week redesigning the processes making a presentation to the steering committee during the next week. The overall approach used was soft systems methodology with additional systems theory interspersed. I want to focus in particular on the use of the viable systems model (Beer, 1975, 1979, 1981, 1985).

Checkland (1981) drawing on general systems theory suggests that each system should have a subsystem concerned with monitoring and controlling the system of which it is a part. He identifies three activities within the subsystem, "know criteria for business success", "monitor the other subsystems", and "take control action". Beer's viable systems model (VSM) contains a more elaborate definition of the mechanisms for control within an organisation. He is also more explicit about the recursive nature of control. I decided that an exposure to the VSM would help the task force members better understand the processes they were identifying. The procedure was as follows. Having made a root definition of an area of the business and identified the current activities, process maps were drawn. Each activity on the map was then classified according to the VSM as to whether it was a system 1 (management of operation), a system 2 (coordination across system 1 operations), a system 3 and 3* (control of system 1 operations), a system 4 (intelligence) or a system 5 (policy). The result was that, on examining the conceptual models, clusters of operational activities were seen to be surrounded by control activities. This greatly enhanced the debate about process redesign by highlighting the fact that major efficiency gains may be possible if the control activities were redesigned. On the other hand, the scope for redesigning the operational processes without addressing the control structure were, beyond a certain point, limited. Taking the operational process as the starting point the task forces worked on several options designed to operate the company in different ways. These were then evaluated and debated by the UK Electricity Management Team.

Comments on Case F

It is not surprising that systems ideas in general and VSM in particular fit in well with SSM, which is, of course, based on systems thinking. The concern in the systems community has been that soft and hard systems approaches do not easily mix (Mingers, 1992). In particular, if an SSM front end is grafted onto a hard systems development process there are three issues. If the same people do both the soft and the hard phase, can they do justice to both paradigms? Are people capable of switching between paradigms? If the soft phase is carried out by appropriate experts in SSM and the hard phase by traditional systems developers, will the benefits of the understanding gained by the soft approach get lost in the handover? These concerns seem to be better addressed when hard analysis or models are embedded in a soft approach. This supports Checkland's position that hard systems thinking lies within soft systems thinking as a special case (Checkland, 1985). However, I would like to maintain the distinction between hard systems methods (the clay) and the traditional process of OR intervention (the putty). Hard methods (clay) embed well in soft methods (plastic); both hard and soft methods need to be embedded in a process which deploys craft skills to maintain coherence, continuity and momentum in the face of disturbances in the environment (putty).

If hard approaches can be embedded in soft but grafting may be problematic, can soft methods be embedded in hard? In my view such an occasion should never arise as hard methods should always be embedded in the putty of an intervention process. The soft process should then also be embedded in the putty and no attempt should be made to embed it in the clay. This approach, which allows hard and soft methods to be used at will so long as they are embedded in the putty of the craft skills of intervention, I shall refer to as the "eclectic" approach. Is there then no limit to the mixing of methods? Yes, the limitations to mixing methods lie in the competence of the consultant and the participants rather than in the methods themselves.

Case G: Market Entry Strategy at Sainsbury's Supermarkets (academic consultancy—soft and traditional OR—catalytic)

In late 1994 Sainsbury's started to form a team to explore the potential of home shopping. I was asked to design and facilitate two workshops, each of one day. The first was held early on before the team had been fully established. The objective was to draw on different areas of expertise within the business, to help form the team and get people thinking about the issues. Each day was structured to achieve an agreed transformation (the state of mind of participants at the beginning of the day to the required state of mind at the end of day, plus tangible outputs in terms of options, costings, strategies and so on).

Day 1—Logistics Workshop   The workshop was attended by 12 participants. After introducing the day, a hat session (De Bono, 1985) was held to debate the merits of the current supermarket format. Then the scope of the remit of the group was explored using SSM. A rich picture was used, and two root definitions were drawn up representing the customers' and the company's viewpoint. The resulting conceptual model was used to identify the key variables to be determined in the design of a home shopping system. These were referred to as design dimensions. Choices along each dimension were defined, in one case using a repertory grid technique (Eden and Jones, 1984). Following the strategic choice approach, six decision schemes were designed by combining the choices along each dimension. After lunch three groups were formed to flesh out and cost each decision scheme. The day had been interspersed with briefing sessions and videos. Time ran out before the final step of evaluating the schemes could be carried out. The next steps were agreed and the group dispersed.

Day 2—Outcomes Workshop   About a month and half later a second workshop was held for the five members of the team to digest the work that had been completed and to work towards recommendations to go into a report scheduled for the following month. The day started with a presentation of the options from the different functional viewpoints of the members of the team. I then introduced some strategy concepts including emergence, basis of competition, interrelationships between value chains, uncertainty (using strategic choice) and risk. Scenarios were then developed and a matrix drawn up of options against scenarios (decision analysis). Each option was then evaluated against each scenario in terms of outcome, learning and uncertainty. To examine how decisions might be made through time against an evolving competitive environment a decision tree was used. Given the uncertainties and the need for exploration in an emergent strategy, a commitment package, including immediate actions, avenues to be explored, decisions to be taken in the future and contingency plans, was drawn up (strategic choice). To plan how the entry strategy might be developed over time, the commitment package was extended over several periods to form a critical path network with identified decision points. The options and the evaluation scheme were subsequently worked on further.

The report was completed by the team and Sainsbury's have subsequently entered the home shopping market on the basis of the team's recommendations.

Comments on Case G

The theme of rapid intervention at Severn Trent Water (Case E) is developed further in this case, which describes the use of soft methods (repertory grids, soft systems methodology and strategic choice) and hard methods (decision analysis, decision trees and critical path networks) to make recommendations on an entry strategy to a new market. Participants happily moved from thinking about and debating different points of view to discussing the "facts" and designing good (hopefully the best) strategies. My role as consultant was essentially catalytic: the participants took away ideas from the workshops and continued with their project. Each workshop was planned. The methods were embedded in workshops which were designed and facilitated using the craft skills of intervention (putty).

This case, by practical example, reinforces the conclusion that hard and soft methods can be used cheek by jowl in one project if embedded in an intervention process. Members of the team strive after objective knowledge where this is feasible and accept views, judgements and assertions as relevant evidence where it is not. The combination allows both analytical insight and creative flair to flourish. Such a combination is the essence of good strategic thinking and good strategy consultancy. Soft and hard OR approaches together form a powerful basis for conducting strategy assignments, an area where OR's contribution has in the past been disappointing (Clark and Scott, 1995; Ormerod, 1993, 1995b).

DISCUSSION

The cases and some of their characteristics are summarised in Table 2.1. They represent a wide variety of contexts within nationalised, privatised and private sectors but as a sample they have some limitations. None of the cases are in the public or not-for-profit sectors. Apart from Case A, all the cases involve strategy determination of one sort or another. In addition, the cases are all concerned with single business units or sections within single business units. Multidivisional, multinational, and global companies provide a different set of

Table 2.1 Summary of the cases presented

Case	Organisation	Consultancy	Paradigm	Activity
A	NCB/North Yorkshire	Internal	Traditional OR	Exploration
B	NCB/CPU	Internal	Mature OR	Decision support modelling
C	National Grid	External	Hard systems	Process support
D	Sainsbury's	External	Soft OR	Process design and facilitation
E	Severn Trent Water	Academic	Soft OR	Catalytic
F	PowerGen	Academic	Soft/hard systems	Process design and facilitation
G	Sainsbury's	Academic	Soft/hard OR	Catalytic

problems, but nothing in my experience suggests that mixing methods in these environments presents additional difficulties. However, my experience outside Anglo-Saxon cultures is limited.

The cases have been introduced in chronological order to allow the development of intervention competence to be assessed. The development of my competence can be traced on the simple two by two matrix shown in Figure 2.4. At the start of my career I engaged in exploratory investigations using hard methods. In consultancy I continued to deploy hard methods but the interventions had to be planned more thoroughly. While in consultancy I started to use soft methods, albeit in a planned way. In academia I have used the soft methods in an exploratory fashion. At each transition from one quadrant of the matrix to another new competences were required. First, to get on the matrix at all, I had to learn the traditional techniques of OR and develop some craft skills of the OR practitioner. Second, I had to learn how to plan effective interventions. Then I had to learn how to plan and facilitate soft OR approaches. Finally, I had to understand the deployment and use of the soft systems well enough to recognise when and how to deploy them in an exploratory investigation. At each stage I perceived myself to be addressing managerial issues from a broad perspective rather than simply solving technical problems. The move to a more facilitative role was one of degree rather than kind. I have never found switching paradigms to be an issue in practice. It always was necessary both to listen to what people say and to look at the factual evidence. The shift in perspective is rather different. In the earlier cases I saw it as my role to pursue the facts and to test the views offered. From the evidence I obtained, and my analysis of the evidence, I offered options and my evaluation of their relative merits. It is then up to the client to take decisions. As a facilitator I see it as my role to ensure that the ownership of

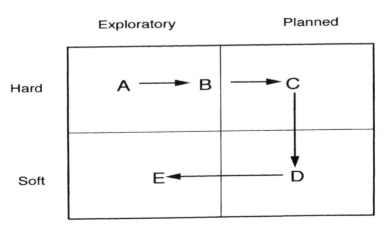

Figure 2.4 Competence development

facts lies with the participants. They must form a view. If they disagree among themselves, they need to resolve the issue by whatever means they find convincing. At the end of the day they have to find a way forward on the basis of what they each believe to be the case. It is my role to design and facilitate a process to bring that about. If that process should require some hard analysis, I am happy to guide such analysis if it lies within my competence. If I feel unable to help I point them to someone else with the appropriate expertise.

The two by two matrix in Figure 2.4 draws attention to the fact that hard approaches can be applied in an exploratory intervention, the result being rather soft in appearance; equally soft approaches can be deployed within a planned intervention, giving a rather hard appearance. It is more usual to think of hard approaches being applied in a planned, methodical way and soft approaches being applied in a looser, more exploratory way. This has not been my experience, as the cases illustrate. The failure of the advocates of soft OR to appreciate the soft, exploratory characteristics of much traditional OR has, I believe, caused misunderstanding.

In designing an intervention an understanding of competence, in other words what is possible, has to be married with an understanding of the intervention transformation required and its context. This understanding needs to be elicited from those involved. Usually this is achieved through discussions with the client. Alternatively it can involve a process of enquiry, forming the first phase of the project. It is very likely that the intervention will be easier to understand and manage if broken up into project phases. The design challenge is to structure the intervention into phases, each with a defined transformation that can be achieved using methods within the competence of the consultant and client participants. In choosing the methods, frameworks such as the system of systems methodologies of Jackson and Keys (1984) can be used or a set of criteria can be developed based on the transformation required and the context. My own preference is to take an eclectic view, mixing methods and parts of methods at will.

Once designed, the intervention is conducted. When the intervention is completed the consultant takes stock of what he or she has learnt, updating the list of intervention competences. The cycle continues from intervention to intervention as illustrated in Figure 2.5. I refer to this as the transformation-competence model (TCM) of the intervention process (Ormerod, 1997), a model based on reflection on practice. This is the model that I now use to design interventions. During the intervention design hard methods (clay) may be embedded in soft methods (plastic) and both must be embedded in a process management based on the craft skills of OR (the putty).

As more OR consultants learn both hard and soft methods the issue of choosing methods and mixing them to support an intervention comes to the fore. In my experience, as I have tried to illustrate in the seven cases in this chapter, there should be no qualms about mixing methods. Indeed, I would

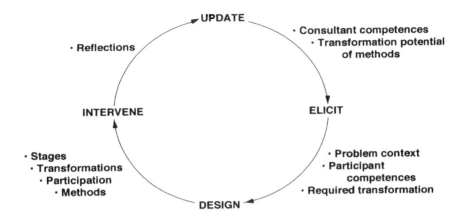

Figure 2.5 The transformation-competence model

encourage OR consultants to adopt an eclectic approach. The key is to hone one's craft skills, learn a number of methods and note when and where they seem to work.

REFERENCES

Ackoff, R.L. (1979a). The future of operational research is past. *Journal of the Operational Research Society*, **30**, 93–104.

Ackoff, R.L. (1979b). Resurrecting the future of operational research. *Journal of the Operational Research Society*, **30**, 189–199.

Beer, S. (1975). *Platform for Change*. Wiley, Chichester.

Beer, S. (1979). *The Heart of Enterprise*. Wiley, Chichester.

Beer, S. (1981). *Brain of the Firm*. Wiley, Chichester.

Beer, S. (1985). *Diagnosing the System for Organisation*. Wiley, Chichester.

Bennett, P.G. (1985). On linking approaches to decision-aiding: issues and prospects. *Journal of the Operational Research Society*, **36**, 659–670.

Breure, A. and Hickling, A. (1990). Coping with unconventional projects: a "socio-technical" approach. In R. Garies (ed.) *Handbook of Management Projects*. Manz, Vienna.

Boothroyd, H. (1978). *Articulate Intervention: The Interface of Science, Mathematics and Administration*. Taylor and Francis, London.

Checkland, P.B. (1981). *Systems Thinking, Systems Practice*. Wiley, Chichester.

Checkland, P.B. (1985). From optimisation to learning: a development of systems thinking for the 1990s. *Journal of the Operational Research Society*, **36**, 757–767.

Clark, D.N. and Scott, J.L. (1995). Strategic level MS/OR tool usage in the United Kingdom: an empirical survey. *Journal of the Operational Research Society*, **46**, 1041–1051.

De Bono, E. (1985). *Conflicts: A Better Way to Resolve Them, Six Thinking Hats*. Penguin, London.

Eden, C. and Jones, S. (1984). Using repertory grids for problem construction. *Journal of the Operational Research Society*, **35**, 779–790.

Eden, C., Jones, S. and Sims, D. (1983). *Messing about in Problems*. Pergamon, Oxford.

Friend, J.K. and Hickling, A. (1987). *Planning under Pressure: The Strategic Choice Approach*. Pergamon Press, Oxford.

Howard, J.V. and Ormerod, R.J. (1977). Models of colliery organisational systems. Invited paper at the Royal Statistical Society Industrial Application Section and Research Conference, UMIST.

Jackson, M. and Keys, P. (1984). Towards a system of systems methodologies. *Journal of the Operational Research Society*, **35**, 473–486.

Miles, R. (1988). Combining "hard" and "soft" systems practice: grafting or embedding. *Journal of Applied Systems Analysis*, **15**, 55–60.

Miles, R. (1992). Combining "hard" and "soft" systems practice: grafting and embedding revisited. *Systemist*, **14**, 62–66.

Mingers, J. (1992). SSM and information system: an overview. *Systemist*, **14**, 82-88.

NGC (1981). The National Grid Company "A Blueprint for the Future". NGC publication.

Ormerod, R.J. (1983). Corporate planning and the use of operational research at the National Coal Board: a personal view. *Journal of the Operational Research Society*, **34**, 461–467.

Ormerod, R.J. (1993). The role of OR in strategy development. *ORiON*, **9**, 71–87.

Ormerod, R.J. (1995a). Putting soft OR methods to work—information systems strategy development at Sainsbury's. *Journal of the Operational Research Society*, **46**, 277–293.

Ormerod, R.J. (1995b). The role of OR in systems strategy development. *International Transactions in Operational Research*, **2**, 17–27.

Ormerod, R.J. (1996a). On the nature of OR—entering the fray. *Journal of the Operational Research Society*, **47**, 1–17.

Ormerod, R.J. (1996b). Information systems strategy development at Sainsbury's supermarkets using "Soft" OR. *Interfaces*, **26**, 102–130.

Ormerod, R.J. (1997). The design of organisational intervention; choosing the approach. *Omega* (forthcoming).

Ormerod, R.J. and McLeod, J. (1983). The development and use of the NCB strategic model. *The Statistician*, **33**, 35–49.

Pidd, M. and Woolley, R.N. (1980). A pilot study of problem structuring. *Journal of the Operational Research Society*, **31**, 1063–1068.

Ward, J., Griffiths, P. and Whitmore, P. (1990). *Strategic Planning for Information Systems*. Wiley, Chichester.

Analysing Litigation and Negotiation: Using a Combined Methodology

PETER BENNETT, FRAN ACKERMANN, COLIN EDEN AND TERRY WILLIAMS

INTRODUCTION

Background

This chapter is based on some consultancy work by members of Strathclyde University's Management Science Department, in the course of which several different types of model were used in combination. We will provide an overview of the work, though certain aspects of the case are disguised in order to respect commercial confidentiality. From it we draw some conclusions—supported by work on this and other projects—about the issues involved in combining methods successfully.

The client for this work, Bravo plc[1], had been involved in a major construction project, at the time close to completion. As happens often enough, the project had gone both over time and substantially over budget, and

---

[1] All names have been changed to respect confidentiality. We have applied the methods described here in the combination outlined, but the description has been simplified and details changed at various points. In addition, the material illustrating the various models used is not necessarily all drawn from the same case.

Multimethodology: The Theory and Practice of Combining Management Science Methodologies.
Edited by John Mingers and Anthony Gill.
© 1997 John Wiley & Sons Ltd.

responsibility for this was disputed. Specifically, Bravo was in dispute with its customer, Cyclops Projects, claiming that Cyclops had acted unreasonably in various ways, for example in changing its requirements at the last minute, and in failing promptly to provide information vital to Bravo's own project management. Bravo was in the process of preparing a legal claim for compensation. The sums of money at this stage were large, at least for the litigants, and the case was expected to be vigorously contested.

In the course of our work, *cognitive mapping* was used throughout as a problem-structuring method, combined (in the earlier stages) with *conflict analysis* of Bravo's negotiations with its customer and (later on) with *system dynamics* (SD) to help quantify the compensation claim. Other papers have described the combination of mapping with each of the other two approaches in various contexts—notably Huxham and Bennett (1985) on mapping and conflict analysis, and Eden, Jones and Sims (1983) and Ackermann, Eden and Williams (1997) on mapping and SD. Many of the issues raised there, and in more general discussions such as Bennett (1985), remain relevant here. In involving both the use of complementary problem-structuring methods and linkage across the so-called "hard–soft" divide, this paper highlights some significant further points about the development of "multimethodology".

The remainder of this section will outline our involvement at the start of the consultancy project. The second and third sections will then describe its two main phases. The first involved the parallel use of cognitive mapping and conflict analysis as problem-structuring methods, the second the development of a quantitative SD model based on the cognitive maps. The fourth section will then draw on this experience and others in discussing the combined use of methods.

Management Science gets Involved

The initial approach from Bravo was based on their own interest in the possible use of Management Science/OR to quantify the compensation claim and validate their own analysis of the history of the project—largely because they were aware of relevant precedents for the successful use of OR models in such a role (e.g. Cooper, 1980; Weil and Etherton, 1990). Specifically, system dynamics modelling was expected to play a significant role in demonstrating how problems with different activities within the project had impacted on each other—such effects often being non-linear and difficult to quantify (Nahmias, 1980). It was also recognised that considerable problem-structuring expertise would be needed in order to bring SD modelling to bear in a credible way. Clarity of problem structuring was vital, as any models produced would have to be comprehensible not only to the clients within Bravo, but to many other relevant actors. Should the case go to court, it was expected that expert witnesses in fields such as design engineering, operations management, and process engineering would be called on to validate various aspects of the model, and indeed that the model would have to be clear and convincing to a judge in court. On top of this, the calibration of any quantitative model would be crucial. As part of the adversarial process, both the internal logic of the model and the assumptions fed into it would inevitably be subject to determined attack. Indeed, those of us involved at the start of the project were initially sceptical as to whether SD models could be made sufficiently "robust" in this sense, as the existence of multiple feedback loops tends to make conclusions highly sensitive to apparently minor changes in assumptions. This scepticism reflected the prior experience of one of the present writers in this field, and is based on concerns expressed by others such as Alonzo (1968) and Berlinski (1976).

At this point it was also not clear whether the case would actually get to court. Though much effort was already going into preparing to fight the case, an out-of-court settlement was still hoped for. This situation recurred throughout the project. Sometimes explicitly, sometimes implicitly, a process of *negotiation* was in train, and the legal preparations could be seen as just one tactic—albeit an important one—within this process.

Following an initial meeting with key members of the client team, the decision was made to start off by building qualitative models, using cognitive mapping as an exploratory tool. This left open the question of later quantification, though previous work (Eden, Jones and Sims, 1983) had already established mapping as an appropriate precursor to SD modelling. At the same time, another part of the exercise would be to model the negotiation process itself, using methods of conflict analysis based loosely on Game Theory.

COGNITIVE MAPPING PLUS CONFLICT ANALYSIS

Mapping the Course of the Construction Project

Cognitive mapping is essentially a means of modelling subjective reasoning, based on the psychology of "personal construct theory" (Kelly, 1955). A map is made up of constructs linked by arrows, expressing particular lines of argument about cause and effect (or means and ends)—"this leads to that, which leads to both *that* and *that* . . .". An example appears in Figure 3.1. Mapping aims to capture each individual's knowledge and "wisdom" in a natural and transparent way, complete with its nuances and complexities. In practice, a map will generally reveal a richly connected network of arguments, with multiple causality. Frequently, one also finds feedback loops expressing a perception of "vicious or virtuous circles". The use of mapping as part of the decision support methodology described here has been pioneered by Eden (1988), and applications have been widespread. When used in this way, it is important to stress the deliberately subjective nature of the exercise: a map is

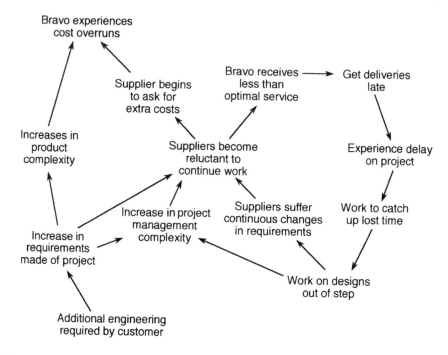

Figure 3.1 Cognitive maps are representations of the various chains of argument presented. As such they take the form of a directed graph where the arrows denote causal relationships and can be interpreted as "may lead to". Each idea (or construct) can have multiple causes (arrows into it) and outcomes (arrows departing) providing insight into their centrality and significance in the map—the more relationships the greater the significance. Therefore the figure shows an extract of a map illustrating a number of interconnecting chains of argument including a feedback loop. The bottom left idea (or construct) "additional engineering required by customer" can be seen as contributing to the "increase in requirements made of the project" which in turn causes "an increase in project management complexity", "suppliers become reluctant to continue work" and "increase in product complexity"—thus suggesting that in this extract it is reasonably central. The feedback loop focuses around the argument that if "suppliers become reluctant to continue work" then this may lead to "Bravo receives less than optimal service" which in turn contributes to "get deliveries late", "experience delay on project", "work to catch up lost time", "work on designs out of step" and finally "suppliers suffering continuous changes in requirements"—thus completing and exacerbating the feedback loop

intended to express a problem-owner's perception of the issues under discussion. The decision support methodology known as Strategic Options Development and Analysis (SODA) (Eden, 1989; Eden and Ackermann, 1997), moves beyond the modelling of individual perceptions to provide *group* decision support, an important element of which is the "merging" of individual maps to produce a group map. This is intended to serve as a jointly owned model for the client group, which is then refined and built on in group workshops. Specialised software, known as COPE (and latterly Decision Explorer) has been developed to allow maps to be explored, manipulated, merged and analysed as a visual interactive modelling exercise in which clients can participate fully.

From individual interviews to a group map

Following the initial meeting with key members of the client team, the first task was to model the views of the senior managers in Bravo most closely involved with the construction project. The focus would be on how the project's progress had been envisaged, and how and why it had been upset by the customer's actions. The results of this round of interviews would then be woven into a single computer-based model, and a series of group workshops conducted to validate and build confidence in this model. This would be achieved through exploring and reconciling conflicting views, determining the key causes of project disruption, and agreeing the key legally sustainable arguments.

From each of the interviews with the senior managers, a cognitive map was created. A typical fragment of such a map is shown in Figure 3.1. Because of the highly technical nature of the material and the need for accurate data, each interview was conducted by two members of the modelling team—one directing the interview and focusing on covering as much of the subject area as possible (while taking rough notes), the other taking detailed notes in the form of a cognitive map and only asking questions of a clarifying nature. In this way, we hoped to capture more effectively the subtlety of the information and arguments put forward, and to identify any ambiguities and contradictions. By working with—and comparing—notes from each meeting, maps of what each individual had said were drawn up.

The maps for each of the managers interviewed were then merged, using the COPE software, to create a model consisting of a *group* map expressing (as far as possible) all the material gathered. This group model—now containing several hundred concepts—was then analysed to find and explore significant clusters of argument, central concepts, and feedback loops (Eden, Ackermann and Cropper, 1992). As will be seen, the results of such analysis later played an important part in the construction of quantitative models. At this point, however, the main concern was to establish a qualitative model that could be agreed as an accurate record, showing the structure of the construction project, and tracing the sources and impacts of disruptions to its progress—especially those for which compensation from Cyclops was being sought. The initial group model was duly presented to the client group for review and further work over a series of workshops, the model being displayed on a projected computer screen, and extended and modified in "real time" as the discussions took place.

Validating the group map

So far, the modelling exercise had followed the standard SODA methodology in gathering individual perceptions and combining them into a group model. Now, however, the methodology was adapted to the specific nature of the consultancy task. It transpired that although our clients were quickly convinced of the *content* of the map, they spent a great deal of time debating its *structure*. In other words, there was little debate—except to clarify phraseology—about individual concepts: rather, discussion focused on how the concepts fitted together. This almost exclusive focus on structure is not normally the case when SODA is being used as a problem-solving methodology to help managers decide on future action. In this case, however, the aim was to develop a "forensic" model, setting out what *had happened* to the project and why. From our client's point of view, the key decisions now to be made were not about managing the remaining parts of their project, but about which arguments about past events could be used in the claim against Cyclops. In this context, checking the precise structure of the model was essential. Significantly, the members of the client team had had distinct roles in the project. Combining their different experiences threw new light on its history, producing a more holistic and detailed picture of what had actually happened. The extended discussions helped to provide extra information as well as validating the model with much more precision than is normal in SODA workshops. Additional interviews were also held with others in Bravo to clarify and validate particular aspects of the model.

Modelling Negotiation Strategy

In parallel with the work just outlined, we had undertaken to assist in the formulation of strategies for Bravo in negotiating with Cyclops. Methods derived from Game Theory—notably Analysis of Options (Howard, 1971, 1987) and Hypergame Analysis (Bennett, 1977, 1980) provide an appropriate format for this, given their concentration on examining the strategies open to each side. In practice, such methods generally go through two rough phases:

- *Problem structuring.* Faced with a complex "mess" of interlinked decisions, a useful first step is often to produce a broad "structured picture" of the relevant parties and the issues over which they interact. Various *levels* of decision within and between organisations can usually be discerned. Such diagrams form an agreed backdrop for more detailed analysis of specific decisions.
- *Formal analysis of specific issues.* The aim in this stage is to consider in specific terms the options available, and the consequences of particular choices by each side. Each actor's preferences are considered, as are the

possible effects of any differences in perception. Analysis allows one to draw conclusions about the stability of different outcomes, and about the bargaining tactics that might support alternative negotiating positions.

Small-scale models can be drawn out by hand, but increasingly user-friendly packages are now available (e.g. the INTERACT package, used here: see Bennett, Tait and Macdonagh, 1994). Their most important advantage is to allow a more flexible approach, in which assumptions can easily be discussed, modified as appropriate and explored within a revised model. Expressed in Analysis of Options format—more convenient in practice than the strategic form of classical Game Theory—the basic "building blocks" of formal analysis are as follows:

● The key *actors* (or "players"), with both a stake in the situation and power to influence it. Within the model, actors may be individual people, or groups or organisations.
● The possible actions or policies open to each, structured in terms of binary (yes/no) *options*.
● The *scenarios* (or "possible futures") that would result from different combinations of options being chosen.
● The various actors' *preferences* for these scenarios, reflecting their respective aims and interests.

This structure can be represented in the form of a *tableau*. An example— using a case with which many readers will be familiar—is shown in Figure 3.2. This particular model was generated in the course of some field research on the Northern Ireland conflict by the first author (Bennett, 1995). There are four (aggregate) actors, the Protestant and Catholic communities within Northern Ireland, and the governments of the UK and the Republic. Each has various options that can be taken up or not: for example, P Comm (Protestant Community) may or may not "Supp PShare" (short for "Support Power-Sharing"). Options taken up or not are given a tick or cross respectively, so that each scenario or "possible future" is shown as a *column* of ticks and crosses. For example, the first column represents a "unification" scenario in which the UK would withdraw and the Republic accept responsibility for the former province, none of the other options being implemented. The preference order for any given actor can be shown simply by arranging the columns, more preferred (by convention) to the left. The ordering shown for illustration was suggested by one source for the Catholic community.

Analysis helps to clarify how the actors are likely to respond to each other's moves. It will also show which scenarios are *stable*. That is, they may

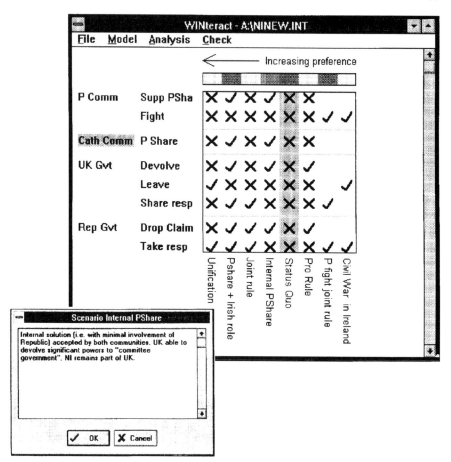

Figure 3.2 Tableau for Northern Ireland analysis showing a typical INTERACT screen (Windows version). Scenarios are displayed in preference order for the highlighted actor, in this case the Catholic Community, more preferrred to the left. Also shown is a typical "details editor" for one of the scenarios. "Joint rule" means that the two governments agree to govern jointly (in this case without an *internal* power-sharing agreement); "Pro Rule" means that power is devolved within the UK to an assembly dominated by the Protestant community (as pre-1970). Note that this model was created in 1993, prior to the IRA ceasefire and subsequent "peace process"

be likely to persist, not because they are necessarily best for anyone, but because any attempt to move away is deterred by other actors' possible responses ("sanctions"). An immediate visual representation of such analysis can be given by drawing up a *strategic map*. Not to be confused with a cognitive map, this shows scenarios as labelled ellipses, and improvements and sanctions as arrows. An example based on the same study as before is shown in Figure 3.3, showing improvements and sanctions from the constitutional status quo.

The basic framework can be extended to take account of further sorts of complexity, for example where the parties may have *differing perceptions* of the situation (for example, they may see different options as possible, or misperceive one another's aims). Formally, one can replace the idea of a single tableau with that of a set of linked tableaux reflecting how each party sees the situation: this constitutes a *hypergame*. If the analyst is working—as here—with one party, one can combine a fairly definite representation of that side's "game" with "what-if" models of how others may see the situation. Comparing the results will be helpful both in identifying the most important uncertainties and in seeking "robust" choices. As will be seen, this was done in a semi-formal way in the case described here.

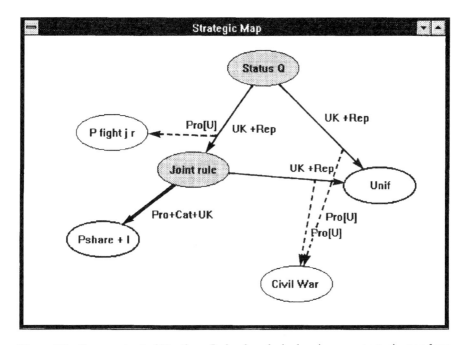

Figure 3.3 Some output of Northern Ireland analysis showing one strategic map from the model in Figure 3.2. Starting from the status quo, the UK and Republic governments could impose joint rule. Against this, the Protestant community has the sanction of "fight", though (with the preferences in this model) this is an *unwilling* threat. From joint rule, both communities and the UK government would prefer a joint move to "Power-sharing with an Irish role". From both "Status quo" and "Joint rule" the two governments have joint improvements to "Unification": in each case the Protestant community can unwillingly threaten an all-Ireland civil war

Structure of the negotiations

Modelling the negotiation was carried out separately from the *cognitive mapping* exercise (see page 64), for reasons discussed in the fourth section. The most significant actors and issues identified are depicted—with some changes to preserve confidentiality—in Figure 3.4. As is usually the case, this was not just a simple two-sided dispute. The eventual operator of the facility under construction (here called Abacus Inc.) had initially raised the finance for the project, largely from bank loans. Abacus had then commissioned Cyclops Projects as "main contractor" to organise and implement the completion of the project. While Cyclops had undertaken a good deal of the work itself, it had contracted out many other parts of the project to other companies including our client Bravo. These in turn had allocated some of the work to subcontractors, and so on. All this is typical of projects involving—as this one did—mixed technologies and expertise.

The cost overruns on the project had thus triggered a cascade of disputed claims, as (sub)contractors attempted to recover the extra costs they had

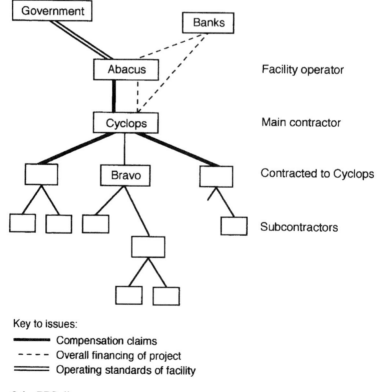

Figure 3.4 PPS diagram

incurred from their customer at the next level up the chain. These claims were logically interdependent, in that settlement of any one would create precedents relevant to the others. Perhaps more importantly, the claims were also financially interlocked, since a significant source of the money required to make the payments envisaged in the major claims were the banks who had provided the initial finance to Abacus. Thus, for a party some levels down the chain, receiving significant additional payment would require more than the existence of a good case against its immediate customer. The latter would only be able to meet the claim by successfully pursuing a claim against *its* customer, and so on up the chain to Cyclops and thence to Abacus, which in turn would have to negotiate for extra funding from the banks.

Four further points served to complicate the picture.

1. Many of the parties labelled as single actors in Figure 3.4 were consortia of separate organisations.
2. Some of the banks funding Abacus had also provided significant finance to Cyclops. As shown in the diagram, there had also been a long-running issue between these three parties about the overall financing of the project, separate to but linked with the more specific disputes just outlined.
3. Cyclops Construction was providing a "turnkey" operation for Abacus. Once the project was complete, the facility would be handed over to Abacus, and Cyclops would have no further involvement with it. None of the other parties thus had any longer-term relationship with Cyclops to consider (or, of course, vice versa)—the maintenance of such relationships generally being a significant spur to the relatively amicable settlement of disputes (see e.g. Fisher and Ury, 1981). Many of the contractors— including our clients Bravo—did have longer-term interests in bidding for future work associated with the facility, for example maintenance and renewal of equipment. But these subsequent contracts would be negotiated with Abacus, not Cyclops. The widely differing nature of the "players" also made it difficult to apply unwritten but generally accepted norms of behaviour specific to a given industry.
4. Figure 3.4 also shows a government department as a significant actor. While not involved in the finance of the project, the government *had* had a significant impact on the progress of the project, by enforcing new and more stringent standards that had not been in the original designs. While such a decision might be understandable, the changing specifications had been a major contributor to project disruption.

Modelling the Negotiation

Initially, the INTERACT software was used "in the backroom" to structure actors and issues, producing an *annotated* version of the PPS diagram of

Figure 3.4. Similarly, a basic options tableau, with information attached to issues, actors, options and scenarios, was stored within the model. (A version of this model is illustrated later on.) This material was accumulated from a variety of sources, including our own background research, and selected elements of the maps. In the latter case, the maps were deliberately scanned for items relevant to—say—each side's preferences, rather than expecting such material to be identified from any formal analysis of the maps. As discussed in the fourth section, this fits in with a "twin-track" approach to combining problem structuring methods.

Although the negotiation model was of some use in helping us think about the context of the legal claim, we decided against introducing our clients to the notation used in the conflict models, as using multiple model types seemed liable to cause confusion. Nevertheless, one key client was sent a summary of material from the model in plain text, including options for the key actors (with commentary), and factors affecting each side's preferences. In this way, we were able to check our initial understanding of the issues. The INTERACT negotiation model itself was also discussed with a member of the legal team, and the material in it periodically updated in case an opportunity arose to use it "live" with our clients. In fact such an opportunity did come about, as a major decision about the negotiation tactics—which had been brewing for some time—came to a head.

Pursuing the claim: legal versus commercial arguments

As already noted, it was far from certain that Bravo's case would go all the way to court. Indeed, there were good reasons for trying to avoid this. One was that the cost of pursuing the case would be considerable. While some costs had already been "sunk" in preparing the case, the expenses would rise sharply once hearings actually began. Perhaps more importantly, the court case would not necessarily provide a quick resolution: hearings would be likely to last many months, while an appeal could go on for years.

Further, the "culture" within Bravo was predominantly that of an engineering concern, and management's prior experience of negotiations, though in some cases considerable, was with "company-to-company" issues. There was frequently tension between what the clients "knew" to be true about their project and the lawyers' advice as to what could be proven legally. Even if these tensions were creative, debate could nevertheless become quite heated.

Thus far, being seen to spend time and money on preparing the legal case had served a dual purpose: as well as improving the chances of success should the case actually go to court, it also provided a way of demonstrating resolve. However, this was not the only pressure Bravo could bring to bear on the other key parties. Independently of the legal claim, Bravo could employ a "commercial argument" in trying to obtain a settlement. The items being supplied by Bravo were vital to the profitable use of the facility. *None of the parties involved in the project*—the operator, the various contractors or the banks—could hope to recoup their costs until Bravo delivered. In fact, few of the items had yet been handed over. Our client was thus in physical possession of vital goods, in principle a strong negotiating asset.

To make use of this position, various tactics were (at least in principle) possible. Outright refusal to continue handing over finished goods would risk legal counter-action by the customer, in addition to known penalties for late delivery. Would the risk nevertheless be worth it? A less drastic alternative might be to slow production—one might legitimately run to a "least cost" production schedule rather than (as had been done so far) straining to achieve prompt delivery. Some of the most relevant options for the key actors were set out as in Figure 3.5 (some changes to the original have been made).

An immediate practical concern for Bravo's negotiators was the relative importance to be attached to such "commercial" ploys, vis-à-vis the preparation of the legal case. It appeared that their feelings about this balance

	1	2	3	4	5	6	"INFEASIBLES"
BRAVO							
Pursue legal claim	✓	×	✓	−	✓	✓	
Suspend delivery	×	✓	×	✓	−	−	×
Slow production	×	✓	×	✓	−	−	
CYCLOPS							
Offer settlement	✓	✓	×	×	✓	✓	
Sue for non-delivery	×	×	×	✓	−	−	✓
ABACUS							
Meet Cyclops' claim, seek funding	✓	✓	×	×	×	✓	✓
Pressure Cyclops to settle with Bravo	×	✓	×	✓	×	−	
BANKS							
Offer new finance	✓	✓	×	×	×	×	×
Pressure Cyclops and Abacus	×	✓	×	−	×	−	

Commentary on scenarios:

1: "claim succeeds" – Cyclops offers realistic settlement, and payment cascades downward
2: "payment under pressure" – commercial pressure "forces" Cyclops to offer settlement, banks agree new finance
3: status quo
4: "deadlock" – dispute escalates as Bravo uses commercial pressure and Cyclops retaliates (column shows one of several variants)
5: "Abacus refuses" – Cyclops offers settlement, but Abacus refuses to fund it (Cyclops unable to pay)
6: "Banks refuse" – Cyclops, Abacus and Bravo reach agreement, but banks refuse funding to implement it

Figure 3.5 Tableau showing examples of possible scenarios (in decreasing preference order for Bravo)

could change rapidly. Our direct use of negotiation analysis was prompted by a sharp swing away from preparing the legal case (one had a sense of our clients having become exasperated with legal arguments at this point), toward reliance on the commercial argument—perhaps even sole reliance. Suddenly, attention switched to the negotiation model.

As a negotiating tactic, the "commercial" argument clearly had some attractions. Nevertheless, our own appreciation of the issue suggested that to pursue this avenue on its own—to the detriment of legal preparations—would be risky, for at least three reasons:

- Bravo's "commercial pressure" would only have a real impact if and when all *other* parts of the project were complete. Having to wait for one contractor to complete is of little consequence if the customer is anyway waiting for another. It was not clear that Bravo would in fact be "last to deliver".
- It was not clear that Bravo could delay delivery of goods in face of counter-pressures from its customer: the proposed strategy effectively presumed an ability to hold out longer in a "chicken" game.
- The commercial argument relied primarily on Bravo's power to delay profitable operation of the whole facility, rather than putting direct pressure on Bravo's own customer. Its effectiveness relied on the assumption that those who would lose most from such delay (primarily Abacus and the banks) could in turn exert enough pressure on parties "down the chain" to persuade them to settle the dispute. However, this was not self-evidently the case.

A session with the chief negotiator, in which we had agreed to run critically through possible choices of strategy, provided the opportunity to air these and other concerns. Given that the session had to be fitted into a fairly brief "window of opportunity", we decided against introducing the tableau model itself. Instead, we built up a strategic map of the situation in front of him, starting from the current situation and setting out possible moves, responses, sanctions and so on.[2] Each aspect in the map was discussed as it was drawn up, and modifications were made at several points. The result was similar to that shown in Figure 3.6, with some changes to preserve confidentiality.

This "on-the-hoof" modelling provided a vehicle for suggesting which were the most critical assumptions underlying alternative choices of strategy, and discussing the confidence with which such assumptions could be made—an exercise in surfacing assumptions somewhat in the spirit of the SAST approach (Mason and Mitroff, 1981), though differing as to specific methods.

---

[2] Though based on a model built up using INTERACT, the map itself was drawn up on flip chart, using card ellipses to represent the scenarios. (The INTERACT software generates strategic maps, but only via the options tableau. Subsequent to this project, software has been developed to allow strategic maps to be drawn up directly on the screen.)

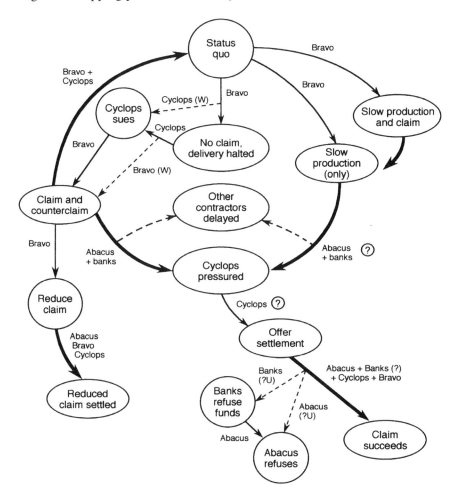

Figure 3.6 Diagram showing improvements between scenarios for single actors (solid lines) or coalitions (thick lines). Sanctions are shown as dotted arrows, W for "willing", U for "unwilling". All arrows are labelled with the actor(s) controlling the move represented. Note that this is a later version of the model, so scenarios do not all match those shown in Figure 3.5

Following the session, a modified version of the strategic map was sent to the chief negotiator. This incorporated both material arising from the discussion and some relevant contextual material taken from the group cognitive map. (Including the latter helped to provide some continuity between the different models presented.) Whether as a result of this intervention or not, Bravo renewed its determination to pursue the legal claim, with "commercial" negotiation continuing in parallel.

At this point, we had left the client with a self-contained "product"—mainly a fully documented set of COPE models structuring the legal claim, illustrating the relevant feedback loops, summarising the key lines of argument, and elaborating specific points in more detail. In addition, we had provided a brief summary of the negotiation analysis. In principle, our involvement could have stopped there had either we or our clients wanted. However, as Bravo pressed ahead with preparations for the court case, further work on this was invited. The decision was made to go ahead and build quantitative models to justify the claim in monetary terms. The work thus entered a new and different phase.

MAPS AND SYSTEM DYNAMICS

As outlined before, our clients' initial interest had been in the possibility of obtaining quantitative analysis to support their claim for compensation. As explained in the first section, they also started with a specific interest in the use of system dynamics models, based on their knowledge of relevant precedents for their use. Given our initial scepticism about the robustness of SD models in this role, we had so far—with their full agreement—provided the clients with qualitative analysis. At the same time, the modelling team kept the issue of quantification under review (discussing, as well as SD methods, alternatives such as discrete-event simulation). As work progressed, the modelling team became more confident that a credibly robust SD model could be built on the foundations of the existing maps, while the clients remained keen to have this done. The task of building such a model was therefore accepted, and consequently the emphasis of the consultancy project changed significantly. The new focus highlights some issues about the linkage of "hard" and "soft" forms of analysis. This topic is discussed further below, while the linkage of mapping and SD in general is discussed more fully in Eden (1994). Though building and validating these was now the main activity, subsidiary investigations of particular aspects of the claim continued (for example, there were further interviews collecting arguments to counter any claim by Cyclops that Bravo's increased costs were due to inadequacies in its own project management).

System Dynamics Modelling

System dynamics simulation modelling, originating in the seminal work of Jay Forrester, was created to help one explore the emergent, dynamic properties of complex systems. People often—it is argued—see events connected by one-way cause-and-effect relationships. They thereby fail to appreciate the holistic structure of the system and to understand the counter-intuitive aspects of behaviour in which the role of feedback is paramount (Forrester, 1961, 1971b;

Sterman, 1989; Richardson, 1991). In principle, the relevance of this to the disruption of a complex construction project was clear enough. Furthermore, advances in computer technology such as the *Stella* package[3]—which was used here—allow one to construct, test and refine complex models *visually*, and hence made them more accessible to non-specialists in SD.

Traditionally, SD modellers have usually sought to provide fully quantified and validated models (see e.g. Coyle, 1977). Recently, however, many practitioners have focused on the systemic *structures* within the system studied rather than on "the numbers" (Wolstenholme, 1993), and on the use of "archetype" models to promote organisational learning (Senge, 1990; Senge and Sterman, 1992). As system dynamics modellers increasingly emphasise the qualitative aspects of their methodology (Lane, 1992; Forrester, 1994), the approach starts to have more in common with "soft" OR. In this case, however, "the numbers" were of paramount importance in supporting a specific claim for compensation. The primary aim was to provide a "demonstrably valid" depiction of alternative scenarios for the progress of a real project—put crudely, *to be able to compare its actual progress with how it would have progressed, had Cyclops not acted unreasonably.* A model that could not recreate the actual progress of the project given the actual conditions would be untenable. Similarly, the model had to quantify the impact of different sources of disruption, responsibility for each of which would be determined by the court. Each individual relationship and value employed in the model had to be defensible in court. This necessity for an accurate forensic model placed this SD modelling exercise firmly in the realm of "hard OR".

To build the SD model required a representation of how the different parts of the construction project impacted upon one another (and hence the knock-on effects of disruption or delay of any particular activity), and of the incoming effects of actions under the control of Cyclops. In qualitative form, a prototype structure existed within the group map. What was now needed was to quantify the picture in a sustainable way.

Building an Influence Diagram

Starting from the revised group map, the first step towards an SD model was to identify all the feedback loops indicating mechanisms through which overruns had built up in the project, together with their immediate "drivers". Using COPE to analyse the map uncovered many significant loops, many of them "nested"—that is, with elements in common but nevertheless representing distinct effects. These clusters of loops were copied from the group map—leaving the map itself intact—and were then used to construct an intermediate

---

[3] Stella is a registered trademark of High Performance Systems Inc., Hanover, NH, USA. The package runs on Macintosh computers.

model in the form of an influence diagram. This differed from the map in showing the loops as *relationships between variables* rather than *concepts in lines of argument*. For example, the concept in Figure 3.1 "supplier begins to ask for extra costs" can be reworded as "additional costs demanded by suppliers", the point being that this is in principle capable of being quantified. It would not be sensible, or logically necessary, to rework every concept in this way. Concepts were therefore omitted which did not have any natural quantifiable equivalent, and which provided either contextual explanation or inessential links in a chain of argument (e.g. "Bravo receives less than optimal service"). The influence diagram was thus a "stripped down" version of the map, containing the set of loops that would represent the logical skeleton of the claim. For a fuller account of the principles involved in moving between these types of models, see Williams et al (1995b).

This influence diagram—an example of what Wolstenholme (1985) calls "qualitative system dynamics"—would then be used as a blueprint for the SD model. While not yet quantified, it provided the structure of variables and their relationships within which quantification could proceed. Meanwhile, the nested structure of the loops gave new insight into how initial disruptions led to escalating problems within the project. Where questions arose about the structure, references could be made back to the COPE group map, or the issue explored with the client group directly. At the same time, the process of constructing the formal SD model continued. Figure 3.7 shows a typical fragment of the SD model itself, dealing with the design stage of the project.

This modelling process was far from linear. As the SD model was built, constant reference was made both to the influence diagram and to the COPE group map to clarify the precise meaning of elements in the SD model. In some cases, information recorded in the SD model was insufficient, and was found to be in contradiction to the arguments expressed in the COPE map. In other cases the map also lacked the necessary information, prompting further meetings with the client group (and others in the organisation), using the existing COPE map as a familiar reference point. The results of such discussions were again incorporated "on the spot" into the COPE group map and thence (if relevant) into the SD model. Conversely, analysing the data in the course of trying to quantify the model sometimes uncovered flaws in the logic originally proposed by the clients. As these were resolved, the group COPE model was updated to reflect a deeper understanding of the issues involved. In this way, the different modelling formats enriched one another.

Refining and Calibrating the SD Model

Further work on the SD model now addressed three primary concerns. The first was that the initial model did not provide the level of detail needed to support a litigation case. This was resolved as new, and more subtle, theories

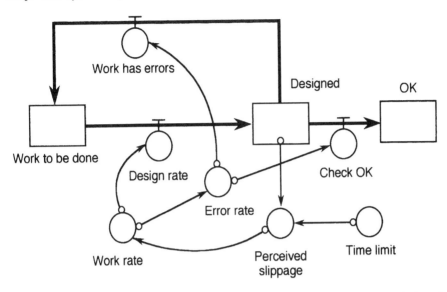

Figure 3.7 System dynamics diagrams are built around the ideas of "stocks" and "flows". This figure shows a stock (the left-hand rectangular box) of design work waiting to be done. The design work is done at a certain rate (the "design rate"), causing the work to flow (the thick arrow) into the stock of "Designed" work. This work is then checked to see whether or not it has errors: a certain proportion flows into the "OK" box and the remainder flows back into the "Work to be done" stock to be re-done. However, rather than simply using constant rates for these flows, system dynamics requires an explanatory model for the various parameters; these are shown by the "auxiliary variables" (circles) and the lines which show which variables have an influence on which. Thus, the rate at which design work is done is a function of the work rate, which itself is a function of the perceived schedule slippage, which is found by comparing the work designed with the time limit. However, an increasing work rate also increases the rate at which errors are made, which changes the proportion which will pass the error check

were discovered about the causes of cost and time overruns. As we tried to match the clients' existing knowledge to the quantitative data, implicit assumptions on the part of the managers concerned were uncovered, and both SD and COPE models updated accordingly.

Second, we needed to ensure that the version of the model incorporating Cyclops' actual impacts on the project "predicted" the project's actual progress. This was potentially of great significance. The SD model had to be built so that it could respond to many possible scenarios vis-à-vis findings on liability. For example, only some of Cyclops' actions might be judged "unreasonable" in court, and the SD model would have to be re-run to show the effects of those particular factors. Unless the model could be shown to predict the actual course of the project, why should anyone believe that modifying it would show how the system would have behaved under hypothetical conditions? By working to attain a reasonable match between model and reality, this issue (as well as the first) was progressively addressed. The "real-life numbers" used to evaluate the model also reflected particular interpretations of reality, and we were often presented with apparently conflicting data. However, multiple perspectives on supposedly objective data are typical, and can help to open up important aspects of the case. Here, having both the group map and the SD model helped set up a useful dialectic from which shared understanding emerged. Sometimes, the existence of alternative interpretations could be managed by finding emergent characteristics common to the different views. In other cases, resolution was achieved only after prolonged debate, sometimes with the use of auxiliary models (e.g. on spreadsheets) to explore the specific issue in question. Throughout, the guiding principle was the requirement for a "requisite model" (Richardson and Pugh, 1981; Phillips, 1984) sufficient for the purpose of making a credible case. In this respect, the legal concept of *best evidence* was highly relevant. In layman's terms, this means that one need only show, not that the data presented is perfect, but only that it is superior (or at least equal) in quality to any other available. Advice on the application of this principle was provided by Bravo's legal team, who remained involved in the modelling exercise throughout.

Third, some of our clients' perceptions appeared "illogical", in the sense of there being unresolved mismatches between the group map and the mathematical logic of the SD model. Such contradictions immediately prompted suspicion about the structure of the SD model, which was reviewed and revised. Occasionally, however, deeper investigation of the model's mathematical logic revealed arguments that were sufficiently compelling to alter the clients' view of the engineering project. In some cases, they concluded that the customer had been less (or more) responsible for problems than had initially been thought. Holistic properties uncovered by SD modelling thus sometimes supported a change in the claim. Often, discussion with the clients became extended and heated, with the modelling team needing to produce smaller OR models (including discrete-event simulation models) to show how their own logic worked. That there was heated debate was not surprising: the clients had good reason to be tenacious in their beliefs, having invested so much of themselves in the project. The debate usually resulted in further learning and an improved model.

In these various ways, confidence was established in two "base" models, one depicting the project as planned, the other depicting its actual course. The model was then run with assumptions set to emulate other intermediate scenarios, to track what would have happened had the project been subject only to some types of disruption. As explained above, these would provide the basis for the claim, matching the possible findings as to Cyclops' liability. Through the combination of the COPE group map to illustrate the feedback loops and the SD model to show their quantitative impact on each other, the clients were able to understand not only the dynamics of disruption and delay but also the methodology of SD itself. The result was to increase confidence that the SD model could be used successfully in court if necessary.

The Settlement

As the work described here proceeded, the deadline for Bravo committing itself to a court claim loomed. In outline, the legal procedure was as follows. First, Bravo as plaintiff, had instructed its lawyers to issue a writ to the court, which the court then served on the customer. As Cyclops declined to accept the claim, there was then a set period of time laid down within which the parties could continue to prepare their respective cases. By the end of this time, unless they had agreed a settlement, they would be committed to proceeding to court (at least, withdrawal would carry large costs). Also during this period, Cyclops would have the opportunity to see Bravo's provisional case, to examine and probe the underlying models for themselves. They could then decide what terms to offer in settlement (if any) having taken a view on the strength of the case facing them.

During this period, the essentials of both the COPE and SD models were thus presented at meetings involving key personnel from *both* sides in the dispute. There were two key meetings. In the first, the modelling work was presented in four stages:

- a simple diagram illustrating the principles of feedback loops, which was then overlayed with a segment of the SD model to demonstrate how the principles applied
- an overview of the key loops in the COPE model, showing the nested structure
- a portion of the SD model, explained in detail to show the process of quantification
- a section of a modified and extended COPE model, this time used to illustrate how two particular events in the project had affected variables in the SD model—this served to clarify how the COPE and SD models related to each other

The linkages between these different aspects of the modelling work, and the ways in which they supported the case, were emphasised throughout—for example, by colour-coding categories of concepts and variables appearing in different models. In the second meeting, the "opposing" team were able to test the robustness of the SD model in more depth by demanding various forms of sensitivity analysis. The COPE model was again used, however, to help interpret the types of change being explored and the results obtained from the SD model.

At this point, Cyclops shifted its position and made an acceptable offer of compensation. Bravo regarded the outcome as highly satisfactory, and our clients were clear that the modelling approach taken had helped significantly in achieving it.

ON COMBINING AND SELECTING METHODS

This section offers some methodological points about the combination of methods both hard and soft, drawn from this and other cases. Some are discussed in more depth in Williams et al (1995a, b) and Ackermann, Eden and Williams (1997), with which this chapter overlaps. The following discussion starts with issues about the combination of soft and hard OR, moves on to the use of different problem-structuring methods and concludes with some general comments about the selection of methods.

Using "Soft" and "Hard" Techniques

The virtues of "softer" methods in general have been much discussed: in general, a greater emphasis on problem structuring does extend the scope of OR in helping tackle "messy" issues (Rosenhead, 1989; Eden and Ackermann, 1997). However, this does not make quantitative analysis irrelevant. Many managers are confronted by issues that may well be messy, but which also have significant quantitative aspects. In the case just described, for example, it was clearly essential to provide a numerical estimate as to how big a claim was justified in different circumstances. By contrast with (say) a libel case, Bravo could not have gone to court demanding "a large but unspecified sum". As we have stressed, the SD model was not only a problem-structuring device but also a forensic model.

In this case, two points are noteworthy from a methodological point of view. First, there was an unusually close correspondence between the hard (SD) and soft (mapping) models (in fact, more direct than that between the maps and the conflict models). The possibility of moving from map to SD diagram is one that had already been explored, and a methodology for doing so established (Eden, Jones and Sims, 1979, 1983). The fact that the SD model was built directly from the group map made it easier to keep continuity in the material presented to our clients, the downside being a danger of carrying over any mistakes from one format to the other.

Second, although the maps preceded construction of the SD model, the latter did not supersede the maps. Rather than simply "front-ending" the harder models with the softer (then discarded), the two continued in use together. We believe that this had three significant advantages:

- *Expressing argumentation.* Despite the improvements afforded by modern visual representations, complex, highly quantified models can be difficult to follow. This was true of the SD model constructed here, not least because it eventually grew to contain several hundred variables. Navigating through this model proved very difficult, especially for those not familiar with the project or the modelling format. The COPE model, with its fuller descriptions and elaborated material, allowed one immediately to illustrate the meaning and context of any of the SD variables in an easy-to-follow form. The full chain of argument leading up to the "final number" could thus be clearly laid out. An "intelligent lay person"—including, in the context of this particular case, the judge in court—could validate the modelling procedure and understand the steps involved. Though the out-of-court settlement prevented this being tried out in court, it may well indicate that Cyclops' advisers were impressed by the clarity of the arguments they were about to face. Our general point is that continued use of soft models alongside hard ones can help make the products of modelling comprehensible to clients and other stakeholders throughout a project. This is not only important in the earlier stages of problem definition.
- *Keeping a record—for both clients and modellers.* The continual updating of the COPE model provided a record of how both our own and our clients' thinking had developed. This documentation was important for two reasons. First, it meant that the modelling assignment could be audited in full in out-of-court discussions or by the judge in court. Second, and of more general relevance, the record of the maps helped everyone—modellers, clients, other advisers, etc.—keep track of our evolving understanding of the issues. Throughout, the COPE group map was used as a knowledge repository and communication medium. Issues of concern identified by the modelling team would often be encoded in map form so they could be discussed in a consistent manner both within the modelling team and with the clients. In this way the continually updated group map acted as a Decision Support System to the modelling team as well as to the clients (Ackermann, Cropper and Eden, 1992).
- *Inconsistency and ambiguity versus precision: a useful dialectic.* While approaches such as cognitive mapping allow one to explore problems in a flexible and transparent manner, there is a corresponding danger of allowing difficult and complex issues to be stated in a vague, ill-defined way—so hiding the very problems that the OR intervention is attempting to clarify. Softer methods may not force clients to face up to implied or potential inconsistencies in their perceived "logic of the situation". In this case, for example, we were often presented with apparent inconsistencies: the views expressed by corporate and plant managers often differed both from each other and from available hard data. Continued use of mapping allowed one to record and explore these conflicting views within a group model, without

"forcing" one to choose between them. In contrast, the SD model could only support one view of the relevant parameters at a time—one had to state assumptions without ambiguity. The dialectic set up between the two types of model was actually very productive. As the SD model was built, the need to impose rigorous logic uncovered gaps in the group map, and vice versa. This constant re-examination and cross-checking of assumptions eventually gave both modellers and clients greater confidence in both types of model.

Despite the intuitive appeal of combining aspects of both soft and hard OR, it is not surprising to find combined use fairly rare in practice. Although OR students increasingly meet material of both types, subsequent professional practice tends to be dominated by whatever methods fit their personal style, are championed within their organisation, or both. By its very nature, this project forced the use of both hard and soft modelling methods, and juxtaposing the different rigours of each proved to be beneficial.

Combining Problem-structuring Methods

At least in its early stages, this project involved the simultaneous use of both Cognitive Mapping and Conflict Analysis as structuring frameworks. Again based both on this case and on others, we offer some comments on attempting to combine problem-structuring methods. As with combining hard and soft methods, the attractions in principle are considerable. In particular, a key issue is that of encouraging creativity. In this respect, models—soft and hard—have a double-edged role. By imposing structures on users' thinking and "forcing" them to address issues that might not otherwise have occurred to them, models may help increase creativity. However, creativity is limited by the mental framework imposed by the modelling method itself—implying that certain types of question will *not* be raised.

Each problem-structuring methodology will highlight certain features, and tend (at least relatively) to ignore others. For example, use of Strategic Choice (Friend and Hickling, 1987) will cause one to look out for, and emphasise, particular forms of uncertainty in the situation facing the client group. Adopting a view influenced by Conflict Analysis will—not surprisingly—lead one to look for conflicts with external actors: questions to the client will concentrate on trying to find out who the key stakeholders are, and what options and preferences they might have. Cognitive Mapping—being based more on a "theory of the mind" than a "theory of the world"—will tend to make fewer presumptions about the nature of the situation facing the client, but more sensitive to differences in problem definition within the client group. Taken as a whole, SODA has much more to say about the *process* of decision making than Conflict Analysis or (say) Decision Analysis, which start from models of the *structure* of decisions. In emphasising the concept of decision, *all* these approaches stand in contrast to methodologies—notably SSM—which take the notion of "system" as prior.

Rather than being incompatible with each other, these different methodologies can be seen as being based on *complementary perspectives*, in the sense of taking different slices through issues (and providing alternative forms of representation). One might therefore hope that exploring these multiple perspectives on the "same" situation can push creativity further. This view of the relationship between methods also suggests using a twin- (or multi-) track approach, with different representations developed in parallel, rather than trying formally to derive one model type from another. Such an approach was used in the project described here, and similarly in others combining mapping with methods including Strategic Choice (Matthews and Bennett, 1986), Hypergame Analysis (Huxham and Bennett, 1985) and Multi-criteria Decision Analysis (Belton and Ackermann, 1997).

Despite the attractions, however, combining methods raises some quite serious challenges. At a purely practical level, expecting clients to relate to different ways of representing issues risks confusion—though some may welcome variety. If different types of model are introduced at once, clients may be overwhelmed, while the sudden replacement of one type by another can cause an awkward discontinuity as clients wonder "what happened to" the former. It may thus be helpful to have one dominant format to which other models can be related. In the case described here, the mapping notation clearly formed the "basic currency"—one could always explain or clarify points arising from any of the other models by referring to a relevant map. Indeed, a case can be made for using mapping as a general method for expressing the argumentation behind *any* other type of model, including those originating within other problem-structuring methods.

At a more philosophical level, the point that each methodology has its own distinctive background and theory has been much emphasised (see e.g. Jackson and Keys, 1984; Bennett, 1985; Cropper, 1990; Tomlinson, 1990; Flood and Jackson, 1991; Brocklesby, 1995). Combining different "techniques" in a purely *ad hoc* way runs the risk of trying to use a method in a way that actually contradicts the assumption on which it is based. To quote Flood and Jackson (1991: 47–48).

> Different methodologies express different rationalities stemming from alternative theoretical positions which they reflect. These alternative positions must be respected, and methodologies and their appropriate theoretical underpinnings developed in partnership.

Accepting that each methodology is based on its own "paradigm"—in some serious sense of the word—has two important consequences for multimethodology.

First, it implies that there is no neutral starting point from which to choose one framework rather than another. This in itself undermines any attempt to impose any top-down formula of the sort "If it's a type A problem, choose method X". Whether it's "that sort of problem" will depend on how you look at it. What one can perhaps do is to try looking at the problem in several ways, to see what insights can be gained from each. This again suggests the benefits of multi-track modelling.

Second, however, even "trying out" different frameworks will not be easy, given the need to be thoroughly at home with the alternative paradigms. A key question is *how much* of the underlying theory one needs to take on board in order to make a "serious" application attempt. Some forms of "multi-methodology" seem to demand not only "literacy" in all the component methods, but also that one should uphold all their underlying assumptions. Is it asking too much for any one practitioner to have full "ownership" of more than one paradigm? Taking up this issue, Brocklesby comments (1995: 1290):

> Paradigm shifts do occur, but when they do it is often a painful experience for the individual concerned, as perhaps decades-old "truths" are discarded . . . Even if it were thought desirable . . . one has to question whether most systems people will have the inclination or the wherewithal to make these sorts of paradigmatic shifts at all, let alone on a regular basis.

The question of whether a synoptic approach—as distinct from a less-rigorous "toolbox pragmatism"—is actually feasible is taken up in further debate (Brocklesby, 1996; Ormerod, 1996). Without pursuing this in detail here, we have some sympathy with Brocklesby's position that theoretical literacy is required, but not "purism" in the sense of only using a method in exactly the way envisaged in some definitive account. There is room for creativity too. But still:

> If we are going to reject something—Checkland's "constitutive rules" for example—surely it is important to know what is being rejected, why it is being rejected, and it is important to know what it is being replaced with. (Brocklesby, 1996: 1320)

This is a position that might be called "reflective pragmatism", paying attention to theoretical underpinnings, while not regarding every aspect of some "standard version" of the methods—each of which itself tends to look less monolithic on closer examination—as sacrosanct. What is also clear, however, is that combining problem-structuring approaches may require as much "interdisciplinarity" as does combining soft with hard. In both cases, dialectic within a *team* of modellers can play a crucial role.

Choice of Methods

Finally, we offer some comments as to how particular methodologies are to be chosen in the context of a particular intervention. It seems helpful to consider this question in terms of two levels. First, what portfolio of methods might a modelling team consider bringing to bear? Second, how might one select methods from within the portfolio?

On the first question, choice of methods is subject to an overriding constraint of *competence*. Whichever theoretical framework is used, modellers engaged in consultancy must (as a matter of professional principle) be able to deliver a piece of work that stands up "in its own terms". Potential clients often come—as in the case described earlier—with quite clear ideas on what modelling skills they are buying. They may approach an individual consultant or a department on the basis of reputation, or through networks of experience precisely *because* they are in search of those skills. In other cases, clients come needing help *with a problem*, but little prior sense of what sort of model might help. Either way, one has to be quite clear what is potentially on offer. (If the modellers are actually using the work to develop a partly formed methodology, this itself has to be made clear.) Having a range of methods available makes no difference in principle to this point, which applies in just the same way as to a single methodology, hard or soft. To use a rhetorical example, if one is only competent to do LP, then that is what one should offer. Provided there are no misunderstandings as to what the client is getting, this may work perfectly well. Clients needing other sorts of modelling simply go elsewhere. (Many readers will, at some point, have referred potential clients to colleagues or to others on the grounds that "this really looks like A's area rather than mine)". A team with a wider range of skills and experience can accept a wider range of work, but still a limited one.

Within the "envelope of competence" of the modelling team, we would argue for a large degree of pragmatism. In particular, it may well be inappropriate to make a once-and-for-all judgement about which methods will be helpful. This in turn means that it may be helpful (if possible) to keep the composition of the modelling team itself under review. Like others in which we have been involved, the intervention described above went through several distinct stages, and the team made some important methodological decisions as it unfolded. We have commented on these as they occurred rather than (we hope) engaging in too much *post-hoc* rationalisation: certainly the final shape of the project was not completely clear at the start, nor could it have been. As noted before, those of us involved at the start had been somewhat sceptical as to how well SD could underpin a legally watertight case. This might be considered somewhat ironic in view of the direction finally taken. However, there is a case to be made for modellers being sceptical of the tools they use, rather than having too rose-tinted a view. They will therefore have rehearsed counter-arguments for themselves—especially valuable when the models are likely to be subjected to determined external attack. This experience, and others reported elsewhere, confirm our belief in the virtues of an adaptive, opportunistic approach, rather than a metamethodology which prescribes a "correct" combination of methods on one's first serious encounter with the problem to be tackled.

Even when the choice of modelling methods themselves is not in flux, cycling between different types of model can bring benefits unattainable by a staged process which fails to recognise continuous interaction between models. This is already emphasised *within* some methodologies—notably Strategic Choice (e.g. Friend and Hickling, 1987) and also SODA itself. We are stressing its application across different approaches. Cycling ensures that data are continually scrutinised and structures examined from a number of perspectives. This is particularly powerful with a modelling team with mixed backgrounds, as those familiar with the "other" method of working ask apparently stupid questions which in fact challenge (too) familiar ways of proceeding.

In conclusion, "multimethodology" is unlikely to become an exact science—nor should it be. While some rules of thumb about what works well may be evolving, choices of method will continue to depend on idiosyncratic combinations of factors to do with the personal styles and preferences of analysts and clients, the time available, gross characteristics of the "perceived issues", past experiences of all concerned, organisational cultures, financial and academic pressures inhibiting or encouraging collaborative working, and so on. Practitioners may need to keep a safety-net of more familiar ways of working at the same time as trying out innovative links. Nevertheless, we believe that such approaches can help develop OR practice more effectively than focusing narrowly on specific methods, thus helping to bring about better matches between problems, clients and methods.

REFERENCES

Ackermann, F., Cropper, S. and Eden, C. (1992). Moving between groups and individuals using a DSS. *Journal of Decision Systems*, **1**, 17–34.

Ackermann, F., Eden, C. and Williams, T.W. (1997). Modelling for litigation: mixing quantitative and qualitative approaches. *Interfaces*, forthcoming.

Alonzo, W. (1968). Predicting best with imperfect data. *Journal of the American Institute of Planning*, **July**, 248–255.

Belton, V. and Ackermann, F. (1997). COPE-ing with VISA—integrated support from problem structuring through to alternative evaluation. *Multi-Criteria Analysis Journal*, forthcoming.

Bennett, P.G. (1977). Toward a theory of hypergames. *Omega*, **5**, 749–751.

Bennett, P.G. (1980). Hypergames: developing a model of conflict. *Futures*, **12**, 489–507.

Bennett, P.G. (1985). On linking approaches to decision-aiding. *Journal of the Operational Research Society*, **36**, 659–669.

Bennett, P. (1990). Mixing methods: combining conflict analysis, SODA, and Strategic Choice. In C. Eden and J. Radford (eds) *Tackling Strategic Problems—the role of group decision support*. Sage, London.

Bennett, P. (1995). Modelling decisions in international relations: game theory and beyond. Mershon *Review of International Studies*, **39**, 19–52.

Bennett, P.G., Tait, A. and Macdonagh, K. (1994). INTERACT: developing software for interactive decisions. *Group Decision and Negotiation*, **3**, 351–372.

Berlinski, D. (1976). *On Systems Analysis*. MIT Press, Cambridge, MA.

Brocklesby, J. (1995). Intervening in the cultural constitution of systems-methodological complementarism and other visions for systems research. *Journal of the Operational Research Society*, **46**, 1285–1298.

Brocklesby, J. (1996). New methods for old: on the take-up of methodological complementarism. *Journal of the Operational Research Society*, **47**, 1318–1322.

Cooper, K.G. (1980). Naval ship production: a claim settled and framework built. *Interfaces*, **10**, 20–31.

Coyle, R.G. (1977). *Management System Dynamics*. Wiley, London.

Cropper, S. (1990). The complexity of Decision Support Practice. In C. Eden and J. Radford (eds) *Tackling Strategic Problems—The Role of Group Decision Support*. Sage, London.

Eden, C. (1988). Cognitive Mapping. *European Journal of Operational Research*, **36**, 1–13.

Eden, C. (1989). Strategic Options Development and Analysis—SODA. In J. Rosenhead (ed.) *Rational Analysis for a Problematic World*. Wiley, London.

Eden, C. (1994). Cognitive mapping and problem structuring for system dynamics model-building. *System Dynamics Review*, **10**(2/3), 257–276.

Eden, C. and Ackermann, F. (1992). Strategy development and implementation—the role of a group decision support system. In R. Bostrom, R. Watson and S. Kinney (eds) *Computer Augmented Teamwork—A Guided Tour*. Van Nostrand Reinhold, New York.

Eden, C. and Ackermann, F. (1997). *The Journey of Strategic Change*. Sage, Chichester (forthcoming).

Eden, C., Ackermann, F. and Cropper, S. (1992). The analysis of cause maps. *Journal of Management Studies*, **29**, 309–324.

Eden, C., Jones, S. and Sims, D. (1979). *Thinking in Organisations*. Macmillan, London.

Eden, C., Jones, S. and Sims, D. (1983). *Messing about in Problems*. Pergamon, Oxford.

Fisher, R. and Ury, W. (1981). *Getting to Yes: Negotiating Agreement without Giving in*. Houghton Mifflin, Boston.

Flood, R. and Jackson, M. (1991). *Creative Problem Solving—Total Systems Intervention*. Wiley, Chichester.

Forrester, J. (1961). *Industrial Dynamics*. MIT Press, Cambridge, MA.

Forrester, J. (1971a). *World Dynamics*. MIT Press, Cambridge, MA.

Forrester, J. (1971b). Counter-intuitive behaviour of social systems. *Technology Review*, **January**, 53–68.

Forrester, J. (1994). "System dynamics, systems thinking, and soft OR. *System Dynamics Review*, **10**, 245–256.

Friend, J. and Hickling, A. (1987). *Planning Under Pressure—The Strategic Choice Approach*. Pergamon Press, Oxford.

Howard, N. (1971). *Paradoxes of Rationality*. MIT Press, Cambridge, MA.

Howard, N. (1987). The present and future of metagame analysis. *European Journal of Operational Research*, **32**, 1–25.

Huxham, C.S. and Bennett, P.G. (1985). Floating ideas: an experiment in enhancing hypergames with maps. *Omega*, **13**, 331–347.

Jackson, M. and Keys, P. (1984). Towards a system of systems methodologies. *Journal of the Operational Research Society*, **35**, 473–486.

Kelly, G. (1955). *The Psychology of Personal Constructs: A Theory of Personality.* Norton, New York.

Lane, D. (1992). Modelling as learning. *European Journal of Operational Research,* **59,** 64–84.

Mason, R.O. and Mitroff, I.I. (1981). *Challenging Strategic Planning Assumptions.* Wiley, New York.

Matthews, L.R. and Bennett, P.G. (1986). The art of course planning: soft OR in action. *Journal of the Operational Research Society,* **37,** 579–590.

Nahmias, S. (1980). The use of management science to support a multimillion dollar precedent-setting government contract litigation. *Interfaces,* **10,** 1–11.

Ormerod, R. (1996). New methods for old. *Journal of the Operational Research Society,* **47,** 1317–1318.

Phillips, L.D. (1984). A theory of requisite decision models. *Acta Psychologica,* **56,** 29–48.

Richardson, G.P. (1991). *Feedback Thought in Social Science and Systems Theory.* University of Pennsylvania Press. Philadelphia.

Richardson, G.P. and Pugh III, A.L. (1981). *Introduction to System Dynamics Modelling with DYNAMO.* MIT Press, Cambridge, MA.

Rosenhead, J. (ed.) (1989). *Rational Analysis for a Problematic World.* Wiley, Chichester.

Senge, P.M. (1990). *The Fifth Discipline.* Doubleday, New York.

Senge, P.M. and Sterman, J.D. (1992). Systems thinking and organizational learning: acting locally and thinking globally in the organization of the future. *European Journal of Operational Research,* **59,** 137–150.

Sterman, J. (1989). Misperceptions of feedback in dynamic decision making. *Organizational Behaviour and Human Decision Processes,* **43.**

Tomlinson, R. (1990). Of tools, methods and methodology. In C. Eden and J. Radford (eds) *Tackling Strategic Problems—the role of group decision support.* Sage, London.

Weil, H. and Etherton, R. (1990). System dynamics in dispute resolution. In *Proceedings of the 1990 International System Dynamics Conference,* 1311–1324.

Williams, T.M., Eden, C., Ackermann, F. and Tait, A. (1995a). The effects of design changes and delays on project costs. *Journal of the Operational Research Society,* **46,** 809–818.

Williams, T.M., Eden, C., Ackermann, F. and Tait, A. (1995b). Vicious circles of parallelism. *International Journal of Project Management,* **13**(3), 151–155.

Wolstenholme, E. (1985). A methodology for qualitative system dynamics. In *Proceedings of the 1985 System Dynamics Conference.* Keystone, Colorado.

Wolstenholme, E. (1993). A case study in community care using systems thinking. *Journal of the Operational Research Society,* **44,** 925–934.

One Size Doesn't Fit All: Reflections on Using Systems Techniques in an Operational Setting

JEREMY BENTHAM

INTRODUCTION

There is a wonderful cartoon in the "Calvin and Hobbes" series by Bill Watterson where the young boy and his tiger companion discuss how the world system really ought to have been designed. Given the obvious quality of their ideas, they conclude that it is incredible that nobody has ever consulted them on the matter! Similarly, I suspect there are many novel perspectives and techniques for examining organisational situations which are rarely heard of outside the immediate group which developed them. I certainly cannot claim to have an overview of the bewildering array of available ideas and insights competing for management attention. Nevertheless, in recent years as a line manager and in staff roles in one of the world's largest business enterprises, I have made use of a small selection of so-called "systems techniques". Personal reflections on some of this practical experience, and the lessons I've drawn from it, will form the focus of this chapter.

Multimethodology: The Theory and Practice of Combining Management Science Methodologies.
Edited by John Mingers and Anthony Gill.
© 1997 John Wiley & Sons Ltd.

A number of different systems thinking concepts, methods and processes have been used by a variety of people in the Royal Dutch/Shell Group of Companies in the past two decades, and some of this work has been widely reported. It would be fair to say that current or former Shell managers and planners have at times been at the forefront of developments in this area. There has been a particular association with the techniques of Scenario Planning (Wack, 1985a, b), Mental Modelling (de Geus, 1988) and, to a lesser extent, Soft Systems Methodology (Checkland and Scholes, 1990). Prompted and encouraged by formal corporate planning processes, training and their use to facilitate dialogue on complex issues, these approaches are familiar to at least the more experienced and senior managers in the company.

While not always being used formally or rigorously, the techniques have helped to create a common vocabulary for strategic learning to support, for example, decisions on business direction and major investments in long-lived assets under conditions of often considerable uncertainty. In highly capital-intensive industries, it is a simple truism that the potential for success is founded on the quality of this type of decision. Putting the assets in place, however, is only the beginning of the story. They also have to be operated effectively, and linked flexibly into their overall business environment. Without this, the benefits accrued through strategic learning will be squandered. As almost anyone with experience in large organisations will testify, however, trying to establish effective learning processes in this operational area can be extremely difficult because of the large number of decisions, people and activities involved.

As a line manager at two European oil refineries in the early 1990s, I was involved with my colleagues in promoting, supporting and implementing a number of initiatives aimed at enhancing performance in such an operational setting. At different times, and in different ways, a cluster of systems thinking techniques was employed in this process, including systems dynamics (SD), soft systems methodology (SSM) and statistical process control (SPC). Some of these interventions would generally be described as successful, while the impact of others was negligible. As described in this chapter, however, where they were effective, the methods applied brought benefits not only from improving the analysis of specific issues, but also appear to have been associated with a general shift in attitudes, perspectives and behaviour in the part of the organisation into which they were introduced.

Introducing and applying systems methods in these circumstances was originally done in an *ad hoc* manner. The techniques selected were simply those with which I was personally familiar and judged potentially useful in isolation. The interventions became progressively more planned, however, as understanding and experience increased. Gradually, the insights born of initial applications were synthesised into a framework providing guidelines for subsequent activity and suggesting the characteristics of techniques which were likely to prove helpful as situations developed further. Much of the later work described below was consciously guided by this framework, and enriched it further. As well as prompting my initial use of extended statistical techniques as analysis tools, for example, it shaped the timing and style of the broader introduction of these methods to provide a shared vocabulary and means for addressing many of the complex situations we faced.

Of course, as a practising manager, my focus in applying any technique is on understanding and ultimately influencing specific situations, so it should be no surprise that context-dependency and change-management will be important features of the framework I will be describing. After giving an overview of some of my more relevant experiences, therefore, I will review them in the light of these considerations, and conclude by presenting some general guidelines for choosing and introducing systems thinking techniques as catalysts for behavioural change in an organisation.

SETTING THE SCENE

By the time I joined our large refinery near Rotterdam, my appreciation of various management-support techniques had been shaped by a number of experiences. In the mid-1980s, I worked in a large central office function which was reorganised according to principles developed through an extensive SSM analysis (see Checkland and Scholes, 1990). Following this, I was part of a team which reviewed worldwide information technology strategy in the company, and then had the opportunity to reflect on both these experiences during a year as a Sloan Fellow at MIT's Sloan School of Management. I concluded that behavioural considerations had received insufficient emphasis in the organisational analyses which had been performed and which guided management's attempts to promote change (see Bentham, 1991). Largely neglecting my own conclusions, however, I subsequently failed in my own attempts to introduce meaningful changes as a manager in a medium-sized refinery! Fortunately, this frustrating experience afforded insights into the operational culture and practicalities of refinery life which I was able to bring to my new role as a manager in the Rotterdam refinery.

Oil refineries can be immensely complex operations with multiple interactions between different production, logistical and commercial activities. The normal variability in activity, along with larger unexpected events, can cause ripples of disturbance to spread across many areas of operation leading to corrective actions which, themselves, have further implications. Although it is an unfortunate term to apply in the oil business, this can lead to what is best described as a "fire-fighting" mentality in which attention is continuously focused on dealing with urgent short-term issues. Insufficient consideration is then given to any underlying matters of which the immediate events are only a symptom, leading to further performance erosion and an increase in short-term issues requiring immediate attention. This sequence of events, along with various behavioural interactions, can be elegantly described using systems dynamics or other causal-loop mapping techniques, and leads to the formation of a stable "culture" in which the bulk of physical, mental and emotional energy is directed towards the "here-and-now". The need to break through these vicious circles and implement more structured approaches was recognised by senior management at the refinery. The question, of course, was "How?"

A FLAVOUR OF THE APPROACHES ADOPTED

In the period under consideration, a number of different steps were taken at the site to institute continuous performance enhancement. These included, for example, the ISO9000 certification of various parts of the business. It became clear, however, that one of the more formidable barriers to improvement remained the fact that a large number of different functional or operational processes are inevitably involved in each of the business processes. With the aim of clarifying and eventually restructuring such interactions, the concepts and methods of Business Process Analysis/Re-Engineering were promoted. Interestingly, the most immediately successful of the various pilot projects initiated was actually one of the more complex, as it crossed several departmental interfaces in very different parts of the business. It involved the commercial and customer transactions of the Trading department, the operation of logistics facilities at the refinery by the Oil Movements department, and the coordination and optimisation of these activities by the Economics and Scheduling department, where I was the relevant manager.

The team involved with this project began by developing a high-level overview of the logically necessary actions required to accomplish the chosen business goal. There were similarities, therefore, between this overview and the sort of conceptual models which result from applying Soft Systems Methodology (SSM). For those readers familiar with SSM, the main differences were that no explicit "worldview" or "root definition" for the model were identified and obviously, therefore, the potential value of investigating the implications of alternative worldviews or root definitions was not explored. An attempt was made to introduce the more general SSM process to the project group, but the relevance was not fully appreciated, and the focus remained on the overview or "Functional Activity Model" as it came to be known.

Each of the logical activities of the main overview was broken down into sub-activities and sub-models. It soon became clear, however, that an unmanageable proliferation of activities in ever greater levels of detail was going to emerge if this process was continued. To return focus to the most relevant issues, therefore, a previously prepared list of concerns was "projected" onto the activity model to highlight the areas where attention was most appropriate. Eventually three linked activities were selected for deeper analysis. Three teams performed detailed work-flow analysis in these areas, and then re-engineered, documented and implemented enhancements. Appropriate attention was paid to ensuring that quantitative feedback on the performance of the new processes was available and, to the satisfaction of all involved, improvements were quite evident.

At the same time, other methodologies were being introduced into the Economics and Scheduling department. From the world of Total Quality Management (see, for example, Grant and Heavenworth, 1988), statistical process control (SPC) run-charting was introduced to monitor deviations of actual plant, logistic and market operations from assumptions and instructions. This was the first time such techniques had been used at the site to focus on broader coordination and planning issues rather than individual well-defined technical production processes. As noted earlier, this was also the first time that the choice, timing and style of introducing a technique were influenced by considering the framework described later in the chapter.

Building on experience with the project outlined above, a functional activity model for the department was also constructed and developed into a handbook detailing activities, responsibilities, information flows, business controls, document controls and interfaces with partners in other areas of the business. This functional model was then supplemented with more general conceptual models based on service partnership and personal development perspectives. In preparing these, I used a more complete SSM approach to view our situation from a variety of perspectives, although it was not until much later that I began to coach others to use SSM themselves. These conceptual models had a rich influence on self-perception within the department through articulating a range of shared understandings of "what we were all about". As an example, a simplified overview of the service partnership model can be seen in Figure 4.1. The acceptance of this model legitimised, for example, the direction of effort towards improved definition and measurement of service transactions with our partners in a way which had not been possible previously when we defined our roles in purely functional terms as professional economists, schedulers, blenders, etc.

Causal-loop analysis and system dynamics concepts were the next techniques introduced into the department. Initial applications were confined to exploring tangible phenomena, but soon members of the department were including the impact of such subjective parameters as "anxiety" and "credibility" in their analyses, and explicitly taking these into account in their decisions and activities. At a later stage, training was requested and given in SSM and a number of techniques for surfacing and exploring the mental maps of different individuals.

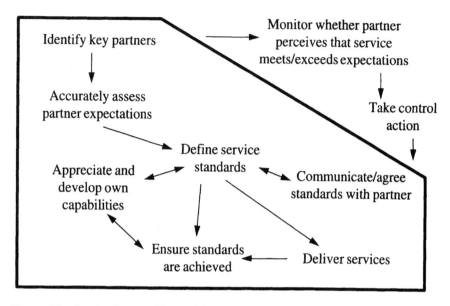

Figure 4.1 Service Partnership model

TRANSFORMATION!

One of the most exciting facets of these developments was the way in which an initial lack of interest, scepticism, and even resistance was gradually replaced by enthusiasm, imaginative application and curiosity about other "exotic" techniques. This was also accompanied by a shift in the climate of attitudes and behaviour. A calmer and more systematic approach began to be adopted in routine activities, and there was a widespread embrace of the quest for structural enhancement. There was also an improved level of understanding of the mutual roles, responsibilities and interactions of management staff and operational staff, an area previously characterised by information blocks and excessive intervention. As an example of the progress, the following is an extract from a presentation on the SPC philosophy prepared by members of the department and given to their counterparts in other departments.

"Management understanding" means "Better use of Management"

Employees: Duty to deliver information in understandable form.
Management: Duty to keep "hands off" if process understood and demonstrably under control.

Besides anecdotal evidence as above, the change in climate was also apparent from the results of an anonymous staff questionnaire. Although an important first step, however, the changes went well beyond this general improvement in the quality of working relationships. There was also a very substantial improvement in functional performance as determined by a wide range of measures (see, for example, Figure 4.2).

QUESTIONS RAISED BY THESE EXPERIENCES

It is almost self-evident that there should be a connection between adopting systems thinking techniques and a shift towards a more systematic and structured view of the environment. It is not surprising that the change in behaviour goes hand in hand with the change in perspective, and that they are mutually reinforcing. A more complex issue to understand, however, is how this virtuous circle was able to be initiated in the first place. A reasonable insight into the contributions of the various methodologies requires, therefore, some examination of the dynamics of organisational change which addresses the following questions.

1. Why were the changes embraced at this site and not in the very similar situation at the refinery in which I had previously worked?

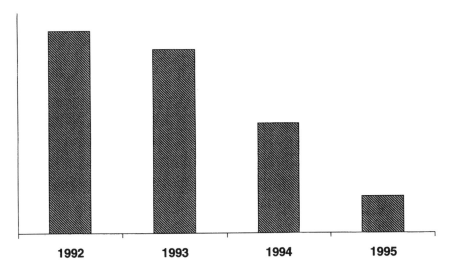

Figure 4.2   Unplanned excursions beyond stock warning limits

2. Why did the Economics and Scheduling department prove to be particularly receptive to these changes?
3. Which systems approaches were most enthusiastically adopted and why? Which methodologies complemented each other?
4. How did the factors build on each other, providing a path to accepting and embracing progressively more abstract and powerful perspectives?

In any kind of complex situation, a wide variety of alternative explanations is possible. Nevertheless, in what follows I have tried to encapsulate the quality of our own specific experience in a consistent way which draws heavily on frameworks derived from the literature.

STIMULATING CHANGES

On the basis of his extensive work on the culture of organisations, Schein (1992) describes the dynamics of change in terms of processes of "Unfreezing", "Cognitive Restructuring" and "Refreezing". To unfreeze the existing culture there must be a sufficient gap between performance and expectations to produce anxiety or guilt. This "disconfirming" data establishes the need for new learning and a redefinition of core assumptions. If and when such changes lead to performance enhancement, their validity becomes accepted and they will gradually become elements in a new cultural pattern.

As Schein (1992) and others have pointed out, however, it is quite possible for members of an organisation to deny the relevance or validity of disconfirming data for very considerable periods, for example by a process of rationalisation which essentially reduces expectations. In addition, the anxiety generated by the performance gap can completely arrest the required learning process because people become too insecure to conduct the experiments needed to generate fresh insights. The treadmill of "doing more of the same" while rationalising unsatisfactory performance becomes, therefore, a substitute for learning and adaptation. Making use of the "Eroding Goals" system archetype described by Peter Senge (1990), the dynamics of this process are illustrated in Figure 4.3.

For change to take place successfully, therefore, Schein (1992) points out that there must be undeniable evidence of the failure to achieve fixed goals and ideals, along with a climate of psychological security in which change can be contemplated without paralysis. Finally, there must be concrete experimentation based on trial and error or the adoption of new role models. This analysis is consistent with the insights reported by Kotter (1995) following an examination of failed transformation efforts.

These considerations provide a reasonable explanation for why the efforts to introduce change into a similar area at my previous workplace had proven

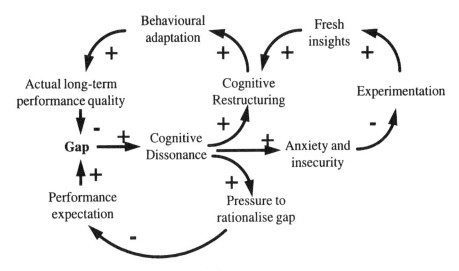

Figure 4.3 Eroding goals structure in change processes

to be largely unsuccessful. On top of my own managerial immaturity, the "case for change" had not yet been unequivocally demonstrated, and so there was little acceptance of the need for changes. More significantly, however, in the face of the performance difficulties which were recognised, a climate of anxiety and distrust had become established which undermined cooperation. Without patient attention to preparing the fertile ground of understanding and repairing previously damaged relationships, therefore, any proposed new working methods simply failed to develop strong roots, received little more than lip-service, and were abandoned at the first sign of difficulty. Early recognition of such organisational malaise is, therefore, essential, and I'm sure each manager will develop their own radar for picking up the signals. For your information, my checklist for recognising organisational character is reproduced in Figure 4.4, and is based on a management text which is now almost two thousand years old!

AIMING FOR THE "LEARNING CULTURE"

Once general organisational malaise has been addressed, however, further action may be required to ensure that the situation is ripe for meaningful learning and progress. The terms "Learning Culture" and "Learning Organisation" may be awfully over-used and abused phrases in current management-speak, but they do provide a useful shorthand description of what needs to be achieved.

Withered/Barren	Fruitful/Fertile
Hatred	**Love**
Discord	**Joy**
Jealousy	**Peace**
Fits of rage	**Patience**
Selfish ambition	**Kindness**
Dissensions	**Goodness**
Factions	**Faithfulness**
Envy	**Gentleness**
Fear	**Self-control**

(New Testament, Galatians 5)

Figure 4.4 Recognising "organisational character"

In considering this, I've again found it useful to follow the lead of Schein (1992) in characterising organisational culture according to a number of key dimensions, summarised in a self-consistent and reinforcing pattern of underlying assumptions. I have previously given an account of applying this type of analysis (Bentham, 1991), and there is no need to examine the methodology in detail at this point. As background information on the type of insight generated by this technique, however, I've included below my summary-level description of the underlying cultural assumptions which appeared to characterise the operational environment at the Rotterdam refinery.

- We are a major production facility in a tough environment. Our mission is to exploit our resources to fight the ongoing battle against the forces of chaos which face us on all fronts.
- We are a traditional hierarchy, and members are obliged to respect the implications of this. Challenge is acceptable, but only from those who have established a highly credible reputation.
- "Truth and wisdom" reside with those who have the most experience/seniority, and who are capable of assertively expressing and acting upon their private knowledge using whatever supporting evidence which might happen to be available.
- The strength of the organisation is "hands-on" expertise. Full membership is achieved through experience or the rapid assimilation of factual knowledge, and translating this into concrete action in recognised situations.

- Individuals have different innate potential for dealing with complex techni-cal, operational and man-management issues. This can be identified early and brought out through experience.
- Roles are well delineated and normally considered the "turf" of the indi-vidual. It is fitting, however, to continually challenge those who have not yet established credibility.
- External relations, and those between departments, are very sensitive with considerable potential for loss of "face". Hard-won credibility should be protected at all times, either by a vigorous response to threats or mutually recognised non-confrontation.

It is of value to compare some of the characteristics of the dominant refinery culture with those of a "Learning Culture" as described by Schein (1992). The dimensions where there appear to be significant differences are summarised in Figure 4.5.

To simplify matters, the most relevant characteristics can be distilled into two summary dimensions. The first of these distinguishes "fragmenting" and "integrating" perspectives, i.e. interpreting situations and events predomi-nantly as discrete and unique or linked and representative. The second makes a distinction between a natural tendency to interpret events from a "mechan-ical or objective" perspective as opposed to a "personal or subjective"

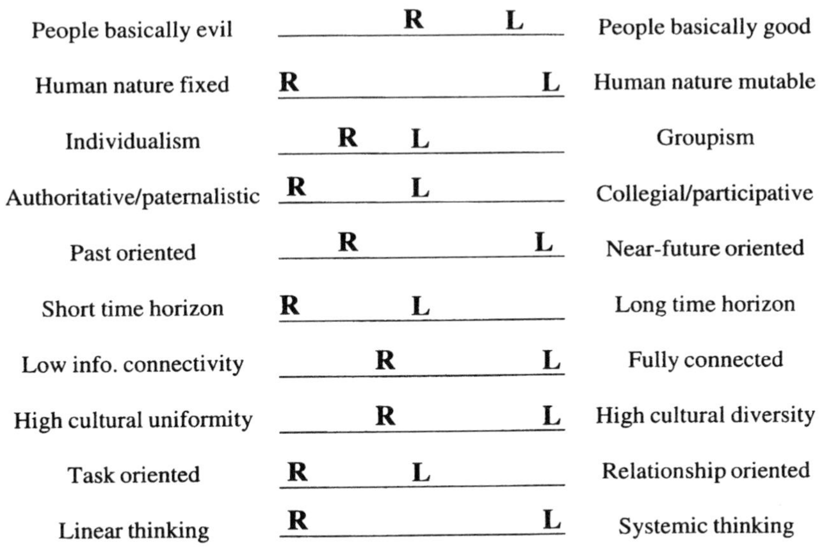

People basically evil		**R**	**L**	People basically good
Human nature fixed	**R**		**L**	Human nature mutable
Individualism	**R**	**L**		Groupism
Authoritative/paternalistic	**R**	**L**		Collegial/participative
Past oriented		**R**	**L**	Near-future oriented
Short time horizon	**R**	**L**		Long time horizon
Low info. connectivity		**R**	**L**	Fully connected
High cultural uniformity		**R**	**L**	High cultural diversity
Task oriented	**R**	**L**		Relationship oriented
Linear thinking	**R**		**L**	Systemic thinking

Figure 4.5 Deviations between assumptions/characteristics of refinery (R) and "Learning" (L) cultures

worldview. Based on the information summarised above, the underlying refinery perspective would be described within this scheme as "fragmenting". There is also a clear tendency towards the "mechanical" orientation.

In contrast, the learning culture described by Schein (1992) and others is relatively integrating on one dimension and more balanced between the poles on the other. The desired and, to some extent, experienced shift in cultural orientation can, therefore, be summarised via the illustration in Figure 4.6.

Using this framework, it is now possible to offer an explanation for the particular receptiveness of the Economics and Scheduling department to change. The cultural pattern illustrated previously describes the general orientation of the refinery, but within this there are a variety of nuances distinguishing different subcultures. The nature of coordination and planning activities, for example, promotes a more polychronic appreciation of the flow of time, a greater focus on the near future and a greater emphasis on relationships as well as tasks. Being closely involved with the very different worlds of refinery operations and trading, the members of the department also have a deep awareness of the very different perspectives which can be brought to bear on the same events and activities. In other words, the subculture found in this type of department is already one small step closer to the learning orientation than the bulk of the organisation and is therefore more likely to be responsive to the changes introduced. Of course, once a process of change becomes established in a part of an organisation having interfaces with many other parts, its influence can be far-reaching.

CUSTOMISATION, CUSTOMISATION, CUSTOMISATION!

As noted previously, the restructuring of assumptions which forms part of the change process is driven by fresh insights. Systems methods can obviously

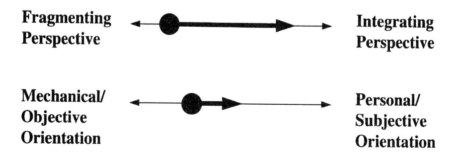

Figure 4.6 Desired shift in underlying orientation

play a role in this. In circumstances where the underlying perspective is predominantly fragmenting, experimenting with these methods can lead to a new appreciation of relationships between events previously treated in isolation, placing them in a context of causal loops and meaningful patterns developing over time. In terms of the framework which has been developed, this will tend to promote a shift of underlying assumptions in the direction of a more integrating perspective. Mental mapping and soft systems methodology also focus attention on the influence of perspective on interpretation and action, and can encourage a shift towards a more balanced position in an organisation with a predominantly mechanical/objective orientation.

To promote these changes, however, requires that the approaches are applied widely and regularly over a reasonable period. They need, therefore, to be accepted by the majority of individuals as relevant working techniques which justify the time and effort involved in learning how to use them. Half-hearted application is unlikely to be successful. In an operational environment with a strong orientation towards the mechanical and fragmenting perspectives, for example, the value of mental mapping and soft system methodologies is not likely to be immediately recognised. This was certainly my experience with previous attempts to introduce systems thinking via such methods. In contrast, however, if people perceive the relevance of an approach, they are more likely to apply it willingly and it is more likely to have a positive impact. In turn, this builds confidence and broadens horizons, enabling further approaches to be introduced, and so on. This dynamic can be described, therefore, as an engine of change contributing to the generation of fresh insights and the reduction of anxiety levels, as illustrated in Figure 4.7.

Although not normally considered a "systems thinking" methodology, the introduction of statistical process control methods provided the required "kick-start" for the Economics and Scheduling department at the refinery. The accent on measured, concrete data was compatible with the mechanical/fragmenting operational culture, while it encouraged the first steps towards an integrating perspective by highlighting trends, patterns and other systems properties. There was the further advantage that the style of data presentation was familiar to those working in a process industry. In addition, SPC made disconfirming data on performance highly visible in a non-threatening manner, emphasising the performance gap without undermining psychological security. Similarly, the construction of a functional activity model was directly appealing within this environment.

These first steps, therefore, were well matched to the needs of the organisation and paved the way towards experimentation with a sequence of increasingly complex and abstract methods which would have been considered alien and irrelevant in the original climate. Over the course of a couple of years, with different individuals progressing at different rates, there was a development from describing the world purely in terms of individual events

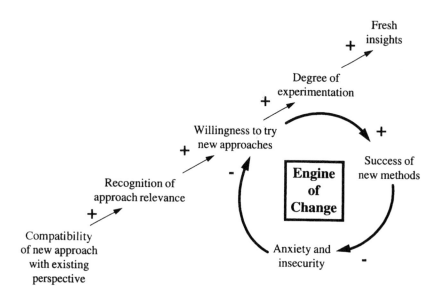

Figure 4.7 Kick-starting the engine of change

through to an appreciation of system archetypes and generic structured metaphors. Statistical methods, systems dynamics, cultural analysis and soft systems methodology all became accepted in the toolkit of the organisation, and each contributed to the desired broadening of horizons and shift in outlook.

A linguistic analogy is, perhaps, useful. To make a successful intervention it appears necessary to appreciate the distinctive "language" used by those involved in a specific situation, and to use this to create an initial shared understanding of that situation. This is often a struggle in itself because there may well be significant underlying differences in the interpretation of apparently shared meanings which may need to be addressed. Attempts to introduce change must, nevertheless, be comprehensible within this basic language, but once accepted will enrich and enlarge the vocabulary. This will enable more complex concepts to be explored and shared, leading to new experimentation and the opportunity to introduce still richer concepts.

FINAL REFLECTIONS

The lessons I've drawn from the experiences outlined above are summarised in the following recommended processes for introducing systems thinking (or any other) techniques as catalysts for behavioural change in an organisation (Figure 4.8).

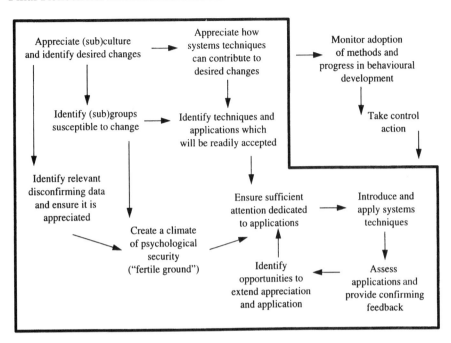

Figure 4.8 Introducing systems techniques

Quite clearly, this does not focus on the philosophical underpinnings of different methodologies, or the different types of issues they can be used to address. While these are interesting and important matters, most techniques are ultimately intended to enhance understanding and support action aimed at changing situations in practical ways. Instead, therefore, the scheme emphasises the broader context of change-management previously described, and the need to match initial approaches with existing characteristics and perspectives.

This scheme clearly suggests that the introduction of different techniques may well be necessary even when addressing superficially similar issues. Similarly, when behavioural change is the goal, I feel it is unlikely that any single approach will have the flexibility to be both culturally acceptable in the early phases of the change process and yet sufficiently stretching to promote a significant shift in perspective. A combination or sequence of techniques may well be more effective, as with the use of functional models, SPC, SD, cultural analysis and SSM described in this chapter. "One size" will certainly not fit all "customers" at all times, and the introduction of any specific methodology needs to be carefully tailored to suit the nature of the overall transformation which is being encouraged.

REFERENCES

Bentham, Jeremy, B. (1991). *METAPHORMOSIS: Transforming Structured Metaphors into Practical Management Tools.* Master's Thesis, Sloan School of Management, MIT, June.

Checkland, Peter and Scholes, James (1990). *Soft Systems Methodology in Action.* John Wiley & Sons Ltd, Chichester.

de Geus, Arie, P. (1988). Planning as learning. *Harvard Business Review*, **66**(2), March/April, 70–74.

Grant, E.L. and Heavenworth, R.S. (1988). *Statistical Quality Control* (6th edn). McGraw-Hill, New York.

Kotter, John P. (1995). Leading change: why transformation efforts fail. *Harvard Business Review*, March/April.

Schein, Edgar, H. (1992). *Organizational Culture and Leadership* (2nd edn). Jossey-Bass, Inc., San Francisco.

Senge, Peter (1990). *The Fifth Discipline.* Doubleday, New York.

Wack, Pierre (1985a). Scenarios: uncharted waters ahead. *Harvard Business Review*, September/October.

Wack, Pierre (1985b). Scenarios: shooting the rapids. *Harvard Business Review*, November/December.

Using Models in Sequence: A Case Study of a Post-acquisition Intervention

ALLENNA LEONARD

INTRODUCTION

This case has been synthesized from several assignments to protect client confidentiality. The acquisition process on which the case is based did in fact combine three methodological approaches to psychological, technical and managerial aspects of the problem situation and drew upon others. The case describes a situation in which multiple models were used to explore and inform an evolving problem situation. The situation exhibited a great deal of variety in both its organizational dynamics and the personal motives and interactions of the individuals. Disturbances buffeted the situation from several sources—some expected and some unexpected. This was due in large part to the fact that the relevant boundaries of who needed to be involved and who needed to be consulted varied from week to week. This made it very difficult to establish a consistent idea of what our assignment was other than to "help" the parties achieve their mutually espoused goals. The particular models were chosen from a functional perspective—to get a grip on the aspects of the relationship that the parties identified as troublesome. Each tackled a different aspect in an attempt to bring requisite managerial variety to the

Multimethodology: The Theory and Practice of Combining Management Science Methodologies. Edited by John Mingers and Anthony Gill. © 1997 John Wiley & Sons Ltd.

situation. The models brought to bear included an interpretive or "soft" tool, a medium-range tool and a problem-solving or "hard" tool. The "critical perspective" in this case was provided by lawyers representing the interests of both parties. Some of their issues came up in conversations both during and after the assignment but no formal modeling of these was done.

There had been a longstanding relationship between the larger of the two organizations and a large general purpose management consultancy. The acquisition had gone forward despite their strong adverse recommendation. When the acquisition ran into the predicted difficulties, the consultancy sought a new and impartial perspective from a cybernetics team, believing that course of action offered the best chance for a favourable outcome. When the cybernetics consultants were engaged, the principals had already agreed to the acquisition but were in the midst of messy negotiations on the details of implementation. They were floundering in miscommunication and misunderstanding and were unsure how many of their disagreements were real and how many were artefacts of disparate styles.

The use of three particular methodologies in this case will be described: Kelly's Repertory Grid, the Critical Path method of project management, and the Viable System Model of organizational structure. Each was used at a different stage and to address a different part of a multidimensional situation. Our efforts were constrained by both the time frame of the assignment, six months, and by the limited channel capacity the participants had available to develop and maintain positive working relationships. Given the limited channel capacity, a major function of the models was to amplify the variety of the team members and attenuate the variety of the situation they were managing.

CASE BACKGROUND

The acquisition involved a start-up innovative company and an established family business. The larger, Knapp Industries, was a third generation manufacturing and distribution company which had a primary business making automobile window glass and a secondary one supplying glass and other products for greenhouses and home gardening. The founder of the firm had been an inventor and tinkerer who was born early in the century—in time to see the transition to an automotive economy. He had over time moved from a general purpose small batch producer to one who concentrated on a dozen products. His son was not a tinkerer, but a businessman. Under his management the company became more focused and prospered. At the time of the assignment, Knapp employed six thousand people in four divisions. Sundial and its inventions were being considered as a possible fifth division. George Knapp, the chairman, president and majority owner, was beginning to look to his twenty-five year old son, Gerald, to take on a role in the firm as he had done as a young man. To date, Gerald had shown little interest in following either in his father's or his grandfather's footsteps. In the absence of a better alternative, and without much enthusiasm, he agreed to join the firm.

George had a gut feeling that most of the products they were offering were competing in mature markets where there was little opportunity for significant expansion. He remembered the postwar excitement of new consumer products which had stimulated Knapp's first growth spurt and thought that the times called for a return to the inventive ingenuity of his father. He also believed that the introduction of a young inventor and his inventions might spark Gerald to take a more active interest as the challenge of applying modern business methods had sparked his own interest some thirty years earlier.

The smaller firm, Sundial, was started by Tim Martin and his high school classmate, Mick Lane. Tim was a twenty-five year old inventor who had already filed more than thirty patents. Sundial had a small production facility to manufacture three of the simpler inventions. It began as a summer project to turn one of Tim's science fair prizes and Mick's entrepreneurial energy into money for university and had grown to employ a production staff of a dozen of their fellow students. Although Tim and Mick had by now graduated from university, their workforce continued to be drawn from a self-replacing pool of engineering students who worked part time while gaining experience related to their field. Tim oversaw production but spent most of his time developing new ideas. Mick handled the marketing and business side. Tim had become frustrated by the fact that the small scale of his operations did not provide enough of a base to launch most of his ideas. He hoped to gain access to a larger laboratory and the capital and production resources which would allow him to bring more of his ideas to market.

George Knapp had met Tim six months earlier at a banquet honoring young inventors. For both men it seemed to be an excellent match. Tim would have the chance to get his more ambitious inventions to market and George would get an opportunity to make a splash by backing a winner and expanding his product line. As an added benefit, Tim and Gerald seemed to hit it off. Within a month, George bought Sundial for Knapp Industries and began to explore his new acquisition. He invited the business press to watch for a new example of technical leadership. George was not interested in Tim's group. He wanted to bring Sundial's production into the Knapp facilities which involved moving operations forty miles to the other side of the city— too far, in any case, for student labor to commute. Mick was the only one with a stake in the business. He chose to accept a cash payment and move to the west coast.

Problems began as soon as George presented his new acquisition to his senior staff. George's idea of the inventor's role was a romantic one which had been formed fifty years ago when he was a child observing his father. He had no idea how much difference there was between launching a new product which was an incremental improvement on an existing one and launching a new breakthrough product. Additional patent work, rigorous testing, design and adaptation of manufacturing machinery, health and safety considerations, environmental impact and market research all needed to be addressed before the new products would be ready for large-scale production. Nor did George find this experience on his management team. For them, "new product" meant existing product with some refinements and improvements which would be handled by the same general production and distribution channels.

The first invention George had hoped to exploit was an auto windshield glass modification which added a coating of pressure sensitive material which would automatically turn the windshield washers and wipers on—or speed them up—in response to rain or splashes from passing trucks. Although related to auto glass, this invention used a number of different technologies and required substantial investment and lead time to bring to market. George had been thinking in terms of months; his advisors told him to think instead of years. This was not the time frame Tim was expecting either.

George had also gotten a somewhat erroneous impression of Tim's social and communication skills based on his essentially casual interactions with him. Few substantive conversations were required for George to see that Tim did not talk the language of business. He neither knew nor cared about much outside of science and technology. His impressive technical knowledge was eclectic and, despite his university degree, mainly self-taught. This was reflected in the range of his patents which were in very different areas although many shared the characteristic of automatic response to changing conditions. Nor was Tim much of a business man; that had been Mick's department. Although Tim turned up on time and wearing a suit for meetings, he preferred to work on his own schedule which involved telephone and on-line chats with contacts around the world and thirty-six hour stretches in the laboratory. He did not welcome unscheduled phone calls or last minute requests as they were likely either to interrupt his concentration or disturb his sleep. Nor did he suffer fools—or those he took to be fools—gladly.

George Knapp found himself with one promising but slightly eccentric new semi-employee and a sheaf of patent applications rather than the fledgling organization he thought would be a new high visibility division. His existing management did not have the technical expertise to direct this operation. Nor, since they had not been consulted, did they have much enthusiasm for it. Despite an amiable social relationship, Gerald had almost nothing in common with Tim.

George set about to remedy this situation and recruited Ken Davis—an engineer who had worked for a large oil company in the north and who had taken early retirement when his installation was amalgamated. George thought it was especially important that a mature hand was on board because he found himself spending more and more of his attention on a horse farm he had inherited from an uncle in Kentucky which had produced a colt that looked like a Triple Crown contender.

George deputized John Beech, his finance vice president, as acting president to run all of Knapp. John was an accountant by training and had proven himself a valuable asset by his strong commitment to achieving cost efficiencies. John did not have much understanding of either Tim's or Ken's fields but he was determined to make the most of his opportunity to move into the top ranks. John turned for advice to the management consultancy partner who had known the company for years and who had tried to talk George out of acquiring Sundial. The obvious recommendation, "Get George back here to raise that puppy he brought home!", was not in the frame. They decided the next best option was to subcontract the job of integrating Sundial into Knapp to a small cybernetics consultancy with an interdisciplinary profile. At a minimum they would understand the principles behind the automatic sensing devices and be able to act as a transducer of the more technical information.

THE INTERVENTION

The problem presented to the cybernetics team was the following: "We have a young guy here with inventions that might make us millions of dollars but we don't know how to get him to focus or how to evaluate which inventions to pursue. He doesn't understand business or our constraints. Help us get him organized and producing."

Tim's view of the problem was quite different. It went more like "Get these guys who don't understand anything I'm doing off my back so I can get on with my inventions. Nobody's going to make any money until we get these things to market."

The first task for the cyberneticians was to listen and learn from both Tim and the Knapp management team. The initial interviews made it clear that each party was operating with a frame of reference which had minimal overlap with that of the other. The discussions between them had run aground because neither seemed to think the facts and arguments offered by the other were relevant to the necessary decisions. It is characteristic of frames of reference that they cannot be falsified. It was up to the cyberneticians to nurture what Donald Schon and Martin Rein call "double vision"; the ability to act from one perspective while holding other perspectives in mind.

In the beginning of this arrangement, both parties began from positions of some strength. Although there was no doubt that Knapp held a larger share of power and resources, Tim's assets of intellectual capital were substantial and he retained ownership of his patents. It was a positive sign that both Tim and Knapp were proceeding on the basis that their interests did overlap and that they could make the relationship work to their joint benefit if they could get the other to understand their point of view.

The cybernetics team was less optimistic. George's active involvement was required to integrate Sundial but it was not forthcoming. Although he had made the decision to bring the cybernetics team in, George made little further direct input. This left no real champion for making the cultural changes necessary to make a new division work. There was contingent support from the Knapp management team, based on their own individual career ambitions, but it was shallow. Gerald, who could have become an advocate when he was transferred to the group from head office, held back. His short experience at Knapp had taught him that he was regarded principally as a conduit to his father—a booster or a tattletale.

The variety of the situation was further complicated by the presence and influence of non-executive family members on the Board of Directors and by the fact that two members of the group had wives working in the headquarters office.

Kelly's Personal Construct Theory

One of the cybernetics team had used George Kelly's (1955) Personal Construct and Repertory Grid (Bannister and Fransella, 1971) and set about to use it as a "neutral" vehicle for Tim and the Knapp management team to explore their different perspectives.

George Kelly was an American clinical psychologist who pioneered travelling mental health clinics in Kansas during the 1930s Depression. He observed huge disparities in the way people responded to seemingly similar, if difficult, circumstances. He concluded that it wasn't the experiences themselves but the constructions placed upon them which predicted behaviour. This posture places Kelly among the constructionists who say that we do not experience "reality" directly but through the lens of our interpretation. His theory was that human beings behaved as "personal scientists" who constructed a world view that enabled them to perceive, predict, and sometimes control their circumstances.

Kelly's formal theory begins with his fundamental postulate: "A person's processes are psychologically channelized by the ways in which he anticipates events." It is followed by eleven corollaries that describe how they are individualized, organized, shared, and applied. Constructs are described as patterns or templates which are tried onto circumstances for fit. They tend to be usefully thought of as scalar measures of bipolar concepts including both evaluative "good–bad" and descriptive "light–heavy" or "light–dark" constructs. Kelly studied classes of constructs and their flexibility. These included the superordinate or overarching constructs that were central to personality, the pre-emptive construct which reduced variety on the basis of a single characteristic, the constellatory construct which encompasses others in a "package deal" and the propositional which is flexible and open to alteration on the basis of new evidence.

Kelly's work emphasizes common thought processes rather than their diverse outcomes. This led to his observation that the main difference between the graduate students he advised and his clinical patients was that the former's world views were more functional. Kelly's ideas have been adapted for numerous uses outside the clinical setting where an inductive approach is useful. Hundreds of studies have been published which have applied personal construct theory to many areas far from the mental health clinic: market research, quality circles, exploring policy options and vocational guidance, among others. There is also an organization—the North American Personal Construct Theory Network—where practitioners may meet to share information.

The Repertory Grid

By far the most widely utilized of Kelly's tools is the Repertory Grid Technique. Kelly had observed that almost everyone tends to utilize a relatively small number (twenty to thirty at most) of bipolar scales to rank their choices and make decisions. When these are elicited from individuals, they can often understand, through the more extensive operational definitions of their criteria which come to light, how they are framing an issue and where their choices are or are not negotiable. The Grid directly explores the relations between topics and the way they are approached in a matrix. The classic way to use the Grid in a non-clinical setting is to ask the subjects to nominate eight to twelve "elements" which represent the main aspects of a situation or its players and invite the subjects to compare and contrast them. This can be done in pairs but is usually done in groups of three for adult subjects. The respondents are asked to nominate a distinction that divides two of their chosen elements from the third. Elements can reflect any type of content: although in most applications they are nouns—proper names, products, or processes. Constructs may highlight an unlimited variety of distinctions although they are most often expressed as adjectives or adverbs. What these distinctions are and their numerical ranking depend on what features of the elements are most salient. It is not necessary for people completing and discussing the results of the Repertory Grid to know Kelly's theories or indeed that it is a tool originally developed in a clinical setting. All that is necessary is to present the tool as helping us speak about the ways that different people talk about the same things.

To take a trivial example, a comparison among the sports of swimming, football and golf might lead to three possible pairings derived from an unlimited number of distinctions leading to different constructs. Football and golf are played professionally; swimming is not. Swimming and football do not require extensive equipment to begin; golf does. Golf and swimming may be done individually and non-competitively; football is played between competitive teams. Which of these is important can vary considerably depending on whether you are sitting on a community recreation board, deciding what to watch on television or looking for a venue to advertise a product.

The cybernetics team thought that a substantial proportion of the misunderstanding between Tim and the rest of the Knapp management group was coming from their different frames and criteria and that discussing those differences in the context of interpreting grid results would be a way of introducing more variety into their perceptions of each other's criteria and perhaps even their own. The team took a list of ten of Tim's product patents and ideas as elements and asked them to spend a few minutes filling out a grid in two separate sessions.

Tim filled out one grid. John, Ken and Peter, a marketing specialist John had recruited with minimal consultation with the other players, filled out the second together. Each was asked to indicate the scales or "constructs" they would use and to rank the products on these dimensions.

The Repertory Grid may be used in formal or informal settings to obtain both qualitative and quantitative results. In this informal case the four people were offered a matrix with the products listed across the top and the dimensions blank. They were asked to do the rankings on a five-point scale with 1 = most similar, 2 = somewhat similar, 3 = neither, 4 = somewhat dissimilar and 5 = most dissimilar. They had selected the products as the most useful starting place. As the purpose was to stimulate discussion, the grids were compared but not analyzed. It was interesting to note that five of the six constructs of the management group could be subsumed under the positive versus negative construct in contrast to three out of six on Tim's grid. This was also reflected in their more consistent rankings of products on the different constructs. This usage would have been too informal for reaching a decision or for a research study but was effective and useful in initiating open ended discussion.

In a clinical or counseling setting with the individual as client, the Repertory Grid is often used at several stages in the intervention to plot the course of change. This is seldom possible in an organizational setting and would not have been appropriate here. The Grid can be used for medium to large populations and analyzed by statistical techniques such as cluster analysis or principal components analysis. If the topic under investigation is not very personal, the same grid may be used for everyone. When the topic is more personal or a greater degree of depth is required, a two-stage process is followed to allow for maximum scope and still have a consistent set of measures to analyze. First, an open ended grid is explored using a representative sample of individuals. From these individual grids, the most frequently appearing elements and constructs are chosen. This grid is then distributed to the study population and the returns analyzed.

These were the ten products at various stages of development that were chosen as elements:

1. pressure responsive windshield wipers
2. outdoor light with vibrating bug repellant feature
3. air filter/fan that would automatically speed up in proportion to particulate matter in the air
4. a device to turn lights on and off randomly within parameters while occupants were away
5. lampshade material which could be adjusted for diffused or directed light
6. automatic garden sprinkler based on sensors of rain, light and soil moisture
7. a combination pill box multi-time alarm clock
8. window blinds that could be automatically adjusted to allow in different light levels
9. an anti-glare, anti-static, anti-radiation computer screen
10. a self-adjusting portable white noise generator

The men were asked to take three of the inventions at a time and indicate a dimension on which they might be ranked. For example, Tim ranked the first triplet "bug repelling light", "computer screen" and "pressure responsive windshield wipers" on the technically innovative versus technically straightforward construct; while the other three ranked it on the simple to manufacture/difficult to manufacture construct.

Tim's constructs included:

technically innovative	vs.	technically straightforward
first to market	vs.	second or later to market
trade-show splash	vs.	trade-show ho-hum
useful	vs.	gimmicky
energy saving	vs.	energy wasteful
environmentally friendly	vs.	not environmentally friendly

The constructs developed by Ken, John and Peter were:

improved product	vs.	existing product
simple to manufacture	vs.	difficult to manufacture
easy to market	vs.	difficult to market
low risk	vs.	high risk
high public relations value	vs.	low public relations value
well packaged	vs.	not well packaged

The resulting discussion proved to be very useful in building an understanding of each other's perspectives although it did not lead to much modification of their own.

Tim's constructs indicated that he was still more focused on the approval of his peers among inventors than on the approval of the market. He was highly idealistic and motivated to protect the environment. Because he had been working with overqualified students, Tim had given little thought to simplicity of manufacture. He had little interest in making incremental improvements to existing products and had never considered packaging the sorts of things he was making as more than a functional consideration.

In contrast, Ken, John and Peter were focused primarily on selling the products in the market and their only construct which touched on innovation was public relations potential. This criterion did match well with Tim's "trade-show splash", energy saving and environmentally friendly constructs. They also found Tim's criterion of usefulness relevant.

When the constructs reflect preferences, grids are sometimes analyzed by adding up the rankings in the elements columns to get a rough order of preference. Although the numerical rankings of these grids do not reflect equivalent measures, it is interesting to note that there was no overlap between the preferred first four products in the two grids.

It would have been interesting to find out how George Knapp would have regarded the situation, but this did not prove possible. Indeed, the cybernetics team never met George; his active engagement had been anticipated at several stages but never materialized. George came home from Kentucky less and less frequently. In the event, his input was limited to occasional comments relayed through Gerald and John. Ken, Peter and John held professional positions that made them risk averse. Ken had worked all his life in a large top-down organization and was accustomed to working with a high degree of consensus among the team. John was very sensitive to the bottom line and saw his own future prospects as depending on maintaining short-term profits. He was very wary of seeing profits drained by new ventures that might not mature for some time, if ever. Peter was the most risk averse of all. He was a new employee and saw that the situation violated almost all the textbook conditions for successful marketing. His attitude was also colored by the fact that he had recently married and taken on a large mortgage. None had either the experience or the instincts of the entrepreneur.

Tim placed little emphasis on risk. Out of any hundred inventions, he guessed that at least one would take off and another twenty or so make money. He thought his own record would be better. Half his science fair prizes had looked marketable and he was learning more every day. He considered a working prototype and a completed patent application to mark a late milestone. His colleagues considered it to be an early one.

The main accomplishment of eliciting and sharing the repertory grid results was that Tim and the others could see and discuss how far apart they were on their expectations and their understanding of the situation. They would have to move closer together if anything were to be advanced. It did help each of

	Wipers	Bug light	Air filter	Security light	Lampshade	Sprinkler	Pill box alarm	Window blinds	Computer screen	White noise	
Technically innovative	1	5	3	4	1	1	5	2	5	5	Technically straightforward
First to market	1	4	5	3	1	1	1	1	5	3	Second/later to market
Trade-show splash	1	3	4	4	2	1	2	1	3	3	Trade-show ho hum
Useful	1	1	1	2	3	1	5	3	1	4	Gimmicky
Energy saving	3	4	3	2	3	3	3	1	3	3	Energy wasteful
Environmentally friendly	3	5	1	2	1	3	1	1	3	3	Not environmentally friendly
Total	10	22	17	16	12	8	19	9	20	21	

Figure 5.1 Tim's grid

	Wipers	Bug light	Air filter	Security light	Lampshade	Sprinkler	Pill box alarm	Window blinds	Computer screen	White noise	
Improved product	1	2	2	3	2	1	4	2	5	2	Existing product
Simple to manufacture	5	3	2	2	4	4	1	3	1	3	Difficult to manufacture
Easy to market	5	3	3	2	4	3	1	4	1	4	Difficult to market
Low risk	5	3	1	2	2	3	1	3	3	3	High risk
High public relations value	1	2	3	2	4	2	1	5	1	3	Low public relations value
Well packaged	3	2	3	1	4	3	1	2	2	5	Not well packaged
Total	20	15	14	12	20	16	9	19	13	20	

Figure 5.2 John, Ken and Peter's grid

them to realize that their criteria of relevance were so attached to their roles and identities. At least it convinced each of them that the other positions were not perverse but typical of the role.

Innovation Planning and Critical Path

The level of uncertainty about what Tim was doing and when it would be ready showed up as a major worry. The Knapp management knew that they did not know enough to evaluate the progress, or indeed the value, of the inventions. They had already spent some money on getting patent lawyers and other scientific experts to look at what Tim had produced. For the most part, these experts had been used as confidential evaluators and had not sat down with Tim to ask questions and follow up on his answers. The expert opinions were sought in isolation from one another and, not surprisingly, did not come together to make any sort of sense. The cybernetics team reviewed the reports and came to the conclusion that unless the experts were invited back, direct comparison was impossible. This was not recommended. The uncoordinated use of outside experts had actually added a great deal of noise to the communications. It was determined that future use of independent experts be confined to answering specific and well-formulated questions..

Critical path

The meetings between Tim and the cybernetics team went smoothly enough. Tim recognized that he would need to be more sensitive to the needs of the business side. He did not need a great deal of convincing to tighten up his documentation and record-keeping so that the subject matter experts who would do the technical evaluations would have something to go on. Nor did he object to starting with one of the simpler inventions. He chose to begin with an anti-glare filter for a computer monitor. This had ranked highly on the Knapp grid and had some market history.

The critical path was developed to include all the tasks which either needed or might need to be done with regular management meetings to monitor and approve progress and next steps. The meetings would provide a channel for management to keep informed about the projects in detail and would keep Tim focused on activities that were on the critical path.

Tim had been manufacturing the screen filter in small quantities and knew that people had been interested in buying it. His new version included a ground wire to draw off static and radiation. He and the team devised a special version of a critical path chart with the various tracks of design and testing and with regular reporting dates identified. It had to take into account not only the standard manufacturing process tracks but also allow for new patent applications, legal liability considerations, different costing scenarios based on choices about where manufacturing would take place, and last, but not least, the highly charged personal relationships which had developed among the group. Right away three basic problems were identified.

First, while Tim had been selling the screens informally in small quantities, the claims that they produced less glare and eye strain were not a big issue. People had simply tried them in the local computer store and bought them if they felt they were better than the unscreened monitor. In short, they had not been subjected to rigorous market or effectiveness testing. While the testing itself was not difficult, Tim found himself operating in an area where standards had not been established. There were no precise definitions of "glare"; it was a combination of the type of light rays, the characteristics of the monitor and even the characteristics of the users and their working environment. Ergonomics and health professionals differed among themselves over the effects of monitor radiation, and some (Bertell, 1985) regarded it as a significant risk. There were no hard data on levels which could potentially damage sight and might lead to discomfort and headaches. Before claims could be made, the performance of the screens against internal if not external criteria would have to be established. But there was no guarantee that any standards set would remain unchanged. Meanwhile, a reading on the product liability risk had been handed over to a law firm. Finally, the glass surface Tim was using needed to be cleaned with optical glass cleaner. How easy would it be to warn a wider variety of users against using regular household window cleaning products?

Second, there were people and technical problems with the manufacturing process. Tim's engineering students were far from typical of the light industrial workforce. There was little in these work arrangements which could be transferred to a mass production mode. Tim's small shop had been laminating the different layers of the screen filters together and fitting the frames and clips one at a time. The materials they used were in metre square sheets and single screen width rolls. Efficient production required laminating multiple materials and using machinery to attach the frames and clips. These machines would need to be purchased or designed and produced. A different work design and manufacturing process would be required and employees would need to be trained. Also, tests would be required to find out if the materials would stretch or break if larger sheets and wider rolls were used. Plans were made to seek advice from sociotechnical systems consultants when more of the parameters were known. Tim accepted that it would not be feasible to duplicate his student group but was anxious that the work design include some of the collaboration and substitution that had helped improve the small batch processes.

Third, these changes would be costly. It would be difficult to justify the investment if enough companies were not prepared to spend enough money to put filters on their monitors. A concurrent effort in market research would need to be done for the product to establish and connect with its target markets.

The initial discussions between Tim and the management team involved establishing the success criteria for the critical path. Time was important, but so was cost. Several stages of the critical path could not be determined until some answers were known. It was decided that the first requirement was a satisfactory exploration and description of whether the existing filter and Tim's modification met whatever standards were in place or were likely to be in place in the near future. If it did, a subsequent step of redesigning the filter would not be required and the group could move on to answering the next questions about whether or not existing machines could satisfactorily laminate the larger sheets of material. When the machines had been investigated, tested and customized, if necessary, it would be possible to design the production line and determine what recruitment and training would be needed to staff it in the several potential production sites. Reliable estimates of the cost of manufacturing the screens could then be made and a tentative selling price established.

When these tasks were laid out in sequence on the critical path, it was possible to see what level of involvement Tim should have in each. Although he would need to be kept informed of progress on each line of inquiry, it was anticipated that Tim's extensive involvement would probably not be required unless the filter needed to be redesigned. This suited Tim, as he did not want to spend a great deal of his time on a product that he had already been selling. He had a working model of the sprinkler and was anxious to develop it further. The sprinkler project was more complex and challenging. There was the advantage here that Knapp already sold standard sprinkler systems through existing distribution channels and that the new one might be well worth the higher cost in areas where there were water shortages. The original expected flagship product, the pressure sensitive wipers, was put on hold until an income stream from the others could be predicted. Tim was not happy about this but agreed that the postponement was probably necessary under the circumstances.

Tim did not have all the equipment in his own laboratory to finish its development, nor did Knapp Industries have the right equipment or atmosphere. The best solution seemed to be to keep the focus of Tim's efforts in his home town and equip a lab for him there. This enabled Tim to retain his engineering student group to work on prototypes but also had the less positive effect of reducing his visibility and presence in Knapp and effectively limiting most of his contacts with them to scheduled meetings and other semi-formal occasions.

Viable System Model Design

Although the cybernetics team had been engaged specifically to help with the new product division, it became clear that some of the issues affecting it were emanating from conflicts elsewhere in the organization. Knapp's growth, especially recently, had been based more on the enthusiasms of George Knapp than any other factor. For the most part, his new directions had been profitable, but expansion had brought discontinuities. The corporation's size, coupled with George's absence, seemed to require another management layer between headquarters and the plants.

The management of Knapp were not familiar with the Viable System Model but were willing to spend some time learning about it because they saw that it might help them solve some other issues which had arisen from changes in their product mix and manufacturing and distribution networks.

Beer's (1966, 1979, 1981, 1985) Viable System Model depicts the structural relationships and communications channels in an organization and between the organization and its environments. It divides the management function into five interacting parts which are repeated at every organizational level from the shop floor to the conglomerate. Any effective management must provide for these five functions. They are: managing the direct connection between the operations selling products or services and their environments; damping oscillation and providing common coordination between different units; managing the here-and-now of the units as a whole for synergy and common goals; making provisions for the future; and keeping the organization's identity in sight and steering an appropriate course between keeping the current show on the road and getting ready for the next one. These management functions are labeled Systems One through Five.

In Knapp's case, the several System One units made different products in different places for different markets. The first question was what division of System One activities would be most helpful. Several seemed possible candidates. After some discussion, the cybernetics team sketched out three versions of the VSM based on three different distinctions between System One activities.

They began with a division that paralleled their current one based on product groups. The products were auto glass (with four plants), greenhouse glass (two exterior, two interior and one combined), hoses and sprinkler systems (two plants), and makers of various plant containers made from glass, wood, plastic and ceramics (six plants—all small). This gave Knapp four product-based System One units, with Sundial's products making up a potential fifth. For the most part, the divisions did not share common suppliers. The auto glass and greenhouse glass were sold primarily to repair shops and contractors, while the other garden products were sold to consumers through retail stores. Employees, especially office workers and management, tended to be long term as Knapp had a policy of promotion from within.

Their System Two activities were primarily oriented toward administration and personnel protocols. Although there were some staff at headquarters, most were located in the facilities.

System Three tended to be focused on the internal distribution of financial resources and information technology and on union negotiations for the roughly 60% of manufacturing employees who were unionized. If this distinction were formally adopted, four new line managers would be appointed for each of the manufacturing lines. Sales efforts which were presently divided between headquarters and the plants could be rationalized. This is where John Beech had been most active in his role as finance vice president and he still seemed to be most comfortable with decisions at this level.

System Four had been dominated by George Knapp, although the individual plants enjoyed considerable autonomy over the planning for their own facilities. Advertising and market research was split between the individual plants which had their own customer bases and headquarters which did some overall advertising for both the contractor and consumer markets.

System Five's identity function was divided between George Knapp and a group of long-time employees who did not necessarily hold high positions. System Five's other role in balancing the present and future activities was only partially filled by George for the top level. The Board, dominated by family members, made only sporadic input. No one in the discussions disputed this conclusion, although there was little they could do about it.

The second model was based on manufacturing locations, by region and country. The disbursed locations had occurred because of both shipping distance factors and the duties involved in cross-border traffic. This latter

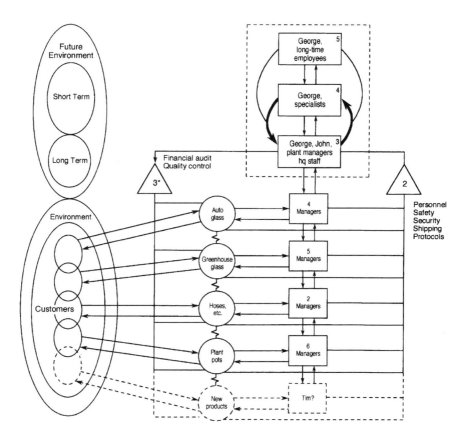

Figure 5.3 Knapp VSM version one

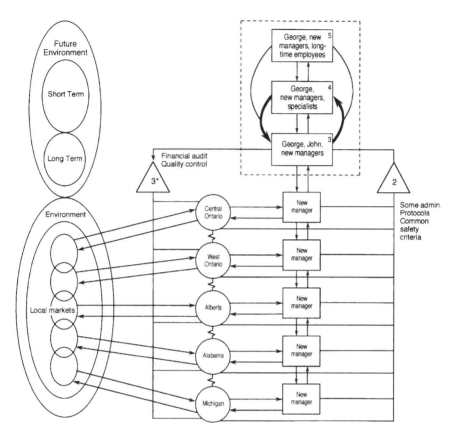

Figure 5.4 Knapp VSM version two

constraint was changing due to the North American Free Trade Agreement but its details had not yet been worked out. Knapp had had its operations split between Canada (Central and Western Ontario and Alberta) and the United States (Michigan and Alabama). Headquarters was near Toronto. This model would give the option of either five or two System One units, but five seemed to offer the more manageable grouping.

Greater cooperation along System Two lines would be possible with sharing of some pick-up and delivery services and the consolidation of some administrative functions. At the System Three level, this distinction would provide the most opportunity for the distributed managers to look for synergy among themselves. This model had the advantage of grouping together plants with the same legal jurisdictions which would enable greater regularization of personnel policies and practices. Although it would not provide as much synergy for sales, it would gain from the common contractual frameworks.

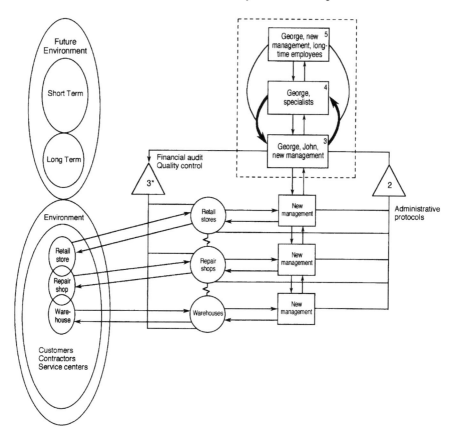

Figure 5.5 Knapp VSM version three

System Four might offer more opportunities for recruitment and training at the regional level and perhaps greater cooperation around local presence on the community charity scene. It would not provide as much help at the level of market research and new technology exploration as those are product based. System Five would absorb a great deal of variety into the regional focus.

The third was based on the type of customers each plant served—particularly whether the end user of the products would be a contractor or an ordinary consumer. This arrangement gave three System One units: retail stores, auto glass repair shops and building supply warehouses. Some of these latter were oriented toward the DIY market but it was decided that this would not require a fourth System One unit.

This arrangement provided the greatest opportunity for sharing supplies and, for the retail products, achieving market synergy. It would also allow sales to be handled more comprehensively. It would concentrate more System Four activities at the System One level—namely advertising, marketing and trade-show representation. As long as George Knapp remained active, System Five would change little. As the months passed, this factor came increasingly into doubt.

Discussions were held looking at these three alternatives and several persistent problem areas surfaced and were explained by the discontinuities between criteria that were based on one distinction being applied across another. While the VSM discussion group—which included John, Ken and several others—was not in a position to make reorganization decisions, it was able to disentangle several persistent problems around employee contracts, insurance requirements and purchasing by handling them "as if" the divisions existed. Also, informal leadership opportunities which had been taken up by the managers of the larger plants were extended by holding more frequent meetings to discuss specific strategies. With all three VSM models, missing or inadequate communications channels were identified and some could be added or enlarged.

The next task of the team was to situate Tim's effort in Knapp's management structure so that they would fit as smoothly as possible. Tim's activities were clearly located in System Four of the whole organization. Until a sufficient amount of the products were marketed and established, the new Sundial focus would have to remain in a business incubator. It would probably be several years before it would be on an equal footing with even the smaller plants with respect to a solid customer base and contributions to overhead.

Several different changes and adaptations were run through the model emphasizing the System Four nature of Tim's effort and how it adapted to or clashed with Knapp's usual constraints. Most of Tim's products were breakthrough products with unknown users and markets. Even when these products were developed and were returning profits, managing them would require different management skills and faster response times than the other divisions. This implied that Knapp would need to expand its overall System Four focus substantially in order to have the variety to cope with Tim's (or later the new division's) proliferation of variety within its lower recursion System Four. Knapp's System Five would need strengthening and an ability to assume a new identity which would encompass the new products and markets.

One point emerged immediately: Tim's inventions crossed all three potential VSM distinctions. Given this, it seemed advisable to attempt to bring Tim into some of these informal product and regional meetings so that he could begin to build bridges with other parts of the corporation which had looked at his projects as a distraction. Tim was not interested in this idea. He regarded the meetings he already attended as cutting into valuable laboratory time.

Trade-show presentations seemed to be the best way to build bridges. Tim could bring and demonstrate prototype products and share some glory and networking with the more pedestrian innovations the established plants produced.

The End of the Intervention

Progress along Tim's critical path and the VSM discussions had continued for several months when everything came to an abrupt halt. George Knapp announced that he was retiring as president and would be moving to Kentucky permanently. Gerald Knapp had also been spending increasing amounts of time there and had become interested in stable management. He enjoyed horses and horse people and was pleased, for once, to be in an environment where his pipeline to his father was not his main asset. Gerald's potential involvement had been a major factor in George's decision to acquire Sundial. Now that Gerald had discovered another interest, that consideration was no longer relevant.

John's "acting" title was removed and he became president. During this time, he had learned a great deal about the difference between what Tim was offering and the Knapp product mix and culture. He requested and received permission to look for a buyer for Knapp's interest in Sundial. With the main portion of the assignment no longer relevant, the contract with the cybernetics team came to an end and was not renewed. It took another three months to find a buyer, during which time Tim finished several of his critical path activities and mothballed the rest. The new buyer was a much larger, high tech firm in California. If Tim's operation had not been sold, his choice not to become more involved with managers of the other divisions could have been a costly one. As it was, it made no difference.

Over the past several years, Tim's association with them had worked out reasonably well, although his hopes for a new division had not materialized. John left Knapp for another assignment within a year. Without the budding new division, Ken and Peter's services were no longer needed. Ken joined the staff of a local community college and Peter found a less prestigious but far more secure position with a large Toronto retailer.

CONCLUSION

Most organizational situations deploy variety along many dimensions including some that are driven by personal agenda and histories which predate the involvement of the individuals directly concerned in a problem. This is especially true of family businesses where parent–child dynamics often result in decisions which would not otherwise have been considered. Of course, family dramas often make for awkward or worse organizational situations because they introduce additional sources of variety. This may make it very difficult for recommendations based on logic or research to be implemented.

Use of multiple models can help to bring more balance into the variety equation by pulling apart some issues which have become tangled. In such situations it is important to establish the consistencies and inconsistencies between values and practices. Once done, plans can be made which are made within these boundaries.

Soft models, with their open ended questions and virtually unlimited scope are the only way into this. If there are enough people involved in a decision-making capacity some of these may be quantified through surveys and other studies, but that is often not feasible. It is a characteristic of models such as the Repertory Grid that they can be used even when situations are quite unstructured. They are extremely effective in illustrating the extent of coherence and permitting discussions to be held which are one step back from the personalities of the individuals. Mid-range models, such as the Viable System Model, come into force when the situation has become somewhat structured—even if the structure is only tentative. Such models have fewer choices and therefore provide greater optical resolution. Once an organization has been assumed, common criteria of viability are brought to bear on alternative arrangements. Even if the organization is not structured along VSM lines, some accommodation needs to be made to align the organization internally and with its external markets.

Harder models, such as critical path methodologies, are most useful when the "what" choices have been made and the search is for the best answer to "how". If the "what" decisions have been made with appropriate input from the involved stakeholders, then achieving buy-in is usually not difficult and subsequent problems are understood in an appropriate context.

In this particular case, no model was able to overcome the difficulties brought about by a disengaging CEO. Like any tools, systems models require a context and some materials. They cannot work in isolation no matter how skillfully applied. It is easy to see in hindsight that this acquisition should never have been made, which was the original advice of the management consultancy. Given that it was made, it would probably not have been impossible if the changes in the family situation had been in the other direction. But that would have been a different story.

REFERENCES

Bannister, D. and Fransella, F. (1971). *Inquiring Man.* Penguin Books, Harmondsworth.

Beer, S. (1966). *Decision and Control.* John Wiley & Sons, Chichester.

Beer, S. (1979). *The Heart of Enterprise.* John Wiley & Sons, Chichester.
Beer, S. (1981). *Brain of the Firm* (2nd edn). John Wiley & Sons, Chichester.
Beer, S. (1985). *Diagnosing the System.* John Wiley & Sons, Chichester.
Bertell, R. (1985). *No Immediate Danger?* The Women's Press, Toronto.
Kelly, G. (1955). *The Psychology of Personal Constructs.* Norton, New York.

Chapter 6

Status and Tendencies of Management Research: a Systems Oriented Perspectives

MARKUS SCHWANINGER

INTRODUCTION

In this chapter the main emphasis is placed on the status and the development of management research. This is not to be recorded in the sense of a snapshot, but to be illuminated as part of the long-term process it forms a part of. Therefore, the tendencies can be dealt with relatively fast and right at the start, because they are inherently of a short-term nature.

Since we are talking about management I shall place two working definitions at the beginning:

First: The term "systems oriented perspective" in the context relevant here is used for an approach to management research and science that is based on systems theory and cybernetics. I shall apply the terms "cybernetics" and "systems theory" more or less synonymously. This simplification is permissible with respect to the subject of "management".

Second: In the categories created by Hans Ulrich (1984), management is about "the design, control and development" ("das Gestalten, Lenken und

Multimethodology: The Theory and Practice of Combining Management Science Methodologies.
Edited by John Mingers and Anthony Gill.
© 1997 John Wiley & Sons Ltd.

Entwickeln") of complex, dynamic, and in the case of organizations, productive, social systems.

This chapter centres on two case studies in multimethodology. Both are of the action research type. The first one, in the third section, draws on the status of systems oriented management research, linking the two paradigms of first- and second-order cybernetics. The second one, in the fourth section, highlights important developments of the systems approach. It reports on a project in which qualitative and quantitative modelling were combined, thereby illustrating a new heuristic for dealing with complex issues in organizations and society: Cybernetic Systems Methodology.

TENDENCIES IN MANAGEMENT RESEARCH

The term "tendency" designates an inclination or a preference. The short-lived character of our time favours the loss of the original meaning of the Latin verb "tendere"—to strive for—or at least makes it take on a one-sided tendency itself: the inclination to a short-term optic.

If on this occasion I specifically abstract from individual educational institutions and consider the research landscape of all German-speaking countries, I notice: within a few years a large number of institutions have sprung up that carry the task of "management research" on their banners, whose activities, however, more often follow the fashion than try to make a well-substantiated contribution to knowledge. For once I do not need to mention any names in this connection. Suffice it to point out that the market is flooded with papers and courses on the topic of "management" satiated like never before with catchwords and slogans.

This harbours the danger that exceedingly important objects of management research are treated far too superficially. "Culture", "strategy", "philosophy", "vision", "the individual in the organization", "integration", etc. are great concerns of our time that are generally not treated with the thoroughness they absolutely require. For the fashions do not only come too late to contribute to mastering a challenge; they would be far too superficial for this, anyway.

So it is the tendency of management research to be tendentious. Its task, however, is to make a long-term coherent effort.

ON THE STATUS OF MANAGEMENT RESEARCH (with a focus on "cybernetics and systems")

This is not the time and place to enumerate everything that is happening in management research at the moment. Therefore, I turn to the subject of the systems oriented perspective right away. This has not only established itself at the University of St Gallen where I am working, but since the middle of the 1980s it has become increasingly popular as a frame of reference for management research in other countries as well, e.g. in Britain and the United States. There are mainly two reasons for this:

First: Dealing with complexity has become the central task of management. For this cybernetics offers specific and effective tools.

Second: "Comprehensive", "holistic" "integral" management is called for. Managerial issues require a synthesis of a growing number of specialized perspectives. Its large connective capability ("Anschlussfähigkeit", to use a term from Luhmann, 1990) renders the systems oriented perspective exceedingly suitable for transduction and thus for integration purposes.

Different Perspectives

As a matter of fact "*the* systems oriented perspective" does not exist. It is rather the case that there are various perspectives developed on the foundation of systemic thinking in order to handle the complexity of organizations. They are all based on the same theoretical foundation—systems theory and cybernetics. But in the course of time a multitude of schools of the systems oriented perspective has developed.

In a publication on the future of systems oriented management research (Schwaninger 1989b) I discussed these developments in great detail. Here only a grossly simplified differentiation between the so-called "hard" and the so-called "soft" systems oriented perspectives can be made. The former are part of the positivistic tradition. In the corresponding schools and works a fact-based rationale, structuralist–functionalist trains of thought, are dominant. They are characterized by the endeavour to represent facts "objectively". Correspondingly, the model design mostly lies with one or few persons, the observer's viewpoint outside the system; following an "instrumental" or "conceptual" rationality. This is why they are also termed "objectivistic" systems oriented perspectives. These are faced by a second group of perspectives that are oriented on hermeneutics and phenomenology. With them the interpretive and discursive modes are dominant. They operate on the basis of what was called "communicational rationality" ("kommunikative Rationalität", see Habermas, 1988) or "cultural rationality". Today an eminent position is held by the "Soft Systems Methodology" according to Checkland; other schools and methods have become known by terms like "Social Systems Science", "Critical Systems Thinking", etc.

In the development towards this variety of perspectives at least two stages can be differentiated. I would like to outline these briefly and also comment on a reproach frequently made.

Stages of Development

One of the main criticisms on cybernetics is expressed in the following line of argumentation: this science was unsuitable for dealing with social systems. Its "instrumental logic" equated companies to machines. This would make it a "manipulative social technology". It is true that this criticism points out a weakness of classical cybernetic works which were rooted in the technological realm. In the course of time, however, a logical differentiation between two different views in cybernetics has emerged. They are referred to as first-order cybernetics and second-order cybernetics, although this is an exceedingly important further development that critics of the systems oriented perspective often tend to ignore. It is shown by the model in Figure 6.1.

In first-order cybernetics the "controller" (manager) stands outside the systems s/he is managing. The system is purposive, i.e. the goals for the system are determined by someone on the outside. First-order cybernetics is the science of directing mainly mechanical and biological systems. Its misapplications demonstrate that it is not suitable to adequately take account of the goal oriented, intentional character of individuals and the multitude of subsystems and stakeholders that constitute organizations. In second-order cybernetics the "controller" (manager) is part of the managed system. The latter is purposeful and it consists of subsystems that follow their own goals.

In first-order cybernetics concepts such as feedback, information exchange, control, regulation and equilibrium play an important part. In second-order cybernetics, the multitude of individual perspectives, the observer that in

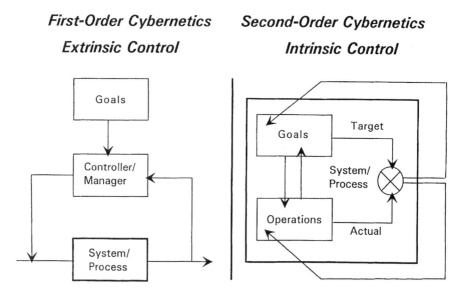

First-Order Cybernetics
Extrinsic Control

Second-Order Cybernetics
Intrinsic Control

Figure 6.1   First- and second-order cybernetics

principle cannot be detached from the system and the concept of self-reference, are of central significance. Heinz von Foerster, the pioneer of a new systems view, defined first-order cybernetics as the "cybernetics of observed systems", and second-order cybernetics as the "cybernetics of observing systems" (von Foerster et al, 1974; von Foerster, 1984).

So much for the various strands of development. However, the differences are not always as striking as this schematical explanation presumes. Behind each of the labels used above there is a multitude of research groups and personalities and quite a few of them are conscious of the limits of their respective approaches. They concentrate on applying their methods to those kinds of tasks they are best suited for. Between the representatives of different schools there exist contacts and cooperations. And, finally, important conceptual developments are also happening.

One example of this is the management cyberneticists who started as early as during the 1950s to apply findings of first-order cybernetics to organizations. In the beginning their papers showed a quantitative, mathematical and partly mechanistic orientation. During the last twenty years or so, however, they have fully integrated the ideas of second-order cybernetics into their repertoire. This is illustrated by recent publications, that show new paths to the future (e.g. Beer, 1979, 1989; Espejo and Harnden, 1989; Espejo and Schwaninger, 1993; Espejo et al, 1996).

Example

The following practical case is meant to show the linkage between first- and second-order cybernetics.

It is the nature of an application oriented science that reflection on theories is only fertile if it interacts with processes of application. From 1988 to 1994 I accompanied several interdisciplinary projects in five industrial organizations together with German and British cybernetics experts. These led to new concepts of organizational structures and management systems on the basis of cybernetic models.

For illustration purposes I shall pick out one significant case, realized in a division of a large corporation of the chemical industry (later on, when the corporation as a whole started a large reorganization programme, all essential innovations of our project were assimilated as guiding concepts and implemented on a corporate scale). What started as an MIS project became a major reorganization project. Together, we—Raúl Espejo, director of Syncho Ltd, a consulting firm based in Birmingham and I, as external consultants—joined in with our internal partner—one of the German "cybernetics experts" mentioned above. He was the director of the focal division, supported by two highly capable men: a deputy with good practical understanding of cybernetics and a young assistant who then became the second cybernetics expert,

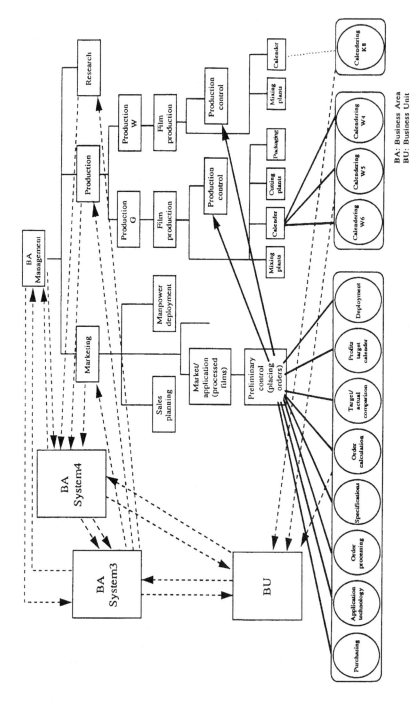

Figure 6.2 Example of organization diagnosis (CyberSyn-Team 1990/91)

BA: Business Area
BU: Business Unit

as the project evolved. Our partners were convinced that the three operating units of the division—two production and one marketing organization—in three different locations should be reorganized cybernetically, to prepare them for challenges to come (enhanced competition was the major one). The point of departure should be a redesign of the management information system (MIS).

The procedure followed in this case was unconventional. First, a core team of MIS and organization consultants from within the firm, and later, the whole group of managers involved in the project, received training in information management and organization design in a cybernetic framework. This was very much based on Stafford Beer's Viable System Model, Raúl's work in MIS and my work on systems oriented management. In the next phase the following operations were carried out:

- A diagnosis of the organization in cybernetic categories was realized.
- An excerpt can be found in Figure 6.2, which reflects very much the view of an internal analyst.
- A recursively cross-linked management information system was implemented whose conceptual (not physical or technical) layout is illustrated in Figure 6.3. This reflects the need to interact easily, expressed by multiple actors who were involved in the design process.

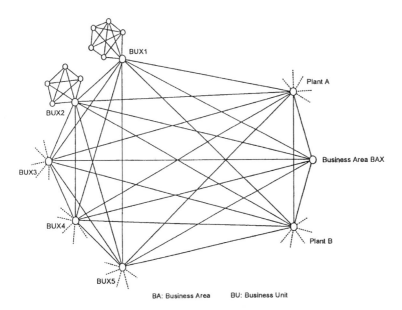

Figure 6.3 Example of a recursively crosslinked information system—conceptual model (CyberSyn-Team 1990/91)

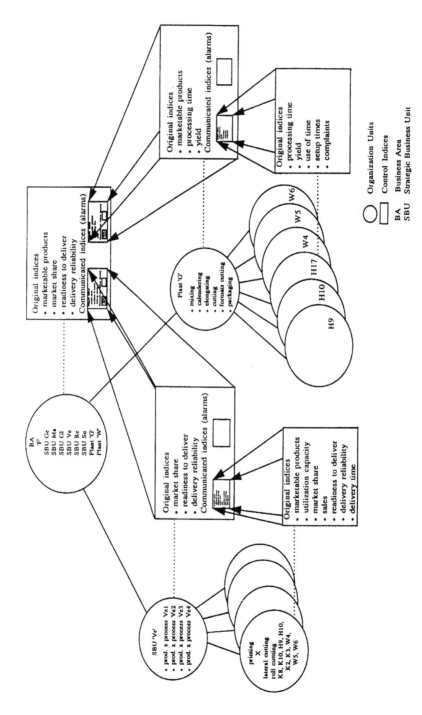

Figure 6.4 Example of index system (CyberSyn-Team 1990/91)

- Finally the users of the new information system defined their own control indices that should prove to be valuable working tools for them in their respective areas of responsibility (Figure 6.4). These indices are meant to emerge basically within the discretion of each actor, and to support autonomy and self-organization. They were defined by managers at all levels themselves, with some external help.
- Eventually, the functioning of the division changed along the lines of the Viable System Model, shifting from an essentially functionalist pattern to a business-process oriented organization, operating in a recursive mode (i.e. the division assuming the structure of a viable system, and containing business units equally conceived as viable systems).

These activities were carried out internally, promoted by the division management, with the support of a "core" team of specialists/facilitators. We interacted with the organization via these promoters,
—the director of the division and his deputy ("power promoters")
—the core team ("change agents").

In regular meetings we gave the internal partners conceptual and technical support. Some of this was provided via written reports. A major "linking pin" function was maintained by the division director's assistant, who did much of the internal analytical work, always in interaction with us—the two external partners. He worked close to his boss and, at the same time, was a very active member of the core team. Through his thorough understanding of cybernetics and good knowledge of the organization's functioning he was invaluable as an amplifier in the process:

1. He amplified the director's (and his own) thinking while acting in the core team.
2. He amplified the external consultants' conceptual knowledge in his interaction with his boss and with the rest of the core team.

Finally, the conceptual input of the external consultants was powerfully amplified via the whole organization by both the power promoters and the core team. An advantage of this indirect approach was that these change agents only amplified what they properly understood and accepted. In sum, they constructed their solutions to their problems, not our solutions to what we thought their problems were.

During the course of this project rather sound solutions were worked out as far as the techno-instrumental side was concerned. But it is only the dimension of human behaviour that renders these solutions valuable. The most ambitious and probably most important aspects of the project were neither the analysis of the organization nor the technical cross-linking or the design of structures and control indices. They are rather to be found:

- in the communication process through which different interpretations of reality interact and "shared meanings" are negotiated;
- in the acquisition of new reference models ("frameworks", "mindsets", "mental models") that assist the users to understand and perceive their role within the organization in the sense of self-control and responsibility with respect to a greater whole;
- in the help to detach oneself from obsolete routines and patterns of behaviour. Some players superficially espoused the "systemic framework" without really changing their established paradigm. In other words, their reductionist or functionalist "theories-in-use" (Argyris, 1992) remained unrevised, albeit their conspicuous enthusiasm for the new models. "Many managers would use cybernetics by intuition, but they do not dare to act like this because it contradicts their models of micro-economics . . . I call this 'terror of wrong paradigm' " (Personal note from a German top manager 13.6.91 and 22.10.96).

The pertinent necessity to reframe one's thinking was a major difficulty in the process. Many members of the organization, although highly trained in disciplines such as physics, chemistry and biology, showed mental "barriers to entry" to systemic thinking. Another difficulty was the opportunism of some players, who superficially espoused the "systemic framework", without really changing their established paradigm. In other words, their reductionist or functionalist "theories-in-use" (Argyris, 1992) remained unrevised, albeit their conspicuous enthusiasm for the new models. However, the director himself, his deputy and his assistant were a strong force: they took on the sophisticated and often frustrating job of fostering systemic thinking via

- learning by the (successful) example and
- training on-the-job

When finalizing our project, we decided to write a book—as a legacy to other managers (Espejo et al, 1996).

In sum, this project became a vehicle for self-organized learning, because it strengthened the autonomy and the self-steering capabilities of the actors involved, while facilitating interaction via an appropriate techno-instrumental infrastructure.

SOME IMPORTANT DEVELOPMENTS

In the following some reservations against system theory and cybernetics will be used to demonstrate how alive this perspective is and how much potential it holds. This will be illustrated by developments under four headings, which were identified as crucial challenges to systems oriented management research, in an early study (Schwaninger, 1989b): "relevance", "dynamism", "humanism" and "synthesis".

Relevance

Again and again cybernetics and system theory have been accused of contributing little towards the solution of problems in organizations. The arguments impute an abstract and vague nature to these theories. These critics tend to forget that earlier fundamental theories such as the theory of thermodynamics and the mathematical information theory, although not translatable right away, have been of eminent significance for actual development. Putting the question "What's the use?" often reveals more about the shortsightedness of the one who is asking than about the relevance of the theory in question. Theorems like Ashby's (1964) Law of Requisite Variety or Beer's Viable System Model was probably of equally fundamental relevance (for managers) as the theories mentioned above (for engineers). It is just that the run-up time for their practical realization is often underestimated.

Today there are numerous applications of these theories taking place the world over. In the recent past some empirical evidence on such applications has been compiled and documented (see, e.g., Espejo and Harnden, 1989; Espejo and Schwaninger, 1993; Espejo, Schuhmann and Schwaninger, 1996).

In many cases there is a large gap between abstract categories of system theory and cybernetics and the conceptions of the realities in organizations. An additional problem is that explanations of economic and corporate cybernetics are often still apprehended to the perspective of machine cybernetics. On the other hand, there are management oriented papers that profess to be based on a "systemic view" or "paradigm", but it is hard to see the connection to these fundamentals.

A faculty team at the University of St Gallen, headed by Professor Knut Bleicher, for the last few years has been trying to take some steps towards bridging this gap. In the project, "St Gallen Management Concept", a framework for research and teaching in the field of general management was newly defined at the University of St Gallen. The fundamental book by Bleicher (1992) was published under the title of *Das Konzept. Integriertes Management (The Concept. Integrative Management)*.

The synopsis of the new St Gallen Management Framework in Figure 6.5 illustrates the aim of a comprehensive, systems oriented perspective:

- in the vertical dimension which ties up the different logical levels of normative, strategic and operative management;
- in the horizontal dimension which suggests a multidimensional integration through activities, structures and behaviour along the three levels;

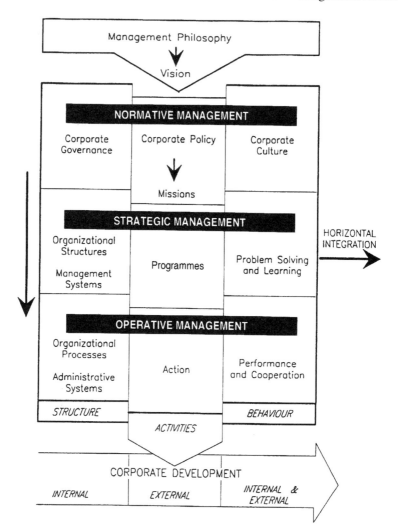

Figure 6.5 Synopsis of the St Gallen Management Framework (Bleicher 1992)

- in the temporal dimension which emphasizes the dynamic aspect of corporate development.

Bleicher's work has already been complemented by publications by Pümpin and Prange (1992), Gomez and Zimmermann (1993), and Schwaninger (1994). At least one more book on the St Gallen Management Framework is planned (Müller-Stewens, in preparation). Feedback from multiple seminars with executives, documents very positive resonance from the business world, which in this context is a good proxy for "relevance".

Dynamism

The so-called "Systemic Thinking" can with its one-sided versions get on the wrong track to astonishingly static views. There is a tendency in human thinking to picture reality in snapshots that will subsequently become stronger but will hardly change at all (cp. von Foerster, 1977). If you cling to the accustomed paradigm, you associate primarily lasting and static configurations with the term "system". Similar to how scientists are increasingly beginning to understand their descriptions—concepts, models and theories—as networks, we today do not regard the reality in organizations as a rigid structure but as a web of relationships that is constantly changing and evolving. The emphasis is not on the picture of the company that "has a structure" but on the conception of an organization that "is a process".

In the next few years management research will have to look much closer into the aspects of change and time such as the learning by organizations, the time constants of structural and cultural transformation, into reaction times, into the beat, rhythm and pulsation of the processes within organizations (cf. Malik, 1993).

In the new St Gallen Management Framework this aspect is already a major factor (cf. Pümpin and Prange, 1992, Schwaninger, 1994, Chapter 7).

Similarly the mathematical theories of dynamic systems should be explored to a larger extent (e.g. fractal geometry, chaos theory, complexity theory). In particular, though, it is the use of simulations of organizations that will increase enormously in importance. The methodology of System Dynamics, for instance, has proven its worth in the most diverse applications in over 35 years of development since Forrester's Industrial Dynamics (1961) (for a recent overview, see Morecroft and Sterman 1994). In a few years' time the survival of many enterprises will depend crucially on (a) whether they are equipped with such models and (b) how good these models are. The example on pages 144 on will revert to this issue.

Humanism

Hearing the words "system theory" and "cybernetics" we often think of tools, computers, forms, information technology. A systems oriented perspective, however, provides much more than just a basis for instrumental, techno-structural devices. It is equally aware of the sociological and psychological, communicative and cultural aspects of social organism. Moreover, it can fertilize processes of "sensemaking" in a positive way.

The perspective of second-order cybernetics corroborates humanistic postulates such as participation, autonomy and meaningfulness of work on structure-theoretical grounds. In a way, it is the recursive theorem on the viability of organizations that so far best substantiates the postulate "Each employee a manager" which in practice often degenerates into a mere slogan (cf. Schwaninger, 1994).

Similarly, under the motto of humane management there is a lot of attention to "employee development", but far too often this means development under purely extrinsic control, among other things with the help of a "delivery of meaning" that easily turns into manipulation. I suggest to move the angle of perception: not enterprises develop employees, but enterprises are developed by employees. For realizing such a view, concepts of the new (second-order) cybernetics can be helpful, for example:

- the evolutionist perspective, e.g. by Umpleby (1986): "A social system in an ecology of competing conceptual systems";
- the perspective from learning theory, e.g. Thomas and Harri-Augstein's approach of "self-organized learning" (1980), that examines organizations under the aspect of the "negotiation of shared meanings";
- the communication-theoretic perspective, e.g. by the authors Winograd and Flores (1986) who understand enterprises as "networks of conversations", with fundamental implications for the design of information systems;
- the constructivist perspective which conceives human action in organization as one of designing new realities and bringing them about (cf. Espejo, Schuhmann and Schwaninger, 1996).

Synthesis

Representatives of the systems oriented perspective have often—whether on purpose or not—taken up positions that are in opposition to more traditional teachings. In one misinterpretation of the evolutionist theory of science they behave as if progress in cognition was only possible if all former theories were dismissed. In doing so they fail to see that many time-tested theories and techniques are still valid, although notice is taken that the scope of their validity may be smaller than assumed so far. Often the old theory is not defeated by the new one but specified, enlarged, connected or integrated. One example is classical mechanics whose laws were not superseded by relativity theory, but remain valid for wide areas.

The representatives of the "Soft Systems Methodology" as well as those of the so-called "hard" systems approaches are learning that in many applications it is imperative to integrate both ways of thinking on a higher level or at least make connections. Specific approaches in this direction can be found in Flood and Jackson (1991), Espejo (1993), Lane and Oliva (1994), and Schwaninger (1995). Major efforts should be made to strengthen interdisciplinary work because it is often so difficult to overcome departmental egotisms. It is essential to tear down barriers to communication and build bridges. Integration capability requires connection capability and connection capability requires, in cybernetic terms, transduction capacity. Exactly these capacities are at the heart of the systems approach, which furnishes a common language to deal with complex issues across disciplines.

Recent developments in systems methodology have also shown that coping with ever more complex situations calls for an integration of the objectivist and the subjectivist frameworks, of communicational and conceptual rationalities, of qualitative and quantitative modelling (Figure 6.6). The categories denoted on the left side of Figure 6.6 are more linked to first-order cybernetics and to the positivistic paradigm, while those on the right side are rather related to second-order cybernetics and to the hermeneutic paradigm (see page 130). All of them are necessary to deal with complexity effectively.

The concept of Integrative Systems Modelling is part of CSM—Cybernetics Systems Methodology—a comprehensive methodology for dealing with complex issues in organizations (Schwaninger, 1996) (as a synonym, the term ISM—Integrative Systems Methodology—has also been used (Schwaninger, forthcoming)).

The scheme in Figure 6.7 outlines the rationale of CSM:

1. It is based on the basic operations of modelling, assessing, designing and changing.
2. These operations deal not only with the substantive issue at hand ("content"), but also the organizational setting in which it is embedded ("context").
3. The operations proceed in an iterative fashion.

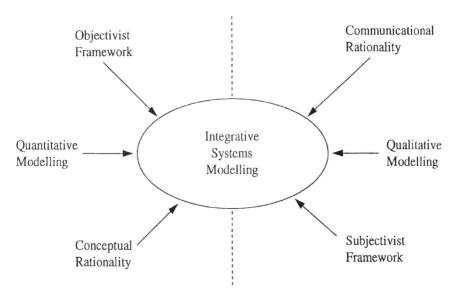

Figure 6.6 Integrative systems modelling marries two paradigms

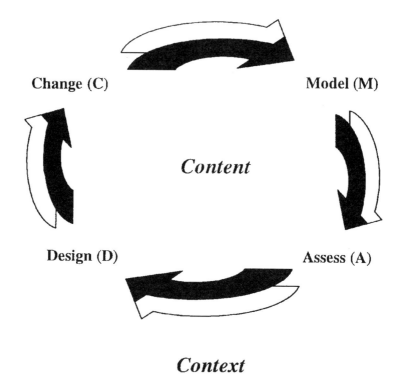

Figure 6.7 Cybernetic systems methodology—an overview (Schwaninger 1996)

An example follows.

Example

The example to be discussed here originates from research for an "integral" approach to management, carried out in relationship with the St Gallen Management Framework (see page 139).

Origins: a concept of integral management

One of the results of this research was a framework for integral management outlining the system of steering variables which is necessary (and sufficient) for an organization to achieve comprehensive fitness. Figure 6.8 depicts the network of goal variables of corporate management within their interrelationships.

It becomes apparent that on the three logical levels—operational, strategic, normative—different rationalities apply. The variables show horizons of

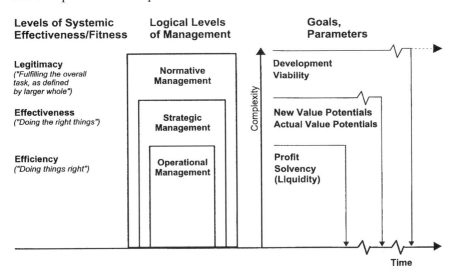

Levels of Systemic Effectiveness/Fitness	Logical Levels of Management	Goals, Parameters

Legitimacy
("Fulfilling the overall task, as defined by larger whole")

Normative Management

Development Viability

Effectiveness
("Doing the right things")

Strategic Management

New Value Potentials Actual Value Potentials

Efficiency
("Doing things right")

Operational Management

Profit Solvency (Liquidity)

Complexity

Time

Figure 6.8 Levels of organizational fitness and pertinent reference values (Schwaninger 1989a)

impact that increase from bottom to top and from there they have the effect of pre-control on the following levels. Today the correlations between the variables illustrated here have only just begun to be corroborated theoretically and empirically, and the same is true for their effects of pre-control (cp. Gälweiler, 1990; Schwaninger, 1989a).

It is also possible to illustrate this model in abstracted form in the categories of a cybernetic control cycle, although it quickly becomes apparent that mechanistic and even biologistical ideas are insufficient to deal with organizational setting.

The control system outlined in Figure 6.9 has several levels and proves that the same process cannot be pre-controlled as well as controlled with the same variables. It is true that the pre-control variables for profits are control variables as well (from a strategic point of view), but their use requires a different rationality and language than that of the operative ones. Another factor is that they are less precise. Analogous to this is the situation where the goal variables of normative management are concerned. On this level control signifies the result of communication processes of multiple constituencies. Here the control variables are not as tangible as on the operative level (costs, revenues) but soft, intangible (and thus susceptible to criticism), and for all that more important. They concern ethical, aesthetic norms and values, cultural patterns and structural principles.

In the same way as hard and soft factors were integrated into this concept, quantitative and qualitative factors should in future be increasingly interconnected in the construction of models.

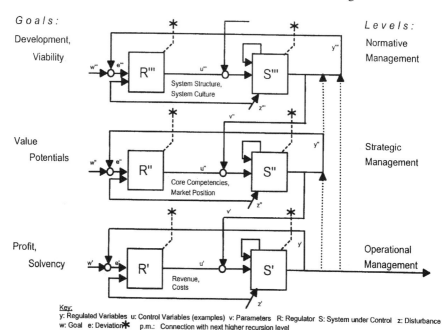

Figure 6.9   Integral management as a multi-level control cycle

If the operative variables can to a large extent be ascertained via established accounts, the strategic and the normative domains are more difficult to access: the relevant knowledge is distributed among many heads. More so, much of it does not (yet) exist objectively, because it can only emerge from a discourse between those who carry such "elements" or "prerequisites". The knowledge gained in such a process is not equal to the sum of elements of knowledge available beforehand. It can be of an entirely new quality which is more a function of synergistic interaction than of mere addition of components. Conclusively, an objectivist model designed by an outside observer would not suffice to portray strategic issues. These are a case for cooperative modelling, in which the two types of rationality—conceptual/instrumental and communicational/sociocultural—have to be "married".

Application: Integrative Systems Modelling

The practice of management confronts paradoxes all the time—perceived contradictions which result from the different meanings one and the same event may obtain depending on the logical level of observation: a cost reduction can make sense from an operative stance, because it "saves" the current profit and loss statement. At the same time, this very cost reduction can be highly detrimental from a strategic point of view, if it impairs a value potential, for example via compromises in the quality or innovation domains.

The different meanings ascribed to phenomena are often at the core of dissent and conflict in organizations. Consequently, collaborative model building meets a growing necessity in management teams, namely those facing turbulent environments.

In the application reported here such a collaborative modelling venture was undertaken, in the case of a RITTS—Regional Innovation and Technology Transfer System (documented in Schwaninger (1995))—as they are being developed, to foster competitiveness, in several regions of Europe. Under the umbrella of a research project (Sprint Project DG XIII/D-4 on Computer Based Modelling, Simulation and Graphic Representation of Technology Innovation Networks) I accomplished the task of helping the newly formed steering committee of the RITTS in Aachen, Germany, in meeting two objectives:

(a) To elaborate a model for supporting that committee's decisions.
(b) To create a platform for cooperation between the parties (companies, personalities and institutions) involved in the RITTS project.

The project consisted of two major modules:

I Building a qualitative model (by means of a soft systems methodology)
II Elaborating a quantitative model (by means of the System Dynamics methodology).

In the first module, we used the Methodology of Network Thinking (MNT—developed at the University of St Gallen and outlined in Gomez and Probst (1987, 1995) and Probst and Gomez (1992)), a soft systems methodology developed for the specific purpose of handling complex issues in organizational settings. In two workshops with members of the steering committee of the RITTS and staff supporting them, the following outcomes were elaborated:

• a list of the perspectives relevant to the Aachen RITTS, their respective objectives and the key factors for their attainment;
• a network model of the factors constituting and driving the RITTS;
• a clear picture of which variables were controllable, and which were not;
• an initial, exemplary set of strategic action programmes.

In these workshops, the soft systems methodology applied proved to be very powerful

• for the purpose of eliciting knowledge from a heterogeneous group of actors;

- leading to better mental models of the complex issues at hand and to a better understanding by the people involved.[1]

Beyond this, the process of applying that methodology—given competent coaching ("moderation")—enhanced the connectivity and cohesion of the group involved, and facilitated the group problem-solving process enormously.

Summing up, applying MNT led to great progress, from a conceptual/ instrumental as well as from a social/communicational point of view. The coordinators of the project asserted that the results were far above their expectations.

The advantage of qualitative systems methodology lies in capturing highly complex issues with a small set of variables: although our model encompassed nine different perspectives (companies, employees, districts, ecology, etc.) it confined itself to 27 variables. With the help of the GAMMA-software (a product of UNICON, Meersburg, Germany, available also in English), these were classified into four categories: "active", "passive", "inert" and "critical".

However, that network-type soft system model would not meet the needs of a decision support model which could allow quantitative simulations and give substantial answers to "what-if" questions. Elaborating such a model was the objective of model II.

Together with José Pérez Ríos, a professor at the University of Valladolid, Spain, subsequently a system dynamics model was elaborated (see Pérez Ríos, 1995; Schwaninger, 1995). In order to get to meaningful qualifications we finally needed roughly 200 variables. This led to a model with seven modules (Figure 6.10). By the end of the project (February 1996) the model had been structurally validated. It demonstrated powerful simulation capabilities and gave counter-intuitive answers to the most demanding questions (e.g. How does ecological consciousness impinge on employment in the region? Which type of budget allocation will have the greatest impact on regional attractiveness?).

Until now, the model had a drawback: it has not been underlined sufficiently with real values from the Aachen region; some validation procedures (e.g. behaviour reproduction test) still lie ahead, and will depend on pertinent funding.

Yet, in principle this project embodies a most valuable synthesis of

- the subjectivist framework with different actors designing their models, and the objectivist framework with the quest for a "best" possible (consensual) model representing a domain of reality shared by a group of actors;

---

[1] "Better" as used here refers to a comparison with an earlier state, as well as with a hypothesized situation in which the other methods commonly used in such situations would have been applied.

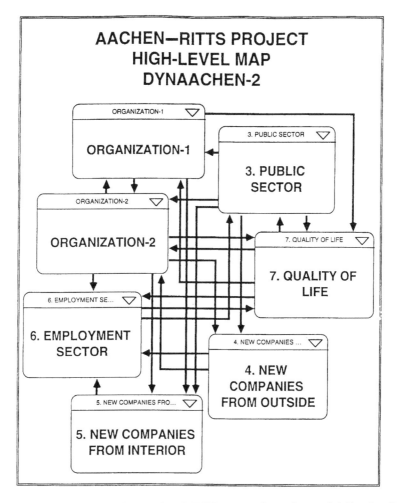

Figure 6.10 Overview of the Aachen-RITTS system dynamics model (for details see Pérez Ríos and Schwaninger 1996)

- the conceptual rationality of a logical representation of pertinent variables with their interrelationships, and the communicational rationality of a group striving to cope with situational complexity;
- the qualitative modelling capturing multiple perspectives in few highly aggregated, "fuzzy" variables with quantitative modelling needing additional formalization, analysis and disaggregation.

It must be emphasized, that the combination of the qualitative MNT modelling and the quantitative modelling was not a mechanical one. The qualitative model of 27 variables and their interrelationships identified in the workshops could not possibly be transformed into the model with 200 variables by any algorithm. The former represented the way of the RITTS actors to model their system-in-focus.

The latter was a translation into a more sophisticated simulation "engine", realized by two experts, on the grounds of

- the substantive knowledge gained in the interaction with those actors;
- theoretical knowledge about invariant structures of complex systems (in this context, the term "system archetypes" is often used);
- knowledge in formal model-building.

The strengths of the methodologies proved to be highly complementary. While relying exclusively on the qualitative model would prove to be insufficient, the same turned out to be a most powerful prerequisite for the SD model. Also, the specific procedure followed in the qualitative modelling process (for details, see Schwaninger, 1995) has led to insights which the traditional, positivistic modelling rationale could not have bred.

OUTLOOK

The systems approach can convey substantial benefits to management research. As a framework, it enables the braiding of a connecting "thread" between different disciplines for innovative synergy. As a methodology it provides powerful metamethods and methods for coping with increasing complexity. However, there is not one systems approach, there are many. There are also conflicts, deficits of communication and maybe even incommensurability between certain "schools" of the systems movement. Generally, a deep gap still yawns between "quantitative" and "qualitative" approaches.

As a demand for holistic, integrated approaches to problem solutions becomes increasingly acute, connecting not only different disciplinary perspectives but also complementary methodologies promises synergies. I have tried to demonstrate that the system oriented perspective constitutes a valuable basis for management research to operate "holistically": in a relevant, dynamic, humane and integrative manner.

This potential power, however, has only been exploited to a small fraction. The reason for this is partly the youth of the perspective and the so far relatively limited diffusion of the pertinent theoretical equipment.

In this contribution, developments towards more relevant and dynamic, as well as humanistic and integrative, contributions have been outlined. On the grounds of a long-range explorative research, possibilities and problems of combining an instrumental logic and a discursive (communicative) logic of systemic problem solving have been discussed.

The systems oriented perspective is still "in its prime". It can make a major contribution to meeting the challenges that arise today provided it develops further. This is why, finally, I would like to name three tasks of systems oriented management research that in my view have high priority.

First, there is a great need for synthesis. It is necessary to make more use of the connective capability of systems theory for the purposes of interdisciplinary work and generally for integration purposes. However, it is also apparent that a synthesis of different systems oriented perspectives is required. It is not enough to build bridges between qualitative and quantitative perspectives. In dealing with complex challenges it is moreover advisable to realize synergies between those methods that spring from the interpretative, hermeneutics of interpretation and those from the positivistic stream of enquiry.

Second, it is necessary to continue to translate ideas from systems theory and cybernetics into statements, concepts and methods that are relevant to management. To achieve this there is, for instance, enormous promise for progress in utilizing recent findings from mathematics and statistics, information technology, behavioural sciences and epistemology. It will be decisive to cast the statements, concepts, etc., in such a way that managers can understand them. This is a transduction task.

Third, it is necessary to pay attention not only to the "How" questions but also to the "What" questions, i.e. the philosophical questions. We have to create much more room for the dimensions of higher orders—the ethical and aesthetical—in the design of our social and also technical systems.

Systems theory makes it possible to build a bridge not only between various specialized disciplines but even between arts and sciences. To "build this bridge" a lot of (practical) experimentation as well as (theoretical) reflection will be needed.

REFERENCES

Argyris, Chris (1992). *On Organizational Learning.* Blackwell, Cambridge, MA.
Ashby, W. Ross (1964). *An Introduction to Cybernetics.* Methuen, London.
Beer, Stafford (1979). *The Heart of Enterprise.* Wiley, Chichester.
Beer, Stafford (1989). The Viable System Model: its provenance, development, methodology and pathology. In R. Espejo and R. Harnden (eds) *The Viable System Model. Interpretations and Applications of Stafford Beer's VSM*, pp. 11–37. Wiley, Chichester.
Bleicher, Knut (1992). *Das Konzept. Integrieres Management* (2nd edn). Campus, Frankfurt/New York. (1st edn: 1991).
Checkland, Peter, B. (1981). *Systems Thinking, Systems Practice.* Wiley, Chichester.
CyberSyn-Team (1990/91). Unpublished documentation internal to firm.
Espejo, Raúl (1993). Management of complexity in problem solving. In R. Espejo and M. Schwaninger (eds) *Organizational Fitness. Corporate Effectiveness through Management Cybernetics.* Campus, Frankfurt/New York.

Espejo, Raúl and Harnden, Roger (eds) (1989). *The Viable System Model. Interpretations and Applications of Stafford Beer's VSM.* Wiley, Chichester.
Espejo, Raúl, Schuhmann, Werner, Schwaninger, Markus and Bilello, Ubaldo (1996). *Organizational Transformation and Learning. A Cybernetic Approach to Management.* Wiley, Chichester.
Espejo, Raúl and Schwaninger, Markus (eds) (1993). *Organizational Fitness. Corporate Effectiveness through Management Cybernetics.* Campus, Frankfurt/New York.
Flood, Robert L. and Jackson, Michael C. (1991). *Creative Problem Solving. Total Systems Intervention.* Wiley, Chichester.
Forrester, Jay (1961). *Industrial Dynamics.* MIT Press, Cambridge, MA.
Gälweiler, Aloys (1990). *Strategische Unternehmensführung* (2nd edn). Compiled, edited and supplemented by Markus Schwaninger. Campus, Frankfurt/New York.
Gomez, Peter and Probst, Gilbert J.B. (1987). Vernetztes Denken im Management, Die Orientierung Nr. 89. Schweizerische Volksbank, Bern.
Gomez, Peter and Probst, Gilbert J.B. (1995). *Die Praxis des ganzheitlichen Problemlösens. Vernetzt Denken—Unternehmerisch handeln—Persönlich überzeugen.* Haupt, Bern.
Gomez, Peter and Zimmermann, Tim (1993). *Unternehmensorganisation. Profile— Dynamik—Methodik* (2nd edn). Campus, Frankfurt/New York. (1st edn: 1992).
Habermas, Jürgen (1988). *Theorie des kommunikativen Handelns.* Edition Suhrkamp, Frankfurt am Main.
Lane, David C. and Oliva, Rogelio (1994). The Greater Whole: Towards a Synthesis of System Dynamics and Soft System Methodology. City University, Business School, Working Paper Series, No. IM/94/DCL2, London.
Linstone, H.A. and Simmonds, W.H.C. (eds) (1977). *Futures Research. New Directions.* Addison/Wesley, Reading, MA.
Luhmann, Niklas (1990). *Die Wissenschaft der Gesellschaft.* Suhrkamp, Frankfurt am Main.
Malik, Fredmund (1993). Understanding a knowledge organization as a viable system. In R. Espejo and M. Schwaninger (eds) *Organizational Fitness. Corporate Effectiveness through Management Cybernetics.* Campus, Frankfurt/New York.
Morecroft, John D.W. and Sterman, John D. (eds) (1994). *Modeling for Learning Organizations.* Productivity Press, Portland, OR.
Müller-Stewens, Günter (in preparation). *Strategische Unternehmensführung.*
Pérez Rios, José (1995). The Methodology of "System Dynamics" and Evaluation of the "IThink" Software. Final Report, Spring Project DG XIII/D-4, October.
Pérez Rios, José and Schwaninger, Markus (1996). Integrative Systems Modelling. Leveraging complementarities of qualitative and quantitative methodologies, in: Proceedings, 1996 International System Dynamics Conference, eds. Richardson, George P. and Sterman, John D., Cambridge, Massachusetts, 21–25 July 1996, Volume 2, pp. 431–434.
Probst, Gilbert J.B. and Gomez, Peter (1992). Thinking in networks to avoid pitfalls of managerial thinking. In Magoroh Maruyama (ed.) *Context and Complexity.* Springer, Berlin/Heidelberg, pp. 91–108.
Pümpin, Cuno and Prange, Jürgen (1992). *Management der Unternehmensentwicklung. Phasengerechte Führung und der Umgang mit Krisen* (2nd edn). Campus, Frankfurt/New York. (1st edn: 1991).
Schwaninger, Markus (1989a). *Integrale Unternehmensplanung.* Campus, Frankfurt/New York.
Schwaninger, Markus (1989b). Zur Zukunft der systemorientierten Managementforschung, Diskussionsbeiträge des Instituts für Betriebswirtschaftslehre an der Hochschule St. Gallen, Nr. 13.

Schwaninger, Markus (1994). *Managementsysteme.* Campus, Frankfurt/New York.

Schwaninger, Markus (1995). From Network Thinking to Integrative Modelling, European Union, SPRINT Project DG XIII/D-4 on Computer-based Modelling, Simulation and Graphic Representation of Technology Innovation Networks. Final Report, University of St Gallen.

Schwaninger, Markus (1996). CSM-Cybernetic Systems Methodology. Working Paper, Institute of Management, University of St Gallen, March.

Schwaninger, Markus (forthcoming). Integrative Systems Methodology. Heuristic for requisite variety. *International Transactions of Operational Research.*

Thomas, Laurie F. and Harri-Augstein, E. Sheila (1980). *Self-Organised Learning. Foundations of a Conversational Science for Psychology.* Routledge & Kegan Paul, London.

Ulrich, Hans (1984). *Management,* edited by Th. Dyllick and G.J.B. Probst. Haupt, Bern and Stuttgart.

Umpleby, Stuart (1986). A Social System is an Ecology of Competing Conceptual Systems. Working Paper, The George Washington University, 28 January.

von Foerster, Heinz (1977). The curious behaviour of complex systems: lessons from biology. In H.A. Linstone and W.H.C. Simonds (eds) *Futures Research. New Directions.* Addison-Wesley, Reading, MA, pp. 104–113.

von Foerster, Heinz (1984). *Observing Systems* (2nd edn). Intersystems Publications, Seaside, CA.

von Foerster, Heinz et al (eds) (1974). *Cybernetics of Cybernetics.* The Biological Computer Laboratory, University of Illinois, Urbana, Illinois.

Winograd, Terry and Flores, Fernando (1986). *Understanding Computers and Cognition.* Ablex, Norwood, NJ.

Chapter 7

Managing a Virtual Organization

ANTHONY GILL

INTRODUCTION

This chapter explores the notion of a virtual organization as a way of managing complexity. Once the concept of a virtual organization (VO) is defined, it is useful to have a way of articulating it and to anticipate the circumstances where it is likely to be used. Multimethodology provides a means for articulating a greater understanding of the VO.

After defining a VO, I then describe the background to a major study of which I was part. This contextual background is given for the real-world surroundings in which such interventions take place. The methods/methodologies used to build the rich picture of the VO for this particular intervention are: Beer's Viable System Model (VSM) for organizational processes; deployment flowcharting (DFC) for business processes; and Warfield's Interactive Management to capture the connectivity of a series of interrelated problems. The chapter ends with a reflection on the process used and conclusions.

What is a Virtual Organization (VO)?

Mention of the words virtual organization is likely to conjure up notions of an organization existing in cyberspace. Just as virtual reality gives the illusion of interacting within some physical space, does this imply that the virtual

Multimethodology: The Theory and Practice of Combining Management Science Methodologies.
Edited by John Mingers and Anthony Gill.
© 1997 John Wiley & Sons Ltd.

organization is also an illusion? Three forms of VO are described: the IT enabled VO, i.e. the geographically dispersed organization integrated by information technology (IT); the network VO, i.e. a set of independent organizations working interdependently for some purpose; and a VO within the Viable System Model (VSM).

Information technology is permitting geographically remote corporate entities to operate in a coordinated manner. Without the technology disparate parts of the organization would not be able to communicate. In some quarters, then, the VO is nothing more than a number of geographically separated parts of an organization "wired" together—the IT enabled VO. This would include the notion of telecommuters working from home and peripatetic workers with their notebook computers linking in periodically to their corporate IT networks. Salesmen logging in their contact management reports and customer orders are an example of the latter category. So are engineers and geologists doing site or field work using notebooks and even mobile phones to log into their corporate systems as a way of maintaining contact with their offices. These work practices are challenging traditional ways of working while reducing office overheads and costs, and result in concepts of "hot-desking" and "hotelling" being applied to knowledge workers (Bredin, 1996).

For others the VO is more than a series of geographically separated parts of the organization wired together. Outsourcing and single sourcing strategies can mean that the VO is a set of independent (in terms of ownership) but interdependent (in terms of strategic intent) companies serving the same market place—the network VO. Benetton is perhaps such an example, although it relies on numerous subcontractors for its garments. So the VO can be a set of organizations that manage a specific supply chain. British Airways has recently been labelled a virtual airline by the press because of its strategic focus on core activities of transporting passengers and cargo. All non-core processes are to be eventually outsourced. Although flexibility and speed of response are key benefits, this model of the VO poses certain problems related to innovation and who controls the VO. Chesbrough and Teece (1996) suggest that "those rushing to form alliances instead of nurturing and guarding their own capabilities may be risking their future". They propose two types of innovation: autonomous and systemic. In matching organization to innovation, management needs to decide if the required capabilities exist externally or need to be created in-house. They accept using the VO where capabilities exist outside and the innovation is autonomous. Where the type of innovation is systemic, caution is the word when trying to ally with an outside organization in order to gain the required capability. While success stories exist, the failures do not make the headlines.

The rest of this section concerns the use of the VO within the VSM. Before the popular notion of the VO emerged, Raúl Espejo proposed its use to solve a particular problem we were working on during 1990. We were carrying out an organizational study using Beer's Viable System Model (Beer, 1979, 1981, 1985; Espejo, 1989a, b) for a large multinational organization. In order to better manage organizational complexity, senior management adopted a three-dimensional matrix structure: market segment; functions; and geography. To solve specific and often ongoing integration issues, unit managers in a particular industry sector set up a Management Action Team (MAT). Our problem related to how to interpret the unfolding of complexity (see Figure 7.1 as an example) for this part of the organization. It was only by using the idea of a VO, that filled a level between the unfolding of viable organizational units, that we could make sense of how the organization as a whole was managed. I will elaborate on this type of problem in the case study later in this chapter.

In general, the VSM is used to explain how complexity is managed by the organization under review and will include an explanation on how communication and control support strategic intent. There rarely is a direct mapping of the organizational chart or matrix onto the VSM. The VSM relies on the principle of recursion based on the primary activities of the organization as a whole: an organizational unit within an organizational unit; a factory within a factory; a cell within a cell. To illustrate this recursive structure, the unfolding of complexity (see Figure 7.1) is used as the graphic device. There are occasions when attempting to determine the unfolding of complexity for the organization that a logical breakdown will occur in this unfolding due to an unexplained gap. This gap, a level of recursion, is an organizational unit logically necessary for the recursive structure of the organization. Sometimes a VO can be used as a tentative hypothesis to fill this gap. In this case, the VO is a mental construct that takes the form of a viable organizational unit. It is not recognized by the organizational members as a viable organizational unit—one that potentially could be hived off. The VO occurs between levels in the "unfolding of complexity", and is itself a level of recursion that will often explain how certain organizational tasks are accomplished.

VOs are likely to be found in large complex functional or matrix structured organizations. Management of VOs is likely to be the responsibility of a group like a MAT or even a committee who are able to command necessary resources to ensure that corporate goals are achieved and integration issues are resolved on an ongoing basis. The emergence of the MAT or equivalent is in response to an "organizational breakdown" where there is a need to work around the structural imperfections of the existing organizational structure and thereby achieve current performance targets. A key aspect of the VO is the sharing of local or tacit knowledge about customers and internal practices. An additional requirement is that members of the VO be well networked into other parts of the formal organization in order that tasks beyond the scope of the VO may be carried out. Thus we have a situation where the MAT are part of a "real organization" but their response, in VSM terms, has been to set up a "virtual organizational unit", although they are unlikely to be aware of this.

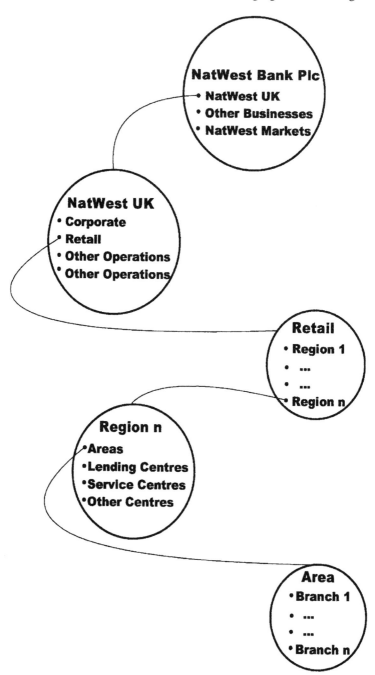

Figure 7.1 Unfolding of complexity

During initial VSM studies, analysts are not likely to establish the presence of a VO. It is only by being aware of certain clues that it may be detected: difficulty in defining structural recursion due to a breakdown in logic; realizing that a group of senior managers from different functional/matrix parts of the organization need to come together regularly to resolve operational issues of coordination and integration. Once the MAT is presented with the VO as a possible recursion level it will formally recognize or reject (by providing additional information) the scenario. Although the MAT may not be able to alter the status quo in the short term, if they accept the VO as a shared mental construct and manage tasks accordingly they are likely to gain significant insights into managing proactively and thereby achieving desired organizational performance. In essence, using a VO in this sense is a diagnostic point in the VSM analysis suggesting that organizational effectiveness may be enhanced by adjustments to organization structure. As soon as the VO is formally recognized through changes to the organization structure this virtual organizational unit ceases to be virtual.

BACKGROUND TO THE PROJECT

Context—the SYCOMT Project

A specific VO that I will articulate has been surfaced during research that has been undertaken (1993–1996) by the SYCOMT consortium which was partially funded by the Department of Trade and Industry's Computer Supported Co-operative Working (CSCW) programme. The academic partner was funded by the Engineering & Physical Sciences Research Council (EPSRC). The consortium members were Lancaster University, NatWest Bank Plc and SYNCHO Ltd, a consultancy specializing in the application of managerial cybernetics in client interventions. In all, the research team involved ten people. Through SYNCHO I was a member of the SYCOMT consortium whose task was encapsulated in the acronym SYCOMT: systems development and co-operative work—methods and techniques.

Until recently, most approaches to systems development were technical. The user had to fit in with the requirements of the technology. Since the introduction of large and expensive mainframe systems often with bespoke software, we have seen the emergence of the mini- and microcomputers. During this time, the user has gained "control" of his or her processing power with the IT department providing support. Off-the-shelf software packages began to proliferate in the working environment often causing compatibility problems between users in the same organization. Corporate directorates were issued in order to standardize software in use. Soon single users of personal computers (PCs) realized that it would be more effective if PCs could communicate with each other and the rapid advances in technology made this possible through the introduction of "local area networks" and "wide area networks". The convergence of telecommunication and computer technologies was at last beginning to happen and internet and intranet technology solutions are becoming widespread. By and large, throughout this diffusion of technology, the user was often a victim of the technology rather than a beneficiary. Yes, having a PC or computer terminal on one's desk may have conferred some form of status but this required a considerable investment in time to get up the learning curve so that beneficial use was possible.

Given that we all work and live in a social environment the issue is how can technology best be exploited to support cooperative work and not how can we adapt ourselves to (the limitations of) technology. In moving from "the technology solution" to "technology as an enabler of cooperative work" we need a far greater understanding of how work is really achieved. This is not to deny that in applying technical solutions workers were not interviewed in order to ascertain their needs. Quite often interviews will surface the espoused view of work rather than what actually transpires (Argyris and Schon, 1978). The ability to capture this latter aspect, i.e. the theory-in-use, in order to develop a good understanding of "how the organizations actually work" is fundamental to good systems design. This was the research question for SYCOMT. In essence, we were developing methods to inform systems development that took account of the nature of cooperative work in a social context. Lancaster University provided skills in the areas of ethnography and computer science. SYNCHO used the management sciences, principally management cybernetics and some current management tools such as deployment flowcharting. NatWest provided access to an area which formed part of a Region within the bank. This afforded us the opportunity to develop a detailed understanding of this part of the bank. Of necessity this chapter covers only a small part of the research carried out and given the nature of the book little mention will be made of work outside operations research and systems.

Context—the Banking Industry

NatWest is one of the major high street banks in the UK. Like all the large banks, it has been undertaking major change programmes as banking is in the throes of a major revolution caused by rapid innovation in the IT industry and increasing national and global competition. The banks are stuck with large mainframe legacy computing systems dating from the 1960s when they were among the first to embrace this new technology. The problem they face is one of migrating to new technology while maintaining customer accounts and records on an ongoing basis. The risks of a "big bang" approach to changing to newer technology are considerable.

Technology has significantly reduced the costs of market entry. First Direct, with its telephone banking service, demonstrates the point. With the proliferation of automated teller machines (ATMs) and cashback offered by all the large food retails chains, the need for high street presence is significantly reduced. This has resulted in the "bricks and mortar" versus technology dilemma. Most have tried to reduce their high street presence by centralizing the "backroom functions".

It is a well-known fact that the UK banking industry is shedding staff at substantial rates and in the course of all this industry rationalization skills requirements have dramatically altered—the shift from "bank tellers' to "sellers of financial products and services". Such a cultural change does not take place overnight. As one may expect issues of low morale caused by fear of job uncertainty are evident. Of course, job uncertainty is not a phenomenon of the banking industry alone. The issues reported in this chapter are widespread in all the banks and are not peculiar to NatWest alone.

Context—the Changing Management Paradigm

> Science is at present undergoing a paradigm shift. The old reductionist ideas suggested that ultimate truth could be discovered by breaking things down into their smallest components and looking at how these ultimate components of matter interact. The reductionist approach is now being replaced by an understanding of the importance of complexity, the way in which very large numbers of seemingly simple things conspire to produce far from simple patterns of behaviour. (Gribbin, 1993)

If *management* were substituted for *science* in the above extract, this would be a fair statement about what is happening in organizations today. Taylorism and scientific management which gave us the functional hierarchy equate to the old reductionist ideas; holistic or process management relates to complexity.

Parkinson's law—"Work expands so as to fill the time available for its completion"—(Parkinson, 1958) bore testimony to this ever increasing organizational complexity. To support his law, Parkinson offers "two almost axiomatic statements, thus: (1) 'An official wants to multiply subordinates, not rivals' and (2) 'Officials make work for each other.' " It has taken the recessions of the 1980s and 1990s and intensifying global competition to begin to dismantle this bureaucracy through the use of outsourcing, flattened hierarchies, outplacement and redundancy. Proactive management of organizational change—continuously adapting to exceed customer expectations—is becoming the norm.

This century has been dominated largely by the management of output, as we moved away from the craftsman in direct contact with the customer to the mass production oriented organization. Managers began to experiment with new ways of organizing so as to maximize production for an apparently limitless market. The "command and control" model developed by the Chinese military some 2000 years ago was adopted by organizations as the way to further efficiency. This hierarchy has functional groups with departments in which the individual performs a repetitive task as the smallest unit of work—the vertical organization.

For most of this century organizations have used a functional structure based on the hierarchical organization chart. This captured the essence of Taylorism and Fordism where the skills expected of the majority of the workforce were physical. While technology has dramatically altered work practices, this structure has hardly changed. Divisionalized forms and matrix structures fail to capture the complexity to be managed. They are little better than the organizational hierarchy which in the words of Beer serves to "apportion blame".

Since then, we have witnessed a shift in management emphasis: Taylorism with its reductionist work practices, though still common today, is losing favour; the focus has shifted from production to selling during the 1950s and 1960s to get rid of manufactured stock; to marketing during the latter part of the 1960s to the early 1980s; until the 1980s and 1990s gave us Total Quality Management (TQM) and a greater focus on *customer needs* (measured by output quality) and *satisfaction* (the judgement that a customer has about a product or service, which is in turn strongly influenced by business processes). The West, which originally helped to modernize Japanese industry and teach quality to the workforce after the Second World War, is now looking East to learn about Kaizen. Earlier this century, Ford made personal transport available to the masses. Now Toyota is teaching the world about JIT (just-in-time inventory) and "lean manufacture" (Womack, Jones and Roos, 1990).

In keeping with the tenets of the Quality Movement, organizations began to use Statistical Process Control charts as a tool to improve the quality of their products. In a similar way, TQM has established the need to define measurable business processes in order to improve them in the drive to increase responsiveness to customers. Through the combination of TQM and the innovative use of technology, especially information technology, to redefine business processes afresh, Business Process Redesign/Reengineering (BPR) emerged as a management idea during the late 1980s (Hammer, 1990; Davenport and Short, 1990; Davenport, 1993). "Process Management" embraces both the philosophy of TQM, with its emphasis on continuous improvement, and the technique of BPR as a vehicle to realign the business in keeping with changes in strategic direction. Under a process oriented approach, a multifunctional team takes responsibility for and has the overview of the process(es) they are accountable for. With well-trained teams working together all parts of the process should be seamlessly linked.

So what is a process? "A process is a specific ordering of work activities across time and place, with a beginning, an end, and clearly identified inputs and outputs: a structure for action" (Davenport, 1993).

In process management terms, four different types of processes need to be recognized:

- Organizational processes—see page 162. These are the regulatory processes prescribed by Beer's (1979, 1981, 1985) VSM to ensure organizational cohesion.
- Business processes—see page 166. These are the customer-related processes that ensure customer satisfaction, and thereby profitability, in the private sector, or meeting "citizen charter" standards in the public sector, thus increasing the chances of the organization's survival.
- Technological processes. These take the form of quantified flow charts as proposed by Stafford Beer (1981). These processes define the "technologies" and material flows used for producing the products and/or services of the organization.
- Information processes. These processes define the information flows necessary to support the data needs of the other three processes and thereby the informational needs of all organizational members.

The latter three processes have similarities to the "three different domains in which to describe activities of an organization: Material Process; Information processes and Business processes" distinguished by Medina-Mora et al (1992). In this chapter, I am focusing on organizational and business processes.

STUDYING THE BANK

Naturally in this account, I will be respecting the commercial sensitivities of NatWest Bank. What is important is the method rather than an account of detailed banking processes. It must also be appreciated that in a three-year study, a change will be apparent as NatWest moves through its transformation process under the vision of "First Choice". In short, problems and issues today are often (dis)solved by tomorrow in keeping with any learning system such as continuous improvement.

To understand the bank's structure and related organizational processes, I am using the Viable System Model. I have focused on the lending process as an example of a business process and have used deployment flowcharting as a way to map this process. This enables business processes to be braided with organizational processes. In the process of doing this a VO is detected. To better understand this VO, Interactive Management (IM) is used to surface related issues within a problem area and thereby communicate and share possible solutions with other organizational members.

I am not giving a full account of the VSM analysis since much of the analysis remains in the domain of "commercial in confidence". Nonetheless, some insights from the analysis will emerge in the course of the chapter. With regard to VSM analysis in general, several cases studies have been reported in the literature (Espejo, 1989a, b; Espejo and Schwaninger, 1993; Brocklesby and Cummins, 1996). The "unfolding of complexity" presented represents a summary of the VSM analysis. Similarly, deployment flowcharting is used in an illustrative rather than exhaustive way. To date IM has not been used as frequently in the UK and Europe as it has been in the Americas and for that reason I am giving a fuller account of our experience in using it. Apart from the problem of space limitations, there is also the issue of client sensitivity in releasing detailed commercial information.

Using the Viable System Model (VSM)—Organizational Processes

A common feature of large organizations is their sheer complexity. Traditionally, they have all been structured around functions with the hierarchical organization chart as the map to establish the pecking order. Beer's Viable System Model (VSM) has been successfully used as an alternative to the functionally driven organization. It is well able to cope with the enormous complexity of the global organization with its vast product range which aims to "think local" by offering customized solutions to specific needs. Additionally, the VSM articulates the "organizational processes" that must be attended to in order to ensure survival over the longer term.

Organizational processes define how the organization "coheres". In effect, the processes help to define the organizational structure. Espejo (1993) writes that "organisation structure is defined by the set of mechanisms constituting the forms of interaction between the people and resources of that organization—where a mechanism is defined as a temporarily stable form of interaction between these parts (i.e. people and resources) which permits them to operate as a whole".

When a medical doctor examines a patient, the doctor is skilled at diagnosing problems based on the comparison with what is known to be a healthy body. The body has a skeleton structure plus various systems: the nervous system; the respiratory system; the circulatory system; the digestive system; etc. All of these "parts and systems" are interconnected to form a unique person. Beer has provided us with the equivalent organizational diagnostic tool—the Viable System Model (VSM). The use of this diagnostic tool is described in Espejo (1989b, 1993).

As the future is unpredictable—consumers influence business outcomes through exercising choice—business units need to be responsive and flexible, i.e. they need to adopt the characteristics of a living system. As business units are created, flourish and die in their attempts to provide products and/or services to customers, the corporate meta-level makes necessary adjustments to accommodate changes in keeping with market realities. Using the VSM as a tool to aid how business units are "plugged in and out of the system" greatly facilitates optimizing the whole and to ensure the creation, maintenance and removal of lifeline linkages and processes in keeping with the life-cycle of the business unit.

The VSM's notion of the "unfolding of complexity" seeks to explain how the various organizational units are embedded in the organization, as well as their relationships with each other and the market place—in short, how the organization goes about its business. The "unfolding of organizational complexity" is shown as a series of recursion levels. Each organizational unit (represented by a circle) is embedded in the next highest level of recursion. Each is viable in the sense that it can survive over time and is directly related to an identified market segment. Each circle contains the five systemic functions of Policy, Intelligence, Monitoring-Control, Coordination and Implementation (Espejo, 1989a). Implementation refers to the primary task or core competence of the organization. The other functions are the vital support or regulatory functions that are essential for viability. At each level of unfolding, the five systemic functions need to occur. The higher recursive levels deal with corporate strategy, the highest level dealing with normative issues (values, beliefs and possibilities for acquisition/divestment and organic growth/decay) and the "grand organizational plan". Lower recursive levels are responsible for balancing their own long-term visions (relative to their operations) with tactical considerations. In this chapter we are using the "unfolding of complexity" as a proxy for the VSM—recalling that each organizational unit is constituted by the five interlinked systems and their relationships to other units.

How these functions are distributed throughout the organization is dependent on the strategic intent and culture of the organization. For a large-scale organization one would expect to see some balance between centralization of resources and the deployment of functions so as to both optimize the organization as a whole and respect the necessary autonomy of each viable unit in order that local problem-solving capability is available to respond to customer requirements. To a large extent, the allocation of resources by an organization determines which organizational units are to be viewed as primary and how the unfolding of complexity is to be enacted. Logically this may not always be done in an optimal way but it may meet the criteria established by management. We are referring to issues of cultural/political feasibility and desirability.

The key organizational processes (Gill, 1995), defined by the VSM, are context dependent and exist at all levels of recursion. They include:

self-regulation; setting a minimal number of "organizational rules"; balancing the Intelligence and Control functions; resources bargaining through the planning process; accountability for achieving agreed plans; coordination of business unit actions to maximize organizational outcomes as a whole; monitoring of lower recursion activities; linking the organization to customers. In short, the organizational processes help in addressing the corporate dual paradox. How do you *continue and change* at the same time? How do you retain *"control"* over the organization as a whole while granting the *autonomy* required for local problem solving?

Interpreting and if necessary designing these processes for the different levels of recursion is a process far removed from the simplistic design of the organization chart. Through "simulating" how the organization works, management can better diagnose and design the preferred structure rather than leave these aspects to the chance that it may emerge at some time in the future. The accelerating competitive environment is unlikely to give organizations time or a second chance to get it right.

Unfolding of complexity

The "unfolding of complexity" is used as a graphical means of illustrating the notion of recursion. We will explain this from the perspective of an Area within NatWest Bank. At the highest level we show NatWest Bank Plc which contains the embedded units of NatWest UK, Other Businesses and NatWest Markets. Within NatWest UK is Retail, Corporate and Other Operations. The Corporate and Retail units unfold into a number of Regions. The Region contains a number of Areas together with the Service Centres and Lending Centres. Branches are shown at the lowest level. This is shown in Figure 7.1 on page 156.

Although branches may be expected to be shown at the lowest level of recursion, Delivery Strategy has removed "backroom" capability from the newer styled branches and centralized resources into Lending Centres, Service Centres and Security Centres. Previously customers going to old style branches had most of their needs provided for directly by the branch which held and maintained their account. Since these branches were autonomous within the operating guidelines of the bank they had the resources and capability to service their customer base directly, i.e. the Branch was viable (in VSM terms) in its own right. Currently, for lending to take place effectively (for the customer), resources need to come from the Branch and the Lending Centre, and, on occasions, from the Service Centre and the Securities Centre in the case of secured loans. New style Branches, now devoid of all the non-customer facing processes, are almost entirely dependent on the support of these Centres in order to jointly serve customer needs. The reality is that these new-style Branches serve customers coming off the street. Telephone and written requests are dealt with by Centres responsible for providing the service.

It emerges as a diagnostic point from the VSM analysis that these new style Branches, on their own, are not viable. In organizational reporting terms, the heads of the new style Branches are managed by an Area Manager. The Area Manager and Managers of the various Centres report to different functional heads within the Region. The necessary overview in VSM terms (i.e. monitoring—control and coordination) of the bank's business processes needs to take place at the level of the Area Manager, Service Centre Manager, Lending Centre Manager, and Securities Centre Manager all of whom have the same customer base in common. At best this overview is happening at the highest levels within the Region which is too remote for effective management of complexity. Viability in VSM terms necessitates effective management and integration of business processes across these new style Branches and the relevant Centre(s). An early outcome of the research was to propose the formation of the meta-level area team (MAT which is discussed later in this section) as a way of managing at the appropriate overview so that the customer may be better served. This overcomes the structural constraints of the bank's functional structure leaving the MAT to manage a *virtual organization*. It is virtual because the MAT are integrating their efforts and resources to serve a common customer base by effectively creating an organizational unit which is viable (in VSM terms) but is not recognized elsewhere in the bank's structure.

Technology has permitted these geographically dispersed units to operate as one. It is also in this sense that I refer to such units as "virtual organizations" and that to support this kind of operation I see the need to have "virtual teams" working together to serve the customer. I would recognize instances of such teams when one or two individuals at the Lending Centre will collaborate with individuals at a Branch on relationship accounts. Through both repeated interactions and by serving customers within the same catchment area, the relationship among members of these teams is likely to strengthen. In this way local knowledge may be shared to better serve clients.

The Area's marketing programme is designed to attract and retain selected relationship-worthy customers by providing a level of service which NatWest Bank staff believe is commensurate with their perceived needs. This process segments the market and provides a differentiated service to the various segments in keeping with life-style marketing concepts. For this marketing programme to be successful good customer contact and relationship management are crucial. Team working between Branch and Centres is crucial for this programme to work.

It should be noted that Delivery Strategy is focused on the internal needs of the bank—primarily cost reduction through limited centralization as a strategy to remain competitive. The marketing strategy is focused on customers. If either strategy is followed to extremes a conflict in resource allocation is likely. I believe that the recognition and development of the concept of the "virtual organization" with its "virtual teams" will satisfy both strategies. For nearly a year I have monitored the progress of the SYNCHO proposed "MAT" (meta-level area team—a virtual team). The prime function of the MAT (comprising Area Manager, Service Centre Manager and Lending Centre Manager—all of whom report to different line managers) has been to coordinate activities between their respective units to better serve customers. This has been possible because of the overview provided by the MAT in considering the total situation. In view of the superior performance of the area as a whole managed by the MAT compared to other areas in the country, the bank is now considering how to formalize the notion of the MAT into its operating procedures. If the virtual organization managed by the MAT is formally recognized and integrated into the bank's structure then it will be part of the formal structure and the virtual organization in the VSM sense ceases to exist. I see this as a key strategy for large, complex organizations: empowered managers at all levels of the organization experiment with cross-functional teams and organizational units to overcome existing structural weaknesses through the creation of virtual organizations that are seen as part of the "unfolding of complexity". If these VOs deliver superior performance in the context of the entire organization then they are to be formalized by inclusion in the formal structure.

Using Deployment Flow Charting (DFC)—Business Processes

The move towards the "horizontal organization" is gathering momentum as more and more organizations from both the public and private sectors begin to embrace process management. Conceptually, this implies integrating all the activities and functions of the business into a series of linked processes in order to provide better products or services for customers. Achieving this may appear to be easy enough for the smaller organization, but what about the large organization?

Business processes are those key customer focused processes that deliver products/services to delight the customer. "In definitional terms, a process is simply a structured, measured set of activities designed to produce a specified output for a particular customer or market. It implies a strong emphasis on *how* work is done in an organization, in contrast to a product focus's emphasis on *what*" (Davenport, 1993). Business processes are generally highly industry specific.

Stewart (1992) describes glimpses of the future organization being developed by McKinsey & Co., the firm of management consultants. This future views the change from the vertical organization, i.e. functional hierarchy, to the process oriented horizontal organization. This organization has multifunctional teams that are accountable for core or business processes that may cross a number of functions. These business processes start and end with the customer. Shapiro, Rangan, Sviokla (1992) capture the ethos with their expression, "staple yourself to an order".

In order to capture and represent business processes, deployment flowcharting, sometimes referred to as matrix or functional flowcharting (Harrington, 1991), is a useful technique. A key element of deployment flowcharting (DFC) lies in its ability to capture the "relationships that shape all processes" (Howard, 1995). Thus processes are sequenced in columns relating to the organizational unit that "owns" the process. The complexity in defining processes can be enormous depending on the amount of detail required and the complexity of the organization itself.

In the SYCOMT research programme, I was keen to explore the link between business processes and organizational processes as prescribed by the VSM. Most initiatives involving Business Process Re-engineering (BPR) or Total Quality Management (TQM) tend to focus on the business processes and use the hierarchical organizational chart as the basis for considering organization structure. This aspect together with the trend towards "delayering" is likely to lead to organizational pain of some kind caused by short-term thinking and an obsessive concern with the bottom line as the only necessary measure of performance. Traditionally, DFC uses functional units as process owners and to head the process column. I was intent on using organizational units that formed part of the "unfolding of complexity" as the process owners. Thus by braiding business with organizational processes I believe that organizations will have a much "richer picture" of themselves and they are more likely to be responsive to and proactively manage change to ensure organizational survival in the longer term. Having access to FlowMap Professional software offered an opportunity to combine the use of the VSM with current techniques for implementing BPR. This I hoped would attract interest in the VSM and thus make it more likely to be considered in organizational analysis. Soft Systems Methodology (SSM) was not initially considered for this flowcharting process. However, during the flowcharting process I became conscious that I was using SSM to resolve dilemmas about levels of resolution.

Flowcharting is a technique that is used by practitioners of both TQM and BPR as a way of capturing and recording business processes. Its popularity is due to the relative ease with which the technique can be learnt and the fact that it has been supported by software tools to graphically capture these processes for nearly a decade. Although there has been some attempt at standardization of the techniques, and in particular the symbols, these attempts have to some extent failed—due, to some degree, to the vested interests of software vendors. Within a single organization, however, there needs to be a single recognized standard approach so that work from different groups may be shared without having to re-invent flowcharting for each different initiative. For any organization that embraces continuous improvement this would seem a basic requirement.

NatWest has carried out a considerable amount of flowcharting itself. However, we did not have access to flow charts that could serve as useful input to our research work. For this reason we produced our own flow charts with the assistance of the NatWest Project Manager, the MAT and staff in the Area where we were carrying out our research.

I had access to a software package called FlowMap which adheres to most recognized standards. The specific technique that I used is called "deployment flowcharting". This enables a matrix approach where processes that are undertaken by a specific organizational unit will all be located under the column heading of this unit. The rows are numbered making it easy to discuss complex charts by referring to processes by column heading and row number. The symbols that I have used are shown in Figure 7.2.

I have used the rectangle to represent a process. Where the rectangle is shadowed this indicates that by double clicking with the mouse on the screen at this point, the user is taken down to lower level processes. By clicking on the reverse shadow effect the user is taken to the next higher process.

FlowMaps for NatWest

Figures 7.3 and 7.4 are shown as an example of the flowcharting work for NatWest. This represents a summary of numerous discussions with various people, particularly the MAT who have taken these FlowMaps away to discuss with members of their staff. Often words have been changed to reflect the language of the bank. Most importantly, I believe that I had the important "buy-in" from the MAT for these processes as they were involved in creating them.

The lending process has not been captured in its entirety. To do this I would have had to involve many other parts of the bank which was beyond the scope of this research project. I have demonstrated the use of deployment flowcharting as a technique. More importantly, I have linked the recursive modelling process of the Viable System Model to deployment flowcharting thus showing how business and organizational processes may be braided.

For the reader unfamiliar with flowcharting I describe the highest level process for Retail Lending. This is shown as Ref#:0 in the chart contained in

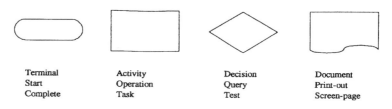

Figure 7.2

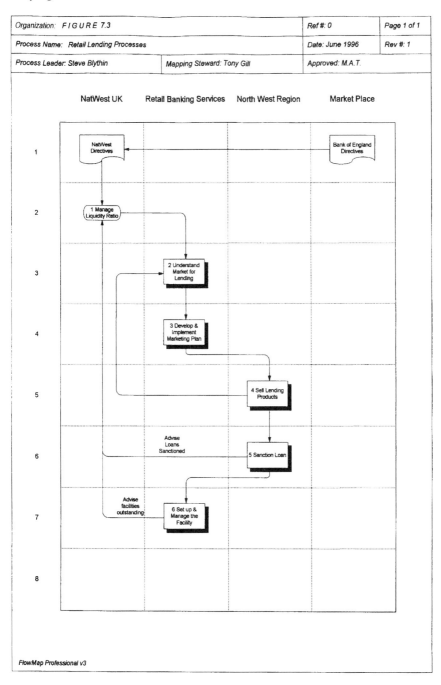

Figure 7.3 Retail lending processes

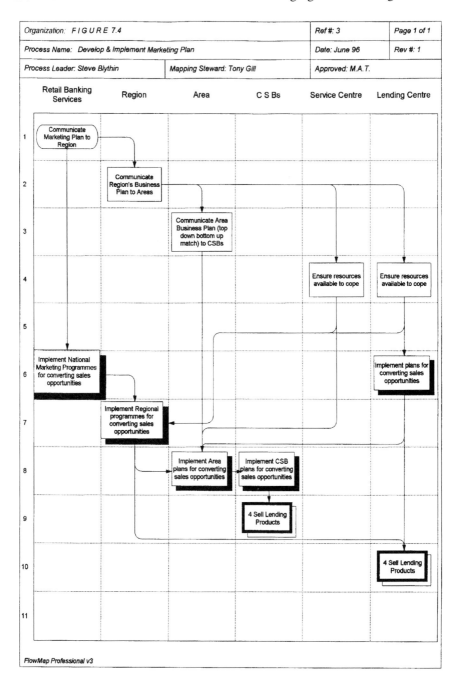

Figure 7.4   Develop and implement marketing plan

Figure 7.3. Public notices, letters or directives from the Bank of England are sent to/noted by NatWest head office. Directives are then sent out to all NatWest operations. In the case of lending, a prime requirement of the bank is to "manage its liquidity ratio". I show this as the start of the lending process within NatWest UK. Retail Banking Services are set lending targets (inputs for the next process) within the parameters required to manage the bank's liquidity ratio. This is indicated by the directional arrow to the process "2 Understand Market for Lending".

Process 2 is a shadowed process which indicates that the process is further decomposed and is shown in Chart Ref#:3 (Figure 7.4). The output of this process is an Aggregate SWOT analysis which can be used as input for the next higher level process—shown by the reverse shadow process. In a similar way, all the remaining higher level processes are decomposed into lower level processes with process charts having the same number as the process. Processes 4, 5 and 6 show outputs which serve as feedback informational loops. Throughout, each process is managed by the organizational unit indicated in the heading of each column. Even customers (or suppliers) who need to fulfil their part of the process can be shown.

It can be noted that all processes have an output and that eventually there is closure to the lending process. One way to envisage all these multiple level processes and their connectivity is to compare them to an architect's isometric projections for a multi-storey building.

The advantage of this approach is its applicability to enabling concepts such as continuous improvement and empowerment. Anyone who wishes to make changes is more likely to "see" the consequences of their actions. During the research I was using the diagnostic mode, i.e. what exists or is current practice. This approach could also be used in the design or "what-if" mode for organizational improvement. By being aware of both organizational and business processes you are aware of the impact of any recommended changes.

Using Interactive Management (IM)—Surfacing Organizational Issues

From our research work in applying the VSM, it was soon apparent that the strategy of centralizing back office functions (known as Delivery Strategy) into various specialized Centres *could* clash with Marketing Programmes (MP) designed to establish and maintain appropriate relationship accounts with its customers. This was a problem facing the VO. I believed that IM (Warfield, 1994; Warfield and Cardenas, 1994) could be used with effect to surface some of the potential issues. Rather than interview key members in the Area to surface issues, I was keen to have a workshop where an interactive discussion would result in a much richer view of the potential problem.

It must also be said that this was undertaken as part of a research programme and getting all the necessary actors together proved to be difficult because of day-to-day work pressures. In effect, we had some three hours for the process which normally would have taken at least a full day. Some shortcuts were required.

Workshop objectives

To help the members of the "virtual organization" (i.e. Branches, Lending Centre, Service Centre and Securities Centre) to articulate and structure the issues of communication, organization and implementation (in relation to current bank strategies) that they are experiencing in working together. This problem structuring should provide a sound platform for the participative development of a structured, prioritized action plan aimed at organizational and system improvement.

Method

The method used, known as Interactive Management (IM), is a participative workshop approach used to help relatively large (12–15 people) diverse groups tackle complex, "thorny" problems in an effective manner. The underlying principle is that the expertise exists inside most organizations to solve the problems with which the organization is faced. What is required is a structure or framework for organizing that expertise (as revealed by a group of key players) into a concerted plan of action that tackles the systemic nature of the problem area.

The approach consists of three main stages: Planning, Workshop and Follow-up. The workshop has the following four main phases structured around a trigger question (loosely based around Nominal Group Technique (NGT)—Delbecq et al, 1975):

- Idea writing—the individual scripting of issues of concern.
- Clarifying ideas—a process of sharing understandings of what the ideas individually represent and (where necessary) rephrasing them to clarify their intent.
- Selection of ideas—a voting procedure for selecting a subset of the total set of issues. The subset represents those issues deemed most critical by the group.
- Structuring ideas—a paired comparison process aimed at discovering the critical relationships among the identified issues and arriving at a structure which reflects the relative impact of each (priority) issue on the wider problem under consideration.

Although the method has been widely used in a variety of organizational contexts and is well documented, this particular application was the first time that the facilitators had used this particular method. Additionally, as far as we know, this was the first time that a method such as this one has been used in the bank. It therefore represents an "experiment" from which important lessons and research issues can be derived by all concerned.

The process in detail and our experience of applying it

Planning stage   The process begins with the planning stage for the workshop. It is essential at this stage for the party with the expertise in applying the process (often an external consultancy) to contract with two roles within the organization concerning objectives and expectations from the workshop. These two roles are the *broker* for the process and the *resource owner*. In some cases these roles are performed by the same person, in others they may be separated. The broker is the immediate point of contact who is able to recognize that a problem exists that may benefit from the application of a particular set of skills or techniques that the service provider has; the resource owner is able to bring the necessary resources (people and their time often being the prime considerations) to the workshop event.

In the case of the Area workshop, the resource owner role was effectively taken by the MAT as a whole and the broker role was split between the MAT and NatWest's project manager for the CSCW project. Therefore, the contracting process took place over the course of two MAT meetings and various discussions with these parties during an intervening period.

One problem we faced was trying to explain in advance the benefits of using an approach that was completely novel to the bank and requires the experience of using it and then reflecting on that experience to completely grasp its utility. One can talk in broad terms about the benefits of involving a diverse group of key participants in a problem situation directly in a structured process aimed at surfacing and structuring the problem elements; however, the downstream benefits of undertaking such a workshop are not easy to envisage from the outset. Common reactions include, "Aren't we just going to be going over old ground and airing grievances which we have no way of dealing with?"; "Wouldn't it be better to be positive—looking for proactive solutions, instead of dwelling on the negative side of things?"; and "Where is all this going to lead?"

The answer to why we need to do a "problematique" before we can go on to develop plans of action, is that until we can fully understand what the problem is (i.e. how the different strands of the problem are interlinked), the chances are that our ongoing "solutions" will indeed just be going over old ground and may even be exacerbating the overall problem without our knowing it!

In effect, we suspect that the MAT's agreement to undertake the workshop was an act of blind faith, a plunge into the unknown which was facilitated by the fact that the "organizational workshop" was annexed to a workshop on "job swaps" (Part 1 of the session) which was the original requirement of the MAT. The downside to this arrangement, however, was the time limitation for the IM session.

The other two factors required at the planning stage are the agreement and commitment of appropriate participants to spend the time at the workshop and approach it in the right frame of mind; and agreement about the phrasing of the key trigger question. Getting the right mix of people to the workshop is crucial. If parties with strong interests in or influence over the problem area under discussion are absent, it can render the exercise of very limited value. One of the benefits of IM is that it can comfortably accommodate a larger group than would normally meet together (6–8 people being a "norm" for group size in most organizations). Having the space for 12–15 participants does allow for a more diverse mix of people representing different facets/strata in the system. Although we believe there were only 11 participants, this objective was largely achieved at the Area.

The trigger question for the workshop was arrived at through discussions with the MAT about what factors were having the most influence on the organization at present. It was decided that the focus of discussion should be broader than that of the "virtual lending team" since for practical purposes lending could not be isolated from the other bank processes. The wording became: "What are ALL the problems involved in implementing Delivery Strategy and the Local Marketing Programme?"

Prior to the workshop, there was some discussion around the word "implementing", as in a sense Delivery Strategy had already happened and the organization was now coming to terms with the consequences of having implemented it. However, the sense that was intended was that Delivery Strategy was an ongoing process that the bank was pursuing. Had there been a problem among participants with this wording, we would have proposed substituting "pursuing" for "implementing", but in the event this did not prove to be necessary. There was also some debate about whether we should aim the issue-surfacing at the *intersect* of DS and MP (i.e. what was involved in managing the inherent tensions between the two), but it was decided that this might prove too restrictive; we wanted to surface issues relating to the "virtual organization" as a whole and therefore left it to the participants whether they wanted to direct their ideas toward DS or MP or the problems of combining the two.

Workshop The workshop began with an outline of the purpose, structure and timings for the IM session. The Idea Writing session was introduced with the following guidelines:

- *One idea per sheet*
  Sheets of A4 paper were circulated and participants were invited to write their ideas down with thick coloured felt tip pens. Each sheet was to contain

one idea only: compound statements were to be split into two or more sheets as necessary.

- *Sheets are unlimited*
No restrictions on the number of sheets each participant could use.
- *No one gets blamed (or rewarded) for ideas*
It is essential to stress and adhere to the confidentiality of the session. It should not under any circumstances be regarded as a covert opportunity to assess personal capability/performance. Participants were asked to contribute frank views for the benefit of the group as a whole and were given assurances that their individual contributions would not be attributed to them after the event.
- *Suspend judgement*
It was stressed that judging/selecting among the ideas would come at a later stage and that it was important to let ideas flow freely in the first stage of the process.
- *Have fun!*
A sense of humour is an important element in creative, lateral thinking and was therefore actively encouraged.

Idea Writing session   The trigger question effectively generated an appropriate volume of ideas from the participants—131 ideas, or an average of 12 ideas per participant. This was very much in line with our expectations. The ideas were immediately assigned a number by the facilitators and then posted around the walls of the room using masking tape.

Clarification/amendments   This stage of the process consisted of reading through each statement on the wall and (in most cases) asking the author to elaborate on the idea for the benefit of helping the group as a whole to understand the full meaning behind the idea. Where it was felt to be advantageous for clarity/understanding, the facilitators added extra words or amended the statements with the consent of the author concerned and the rest of the group. This is the clarification method proposed by Professor John Warfield (1994), the inventor of IM.

This process was the most time consuming of all. In retrospect, we feel that this process would be greatly improved if the participants were themselves encouraged to amend/sharpen their statements before they are posted up on the walls. In many cases, the process of transforming single word ideas and queries into structured problem statements that are context-explicit could at least be begun by the authors, thus saving on the total time spent in "translating" with the whole group. However, there is a balance to be struck, bearing in mind the following objectives:

- The desirability of having "uncensored" ideas for the group as a whole to explore.

- The desirability of generating discussion around the ideas to foster understanding/teamwork.

If the process becomes too cut-and-dried and free of personal interactions, the value of the session could be significantly reduced. Therefore, the aim should perhaps be to get the participants to make first revisions on an *ad hoc* rather than a systematic basis and allow the space for discussions and making further amendments on the wall as necessary.

The amendment process also consists of de-duplicating ideas where the statements are genuinely identical. A total of 18 items were removed at this stage of the process through de-duplication. However, we found it difficult to do this exercise comprehensively due to the time shortage. The result was that in the next phase of the process, people were in some cases voting for alternative wordings for the same basic concept. This may be acceptable in the sense that they can choose the actual wording that they prefer, but it did present problems when two very similar statements each received some votes and thus went on to the structuring stage. More time could be devoted to de-duplicating if the statement revisions were handled as suggested above.

Where a very large number of problem statements is generated (as in this case), a further stage of idea-clustering is often advisable to make it easier for people to grasp the full range of issues generated by the group. *However, the voting process (see below) is still based on individual issues, not generic cluster/ theme headings.* The cluster headings may subsequently be overlaid on the problematique to provide another view on the data.

Due to the time shortage, we were aware from the outset that it would be unrealistic to plan to insert a clustering stage into the process. Therefore, having clarified and de-duplicated the statements with the group as far as possible, we proceeded straight to the voting stage.

In order to present the full list of idea statements a little more "digestably", we decided to do a tentative clustering exercise after the event to see what overall themes might have emerged from this exercise. This exercise was performed as follows. All the idea statements were numbered as they went up on the wall. After the event, the statements were typed up in numerical order. A scan through the list began to suggest some common themes/headings to the facilitators and names were invented to encapsulate these themes. The statements were then grouped under these headings.

It must be emphasized that there is no one "correct" way to group the data and a great deal of the value of a clustering exercise is lost by doing it "off-site" without the participation of the group. There will no doubt be different views on where certain items should reside. Nevertheless, we felt that in 80–90% of cases, people would have no difficulty in accepting the assigned groupings and that it would be easier for them to sift through the data, recognizing their own inputs, than if the issues were presented as a random, unsorted list.

Voting   The voting stage consists of each participant having a strip of adhesive markers (four in this case) to distribute among the statements he or she considers to be the most critical of all. This process happened in a very short time. Hopefully, this did not reflect a lack of concern with the process on the part of participants.

Structuring process   This phase of the process involved the group answering "yes" or "no" to the iterative question, "Does Problem X significantly aggravate Problem Y?" It was taxing for the group to remain focused on the task at this late stage of the day; however, the cooperation was good and the process resulted in some interesting debates taking place. In one or two instances, minor text changes were agreed on the spot. These might have been ironed out in the previous clarification stage, but as the meaning of the statements was not drastically altered, this did not appear to affect the integrity of the process.

Although the computer was unable to generate the problematique on the spot, the DOS-based program was fast to use and did not cause significant delays. The large-scale monitor was also fairly easy to read from a distance. Therefore, this phase of the process appeared to have run satisfactorily.

Interpreting the Problematique

A copy of the problematique resulting from the workshop is shown in Figure 7.5. The diagram shows the relative impact of each problem that was voted a priority on the other problems in the priority set. The arrows in the diagram represent the relationship "significantly aggravates". Where two or more issues share a single box, those issues have a mutually aggravating influence on each other (i.e. the issues should be treated as an interlinked *cluster*, as opposed to individually).

I would stress that the shortage of time in the workshop for discussions/clarification/logic testing has meant that the problematique cannot be viewed as a technically flawless product. Nevertheless, some clear messages do emerge from studying the flows in the diagram in overview. We (the facilitators) offer the following pointers not as a definitive interpretation of the model, but as a starting point for analysing the implications of the workshop findings to the Area.

To the extreme left of the diagram, the two fundamental drivers aggravating the problem of implementing DS and MP are shown as "Technology that is not state of the art" and "Staff training does not include how to communicate/behave in new environment". There are 13 factors that are directly or indirectly impacted by the technology issue and 19 factors that are directly or indirectly impacted by the staff training issue. "Lack of teamwork" lies in a pivotal position between these two key drivers. This would suggest that teamwork

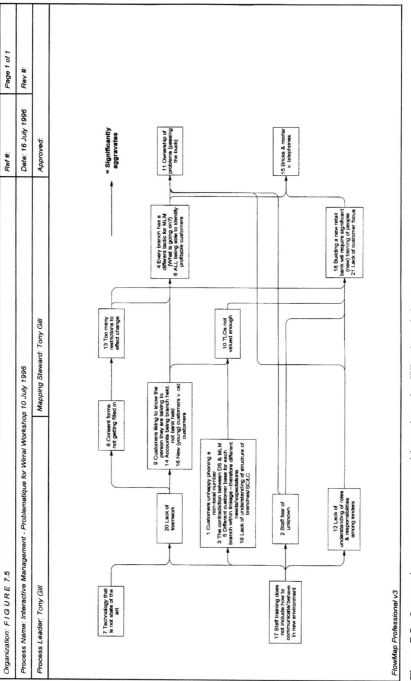

Figure 7.5 Interactive management—problematique for Wirrel workshop

in the DS/MP environment (where people are geographically separated) is a function of having *appropriate* training and good technology support.

Lack of clarity/understanding about new roles and responsibilities in the new structure is probably the next most pivotal issue (problems 19 and 12 are both concerned with this). It is derived from the training issue and has significant impacts across the problematique. A role that appears to have particular significance in the new organization structure is the Telephone Liaison Officer (TLO) role. Improving the perceived value to the organization of this role will help the bank to address a number of the issues connected to the transition to a new retail banking environment where the telephone has a strong role to play.

At the extreme right of the diagram are two symptoms that are being aggravated by a large proportion of the other elements of the structure: "Ownership of problems (passing the buck)"—impacted directly or indirectly by 12 other factors—and "Bricks & mortar v. telephones"—impacted directly or indirectly by 19 other factors. The problematique indicates that trying to address either of these issues "head on" is unlikely to work: staff will not be willing to take ownership of problems until issues like fear have been addressed (through training), until there is more coherence in the application of MP, and until they have flexible IT systems that allow them to understand and communicate with the customer base and operate as a mutually supportive team. Equally, resolving the issue of balancing/migrating between the old world (bricks and mortar) and the new (telephone lines) will require that all the other factors in the structure (bar ownership of problems) are first addressed.

How does the problematique relate to the thematic clusters?

The thematic clusters are a convenient way of viewing the full set of issues that emerged from the workshop. The clusters (not shown) give another approximate indicator of the strength of views on a particular theme, although the significance of this ordering to the overall problem analysis should not be overemphasized. It is interesting to note that all but nine of the 24 clusters have at least one representative element in the problematique.

We surmise that the clustering can be used as a form of quality check on the problematique in answering the question, "Does the problematique contain a reasonable spread of the original issues generated by the group?" Broadly speaking, it would appear that the voting process did result in a fair spread of the original issues being featured in some way in the problematique. Where there are significant "gaps" or issues that people feel strongly about in retrospect, these can be picked up at the next stage of the process.

Tentative conclusions

A key theme to emerge from both parts of the workshop is that of training: not only the *quantity* of training that people receive but also the *nature* of that training. Setting training in the context of developing the whole individual to act effectively in the new environment of the bank appears to be key. This means addressing the softer behavioural issues to do with the context of work, as well as attending to traditional areas of training, i.e. technical job content. It also means widening the concept of training/development to incorporate experiential learning, coaching and different forms of group work that perhaps have nothing to do with attending formal training courses. The business case for investment in this area is reinforced when the impact of staff training across the total problem structure is examined.

Technology investment is clearly a key enabler of effective teamwork but we would suggest that this relationship should be handled with care: it does not follow that a higher spend on IT systems will automatically improve teamwork across the organization, or that inadequate technology can always be blamed for a lack of team focus. Addressing the softer human communication issues in an effective manner may go a long way towards overcoming the shortcomings of existing technological solutions and preparing the ground for an effective uptake of new technologies as and when they come on stream.

Outputs from the workshop generally meet the researchers' expectations and will be fed into the bank's ongoing improvement and redesign activity. It is deliberate and noteworthy that we were using computer-assisted facilitation software to manage the structuring of the problem matrix. It is through this software that we have been able to generate the problematique. This DOS-based version of the software was provided to Anthony Gill by Professor John Warfield of George Mason University, USA, who was responsible for managing its development.

The specific outputs from the workshop include: presentations and ideas generated from the "job swaps" programme; the problematique and the listing of all the ideas generated grouped under common themes; rich conversations during the workshops and no doubt after the workshop. The area will thus hopefully have a much clearer common understanding of the full scope of its key problems and how those problems are interrelated. Ideally, what is required is to develop a prioritized set of action options that effectively address the key problem areas identified in this workshop in terms of the leverage or influence available to those working in the Area.

As a process observation, we would also like to mention an issue that emerged strongly from the group interactions. The Securities Centre would appear to be operating in relative isolation from the other entities in the Area structure, which undoubtedly affects the ability of the whole "virtual organization" to function effectively. This factor has not been explicitly brought out by the problematique, but we feel that the issue of the actual and potential role of the Securities Centre in the new structure requires attention.

A VERY RICH PICTURE?—REFLECTIONS AND CONCLUSIONS

Process management is offering organizations a way to fundamentally alter the way they do business. It is about empowering people and letting them take responsibility for the processes that they manage. Process management embraces the principles of continuous improvement on the one hand and BPR on the other. When used with the VSM as a structure to manage complexity it provides a powerful framework with which to understand how the organization works. It enables the braiding of business with organizational processes. This holistic approach offers an alternative to functional hierarchy as organizations realign their businesses to the market place. I believe that this braided process approach enables what Useem calls "building high-performance systems".

Customers are demanding products/services of increased quality, shorter lead times, at a more competitive price. If you cannot meet these demands, competitors will. Customer satisfaction, on the other hand, manifests itself through effective business process. Product quality alone is no longer sufficient as a competitive differentiator. Shareholders are restless in their desire for greater returns on their investments. I support Useem's (1996) view that "Global competition + shareholder pressure = high performance organizations". Essentially it will mean that if you survive, you are a high performance organization. Time is running out for unfit global players.

In our CSCW research programme we have used the VSM to build an understanding of how the bank operates. In the organizational analysis using the VSM in diagnostic mode, we have surfaced several areas of concern. In this chapter, I have focused on one specific area of concern—the notion of a virtual organization managed by the MAT of a specific geographical area of the bank as a way of overcoming the constraints of the bank's organization structure. I was able to monitor the progress of the MAT in their efforts to manage this virtual organization. By the end it was rather rewarding to witness the teamwork of the Area Manager, Lending Centre Manager and Service Centre Manager—the MAT—in managing the VO. To give other members of the VO a better understanding of the overall tasks they were performing, the MAT implemented the cybernetic team suggestion of "job swaps" i.e. short-term job rotation. At the Service Centre in keeping with my suggestion, the Shapiro, Rangan and Sviokla (1992) "Staple yourself to an Order" idea for job swaps was adopted. At various times during the course of this year, I had drawn attention to the potential for conflict between Delivery Strategy and the Local Marketing Programme. I believe that it is possible to engage in both strategies, provided attention is paid to the management of resources for achieving both strategies and that adequate performance measures are in place. In order to gain a better understanding of this potential for conflict I secured agreement from the MAT to run part of an IM workshop together with another member of the cybernetic team so that we could develop a problematique. This was well received and followed up by a further workshop to explore how to overcome some of the problem areas.

Although considerable other work has been carried out by various members of the SYCOMT consortium, particularly for the purpose of informing systems development, the emphasis of this chapter has been to highlight two systems approaches used in the same study to complement each other—to build a richer picture. The bank has already benefited from the SYCOMT research by being able to capture best practice from the area under review which can be replicated in other areas. The idea of the MAT is likely to be rolled out to other areas. An interesting question remains: will the Bank adjust its organization structure to formalize the VO?

REFERENCES

Argyris, C. and Schon, D. (1978). *Organizational Learning: A Theory of Action Perspective.* Addison-Wesley Publishing Company, Reading, MA.

Beer, S. (1979). *The Heart of Enterprise.* John Wiley & Sons Ltd, Chichester.

Beer, S. (1981). *Brain of the Firm* (2nd edn). John Wiley & Sons Ltd, Chichester.

Beer, S. (1985). *Diagnosing the System for Organizations.* John Wiley & Sons Ltd, Chichester.

Bredin, Alice (1996). *The Virtual Office Survival Handbook: What Telecommuters and Entrepreneurs Need to Succeed in Today's Nontraditional Workplace.* John Wiley & Sons Ltd, Chichester.

Brocklesby, J. and Cummings, S. (1996). Designing a viable structure. *Long Range Planning,* **29**(1), 49–57.

Chesbrough, Henry W. and Teece, David J. (1996). When is virtual virtuous? Organizing for innovation. *Harvard Business Review,* January–February.

Davenport, Thomas H. and Short, James E. (1990). The new industrial engineering: Information Technology and Business Process Redesign. *Sloan Management Review,* Summer: 11–26.

Davenport, T.H. (1993). *Process Innovation: Reengineering Work Through Information Technology.* Harvard Business School Press, USA.

Delbecq, A.L. et al (1975) *Group Techniques for Program Planning.* Scott, Foresman and Company, Glenview, Illinois, USA.

Espejo, R. (1993). Management of complexity in problem solving. In R. Espejo and M. Schwaninger (eds) *Organisational Fitness: Corporate Effectiveness through Management Cybernetics.* Campus Verlag, Frankfurt am Main.

Espejo, R. and Schwaninger, M. (eds) (1993). *Organisational Fitness: Corporate Effectiveness through Management Cybernetics.* Campus Verlag, Frankfurt am Main.

Espejo, R. (1989a). The VSM revisited. In R. Espejo and R. Harnden (eds) *The Viable System Model.* John Wiley & Sons Ltd, Chichester, pp. 77–100.

Espejo, R. (1989b). A cybernetic method of study organisations. In R. Espejo and R. Harnden (eds) *The Viable System Model.* John Wiley & Sons Ltd, Chichester, pp. 361–382.

Gill, A. (1995). A life-line for those abandoning check-list management. In K. Ellis et al (eds) *Critical Issues in Systems Theory and Practice*. Plenum Publishing Corporation, New York, pp. 454–550.

Gribbin, J. (1993). Aiming at the whole truth. *The Sunday Times*, 31 January 1993, page 6.8 Books.

Hammer, M. (1990). Reengineering work: don't automate, obliterate. *Harvard Business Review*, July–August, 104–112.

Harrington, H.J. (1991). *Business Process Improvement: The Breakthrough Strategy for Total Quality, Productivity and Competitiveness*. McGraw-Hill Inc., New York, NY.

Howard, D. (1995). *Deployment Flowcharting of Business Processes*. (Booklet available from Management-NewStyle, PO Box 281, Chislehurst, Kent.)

Medina-Mora, R., Winograd, T., Flores, R. and Flores, F. (1992). The action workflow approach to workflow management technology. In *CSCW 92 Proceedings* (November). Toronto, Canada. Sponsored by ACM SIGCHI & SIGOIS.

Parkinson, C.N. (1958). *Parkinson's Law*. John Murray, London.

Shapiro, B.P., Rangan, V.K. and Sviokla, J.J. (1992). Staple yourself to an order. *Harvard Business Review*, **70**(4), July–August, 113–122.

Stewart, T.A. (1992). The search for the organization of tomorrow. *Fortune*, 18 May.

Useem, M. (1996). The true worth of building high-performance systems. *Financial Times* series *Master Management Part 10*, 12 January 1996.

Warfield, John N. (1994). *A Science of Generic Design: Managing Complexity through Systems Design* (2nd edn). Iowa State University Press, Ames, IA.

Warfield, John N. and Cardenas, A. Roxana (1994). *A Handbook of Interactive Management* (2nd edn). Iowa State University Press, Ames.

Womack, J.P., Jones, D.T. and Roos, D. (1990). *The Machine that Changed the World*. Rawson Associates, Macmillan Publishing Company, New York, NY.

Part 2
Cognitive Aspects of Multimethodology

Commentary

In the first part of the book we have seen a range of real examples of multi-methodology, some of which have been across different paradigms. We now move away from the practice to consider some of the theoretical and philosophical issues underlying multi-paradigm methodology and research. This part covers the cognitive aspects of multimethodology, that is, the kinds of knowledge that are needed for multimethodology, and the cognitive capabilities required for multi-paradigm work. The third part of the book explores possible philosophical and theoretical frameworks to support multimethodology.

Using a methodology, any methodology, effectively requires a range of knowledge, skills and experience that take time to develop. It requires not just textbook, explicit knowledge, but that *tacit* knowledge of how to do things in practice that generally only comes with experience. This is hard within one paradigm—becoming an *expert* in mathematical programming and simulation and forecasting will take a long time—but becoming an expert across different paradigms, and being able to switch easily from technical to social skills, introduces a new order of difficulty. These are the issues considered in this part of the book. First, from the cognitive viewpoint of the individual person trying to develop such skills, and second, from the perspective of the type of technological systems that may be useful in supporting multimethodological work.

These themes are echoed elsewhere in the book. For instance Richard Ormerod (Chapter 1) views his case studies as stages in the development of his own personal competence as a practitioner able to work in different paradigms. While Mingers (Chapter 15) sees the individual competency issue as one of the main reasons for bringing the individual agent to the fore within multimethodology.

John Brocklesby is concerned with the individual users of methodologies, or multimethodologies, and the extent to which the difficulty of working in

Multimethodology: The Theory and Practice of Combining Management Science Methodologies.
Edited by John Mingers and Anthony Gill.
© 1997 John Wiley & Sons Ltd.

substantively different paradigms poses feasibility problems for multi-methodology. It seems clear that the different paradigms do make different demands on users—developing a complex, technical computer system requires very different skills and competencies from facilitating a meeting of managers with conflicting views. Equally, some people seem to be much more at home in one world rather than another. Is it really possible for everyone to move comfortably between different paradigms? What factors would enable or hinder this process? Brocklesby bases his contribution on the cognitive theories of Maturana and Varela who see cognition not as abstract mental processes but as involved, engaged, activity in the world.

After briefly outlining the theory, Brocklesby concentrates on the case of developing an agent who usually works in only one paradigm to someone competent in multiple-paradigm working. This transformation is conceptualised in four stages—becoming aware of other options; wanting to enter a new paradigm; becoming competent in the paradigm; and moving easily between paradigms. The conclusions are that there are many obstacles to be overcome, but that becoming multimethodology literate is a competence and ability that can be developed given sufficient determination.

David Skyrme's chapter addresses the role of information and knowledge in successfully applying multimethodology in practice. After discussing his experience of the gap between textbook methodologies (especially hard ones like SSADM) and real organisational situations, Skyrme argues that the effective use of a methodology relies on *tacit*, experiential knowledge as much as explicit, textbook knowledge. Such knowledge is generated in the early days of the development of a methodology and then needs to be diffused to a wider audience. This is part of a wider concern—the management of information and more especially *knowledge* within the organisation as a whole.

Skyrme goes on to focus specifically on the role that IT can play in the generation, maintenance and dissemination of knowledge in organisations suggesting that the use of methodologies may be a good starting point for such developments. He concludes with what is effectively a requirements list for the development of knowledge management software specifically tailored for the use of multimethodology.

Chapter 8

Becoming Multimethodology Literate: an Assessment of the Cognitive Difficulties of Working Across Paradigms

JOHN BROCKLESBY

INTRODUCTION

Multimethodology, the idea of combining methodologies and techniques from different paradigms, is gradually becoming popular currency in management science, operational research, and systems circles (referred to hereafter under the collective term "MS"). Whereas a decade ago there was much talk about the confrontational posture adopted by the proponents of the various paradigms, and about paradigm incommensurability, today there are signs of a new ecumenical spirit in MS based upon inter-paradigm exchange. Previously there was a belief that an agent simply had to make a choice between the paradigms; you make a choice—be a hard-nosed realist or be a humanistic idealist but you cannot be both. Today, there is some sense that, at a personal level, an accommodation—or some form of complementary posture—is possible. Multimethodology, as some practitioners have known all along, is even in danger of becoming academically respectable.

Multimethodology: The Theory and Practice of Combining Management Science Methodologies.
Edited by John Mingers and Anthony Gill.
© 1997 John Wiley & Sons Ltd.

It is not difficult to see how multimethodology can enhance the efficacy, efficiency, and applicability of MS. Being literate across a number of paradigms allows an agent to deal with a broad range of issues, and to enter a problem situation with fewer preconceived ideas about how it will be handled than may be the case when their expertise is garnered from one or perhaps two methodologies from the same paradigm. Moreover, multimethodology provides the agent with the wherewithal to manage themselves the complete cycle of intervention from initial diagnosis of the problem to taking action of some sort (Jackson and Keys 1984; Bennett, 1990; Bennett and Cropper, 1990; Flood and Jackson, 1991; Jackson, 1991; Mingers and Brocklesby, 1996).

So ostensibly it makes sense. But how feasible is it? It is one thing to say that there has been some degree of accommodation between the various MS paradigms because the combatants no longer completely ignore one another, or because it is now possible for "alternative" researchers to publish in dominant paradigm journals. But, for an individual agent, multimethodology demands a form of accommodation that is altogether more daunting. Reorienting educational programmes with the intention of creating a new breed of management scientist who can routinely traverse the boundaries of the various paradigms is, itself, a difficult enough proposition, but transforming someone who has been thoroughly socialised in a single paradigm and has years of investment in a particular approach is an even more ambitious project. For example, someone who has been trained in hard systems and who is thoroughly steeped in its ways, can hardly expect to achieve instant success if they choose to practise soft systems. The underlying beliefs that sustain the soft systems paradigm are fundamentally different, as are the various techniques. Shifting from the soft to the hard paradigm is no less problematic; indeed it may be more so.

Yet these sorts of personal transitions are not uncommon. Virtually all of us know of someone, often a practitioner, who seems to be able to work in two or more paradigms. And there are enough well-known management scientists around—Ackoff, Beer, Churchman, Checkland, Flood, Rosenhead, to name a few—who seem to have successfully transitioned from one paradigm to another. There seems little doubt that these people are eminently capable of doing multimethodology research, even if they do not always choose to practise it. But what about the rest of us who primarily operate within a single MS paradigm? What needs to happen to make us equally proficient? And how feasible is this?

There are a number of feasibility issues that arise in connection with multimethodology (see Mingers and Brocklesby, 1996). Here I shall concentrate upon cognition, and I shall do so using the ideas of the Chilean biologists Humberto Maturana and Francisco Varela. Why, it may be asked, Maturana and Varela? The answer to this question has to do with their somewhat unusual conceptualisation of cognition. Whereas conventional wisdom has it that cognition is primarily a mentalistic process that can be seen as a separate and discrete human activity, to these authors it is *involved, engaged activity in the world*. This, one could argue, is what management science is all about—being involved, engaging with problems, and acting to bring about an improvement in the *practical* affairs of organisations and their members. Such a perspective on cognition, therefore, seems befitting.

There are some assumptions underpinning the discussion that require clarification at the outset. I do not consider these to be especially unreasonable, but as they are unsubstantiated (in a scientific sense), they do require comment before I enter the main discussion. The first assumption is that many management scientists operate exclusively within a single paradigm. The majority lean towards the so-called "hard" (systems or OR) paradigm, a much smaller number the "soft" paradigm, and there are a few committed enthusiasts energetically developing an agenda for the "critical" paradigm. As for the rest, there are some (mainly, but not exclusively, practitioners) who operate across two or more paradigms, and there are others who enrich their work in one paradigm by incorporating tools or techniques from another. A further group use a hodgepodge of diverse techniques according to no particular set of theoretical or philosophical principles, and do not feel under any obligation to justify their choices other than on purely pragmatic grounds.

Of course this hard/soft/critical classification is not sacrosanct. While abstractions and labels can be handy, it is important to remember that they are applied from an *outside* perspective, so cleaving MS along such lines does not mean that this represents its "true" state. In a sense, the distinction, like all distinctions, is part fiction. There may be more useful ways of dividing the terrain waiting to be invented. What is more important, labelling someone hard, soft, or critical, does not—in any sense—convey a complete picture of how that individual practises MS. No two management scientists are completely alike—they are all different in some regard. To say that someone operates according to the logic of the hard systems paradigm because they believe in a transcendental reality, or that someone else does their work in the soft paradigm because they believe in multiple socially constructed truths, defines them only at the grandest ontological level. At the operational level of practice this categorisation is less useful because here the situation is more complex. A rather straightforward basic assumption about the nature of the world can generate extremely rich and complex behaviours. Yet despite this, the paradigms that have entered the discourse of MS do provide an important source of consensuality about the high level options—the various deductive systems of rules—that are available to management scientists. Providing we understand that the *actual* practice of MS is shaped by the lived experience, concerns and interests of whoever is doing it, the traditional characterisation of the discipline is a useful heuristic device.

The second assumption that I am making here, is that although I suspect that today most management scientists have at least heard of some of the various methods and techniques originating in paradigms different to their own, many do not have an acute sense of their own paradigm alignment. This is not a particularly contentious statement because, as we shall see shortly, it is in the nature of paradigms that they operate tacitly. One could argue that this applies to members of most disciplines and professions. However, whereas in some other fields—organisation theory would be a good example—there has been an explosion of reflexive awareness about paradigms, metaphors, discourse and genealogies over the last decade or so, the practice of MS continues to be almost exclusively technical. My feeling, therefore, is that most management scientists would rather continue to focus directly on pragmatic concerns, rather than be distracted by philosophical abstractions (see Ormerod, 1996). But we cannot be presumptuous about this. Doubtless there are many academic and practitioner management scientists who realise that it is only by constantly re-examining and questioning the foundational assumptions of various theories and practices that the discipline can avoid becoming trapped within a limited range of conceptual possibilities. There are limits, for example, as to what can be achieved by simply inventing more and better techniques or refining existing ones. Some philosophically inclined colleagues may even relish the opportunity of reflecting upon paradigms and other weighty matters as a worthwhile end in itself. So while many in the discipline may choose to downplay the importance of debates about paradigms, and to baulk at the prospect of reflecting upon their own role in such terms, I do acknowledge that others will be acutely conscious of their own standing within a paradigm, and will know a great deal about others.

There is another issue that requires comment before I enter the main discussion. This pertains to the particular form of multimethodology used here. Throughout the chapter there is an assumption that there is a one-to-one correspondence between a paradigm's philosophical assumptions, "its" methodologies, "its" techniques and "its" tools (see Mingers and Brocklesby, 1996 for a definition of these terms). This is not an unreasonable assumption. For example, we tend to associate soft systems methodology with the interpretive philosophical tradition, and we associate techniques such as rich pictures and conceptual models with SSM. Various techniques for reflecting on systems boundary judgements are normally linked with the critical systems heuristics methodology, and it with the critical paradigm. Software tools such as "I Think" or "Stella" have been designed to support system dynamics modelling, and system dynamics has largely been developed within the hard systems paradigm.

In effect, I am distinguishing a complex unity—*paradigm*—whose *organisation* involves the particular relationship among the components just described. Organisation is a term that Maturana uses to refer to the relations between the components that define a composite unity as a unity of a given kind. Thus, for example, the unity "table" is constituted by there being a particular relationship between the top surface and the legs. The organisation of the unity *paradigm* (as used here) involves a recursive one-to-one relationship between MS philosophical principles, methodology, techniques and tools. Another term of Maturana's—*structure*—describes the way in which the relations that constitute the organisation of a unity are actually realised. Through this operation we are able to distinguish hard, soft, and critical MS as paradigms that embody different structures (different philosophies, methods, techniques, and tools), yet which conserve the invariant set of relations between the components. Similarly when someone observes a management scientist moving from, say, hard to soft systems, provided what is distinguished is still "management scientist", then it can be said that there has been structural change with a maintenance of organisation.

Although defining the organisation of the unity paradigm this way is acceptable as a theoretical construct, in practical terms the relationship between philosophical principles and research practice is much less straightforward. Many would argue that there is a strong connection between a paradigm and methodology (see Jackson, 1991, for example), but there are no compelling reasons why an agent should not apply techniques and tools in the service of different philosophical principles or in isolation of the theories that spawned them. In MS, for instance, an agent can employ cognitive maps without necessarily subscribing to Kelly's theory of personal constructs; the Viable System Model can be detached from the various cybernetic concepts such as negative feedback and requisite variety. There is, it seems, no necessary connection between meta-beliefs and techniques (see Firestone, 1990 and Smaling, 1994 for a discussion on the dialectic interplay between philosophical principles and the conduct of research).

The main implication of maintaining this one-to-one relationship between philosophical principles and methodology/technique/tool, through the discussion, is that we are examining the feasibility of multimethodology from what amounts to a worst case perspective. It means that when two methods are combined, so are two sets of philosophical principles. Other multimethodology options such as borrowing a method or technique from a non-preferred paradigm and then employing it in support of one's preferred philosophical standpoint, are somewhat less ambitious.

Having laid out the groundwork for the discussion, let us now rehearse Maturana's main proposition. (The original source material is Maturana and Varela, 1980, 1987; Maturana, 1980, 1988, 1990. Concise secondary accounts are available in Mingers, 1989a, 1989b, 1990, 1991, 1995.)

MATURANA'S BASIC PROPOSITION ON COGNITION

This section begins with Maturana's delineation of the process through which cognition works. This is followed by an outline of what—in humans—it depends upon. Opening the discussion in this way helps in appreciating Maturana's somewhat unconventional view on what cognition is. A more comprehensive picture of this theory will develop as I add to and elaborate upon these points in the main body of the chapter. In order to encourage readers to persevere with what appears to be a rather abstract body of theory, I wish to reiterate the point made earlier, namely that Maturana's perspective on cognition is, I believe, particularly relevant to the primary concern of most management scientists which revolves around taking *practical action* in situations of concern.

How does cognition work? For Maturana, humans engage the world in which they operate through the process of *observation*. This involves making distinctions in which an environment is divided into some "unity" with defined boundaries, and a "background". Unities may be material entities such as a chair or a computer, or they may be abstract such as a particular worldview or problem definition. Observation, Maturana claims, is at the root of our living and it has important consequences. It circumscribes all knowledge, all explanations and, importantly, all discussion (hence Maturana's widely quoted declaration that "everything said is said by one observer to another"). It determines how we experience the world, and how we live our lives.

What does knowing depend upon? Knowledge emerges from our capacities of understanding, and in this regard there are two sets of qualification pertaining to any particular act of distinction. First, since observation largely occurs through language, it is relative to the languaging subject, his/her history, and—because human interaction gives rise to shared linguistic descriptions—the history of interactions among the various communities to which they have belonged. We constitute reality with our distinctions through language, and the *recurrent conversations* that characterise human communities are potentially an important source of consensuality about such distinctions.

Second, knowing depends upon our biology (Maturana always speaks as a biologist). Any attempt, therefore, to understand an aspect of human endeavour such as cognition must acknowledge a human being's fundamental existence as a biological entity coupled to a medium. Our cognitive abilities, Maturana claims, arise out of, and are circumscribed by, the biology of our human condition. Biologically, there are limits to what our human condition allows us to distinguish. We cannot smell, see, hear, taste, or feel beyond the parameters imposed by the respective *sensing spaces* in our bodies. Although the concreteness of our daily experience hints at our existing in a world of objects, Maturana rejects this. Even if there was such a thing, he claims, it would not be accessible to humans. Our experience comes to us mediated by our sensory and mental apparatus. What we can experience depends on the nature of our faculties, what our faculties can handle, and what they do to what they handle.

The main implication of this is that humans—indeed all composite systems—are *structure determined*—". . . everything that happens in them happens as a structural change determined . . . either in the course of their own internal dynamics or triggered but not specified by the circumstances of their interactions" (Maturana, 1990: 13). In other words, whatever happens to us has to do with *us*. The way we operate depends largely upon how we are made. It depends upon the properties of our internal components and the specific way in which these are "put together".

Structural determinism should not be taken to mean that a system's environment is unimportant, or, indeed, that structures are static. In fact, Maturana claims that we become intimately connected, or *structurally coupled*, to our environments. This alludes to a relationship of *natural drift*—born of recurrent historical interactions—where environmental forces trigger (i.e. release) structurally determined changes in us, and where our actions trigger structurally determined changes in the environment. The key word here is *trigger*. An environmental perturbation acting on a system cannot determine what happens to it. Nothing external to a system can determine what happens to it. No external force can determine its own effect. The system *itself* determines what environmental forces are recognised as triggers and what outcomes are possible.

In simple terms, Maturana's position is that the cognitive process that creates our knowledge of the world is entirely circumscribed by the process of observation. This means that we cannot separate the observer and the observed, nor the subject from the object, nor the knower and the known. The part of cognition which is bound to our biological functioning is universal for our species, the part which is bound to our languaging is culture specific.

We are now in a position to outline Maturana's view on what cognition is. By insisting that knowledge is underpinned by biology and languaging, Maturana portrays a resolutely anti-representational epistemology. He rejects the commonsense notion that we are "in here", and that a world independent of mind is "out there". Cognition, he claims, is not a matter of transforming external data of a transcendental reality—*a universe*—captured through our senses into mirror images in the brain. Instead, what we know of as "reality" is an active projection of our own cognitive structure. That things appear to us in a certain way does not mean that is how they are in themselves; in effect, we see the world in terms of ourselves. Maturana is emphatic in his insistence that all we ever have access to is that which we experience; and, to this end, he urges us to qualify any reference to reality by putting *objectivity in parentheses*.

This raises an important question. If we cannot measure the veracity of mental representations against the benchmark of a transcendental reality (conventional epistemology), how do we assess someone's knowledge? Maturana does not answer this question directly. Instead of saying what cognition or knowledge is, he focuses on how we can recognise it. He claims that the only way to assess someone's knowledge is through their action. If we observe someone (including ourself) acting effectively in some domain then we can assume that they have knowledge relevant to it. Moreover, the claim "I know" is verified through effective action in some domain, not through reference to objective knowledge. So, according to Maturana, all living systems (including those without a nervous system) are cognitive "knowing" systems because, to an observer, they display "adequate behaviour". Whereas we are accustomed to thinking of cognition as a mentalistic process that involves us manipulating information about the environment, here cognition is viewed as an integral part of, and is constituted by, our normal everyday activity (this point is taken up in more detail in the final part of the chapter). To all intents and purposes, cognition *is* effective action.

This, then, is the briefest outline of Maturana's cognitive theory, but it is enough to get us started, and we can now turn our attention towards the main issue under discussion. But, before we do, there is one final matter that is worthy of comment. This concerns the role which personal choice and intent plays in bringing about change. Put simply, the question is the extent to which personal transformation just happens, or whether people can take charge of their own destiny and make it happen. Maturana chooses to emphasise the former. Life, he argues, is basically a purposeless drift in which people constantly change according to their structural determinism in response to various internal and external perturbations as they drift naturally through a medium. Under this view, changes do not have to be foreshadowed. Indeed they do not have to be languaged at all. Even if they are languaged, this should not be taken to mean that the individual is in control because the conversations that people have with others, and with themselves, that contain terms such as "choice", "intent" and "self-control" often take place after the change, not before it. In other words, these conversations are reformulated explanations of what, to all intents and purposes, may well have just happened. On this count Maturana is probably right, there being little doubt that many day-to-day changes do occur in this imperceptible unknowing way. But this is not to say that individuals are impotent in the face of change. Thinking about one's predicament is a source of perturbation that can trigger a structurally determined response. In this sense, it can be said that people are, at least to some extent, in charge of their own destiny. Always, however, this is subject to their structural determinism. People can think, plan, and make decisions, but, ultimately what a person *does* depends on their structure at any moment. This is an important point to remember because in the next section I outline a process that endows agents with a degree of latitude in deliberately engineering changes in the way they do management science, that Maturana would almost certainly find hard to accept.

Because the process of transforming an agent whose current predilection is to do research within a single paradigm into someone who is capable of doing multimethodology is highly complex, I have chosen to conceptualise it as involving a progression through four key stages. First, the agent reflects upon his or her current predicament, i.e. they *become aware* that their hitherto preferred approach to MS is underpinned by particular sets of distinctions, and that there are other options available. Next the agent decides that he or she *wants to enter a new paradigm*, i.e. they see some value in acquiring its knowledge, its skills, its methods, and its techniques and tools. Third, while the motivation to learn a new paradigm is necessary, this, in itself, is not sufficient. The agent has to be *able to perform effectively* in the new paradigm, i.e. he or she must already possess, or be able to acquire, the various cognitive skills that are required. Progression through these three stages takes the agent from one paradigm to another. Thereafter, multimethodology introduces a further requirement—the ability to *move easily between paradigms*. These, then, are the key activities involved in bringing about the specific transformation under discussion. Obviously they could be further decomposed, but this is not attempted here.

BECOMING PARADIGM CONSCIOUS

This section begins by outlining the reasons why, ordinarily, people often do not consciously reflect upon their paradigm alignment. Next, several circumstances that *can* trigger such awareness are discussed. The section concludes by outlining the reasons why we cannot assume that an individual who becomes paradigm conscious will subsequently seek to investigate other options.

The Closure and Self-referentiality of Paradigms

In Maturana's terms, any unity whose components include a particular philosophical position that is embedded in various methodologies, techniques, and tools, is an increasingly differentiated hierarchy of distinctions, distinctions within distinctions, and so on. At each level an agent has access to a consensually validated language, and a template for seeing and dealing with the world in a particular way. Efran, Lukens and Lukens (1990: 45) describe such domains of distinctions as the "sandboxes" in which we play life's games. Each one is self-contained—it has its own boundaries, vocabularies, and grammars of interaction. We can see this in the case of the three MS paradigms. Clearly there are points of intersection; hard, soft, and critical systems methodologies, for instance, all employ concepts such as transformation process, boundary, feedback, and so on. However, by definition, each paradigm is separate and distinct; it is a closed domain of potentially unique distinctions. These distinctions are helpful and necessary because they provide people with a way of dealing with what otherwise might be an overwhelmingly complex situation; paradoxically they are also a trap. While paradigms, as domains of distinctions, are helpful in providing people with ways of seeing, they can unwittingly blind people to alternative possibilities. They provide insight and illumination, but also produce silences around certain issues and themes. Hard MS, for instance, is silent on the question of plural definitions of problem situations; soft MS is silent on the issue of structured inequalities; critical MS does not provide much help in dealing with complex technical problems. Consequently, when agents—operating within any of these paradigms—have experiences that do not dovetail within its preferred distinctions, the experiences must be reshaped, discounted or ignored.

In itself, the cognitive closure of a paradigm is not necessarily a major issue. It is only when the agent fails to recognise this closure that it becomes a matter of concern. Yet this is quite common, our normal mode of bonding with a paradigm being tacit and unreflective (Burrell and Morgan, 1979; Margolis, 1993). As Maturana puts it: ". . . as a consequence of their manner of constitution, cognitive domains are closed operational domains: an observer cannot get out of a cognitive domain by operating in it. Similarly an observer cannot observe a cognitive domain by operating in it" (1988: 61). The difficulty is that we can become so wedded to paradigms that we fail to see their "blind spots". Maturana would view this as a natural consequence of our predilection to operate according to the *objectivity without parentheses* explanatory path—the paradigm "reflects the way things are"—and because we gradually grow into the paradigm's language we fail to see how it creates a particular way of seeing.

When a commitment to some paradigm is reinforced by an organisational or professional culture, the chance that a member of that culture will question or challenge the paradigm's preferred sets of distinctions is even less likely. Like paradigms, cultures and subcultures uphold established patterns of distinctions that have been socially created and legitimised over time. Essentially cultures are the arenas where the conversational enactment of preferred sets of distinctions takes place. Like any other discipline, MS is made up of a number of discernable subcultures that act in this manner. Some—based around OR groups, consultancies, or university departments—embrace a number of different paradigms. But some groups are less eclectic. Most of these lean towards the hard paradigm, attracting people with sophisticated quantitative skills. In the other paradigms, Lancaster, in the 1970s and 1980s, was rightly seen as the hub of soft systems thinking; and, more recently, Hull has attracted a cadre of people committed to developing the critical paradigm.

This sort of specialisation is not necessarily a bad thing; pooling a number of specialists in a single location can be an important development strategy. But there are some pitfalls. Through recruitment, training, reward, and other socialisation processes, these narrowly focused subcultures encourage people to "fit in", and when alternative viewpoints are unavailable, assumptions go unexamined, and people are often in a poor position to question the premises on which accepted practices rest.

Circumstances Triggering Paradigm Consciousness

Let us now consider the question: if paradigms are closed operational domains, how can they be brought to our attention? If a paradigm is hidden, can it be studied? If a paradigm connotes a particular way of observing, can this be observed, and if so how?

Breakdowns in structural coupling

In promoting the inseparability of knowledge and everyday action, and of mind and body, Maturana clearly accedes to the view that much of what is taken to be cognition occurs automatically—that is, without conscious attention. Switching to a mode in which one consciously reflects upon behaviours that have become obvious, regular and acceptable, and therefore invisible, requires some form of trigger. This occurs when there is a breakdown in structural coupling.

Here Maturana echoes Heidegger's (1927) renowned claim that the separation between knowing subject and known object only occurs when something goes wrong, and that adequate completion of many of the mental and physical tasks that arise in everyday life does not require conscious thought. Other social scientists (Mills, 1940; Schutz, 1964; Louis, 1980; Wong and Weiner, 1981; Schon, 1983; Hastie, 1984; Lundberg, 1985; Margolis, 1993, for example) have also implicated failure or breakdown in engaging active or conscious thinking about everyday behaviour. When things do go wrong, or when an agent is surprised or perplexed by some unpredicted outcome, it can trigger a delving into what otherwise would remain hidden, and this can be the precursor for change. This perhaps explains why many management scientists who operate within the soft or critical paradigms were not actually trained in them. In many cases their introduction to soft or critical MS came about because they had become increasingly disaffected with the dominant paradigm, realising that it fell short in preparing agents for the full gamut of problems likely to be encountered in practice. One can understand this. The various methods, tools, and techniques of the hard paradigm, for example, provide plenty of ammunition for dealing with the material aspects of problem situations, but they provide little in the way of guidance for someone who has to deal with social and personal issues (see Mingers and Brocklesby, 1996). Such guidance must be sought from within the soft and critical paradigms.

Another important repercussion of becoming disaffected or experiencing a breakdown in structural coupling with a paradigm is that it may lead the agent to question, possibly for the first time, the veracity of the claim that the social consensus surrounding a paradigm's body of knowledge somehow represents proof of the truth. Such awareness can open up space for the agent to embrace other paradigms. Once someone has discarded the idea that a particular paradigm lays out "the way things are", moving from one to another is less problematic because it does not have to carry with it the connotation that the truth is somehow going to be jettisoned. If people can come to appreciate that paradigm switching merely exchanges one reality in a multiverse of realities for another, and that ultimately one's alignment is a matter of choice, then they have an intellectual conduit through which they can move from one paradigm to another with much less fear.

Experiences in other cognitive domains

The second circumstance that can precipitate a greater level of paradigm awareness is through an experience in some other cognitive domain. Maturana claims that at any moment our "bodyhood" is at the intersection of simultaneous intersecting conversations, ". . . our present as human beings is always a node in a network of conversations . . ." (Maturana, 1988: 53). In our daily life we populate many different domains. Although these are independent as domains of conversations, they are realised through our bodyhoods, so potentially they influence each other. What happens to us in one, has consequences for our participation in the rest. This is an important point, it being easy to forget that management scientists are not *just* management scientists. All of us operate in multiple domains; that is, we participate simultaneously in various conversations not only as management scientists, but also as engineers, economists, mathematicians, quality experts, academics, parents, teachers, managers, community workers, trade unionists, and in myriad other ways. In fact very few management scientists have been trained just as management scientists. Most enter the field from the outside, so to speak. Thus we all have a rich source of interactions that can trigger our reflecting upon the way we participate as management scientists. Whenever an agent has an encounter outside a particular domain, it triggers structural changes in him or her. Some of these encounters, in Maturana's terms, will be *orthogonal*, i.e. contrary to the rules under which he or she participates as a management scientist. Upon returning to the domain of management science their participation alters, and this, in turn, can trigger structural changes in the domain itself. It is part of the dynamic through which fields like management science are constantly changing.

External initiatives

A third possibility is when an external agent requests it. This could take the form of a direct request to reject one paradigm in favour of another, or it could involve an external agent—say a teacher, an author, or an OR group leader—providing the agent with a contextual framework that allows them to understand where they stand in relation to various paradigm categories. This circumvents the paradigm's cognitive closure, thereby bringing it into focus. As Maturana (1988: 61) puts it, ". . . an observer can get out of a cognitive domain, and observe it, only through the recursive consensuality of language by consensually specifying another cognitive domain in which the first one is an object of distinctions". Examples of such sense-making devices to account for and locate various paradigms include Burrell and Morgan's (1979) "sociological paradigms", Pepper's (1942) "world hypotheses", and, most obviously, the "hard/soft/critical" framework used here.

In summary, although there are grounds for believing that the paradigms that buttress the way people do MS often remain hidden, breakdowns in structural coupling, experiences in other domains, and direct initiatives can make them accessible. These events can be instrumental in bringing about a change in someone's paradigm alignment, although one should not assume that will happen immediately. For example, when someone decides *not* to act on a speaker's suggestion that they adopt some new methodology or other, this does at least show that the message has been heard. Should the speaker repeat the same message at a later date, it will act on a different structure, so one cannot assume that events that fail to trigger an expected response at a particular point in time will not ultimately be successful.

Although the events just described can bring paradigmatic concerns into focus, there are two important caveats worth mentioning. First, we must be wary of attributing too much influence to external agents. Because individuals are structure-determined systems who hear what they hear not according to what is said, but according to their own structural determinism, then the influence of any speaker on a listener is severely proscribed. External agents *can* induce others to reflect on their predicament, but this will only happen if the listener's structure allows it, and if certain other conditions are met. These are discussed in the final section of the chapter.

Second, we have to be clear about what emerges when people *do* reflect on their paradigm posture. Were Maturana to address this question his answer would almost certainly reflect the pre-eminence that he always gives to his observer-dependent epistemology, ". . . we are already languaging living systems doing what we do, including our explaining, when we begin to explain what we do, and that we are already in the experience of observing when we begin to observe our observing" (1980: 12). So when we reflect on something we do so as structurally determined observers, and language provides the operational mechanism for this. People cannot refer to themselves, or anything else for that matter, outside of language or their structural determinism. Even the distinction "*I*" occurs through language, so language is required to experience ourselves. In reflecting on our paradigm preferences we use language to make distinctions of our distinctions, and our experiential situation is the context within which this occurs. As Maturana (1988: 59) puts it, ". . . the observer constitutively cannot make distinctions outside the domain of operational coherences of his or her praxis of living". We cannot, therefore, step outside of our existence and come up with some objective view.

Of course, in attending to the context in which our experience is embedded we can make every effort to be objective, but inevitably there are limits on what is possible. Observing naively, that is, separating the influence of one's linguistic structures from that which is seen, is virtually impossible once language, words and symbols become an integral part of a person's experience. An agent may concur that reflecting upon their own habitual thought patterns and preconceptions is a worthwhile activity. However, this does not diminish the difficulty that they face in accomplishing this task without any resulting interpretations being themselves grounded in, and constrained by, the paradigm which is being reflected upon.

COMMITTING ONESELF TO A NEW PARADIGM

At this stage in the argument, let us assume that despite the countervailing tendencies just mentioned, our notional agent is now more aware of his or her paradigm alignment than before, let us assume that they now know about other paradigms, and let us assume that they are contemplating whether or not to examine these further. Many members of the present management science community will be able to identify with this situation having reflected upon the possibility of moving from one paradigm to another at some stage or other during their careers. Basically, what happens next depends upon the sort of life the agent leads, and the sort of person they are.

The Agent's Experiential Situation

To illustrate the importance of an agent's experiential situation in this matter, consider the experiential domains of academic and practitioner management scientists in relation to matters concerning methodology and research preferences. Tenured academics can generally do whatever they want, and many exercise this freedom by choosing to specialise in one or perhaps two methods from a single paradigm. To an academic, specialisation can make sense because it satisfies both personal and career-related needs. It can lead to a public and a self-realisation that one has achieved some sort of expert status, and, arguably, it can open up publishing opportunities. Some academics might reasonably claim that while multimethodology is a good idea in principle, they fear the consequences of becoming a "jack of all trades and master of none".

Better, they might claim, to be secure in one paradigm, than risk drifting aimlessly in every paradigm.

It is manifestly clear that the experiential world of most practitioners is different to that of most academics. Academics can shun multimethodology for the reasons just mentioned, but practitioners may have good reason to take it seriously. Whereas academics can be choosy about their methodological preferences, practitioners often have to turn their hands to whatever work opportunities are available, and this might mean that they have to be more methodologically versatile. Of course, some hard MS practitioners do approach problem situations from a single methodology perspective, but we must be careful about what we conclude from this. One of the differences between academics and practitioners is that the liquidity of the practitioner's employment depends more on the results that they obtain, than it does on their methodological prowess. The constant pressure to function effectively and "produce the goods" almost mandates that the practitioner grapples with the ever-present social, political, and personal issues that impinge on problem situations where they seek to intervene, even though their technical training and methodological fitness may fall short in preparing them for this. Not all academics are subject to these sorts of pressures.

Some experienced practitioners might reasonably claim that they can explore and deal effectively with these diverse cross-paradigm issues in an *ad hoc* or intuitive manner, and that little would be gained by having recourse to formal methodologies. It would be churlish to deny this possibility because, as I discuss in the final section, expert performance relies heavily upon intuitive behaviours. But not all practitioners will feel confident that they can simply trust their instincts in dealing with matters for which their formal training leaves them ill-prepared. It is hard to imagine that those who lack confidence in this regard would not appreciate the benefits of multimethodology.

This broad comparison of the different lives led by academic and practitioner management scientists is just one example, but it does serve to illustrate the point that the take-up of multimethodology depends very heavily upon an agent's experiential situation. For some, it will make a great deal of sense and it will trigger a positive response. For those with different interests, with different values, with different *structures*, it may turn out to be just another environmental perturbation that is largely inconspicuous.

The Agent

Equally important in estimating the likely take-up of multimethodology is the agent themselves. As Lincoln (1990: 67) claims, ". . . fooling around with a new paradigm is an intensely *personal* process, evolving from not only intellectual but also *personal, social, and possibly political* transformation . . .". If this is so, then we can hardly expect agents to be equally comfortable in all three MS paradigms. The degree of comfort experienced in a paradigm depends, for example, upon the agent's values and beliefs, their personality, and their preferred cognitive style. Again, it can be said that it depends upon their structure.

Maturana places a great deal of emphasis on emotion, and focusing on emotion helps to demonstrate the point that the feasibility of multimethodology depends a great deal upon the actual agent who is expected to do it. It is now widely accepted that different human interests underpin the production of knowledge, and each interest contains different dispositions towards the world (see Habermas, 1974; Jackson, 1991). In MS we have come to associate the hard paradigm with the *technical interest* that an agent might have in the prediction and control of some real-world system (see Flood, 1990; Jackson, 1991). This would seem to best suit those whose emotional predisposition is towards curiosity—of the "getting to the bottom of a problem" sort—and whose predilection is to want to invent new systems or make existing systems work better.

The soft MS paradigm has been associated with the so-called *practical* interest. Here the technical rigour that one associates with the hard paradigm gives way to relevance. It is a place for those whose emotional preference is to facilitate intersubjective understanding, and would seem to suit best those who enjoy helping people with divergent viewpoints, who are keen on better understanding their own position as well as those of others, and who believe that accommodation and commitment to some sort of action is a more realistic objective than always seeking technically correct solutions to predetermined problems.

The critical paradigm almost obliges the agent to have some degree of empathy for the underdog, and (at least in the traditional guise of critical theory) to harbour noble dreams about creating a more equitable society. Here the agent's curiosity is geared towards the *emancipatory* interest which seeks to recover ideas and thought that become distorted through power relations.

If we accept that each paradigm has its own set of explicit and implicit operational premises (values, accepted truths, emotional and political predispositions, etc.), we are forced to admit that journeying between paradigms is not a simple matter. At the extreme, it has been described as requiring a quasi-religious Paulinian conversion (Jackson and Carter, 1991), and as an odyssey that involves severe, even traumatic, philosophical and value dislocations (Guba, 1990). This may be overstating the case somewhat, but such statements do serve to reinforce the point that when the *actual* people who might be expected to do multimethodology are brought into the picture, moving between paradigms is much more than simply an exercise in intellectual musical chairs. Whereas moving from one paradigm to another sequentially over time is difficult, operating concurrently across two more may be even more problematic. It is understandable therefore, that while some may decide to fully embrace the possibilities of employing methods from different paradigms, others might choose not to subject themselves to the various personal demands and stress that it would involve.

In summary, the main argument of this section has been that there are a number of good reasons why someone who is paradigm conscious, and who understands the rationale behind combining methods from different paradigms, will nevertheless conclude that the costs outweigh the benefits, and that they do not wish to pursue the matter any further. Leaving any cognitive domain can be a painful operation involving abandoning (if only temporarily) old views. Not everyone will want to do that, particularly when there is uncertainty about what another domain will bring. For those who *are* persuaded that exploring a new paradigm is worthwhile, the next concern is whether they are able to translate their intent to perform according to the logic of a new paradigm into effective action.

ACTING EFFECTIVELY IN A "NEW" PARADIGM

In some respects, making the decision to explore a new paradigm is straightforward. It is simply a case of wanting to move into a different intellectual neighbourhood. Maturana makes clear (1988: 33) that we *can* expand or change our cognitive domains, and that we can even participate in nonintersecting and *contradictory* cognitive domains as is the case with different paradigms. Thus he claims (1980: 13) that, ". . . a man can be a member of a family, a club, a political party, or a religious brotherhood, however dissimilar or antagonistic these social systems may be . . . and do so apparently without contradiction . . .".

This statement, however, does not convey any sense of the extent to which an agent is *able* to meet the demands of a new paradigm. Certainly people can move from one cognitive domain to another, we do that all the time. But moving from one MS paradigm to another is not like finishing a game of chess and starting a political discussion. It is not simply a case of operationalising a new set of linguistic tools. New rules for what is considered knowledge and truth have to be inculcated, and new skills and practices have to be learnt.

Acquiring a Paradigm's Propositional and Commonsense Knowledge

At this stage in the discussion it is worth restating Maturana's declaration that there is an intimate connection between cognition and action. Recall his conceptualisation of cognition as effective action. Recall also his view that cognition is an integral part of our normal everyday activity. It is not, as many of us are inclined to believe, "detached cogitation, but situated practical action" (Mingers, 1995: 109). What then does it take to *act effectively* in a new paradigm?

To answer this question let us rehearse how, ordinarily, humans relate to the world. As we have seen, Maturana concurs with Heidegger whose position Mingers describes as follows:

> Our natural attitude, our being-in-the-world, cannot be expressed in, nor does it consist of, conscious beliefs, ideas, rules and intentions. Rather it is *a sub- or pre-conscious* attitude *socialized into us* and *embodied in our actions and skills.* Being, our way of interpreting and dealing with the world, is inherent in the practices of our culture and society and is continually enacted by us in an unmindful way. We cannot uncover the beliefs or intentions behind what we do, for there are none; there are only skills and practices." (Mingers, 1995: 108 emphases added).

Let us examine these points in more detail. The issue of our pre-conscious attitude to the world has been pursued extensively by other philosophers, the most notable being Maurice Merleau-Ponty. And it is Merleau-Ponty's ball that Maturana's colleague, Francisco Varela, picks up and runs with. In their 1991 work, Varela, Thompson and Rosch identify two types of knowledge: "propositional" and "commonsense". The case of learning to drive a car is used to illustrate the difference between the two.

When someone first learns how to drive they have to learn how to start the car, change gears, use the steering wheel, use the brakes. They also have to know about and abide by the various rules and regulations that are designed to prevent accidents. For someone new to driving there is a great deal of such propositional knowledge to be learnt, although with practice most people pick up "the rules" of driving very quickly. Because it is relatively easy to specify all possible states in these task domains, even robots can be designed to drive a car and follow the road code.

The driving world, however, does not end at the point where one has mastered the various actions that are required to turn on the ignition, steer correctly, and know that it is wise to stop at red traffic lights. Unlike games such as chess or snooker (where there are fewer possible states) driving is a task domain that "has the structure of ever-receding levels of detail that blend into a non-specific background" (Varela, Thompson and Rosch, 1991: 147). This background includes a complex array of variables such as weather condi-tions, road surface, local driving customs, pedestrians, the mood of the driver and passengers, and so on. Knowing *how* to drive a car properly—*effective action* in this cognitive domain—"depends upon acquired motor skills and *the continuous use of commonsense or background know-how*" (Varela, Thompson and Rosch, 1991: 147 emphasis added).

As in the case of driving a motor vehicle, few of our "lived worlds" in MS have predefined bounded environments, although from my vantage point, some are more bounded than others. Hard MS—linear programming or producing a spreadsheet, for example—has a highly sophisticated and explicit set of rules that can be transmitted. Although the rules still have limited jurisdiction, once understood, producing outputs is relatively straightforward. Soft MS, in contrast, is manifestly different. The propositional knowledge that is required to create rich pictures, produce root definitions, and construct cognitive maps can be acquired from textbooks; but effective soft MS involves working directly with people, and responding, often in real time, to the exigencies of whatever situation develops. Unfortunately these relationship-managing skills are difficult to capture in a propositional format. SSM is a much vaunted methodology, but one could argue that the coupling between the agent and the people in the problem situation is a greater critical success factor than is the methodology itself. The propositional content of SSM may be important, but people still have to rely upon their experiences and creativity in defining whatever it is that they have to deal with. These "ready-to-hand" skills and commonsense understandings have to be learnt somehow, but because "the unmanageable ambiguity of background common sense is left largely at the periphery of the inquiry" (Varela, Thompson and Rosch, 1991: 148), they rarely have chapters assigned to them in textbooks, neither are they regularly discussed at conferences. In relation to SSM, one could argue that there is a distressingly wide gap between what management scientists write about and what they do.

Maturana might even claim that because highly complex actions can be executed without the generation of an observer to appreciate and evaluate them, "giving voice" to all aspects of the MS "experience" is unattainable. As (self) observers we become aware of some of our action patterns, but because only highly abstracted and selected aspects of our operations are ever languaged, much of what we do remains unnoticed in the background. The basics may be simply so obvious that we do not see them. Even if we do notice, we are subject to our structural determinism, so whereas the actual experience of doing something is spontaneous, thinking about and then articulating it is a reformulated activity that occurs post-event within this constraint. The same logic applies when we ask experienced practitioners what worked for them. They don't know; they only know the story of what worked for them.

Soft MS may provide the best illustration, but the same logic applies to all three MS paradigms. Acquiring propositional knowledge is only the first stage in becoming effective. Dreyfus (1996)—who also pays intellectual homage to Merleau-Ponty—agrees that "instructor provided" (propositional) knowledge is sufficient only to get someone started in a task domain. That which is learnt from teachers/textbooks/journals, etc., mainly concentrates on detached uninvolved rule-following behaviour leading to reasoned responses. Typically it lays out ways of decomposing task environments, differentiating commonly occurring situational features, and it produces rules for dealing with these. This is very useful for the novice, but it capitulates in the face of the potentially vast number of situational factors that must be faced, especially when these differ in subtle, nuanced ways. Neither can it provide perspectives for prioritising these, i.e. in deciding what is important and what is not. Competency or proficiency in such circumstances requires active involvement, practice and experience of a large number of cases. Becoming expert, where reasoning gives way to intuition, is even more demanding. This requires a gradual accumulation of a vast number of situational discriminations, associated responses, and acquired feedback on the success or failure of these. Experts, with this sort of experience, know intuitively what needs to be done in a situation and how to do it. They resort to rule-following behaviour and reasoned responses only when things do not turn out as expected.

The concept of *enaction* or *embodied cognition* articulated by Varela and his colleagues adds another piece to this jigsaw. Enaction further develops the idea that knowledge is constituted in our actions. As an individual confronts new situations various experiences are gained through thinking, sensing, and *moving*. This means that the way we experience (and "bring forth") the world is very much an *active* construction involving the whole *body*. Effective action depends upon having a body with various sensorimotor and orienting capacities that allow an agent to act, perceive, and sense in distinctive ways. If the agent's body has not learned how to orient itself in such a way that the relevant cues are picked up then they run the risk of "missing" that which others might pick up. Again, I suspect that this is a major critical success factor in soft MS where the agent has to respond expeditiously to the demands of the situation paying due regard to the needs of those involved. The problem is that these sorts of orienting credentials are not easily taught. They grow out of accumulated lived experience of certain kinds of activity. They are entrenched in the day-to-day experience of acting in the world, and they become entangled in various ways in expert practice.

The main point of this section is that while the newcomer has to acquire relevant propositional knowledge, this is only the very first step in becoming proficient in a new paradigm. Really "knowing" the paradigm—acting effectively in it—makes more substantial demands, and these can only be satisfied through active bodily involvement, experience and practice. Any claim, then, that an agent is effective within a paradigm must speak about their whole "being", about how they enact their daily existence in the fullest possible sense, not just about "what they know" in a conventional sense. What counts is not what someone says they know or what they say they can do, it is what they actually do. Some might argue that the thoroughly universal nature of any paradigm means that it literally permeates every act associated with the sort of work a management scientist might do, such that in moving from one paradigm to another, a totally new *"being-in-this-world"* has to be enacted. If this is so, the difficulties of bringing it about are self-evident. Consuming relevant propositional knowledge helps, but because the "rules" of any paradigm are woven so completely and unobtrusively into the fabric of everyday life, they are notoriously difficult to explain. Ultimately one has to find ways of being there and doing it.

Finally, let us not underestimate the difficulty of learning new propositional knowledge, which can itself pose a formidable barrier. How many management scientists, for example, who enter the discipline through the soft or critical paradigms and lacking a background in mathematics or statistics, take up the challenge of learning sophisticated quantitative techniques? Not many. Virtually all who are known to be competent across the hard/soft divide graduated from the hard to the soft paradigm.

Resocialising Oneself

Assuming that an agent is able to gain the sort of practical lived experience that exposes them to a paradigm's commonsense knowledge, the next potential difficulty concerns the question of whether someone who has been thoroughly socialised in one paradigm can prevent its unwelcome intrusion into another. Basically, the issue is that the structural change involved in learning a new paradigm is but one moment in an ongoing history of structural couplings. Hence it would be rather naive to believe that a new coupling completely supersedes that which preceded it.

Operating effectively in a new paradigm, then, may be said to require both a learning and an *un*learning. Indeed, as much training and effort may be required in letting go of established and habitual ways of doing and thinking about things, as is required in learning the new paradigm. Consequently, a manifest switch from one paradigm to another need not mean that there has been a complete eradication of established behaviours. Contexts may remain in which there is a residue of the "old" or the "other" behaviours. These can reassert themselves, as happens, for example, when reformed smokers or drinkers revert to their old habits at times of stress, or when an "unlearned" accent suddenly reappears when a person is "not on duty". One suspects that the same may be the case for those who claim to have moved from one paradigm to another, or who claim to be able to switch easily from one paradigm to another. At a superficial level this may appear to be the case, but deeper investigation may reveal that long-held basic assumptions—even beliefs, values, and behaviour patterns—are still influential.

In extreme cases, there may be so much intellectual baggage that the odds of someone completing a successful transition are somewhat remote. The choices that people have depend a great deal upon their past experiences. We are all contextually and historically situated actors and our autonomy and freedom to move is often severely constrained. Our thrown-ness, our historical couplings, makes certain decisions and paths for the future unlikely or even impossible. Darwin, for example, despaired of converting any but young uncommitted naturalists to his theory of evolution (see Guba, 1990). Despite this, we can confront and own up to our thrown-ness, and we do achieve some sense of liberation in recognising why this is so, and, in this way, we do broaden our horizons to some extent. By recognising the flow of our thrownness, by not just unconsciously accepting it, we may seek to redirect it to a degree. As Efran, Lukens and Lukens (1990: 196) put it, ". . . the future is never just the past with some more time added . . . language always creates new and different possibilities".

MOVING EASILY BETWEEN PARADIGMS

Having learned how to act effectively in a new paradigm, the final concern is whether the agent can move easily between the new and old paradigms. While the success of multimethodology depends upon the agent becoming competent in using methodologies from new paradigms, this must not detract from their performance in the original preferred paradigm because they must be able to move from one domain to another as attention shifts from issue to issue, or as the intervention proceeds through various stages. Of course, one could claim that this is a redundant question since acquiring new skills and learning new practices need not entail losing existing competences. But again, the issue is more complex than this.

Maturana's concept of orthogonal interaction, discussed earlier, sheds some light on the difficulty. When someone interacts outside a particular domain in a way that is different—or *orthogonal*—from what the domain's "rules" specify—as one would, for example, in moving from hard to soft MS—the interaction triggers structurally determined changes in the individual. The individual then returns to the original domain and participates differently in it. Thus, a hard systems management scientist who returns to hard systems practice after having discovered the soft paradigm is not the same person who left the hard paradigm in the first place. It is impossible to remain untouched by this sort of orthogonal interaction, and whether the agent is aware of it or not, there will be practical implications for them, as there will for the various communities to which they return. Each community will be triggered as a result of the various orthogonal interactions of its members, and will change according to its own structural determination. As for a hard systems practitioner undergoing orthogonal interactions in the soft paradigm, the sorts of changes that immediately spring to mind include the agent no longer being able to accept unquestioningly the concept of "problem" as an objectively independent concept, and no longer being able to ignore or negate the subjectivity—or worldview—that underpins a particular system and the various boundary judgements that it contains. These difficulties are manifest when the soft paradigm intrudes on the hard, but problems could arise when the assumptions of any paradigm intrude upon and detract from the application of a methodology from another paradigm.

In signalling a way out of this difficulty Maturana's perspective hints at an alternative philosophical basis for the "multi-paradigm" genre of multimethodology that has been the focus of discussion here. Maturana (see Mendez, Coddon and Maturana, 1988) claims that one of the reasons why people have problems is because they operate in multiple domains, or, as Efran, Lukens and Lukens (1990: 146) put it, different "clubs". The rules of one coupling run counter to the rules of another, such that the individual lives in "emotional contradiction". If this is what may happen when an agent is asked to perform concurrently across each of the three major MS paradigms, what can be done about it? "The solution [Maturana claims] . . . lies in moving away from the opposition and changing the nature of the question, to embrace a broader context" (Efran, Lukens and Lukens, 1990: 147). The aim of this perspective-widening process is to move to a larger, more encompassing frame.

Such a possibility has already been canvassed in MS. Whereas multi-paradigm multimethodology would have an agent move from one paradigm to another depending upon which methodology, or part thereof, is being used at any moment, an alternative possibility has methodologies originating in different paradigms being employed in the service of a *new* paradigm. The defining feature of such a paradigm is that it can dissolve the competing objective–subjective duality of the original paradigms by incorporating these perspectives within a broader ontological framework. It is not appropriate to delve into this matter here, save to point out that, in the MS context, this option was first raised by Midgley (1989, 1990, 1992). In Mingers (1995), and Mingers and Brocklesby (1996), it was developed further through reference to the work of philosophers such as Bhasker and Giddens.

It seems to me that putting various methodologies to work in support of this new paradigm is desirable because it provides a way of avoiding having to choose between one of the three existing paradigms, or having to constantly adjust one's assumptions as one moves between them. This option, therefore, accords with Maturana's suggestion that in dealing with conflict we should "create a new domain of reality where the two parties can coexist" (Maturana, 1988: 62). For those who are keen on multimethodology it provides the authority to throw away the old rule books and play by new rules. The new rules circumvent the need to be constantly adjusting one's philosophical position depending upon which methodology or technique is being used at any moment in time, which, as we have seen, can create difficulties.

CONCLUDING COMMENTS

The main conclusion of this chapter is that the process of transforming an agent who works within a single paradigm into someone who is multi-methodology literate is perhaps an unlikely, although by no means impossible, proposition. For it to happen, a number of obstacles must be overcome. First, the agent must become paradigm conscious. This is difficult because of the cognitive closure of paradigms, and, because the insights accruing out of self-observation are bounded by people's experiential situation. Second, the agent must believe that a new paradigm offers them something worth having, and it must fit with their personality, emotional and political predilections. Third, effective performance in a paradigm necessitates learning its common-sense, as well as its propositional, knowledge. This can be difficult if the agent's previous history of structural coupling has not led them to develop, or have the capacity to acquire, the full range of embodied skills that this re-quires. Even if the agent is capable of learning such skills, appropriate prac-tice and apprenticeship is required, and old habits have to be unlearned. This involves a major resocialisation, and there is no escaping the time and effort that is required. Finally, moving easily between paradigms can be problem-atic, although this can be facilitated by the agent adopting one or other of the broader philosophical perspectives that nullify the competing ontological as-sumptions of the traditional hard and soft paradigms.

I would like to end the chapter by reflecting briefly on the role that an external agent might play in encouraging others to contemplate the personal journey just described. In this regard, it would be easy to conclude that if people's experiential situation made multimethodology or the exploration of a new paradigm a sensible option for them, then it would happen anyway, and that external agents should not seek to influence people's own judgements about what is good for them. While being sympathetic to this view, one has to acknowledge that sometimes external agents can help us to see new ways in which we can improve how we live our professional lives (on our terms, not on theirs). On this point, those seeking to persuade fellow management scientists to explore beyond their favoured paradigm, or take up multimethodology, can extract some useful guidance from Maturana's work.

The first lesson is that it is inadvisable to set out with the deliberate inten-tion of getting people to "join" the multimethodology "club". A more pru-dent approach is first to put objectivity into parentheses, and then, as Dell (1985) puts it, to become a *scholar of structural determinism*. This allows a better grasp of what messages will act as triggers and which have a high probability of leading to favoured outcomes. Instead of just marshalling the so-called "facts", a speaker must know the target audience, understand its various meanings, its values and priorities, and communicate with it on its terms. Someone who appreciates the culpability of language has an advantage here. The listening of the participant and the language they use reveals both their structure and the world they bring forth. Hence language becomes a key instrument for eliciting structural change.

Second, the speaker has to ensure that his or her interactions do not simply confirm the system that they are trying to disintegrate. Getting around this problem requires that he or she choose an adequate orthogonal interaction (intervention, statement, interaction, etc.) that is outside the domain of conversations that defines the existing system, but which takes place in the domain of existence of whomever is subject to it. Thus, for example, in attempting to persuade someone with a leaning towards the hard MS paradigm to broaden their perspective one should avoid speaking in terms of *problems* and *solutions*. Ultimately this would be self-defeating because this is the language of the hard paradigm and using it would merely serve to bolster that which is being questioned. The trick is to use language that is outside the domain of conversations that defines the existing system, but which takes place in the domain of the listener's existence. One could speak with some confidence in terms of *issues* and *accommodations*—the language of soft MS—to an audience that is used to thinking in terms of *problems* and *solutions*, knowing that one is building upon some relevant experience that the listener can relate to. It is hard to imagine that even the most laboratory-closeted hard management scientist would not have some such relevant experience.

Third, the speaker must be sensitive to people's emotional as well as their rational attachments to their paradigms. As Maturana puts it, cognitive requests made by a speaker to a listener can only ". . . operate as *invitations* to enter in the same domain of reality as the speaker" (1988: 62, emphasis added). Requests cannot operate as demands for obedience. People cannot be "strong-armed" into renouncing their personal realities. The management science community needs to hear this because in recent years the literature has resounded to various conversations of recrimination, accusation, and characterisation (see, for example, Ackoff, 1982; Checkland, 1982; Churchman, 1982; Jackson, 1982; Checkland, 1992; Flood, 1993; Tsoukas, 1993) that testify to the emotional commitment of people to their definitions of reality. Clearly the emotional factor must be incorporated within any strategy that is designed to bring about changes in the way management scientists approach their work.

Finally, a speaker who seeks to intervene having regard to the possibility of bringing about change in a listener, has to weigh their actions alongside Maturana's claim that "all manners of living are operationally legitimate" (Maturana, 1990). If a speaker accepts the premise that nothing can be proven objectively correct, the question has to be asked—on what grounds can anyone promote multimethodology over single paradigm research? The answer to this question is simple. If objectivity is placed in parentheses, all paradigms are indeed operationally legitimate in the *biological domain*, i.e. any set of distinctions made by a person's nervous system is legitimate. But it does not follow that they are equally desirable for everyone in the *human domain of coexistence*. Here, in this domain of values, it is a matter of preferences. No one, therefore, can claim any transcendental objectivity as a foundation for influencing others. People have to take personal responsibility for their preferences and whatever they may espouse, and this applies as much to multimethodology as it does to any other idea for "improving" the practice of MS. Those who promote it, do so not because it is the harbinger of some new objectively correct way of doing MS, but because it makes sense to *them*, given *their* history of interactions, within *their* praxis of living. Notwithstanding this, agents who are wedded to a particular paradigm or method, can still be asked to clarify their desires, and to reflect upon options that they would not have generated themselves. Under this style of interaction the aim of the external agent is not to change or manipulate the existence of the other, but to invite the other to put objectivity in parentheses.

For those who, hitherto, have uncritically accepted the transcendental "rightness" of their own preferred paradigm, the awareness that objectivity is biologically unattainable, and that in the end it all comes down to values and preferences, may trigger a change in their thinking. Even if it does not, and they decide to stick with what they know, at least knowing about competitors provides a platform from which to examine unexamined assumptions. When there are no alternatives people are not in a good position to know what they have, so the presence of alternatives forces them to present their position, to defend it, and thereby understand it better. Moreover, it invokes a sense of humility as they become aware of the precarious quality of their knowledge.

REFERENCES

Ackoff, R.L. (1982). On the hard-heartedness of M.C. Jackson. *Journal of Applied Systems Analysis*, **9**(1).

Bennett, P. (1990). Mixing methods: combining conflict analysis, SODA, and strategic choice. In C. Eden and J. Radford (eds) *Tackling Strategic Problems: The Role of Group Decision Support.* Sage, London, pp. 99–109.

Bennett, P. and Cropper, S. (1990). Uncertainty and conflict: combining conflict analysis and strategic choice. *Journal of Behavioural Decision Making*, **3**, 29–45.

Burrell, G. and Morgan, G. (1979). *Sociological Paradigms and Organisational Analysis.* Heinemann, London.

Checkland, P. (1982). Soft systems methodology as process: a reply to M.C. Jackson. *Journal of Applied Systems Analysis*, **9**(1), 37–39.

Checkland, P. (1992). Systems and scholarship: the need to do better. *Journal of the Operational Research Society*, **43**, 1023–1030.

Churchman, C.W. (1982). Reply to M.C. Jackson. *Journal of Applied Systems Analysis*, **9**(1), 35.

Dell, P. (1985). Understanding Bateson and Maturana: toward a biological foundation for the social sciences. *Journal of Marital and Family Therapy*, **11**(1), 1–20.

Dreyfus, H.L. (1996). The current relevance of Merleau-Ponty's Phenomenology of Embodiment. In H. Haber and G. Weiss (eds) *Perspectives on Embodiment*. Routledge, New York and London, pp. 56–62.

Efran, J., Lukens, M. and Lukens, R. (1990). *Language, Structure, and Change—Frameworks of Meaning in Psychotherapy*. W.W. Norton and Co. Inc., New York.

Firestone, W. (1990). Accommodation: toward a paradigm–praxis dialectic. In E.G. Guba (ed.) *The Paradigm Dialog*. Sage, Newbury Park, CA, pp. 105–124.

Flood, R.L. (1990). *Liberating Systems Theory*. Plenum Press, New York.

Flood, R. (1993). Checkland and scholarship: the need to do better. *Journal of the Operational Research Society*, **44**(6), 632–633.

Flood, R.L. and Jackson, M.C. (1991). *Creative Problem Solving*. John Wiley & Sons, Chichester.

Guba, E.G. (1990). *The Paradigm Dialog*. Sage, Newbury Park, CA.

Habermas, J. (1974). *Knowledge and Human Interests*. Heinemann, London.

Hastie, R. (1984). Causes and effects of causal attribution. *Journal of Personality and Social Psychology*, **46**, 44–56.

Heidegger, M. (1927). *Being and Time*. SCM, London.

Jackson, M.C. (1991). *Systems Methodology for the Management Sciences*. Plenum Press, New York and London.

Jackson, M.C. (1982). The nature of soft systems thinking, the work of Churchman, Ackoff, and Checkland. *Journal of Applied Systems Analysis*, **9**(1), 17–28.

Jackson, M.C. and Keys, P. (1984). Towards a system of systems methodologies. *Journal of the Operational Research Society*, **35**(6), 473–486.

Jackson, N. and Carter, P. (1991). In defence of paradigm incommensurability. *Organization Studies*, **12**(1), 109–127.

Lincoln, Y. (1990). The making of a constructivist: a remembrance of transformations past. In E.G. Guba (ed.) *The Paradigm Dialog*. Sage, Newbury Park, CA, pp. 67–87.

Louis, M.R. (1980). Surprise and sense-making: what newcomers experience in entering unfamiliar organizational settings. *Administrative Science Quarterly*, **25**, 226–251.

Lundberg, C. (1985). On the feasibility of cultural intervention. In L.F. Moore et al (eds) *Organisational Culture*. Sage, Beverly Hills, CA, pp. 169–186.

Margolis, H. (1993). *Paradigms and Barriers—How Habits of Mind Govern Scientific Beliefs*. University of Chicago Press, Chicago, IL.

Maturana, H. (1980). Man and society. In F. Benseler, P.M. Hejl and W.K. Kock (eds) *Autopoiesis, Communication, and Society: The Theory of Autopoietic Systems in the Social Sciences*. Campus Verlag, Frankfurt, pp. 11–32.

Maturana, H. (1988). Reality: the search for objectivity or the quest for a compelling argument. *Irish Journal of Psychology*, **9**, 25–82.

Maturana, H. (1990). Science and daily life: the ontology of scientific explanations. In W. Krohn, G. Kuppers and H. Nowotny (eds) *Selforganization: Portrait of a Scientific Revolution*. Kluwer Group, Dordrecht, pp. 12–35.

Maturana, H. and Varela, F. (1980). *Autopoiesis and Cognition: The Realisation of the Living*. Reidel, Dordrecht.

Maturana, H. and Varela, F. (1987). *The Tree of Knowledge—The Biological Roots of Human Understanding*. Shambhala, Boston, MA.

Mendez, C., Coddou, F. and Maturana, H. (1988). The bringing forth of pathology. *Irish Journal of Psychology*, **9**(1), 144–172.

Merleau-Ponty, M. (1961). *Phenomenology of Perception*. Routledge & Kegan Paul, London.

Midgley, G. (1989). Critical systems: the theory and practice of partitioning methodologies. In *Proceedings of 33rd Annual Meeting of the International Society for General Systems Research*. Edinburgh, pp. 123–129.

Midgley, G. (1990). Critical systems thinking and methodological pluralism. In *Proceedings of 34th Annual Meeting of the International Society for the Systems Sciences*, pp. 86–107.

Midgley, G. (1992). Pluralism and the legitimation of systems science. *Systems Practice*, **5**(2), 147–172.

Mills, C.W. (1940). Situated actions and vocabularies of motive. *American Sociological Review*, **5**, 904–913.

Mingers, J. (1989a). An introduction to autopoiesis—implications and applications. *Systems Practice*, **2**(2), 159–180.

Mingers, J. (1989b). An introduction to autopoiesis: a reply to Fenton Robb. *Systems Practice*, **2**(3), 349–351.

Mingers, J. (1990). The philosophical implications of Maturana's cognitive theories. *Systems Practice*, **3**(6), 569–584.

Mingers, J. (1991). The cognitive theories of Maturana and Varela. *Systems Practice*, **4**(4), 319–338.

Mingers, J. (1995). *Self-Producing Systems—Implications and Applications of Autopoiesis*. Plenum Press, New York and London.

Mingers, J. and Brocklesby, J. (1996). Multimethodology: towards a framework for critical pluralism. *Systemist*, **18**(3), 101–132.

Ormerod, R. (1996). Viewpoint: new methods for old. *Journal of the Operational Research Society*, **47**, 1317–1318.

Pepper, S.C. (1942). *World Hypotheses*. University of California Press, Berkeley, CA.

Schon, D. (1983). *The Reflective Practitioner: How Professionals Think in Action*. Basic Books, New York.

Schutz, A. (1964). *Collected Papers 2: Studies in Social Theory*. Martinus Nijhoff, The Hague.

Smaling, A. (1994). The pragmatic dimension—paradigmatic and pragmatic aspects of choosing a qualitative or quantitative method. *Quality and Quantity*, **28**, 233–249.

Tsoukas, H. (1993). "By Their Fruits Ye Shall Know Them": a reply to Jackson, Green and Midgley. *Systems Practice*, **6**(3), 311–318.

Varela, F., Thompson, E. and Rosch, E. (1991). *The Embodied Mind—Cognitive Science and Human Experience*. MIT Press, Cambridge, MA.

Wong, P.T.P. and Weiner, B. (1981). When people ask "why" questions, and the heuristics of attributional search. *Journal of Personality and Social Psychology*, **40**, 650–663.

Chapter 9

Multimethodologies— the Knowledge Perspective

DAVID J. SKYRME

INTRODUCTION

In my work as a manager and consultant, I have continually been struck by the gap between theory and practice in the areas of development and change, such as strategic planning, new product development, systems development and organisational change. I have also been keen to apply new methods and computer tools to help with these demanding processes. Generally, like many other managers, I have been disappointed more times than not.

Academics and consultants have offered various methodologies as ways of improving outcomes, whether in new systems, processes or products. Yet many of these methodologies have failed to gain widespread acceptance in organisations. Furthermore, those that have are often criticised for being too rigid and inflexible. The notion of adopting a multimethodology approach, even at the level of using selected parts of different methodologies in the same situation, appears to offer a means of adding choice and flexibility. But what will determine whether such an approach will be any more successful than those of single methodologies?

This chapter argues that if we are to be more successful in practice at applying methods and tools, of whatever type—hard or soft—then a new

Multimethodology: The Theory and Practice of Combining Management Science Methodologies.
Edited by John Mingers and Anthony Gill.
© 1997 John Wiley & Sons Ltd.

perspective is needed by both proponents and users. That perspective is understanding the role of information and knowledge.

I start by outlining some of the differences between methodologies in theory and methodologies in use. The nature of information and knowledge is then considered. This is related to the development and use of methodologies. This theme is then developed to indicate that by explicitly recognising and managing information and knowledge, the outcomes of a methodology can be improved. The role of information technology in capturing and diffusing information and knowledge is then explored. The chapter concludes with some suggestions on how multimethodologies should be packaged, and the requirements of a good information and knowledge management infrastructure to support their effective use. Throughout, I draw heavily on my practical experience and observation.

THE THEORY–REALITY GAP

My first exposure to such gaps was in the early 1980s when trying to apply the planning and decision-making methods described in virtually all corporate planning textbooks at the time. They described how managers were supposed to think and how product developers were supposed to plan new products. Although the methods described might have worked in some organisations, in the fast moving environment of the computer industry, the textbook approaches never seemed to work. It was some relief, therefore, when I first came across Isenberg's article "How manager's think" in 1984 (Isenberg, 1984). He described intuition, sensing context and other apparent non-rational behaviours. Similarly, the process of innovation that until the late 1980s had been described in mainstream literature as a neat linear process, is, as we know now, a much more iterative process, haphazard and with complex interactions and involvement of quite large networks (see, for example, Riemans (1992), and the UK Economic and Social Science Research Council (1995) which produced a series of leaflets describing such results in a way more easily accessible to the practising manager).

In the light of this knowledge, it should therefore not be surprising that methodologies, many of which were after all developed from a systematic and logical engineering perspective, would also fall foul of management reality. This was brought home to me time and time again in two research projects with which I was involved. The first, the hybrid manager (Skyrme, 1995), analysed the gap between the IS (information systems) function and the business. The logical rationality of information systems professionals created tension with the pragmatic instinctive behaviour of business managers. The former used structured methodologies like SSADM (Structured Systems Analysis and Design Methodology, originally developed by the UK government's Central Computer and Telecommunications Agency) in developing new systems, and often forced businesses to sign off on a requirements specification before programming would commence. Yet the business managers, whom these systems were supposed to serve, continually wanted to adapt their requirements to meet changing business imperatives. No wonder that today there is a significant interest in RAD (rapid application development) methods where IS specialist and user can sit together and mutually develop and explore IT solutions to business problems in an iterative manner.

The second project—SOFTCASE[1]—was an investigation into the use of systems development methods (such as SSADM) and how well they took account of organisational and human factors. Early on it was found that although junior analysts tended to "go by the book", experienced analysts were much more pragmatic. They tend to use the bits of the methodology as it suited them, "dipping and diving into the workbook, as appropriate".

Both of these examples illustrate how the real world does not seem to harmonise with the tidy logical world of methodologies. Real situations are "messy" and call for a variety of approaches that are very context dependent, and may change almost daily. That is what attracted me as a strategic planning manager to the "soft" methodologies and their accompanying tools, such as Checkland's Soft Systems Methodology (SSM) and Eden's cognitive mapping software COPE. In different situations they had the advantages of broadening the participant's range of discussion and thinking about the business situation. However, at least the way we used them, they still failed to sit each alongside the conventional management decision processes they supported. Although they generated useful "rich pictures", the information generated did not flow seamlessly between the different actors and the different stages of strategic decision making.

Another example of the clash of methodological nicety and real-world reality is the business research projects that I supervise. The simplistic textbook approach of problem/hypothesis formulation, data collection, analysis and report writing comes drastically unstuck, as many of my students know to their cost, when their organisation sponsor changes or their subject of analysis (the department or organisation) gets restructured or even closed during the course of a project!

From such experiences, I believe that to try and apply a single methodology, however appropriate it may seem to its proponents, does not reflect the richness, diversity and interdependence of most real-life situations. Therefore a multimethodology approach, which uses techniques from many other

---

[1] SOFTCASE, a project under the UK's Joint Framework programme, developed tools to address the human and organisational factors in the development of computer systems. Findings of the initial research on use of systems development methodologies were published as a report, see Maclaren et al (1991).

methodologies, would seem to have many attractions. The challenge then is twofold. First, how to "mix 'n match" the most appropriate parts of different methodologies and techniques. Second, how to do this with some degree of cohesiveness, when you are using a diversity of tools from different pedigrees and perspectives. My argument is that the unifying glue is information and knowledge.

THE INFORMATION AND KNOWLEDGE PERSPECTIVE

Encapsulated Knowledge

Anyone who uses a methodology is, in effect, using the results of the experience of others faced with similar situations. The developers of a methodology have captured some of this experience and have codified the "best practices" into a process framework. It typically distills this knowledge into a workbook with guidelines, process descriptions and checklists. What is written in the workbook is the basic, but only the basic, information needed to carry out the methodology.

However, as any newcomer to a methodology knows, this is only part of the knowledge needed to use it effectively. An experienced user will know how to apply it effectively. He or she will be sensitive to the working context, the personal biases of those providing information and the needs of the various stakeholders. Much of this extra knowledge will not be found in the documentation.

This difference between methods or procedures as written in manuals and what actually happens in practice is apparent in most organisations today. Other than in highly bureaucratic organisations, employees in most organisations are encouraged to do "what is right for the customer", within a general set of guidelines. Achieving successful results in most business activities depends more on the "tacit" knowledge (a concept first introduced by Michael Polyani (1966) to describe the idea that "we can know more than we tell") of the workers rather than the explicit knowledge that is codified in written documents or computer procedures. This facet of the workplace is one that is receiving considerable attention as organisations start to realise the pivotal role of knowledge in business. Nonaka and Takeuchi (1995) in their book *The Knowledge Creating Company* emphasise this distinction between "explicit" and "tacit" knowledge. They describe "explicit" knowledge as formal and systematic:

> Explicit knowledge can be expressed in words and numbers and can be easily communicated and shared in the form of hard data, scientific formulae, codified procedures or universal principles.

Such knowledge is seen as "only the tip of the iceberg". "Tacit" knowledge on the other hand is described as:

> something not easily visible and expressible. Tacit knowledge is highly personal and hard to formalise. Subjective insights, intuitions and hunches fall into this category of knowledge. It consists of schemata, mental models, beliefs, and perceptions so ingrained we take them for granted.

The transfer of tacit knowledge involves complex processes, including the conversion from tacit to explicit, and vice versa. Boiset (1995) has expanded on the notion of tacit–implicit by adding a dimension of diffusion. He thus maps knowledge into C–D space, with the two dimensions being degree of codification and diffusion. In practice, any widespread take up of new ideas, whether they be new products or process innovations, such as a methodology, will need to evolve through the phases of moving from uncodified to diffused (Figure 9.1).

This figure indicates that in the early days of development, there will be a divergent range of views and knowledge. Once knowledge starts being articulated, the codification process begins, such that a particular domain of knowledge becomes more consistently described.

Readers familiar with innovation and product development will recognise Figure 9.1 as an example of the generic "concept–prototype–product commercialisation" process. Many widely practised methodologies have followed such an evolution. This pattern is the result of "packaging" the knowledge of many specific experiences into a more generalised approach. Over time they tend to become very formalised and structured (e.g. SSADM).

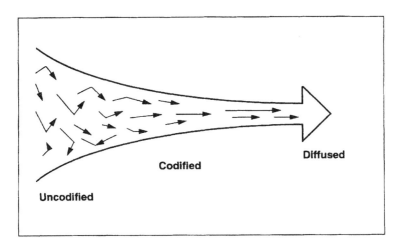

Figure 9.1 The evolution of knowledge

However, the mere act of codification often results in the loss of richness that went into the original design of a product or process (Figure 9.2). For example, ask a salesperson about particular detailed functions of a product and its applications, or why certain features are present. At best they might point to the detailed user manuals, but quite often you might need to talk to the design team directly. I recall one office software product in my time at Digital, where a significant amount of behavioural and observational research of office users had led to inclusion of certain design features, but whose awareness among the user and sales community was very low.

Consider also the utility of a product without access to its user manual or another experienced user. The depth of tacit knowledge, going far beyond the manual, is very apparent in industries like the oil industry. Companies fly their experts all over the world to carry out delicate service or repair work, even though the manuals are available on site. Who, with one of their oil wells on fire, would prefer local operatives to work from the on-site manuals, rather than flying in someone like Red Adair?

In a recent process example, the insurance company CIGNA were able to improve significantly their processes (and also their financial results) by a concerted effort to identify and capture more of the knowledge possessed by their best underwriters, but not previously encapsulated into day-to-day operational procedures.

Such examples of loss of knowledge through codification abound in business today. Further, difficulties are increasing due to the rate of change in the surrounding environment. Products have shorter life-cycles. Processes that seemed eminently sensible when designed only a short while ago do not

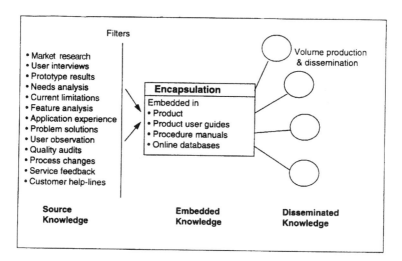

Figure 9.2 Loss of knowledge in products and processes

seem to gel with current market needs. So where does all this knowledge, not encapsulated into current products and processes, reside? It will be found in places such as minutes of development meetings, designer's working notes, but most likely in the minds of all those involved in the codification process. Therefore, unless the person using the product or process can tap into this wealth of contextual knowledge, their effectiveness is likely to be limited.

This, in my experience, accounts for much of the poor usage of methodologies. If there isn't a box in the method to describe this vital contextual knowledge, then it doesn't get recorded.

For methodologies to be widely used and effective, then both the explicitly written information plus a significant amount of tacit knowledge must be widely diffused.

This tacit knowledge may be acquired by users in various ways. Some is transferred to the novice through training, especially if the trainer is also an experienced user. In many crafts the apprenticeship model, where someone works under the tutelage of an experienced user, is common. When we look at which systems methodologies, such as SSADM and Yourdon, have been successful in the market place, most have achieved their position through concerted efforts on a number of fronts:

- User oriented documentation—quality workbooks, with plenty of emphasis on process—how to carry out a procedure, factors to consider.
- Guidance notes—the context in which certain procedures are valid, the settings needed, the skills needed by the practitioner.
- Extensive training—lengthy courses, with hands-on practice under the tutelage of an expert.
- On-hands assistance from experienced users (e.g. consultants).
- Effective marketing, that also includes exposure to practical applications.
- A supportive infrastructure—advice lines, good channels of communication back to developers and originators.

If getting a "hard" methodology accepted in the market place requires all this, achieving acceptance of "soft" methodologies is an even greater challenge. Much of the diffusion will require the passing of knowledge face to face, as takes place in many management change programmes. The fact that many of the "soft" methodologies such as ETHICS, SSM, etc. originated in academic environments adds further difficulty. Often the academic interest finishes after the first publications or pilot implementations. It is instructive to note the time and effort it has taken Colin Eden to get SODA (strategic options development and analysis) and its associated software package COPE (a conceptual mapping tool) to even the limited market position they enjoy today. He has achieved this through complementary efforts—trained facilitators, extensive publishing, wide exposure to non-academic audiences, and to a large measure the active participation of himself in person in promoting the methodology and acting as a facilitator. All are channels to take the tacit knowledge into the user community.

Knowledge in Use

Similar considerations of knowledge diffusion apply to methodologies in use. In all methodologies, information is acquired and knowledge is elicited from and shared by participants. These are processed in various ways to generate new knowledge that guides the users to an appropriate solution. The general pattern is that shown in Figure 9.1—from divergent thinking to convergent thinking. However, most methodologies are better suited to only one part of the spectrum. The "soft" methodologies and tools, such as conceptual modelling, come into their own in the process of exploring and articulating uncodified knowledge. On the other hand, a systems dynamics approach and simulation techniques are a better fit once codification has taken place. In practice, few methodologies provide a direct flow of information along the spectrum from one end to the other, or allow easy mixing of "hard" (structured) and "soft" (unstructured) information.

In an ideal world, information and knowledge will be neatly codified and flow seamlessly back and forth through the various stages and iterations. In the real world, information gets filtered out and lost, people change jobs and important tacit knowledge fails to get considered. In hard methodologies, if knowledge of importance to the user does not fit the method, the chances are it is overlooked or discarded.

For example, many of the problems with the development and implementation of computer systems have been attributed to the IT-business culture gap mentioned above. Many complaints about the IT systems resulting from the use of a methodology concern their "rigidity and inflexibility", or their inability to cope with the ever-increasing number of "exceptions". Many of the problems can be traced back to the processes of requirements analysis and "force-fitting" solutions into pigeonholes. As many customers know to their cost, most software houses and contractors of many types of project tend to make their profits not on the initial specification but on all the changes that take place during the course of the project.

The growing disillusionment with outsourcing is another example of how too much a focus on explicit (codified) knowledge can lead to ultimate dissatisfaction. Extensive effort is usually spent between the two parties—user and supplier—to define in precise detail what is to go into the contract. Later on, requirements change, the systems are not used as predicted and expensive renegotiations take place. Similarly, change of personnel can also have dramatic impacts. Kumar and Willcocks describe the experience of outsourcing development by Holiday Inns of America to a software house in India. All went well until key personnel on both sides changed. Then things started going very wrong. This was attributed first to the change in personnel, but also to the different approaches implicit in the way the two parties worked:

> While in the past Daniel [project manager] could rely on the Indian project manager's and team's intimate understanding of the project requirements, the new staff needed detailed specifications.
> The work style of Indian programmers and analysts was very different from that of their American counterparts. Compared to most US professionals who had acquired their expertise on the job, most of the Indian professionals had formal graduate level training in development methodologies. Thus, while the work style of the Americans relied upon informal learnt practices and improvisation, the Indian workstyle reflected a greater degree of methodology formalism. (Kumar and Willcocks, 1996)

This concern of organisations of retaining and tapping into tacit knowledge is one of the factors driving the growing interest in a more systematic approach to its identification and management. By capturing such tacit knowledge, companies hope to retain such knowledge in "organisational memory", so it can be reused and not lost. When properly practised some significant bottom line advantages have been achieved, such as:

- Avoiding expenditure on external research: "if we only knew what we know we could save a fortune".
- Sharing best practices for continual improvement, e.g. CIGNA's approach in claims processing has helped turn from loss to profit.
- Reducing time-to-market for new products—pharmaceutical companies in particular are taking a more systematic approach to knowledge management in clinical trials.
- Customer service—identifying known solutions to problems to make help desks more efficient.

In a similar way methodologies are likely to increase their bottom line contribution to the business if the knowledge used and generated during their use can be better managed for later reuse (such as in the roll out of the solution the methodology is creating). We must be wary of using methodologies in a way that generates isolated "islands of information".

INFORMATION AND KNOWLEDGE COMPONENTS

Let us now examine aspects of information and knowledge in a little more depth. This will give some indications of how it can be better managed.

Information–Knowledge Hierarchy

Several writers have described a hierarchy along the lines of data–information–knowledge–wisdom. In practice there is often much overlap of the terminology. Quite a few consider information as "explicit" knowledge. Thus, what some describe as a "knowledge map" would be described by others as an "information map". Whatever the precise definitions, somewhere along the data–wisdom spectrum is a significant discontinuity (Table 9.1).

Whereas information is tangible, easily codifiable and lends itself to computer representation and manipulation, knowledge is much more a cognitive entity, associated with the human mind and very context dependent. Within the domain of tacit knowledge, several distinct types have been described and defined. Savage (1990) describes the following categories:

- *Know-how*—skills, processes and techniques that get things done
- *Know-why*—understanding the wider context
- *Know-who*—who has expertise that can help
- *Know-what*—the ability to discern key factors and patterns
- *Know-where*—where things can and should happen
- *Know-when*—a sense of timing; the most appropriate time to intervene

Understanding all of these for each stage of use of a methodology is one key to increasing its effectiveness. Knowledge in each of these categories will need to be put into the language and terminology of the situation and its actors. For example, a business systems change may need to articulate them according to some of the following parameters:

- *Know-how*—how the company's key business processes work, how users implement systems and processes in practice (as opposed to how they are supposed to run them!)
- *Know-why*—understanding the rationale behind the intervention, which may well be a complex mix of the agenda of multiple stakeholders
- *Know-who*—who has worked successfully with these people before, whose judgement and opinions do they value and trust

Table 9.1 A comparison of information and knowledge

Information	Knowledge
Tangible—informs humans	Human process—thinking/awareness
Processing changes representation	Processing changes consciousness
Physical objects	Mental objects
Context independent	Context affects meaning
Entity	Awareness and intuition
Easily transferable	Transfer requires learning
Reproducible at low cost	Not identically reproducible

- *Know-what*—what aspects are important in a good hierarchy or ends–means chains, e.g. which customers, products, markets, competitors, technology trends
- *Know-where*—which situation might provide the best initial pilot or test, which would be necessary for widespread acceptance
- *Know-when*—the right time to carry out different steps in the process

In my experience, it is this last type of knowledge that represents some of the finest management judgement, since mistiming an intervention is often a primary cause of failure. In one case, development of a new skills database system took place at a time of organisational uncertainty and an impending round of redundancies and failed to gain acceptance. Yet an almost identical system succeeded at a different time and place in the same organisation. It is important that practitioners understand the needs of all their stakeholders—their priorities, "blockages", personal ambitions and other distractions on their time.

This deeper awareness and knowledge surrounding the use of a methodology is something that many consultants understand. They learn to "gain entry" and keep any intervention locked into "business imperatives". They keep close contact with key stakeholders, any of whom may, and often do, change during the course of an assignment. Where in a simulation or a viable systems model is such knowledge stored? Look at current methodologies and their tools and see how well they can capture such information. It is this rounded knowledge of the situation within which a methodology is used that its successful practitioners must develop and the methodology itself support.

Information and Knowledge Processes

Supporting every business and management process—and a methodology is such a process—are allied information and knowledge processes. Some methodologies, particularly those involved with systems development, place great store on recording information. They use devices such as data flow diagrams (DFDs), entity-relationship diagrams and so on. Again, my experience and the SOFTCASE research on using such methodologies suggests that they often miss important uncodifiable information, and go into far too much detail at the wrong time. They can actually widen, rather than close, communication gaps between developer (methodology user) and end user. For most methodologies, an important issue is to understand clearly how its underlying processes capture and deploy the information and knowledge relevant to the end-user. One way of investigating this aspect is to consider a generic information/knowledge value chain (Figure 9.3).

These processes are similar for information and knowledge, except that knowledge processes are much more human related and haphazard compared

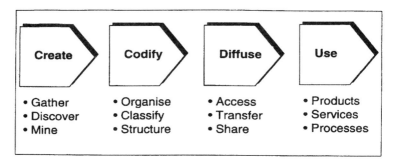

Figure 9.3 Outline of a generic information and knowledge value chain

to information processes. Thus storage in knowledge databases will often be "pointers to people" rather than the codification of knowledge *per se*.

For each part of the value chain there are a growing number of specific techniques and a growing role for computers. Among the techniques are information audits for identifying sources and use of information, developing thesauruses for classifying information and information mapping for identifying owners and accessibility of "information resource entities". In computing there are technologies such as data mining to discover patterns in large quantities of company information, or groupware such as Lotus Notes to aid sharing of information across departments.

It is our contention that many methodologies lack attention to these aspects, in their design and their deployment. How many of the individual methodologies mentioned throughout this book address the diffusion of the wealth of knowledge unearthed during its use? The main proposition of this chapter is that, if these information and knowledge processes were explicitly addressed at each stage of the methodology, then they would be more effective, both in terms of process and outcomes.

Evidence to support this proposition comes from parallels in general management. Various writers have highlighted the growing role of information and knowledge resources as an ingredient in organisational success. Drucker (1993) has highlighted the role of knowledge work, Hamel and Prahaled (1990) of "core competencies", Quinn (1992) of "enterprise intelligence" and the Hawley report (1995) the management of intangible assets such as information. Such concepts are being turned into practice through the emerging and potentially converging disciplines of information resources management (IRM) and knowledge management.

Information and Knowledge Management

IRM is an evolution of the movement to focus on information as a resource in its own right. Whereas many of the implementations of information systems in companies are based on the work of systems analysts and technology professionals, IRM has its roots in information science of the library science variety. Among its main exponents are Aslib, the UK-based society for information professionals, whose special interest group, the IRM Network, has been advocating the five pronged Willard (1993) model:

- *Identification*—What information is there? How is it identified and coded?
- *Ownership*—Who is responsible for different information entities and coordination?
- *Cost and Value*—The basis for making judgements on purchase and use.
- *Development*—Increasing its value or stimulating demand.
- *Exploitation*—Proactive maximisation of value for money.

These precepts can be applied at several levels in an organisation. At the strategic level, they can lead to company-wide programmes to identify and value key information used in the business. They can also result in the development of general information policies, and frameworks for information ownership and use in an organisation. At a more detailed level, in support of a specific business activity or process, they can be applied to the practicalities of identifying and collecting key information and keeping it updated and relevant. In turn, these lead to the development of systems, including computer-based systems, for storing and disseminating information.

A second emerging strand is that of knowledge management. From a phrase used by a few cognoscenti five years ago, it is rapidly entering the mainstream of consciousness of many managers. Tom Stewart (1991, 1994) has popularised the concept in various articles in *Fortune* and it hit the conference scene in a major way in 1995–96 with over 20 major conferences devoted to it in this period. Knowledge management is based on the recognition that value and competitive advantage come from a better understanding of intellectual capital, such as:

- structural knowledge—knowledge in organisational processes
- customer knowledge—customer relationship, assets such as patents
- human knowledge—competencies and specialist skills

Many companies are becoming knowledge intensive—pharmaceutical companies, software companies and management consultancies being obvious examples. Their balance sheets in conventional accounting show a book value (based on tangible assets) often at least 10 times less than their market capitalisation. Companies like Microsoft have higher market values than companies like General Motors.

Knowledge management practices are therefore based on the identification of these different knowledge assets (competencies, process knowledge, etc.)

and their better deployment and use. The kinds of practice increasingly being deployed include:

- Knowledge mapping—identifying the sources of critical knowledge
- Knowledge databases—storing information about sources of knowledge (especially pointers to people)
- Knowledge sharing—creating mechanisms to improve sharing, ranging from cross-functional teams to groupware solutions
- Knowledge development—better ways of creating new knowledge, innovating new products
- Knowledge exploitation and protection—encapsulating knowledge in a form that can generate additional revenue, such as in higher value "intelligent" products, customised services and technology licences

While few organisations are whole-heartedly embracing the full gamut of IRM and knowledge management techniques, there is growing evidence of significant adoption of specific techniques and supporting technologies. The growth of Lotus Notes and internal Internet networks (an Intranet) are prime examples. What has yet to happen is the systematic adoption of these disciplines into everyday activities. Moreover, their inclusion into the support of methodologies would seem a natural place to start.

A New Perspective on Methodologies

At a broad level a methodology is a collection of methods. Each method or technique encapsulates some basic process knowledge that is applied to a specific part of the problem in hand. Also surrounding the methodology, as we have already noted, is a significant amount of tacit knowledge, the experience of the user in applying this methodology in a variety of circumstances.

The advantage of a methodology, such as SSM, as opposed to a library of methods, is that the tools and techniques you need are put into a cohesive whole and offered to the user at an appropriate stage. In other words, the knowledge, or at least some of it, is conveniently packaged. A user trained in system dynamics, for example, is likely to have experience of a range of techniques to cover the problem in hand. On the other hand, a limitation of the single methodology approach is that the specific tools offered may not be the best in a given situation or even the best of its class. In my experience, breakthroughs in interventions have often come when an experienced facilitator facing a problem situation has broken away from a methodology and chosen a tool from elsewhere in their "kitbag of techniques". I particularly remember one such breakthrough in the design of an Internet web site, where the breakthrough was achieved by visiting an earlier stage in the method and using a novel adaptation of an existing matrix. How can this sort of knowledge, not conveniently packaged, be made available when and where it is needed?

Together with our user interviews in SOFTCASE, that suggested pragmatism and "dipping and diving" into the techniques as needed, an obvious conclusion is that rather than a methodology, many interventions will be the skilled linkage of a variety of tools and techniques. This is necessary to cope with situation variety and a dynamic that more rigid methodologies have difficulty coping with. However, we can draw, as done in Chapter 1 by Mingers, a generic model of a methodology, which has the following common phases:

- Exploration—exploring ideas, generating concepts
- Analysis—organising information, calculating
- Implementation—disseminating and communicating information

Supporting each of these are the generic information and knowledge processes described earlier, and for given situations context specific knowledge in the minds of the actors. Applying the information and knowledge perspective to the generic aspects of any methodology, one can conclude that what makes it work effectively is the carrying forward and sharing of information and knowledge gained at each stage.

Specific information may well be recorded in completed worksheets. But much knowledge is also held in the minds of participating developers and users. If a developer leaves a project, as we saw in the Holiday Inns example, it can have disastrous effects. Therefore the success of a multimethodology depends on having in place mechanisms to carry information and knowledge from one method to another in a systematic way. The quantity and diversity of knowledge processed in many situations takes this beyond individual human capabilities. Hence computers have an important role to play in the information and knowledge processes that support a multimethodology.

THE ROLE OF INFORMATION TECHNOLOGY

Virtually every business activity today makes extensive use of information technology in routine transactions and procedures. However, its take-up for less structured activities, such as knowledge work and management decision making, has been less forthcoming. There is, however, an unfolding trend in the focus of new developments of the applications of IT in business (Figure 9.4). IT's role evolved in the 1980s from one of computation to one of information handling and communication, for example through access to databases and the use of electronic mail. Our terminology has also changed in step. Where once we talked of "data processing" we now talk of "information systems".

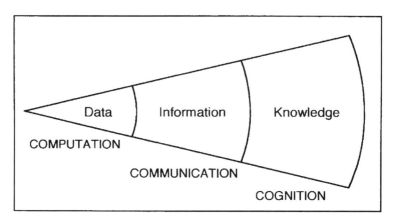

Figure 9.4 Evolutionary phases of information technology use

Compared to just a decade ago, computers today are

- more pervasive (the majority of people in organisations have access, typically through personal computers)
- more functional (today's personal computers have more capabilities and features than yesterday's expensive mainframes)
- more connected (many are part of the networks, either local area networks—LANs—or increasingly networks, like the Internet, that provide global connectivity)
- multimedia (colour graphics, sound and video are becoming the norm, rather than an add-on option)

Many criticisms of computer systems of the earlier type (of which many are still being developed) were that they were too inflexible and rigid. This is because they are pre-programmed to handle specific occurrences. In a more dynamic world, systems must be more adaptable to changes in the environment in which they work. There is a parallel here in methodologies!

Even as the second phase of IT evolution, widespread communications and information, gains maturity, a new focus is already apparent. Many of the emerging competitive applications are to do with supporting knowledge work and the processes of human cognition. Knowledge work is much more human related and unstructured compared to information processing. Supporting knowledge activities processes with IT therefore needs an approach based not on making "thinking machines" (the artificial intelligence paradigm that failed to fulfil its promise of the early 1980s) but on using machines to help "thinking humans". In this role computers augment human knowledge processes—the creation, exchange and application of new knowledge in products, services and processes.

One of the ways that computers help human knowledge processes is through a growing class of knowledge support software tools. These may be tools that support specific activities in the knowledge value chain. Examples include data mining (extracting knowledge from data warehouses), decision support (prioritising options) and conceptual mapping (tools, such as COPE or IDONS).

There is also a separate class of knowledge support software, that which is more infrastructure related. It provides the mechanisms for collaborating in knowledge development and sharing over electronic networks. Perhaps the best example of such software is the so-called "groupware" product Lotus Notes, which provides shared databases of electronic communications, public information and workflow.

The challenge is to use such tools and infrastructure to better manage the flow of knowledge during the application of a methodology.

Software Tools for Methodologies

A growing number of methods have computer software built in, or as an integral part of the method. Examples include STRATPLAN, a system for strategic planning, and CASE tools for software development. Such software supports their methodology in two main ways, content and process:

- They store results and basic information; thus information is carried from one stage to the next; solutions to new situations or problems can be based on similar existing solutions.
- They guide the user through process: they have defined steps; they quite often place prerequisites or restrictions on what data are allowed to be entered, and when they can be entered, and by whom.

Other features commonly found include:

- Hierarchies—providing different levels of granularity, for example grouping comparable products into a generic product type.
- Multiple views of same information—allowing, for example, a group of managers to view information in the way of most interest to them, e.g. customers, products, markets, actors (who has what responsibilities).
- Help files—providing methodological or contextual help—thus Product Planning Adviser can give textbook theory and examples of product utility functions and what pricing options to use.
- Level of use—providing different options and levels of functionality for novices, intermediate and advanced users.
- What-if analyses—allow users to explore different options without violating the integrity of the current process data.

In my analysis of tools that support knowledge activities I have noticed some recurring characteristics:

- Many are good at one facet of knowledge activity, but are rarely best in class for all aspects.
- Most are developed by small specialist suppliers, often from an academic background, and have little marketing effort; most have worldwide sales in their hundreds, rather than thousands.
- Many are closely bounded—thus they are not amenable to modification or cannot access common facilities such as Window print drivers (which causes difficulties when a new printer is installed).

Many of the criticisms of applicability levelled at single methodologies also apply to such software. Too many packages are rigid, inflexible, and not easily adaptable. Thus when considering how we can use the obvious potential of IT to support a multimethodology, we must take account of shortcomings, seen in many of these computer packages:

- They are not integrated (no easy way of taking the output from one tool to the input of another).
- They lack more general import/export facilities, e.g. from databases, spreadsheets, word processing documents.
- There is no common accepted terminology and information structuring (schema, thesaurus).

The explosive growth of Intranets in companies gives us food for thought. Why have they succeeded in gaining rapid widespread acceptance when many individual computer applications have not? Part of the answer is that it is an infrastructure solution. But it is also because Intranets overcome many of the limitations just mentioned. They use open standards, they are based on a client-server approach, with a low cost client, and the client software (the browser) is intuitive and easy to use.

From these observations, and drawing on data from usability studies and other research, we can state some essential requirements for effective knowledge tools to support a methodology:

- Systems must allow information sharing while maintaining a degree of integrity and activity history.
- Thus they are most likely to be client-server systems that run over a network—in other words, they must fit seamlessly into an existing infrastructure.
- Users must be able to enter and start at (almost) any point.

- Users must be able to move to subsequent stages without completing all the information entry for the current stage.
- There must be good cues, so that the user can easily identify where they are in the overall context of the methods.
- There must be good export/import facilities, so information can flow relatively seamlessly from one tool to another without rekeying (while researching this chapter I discovered at least one Windows package that did not even allow a simple cut and paste!).
- To print what is on the screen (in another case, one package has very good schematics that cannot be printed).
- Good error recovery—a single mistyping is not disastrous (in my experience too many still commonly crash Windows systems and do not have autosave facilities).

These truisms are well known by professional software developers, but unfortunately too much of the software for methodologies often seems to be at the amateurish or experimental phases. The wider issues, though, are the overall information and knowledge management functions that should be carried out alongside any individual tool.

Methodology Knowledge Infrastructure

A methodology knowledge infrastructure is needed at two levels—one for the use of the methodology and one for each project using the methodology. For each, an approach based on the knowledge value chain offers a good starting point. Here are some examples of the knowledge management activities that are required:

- Information mapping—identification of sources of information and knowledge; for example, a database of methodologies used within the organisation and who has experience of using them in different situations.
- Reference aids—catalogues of information types, the classification scheme, a directory of expertise and skills, contact details of external methodology experts.
- An information or knowledge store—repositories for one or more projects; examples of "best practice" in using various tools and techniques, in-depth case studies and other aspects of organisational memory (case lists with conditions and outcomes).
- Dissemination and use—provision of appropriate mechanisms for communications and coordination; electronic mail, groupware (computer conferencing) for debating issues, desired new features, problems solving, etc., and especially the use of a company-wide facility such as Lotus Notes or an

Intranet, which allows knowledge sharing across functional (and geographic) boundaries.

• Expert networks—development of the above into mechanisms for dialoguing with external experts, and other organisations using similar methods and doing similar work, e.g. closed Internet groups.

Other elements of a knowledge infrastructure include the prerequisite computer and communications hardware and services (the hard infrastructure) as well as information and organisation policies, including reward systems that support knowledge sharing (the soft infrastructure).

These aspects illustrate that computers, or rather information and knowledge networks, can act as process aids and information stores that can enhance methodology processes of all types in a general intervention. In effect, they allow users to break free from the constraints of most methodologies by developing an information and knowledge base that grows in value each time a methodology is used. They enable knowledge sharing and exchange within a human network.

Issues and Challenges

Developing such an infrastructure is not without difficulties. Thus many users of electronic mail and conference systems complain of information overload, since the information in these files seems to grow haphazardly with every person's input. Also, too frequently the "politics" of information—who hoards it and who uses it as a vehicle of power—cannot be ignored.

Several things are needed to address these challenges. One is the need to systematically identify, codify and store information about knowledge. This is a carefully balanced management tightrope. On the one hand, as indicated above, knowledge managers must overcome the free-for-all where knowledge simply accumulates. On the other, they must avoid the pitfalls of a centrally managed and highly structured enterprise-wise database, which is likely to prove inflexible and need significant maintenance. An ideal intermediate situation is one where information is "refined" and a network of users assumes responsibility for orderly management of some domain of knowledge. That is, subject matter experts synthesise the relevant knowledge that flows in the networks and into conference files, and add some structure and qualifiers. These qualifiers could include quality measures such as likely accuracy, reputation of source, date of last update, as well as details of originator and pointers to further expertise. In other words, they have turned unrefined databases into "knowledge bases". The "knowledge bases" of the major consultancies, such as Price Waterhouse's KnowledgeView®, are starting to demonstrate this midway course between highly formal and structured and totally informal and unstructured.

Perhaps the greatest need, though, is recognition at the highest levels within an organisation of the value of knowledge as an adjunct to development and transformation processes including the use of methodologies. An indication of this recognition is that some organisations are creating a post of Chief Knowledge Officer, whose role is to promulgate good knowledge management practice, to develop a knowledge infrastructure and to create a culture of widespread knowledge sharing.

Implications

This chapter has stressed the importance of managing the information and knowledge associated with methodologies. The ease with which they can be accessed and processed at different stages of a methodology is a fundamental factor in achieving a successful outcome. Perhaps the key point to make is that the knowledge is context dependent. Much of it exists and has legitimacy outside of a given methodology. A methodology gives it some structure to hang on. But what if we completely reverse our perspective and say that the information and knowledge should be the focal point for management, and that the individual components of a methodology are merely convenient processing algorithms?

This perspective has the merit that it focuses on knowledge *objects* (e.g. knowledge of markets, competitors, processes), something that most managers are more attuned to than long-winded procedures. These objects then need to have relevant parts of methodologies they can call on for processing.

Adopting the knowledge perspective advocated here has several important implications for developers, researchers and users of multimethodologies.

1. Methodologies need to be decomposed into their basic units. Thus each methodology would be a seamless toolkit that allows "dipping and diving" into appropriate techniques to support a multimethodology. In fact, one can foresee that in the future, methodologies as such might not exist. There may be in place method components or "technique objects", that will be tradable commodities in their own right.
2. Each unit should have an associated information and knowledge dimension. The individual tools and methods within a methodology need facilities to record information and knowledge in ways meaningful to the user. These may be relatively unstructured and be in the form of working notes, or pointers to documents, databases, people, etc. Examples may include contact details for experts in each aspect of the methodology, results of its use, etc. Information must also be easily transferable to other units in other methodologies, hence the need for some common standards.
3. These information and knowledge aspects should in turn be part of a wider coherent information and knowledge infrastructure, and not specific to the given methodology or tool. This infrastructure should cover strong "hard"

(computer and communications support) and "soft" (information and organisational) aspects.

4. A multimethodology is likely to have some "road maps", "preferred routes" or "suggested paths". These may be linked into context specific integrated high level processes, such that they can be used in the familiar monomethodology way in those cases where it might still be appropriate.

5. Recording information about process and outcomes is as important as recording information relevant to the task in hand.

6. Most methodology interventions should be conducted by multidisciplinary teams rather than experts in the detail of the methodology. Such teams should include experienced facilitators, who manage the process, and information/knowledge managers who structure and manage the richness of knowledge generated by the process.

7. Senior management needs to participate in the methodology. Poor acceptance of many of the outcomes—the systems and interventions—can often be traced to lack of ownership of the solution.

In effect, I am implying that methodologies will follow the path of current philosophy in computer applications development. Rather than being self-contained processes, methodologies will be decomposed into knowledge and information objects, that users string together in a dynamic way according to their immediate needs.

These high level implications have important repercussions. Methodology developers must significantly rethink the way that they package methods, how they develop the basic method objects and how they transfer the associated "tacit" knowledge. Users must start thinking of the underlying tools and techniques and of managing the flow of information and knowledge. Managers, who may have taken a hands-off stance with methodologies, must relish the challenge of dipping and diving into methods, just as they do with "the numbers" today. Further, knowledge management is an important new agenda item for them. Finally, researchers should focus more on methods in use, rather than on new methodology development. Developing a better understanding of the knowledge and behavioural dimensions is also important.

SUMMARY AND CONCLUSIONS

This book has two main themes—choice and adaptability. Choice is about mixing and matching. Adaptability is about coping with the dynamics of the environment, even during the course of a project. How does the knowledge perspective help?

There are many parallels with large-scale systems development and their frequent failure. Wholesale top-down solutions are fraught with difficulties.

Rigid inflexible systems cannot cope with the changing dynamics of the business environment. Solutions are to be found in defining some basic standards, especially for information exchange, providing basic building blocks and supporting end-users in developing their own solutions. Just as closed proprietary systems are giving way to open client-server systems, so methodologies must abandon their closed boundaries and be open to more flexible arrangements of their basic components. Just as computer systems are moving from a process perspective towards an object oriented one, so must methodologies. These new architectures provide the building blocks and the connections that give choice and adaptability.

Adding the perspective of information and knowledge is a powerful way of understanding how to improve development and use of methodologies. Today's methodologies represent codified knowledge, used in a specific kind of situation, and frozen in time. The knowledge perspective shows the importance of connecting users to tacit knowledge—knowledge in the heads of other users and developers. The use of a knowledge infrastructure shows how computer technology, such as knowledge bases and groupware, can aid knowledge flows from developer to user, between users and allows sharing of ideas, case histories and best practice.

However, it is fair to conclude, from my own observations and experience, that general management appreciation of the nuances of methodologies in organisation strategy and decision making is relatively low. Similarly, the use of computer supported methods for management processes (change interventions) is also in a very embryonic state. We may thus conclude that however compelling a case this book makes for a multimethodology approach it may take 10 years or more before widespread application in business. However, with knowledge management clearly on today's management agenda, adding the knowledge perspective to a multimethodology may provide a quicker route to wider acceptance than would otherwise be achieved.

REFERENCES

Boiset, M.H. (1995). *Information Space: A Framework for Learning in Organisations, Institutions and Culture*. Routledge, London.

Drucker, P. (1993). *The Post Capitalist Society*. Harper Business, NY.

Economic and Social Science Research Council (1995). *Research in Innovation*.

Hamel, G and Prahaled, C.K. (1990). The Core Competence of the Corporation. *Harvard Business Review*, May–June, pp. 79–91.

Hawley (1995). *Information as an Asset: The Board Agenda*. The Hawley Committee, KPMG IMPACT, London.

Isenberg, D. (1984). How managers think. *Harvard Business Review*, **62**(2), 81–90.

Kumar, K. and Willcocks, L. (1996). Offshore outsourcing: a country too far? RDP96/1, Templeton College, Oxford.

Maclaren, R. et al (1991). *Systems Design Methods—The Human Dimension*. Digital/NCC.

Nonaka, I. and Takeuchi, H. (1995). *The Knowledge Creating Company.* Oxford University Press, New York.

Polyani, M. (1996). *The Tacit Dimension.* Routledge & Kegan Paul, London.

Quinn, J. (1992). *The Intelligent Enterprise: A Knowledge and Service Based Paradigm for Industry.* Free Press, NY.

Riemans, W.G. (1992). *Managing Innovation within Networks.* Routledge, London.

Savage, C. (1990). *Fifth Generation Management.* Digital Press, pp. 203–204.

Skyrme, D.J. (1995). The hybrid manager. In Michael J. Earl (ed.) *Information Management: The Organizational Dimension.* Oxford University Press, Oxford.

Stewart, T. (1991). Brainpower. *Fortune,* 3 June.

Stewart, T. (1994). Your company's most valuable asset: intellectual capital. *Fortune,* 3 October.

Willard, N. (1993). Information resources management. *ASLIB Information,* May, pp. 201–205.

Part 3
Theory of Multimethodology

Commentary

In the first part of this book several practitioners illustrated their use of multimethodology in practical situations. Driven by the demands of a particular engagement, different methodologies or techniques were combined together in some way to improve the effectiveness of the intervention.

The only people who have made a serious attempt to develop a philosophical and theoretical approach to the problem of using different methodologies from disparate paradigms are Bob Flood and Mike Jackson, and their colleagues, at Hull and Lincoln. This work has generally been termed critical systems thinking (CST) and includes the meta-methodology total systems intervention (TSI). It is not surprising, therefore, that almost all the theoretical contributions orientate themselves in some way towards this work, whether by developing it further in the light of debate and comment, or by proposing alternative directions. Although these chapters present a plurality of visions, one can clearly identify a set of common issues that surround the idea of multi-paradigm pluralism that the authors generally feel the need to address.

The first issue is that of paradigm incommensurability. As discussed in Chapter 1, most social science disciplines developed into a set of apparently mutually incompatible paradigms. Proponents of this thesis argue that a paradigm is, in itself, reality-constituting. That is, it shapes the way we may experience and deal with reality. It specifies what types of entities exist, what form of access we have to them, how we should generate knowledge, and how we might thereby act. As the paradigms differ fundamentally on these issues, it is not possible to consistently accept more than one paradigm. Within CST/TSI, the stance taken was that each paradigm should be respected in its own right; that the assumptions that each made were more or less appropriate to particular contexts; and that therefore it was a matter of choosing the most appropriate paradigm. With this logic, it could be argued that there was never really a need to contrast or play off one against another. However, with multimethodology this is not the case, for we must explicitly bring methodologies

Multimethodology: The Theory and Practice of Combining Management Science Methodologies.
Edited by John Mingers and Anthony Gill.
© 1997 John Wiley & Sons Ltd.

from different paradigms into play within the same intervention or piece of research. How is it then possible to reconcile the inevitable contradictions between them? Is one paradigm taken as dominant and the others subservient? Do we try to be meta-paradigmatic and stand outside all of them; or must we generate a new paradigm that in some way subsumes all the others?

The second issue is the nature of critique. Although a *critical* perspective is not identical to a *multimethodological* perspective, because of its history of development multimethodology does stem from critical systems thinking. However, this too raises many questions. To what extent is CST a satisfactory practical interpretation of Habermasian critical theory? To what extent can or should multimethodology rely on Habermas's theory of knowledge-constitutive interests given that this has been largely abandoned by Habermas himself? What of the serious questions for any form of rational critique posed by postmodernist thinkers such as Foucault and Lyotard? Are not all forms of rationality and knowledge fatally compromised by their intimate connection with power? Can there be any grand theory of the social world to provide a critical framework or are they all merely stories told from particular perspectives? Can there be any external point from which we can maintain a critique or are we inevitably constituted through the prevailing discourses of power?

The third and related issue is that of theory versus pragmatism. Given that multimethodology embraces a plurality of paradigms and methodologies the question obviously arises as to how to choose between them in particular situations. Postmodernists such as Taket and White, and many of the practitioners in Part 1, tend to be very pragmatic on this issue – if it seems to work, or it feels right, that's fine, let's not worry about the theory. On the other hand, theorists argue that such an approach is likely to be ineffective. *Ad hoc* combinations of methodologies may work poorly or not at all. When they do seem to work one does not know *why* they worked, or the circumstances in which they will work again, or whether some other combination might have done better. So, is it possible to have a pluralistic approach that does not relapse into unthinking pragmatism?

The notion of *pluralism* is itself a feature of these chapters. Within CST/TSI the main term used was *complementarism*, emphasising the way in which the different methodologies were seen as complementary to each other. But now Midgley, Jackson, Taket and White, and Mingers all consciously use *pluralism* to emphasise the use of a plurality of perspectives and methodologies. They do, however, differ in their approach to pluralism. Midgley concentrates on methodological pluralism and the *design* of mixed methods; Jackson argues for pluralism as a meta-methodology – an extension to TSI; Taket and White, from a postmodern position, argue for pragmatic pluralism at many levels and not based on an underlying theory; while Mingers suggests a critical pluralism that tries to fuse some of the insights of both Habermas and Foucault.

Finally, an issue that arises particularly in the context of multimethodology is that of the real user of methodologies—the agent in a particular intervention. This is for two reasons. First, as shown in Part 2, multimethodology requires users to be skilled in several methodologies and to be able to work in a variety of paradigms. Clearly, this may pose feasibility problems for potential users and, at the least, a particular user's skills, knowledge, values, and experiences will be important factors in methodology choice. Second, it is increasingly difficult to maintain that a particular theory or framework can *impose* its commitments on its users, or that it should assume some ahistorical, abstract subject rather than a particular, culturally situated and gendered person. Rather, it will be a particular person, with their own commitments, values, desires, and concerns, who will drive the intervention and methodological usage.

All of these questions are considered in the following chapters.

Gerald Midgley begins this part with an interesting and comprehensive review of the Hull critical systems tradition from the specific viewpoint of its approach to mixing methodologies. He discerns five substantively different strands within the work associated with Hull and Humberside. For each one, Midgley outlines the position and then considers the key problems associated with methodological pluralism—the philosophical underpinnings and the view on paradigm incommensurability. The five different strands are: Jackson and Key's system of systems methodologies; Flood and Jackson's first version of TSI; Midgley's own creative design of methods; Gregory's notion of critical appreciation; and Flood's second version of TSI, further developed with Romm. In each case Midgley highlights (and in some cases has to, himself, construct) what the approach assumes at a philosophical level, particularly concerning incommensurability, and the debate between Habermas and Foucault concerning the possibility and nature of *critique*.

None of the approaches is seen to be wholly successful and in the final part of the chapter Midgley outlines his own developing approach to systemic intervention. This takes the view that *critical* intervention *is* possible and should be seen as taking place within a dynamic interaction between the *subject* (not necessarily an individual but any group to which an identity can be ascribed) and the *power–knowledge formations* that frame the identity of the subject. The approach is operationalised in the form of a three-stage methodology involving *critique*, *judgement*, and *action*.

Bob Flood and Norma Romm continue the theme of the development of critical systems thinking by considering how a variant of CST (that offers what might be considered a deeper intended meaning for TSI users)—what they call "triple loop learning"—relates to multimethodology. In fact, they are not entirely comfortable with the term "multimethodology", preferring to stay with the earlier concept of complementarism. The chapter begins with a philosophical review of the notion of *meta*-theory and its relation to complementarism dealing thoroughly with the question of incommensurability. This begins with a historical survey covering the Enlightenment, Kuhn and Habermas, through to the postmodernism of Foucault and Lyotard. The idea of complementarism is then explored in theoretical and methodological terms in both natural and social science.

After this review, Flood and Romm develop their own position that they call "diversity management". This attempts to navigate the waters between realism and constructivism by developing "castles made of sand that slip into the sea"— coherent theoretical constructs that may be helpful as guides for action, but that do not claim correspondence to some external reality. This theoretical position is embodied in the methodological idea of triple-loop learning. Single-loop learning addresses only a single general issue. This issue could be about design—*how* should our organisation work? Or it could be about debate—*what* should we be doing? Or it could be a concern with power and legitimacy—*why* are we doing this? Double-loop learning recognises that these three questions may conflict and tries to reconcile, particularly, the tasks of design and debate. Triple-loop learning is concerned with managing all three issues together, in a way that leads to responsible and reflective intervention.

Martin Spaul provides a counterpoint to many of the theoretical contributions by challenging the way in which critical systems thinking has drawn, rather unthinkingly, upon the critical theory of Jürgen Habermas as an underpinning. In an erudite contribution Spaul first argues that CST has adopted Habermas's work, in particular his theory of knowledge constitutive interests, for largely epistemological purposes in order to support the idea of methodological complementarism. For this to succeed, the underlying theory must be sustainable, and the particular interpretation or application must work. However, it is not clear that either of these conditions has been met. Habermas's theory has been strongly criticised, and it is debatable as to the extent to which its very abstract tone can be effectively translated into particular historical and social contexts.

Spaul goes on to consider how Habermas's later work—the theory of communicative action and the system/lifeworld model—might inform a critical management science. Such an approach would have to move away from a primary concern with particular interventions in specific situations, towards the formation of a broad "alternative social movement" (like, for example, environmentalism) that would provoke debate and questioning about management and working practices from a lifeworld perspective.

Leroy White and Ann Taket also provide an alternative vision to that of the traditional Habermasian version of critical systems thinking. Their approach is informed by the concerns of postmodernism, and particularly by Nietzsche. In their chapter they provide both theory and several examples from their own practice. In the first section they portray both traditional OR and critical systems as having a "will to methodology", that is, an approach that aims to control and tame the diversity and plurality of the world through scientific conceptions of truth and rationality. Even multimethodology, which is clearly pluralist in its support for mixing together different methodologies, aims for a formalistic and rationalistic basis for dealing with diversity.

In the second section White and Taket outline their position of "pragmatic pluralism". While this approach embraces multimethodology, i.e. mixing and matching, it does so in a postmodern rather than rationalistic spirit. They argue for a pluralism at many levels—in the choice of methodologies, the roles of the interventionists, the modes of representation, and the nature of the client. Choices about these matters should be made in terms of how they *feel*, and the extent to which they encourage diversity, freedom, and empowerment, rather than their supposed efficacy or truth. This approach is illustrated in two case studies of the authors' work in community OR.

Michael Jackson concentrates specifically on the nature of *pluralism* in systems thinking. This amounts to a rethinking of the development of critical systems thinking to bring out its pluralist nature and to consider future developments from this perspective. In the first section Jackson re-views the history of CST, from the system of systems methodologies through to TSI, recognising that, although there were many strengths, it fell short of fully embracing pluralism in the sense of mixing parts of methodologies within the same intervention, and did not fully resolve the question of its status as a meta-methodology. The next section reconsiders the five commitments of CST in the light of recent developments, especially postmodernism, and is followed by a discussion of pluralism in other disciplines such as organisation theory, information systems, and evaluation research.

In the final section, Jackson puts forward his own preferred version of pluralist systems thinking. This revolves around four assumptions: that pluralism must allow a mixing of different methodologies and techniques within an intervention, and allow the situation to be seen from different perspectives; that it must accept and manage a degree of paradigm incommensurability rather than assume it away; that it should encourage the use of methodologies from a diversity of paradigms; and that it must encourage the use of the widest possible range of methodologies without lapsing into pure pragmatism.

John Mingers also aims to reformulate the notion of critical systems thinking in a pluralist manner while retaining its critical edge—thus "critical pluralism". His argument is that CST as so far developed, culminating in TSI, does not really address the question of mixing parts of methodologies from different paradigms. Furthermore, there are a variety of issues and debates internal to the CST paradigm. Of even greater significance are the issues raised, particularly by postmodernists, that call into question any form of rationally based critique. The first section of the chapter highlights the issues internal to CST, while the second section points out the external criticisms, each of which is answered briefly.

The main section then develops, in outline, a version of critical pluralism that addresses the issues identified earlier. Drawing both from recent work by Habermas concerning discourse ethics, and from Foucault's view of the nature of critique and the technologies of self, Mingers identifies the role of the agent or user of methodologies as being central for critical pluralism. Usually downplayed in favour of abstract theoretical or methodological considerations, it is the agent(s), embodied and embedded in a particular social context, whose desires, values, commitments, skills and experience, and limitations and weaknesses drive critical interventions.

Chapter 10

Mixing Methods: Developing Systemic Intervention

GERALD MIDGLEY[1]

INTRODUCTION

Recently, there has been a growing interest in mixing methods to maximise flexibility and responsiveness during interventions. This is a practice that has been explored extensively over a thirteen-year period by a number of authors working in the area of critical systems thinking. The purpose of this chapter is to review some of the contributions made by critical systems thinkers over this time, and then to further develop our understanding of systemic intervention. We will find that this developed understanding of systemic intervention embraces aspects of all the previous models of good practice in critical systems thinking, but goes beyond them in several key respects.

Now, critical systems thinking is an approach to systems practice that was first developed in the early 1980s, and has since been debated widely in the literature. Recently, several authors have reflected on significant contributions to this debate, and have suggested that it can be described as an evolving discourse around three themes: *improvement*, *critical awareness*, and *methodological pluralism* (Midgley (1995), developing the work of Schecter (1991)

[1] This chapter was written on a research visit to the Departamento de Inginería Industrial, Universidad de Los Andes, Bogotá, Colombia. I am grateful for the support of the staff of that department, and for the funding provided for my visit by Colciencias.

Multimethodology: The Theory and Practice of Combining Management Science Methodologies.
Edited by John Mingers and Anthony Gill.

and Flood and Jackson (1991a)).[2] It is the third of these themes, methodological pluralism, that we will be concerned with here. However, rather than dealing with the totality of the critical systems literature on methodological pluralism (which is vast), I will focus attention on the practice of mixing methods. For this reason, I will omit discussion of pluralist ideas that focus solely on the categorisation of methodologies and their underlying rationalities without discussing how methods might be interrelated (e.g. Ulrich, 1988). I will also leave out work which focuses on the theory and practice of mixing methods, but does not yet offer adequate philosophical underpinnings (e.g. Midgley, 1992a).

Unsurprisingly, a number of different ideas have evolved over the twelve years. In all, I have identified five discrete approaches. Over the coming pages, I intend to review each of these in turn before moving on to suggest further developments. While the review process will inevitably highlight differences between the approaches, I believe it is also important to consider what they have in common. I will therefore say a little about the agenda that is shared by critical systems thinkers before discussing the five approaches themselves.

COMMON CONCERNS

Critical systems thinkers are concerned to develop methodological pluralism in a theoretically informed manner. Several papers have been written contrasting methodological pluralism with atheoretical pragmatism (Jackson, 1987a; Flood, 1989a, b, 1990; Midgley, 1989a).[3] This is defined by Jackson (1987a), building upon previous work by Reed (1985), as follows:

> The pragmatist strategy is to develop management science by bringing together the best elements of what may appear to be opposing strands [of management and systems thought] on the criterion of what "works" in practice. Pragmatists are distrustful of theory, believing that the wranglings to which it gives rise distract attention away from management science practice . . .. Pragmatists, therefore, do not worry about "artificial" theoretical distinctions. They concentrate on building up a "tool kit" . . .. Proven techniques from different strands of management science are employed together in the course of problem-solving

---

[2] In the literature, improvement is sometimes described as "emancipation" (e.g. by Flood and Jackson, 1991a), but I have specific reasons for not using the term (see Midgley, 1995). Also, an alternative name for methodological pluralism sometimes found in the literature is "complementarism" (e.g. Flood and Jackson, 1991b).

[3] "Atheoretical pragmatism", as these authors have defined it, should not be confused with American pragmatism, which is actually one of the philosophical traditions that has informed the development of critical systems thinking (and from which, as Brauer (1995) notes, we still have much to learn).

if the situation warrants it. The choice of techniques and the whole procedure is justified to the extent that it brings results in practice. (Jackson, 1987a: 462)

Flood (1989a) adds the following:

> The pragmatist may be seen as someone who has a systems tool bag . . . which . . . is used in an analogous way to cathedral building of old. The craftsmen were able to build complex structures using their own tool kit but had no idea why the thing stood up, why a beam fixed one way cracked but fixed another way did not. They only knew how to do it from the practice of trial and error . . . .. (Flood, 1989a: 78–79)

Critical systems thinkers have criticised atheoretical pragmatists on a number of grounds. The following points have been distilled from the works of Jackson (1987a) and Flood (1989a). First, the trial and error approach means extensive and costly experimentation in the social domain. Theory is needed to develop understandings of *why* methods sometimes work and sometimes do not, so that people can learn more effectively from their mistakes. Second, pragmatists without a common theoretical language find it difficult to pass their knowledge on to others—theory enables communication between practitioners and even across disciplines. Third, what may appear to "work" in the short term might have disastrous consequences in the longer term; theory is needed to expand our understandings of what it means for a method to "work". Finally, because pragmatists are not concerned with the *terms* in which methods "work", their activities may unwittingly lend support to authoritarian practices—after all, methods often work "not because they are the most suitable for the situation in which they are employed, but because they reinforce the position of the powerful, and implementation is therefore enforced" (Jackson, 1987a: 464).

The kind of methodological pluralism pursued by critical systems thinkers is *superficially* similar to pragmatism in the sense that both pragmatists and pluralists are concerned with developing a flexible and responsive practice of intervention. However, the two approaches part company when it comes to theory. As we shall see over the coming pages, all the authors who have explored the practice of mixing methods have striven to demonstrate philosophical and theoretical coherence. Some have had criticisms levelled at them, but their success in achieving coherence is for you to judge. Because, in some cases, the literature discussing the pros and cons of the perspectives is extensive, it will not be comprehensively reviewed: only those criticisms made by authors advancing an alternative pluralist perspective will be detailed, so the reader can see some of the thought processes lying behind the emergence of new approaches. However, references to other criticisms will be provided so that people wanting detailed critiques can find them. Let us begin, then, by reviewing the first of the five perspectives.

THE SYSTEM OF SYSTEMS METHODOLOGIES

The first critical systems thinkers to consider the issue of methodological pluralism were Jackson and Keys (1984). They were concerned to show that different systems methodologies have different strengths and weaknesses, making them suitable for application in different circumstances. Their approach was quite straightforward: they simply developed a grid with four boxes, representing four different types of perceived problem context, and then aligned different systems methodologies with each of them. These four boxes were later expanded to six by Jackson (1987b), and the authors called the resulting grid of contexts a "system of systems methodologies". This has been described in the literature using a number of different terminologies. In producing my own description over the coming pages I have chosen to adopt the terminology of Flood and Jackson (1991b), which is now the most widely used.

The grid defining the six contexts of application in the system of systems methodologies has two axes, and is presented here in Figure 10.1. One axis is labelled *Participants* (referring to perceptions of the relationships between participants in the problem situation) and the other is labelled *System* (referring to perceptions of complexity).

Let us look at each axis in turn, starting with Participants. The Participants axis has three states: *unitary* (a perception of full agreement between participants on definitions of the problem situation), *pluralist* (a perception of disagreement between participants) and *coercive* (a perception of disagreement that is masked, or potential disagreement that is not being allowed to surface, due to power relationships between participants). The System axis has two states: *simple* (easy to understand) and *complex* (difficult to understand).

The six contexts in the system of systems methodologies are arrived at by cross-referencing the two axes, and these can be labelled simple–unitary, complex–unitary, simple–pluralist, complex–pluralist, simple–coercive and complex–coercive. Various systems methodologies have been aligned with these different contexts: see Jackson and Keys (1984), Banathy (1987), Oliga (1988), Flood and Jackson (1991b) and Midgley (1992b, 1996) for details. In broad terms, when Jackson and Keys (1984) and subsequent authors conducted this alignment of methods with their ideal contexts of application, "hard" (quantitative, modelling) methods were said to be most appropriate for the unitary contexts, "soft" (debating) methods were regarded as best for pluralist situations, and "emancipatory" (confrontative, boundary-challenging) methods were aimed at coercive contexts.

These were not arbitrary alignments. Quantitative modelling methods were said to be best suited to unitary contexts because formulating a picture of "the truth" in response to a set of questions will only be of relevance to those people who agree that this is the *right* set. If there is disagreement over what

System

		Simple	Complex
	Unitary	Simple-Unitary: key issues are easily appreciated, and general agreement is perceived between those defined as involved or affected.	Complex-Unitary: key issues are difficult to appreciate, but general agreement is perceived between those defined as involved or affected.
Relationships between Participants	*Pluralist*	Simple-Pluralist: key issues are easily appreciated, but disagreement is perceived between those defined as involved or affected.	Complex-Coercive: key issues are difficult to appreciate, and disagreement is perceived between those defined as involved or affected.
	Coercive	Simple-Coercive: key issues are easily appreciated, but suppressed disagreements are perceived between those defined as involved or affected.	Complex-Pluralist: key issues are difficult to appreciate, and suppressed disagreements are perceived between those defined as involved or affected.

Figure 10.1   The system of systems methodologies

the basic issues are (i.e. the context is pluralist), then this will not be addressed by provision of a simple set of facts that are oriented to answer questions that only some people regard as important. Similarly, if we are dealing with coercion, the facts provided will simply strengthen the hand of those who have control over what issues are addressed by allowing them to pursue their aims more effectively. When there is genuine agreement on the nature of the problem, however, then quantitative modelling methods do provide useful answers.

In contrast, debating methods were aligned with pluralist contexts because, when there is open and non-coercive disagreement, debating methods can be helpful in providing a basis for mutual understanding and decision making. However, when there is agreement on what the problems are (i.e. the context is unitary), then there are few differences between viewpoints to explore, so debating methods become redundant. Debating methods are equally unhelpful in coercive contexts because open disagreement is not easy to surface, and the intervention can simply end up supporting the dominant vision.

In contrast once again, confrontative, boundary-challenging methods were aligned with the coercive contexts because, when mutual understanding is difficult to achieve and a necessity for "taking sides" arises, these methods can help in subjecting dominant visions to dialectical challenge. When there is agreement on the right course to pursue (i.e. the context is unitary), such dialectical challenge will usually be redundant. Alternatively, if we try to use emancipatory methods when disagreement is open (i.e. the context is pluralist), then their challenging nature may well threaten the potential for mutual understanding that could make conflict easier to handle in other ways.

We therefore see that each type of methodology in the system of systems methodologies has its strengths, but each also has significant weaknesses. This gives rise to the possibility for methodology *choice* following diagnosis of the problem context. It also provides a means to consider how to *mix* aspects of different methodologies. Jackson and Keys (1984) talk about this in the following terms:

> Some problem contexts will, of course, not fit exactly into any one of the . . . categories. Faced with such an intransigent problem context, the problem solver may still gain benefits from the analysis. It will be possible, using the analysis, to see how a particular methodology might be extended by making use of aspects of other approaches. For example, a problem solver who is armed with a soft-systems methodology appropriate for a systemic-pluralist [complex-pluralist] context may find it possible to "harden up" his methodology for a problem context which has some mechanical-pluralist [simple-pluralist] aspects. The resolution of conflict over objectives may be helped by the use of a quantitative approach to aid the decision makers in investigating the effects of their own preferred solutions relative to the solutions of others. (Jackson and Keys, 1984: 484)

The authors also refer to the possibility of dynamism in the problem context, necessitating movement between methodologies (although it must be said that this is only mentioned in passing):

> The emphasis is on the key variables in problem contexts which can, in changing their character, lead to qualitative changes in such contexts, affecting the problems therein and thereby demanding a significant re-orientation in problem-solving approach. (Jackson and Keys, 1984: 474)

Before moving on to look at the philosophical underpinnings of the system of systems methodologies, one final point needs to be made. Jackson (1990) stresses that the system of systems methodologies is most expressly not a "rule book" to be followed systematically. Indeed, he is highly critical of authors (e.g. Banathy (1984, 1987, 1988) and Keys (1988)) who treat it in this way. Rather, it should be regarded as *an ideal of research practice that is useful for critical reflection on methodology choice*. Let me explain. Ideals are theoretical constructs, and to be critically reflective is to question assumptions. By saying that we should be critically reflective about methodology choice, Jackson is suggesting that there is a need to look carefully at the situations we are going into, trying not to take too much for granted. We also need to consider the possible consequences of the methods we might use, and select our approach accordingly. So, by saying that the system of systems methodologies is an ideal that can be used to guide critical reflection, he is saying that the theoretical insights it provides can offer *direction* to our thinking, but should not *determine* it. Jackson (1990) recognises that practical situations may require compromises with what we might like to do with methods in an ideal world, and researchers must think critically about how they should manage non-ideal situations.

Philosophical Underpinnings

In the introduction to this chapter, I noted that critical systems thinkers are not only concerned with the "practical" aspects of methodological pluralism, but also its philosophical underpinnings. The system of systems methodologies has been underpinned by an epistemological theory (a theory about the nature of knowledge) originally proposed by Habermas (1972). Habermas calls this the "theory of knowledge-constitutive interests". This was first discussed in the critical systems literature by Mingers (1980) and Jackson (1982), but Jackson (1985a) was the first to relate it to the system of systems methodologies. Now, Habermas's work is immensely broad, and cannot be summarised adequately in a few paragraphs. However, Jackson (1985a) offers his own understanding of the theory of knowledge-constitutive interests:

> According to Habermas there are two fundamental conditions underpinning the socio-cultural form of life of the human species—"work" and "interaction".
>
> "Work" enables human beings to achieve goals and to bring about material well-being through social labour. The importance of work to the human species leads human beings to have what Habermas calls a "technical interest" in the prediction and control of natural and social events. The importance of "interaction" calls forth another "interest", the "practical interest". Its concern is with securing and expanding the possibilities of mutual understanding among all those involved in the reproduction of social life. Disagreement among different groups can be just as much a threat to the reproduction of the socio-cultural form of life as a failure to predict and control natural and social affairs.
>
> While work and interaction have for Habermas . . . pre-eminent anthropological status, the analysis of power and the way it is exercised is equally essential, Habermas argues, for the understanding of all past and present social arrangements. The exercise of power in the social process can prevent the open and free discussion necessary for the success of interaction. Human beings therefore also have an "emancipatory interest" in freeing themselves from constraints imposed by power relations and in learning, through a process of genuine participatory democracy, involving discursive will-formation, to control their own destiny. (Jackson, 1985a: 523)

While Jackson was the first to claim that this theory could be used to underpin the system of systems methodologies, we should note that there has been a difference of opinion between Jackson (1985a, 1991a) and Flood (1990) concerning how this underpinning should be achieved. A review of their individual positions can be found in Midgley (1992b). To keep matters simple, I will concentrate on the position that has been discussed most widely in the literature—that proposed jointly by Flood and Jackson (1991b). In short, they suggest that " 'hard' and cybernetic systems approaches can support the technical interest, soft methodologies the practical interest, and critical systems heuristics can aid the emancipatory interest" (1991b: 49)

To explain in more detail, "hard" and cybernetic systems approaches are those which have modelling as their central activity. In relation to the theory of knowledge-constitutive interests, these methodologies are viewed as supporting one particular human interest—our technical interest in predicting and controlling our environment. In contrast, "soft" methodologies involve managing debate between people so that learning may be facilitated, ideas evaluated, and plans for action developed. In relation to the theory of knowledge-constitutive interests, these too are seen as supporting one interest—this time, our practical interest in achieving mutual understanding. Finally, critical systems heuristics is concerned with subjecting assumptions in planning to ethical critique. It asks both the researcher and participants in dialogue to address a number of questions concerning the issue of whose views should enter into the planning process, and how this should be achieved. According to Flood and Jackson (1991b), this can support the remaining human interest—our emancipatory interest in freeing ourselves from restrictive power relations.

The Paradigm Problem

One further aspect of philosophy needs to be discussed before we can conclude this section. This is the attitude assumed by the creators of the system of systems methodologies to the *paradigm problem*. The paradigm problem can be summarised as follows. All systems methodologies make different philosophical and theoretical assumptions—i.e. they are born in different paradigms—so if we wish to mix them, or bring them together in a framework, we have to justify this at the level of philosophy. Some authors (e.g. Burrell and Morgan, 1979; Jackson and Carter, 1991) claim that philosophical paradigms are irrevocably incommensurable. This might lead one to suppose that methodological pluralism is a non-starter. Others claim that rational analysis may bridge the paradigm gap, allowing for a "unification" of paradigms (Reed, 1985), or that communication across paradigm boundaries is possible even if unification is neither feasible nor desirable (Willmott, 1993). Proponents of methodological pluralism claiming theoretical coherence must inevitably develop a position on the paradigm problem, otherwise they risk being accused of theoretically contradictory eclecticism.

Two authors, Flood (1989a, 1990) and Jackson (1990, 1991a, 1993a), have been prominent in tackling this issue in relation to the system of systems methodologies. Their basic argument is that it is Habermas's (1972) theory of knowledge-constitutive interests that allows complementarity. The various paradigms are aligned with the three interests in the manner described above. Flood (1990) says that critical systems thinking, in its embodiment of the system of systems methodologies and the theory of knowledge-constitutive interests, is "meta-paradigmatic"—clearly indicating his belief that critical systems thinking can govern the use of other systems paradigms. Jackson has been engaged in a long-running debate over the paradigm problem with various authors (see the references to critics provided in the Summary of this section), and has developed his position over the years in response to their comments. He has recently suggested that the system of systems methodologies does not have to

> decide whether the issues, or problems, or systems of concern are "in the world" or whether they are in the minds of those conducting and participating in the analysis. As is demanded by its radical complementarism, since it embraces methodologies with varying ontological and epistemological presuppositions, it is agnostic on this matter. (Jackson, 1993a: 292)[4]

And,

> . . . systems methodologies can be related to different paradigms, each of which will constitute and frame social reality in its own way. Nevertheless, rather than these paradigms being incommensurable, it is possible to see them as complementary on the grounds of the three essential human interests identified by Habermas—the technical, the practical, and the emancipatory. The paradigms should guide knowledge production and the systems methodologies should be put to work, in an informed manner, in the service of appropriate human interests. (Jackson, 1993a: 290–291)

Summary

In concluding this section, we see that the system of systems methodologies critically aligns systems approaches with contexts for use, and supports this alignment with an epistemological theory of universal human participation in work and interaction. It is the notion that work and interaction are fundamental to the human condition which gives rise to our interests in prediction and

---

[4] This comment was actually made in defence of Total Systems Intervention (Flood and Jackson, 1991b), a meta-methodology that *includes* use of the system of systems methodologies. However, it is reasonable to suppose that Jackson would take the same view if he were discussing the system of systems methodologies on its own.

control, mutual understanding and freedom from oppressive power relations. Complementarity between paradigms is granted by this theory. While the main focus of the creators of the system of systems methodologies has been choice between whole methodologies (see Carter et al (1987) and Flood and Jackson (1991b) for some practical examples), they do acknowledge that research contexts may appear sufficiently complex or dynamic to warrant "hardening" soft methodologies or "softening" hard ones. In these cases, they say that the system of systems methodologies can still provide guidance.

Before moving on to the second of the five approaches, I will provide some references to criticisms of the system of systems methodologies and its underlying philosophy which the interested reader might like to follow up. See, in particular, Gregory (1990, 1992), Midgley (1990a, b, 1992b, c, 1995), Mansell (1991), Mingers (1992a–c, 1993), Tsoukas (1992), Jones (1993) and Dutt (1994). However, in consulting these, it will be important to read several replies that have also been written in defence of the system of systems methodologies: see, for example, Jackson (1992, 1993b, c) and Schecter (1993).

TOTAL SYSTEMS INTERVENTION (VERSION ONE)

The second approach to mixing methods that I will address is Total Systems Intervention (TSI). Although another approach (the creative design of methods, to be discussed in the next section) emerged in between the system of systems methodologies and TSI, it makes sense to review TSI first because it includes the system of systems methodologies within it. However, before reviewing TSI, I first need to point out that there are actually two versions in the literature: the first (Flood and Jackson, 1991b) has now been superseded by the second (Flood 1995a). This section will only be concerned with the first version, which I will call TSI(1). The second version will be reviewed later because, in my opinion, it has a sufficiently different view of mixing methods to warrant being described as a separate approach.

TSI(1) is described by Flood and Jackson (1991b) as a "meta-methodology" because it offers direction to systems practitioners wishing to choose between methodologies, and relate them together, in a theoretically informed manner. There are three "phases" to the meta-methodology of TSI(1): *creativity*, *choice* and *implementation*. Each of these is described below, starting with creativity.

The *creativity* phase assumes that each of the main systems methodologies embraced by TSI(1) embodies a particular "metaphor of organisation" (here Flood and Jackson (1991b) follow Morgan (1986)). For instance, implicit in system dynamics is the view that organisations are like machines. Cybernetic methodologies, on the other hand, look at organisations as if they are organisms adapting to their environment, or alternatively they talk about organisations as if they have the same capacity to learn as the human brain. In contrast, soft systems methodologies assume a culture or a coalition metaphor, and emancipatory methodologies (such as critical systems heuristics) view organisations as if they are prisons. Seven metaphors are identified in all. According to Flood and Jackson (1991b), these metaphors are helpful because their use in debate can enhance creativity. Participants can use them to think in different ways about the issues with which they are concerned. For example, they may explore the possibility that their organisation is "broken" (the machine metaphor), finds learning difficult (the brain metaphor), or is failing to grow (the organismic metaphor). The output of the creativity phase should be the identification of a key metaphor, or a set of key metaphors related together, that seems to be particularly apt in describing the "problems" facing the organisation.

The *choice* phase then follows. To choose an appropriate methodology, or set of methodologies, the metaphors generated during the creativity phase are mapped onto the system of systems methodologies. The usual mapping of metaphors is represented in Figure 10.2 (taken from Flood and Jackson, 1991b, p. 42). Flood and Jackson stress that "the choice of systems methodology *should be informed* by the system of systems methodologies, *it should not be determined* by it" (1991b, pp. 42–43, emphases in the original).

Having chosen a methodology, or methodologies, TSI(1) asks the practitioner to move to their *implementation*. The implementation of systems methodologies yields change proposals.

Now, for ease of presentation, I have described the relationships between creativity, choice and implementation in a linear fashion. However, it is possible to move between these in any order, and indeed there may be a need to undertake each phase more than once (for example, if addressing one problem gives rise to another). The process of TSI(1) is therefore more appropriately seen as a multi-directional activity cycle.

TSI(1) embodies a very particular view of the practice of mixing methods. In fact, it is not methods that are mixed at all, but method*ologies*. Even the

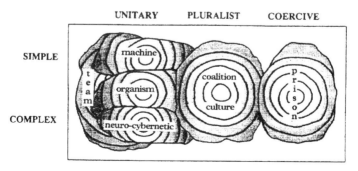

Figure 10.2 Metaphors mapped onto the system of systems methodologies (Flood and Jackson 1991b: 42)

word "mixed" is rather misleading. During the creativity phase, TSI(1) asks for "dominant" and "dependent" metaphors to be identified. The significance of this is explained by Flood and Jackson as follows:

> The outcome (what is expected to emerge) from the creativity phase is a "dominant" metaphor which highlights the main interests and concerns and can become the basis for a choice of an appropriate intervention methodology. There may be other metaphors which it is also sensible to pursue into the next phase. The relative position of dominant and these "dependent" metaphors may indeed be altered by later work. (Flood and Jackson, 1991b: 51, emphasis removed)

Therefore a dominant methodology is chosen, but other issues might need to be dealt with through the use of dependent methodologies. In this way, methodologies are *related together*, but methods are not truly mixed.

Philosophical Underpinnings and the Paradigm Problem

There is little to say about the philosophical underpinnings of TSI(1) and its attitude to the paradigm problem that has not already been said earlier in relation to the system of systems methodologies. TSI(1) is described as a meta-methodology because it is a methodology which guides the researcher in making choices between other methodologies. As with the system of systems methodologies, this approach to the paradigm problem is supported with reference to Habermas's (1972) theory of knowledge-constitutive interests.

Summary

In summary, the meta-methodology of TSI(1) asks people to move between creativity (about the problem situation), choice (of methodologies) and implementation (to yield change proposals). As with the system of systems methodologies, complementarity between different systems paradigms is granted by the theory of knowledge-constitutive interests (Habermas, 1972). Methodologies are not so much "mixed" in TSI(1) as "related together": people are required to decide which should be regarded as dominant and which should be treated as dependent.

Before moving on to the third of the five approaches to be reviewed, it remains for me to provide references to the work of critics. Many of the criticisms raised against the system of systems methodologies can also be seen as applicable to TSI(1), but in addition the following may be of interest: Elstob (1992), Ghosal (1992), Gregory (1992), Taket (1992), Tsoukas (1993a), Green (1993a), Brocklesby (1994), Cummings (1994) and Flood (1995a, b). Once again, however, it would also be advisable to consult papers written in defence of TSI(1): see, for example, Jackson (1993a), Green (1993b) and Ho (1994).

THE CREATIVE DESIGN OF METHODS

The third of the five approaches to mixing methods was developed following reflection upon a particularly complex intervention (Midgley, 1988, 1989b, 1990a; Midgley and Floyd, 1988, 1990). Midgley problematised the notion of simple methodology choice, arguing that *most* research situations are perceived as sufficiently complex to warrant the use of a variety of methods. Therefore, it is more useful to think in terms of the *design of methods* than simple choice between "off-the-shelf" methodologies.

This line of research gave rise to the concept of "creative methodology design" (Midgley, 1990a), which was later changed to the *creative design of methods* (Midgley, 1997a) to avoid confusion between method and methodology. This involves understanding the problem situation in terms of a series of systemically interrelated research questions, each of which might need to be addressed using a different method, or part of a method. These research questions are not necessarily determined as a complete set in advance, but may evolve as events unfold and understandings of the situation develop. A particularly important idea in the creative design of methods is that the method that is finally designed is different from the sum of its parts (Midgley, 1997a). It is not simply a matter of "stitching" other people's methods together in an additive fashion: a *synthesis* is generated that allows each individual research question to be addressed as part of a whole *system* of questions.

Midgley (1989b, 1990a) makes it clear that it is important to develop the research questions in dialogue with stakeholders, but that researchers should also take care to allow people time and space to surface issues confidentially. This confidential space is needed to facilitate the identification of power issues that people might not be willing to discuss openly. Here, the researcher cannot avoid taking a lead in guiding the development of the research (Midgley, 1989b): the need to talk with people individually and confidentially places the researcher in a unique position of responsibility. He or she must manage the possible tensions between his or her own, and various stakeholders', different viewpoints.

Now, when this approach was first developed it was conceived as an improvement of the system of systems methodologies.[5] The interlinked research questions generated in the intervention described in Midgley (1990a) were produced through reflection on the problematic situation *in relation* to the system of systems methodologies. However, in the most recent incarnation of the creative design of methods (Midgley, 1997a), the system of systems methodologies is not mentioned. While the reasons for this were not made explicit in that work, they can be detailed now.

---

[5] An improvement was thought to be necessary because the issue of the researcher's responsibility was not addressed in earlier descriptions of the use of the system of systems methodologies. The system of systems methodologies was also criticised for paying insufficient attention to the dynamism and complexity of most research situations (Midgley, 1990a).

First, as Gregory (1992) argues, the system of systems methodologies encourages people to accept only one interpretation of each methodology. Flood and Romm (1995a) have demonstrated that it is actually possible to use methods for a variety of purposes, some of which go beyond those they were originally designed for. By placing the methodologies in boxes, alternative interpretations and uses which may be quite justifiable are discouraged. That this is indeed the case is demonstrated by the fact that there has only been one change in the structure of the system of systems methodologies (Jackson, 1987b), and only a handful of changes in the alignment of methodologies with the boxes, in its thirteen-year history. This is despite repeated calls for further critical reviews of both individual systems methodologies and the framework itself (e.g. in Flood and Jackson, 1991b).

Not only does the system of systems methodologies "freeze" interpretations of methodologies in an unnecessarily restrictive manner, but it cannot easily take account of the methodological developments that occur when researchers learn from other perspectives (Gregory, 1992). A classic example is system dynamics, which has always appeared in the system of systems methodologies in the "simple-unitary" box. However, recent research on system dynamics has suggested that, rather than claiming that the model represents reality (the traditional view), it is more useful to focus on the modelling *process* as a vehicle for the development of learning and social coordination (see, for example, de Geus, 1994). System dynamics practitioners have therefore changed their understanding of "system" to one that is much closer to soft systems thinking, and presumably this new way of using it makes it *equally* applicable to unitary and pluralist contexts.

Finally, the system of systems methodologies is problematical in the way it confines the business of making critical boundary judgements (in the form of Ulrich's (1983) methodology of critical systems heuristics) to simple-coercive contexts. This means that, in practice, critical reflection on, and discussion of, boundary judgements will only happen on an occasional basis. Of course, I am not suggesting that critical systems heuristics gives us all we need to enact critical awareness (several criticisms can be raised against it, as Jackson (1985b, 1991a), Willmott (1989), Ivanov (1991), Flood and Jackson (1991b, c), Mingers (1992a), Romm (1994, 1995a, b), Brown (1996) and Midgley (1997b) have all pointed out), but the question remains, "how is the commitment to critical awareness enacted in situations where coercion is *not* identified?"

Now, this last criticism of the system of systems methodologies not only indicates (to me) the need for a rethink about its use, but also suggests that further work should be done on the practice of making critical boundary judgements. Midgley (1995) takes a first step here by proposing support for Ulrich's (1993) argument that methods to aid critical reflection on making boundary judgements should be used to enhance critical thinking up-front—both when we enter into interventions, and as an integral part of the whole inquiry process.

I say that this is a "first step" because Ulrich's critical systems heuristics is currently the only method we have for this: there is still a crying need for further research, both to enhance critical systems heuristics (in theory and practice) and to develop other approaches to making critical boundary judgements. Encouragingly, research along these lines is already well under way (see, for example, Cohen and Midgley, 1994; Gregory, Romm and Walsh, 1994; Flood, 1995a; Flood and Romm, 1995a; Midgley, Munlo and Brown, 1997).

Now, defenders of the system of systems methodologies may well reply by saying that boundary critique is redundant in situations where coercion has not been identified. However, the most immediate question that springs to mind is, "how do we identify coercion?" and related to this, "whose views do we take into account?" Answering these questions will involve the researcher and other interested parties in *making critical boundary judgements*. In other words, making up-front boundary judgements cannot be avoided in *any* research situation. Failure to realise the full implications of this will inevitably result in some of the most important boundary judgements—those which determine who the researcher will talk to and how the initial remit of the work will be defined—being made in an uncritical manner. Therefore, when generating research questions for the creative design of methods, it is important to prioritise boundary questions.

Philosophical Underpinnings

Possible philosophical underpinnings of the creative design of methods have also been explored. A move away from the theory of knowledge-constitutive interests was considered to be necessary following two critiques: a critique of the use of the theory of knowledge-constitutive interests to underpin methodological pluralism (Midgley, 1989a, b), and a critique of the legitimacy of the theory of knowledge-constitutive interests itself (Midgley, 1992b). I will give brief details of each of these critiques before going on to present the alternative perspective that has been developed.

First, both Flood and Jackson seem to see the theory of knowledge-constitutive interests as something that can take us above and beyond inter-paradigm debate. This is important because, were we to claim that a pluralist theory was in some sense "meta-paradigmatic", as Flood (1990) does,[6] we would be heading for the same trap that Jackson and Carter (1991) identify in their critique of systems theories of the unification of science: creating a new Grand Truth that is beyond question, and which seeks to invalidate any ideas that oppose it. Let me explain.

---

[6] Flood has recently changed his view on this, and (in partnership with Romm) has developed a more sophisticated vision of the relationship between paradigms (Flood and Romm, 1995b). This will be discussed more fully later.

As individuals trying to embrace diversity, we are inevitably selective. We cannot be aware of either the existence or the relevance of all methodological positions. Having attempted to be as comprehensive as possible in making our selection, we then "freeze" this diversity into an epistemological system of categorisation. However, if we try to claim that this system of categorisation is meta-paradigmatic, we are dismissing the possibility that others could legitimately disagree with it. It will therefore no longer be open to change and further development.

Now, when it was first published, this critique made me aware of the need to be explicit about the paradigmatic nature of my own work on pluralism, but was not the only spur to move towards a new position. While the theory of knowledge-constitutive interests may be internally coherent, I had doubts about its legitimacy (Midgley, 1992b). The problem is that the theory of knowledge-constitutive interests describes the relationship that human beings have with the non-human environment as one of "prediction and control". If this is used to inform the development of systems science, it is likely to reinforce the humanist assumption that the natural world is a resource for human control and consumption. It is far better to view human beings as having an interest in preserving and/or building a sustainable, interactive relationship with their non-human environment. For further details of this argument, see Eckersley (1992) and Midgley (1992b, 1994).

So let me now describe the alternative philosophical ideas that these critiques gave rise to. Like Jackson (1985a), I also chose to draw upon the work of Habermas to build a pluralist theory—only I focused on his later work (Habermas, 1976, 1984a, b) which offers an analysis of rational argumentation. Habermas claims that there are four implicit validity statements inherent in any sentence intended for communication. Giddens (1985) summarises his position neatly:

> When I say something to someone else, I implicitly make the following claims: that what I say is intelligible; that its propositional content is true; that I am justified in saying it; and that I speak sincerely, without intent to deceive. (Giddens, 1985, p. 99)

The first of these implicit claims, that what I say is intelligible, is simply a precondition for effective communication. However, the other three, when made explicit, can all be questioned and justified through rational argumentation.

It is these three claims that refer directly to three "worlds": the claim that my statement's propositional content is true relates to *the external natural world*; the claim that I am justified in making it relates to *our social world*; and the claim that I speak sincerely relates to *my internal world*. These "worlds" do not have a concrete existence separate from the use of language to describe them, but inevitably come to be *viewed* as separate through the process of rational argumentation where people make and challenge validity claims, focusing on one of these "worlds" at a time. It is the nature of language that makes us differentiate the "natural", "social" and "internal" when we enter discourse.

It is important to be clear about a key implication of Habermas's notion that all three validity claims are already inherent in any act of communication. Although a statement may *appear* to be about just one "world" (the object external world, the normative social world, or the speaker's subjective internal world), in fact a position on the other two is always implied in it. This allows the hearer to mount one of three types of challenge, regardless of which "world" the original statement appeared to refer to: a challenge to its propositional content, its normative acceptability, or the sincerity of the speaker.[7]

In developing philosophical underpinnings for methodological pluralism from this work, I suggested that it is possible to make, and challenge, *truth* statements (about the objective external world), *rightness* statements (about our normative social world) and statements about an *individual's subjectivity* (a person's subjective internal world). I then suggested that all existing systems methods prioritise the investigation of one of these kinds of statement. "Hard" and cybernetic methods primarily allow us to investigate and make truth statements—they attempt to model reality. They may deal with issues of rightness and subjectivity along the way, but these are subordinate concerns. In contrast, "soft" systems methods primarily encourage us to investigate and make decisions on rightness issues. They attempt to structure debate so that a group of people can figure out the right way forward.[8] While issues of truth and subjectivity will often be explored too, these are once again subordinate concerns. There are also a set of methods that are primarily oriented towards helping us understand subjective positions. These include personal construct theory (e.g. Kelly, 1955) and cognitive mapping (e.g. Eden, Jones and Sims, 1983), both of which seek to build a picture of a single individual's unique perspective. Again, truth and rightness issues may have a bearing on the use of these methods, but they are inevitably treated as subordinate concerns. It

---

[7] In Habermas's view, this is what good rational argumentation is all about: making distinctions between the objective, normative and subjective, and thus challenging the unseen assumptions of the speaker who is generally only aware that he or she is making a statement about one of the worlds. However, although I am drawing upon the work of Habermas here, I feel that it is important for me to make it clear that I disagree with his view of "good" rational argumentation. I will be exploring this issue in more detail later on.

[8] Given that several authors (e.g. Mingers, 1980; Jackson, 1982) have criticised soft systems thinking for ignoring moral (or power) issues, it might appear strange for me to suggest that soft systems methods encourage us to investigate and make decisions on rightness. Some (e.g. Flood, 1995a) say that soft systems methods focus on questions of "how" things should be done, not whether those things are right. However, I use the term "rightness" in its broadest sense: the general form of a rightness question is, "given an interpretation of the context in which a choice is to be made, including the possible consequences of that choice, what is the right path to take?"

should be noted that this is a highly summarised account—a more detailed version is provided in Midgley (1992c).[9]

The Paradigm Problem

It should already be possible to discern from the above that my own approach to the paradigm problem is substantially different from that of Flood (1989a, 1990) and Jackson (1990, 1991a, 1993a): I have argued that critical systems thinking cannot be "meta-paradigmatic" given that critical systems thinkers make assumptions about human knowledge that are alien to, and incommensurable with, assumptions made by the proponents of other systems paradigms. In my view, critical systems thinkers are trying to establish the foundations for a *new* paradigm. Interestingly, Flood (1990) accepts the incommensurability argument: he suggests that it is possible to have methodological *commensurability* while acknowledging theoretical *in*commensurability. However, it would seem to me that this stands in opposition to his claim that critical systems thinking is "meta-paradigmatic": it means that, if critical systems thinking is indeed theoretical in nature, we must recognise that it is incommensurable with other perspectives based on different theoretical assumptions. This does not mean that critical systems thinkers cannot learn from other paradigms, or that the proponents of other paradigms cannot learn from critical systems thinking (Gregory, 1992), but it does make the claim to a meta-paradigmatic status problematic.

Now, my understanding is that this claim came about through the wish to promote a form of methodological pluralism where no one methodology was seen to dominate. However, if we take on board the idea that the ethical critique of boundary judgements is of central importance, then there is no longer a need to describe methodological pluralism in this "neutral" manner. We can accept that there may be many different visions of methodological pluralism, including one which rests on the assumptions of critical systems thinking outlined in this section on the creative design of methods, and our task is then to justify why any one is preferable (Midgley, 1992c).

Summary

In summary, the creative design of methods involves the development of a dynamic set of interrelated research questions, each of which might need to be addressed using a different method, or part of a method. In generating the research questions, the need for critical thinking and debate about boundary judgements is crucial. As making boundary judgements may well involve

---

[9] Also see Ulrich (1983) and Fairtlough (1989, 1991a) for the views of two other critical systems thinkers who have used Habermas's later work to inform systems practice.

considering issues of power, the researcher must take some responsibility for ensuring that people have confidential spaces to explore sensitive issues. Complementarity between methods is granted by a theory of the use of language, where different methods are seen to address different kinds of question. However, embracing this theory of language means accepting that we cannot be "meta-paradigmatic": the principles of the creative design of methods form the foundation stones for a new paradigm.

The creative design of methods has not yet been subject to criticism in the systems literature, although my approach to resolving the paradigm problem has (see Tsoukas (1993b) and Jackson (1997) for details). Let us now move on to the fourth of our five approaches to the theory and practice of mixing methods.

CRITICAL APPRECIATION

The notion of critical appreciation was first introduced into the literature by Gregory (1992) following her critique of the system of systems methodologies, TSI(1) and their common underlying philosophy. This critique was described in the previous section, and involved the observation that the system of systems methodologies and TSI(1) are insufficiently dynamic. By suggesting that each kind of systems methodology ("hard", "soft" and "emancipatory") supports just one of the three knowledge-constitutive interests, a meta-theory is produced that encourages people to resist other interpretations of the methodologies.

So, let us summarise Gregory's own ideas. First, she talks in terms of "discordant pluralism" to differentiate her own understanding of methodological pluralism from that offered by Jackson (1987a) and Flood and Jackson (1991b). These authors view the various systems methodologies as "concordant" in the sense that a meta-theory can be provided to make them appear complementary: the differences between the methodologies are only important in as much as they indicate what alignments should be made with the system of systems methodologies. In contrast, Gregory (1992, 1996) believes that the differences between the methodologies should not be "rationalised away" through the use of a meta-theoretical structure. She therefore wishes to preserve discord and learn from it.

Gregory (1992, 1996) uses a metaphor, borrowed from Bernstein (1991), to explain her understanding of pluralism. This is the metaphor of "constellation". A constellation of methodologies, like a constellation of stars in the sky, is not ordered in a regular fashion, changes over time, and can be seen from many different angles. Each researcher can develop his or her own constellation of methodologies in discussion with others who likewise have their own constellations. There is no attempt to bring once-and-for-all theoretical unity to the constellation, except insofar as a "snapshot" taken at a moment in time will reveal certain regularities of ordering that are visible because of the dominance of a temporary theoretical perspective.

On its own, Gregory's vision of discordant pluralism might be difficult to differentiate from atheoretical pragmatism, where people pick and mix from the various methodologies without theoretical reflection. This is where the theory of critical appreciation comes in. The theory of critical appreciation suggests that there are four dimensions of critical research practice: empirical–analytic (based on experiment and observation), historical–hermeneutic (two way communication with others), self-reflection (revealing one's own assumptions) and ideology-critique (revealing assumptions at the level of society). Gregory (1992) argues that all four of these aspects should be built into research for it to be considered critical. The relationships between them are illustrated in Figure 10.3: essentially, it is possible to move from any one aspect to any of the others. At first sight, this might appear to be a "meta-ordering" imposed on the discordant pluralism described above. However, Gregory side-steps this trap by refusing to align existing methodologies with the four dimensions. She hands over to individual researchers, in debate with others, the task of developing specific methodological expressions of her theory of critical appreciation.

Gregory (1992) makes it clear that the practice of mixing methods is at the heart of her approach: interventions must draw upon and mix different methods so that empirical–analytic study, historical–hermeneutic inquiry, self-reflection and ideology-critique can all be included—no single method is currently able to offer adequate support to all four of these aspects of the critical research process.

Philosophical Underpinnings

Now, the reader may be left wondering why critical research might require the four dimensions already outlined. To ground this claim, Gregory (1992, 1994) enters the realm of epistemology to produce a theory of self-society dynamics.

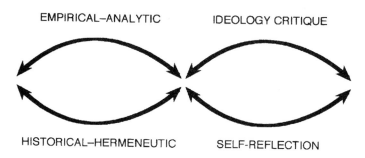

Figure 10.3 The critical appreciation process

She argues that the self and society are engaged in many dynamic relationships. The individual acts (often with others) to change or maintain society, yet social processes transform or constrain the knowledge that any individual may have, and thereby the actions s/he may take. Self and society can therefore both be seen as playing a part in maintaining or transforming the other: neither the self nor society is prime. This gives rise to the claim that both self-reflection *and* ideology-critique are necessary: the first to help the individual understand his or her own role in maintaining or transforming social processes, and the second to understand the way social processes shape consciousness (including the individual's own). Now, both empirical–analytic and historical–hermeneutic study are necessary because observation and two-way communication are the two means that individual human beings have to develop their understanding beyond mere reorderings of their current knowledge. Self-reflection and ideology-critique without observation and two-way communication are therefore limited activities. Similarly, observations and communications are limited if they are not related to self-reflective activity and ideology-critiques: without the latter, there can be no appreciation of the context in which observations and communications are understood.

The Paradigm Problem

Gregory's (1992) thinking on the paradigm problem is very similar to Midgley's (1989a, b, 1992b), only she has taken it one stage further. Like Midgley, Gregory insists that it is impossible to transcend the paradigm debate: each attempt to do so must inevitably involve researchers in making new paradigmatic assumptions. However, she moves our thinking on by examining the nature of communication between people based in different paradigms. Every time one person listens to another whose thinking is based in another paradigm, he or she can only interpret what they are saying through his or her own terms of reference. However, this does not mean communication is impossible—just that care is needed not to be either dismissive or to think that full understanding has been achieved. If care is taken to *appreciate* the other, in the knowledge that full understanding in the other's own terms is impossible, then one's own learning can be enhanced. This way of thinking moves the debate on because it allows us to see paradigms in relation to the perspectives of individuals. Learning through appreciating the viewpoints of others can feed back (via communication with one's peers) to transform one's own paradigm.

Summary

We see that Gregory's (1992) thinking on methodological pluralism is similar to that of the previous authors', but only in the sense that it is grounded in theory—a theory of the dynamic relationships that exist between self and society, with each contributing to the formation of the other. However, while this theory gives rise to methodological guidelines, and the practice of mixing methods is promoted, it does not result in a restrictive categorisation of existing methodologies. On the contrary, Gregory wants individual researchers to develop their own constellations of methods and methodologies, being mindful of the differences between them as well as possible similarities. In doing so, she asks researchers to engage in a critical appreciation process: to observe, converse with others, self-reflect and conduct critiques of society. While it is not possible to transcend paradigms and take a "neutral" view of them, it *is* possible to develop one's own paradigm by appreciating the views of others and allowing that appreciation to feed back into one's own paradigmatic community.

Gregory's work on critical appreciation has not yet been subject to critique in the systems literature, so we can move straight on to detail the fifth and final perspective on mixing methods being reviewed here.

TOTAL SYSTEMS INTERVENTION (VERSION TWO)

Earlier, I reviewed the first version of Total Systems Intervention—TSI(1). It is now time to deal with the second version which is different in a number of key respects. I will call this second version TSI(2). This was developed by Flood (1995a) in response to criticisms of TSI(1), and specific details of these criticisms and the changes made can be found in Flood (1995b). TSI(2) is represented diagrammatically in Figure 10.4.

TSI(2) is still a meta-methodology based around the tripartite division of *creativity* (about the problem situation), *choice* (of methods) and *implementation* (producing change proposals). One significant development, however, is that the structure of TSI(2) is regarded as *recursive*. In other words, within each of the phases, the structure is replicated. So, for example, when we're being creative about the problem situation, we should consider the need to be creative about our approach to the creativity task itself, choose an effective creativity-enhancing method, and then implement it. All of the phases of the TSI(2) approach are represented at the micro-level within each macro-level phase.

We should also note that both the creativity and choice phases are significantly transformed. First, the creativity phase is no longer concerned solely with metaphorical analysis. Flood (1995a) has accepted the criticism made of TSI(1) that the six metaphors used to explore the problem situation are overly limiting. TSI(1) did not give sufficient encouragement to participants in debate to generate *their own* metaphors. The result is that the problem situation is generally seen in terms of one or another existing systems perspective—

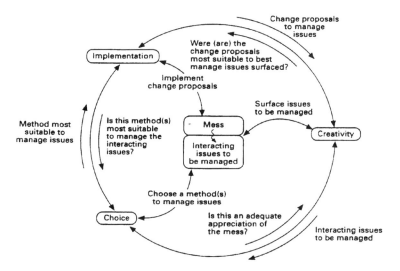

Figure 10.4   The process of TSI(2) (Flood 1995b: 178)

there is no incentive to develop new perspectives, as there is if novel meta-phors are generated. The creativity phase in TSI(2) now involves three things: "divergent" metaphorical analysis (allowing people to generate their own metaphors); the use of creativity-enhancing techniques (such as brainstorm-ing, idea-writing, etc.); and an understanding of the "ergonomics of reflec-tion" (the notion that people need time and space to think if they are going to be creative). See Flood (1995a) and Ragsdell (1996) for further details.

The choice phase is also transformed. First, the System of Systems Meth-odologies has been abandoned. Earlier, I explained why Gregory (1992) and Midgley (1997a) abandoned the system of systems methodologies, but Flood (1995b) has a different reason for doing so. He has found that it is difficult to communicate the framework effectively to practising managers. One of Flood's main concerns, especially in his (1995a) work, is to make TSI access-ible to a non-academic audience. In TSI(2), Flood (1995a) has replaced the system of systems methodologies with a much more basic framework that simply categorises four domains in which systems practitioners seek to inter-vene: organisational process, organisational design, organisational culture and organisational politics. He then argues that each systems method has a do-main in which it is most effectively used, and our task is to align methods with domains accordingly. Flood also argues that it is important to consider what changes might be needed in *each* of the four domains, not to concentrate solely on one domain to the exclusion of the other three.

At first sight it would seem that Flood has just replaced one restrictive framework with another. However, I would suggest that this is not the case.

Flood (1995a) argues that there are three "modes" in which TSI(2) should be used: the problem-solving mode (during interventions), the critical reflection mode (where the TSI process is used to evaluate interventions post-operatively in order to improve TSI itself) and, crucially, the *critical review mode*. The critical review mode, initially proposed by Flood (1995a) and substantially developed by Wilby (1996), represents a significant innovation because it asks researchers to use the TSI process to evaluate other methodologies in order to integrate them into the repertoire of TSI. In this way, individual researchers can, in Gregory's (1992) terms, generate *their own* "constellations" of methods and methodologies. While Flood (1995a, b) and Wilby (1996) still advocate the framework that categorises four domains of organisation (process, design, culture and politics), Flood (1995c) goes further to suggest that *new* frameworks can be developed using the TSI process that are sensitive to local cultural needs. Therefore, his four categories are just that—*his* categories. They may be useful for some practitioners, but others who find them restrictive are encouraged to develop their own.

Another significant development in TSI(2) strikes right to the heart of the subject of this chapter. There is no longer a focus on relating whole methodologies together, as there was in TSI(1). Rather, the researcher is encouraged to mix methods flexibly. Flood (1995a) emphasises that one of the most important aspects of a methodology is its *principles*. In his view, as long as a researcher remains faithful to the principles of a given methodology, he or she can draw upon any method, or any combination of methods, and the intervention will be a valid application of that methodology. The assumption is that "methods" and "methodology" are separable.

This way of thinking is further developed by Flood and Romm (1995a) who argue that methods can be used for many purposes: every method has a "given and immediate purpose", the one it was originally designed for, but may nevertheless be used in other ways. Flood and Romm are particularly concerned to demonstrate that it is possible to use a diverse variety of methods to tackle coercion, including many (such as those originating in the cybernetic and soft systems paradigms) that have actually been criticised for their *inability* to deal with coercive situations. According to Flood and Romm (1995a), the key to using methods for purposes other than those for which they were originally designed is to operate them *using the principles of a different perspective*. This is what they call their "oblique" use. In their own words,

> When the . . . practitioner proceeds by operating a method obliquely, s/he operates it with knowledge drawn from his/her experience of, and insight into, what other theoretical positions can offer. (Flood and Romm, 1995a: 390)

Taking coercion as an example, they argue that it is possible to address it obliquely using methods of organisational redesign and participative planning—but only if the intervener employs emancipatory principles and retains an awareness that the main purpose of the intervention is to address power relationships. If awareness of the power issue is lost, the original theoretical assumptions of the approach will resurface and dominate the intervention, resulting in an organisational redesign or plan that fails to address the coercion. Flood and Romm (1995a) give a number of practical examples of the oblique use of methods, most of which involve mixing methods to achieve the desired results—the "desired results" being defined in terms of methodological principles.

Philosophical Underpinnings

Flood (1995a), which is the main reference source for TSI(2), is primarily aimed at practising managers, so there is scant discussion of philosophy within it. Nevertheless, Flood says that its philosophical underpinnings can be found in an earlier work (Flood, 1990). In that earlier work, he offers a general theory of critical thinking which he calls "liberate and critique". I will summarise this theory before going on to suggest how it might underpin TSI(2).[10]

Central to the theory of liberate and critique is an integration of the very different views of power championed by Habermas (1972) and Foucault (1972, 1976, 1980). I will describe each of their perspectives in turn before demonstrating the nature of Flood's integration of their work. Please note that the writings of both Habermas and Foucault are detailed and complex, so it is impossible to do them justice in a few paragraphs. What is important for the purposes of this chapter, however, is to follow *Flood's* representation of their ideas (although I will inevitably have to simplify this too, as Flood's representation is quite densely argued).

Let us begin with Habermas. The concept of an "emancipatory interest" in freedom from restrictive power relations, which is central to Habermas's (1972) thinking, presupposes that it is indeed possible to be free of the effects of power. Power is "owned" by some people who exercise it over others. It is also seen as a negative, oppressive force. People are thought to be *subject* to the oppression of others, both in terms of observable social relations and ideological rationalisations of these. There is therefore a need for emancipation, both from the power relations themselves and the "false consciousness" (ideology) that supports them.

Foucault's understanding of power could hardly be more different. For Foucault, power is not "owned" by anybody. It resides in the development of forms of knowledge which people use to order their social relationships. What

---

[10] The exact relationship between Flood's (1990) and (1995a) pieces of work appears to me to be unclear, so what I will present will be my own interpretation of the relationship. It remains to be seen whether this is the same as, or different from, Flood's.

appears on the surface to be one person exercising power over another is actually the *end result* of a process of knowledge formation in which certain social practices come to be legitimated. Hollway (1991) provides an interesting example of this: what is perceived as the "power" of the manager over the worker is a result of the formation of knowledge about what "management" actually is.

These two views of power have very different implications. On the one hand, for Habermas, the ability for human beings to make truth claims is a vital aspect of the rational practice of exposing ideology. On the other hand, for Foucault, knowledge and power are so intimately linked that there can be no acceptable criteria for the establishment of truths. For Habermas, it is possible for the "force of the better argument" (1984b, p. 145) to prevail in rational debate. For Foucault, what constitutes a "better argument" is determined by the rules of rationality being employed: there are no external standards of rationality against which to judge arguments, as any such standard will itself be a manifestation of power–knowledge formations.

Now, I have said that Flood (1990) has striven for an integration of the different perspectives of Habermas and Foucault. He has approached this through a consideration of two key aspects of critical systems thinking: critical awareness and pluralism. To take critical awareness first, Flood (1990) argues that to be critical we must hold onto the possibility of comparing and contrasting different knowledges. It is because some forms of knowledge come to dominate social relationships, and others come to be suppressed, that Foucault identifies the *liberation of suppressed knowledges* as essential to the critical endeavour. Having identified (with Foucault) a need for the liberation of knowledges, Flood moves on to a Habermasian examination of the critical systems notion of pluralism. Habermas offers us the chance to critique liberated knowledges *in more than one area of human interest*: the totalising power of a dominant form of knowledge distorting one interest can be challenged by growth of knowledge relating to the others. This is summarised by Flood (1990) as follows:

> Interpretative Analytics [the label given to Foucault's perspective by Dreyfus and Rabinow (1982)] can release rationalities, thus helping to grow diversity. Habermas's critical theory accepts openness and conciliation and welcomes this diversity. Knowledge-constitutive interests then deal critically with the tensions between rationalities. (Flood, 1990: 48)

This represents an interesting juxtaposition of Foucault's and Habermas's ideas, but not yet an integration. While the two authors actually share much common ground (see Fay (1975) and Smart (1983) for comparisons), Flood still faces the fundamental problem of reconciling their different views on the nature of power. Habermas maintains that any analysis of power relations is dependent on the ability to make a (critical, non-absolute) claim to know truth, whereas Foucault says that all "truths" are themselves manifestations of power–knowledge formations. Flood (1990), however, believes that a reconciliation is achievable,

> via the notion that truth is dependent on power and that there is a need to liberate discourse. We then employ Habermas's ideal by looking for the truth of judgement according to our interest, explicit ideology and critical analysis. In this process, however, we drop the idea that truth comes about from the force of the better argument. (Flood, 1990: 50)

In essence, integration is achieved at the expense of Habermas's view of power. Here, then, we have the theory of liberate and critique with which Flood (1995a) would like to underpin TSI(2). My interpretation of this underpinning is that the liberation of knowledges is achieved through processes of *creativity*, and the critique of those knowledges leads to *choice* between methods for *implementation*.

The Paradigm Problem

The view taken of the paradigm problem in TSI(2) differs significantly from that taken by the authors of TSI(1). Flood and Romm (1995b) address the paradigm problem explicitly. They acknowledge the argument that any attempt to embrace methodological pluralism will involve the researcher making assumptions that other methodologists may not agree with. It is therefore very difficult to suggest that there is genuine commensurability between paradigms: there is no position outside the paradigm debate from which to achieve this commensurability. Nevertheless, it *is* still possible to learn from a variety of other people, not only about methods but also about methodological principles, and thereby choose the "most appropriate" approach to each intervention depending on the circumstances and the wishes of the researcher and participants. Because Flood and Romm (1995b) see both sides of this argument, they refuse to talk about either paradigm commensurability *or* incommensurability. Instead, they express the irony of the problem with the phrase "paradigm (in)commensurability" (note the "in" is bracketed).

Summary

In summary, TSI(2) is built around the concepts of creativity, choice and implementation, but unlike TSI(1) it specifically encourages the practice of mixing methods. Furthermore, it gives the researcher the opportunity to develop his or her own pluralist framework and toolkit of methods in response to local need. It also encourages reflection on the adequacy of its own process. TSI(2) is underpinned by the theory of "liberate and critique" which suggests that some forms of knowledge dominate others. Hence, there is a need to liberate suppressed knowledges (through creative exploration) before critiquing those knowledges in order to move towards the choice and implementation of appropriate methods. Of course, the twist in TSI(2) is that, in offering a meta-methodology to promote methodological pluralism, it inevitably embodies assumptions that set it against other methodological approaches which disallow pluralism. It therefore embraces the irony of "paradigm (in)commensurability".

The only task remaining is to provide references to criticisms of TSI(2). For a critique of the philosophy of liberate and critique, see Fairtlough (1991b). For some further thoughts on the oblique use of methods (the use of methods for purposes other than those they were originally designed for), see Midgley (1997a). It is also worth consulting other authors who have related the work of Foucault to critical systems thinking, particularly Mingers (1992a, b) and Valero-Silva (1994, 1995a, b, 1996).

DEVELOPING SYSTEMIC INTERVENTION

Having reviewed all five of the approaches to the theory and practice of mixing methods thus far developed by critical systems thinkers, I will now go on to look at how we might use some of their insights to further develop our understanding of systemic intervention. Over the coming pages I will develop a skeletal vision of a new critical systemic understanding of the theory and practice of mixing methods that will hopefully act as an agenda for future research. This time, however, I will begin with philosophy, move on to discuss the paradigm problem, and finally deal with methodology.

Philosophical Underpinnings

The system of systems methodologies and TSI(1) were both underpinned by Habermas's (1972) theory of knowledge-constitutive interests, and the creative design of methods was underpinned by a development of Habermas's later work on language (1976, 1984a, b). However, Flood (1990) has introduced a spanner into the works in the form of Michel Foucault. The Foucaulvian critique of the Habermasian notion of power is important, not least because it challenges the idea that we can cling to quasi-objective criteria of rationality that we can then judge claims to knowledge against. For Foucault, any such criteria are themselves the product of power–knowledge formations, so those who take a Habermasian line are simply judging one power–knowledge formation by the standards of another.

For me, this makes sense. Even when I drew upon Habermas's theory of language to underpin the creative design of methods, I rebelled against his notion of "good" rational argumentation (Midgley, 1992c). Habermas (1984a,

b) says that "good" argumentation is to do with extricating the three "worlds" (natural, social and internal) from one another in any analysis. Some cultures, he maintains, have a prevailing "worldview" which collapses two or more of the "worlds" together. For instance, the rights and wrongs of social relationships might be seen as an extension of nature in some cultures because the dominant view of both is governed by some form of myth. What is considered *right* is therefore taken for granted because of what is considered to be *true*, and both are "solidified" in myth. Habermas believes that such worldviews represent an intrinsic restriction of "good" rational argumentation: "myth binds the critical potential of communicative action, stops up, so to speak, the source of inner contingencies springing from communication itself" (Habermas, 1984b, p. 159). In contrast, I suggest (Midgley, 1992c) that what constitutes "good" argumentation has to be defined in the context of other discourses we regard as important. It is therefore possible for us to claim that, in some contexts, extricating the three "worlds" from each other might be necessary, while in others it might not be. We therefore escape Habermas's inevitable—and I would say ethically questionable—conclusion that forms of rationality other than the most "advanced" Western rationality must in some sense be "poorer".

However, in moving away from a strictly Habermasian understanding of rationality, I believe that there are two significant pitfalls we must avoid. First, I do not wish to join Flood (1990) in seeking a union between Habermas and Foucault. I would argue that Fairtlough (1991b) is right when he says that a "union" is never really achieved in Flood's work (indeed, Flood (1990) acknowledges that there are still significant tensions in his argument). What he produces is more of a juxtaposition of ideas. My own belief is that unification is a holy grail that will remain forever out of reach. Also, like Bernstein (1991) and Gregory (1992), I suggest that we can *learn* from a juxtaposition of the two authors' work, so we should not attempt to eradicate their differences. In learning from Habermas and Foucault, it may be possible to develop a *new* set of ideas—and shortly, this is what I intend to do.

The second pitfall that I believe we need to avoid when treading this path is the risk of moving away from thinking in terms of intervention to thinking in terms of "pure" critique divorced from any context of action. Because taking action inevitably involves making assumptions about social reality, and because the realisation that there is no "foundational" standard of rationality to judge knowledge against means that the formation of these assumptions will inevitably be influenced by the operation of power, there is a danger of succumbing to pessimism about whether there are any worthwhile possibilities for change. Some may claim that the only truly critical practice is a constant overturning of assumptions, ultimately resulting in a paralysis of intervention because of an unwillingness to take anything for granted, however temporarily.

I would suggest that there are two reasons why people might be tempted to succumb to this pessimistic attitude. The first is that they may still be carrying around some old assumptions about power; in particular, that it "taints" knowledge. If power is seen in this negative sense, then the realisation that it is inescapable will result in disillusion with all forms of knowledge. Instead, we need to accept that it is a matter of judgement whether power is perceived as positive or negative. It is possible for change to be pursued on the basis that a power–knowledge formation regarded as negative can be challenged by the promotion of another that is positively valued. And, of course, the "valorisation" of any power–knowledge formation is open to critical review at any time.

The other reason why people might be tempted to succumb to a pessimistic language of "pure" critique stems from an interpretation of power–knowledge as *forming* our personal and social identities, not interacting with them. Foucauvian critique is dependent on the possibility of revealing the power–knowledge formations that have "made" us. It is easy, when considering this idea, to lose the sense in which we, as individuals and as groups, "make" power–knowledge. We need to maintain the notion of the subject *intervening* in power–knowledge formations in order to preserve the idea of critical action.

The starting point for developing my own philosophical position, then, is the relationship between the *subject*, which acts on power–knowledge formations, and the power–knowledge formations which *frame the identity* of the subject. You may recall Gregory's (1992) theory of self-society dynamics, in which the individual acts (often with others) to change or maintain society, yet social processes transform or constrain the knowledge that any individual may have, and thereby the actions s/he may take. I propose a similar dynamic, only between the subject and power–knowledge rather than the self and society. The difference is important. The term "self" suggests an individual human being, while a "subject" can be any individual, group, community or society that has an identity ascribed to it. Similarly, the term "society" suggests a large-scale collection of people, while "power–knowledge" is that which *gives meaning* to this collective identity (among other identities). Both self and society therefore end up on the same side of the dynamic, creating and being created by power–knowledge. The form of a subject–knowledge dynamic is represented in Figure 10.5.

However, we should not be tempted to regard subject–knowledge dynamics as "observable" in Popper's (1959) sense of independent observation, where the observer is assumed to play no part in constructing the observed. We are ourselves part of the dynamics: every subject is an *identified* subject, and every power–knowledge formation is also *identified* as such. Introducing the concept of "identification" makes it clear that "pure" critique, divorced from any context of action, is an illusion. This is because *identifying something requires*

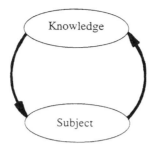

Figure 10.5 Subject–knowledge dynamics

an act of judgement (whether conscious or unconscious). "Acts", of whatever type, are by definition interventions. The *act* of identifying either a subject or the power–knowledge conditions giving meaning to the subject, is therefore itself an intervention. Consequently critique, which in my terms involves the identification of alternative possibilities for knowledge and identity, must also be a form of intervention (see Romm (1995b) for some further thoughts on knowledge as intervention).

The centrality of the concept of intervention is further reinforced when we consider that the choice made by the intervener at any particular moment to self-reflect (to focus on his or her *own* identity, or the power–knowledge formations giving meaning to that identity) also involves an *act* of judgement, and is therefore interventionary. Indeed, acts of self-reflection are qualitatively similar to other acts, such as acts of observation or communication that form a significant part of systems methods.

There is one final point that should be made before moving on. We should note that preserving the notion of the subject that plays an active role in maintaining or transforming power–knowledge formations allows us to avoid one of the most important criticisms Habermas (1985) levels at Foucault. Habermas's argument, in simplified form, is that, by viewing power in association with knowledge rather than in the hands of particular people, there is no longer any justification for overthrowing oppressors. In the perspective outlined here, the fact that power–knowledge formations are valorised, and the fact that subjects can reinforce or challenge these formations, allows us to evaluate the actions of subjects in terms of their perceived positive or negative effects on power–knowledge. Acting against perceived oppressors is therefore quite justifiable: by challenging the offending subject we may indeed have an impact on the power–knowledge which facilitates the continuance of the oppression (although such a result cannot be guaranteed).

So far, I have presented the "bare bones" of a philosophy that I believe will be useful in helping us develop our understanding of systemic intervention, and in particular the theory and practice of mixing methods. Before moving on to methodology, however, let me first address the paradigm problem.

The Paradigm Problem

It is clear from earlier discussions of the paradigm problem that most authors (Jackson, 1993a excepted) now recognise that there is no neutral space outside the paradigm debate from which to argue for methodological pluralism. For Midgley (1989a, b, 1990b, 1992c), this means accepting that critical systems thinkers are trying to establish the foundations for a new paradigm. It is therefore inappropriate to claim that we can contextualise other paradigms. Rather, we "import" ideas and methods from other paradigms, reinterpreting them in our own terms. Flood and Romm (1995b) see the irony of the claim to pluralism given the inevitability of these acts of reinterpretation, so they talk in terms of "paradigm (in)commensurability". Paradigms are commensurable in the sense that we can draw upon ideas from a variety of sources, but they are also *in*commensurable in the sense that we can never appreciate those ideas exactly as their original advocates do.

Now, it seems to me that resorting to a phrase like "paradigm (in)commensurability" expresses the irony of the paradigm problem very well, but it also indicates the "bluntness" of the language of paradigms in helping us deal with the relationships between our own ideas and the ideas of others. When Kuhn (1962) first popularised the term "paradigm", his insights were revelatory for many philosophers of science: previously, science had been seen as an activity that allowed incremental progress by continually developing our store of knowledge. However, this older view did not take account of the experiences of scientists who often found themselves involved in lengthy theoretical debates with others. When new knowledge came along, old ideas didn't die easily: they were often defended by their advocates for years to come. When Kuhn suggested that different groups of scientists make different paradigmatic assumptions, and that one view eventually *replaces* the other (rather than simply building upon it), this seemed to explain the difficulties people experienced in convincing others of their point of view. For this reason, I would suggest that the language of paradigms has been very important.

Nevertheless, the first indications of its bluntness were identified quite early on. For instance, Masterman (1970) points out that Kuhn uses the term "paradigm" in a large number of different ways—Kuhn cannot explain every aspect of his position without doing so. While the language of paradigms has certainly generated insights, and I have used it on a number of occasions myself, I now wish to argue that its inadequacies become transparent in the light of a consideration of subject–knowledge dynamics. If subjects play an active part in the process of maintaining or transforming power–knowledge formations—and the term "subject" represents any participant in this process that is *identified* (whether this is an individual, a group, a community or a society)—then our language must be capable of describing the assumptions made by any of these. The term "paradigm" usually refers to a set of assumptions made by a scientific community, not any other kind of subject. The vagueness of the term already becomes problematic when we ask questions like "how many people, or groups of people, does it take to make a scientific community?" But once we go to the level of the individual who is building his or her own unique perspective, the language of paradigms has severe limitations.

It is for this reason that I believe Gregory (1992) has made a vital contribution in focusing on what happens when the *individual researcher* seeks to learn from another. As explained earlier, she argues that every time one person listens to another whose thinking is based in a different paradigm, he or she can only interpret what they are saying through his or her own terms of reference. However, this does not mean communication is impossible—just that care is needed not to be either dismissive or to think that full understanding in the others' terms has ever been achieved. Note that Gregory still refers to people's ideas being based in different paradigms. However, I would argue that, even when we are talking about people who claim to share the *same* paradigm, the basic point still holds that communication between people is possible, but each interprets the other's ideas in his or her own terms. We might wish to retain the concept of "paradigm" to refer to major differences between research communities on basic assumptions (while recognising that what constitutes a "research community" will remain open to challenge), but I suggest that introducing the idea of individuals learning from one another significantly enhances our understanding. The paradigm problem has been tackled, then, by complementing our thinking about paradigms with a theory of how researchers from different backgrounds can learn from each other, but only in their own terms.

Methodology

So far in this section I have proposed some philosophical developments and a new approach to the paradigm problem. We can now begin to look at how the *methodology* of systemic intervention, in particular the theory and practice of mixing methods, might also be developed.

We can begin by asking how the idea of subject–knowledge dynamics might help us understand the nature of critical action. For a start, we are subjects ourselves. We are therefore caught up in processes of maintaining and challenging power–knowledge formations on a day-to-day basis. There is no escape from this. But, if there are different possibilities for knowledge and identity, we can make value judgements about which forms of knowledge we wish to promote, which identities we wish to accept, and what we want to reject and challenge. This, essentially, is the basis of critical action, which can be represented as a *cycle* of critique, judgement and action (Figure 10.6).

There is a smooth line running from *critique* (revealing different possibilities for knowledge and identity), through *judgement* (choosing between

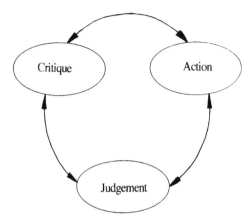

Figure 10.6 The critical action cycle

alternative knowledges and identities), and on again through *action* (based on the judgements already made). Each of these aspects of critical action can be seen in terms of systems methodology. Let us look at them in turn, starting with *critique*.

Critique, when translated into the terms of systems methodology, is about exploring different possible boundary judgements (see also Churchman, 1970, 1979; Ulrich, 1983; Midgley, 1992d). If one widens the boundaries of exploration, one is likely to sweep in new forms of knowledge. These in turn allow the exploration of different possible identities for the people involved. A simple example should demonstrate. Let us say that a researcher is working with a car manufacturer. If she sees what she is doing as working with an organisation in a business environment, she will probably draw upon economic forms of knowledge, and the likely identity people will adopt is the traditional identity of "manager". Alternatively, if she decides to see the organisation as part of a natural environment, she is more likely to draw upon ecological forms of knowledge, enabling people to opt for the identity of "conservationist" or "planetary steward". Similarly, if she sees the organisation as part of a local community, she is likely to sweep in considerations of social justice, enabling people to adopt the identity of "community leader" or "good employer". So, exploring boundaries allows for the consideration of different forms of knowledge and different social identities.

Now, there are a number of different approaches to exploring boundaries, but they basically fall into two categories: those that focus on *what* is included, excluded and marginalised in analyses, and those that focus on *who* should participate in discussion about what is to be included.

There are several different techniques that can be used to explore the "what" and "who" questions. In terms of *what* should be included, it is possible to use some of the questions from Ulrich's (1983) methodology of critical systems heuristics, which are specifically designed to stimulate debate about boundaries. It is also possible to use creativity enhancing techniques, such as brainstorming and idea-writing, which allow for new issues to be swept in (Flood, 1995a).

However, it is important to remain aware that the question of *who* should participate in discussions is just as important as *what* is discussed. This is because different stakeholders already start with different identities, suggesting that they may be able to draw upon different forms of knowledge. Once again, Ulrich (1983) has some boundary questions relating to who should be involved, but there are also other techniques that can be employed to sweep in different stakeholder views. One method that Midgley and Milne (1995) use is expansion of the community of stakeholders through a rolling programme of recommendations, where each stakeholder recommends others with different views until the only people being recommended are those already identified.

It is also important to consider *how* stakeholders can best become involved in the process of boundary setting. In some cases, when open communication seems possible, group work with a variety of stakeholders might be preferable so that they can learn from one another and develop their views. However, in other situations (such as when there is a reluctance on the part of some people to talk openly), discussions might need to be held in individual interviews or single stakeholder groups to allow people space to explore different perspectives confidentially. One thing I must stress here is that critique based on boundary exploration does not *free* people from the effects of power. It simply gives people more scope to judge who they are, what situation they are in, and how they should act in a manner they regard as positive.

Next we can consider *judgement*. In Figure 10.6, judgement is the pivot between critique and action. Having developed some interpretations through critique of the situations people find themselves in, a process is needed to judge which forms of knowledge and identity should be promoted (i.e. what boundaries to accept, albeit temporarily) and, following on from this, which methods should be used to pursue action. This process is the creative design of methods discussed earlier. Issues related to choice between boundaries and the pursuit of action are expressed in the form of research questions. Typical questions might be, "should we involve clients in reviewing our strategy?", "if we do this, what will the effects be?" and "how should we proceed?" Over the course of an intervention, numerous questions are likely to emerge. Some will be answered directly, but others will require the use of systems methods to explore possible answers.

The creative design of methods allows us to generate a set of dynamically evolving questions and a set of methods following from these, but there will not necessarily be a one-to-one correspondence between questions and methods. Usually, a synthesis of methods needs to be produced that is different from the sum of its parts (Midgley, 1997a).

So, we have dealt with *critique* (exploring different possibilities for knowledge and identity) and *judgement* (about which knowledges and identities to promote and what forms of action should be taken). It now just remains to say that *action* is taken based on the judgements already made about appropriate methods. Of course, the whole cycle can be re-entered, or can be operated in reverse order, as and when it is considered appropriate to do so.

CONCLUSION

Over the course of this chapter I have reviewed five different approaches to mixing methods that have been developed in the literature on critical systems thinking. This represents quite a substantial resource of ideas, and I have attempted to use this resource to reflect on the possibility of further developing systemic intervention and the theory and practice of mixing methods. I have produced the skeleton of an approach to systemic intervention that is true to the spirit of critical systems thinking, but also incorporates some new ideas. In particular, I have outlined a philosophical perspective—"subject–knowledge dynamics"—that respects the Foucaulvian insight into the relationship of power with knowledge. However, it avoids the trap of pessimism about knowledge and action by clarifying the need to see relationships between subjects and power-knowledge as co-constructive. The idea of the active, intervening subject is therefore preserved. This then allows for a fresh approach to the language of paradigms, which can be supplemented by an understanding of communication between individuals (people can only interpret the ideas of others in their own terms, but this does not mean that their perspectives remain unchanged). Finally, I have argued that these ideas suggest the need for a methodology that seeks to open minds to alternative knowledge sources and ways of defining subjects' identities and roles. The practice of critically exploring boundaries (of knowledge, and of the involvement of subjects in generating that knowledge) is therefore essential. Once different possibilities for knowledge have been opened up, judgements about ways forward can be made. These judgements involve the generation of a dynamic system of research questions, and methods can be selected, (re)designed and related together in response. Lastly, we should note that the action that flows from the implementation of the methods may give rise to the emergence of new issues, and the cycle of intervention may therefore be resumed. My hope is that this skeletal outline of a new systems methodology will inspire further critical and systemic research, and I look forward to a continued development of the ideas.

REFERENCES

Banathy, B.H. (1984). *Systems Design in the Context of Human Activity Systems.* International Systems Institute, Carmel, CA.

Banathy, B.H. (1987). Choosing design methods. In *Proceedings of the 31st Annual Meeting of the International Society for General Systems Research*, held in Budapest, Hungary, pp. 54–63.

Banathy, B.H. (1988). Matching design methods to system type. *Systems Research*, **5**, 27–34.

Bernstein, R.J. (1991). *The New Constellation.* Polity Press, Cambridge.

Brauer, T. (1995). Do brahmins dream of electric sheep? In B. Bergvall-Kåreborn (ed.) *Systems Thinking, Government Policy and Decision Making.* International Society for the Systems Sciences, Louisville, KY.

Brocklesby, J. (1994). Let the jury decide: assessing the cultural feasibility of Total Systems Intervention. *Systems Practice*, **7**, 75–86.

Brown, M. (1996). A framework for assessing participation. In R.L. Flood and N.R.A. Romm (eds) *Critical Systems Thinking: Current Research and Practice.* Plenum, New York.

Burrell, G. and Morgan, G. (1979). *Sociological Paradigms and Organizational Analysis.* Heinemann, London.

Carter, P., Jackson, M.C., Jackson, N. and Keys, P. (1987). Community OR at Hull University. *Dragon*, **2**, special issue.

Churchman, C.W. (1970). Operations research as a profession. *Management Science*, **17**, B37–B53.

Churchman, C.W. (1979). *The Systems Approach and its Enemies.* Basic Books, New York.

Cohen, C. and Midgley, G. (1994). *The North Humberside Diversion from Custody Project for Mentally Disordered Offenders: Research Report.* Centre for Systems Studies, Hull.

Cummings, S. (1994). An open letter to Total Systems Intervention (TSI) and friends: a postmodern remedy to make everybody feel better. *Systems Practice*, **7**, 575–587.

de Geus, A.P. (1994). Modeling to predict or to learn? In J.D.W. Morecroft and J.D. Sterman (eds) *Modeling for Learning Organizations.* Productivity Press, Portland, OR.

Dreyfus, H.L. and Rabinow, P. (1982). *Michel Foucault: Beyond Structuralism and Hermeneutics.* Harvester Press, Hemel Hempstead.

Dutt, P.K. (1994). Problem contexts—a consultant's perspective. *Systems Practice*, **7**, 539–550.

Eckersley, R. (1992). *Environmentalism and Political Theory: Toward an Ecocentric Approach*, UCL Press, London.

Eden, C., Jones, S. and Sims, D. (1983). *Messing About in Problems.* Pergamon, Oxford.

Elstob, M. (1992). Review of "Creative Problem Solving: Total Systems Intervention" by R.L. Flood and M.C. Jackson. *Kybernetes*, **21**, 62–63.

Fairtlough, G.H. (1989). Systems practice from the start: some experience in a biotechnology company. *Systems Practice*, **2**, 397–412.

Fairtlough, G.H. (1991a). Habermas' concept of "lifeworld". *Systems Practice*, **4**, 547–563.

Fairtlough, G.H. (1991b). Review of "Liberating Systems Theory" by R.L. Flood. *Systems Practice*, **4**, 263–271.

Fay, B. (1975). *Social Theory and Political Practice.* George Allen and Unwin, London.

Flood, R.L. (1989a). Six scenarios for the future of systems "problem solving". *Systems Practice*, **2**, 75–99.

Flood, R.L. (1989b). Archaeology of (Systems) Inquiry. *Systems Practice*, **2**, 117–124.

Flood, R.L. (1990). *Liberating Systems Theory*. Plenum, New York.

Flood, R.L. (1995a). *Solving Problem Solving*. Wiley, Chichester.

Flood, R.L. (1995b). Total Systems Intervention (TSI): a reconstitution. *Journal of the Operational Research Society*, **46**, 174–191.

Flood, R.L. (1995c). Plenary address to the 1st annual China–Japan–UK conference on systems methodology, held in Beijing, China, on 23–25 May 1995.

Flood, R.L. and Jackson, M.C. (1991a). *Critical Systems Thinking: Directed Readings*. Wiley, Chichester.

Flood, R.L. and Jackson, M.C. (1991b). *Creative Problem Solving: Total Systems Intervention*. Wiley, Chichester.

Flood, R.L. and Jackson, M.C. (1991c). Critical systems heuristics: application of an emancipatory approach for police strategy toward the carrying of offensive weapons. *Systems Practice*, **4**, 283–302.

Flood, R.L. and Romm, N.R.A. (1995a). Enhancing the process of choice in TSI, and improving chances of tackling coercion. *Systems Practice*, **8**, 377–408.

Flood, R.L. and Romm, N.R.A. (1995b). Diversity management: theory in action. *Systems Practice*, **8**, 469–482.

Foucault, M. (1972). *The Archaeology of Knowledge*. Tavistock, London.

Foucault, M. (1976). *The History of Sexuality, Volume 1: An Introduction*. Penguin, London.

Foucault, M. (1980). *Power/Knowledge: Selected Interviews and Other Writings—1972–1977*, C. Gordon (ed.). Harvester Press, Brighton.

Ghosal, A. (1992). Review of "Creative Problem Solving: Total Systems Intervention" by R.L. Flood and M.C. Jackson. *SCIMA*, **21**, 39–40.

Giddens, A. (1985). Reason without revolution? Habermas's theorie des kommunikativen handelns. In R.J. Bernstein (ed.) *Habermas and Modernity*. Polity Press, Cambridge.

Green, S.M. (1993a). Total Systems Intervention: a practitioner's critique. *Systems Practice*, **6**, 71–79.

Green, S.M. (1993b). Total Systems Intervention: a trial by jury. *Systems Practice*, **6**, 295–299.

Gregory, W.J. (1990). Critical Systems Thinking and LST: how "liberating" are contemporary critical and liberating systems approaches? In *Toward a Just Society for Future Generations. Volume I: Systems Design*. Proceedings of the 34th Annual Meeting of the International Society for the Systems Sciences, held in Portland, Oregon (USA), 8–13 July, 1990.

Gregory, W.J. (1992). *Critical Systems Thinking and Pluralism: A New Constellation*. Ph.D. thesis, City University, London.

Gregory, W.J. (1994). Critical appreciation: thinking, speaking and acting critically. In B. Brady and L. Peeno (eds) *New Systems Thinking and Action for a New Century, Volume II*. International Society for the Systems Sciences, Louisville, Kentucky, pp. 1555–1574.

Gregory, W.J. (1996). Dealing with diversity. In R.L. Flood and N.R.A. Romm (eds) *Critical Systems Thinking: Current Research and Practice*. Plenum, New York.

Gregory, W.J., Romm, N.R.A. and Walsh, M.P. (1994). *The Trent Quality Initiative: A Multi-Agency Evaluation of Quality Standards in the National Health Service*. Centre for Systems Studies, Hull.

Habermas, J. (1972). *Knowledge and Human Interests*. Heinemann, London.

Habermas, J. (1976). *Communication and the Evolution of Society* (English ed., 1979). Heinemann, London.

Habermas, J. (1984a). *The Theory of Communicative Action, Volume One: Reason and the Rationalisation of Society*. Polity Press, Cambridge.

Habermas, J. (1984b). *The Theory of Communicative Action, Volume Two: The Critique of Functionalist Reason*. Polity Press, Cambridge.

Habermas, J. (1985). *The Philosophical Discourse of Modernity: Twelve Lectures* (English ed., 1987). Polity Press, Cambridge.

Ho, J.K.K. (1994). Is Total Systems Intervention (TSI) no better than common sense and not necessarily related to Critical Systems Thinking (CST)? *Systems Practice*, **7**, 569–573.

Hollway, W. (1991). *Work Psychology and Organizational Behaviour: Managing the Individual at Work*. Sage, London.

Ivanov, K. (1991). Critical Systems Thinking and information technology. *Journal of Applied Systems Analysis*, **18**, 39–55.

Jackson, M.C. (1982). The nature of soft systems thinking: the work of Churchman, Ackoff and Checkland. *Journal of Applied Systems Analysis*, **9**, 17–29.

Jackson, M.C. (1985a). Systems inquiring competence and organisational analysis. In *Proceedings of the 1985 Meeting of the International Society for General Systems Research*, pp. 522–530.

Jackson, M.C. (1985b). The itinerary of a critical approach: review of Ulrich's "Critical Heuristics of Social Planning". *Journal of the Operational Research Society*, **36**, 878–881.

Jackson, M.C. (1987a). Present positions and future prospects in management science. *Omega*, **15**, 455–466.

Jackson, M.C. (1987b). New directions in management science. In M.C. Jackson and P. Keys (eds) *New Directions in Management Science*. Gower, Aldershot.

Jackson, M.C. (1990). Beyond a System of Systems Methodologies. *Journal of the Operational Research Society*, **41**, 657–668.

Jackson, M.C. (1991a). *Systems Methodology for the Management Sciences*. Plenum, New York.

Jackson, M.C. (1991b). The origins and nature of critical systems thinking. *Systems Practice*, **4**, 131–149.

Jackson, M.C. (1992). With friends like this . . .. A comment on Mingers' "Recent developments in critical management science". *Journal of the Operational Research Society*, **43**, 729–731.

Jackson, M.C. (1993a). Don't bite my finger: Haridimos Tsoukas' critical evaluation of Total Systems Intervention. *Systems Practice*, **6**, 289–294.

Jackson, M.C. (1993b). The System of Systems Methodologies: a guide to researchers. *Journal of the Operational Research Society*, **44**, 208–209.

Jackson, M.C. (1993c). How to cause anguish without even trying: a reply to Graham Jones. *Journal of the Operational Research Society*, **44**, 848–849.

Jackson, M.C. (1997). *Towards Coherent Pluralism in Management Science*. Lincoln School of Management Working Paper 16, University of Lincolnshire & Humberside, Lincoln.

Jackson, M.C. and Keys, P. (1984). Towards a System of Systems Methodologies. *Journal of the Operational Research Society*, **35**, 473–486.

Jackson, N. and Carter, P. (1991). In defence of paradigm incommensurability. *Organization Studies*, **12**, 109–127.

Jones, G.C. (1993). OR practice, systems methodologies, and the need to do better. *Journal of the Operational Research Society*, **44**, 845–848.

Kelly, G.A. (1955). *The Psychology of Personal Constructs. Volume One: A Theory of Personality.* W.W. Norton, New York.

Keys, P. (1988). A methodology for methodology choice. *Systems Research*, **5**, 65–76.

Kuhn, T. (1962). *The Structure of Scientific Revolutions.* University of Chicago Press, Chicago, IL.

Mansell, G. (1991). Methodology choice in a coercive context. *Systems Practice*, **4**, 37–46.

Masterman, M. (1970). The nature of a paradigm. In I. Lakatos and A. Musgrave (eds) *Criticism and the Growth of Knowledge.* Cambridge University Press, London.

Midgley, G. (1988). *A Systems Analysis and Evaluation of Microjob—A Vocational Rehabilitation and Information Technology Training Centre for People with Disabilities.* M.Phil. thesis, City University, London.

Midgley, G. (1989a). Critical systems and the problem of pluralism. *Cybernetics and Systems*, **20**, 219–231.

Midgley, G. (1989b). Critical systems: the theory and practice of partitioning methodologies. In *Proceedings of the 33rd Annual Meeting of the International Society for General Systems Research (Volume II)*, held in Edinburgh, Scotland, on 2–7 July 1989.

Midgley, G. (1990a). Creative methodology design. *Systemist*, **12**, 108–113.

Midgley, G. (1990b). Critical systems and methodological pluralism. In *Toward a Just Society for Future Generations, Vol. I. Systems Design*, Proceedings of the 34th Annual Conference of the International Society for the Systems Sciences, Portland, Oregon, 8–13 July, 1990.

Midgley, G. (1992a). Power and languages of co-operation: a critical systems perspective. In *Sistemica '92: Ira Conferencia Internacional de Trabajo del Instituto Andino de Sistemas (IAS)*, held in Lima, Peru, on 23–28 August 1992.

Midgley, G. (1992b). *Unity and Pluralism.* Ph.D. thesis, City University, London.

Midgley, G. (1992c). Pluralism and the legitimation of systems science. *Systems Practice*, **5**, 147–172.

Midgley, G. (1992d). The sacred and profane in critical systems thinking. *Systems Practice*, **5**, 5–16.

Midgley, G. (1994). Ecology and the poverty of humanism: a critical systems perspective. *Systems Research*, **11**, 67–76.

Midgley, G. (1995). What is this thing called critical systems thinking? In K. Ellis et al (eds) *Critical Issues in Systems Theory and Practice.* Plenum, New York.

Midgley, G. (1996). Evaluation and change in service systems for people with disabilities: a critical systems perspective. *Evaluation*, **2**, 67–84.

Midgley, G. (1997a). Understanding methodology choice in TSI: from the oblique use of methods to their creative design. *Systems Practice*, **10**, 305–319.

Midgley, G. (1997b). Dealing with coercion: critical systems heuristics and beyond. *Systems Practice*, **10**, 37–57.

Midgley, G. and Floyd, M. (1988). *Microjob: A Computer Training Service for People with Disabilities.* Rehabilitation Resource Centre, London.

Midgley, G. and Floyd, M. (1990). Vocational training in the use of new technologies for people with disabilities. *Behaviour and Information Technology*, **9**, 409–424.

Midgley, G. and Milne, A. (1995). Creating employment opportunities for people with mental health problems: a feasibility study for new initiatives. *Journal of the Operational Research Society*, **46**, 35–42.

Midgley, G., Munlo, I. and Brown, M. (1997). *Sharing Power: Integrating User Involvement and Multi-Agency Working to Improve Housing for Older People.* Policy Press, Bristol.

Mingers, J. (1980). Towards an appropriate social theory for applied systems thinking: critical theory and soft systems methodology. *Journal of Applied Systems Analysis*, **7**, 41–50.

Mingers, J. (1992a). Recent developments in critical management science. *Journal of the Operational Research Society*, **43**, 1–10.

Mingers, J. (1992b). Technical, practical and critical OR—past, present and future? In M. Alvesson and H. Willmott (eds) *Critical Management Studies*. Sage, London.

Mingers, J. (1992c). What are real friends for? A reply to Mike Jackson. *Journal of the Operational Research Society*, **43**, 732–735.

Mingers, J. (1993). The System of Systems Methodologies—a reply to Schecter. *Journal of the Operational Research Society*, **44**, 206–208.

Morgan, G. (1986). *Images of Organisation*. Sage, London.

Oliga, J.C. (1988). Methodological foundations of systems methodologies. *Systems Practice*, **1**, 87–112.

Popper, K.R. (1959). *The Logic of Scientific Discovery*. Harper, New York.

Ragsdell, G. (1996). Creativity and problem solving. In R.L. Flood and N.R.A. Romm (eds) *Critical Systems Thinking: Current Research and Practice*. Plenum, New York.

Reed, M. (1985). *Redirections in Organizational Analysis*. Tavistock, London.

Romm, N.R.A. (1994). *Continuing Tensions between Soft Systems Methodology and Critical Systems Heuristics*. Centre for Systems Studies, University of Hull, Working Paper Number 5.

Romm, N.R.A. (1995a). Some anomalies in Ulrich's critical inquiry and problem-solving approach. In K. Ellis et al (eds) *Critical Issues in Systems Theory and Practice*. Plenum, New York.

Romm, N.R.A. (1995b). Knowing as intervention: reflections on the application of systems ideas. *Systems Practice*, **8**, 137–167.

Schecter, D. (1991). Critical systems thinking in the 1980s: a connective summary. In R.L. Flood and M.C. Jackson (eds) *Critical Systems Thinking: Directed Readings*. Wiley, Chichester.

Schecter, D. (1993). In defence of the system of systems methodologies: some comments on the Mingers/Jackson debate. *Journal of the Operational Research Society*, **44**, 205–206.

Smart, B. (1983). *Foucault, Marxism and Critique*. Routledge and Kegan Paul, London.

Taket, A. (1992). Review of "Creative Problem Solving: Total Systems Intervention" by R.L. Flood and M.C. Jackson. *Journal of the Operational Research Society*, **43**, 1013–1016.

Tsoukas, H. (1992). Panoptic reason and the search for totality: a critical assessment of the critical systems perspective. *Human Relations*, **45**, 637–657.

Tsoukas, H. (1993a). The road to emancipation is through organizational development: a critical evaluation of total systems intervention. *Systems Practice*, **6**, 53–70.

Tsoukas, H. (1993b). "By their fruits shall ye know them": a reply to Jackson, Green, and Midgley. *Systems Practice*, **6**, 311–317.

Ulrich, W. (1983). *Critical Heuristics of Social Planning: A New Approach to Practical Philosophy*. Haupt, Berne.

Ulrich, W. (1988). Systems thinking, systems practice and practical philosophy: a program of research. *Systems Practice*, **1**, 137–163.

Ulrich, W. (1993). Some difficulties of ecological thinking, considered from a critical systems perspective: a plea for critical holism. *Systems Practice*, **6**, 583–611.

Valero-Silva, N. (1994). Michel Foucault: power, knowledge and the "critical ontology of ourselves". *Systemist*, **16**, 211–223.

Valero-Silva, N. (1995a). The philosophical foundations of critical systems thinking: beyond Habermas, towards Foucault. In K. Ellis et al (eds) *Critical Issues in Systems Theory and Practice.* Plenum, New York.

Valero-Silva, N. (1995b). A reflection on the work of Michel Foucault and its implications for critical systems thinking. In B. Bergvall-Kåreborn (ed.) *Systems Thinking, Government Policy and Decision Making.* International Society for the Systems Science, Louisville.

Valero-Silva, N. (1996). A Foucauldian reflection on critical systems thinking. In R.L. Flood and N.R.A. Romm (eds) *Critical Systems Thinking: Current Research and Practice.* Plenum, New York.

Wilby, J.M. (1996). Developing Total Systems Intervention (TSI): the critical review mode. *Systems Practice,* **9**, 231–261.

Willmott, H. (1989). OR as a problem situation: from Soft Systems Methodology to critical science. In M.C. Jackson, P. Keys and S.A. Cropper (eds) *OR and the Social Sciences.* Plenum, New York.

Willmott, H. (1993). Breaking the paradigm mentality. *Organization Studies,* **14**, 681–719.

Chapter 11

From Metatheory to "Multimethodology"

ROBERT FLOOD AND NORMA ROMM

INTRODUCTION

In this chapter we will introduce our thinking on the issue of so-called "multi-methodology".[1,2] This we do in two main parts. First, we review key meta-theoretical debates and identify our complementarist[3] position in (beyond)

---

[1] The reader who wishes to get straight to the practical implications of the following theoretical work can move right away to the section on triple loop learning (see page 312). We hope then that the reader will engage in our theoretical discussion to some extent since this helps to sensitise us to fundamental issues that make triple loop learning so important. We have done our best to make the theoretical section accessible to non-theoreticians by extracting supporting points to our argument from the main framework of the chapter and lodging them in footnotes.

[2] This chapter presents a possible deeper intended meaning of the approach to "problem solving" called Total Systems Intervention (TSI). A full methodological account of TSI was first published by Flood and Jackson (1991a). This was supported at that time by a (meta)theoretical and historical account of critical systems thinking from where TSI was conceived (Flood and Jackson, 1991b). Recent developments in TSI are reported in Flood (1995), and then in Flood (1996a) where the desirability of a name change to Local Systemic Intervention is introduced. Why Local and Systemic are more relevant terms than, respectively, Total and Systems, is in a way another side to the argument of this chapter. People wishing to explore all sides of the argument in this chapter are referred to Flood and Romm (1996a). People wishing to sample recent work in critical systems thinking are referred to Flood and Romm (1996b).

[3] Complementarism is an attempt to preserve diversity in different spheres of thought and action.

Multimethodology: The Theory and Practice of Combining Management Science Methodologies.
Edited by John Mingers and Anthony Gill.
© 1997 John Wiley & Sons Ltd.

them. The review entails analysing metatheory in the domains of philosophy and the history of knowledge, and then theory and methodology. This we do by providing a section on each one. Second, we build on the findings of the first part by introducing our complementarist brand of metatheory, that we call "diversity management", before reviewing our complementarist brand of "multimethodology", that we call "triple loop learning".[4] This we do by providing two more sections, one on each brand. So, we have chosen to progress from metatheory in the first part of the chapter to "multimethodology" in the second part. The two parts (in four sections) are put between background thinking to start with and their summary in the concluding section.

In our background thinking we move very quickly between important milestones in understanding about the notion and validity of knowledge. This at least helps us to raise a structure with scions on which we hang more detail as we move from metatheory to "multimethodology". So, let's start at a pace and get straight into the background.

BACKGROUND

Until the eighteenth century the Christian church in Europe determined the nature of knowledge of the world and the position of people within society. The Church elevated a religious philosophy based on theological speculation that generated ideas which cannot be proven or disproven. A literal faith in the Scriptures was called for, for the good of all people. In the eighteenth century the counter-project of Enlightenment was launched. Enlightenment theorists argued that human thought is able independent of the Scriptures to understand and/or control the world. Enlightenment for the most part was built on a mode of thought termed critical scientific rationalism. The idea of critical scientific rationalism was to seek out scientific truth that would support human progress and hence lead to emancipation. The human condition would be improved through human reason (rationality) and human experience (empiricism). Reason and empiricism would facilitate the rational organisation of society.

As the project of Enlightenment progressed, ideology critique took up a

---

Preservation of diversity enhances chances people have to manage intelligently and responsibly the most exacting issues that arise in organisational and societal affairs. The question for complementarism is, How can theoreticians and interventionists find a way that satisfactorily allows us to theorise and act with *different notions of the world* at the same time whilst maintaining overall emancipatory practice?

[4] We are not the first to use the term. For example, Swieringa and Wierdsma (1992) refer to it as a way of reflecting on possible principles to be adopted. Our conception of triple loop learning was developed in the light of issues that we raise in this chapter.

leading position in social science research. It was argued that ideas serve the interests of power and that this led to there being a ruling class with ruling ideas. "The ruling ideas of each age have ever been the ideas of the ruling class" (Marx and Engels, *Communist Manifesto*, 1888, English translation). For Marx and Engels, the promise of rational scientific inquiry was to disclose truths that lay behind false conceptions of the past (cf. Simons and Billig, 1994). Marx and Engels' critical interest in Enlightenment urged laying bare and challenging dominant ideology and hence become liberatory in this sense too.

In recent times much doubt has been cast over the feasibility of rational scientific thought and ideology critique. Commentators pointed out, for example, that Marx and Engels' contribution to the project of Enlightenment was subject to its own ideology, one that "put an innocent trust in the power of reason and an optimistic faith in modernity" (Simons and Billig, 1994: 2). New studies continued the search for a sound, stable, and fair modern world. Recently, the concrete foundations of castles of modernism have worn away, crumbling into sand as they are weathered by a postmodern critique.

The postmodern critique of modernism undermines the idea of truth by raising dilemmas, doubts, and suspicions about all truth statements, and maintains that it is not possible to lay open ideological chimera. It paints the dark side of modernism. It is not possible, through modernism, to emancipate people from whatever system dominates their lives, be it Scriptures or ideas of a ruling class (which in some cases are the same thing). The project of Enlightenment had "failed". In a short-lived victory, postmodernism seemed to conclude that the essence of emancipation is, anything goes. With this goes solidity of thought, leaving a fluid and diverse world of many equally valid truths. Ironically, then, choices in a postmodern world can easily be colonised by the ruling class or its equivalent. It is this whimsicality and dark side to postmodern thought that provides modernism with a second chance; a chance to come up with a reworked account of ideology critique that provides a retort to an unfettered postmodern critique. The reworked account, however, will not be a reinstatement of modernism. The critique will tack its course between modernism and postmodernism, succumbing to neither. It unveils a post-critical position that we put forward as an essential argument which any coherent approach to "multimethodology" must, indeed will, reflect.

Milestones in understanding about the notion and validity of knowledge are now in position, setting us up for a detailed investigation into metatheory. We start our metatheoretical investigation in the domain of philosophy and the history of knowledge. The presentation, as in the background, stretches from Enlightenment to postmodernism, but on the way we spend more time, especially with a number of the better known scholars whose arguments are central to understanding complementarist metatheory and, ultimately, complementarist "multimethodology".

PHILOSOPHY AND THE HISTORY OF KNOWLEDGE

The Enlightenment

The philosophy of the Enlightenment is often understood to present a (meta)theoretical dictum. Enlightenment as mentioned in the last section came to the fore in the eighteenth century. The aim was laudable; to free people from unreason, from the idols of their mind, specifically, from the dogmas of tradition and religion, so that rational understanding of the world could ensue. The Enlightenment fought for rational analysis, seeking to identify natural connections between empirical events and, further to this, to make predictions about future events. It opened up ways for people to rethink their hitherto traditional relationship to the world.

However, the Enlightenment has been (ab)used to justify scientific developments and discoveries by grounding them in a supposed absolute foundation for knowledge construction. It was linked to a strong belief that it is necessary to adjudicate with reference to known criteria, which the Enlightenment defines. In this sense it became a metatheory that sought to provide and impose an overarching scientific methodology for theory development. The Enlightenment has a dark side.

Our lobby room for discussion entertains tension between the Enlightenment and speculative theology. Attendance in the lobby room enables researchers to confirm the profoundly different ways in which people do come to relate to their world. This corroboration was exploited by Thomas Kuhn whose metatheory about scientific progress is discussed below.

Thomas Kuhn

Many intellects, ranging from Frankfurt School authors such as Horkheimer and Adorno, to postmodern writers such as Foucault and Lyotard, have pointed out that the Enlightenment tradition became associated with forms of positivism. Positivism promised ingredients that would make concrete knowledge. The positivist belief in scientific progress towards concrete knowledge was challenged radically in Kuhn's famous and much quoted book *The Structure of Scientific Revolutions*. We incorporate Kuhn's argument in our story because it has a particular bearing on our brand of metatheory.

Kuhn cast new light on the so-claimed relentless progress of science. He argued that progression realises modes of doing science and, consequently, of understanding the world, that constitute incommensurable paradigms. He offered a metatheoretical solution to the diversity of modes of approach, arguing that through scientific revolutions new paradigms become dominant in a recurring cycle of normal and extraordinary science.[5] Normal science is where a dominant paradigm progresses in sophistication. Extraordinary science is where anomalies found in a dominant paradigm, often discovered in the process of sophistication, are exploited in a revolutionary process that dislodges the normal science paradigm from dominance and replaces it with a new one. Another period of normal science ensues as the new paradigm progresses in sophistication.

Ultimately, for Kuhn, there is no Archimedes point from which to judge superiority of paradigm. Competing paradigms employ languages and criteria of assessment to judge validity that are incommensurable. Kuhn (1970: 148) states his point as follows: "The competition between paradigms is not the sort of battle that can be resolved by proofs." Although proponents of a new paradigm may claim that they are able to solve theoretical crises which they see as characterising the old paradigm, the issue, Kuhn continues, is not hereby resolved. It cannot be resolved when "the issue is which paradigm should in the future guide research on problems many of which neither competitor can claim to resolve completely" (Kuhn, 1970: 157). Hence "a decision between alternative ways of practising science is called for". Kuhn suggests that this decision cannot be resolved by simply assessing the comparative ability of the paradigms to address issues agreed to constitute problems, for one of the issues at stake is how the problems should be addressed. As he puts it: "If there were but one set of scientific problems, one world within which to work on them, and one set of standards for their solution, paradigm competition might be settled more or less routinely by some process like counting the number of problems solved by each" (Kuhn, 1970: 147). For Kuhn, there is no one set of scientific problems, no one world, and no one set of standards for deciding between paradigms. Nevertheless, Kuhn holds out, this does not make proponents of old paradigms entrenched in a process of normal science completely deaf to arguments advanced by those proposing new types of science.

Kuhn's incommensurability[6] thesis is not a statement to the effect that

---

[5] Kuhn's commentary refers largely to theories generated by empirical natural scientists. However, he also offers a brief commentary on the way that students of social science face a diversity of perspectives (Kuhn, 1970: 164–165). The diachronic existence of a diversity of perspectives in social science has implications for the notion of evaluation. Kuhn does not elaborate on what these implications may be—but we pick up on some of these issues below.

[6] Debates in metatheory have yielded two theses: a commensurability thesis and an incommensurability thesis. Commensurability promises to hold in the frame many different paradigms. However, it poses a dilemma for practically minded researchers. The dilemma begins with the question, On what basis can choice be made between paradigms? All answers to this question are contingent on the meaning they ascribe to commensurability. One seemingly reasonable

researchers working in one paradigm are naturally deaf to arguments from researchers of other paradigms (Kuhn, 1970: 152). Deafness, he seems to think, is an example of excessive "pigheadedness"; a characteristic he leaves largely undefined. In the context in which he describes it, pigheadedness implies a propensity to close off one's thinking entirely and to resist indefinitely any thought of entertaining an alternative way of seeing or doing things. This propensity may be related to "productive careers" of researchers committed to an established tradition of normal science. And so, Kuhn argues, it is sometimes necessary for established and resistant opponents to die before a new generation of thinking can be fully brought to bear on the scientific enterprise (Kuhn, 1970: 151).

Interestingly, although Kuhn refers to incommensurability between different research traditions, he still speaks of progress in the process of doing science (Kuhn, 1970: 170–171). In keeping with his focus on the paradigmatic nature of discovery, he argues that progress does not imply progress toward the truth about the world. This is not possible since he insists that the world is paradigmatically defined. However, Kuhn hints, there are other ways of assessing progress. One criterion, for example, is whether forms of science help the community of scientists to evolve their knowledge and appreciation of research issues.

Kuhn is clear, then, that the best he can do with his incommensurability thesis is hint at the need to consider alternative views of scientific advance. He was reluctant to "specify in any detail the consequences of this alternative view of scientific advance" (Kuhn, 1970: 171). Consequently, many people have laid siege to his argument because it is regarded as simply relativistic. The theory of scientitfic revolutions seems to conclude that since there are no common standards by which to assess the relevance of paradigms, there are no standards at all. Yet, Kuhn may not have to surrender his argument so quickly, as we find a route of escape in a reference to the process of social science (Kuhn, 1970: 164).

When contrasting natural and social science, Kuhn concludes that in the latter enterprise the process of solving problems takes on a new meaning. He observes that social scientists "often tend, as the former [natural scientists]

_____

assumption on this score defines commensurability in terms of measurement by a common standard; or, in other words, the reconciliation and integration of different spheres of thought and action. Integration, however, carries more than a suggestion that the spheres must end up denatured, being reduced in meaning to comply with determining factors set in the measurement standard. Action is possible following choice of measurement standard, but this, it seems, immediately introduces reductionism rather than commensurability. The dilemma gets more complicated when turning attention to incommensurability. Incommensurability, of course, means that there is no common measurement standard, no possible way of comparing paradigms. They are fundamentally different and that is that. Action following choice of paradigm, therefore, can result in only one thing if practice is not to be contradictory. The result of choice appears to be a somewhat arbitrary adherence to a preferred paradigm. We choose to speak of (in)commensurability and that we will explain a little later.

almost never do, to defend their choice of a research problem—e.g. the effects of racial discrimination . . . —chiefly in terms of the social importance of achieving a solution".

What is considered important is contentious indeed. Consequently, in the social sciences, revolutionary switches to new paradigms are less likely to be able to destroy traces of old paradigms. Thus a student of social science is faced with a diversity of paradigms and "has constantly before him [*sic*] a number of competing and incommensurable solutions that he must ultimately evaluate for himself" (Kuhn, 1970: 165). Kuhn's statement is significant. He recognises that in the social sciences people are called upon to make choices whenever they address social issues. With Kuhn's route of escape we show in our discussion how the apparent relativism of his metatheory can be revised to lend credence to an enhanced process of choice making by researchers evaluating competing solutions.

We have paid special attention to Kuhn's argument because it provides a useful backdrop to our brand of metatheory. We believe that the term incommensurability is useful insofar as it allows us to keep in consciousness diversity and radical differences in position, which open up a wide set of theoretical choices. This alerts researchers to the nature of theoretical alternatives as alternatives and encourages researchers to encounter theoretical differences in choice making. Our metatheoretical stance is also informed by other researchers interested in the philosophy and history of knowledge. We continue our narrative by referring to such researchers, beginning with Jürgen Habermas.

Jürgen Habermas

Casting new light on Kuhn's argument, that understanding is *theory-based*, Habermas's (1971) *Knowledge and Human Interests* sets out to demonstrate that knowledge is *value-based*. Habermas contends that knowledge is a feature of people's existence that cannot be divorced from their values. He argues that knowledge and action are inextricably connected because knowledge is always tied to some purpose. Taking stock of the whole project of empirical–analytical science, applied to both the natural and social worlds, Habermas detects that the project is rooted in values and, he expresses with concern, that values are tied to the administrative apparatus of control and its purpose. The purpose of this apparatus is to use scientific inquiry to predict and control natural and social processes. The result is that empirical–analytical science controls people and reduces the human species in its potentialities. Empirical–analytical science operates within and suffers from restrictions inherent in its mode of doing (social) science research.

Habermas contends that counter-efforts to operate an interpretive approach slip into an empiricist outlook. They make meanings objects of investigation in an attempt to encase and to grasp given meanings.[7] They fail to recognise, however, that social suppression of discursive communication fixes casing around meaning. They fail to engage in quests to remove the casing. And they fail to address the question of standards of discursive engagement. The practical purposes which Habermas associates with both early and contemporary interpretive theory are linked to an agenda unable to question its own interests and purposes in the social arena. Interpretive theory has a dark side.

Habermas's metatheoretical solution in his *Knowledge and Human Interests* makes provision for the exercise of different human interests under the control of critical and conscious self-reflection. We must take control of our historical destiny through discursive reflection on goals being sought in the process of knowledge construction. The quest is to engage consciously and discursively in human interests.

Habermas's (1984, 1987) later work on the ideal speech situation continues, although from another angle, his suggestion that the human species has the potential to develop its historical path through discursive encounter. Here, however, he raises more starkly the uncertainty of the tension between a "system" which seems to be buttressed by scientific technological knowledge construction and a "lifeworld" where people are able to raise continually the question why specific foci for knowledge construction are chosen. Habermas (1993: 94) argues, albeit ambivalently, that it is possible in discursive encounter to reach consensus about values to be pursued and priorities to be set. He also suggests that such consensus seeking may be trammelled by the force of administrative technical standards of rationality and knowledge creation which can come to colonise the "lifeworld" (see Brand, 1990; Habermas, 1993: 168–170). This implies that the tension between valuation of standards is likely to be a continuing one as people attempt to engage with what he calls the project of modernity (Habermas, 1981).

However Habermas's metatheory is interpreted, it is relevant to our complementarist endeavour because it recognises and differentiates between different human interests and purposes. An important question remains, though. How can we make choices between interests and purposes while remaining accountable? Habermas accepts tension will enter the process of choice

---

[7] We have not included in our narrative the interpretive argument—popularised by Weber in the social sciences—about the distinctiveness of the subject matter of the social sciences. Since Weber's seminal writings around the start of the twentieth century, the so-called interpretive tradition has been operative in various forms of phenomenology and ethnomethodology in social theory. Its metatheoretical account of the relationship between different theories largely followed the rationale that better theoretical accounts could be determined with reference to their ability to account better for meaning-constitution in social reality. In this sense the interpretive argument still bears the mark of Enlightenment roots, with the quest for better understanding grounded in reality. What is relevant for our narrative is that the interpretive school highlighted another distinct way of doing (social) science.

making, but places accountability firmly in a process of consensus seeking. But, can choices always be made by consensus? The reader's everyday experience might demonstrate that it is rare for everyone to agree on purposes to be pursued. This is true even if consensus is sought in a critical rather than regulative way. Habermas (1993: 94) admits this but, it seems to us, leaves the issue hanging in the air. People's defence of choices that are not consensually grounded, then, appear to have no grounding at all.

The status of positivist definitions of empirical–analytical science in relation to the ability to offer progressively better, objective representation of the world, was questioned from yet more angles. The late 1960s and 1970s saw a proliferation of texts positing different answers to the metatheoretical questions raised above. This led to considerable debate between those advocating forms of positivism and their challengers. One such debate known as *Methodenstreit* is briefly reviewed below.

Methodenstreit

German social scientists entered a debate known as *Methodenstreit* (cf. *The Positivist Dispute in German Sociology*, 1969, edited by Adorno *et al*). This debate characterises some of the points of tension surrounding social science research. Tension sparked between those who argued for a positivist, value-free methodology adopted from the natural sciences,[8] and those who believed the social sciences should develop its own methodology that acknowledges the influences of values on theoretical interpretation.

In one sense it can be claimed that positivists won the dispute. The dominant epistemological position subsequently expounded in the social science literature was and remains positivism. Positivism reduced metatheory to justification of forms of empiricist approaches to doing science. Empirical evidence came to be seen in most circles as the ultimate arbiter between theories.

An interesting commentary on the victory raises new issues for metatheory. The commentary says that the victory hardly came about because of the

---

[8] The definition of positivism used here and indeed by those criticising its premises in the *Methodenstreit*, embraced versions of inductivism as well as (Popperian) hypothetico-deductivism. The inclusion of Popper under the positivist category by non-positivists in the dispute—such as Habermas—was later followed up by other critics of the position. These included people from the so-called Marxist realist camp, such as Benton (1977) and Keat and Urry (1982). What the Popperian position added to the discussion about science was that specific statements could never be verified with certainty—but only tentatively corroborated (cf. Romm, 1991: 38–39). What he argued though is that we can know when a set of statements (a theory) is better than another in offering a truer representation or explanation of reality. This is linked to his assertion that false statements can be weeded out. Realist argumentation, however, questioned the Popperian account, arguing that it was still too positivistically oriented to finding out about laws in natural and social reality, rather than trying to explain these in terms of hidden mechanisms.

strength of the better argument. A more plausible explanation might be located in direct and indirect tactics and strategies of institutional forces where vested interests in maintaining positivism as dominant come into play (Bourdieu, 1975; Bleicher, 1982; Ashley and Orenstein, 1985). For example, applications for grants to support social science research are in the main handled and vetted by researchers whose reputations are built on published work of a positivist ilk. Picou, Wells and Nyberg (1978) identified funding structures as a cause of theoretical closure and methodological monism. Editors of many, if not most, key journals are researchers of the same type, whose preferences for referees, and papers to publish, are influenced by a commitment to positivism. Morgan (1984) talked about academic institutional constraints that prevent innovation.

These factors and others may be responsible for the positivist content of much of today's social science literature. The influence of these forces are of great importance to metatheory because they force a paucity of theoretical options. Furthermore, the idea that these forces are of significance adds another dimension to both Kuhn's[9] and Habermas's arguments. Tactical and strategic dimensions demand tactical and strategic solutions, ones that we introduce below.

Postmodernism

Postmodernism challenges the foundations of modernist thought. The postmodern critique of modernism undermines its idea of truth and fairness through reason by raising dilemmas, doubts, and suspicions about all truth statements. Forerunners of postmodern thought include Feyerabend and Quine. Challenges such as those propounded in Feyerabend's (1975) widely cited *Against Method*, and Quine's (1964) *From a Logical Point of View*, managed to gain some momentum, at least in lobby rooms where the philosophy of natural science and social science were being debated. They helped to keep alive a critique of the positivist view of science and metatheory.

Feyerabend's shocking metatheoretical contention stated that in the realm of methodology, anything goes. He highlighted a number of core developments to support his case.

- Already in 1975 Feyerabend was struck by the proliferation of theories that gave rise to much theoretical diversity.
- A consequence of theoretical diversity was recognition in some quarters of the importance of non-rational factors in the development of science.

---

[9] Kuhn does mention issues such as career-linked adherence to paradigms, but he does not make a play on this. Instead he concentrates on how conversion to new ways of thinking may occur (Kuhn, 1970: 155–159).

- Another consequence of theoretical diversity was a need to reject the empiricist criterion of cognitive significance because of incommensurability between modes of understanding our experience.

Western science ignored such issues in its relentless quest for objective knowledge. Feyerabend thus concluded that, ultimately, Western science has become a new form of dogmatism. Furthermore, he criticised Western science for being over-intellectual and hence elitist. Western science has a dark side.

Feyerabend's metatheoretical solution did not go as far as rejecting science or scientific practice(s). He did, however, criticise the elevated status of science. He aimed to sensitise scientific practitioners and other members of society to the danger that science is a potential instrument of coercion. This will always be a concern if science continues to be seen as a process of antiseptically discovering truth by testing theories against evidence. The shockwaves of Feyerabend's understanding of modern science kindled debate about the possibility of doing science in the light of, what he argued to be, the impossibility of adjudication between theoretical and methodological choices. Quine had pre-empted this debate. Quine challenged the distinction between so-called synthetic (empirically grounded) and analytic statements. He argued that any empirical piece of evidence can be accounted for in a theory by altering the pattern of the web of concepts that make up the theory (cf. Quine, 1964; Quine and Ullian, 1978). Webs of belief can be respun to account for supposed evidence.[10] The credibility of the positivist idea of using evidence as a way of testing theory was therefore strongly challenged by Quine.

So, Feyerabend kept alive debate in natural and social science research by shocking the dominant empiricist view, saying, when it comes to method, anything goes. Quine also kept the debate alive by writing shocking accounts of logic. Both contributions are relevant to our debate for this reason.[11]

The challenge known as postmodernism, as stated, raises queries about the

---

[10] Thus, for example, even the so-called deduction that the apparent observation of a black swan falsifies the statement that "all swans are white" is not clear-cut. Observation that it may be a swan is already imbued by theoretical conceptualisation. We can adjust the web of theory to account for, say, the existence of this creature, no longer called a swan, or we can incorporate black swans into the category of swans. It thus becomes unclear whether the statement "all swans are white" is a so-called synthetic (refutable) one or an analytic one. The time-honoured analytic/synthetic distinction was thus challenged in Quine's formulation.

[11] As pointed out above, positivists did not relinquish their elevated status in society, nor did they compromise the quest to ground theoretical statements with reference to evidence. Consequently many if not most scientists and philosophers of science continue in their privileged positions to ground their quest for good and sound theorising in a narrative that offers criteria for choosing between theories. Responsibility for choice can then purportedly be placed in the hands of the scientific community.

project of modernity, which it links to the Enlightenment and many subsequent writers. Postmodern thought[12] characterises modernism as a failed attempt to ground the search for knowledge in some absolute foundation. Postmodern writers argue that absolute foundations are illusory involving an infinite regress. The postmodern challenge extended to Marxist oriented realist argumentation, which tried to make a case for using (social) science to explore hidden structures of causality (that were argued to lie at the basis of exploitative social relationships). Marxist realism was challenged, along with other quests for representational knowledge, because it was felt that the knowledge developed would be used to legitimate forms of recommended action as obviously based on knowledge about real causal mechanisms. The postmodern challenge also extended to nonrealist Marxist argumentation concerning possibilities for envisioning the emancipatory potential of humankind. It was felt that the grand narrative of emancipation woven within this scheme of thought might fail to make provision for a toleration of real alternatives (by excluding a toleration of incommensurability). Habermas's so-tagged grand narrative was targeted on this score.

For postmodern thinkers, thought can be defined as "that which allows us to step back from this or that way of acting or reacting, to present it as an object of thought and question it as to its meaning, its condition, its goals" (Foucault, 1984: 334). Thinking encourages toleration of incommensurable and adversarial positions.[13] Thinking defines a relationship with other people that is not grounded in an attempt to reach consensus. Ethical and intellectual integrity cannot be gained by justification of actions through mandates from religion, law, science, or indeed social agreements (cf. Dreyfus and Rabinow, 1982: 121). A similar concern is epitomised in Lyotard's (1984) insistence that knowledge and action formulated and legitimated with reference to metanarratives is totalising thought best linked to social totalitarianism (cf. Readings, 1991: 109; Hassard, 1993: 124). Postmodern incredulity with metanarrative provides a refreshing account of living with and making sense of diversity although it does have its own dark side (cf. Jackson and Carter, 1991: 110–111; Gergen, 1992: 222–223; Hassard, 1993: 69–75; Spaul, 1993: 151;

---

[12] There are many definitions and strands of postmodern thought. In this chapter we consider both Foucault's and Lyotard's arguments to help map the postmodern mentality. We focus on their contributions to highlight the narrative character of knowledge and the problem of absolutism which, they argue, is linked to the terror of political domination. See also Leroke (1994) for an account of the links between Foucault's postmodern position—grounded in poststructuralism—and Lyotard's postmodernist position as a critique of the project of modernity.

[13] Foucault (1984: 378–379) insists that the ideal of consensus must not become a regulatory principle, though it could be a critical one in the sense that it emphasises patterns of domination built in nonconsensuality. Lyotard (1990: 340) wishes to remind us that any consensus is based on the playing of the present players and reflects only a provisional contract.

Taket and White, 1993: 737).[14,15] It has strongly influenced our metatheory of diversity management and our "multimethodological" principles of triple loop learning.

Details of metatheory encountered in the domain of philosophy and the history of knowledge are now hung around the milestones positioned at the start of this chapter. Arguments were surfaced by calling in on a number of better known metatheorists. We now want to penetrate deeper and do so by entering the domain of theory and methodology. In this domain we visit disciplinary locations and report on relevant discussions encountered therein.

THEORY AND METHODOLOGY

The Natural Sciences

Metatheory in the natural sciences arguably has its roots in Bohr's complementarity theory (Bohr, 1932). Its most famous exposition is in physics and deals with the theory of light. At one time light was a little-understood phenomenon. Physicists brought forward an explanation of light by drawing parallels between the behaviour of light and the behaviour of water waves. From this parallel came the wave theory of light. This parallel, however, provided only a partial explanation. Some properties of light do not conform to the theory of water waves. A second parallel was drawn between light and moving particles. Some of the behaviour of light, not explained by the wave theory, was explained by the moving particle theory. So two analogies/theories had been drawn. The first analogy/theory reasoned that light behaved like waves. The second analogy/theory reasoned that light behaved like moving particles. Bohr called this dual analogy/theory "the wavicle theory of light" and from this was born in the natural sciences the idea of complementarity between theories.

---

[14] Postmodernists often shy away from using terms such as theory and metatheory. For postmodernists they imply metanarrative. But we are not averse to either theory or metatheory and we do not take issue with people who construct them, as long as they do not then take the construction too literally. Without theory, we argue, one cannot make considered choices. Some postmodernists admit that their project is not anti-theoretical—for example, Hassard, Gergen, and others, who argue that new theoretical visions may help provide cultural resources to allow us to move forward (e.g. Hassard, 1993: 135). Huyssen (1990: 271) also shows that these efforts are linked to a critique of tendencies to associate postmodernism with an "anything goes" attitude. Jackson and Carter (1991) offer some theoretical guidelines for embracing emancipation, now locally defined.

[15] Freundlieb (1989) points to a difficulty raised by the postmodernist suggestion that argument itself takes place in terms of criteria that may not be agreed by the players. He notes that it is unclear how this reservation about argument relates to their own proffered arguments. Postmodernist writers themselves offer arguments in support of their statements (e.g. their statements concerning the textual character of social reality; the necessary deferment of all meaning construction; and the importance of preserving variety).

Similar lines of thought have been advanced in other domains of science such as biology. For example, Manier (1969) reckoned that, to capture the real flavour of biological science, researchers should refuse to be satisfied with analysis of singular paradigms, no matter how lucid. Favouring paradigms, Manier claimed, results in theoretical reduction, reducing chances of theoretical explanation of complex phenomena. Manier made reference to pioneering work in genetics, in particular T.H. Morgan's success, and attributed this to Morgan's willingness to patiently entertain theoretical alternatives. Manier then turned to Wm. Bateson, another leading geneticist, who was unwilling to accept the utility of theoretical diversity which, Manier goes on, led to theoretical closure and rejection of evidence that ultimately gave fame to the powerful chromosome theory of the gene.

In Bohr's and Manier's works, complementarist arguments are formulated that support the sentiment of holistic thinking, vindicated by the benefits of consciously recognising value in diversity of viewpoints. Their arguments, however, are couched in terms that imply criteria for scientific progress can be established and that it is feasible to know when better theories are contrived. Scientific progress of that kind was challenged on various scores relevant to our final argument (see pages 308–312). For example, it implies progress toward the truth about the world which we, ironically, cannot tolerate in our theory of diversity management. The irony is toleration of the intolerable.

Our brief foray into the natural sciences turned up little supplementary support or otherwise to our argument. However, the issue appears much stickier in the social sciences. As Kuhn pointed out, there is a social importance to solutions and what is important is contentious indeed. This gumminess has led to a much more wide ranging debate about complementarism in the social sciences.

The Social Sciences

Picou, Wells and Nyberg (1978) researched the theories and methodologies of rural sociology. Historically, they argue, rural sociology has been atheoretical.[16] The first metatheoretical inquiry they encountered was Bealer (1975). Bealer talks in terms of Kuhnian theory. The normal science dominating rural sociology at that time was structural functionalism. Disciplinary theory of rural sociology was subject to theoretical closure and methodological monism. For Bealer, this suggested a crisis of discipline stasis with all problems being

---

[16] Which in terms of our argument presented above is not possible because on reflection any research programme will be found to have assumptions that indicate a theoretical position. A more insightful observation we believe is that historically rural sociology has been somewhat non-reflective in regard to its premises.

forced rigidly into the mould of a structural functionalist paradigm. To escape from this stasis, Bealer suggested a new rural sociology founded on theoretical and methodological diversity. Here Bealer endorses diachronic existence of multiple paradigms, that Kuhn identified as a feature of social science, rather than pushing from a revolutionary shift to a new perspective in which scientists would again practice uni-paradigm normal science.

Bealer does not take into account forms of resistance introduced in the last section capable of putting a stranglehold on his call for diversity. Resistance is most likely to originate from those wedded to the structural functionalist option. Career prospects and research funding prospects are often tied to the dominant option. This might involve micropolitical forces such as the ones Foucault identifies. Reflection on this sort of explanation suggests ways open for intervention other than the theory-centred one which Bealer offers here. Being aware that "might" can be embroiled in monolithic research programmes adds insight into tactics that can be employed to nurture diversity.

In a review of theoretical diversity in organisational analysis, Nurse (1988) sensed a political statement in the way Burrell and Morgan (1979) deliberated about choice of theory for conducting research. He minuted with favour Burrell and Morgan's aversion to integrated consensual approaches. The co-workers encourage analysts to step outside of their favoured theoretical position and from there piece together a richer appreciation of what other theories have to offer. Following Driggers (1977), Nurse believed that it is possible then to harvest a plentiful crop of theoretical development by purposely confronting opposing perspectives with each other.

Continuing along these lines, Nurse worked out ways of posing questions about organisations, work, the production of relations in society, and of generating knowledge about these phenomena. He called for different theories to study the different phenomena and the kinds of (insoluble) issue they generate. There is, he argues, value in theoretical diversity because it leads to differing conclusions about organisational realities and is of practical significance because it broadens options for organisational intervention.

Morgan (1980) too is keen that organisational theorists recognise the existence and validity of rival modes of research practice. The research process, he says, belies assessment in terms of neutral criteria and always proceeds in the image of some metaphor that excludes other images.[17] Yet all studies involve some choice making precisely because of the exclusionary nature of metaphors (theories). The quality of research choices, that are inevitable, improves in line with researchers' ability to recognise the partial character of

---

[17] The metaphorical nature of theory and the implications for theory construction are examined by Morgan (1984) and has informed his account of the diversity of approaches to organisational analysis (see also Morgan, 1989).

any study. Morgan (1980: 612) argues recognition of that kind "cautions against excessive commitment to favoured points of view". The aim is to prevent "premature closure" to alternatives (Morgan, 1980: 613). As Jackson and Carter (1991: 116) recognise, Morgan here accepts and indeed hopes that divergent theoretical perspectives will exist in perpetuity and that the tension between them will never be dissolved.[18] Reed (1985) wanted to wrap a methodology around these ideas encouraging diversity to strike a sensible balance between incremental conceptual integration (tension dissolution) and theoretical proliferation (tension generation).

Also writing about organisational studies, Gergen (1992: 215) argues that it is incumbent on theorists to entertain a sense of ludic humility in their judgements. This reminds theorists of the constructed character of their insights. They are constructors of narratives. Awareness of this retains in the minds of all concerned a mindfulness that insights are not constructed on "vindicating foundations" (Gergen, 1992: 215). Hassard (1993: 127) also points to this need for self-reflexivity, continually retaining a "suspicion of our own intellectual assumptions", so that our own discourse will then not serve to suppress "the possibility of a multitude of alternative voices" (Hassard, 1993: 128).

Ackroyd (1992) is another author who appreciates the reality of institutionally located theoretical conflict and controversy. He stands firm against a paradigm mentality. This type of mentality leads to polarisation which debilitates efforts to improve the calibre of organisational knowledge. It leads to fragmentation. It fractures knowledge into a competing set of theoretical factions. Unity must not be forced, however. Instead, Ackroyd plays his hand, there should be a limited synthesis between competing approaches and empirical research projects to correlate relevance of approaches to improved organisational practice.

Ackroyd (1992: 116) admits that there are points of intellectual as well as moral tension when riding the pro-diversity bandwagon. However, this does not mitigate against the relevance in riding with such research practice. On the contrary, he notes, "A case can be made that growth areas in social science have always centred on points of intellectual as well as moral tension, and it is this that gives vitality to schools of thought."

Of further interest to us is Ackroyd's secured focus on the principle of practical relevance. Our brand of complementarism also has a practical strain. Triple loop learning is a testament to that. Only we lend even more credence to tensions involved in demonstrating relevance. We concentrate on exploring tensions by linking them to a quality of reflexive research coupled to widely

---

[18] Jackson and Carter (1991: 120) argue that a simple acceptance of diversity is likely to lead to a position where a middle ground option becomes the favoured one. They are worried about the implicit assumption of equality of power between the discoursers. Their concerns relate to questions of micropolitics that have been raised by Foucault.

informed local decision making. (See Flood and Romm, 1996a for an account of this process in relation to design, debate and what we call might–right management.)

Gouldner's time honoured definition of reflexivity (1973—in *The Coming Crisis of Western Sociology*) has strongly shaped our own appreciation. Gouldner judged that a quality reflexive approach looks

> . . . to the deepening of the self's capacity to recognise that it views certain information as hostile, to recognise the various dodges that it uses to deny, ignore, or camouflage information that is hostile to it, and to strengthening of its capacity to accept and to use hostile information. In short, what Reflexive Sociology seeks is not an insulation but a transformation of the sociologist's self, and hence of his [*sic*] praxis in the world. (Gouldner, 1973: 495)

Gouldner likens the process of getting to know the world as a continuous process of self-discovery. In Gouldner's process theorists discover miscellaneous dodges that they use to avoid information hostile to how they prefer to know the world. Wanting to dodge the dodges, Gouldner schemes what he called knowing as awareness. Knowing must include an awareness of the fragility and anomalous character of theoretical and attendant moral judgements.

Other sagacious commentaries assume different angles on reflexivity.

Brown (1977) in his *Poetic for Sociology*, using poetic terms, deliberated over the use of irony as a way of avoiding excessive theoretical commitment to singular points of view. Irony, Brown (1977: 173) suggests, serves a "critical and self-reflective function for professionals". He isolates a number of forms of irony, all of which involve juxtaposing apparent opposites to nurture a grasp of unexpected yet valued associations that may result (Brown, 1977: 174).

Wexler, operating in the field of education, launched his own offensive to secure the potential in diversity. Potential can be secured from the moment that researchers recognise disjunction in all theoretical accounts of organisational and societal affairs. He wants to install a mentality where people can reconfront their starting position with cognitive armoury issued by different interpretations. It is this self-encounter that may prevent reification of theory into fixed signs and solidified consciousness (Wexler, 1987: 179).

Reflexivity has thus been championed in many disciplines in the social sciences, although not necessarily in their mainstream! It enables and prepares theoreticians and practitioners for the enriching process of confronting alternatives. Reflexivity is indeed a means by which disciplines are able to retain and encourage diversity and tension. Still, other than calls to reflexivity there has been little work done on isolating ways of managing diversity. This is where triple loop learning registers its credentials as we shall see later on.

We have now concluded our metatheoretical reasoning and, indeed, the first part of this chapter. In the second part we will draw to the surface our own position in a complementarist metatheory we call "diversity management" that wells up in the forerunning presentation. Once this has been achieved we will explain our preferred complementarist "multi-methodological" expression of "diversity management" that we call "triple loop learning".

DIVERSITY MANAGEMENT

Diversity management is about managing the increasing diversity of issues that confront humankind[19] in contemporary organisational and societal affairs. Initially this meant people managing the increasing diversity of issues they confronted by increasing the diversity of types of model, methodology and theory available to address those affairs. Diversification, however, created a brand new issue to be managed—how to choose between the models, methodologies and theories. Consequently, the emphasis in diversity management switched to people managing the increasing diversity of models, methodologies and theories that continue to come to the fore, thus improving management of the increasing diversity of issues confronted. Diversity therefore means that more choices are made available for people to manage organisational and societal affairs. Management means that these choices, which after all have to be made, are thought through intelligently and made responsibly. Intelligence and responsibility are the defining features of triple loop learning, which is mapped out in the next section.

Diversity management understands well that no argument is dilemma free. For every argument put forward, it is possible to locate barby dilemmas in its solutions. This is also true of our complementarist assertions. However, we propose that a strength of our complementarist argument is that it actually increases awareness of the existence and barbiness of dilemmas so that they can be handled carefully, rather than be ignored, or blindly dodged, with cutting consequences. The principal dilemma facing diversity management is how to manage the diversity of theoretical voices that we hear.

Management of the diversity of theoretical voices for us begins with a mentality of toleration. Yet toleration must be supplemented by a metatheory that accounts for choice making at the level of methodology practice. Toleration must allow for comparison between theories through some form of

---

[19] Issues of humankind to us refer to physical, biological and social cares. That is not to say that the physical and biological worlds are there for human exploitation. For example, ecological issues may be issues to be cared about not solely in terms of human needs. No matter how these issues are seen, humankind must take some responsibility for their care.

argument. At the same time it must be recognised that comparison itself requires defining criteria to effect comparison as a basis for and as part of choice making. The deliberations involved in this process are necessarily fragile. Nevertheless, when a methodological choice is made by interventionists, it is vital that they hold a definite theoretical image in mind that directly informs the action. For this reason, theoretical development, or theorising, is not in itself dangerous, as long as interventionists are aware of the constructed character of their theoretical images.

Recognition of the constructed character of theories installs in interventionists theoretical sensitivity so that they can take on board news that fails to accord with an initial theoretical image that normally influences them. This implies a reflexive quality of re-evaluating favoured images and hearing news and information from other perspectives. Informedness does not, however, imply that the character of the news is directly translatable between the languages of the theories. This is precisely why the theorists need to loop between alternative visions to take on board new information and to recognise it as different news. This loopiness does not mean that action is thereby stalled. Invoked knowledge makes explicit details of any theoretical vision chosen for the purpose of intervention. Practitioners, therefore, are able to make choices intelligently and live with the consequences of chosen actions as a matter of personal responsibility.

Theorising is thus important, but how can theory actually lead to intelligent and responsible choice making? Jackson and Carter (1991: 110) suggest that once we accept the necessary impact of knowledge in and on the world, different knowledge claims should, ideally, "be resolved in the light of their implications for social praxis".[20] Other postmodernists too suggest that the hallmark of good theory is whether "it supports patterns of relationships we feel have positive rather than negative consequences for social life" (cf. Hassard, 1993: 134–135). Yet, once again we are left with a dilemma, questioning exactly how decisions are to be made in accordance with these laudable abstractions.

Yet more dilemmas pop up. For instance, how can choice making of

---

[20] Understanding that theorising affects and enters the conduct of social life has a long history in (meta)theory. Radnitsky (1974: 51), for example, argues that "it is characteristic of the human sciences that their theories have direct implications for the *praxis* of life". Images of people are built into our theorising, which thus becomes linked to endorsing forms of social existence. The interconnection between theory and praxis, though more starkly evident in social scientific theorising, can be extended to theorising about the physical world. Norgaard (1989) offers a classic example of theorising affecting the physical world. Agroecologists recognise that traditional agricultural systems are products of the beliefs of the culture—their theories. Micro-organisms through insects have evolved characteristics in response to the selective pressures of human intervention in plant management that has come about from dominant theories (Altieri, 1987). All of this means, for us, that judgement on a theoretical vision is related to judgement about which actions are defensible.

interventionists be vindicated after admitting that standards for choice making differ? For a champion of cybernetics, standards are primarily linked to purposeful design and organisation. For a champion of systemic interpretivism, standards are linked to the provision made for accommodation between people to be reached through a process of debate. And for a champion of critical systemic modernism, some normative standard will be called upon to measure the quality of debate, assessing the extent to which dominant forces shape the debate. And if we accept this fluidity in criteria employed to make judgements, then how can interventionists, if at all, become involved in meaningful action? There is a need to establish a base for judgements, so that interventionists do not enter into an anything goes romp. Diversity management must provide a base of guidelines for choice making.

Diversity management argues that critique and self-critique can lead to a quality of choice making that avoids relativism as well as absolutism. In diversity management, *choice is a post-critical moment when results of critique are harvested so that decisions can be made.* Purposes are selected that are judged worthy to pursue. Judgement cannot be absolutely vindicated. It is, however, likely to be better if there is explicit recognition that choices adopt decided purposes. Habermas makes relevant assertions here. He suggests that normative purposes are better insofar as their normative content is less "crypto". At least their content is opened up for discussion and partial assessment.

The word partial is deliberately added in the above assertion. It commissions the tension between a modernist and postmodernist position. Postmodernists wish to emphasise that all judgements are fragile. Arguments used to vindicate judgements are never foolproof. Judgements are easily ruled by dominant modes of reasoning in society and this, at least, has to be kept in mind by those willing to pursue a complementarist agenda. Choice making needs to be guided by a sensitivity to power that is (often invisibly) built into knowledge and action-based decisions.

So, where does all this reckoning lead us? Are we any nearer to helping theoreticians and interventionists managing choices that they face? We believe that awareness of the theoretical and methodological work done, if treated with a sensitivity to some of the dilemmas raised, is the first step toward guidelines for better choice making and hence diversity management. It provides a framework within which theoreticians and practitioners can evaluate purposes that may be aligned to any theory, methodology or model. It helps those people to consider the relevance of different purposes and the way that they may be accorded priority by different people (or groups) at distinct places and distinct points in time. People's choices obviously will be a matter of judgement, but their defence rests on a broader framework that arranges purposes in relation to one another. This allows for some measure of debate between theoreticians, practitioners, and indeed any other people, about the relevance of possible choices that they can make.

What is important, in these debates, is that we do not substantiate judgements by reference to so-called external reality or to consensual agreements about reality as if these realities have authority. We follow Foucault and Lyotard in their suggestions that the authority of such realities should be replaced by patterns of thought that are able to admit their own premises. With diversity management theoretical underpinnings are called purposes, which then can become explicit moments of any research investigation or intervention.

Nevertheless, we expect that positivists, realists and modernists, of various kinds, are likely to argue that our approach borders too close to a relativist position, where theoretical and methodological judgements cannot be substantiated. Our reply is that we are devising theoretical and methodological tools that allow us to build castles made of sand. Our sand castles are theoretical images that call forth specific purposes for action. Our range of sand castles allows life to ensue in a variety of ways, as different methodological decisions are made. They can be used as guides for action, for now. All the evidence we have brought forward suggests that castles made of sand slip into the sea, eventually.

Our counter-argument to positivists, realists and modernists, is that meta-narratively grounded theorising of their type is too forceful in this respect. Building concrete castles, as they do, is a dangerous activity. It does not guard against the dangers of monolithic thought, or put in terms of our metaphor, against the dangers of building concrete castles in which everybody will have to live, and live according to the laws of the castle. Tolerance of diversity surely is a more curative tonic, even though it means managing diversity of criteria by which to judge theoretical and methodological choices.

Discussion in this chapter encourages us to reconsider the question of incommensurability between theories, methodologies and models, whose diversity and difference are endorsed in our complementarist framework. We accept incommensurability between options for presencing the world and relating to it. We suggest theoreticians and interventionists think in terms of theoretical and methodological (in)commensurability. The bracket within the term (in)commensurability points to tension in consciousness; between knowing that choices at the moment of action exclude other possibilities, but being able to submit a defence for decisions made. There are tensions involved in trying to maintain a position that neither "accepts differences between paradigms but slips into a paradigm mentality", nor "denies differences between paradigms". The bracket within the term (in)commensurability suggests a way of managing, while not denying, or evading, this tension.

In the following section we translate our complementarist metatheory (developed through our investigation of literatures on philosophy and the history of knowledge and literature on research agendas in fields of study) into a complementarist approach to so-called "multimethodology" that we call "triple loop learning". Before advancing the details of our proposal, it is pertinent to highlight some crucial connecting nodes between our meta-theoretical discussion and our complementarist approach to multimethodology (triple loop learning).

One point of connection lies in our suggestion that those operating multi-methodology (or in our terms triple loop learners) need to have *some awareness of debates* revolving around processes of knowledge construction. We offered a narrative above that introduced some focal points in such a debate. The point of doing so was—at least—to bring to consciousness (and keep in consciousness) a reminder that there is no fool-proof way of defining *the* route to knowledge creation (or learning). A consciousness of this enables triple loop learners to operate in recognition of the requirement not to preselect continually a favoured way of knowing (a loop of learning). As we shall see below, this is vital to triple loop learning and its way of embracing so-called "multimethodology".

There is furthermore a crucial point of connection between our discussion of possibilities for reflexive theorising as a way of exercising ludic humility in fields of study and our argument regarding triple loop learning. This point of connection lies in our proposal concerning what *nonobsessive practice* involves. In our exposition of triple loop learning it is spelled out that such nonobsessiveness requires a reflexive (rather than fixated) approach towards any way of defining purpose. This does not preclude (and indeed specifically includes) an acceptance that at decision points certain courses of action have to be activated in order to embrace the need for choice. We show in our discussion why we believe that action without obsession is both possible and desirable and also how this fits with a mentality of toleration of diversity.

TRIPLE LOOP LEARNING

Triple loop learning is about increasing the fullness and deepness of learning about the diversity of issues and dilemmas faced. It is about ways of managing them. It is the dénouement of single loop learning and double loop learning.

Single loop learning will be most familiar to the reader as means–end thinking. Ends are set and then a search begins for the best means of meeting those ends. The general issue is, How should we operate to meet best those ends? Other definitions of ends are either not recognised or not valued. The consciousness of single loop learners is non-reflexive leading to an obsession with the best means to meet their defined ends. Single loop learners are task oriented, oriented exclusively to identifying the best means to meet their defined ends. Identification of ends and the best means to achieve them is not considered to be problematic. We recognise three main types of single loop learning, each one being an obsessive use of one of our three loops (see Figure 11.1).

The first type of single loop learning in broad terms is about process design and organisational design (Figure 11.1(a)). Subject areas include process-based approaches like Business Process Reengineering and Quality Management as well as a range of design proposals that create structural arrangements within which processes flow. The centre of learning asks, *Are we doing things right?* The question is clearly, *How* should we do it? Ends, for example, with Business Process Reengineering are to defunctionalise organisations and rebuild them on a small number of core business processes. The means then is a search for a radically improved set of processes to do this, measured in terms of efficiency. For Quality Management, broadly speaking, ends are to make customers happy. The means then is incrementally and continuously to improve the efficiency of the processes that produce the ends. For people concerned with organisational design, the ends come in the form of models, each claiming to offer the most effective rules of organisational design. The means are a search for principles of implementation to produce the right way of achieving those ends.

The second type of single loop learning in broad terms is about processes for debate (Figure 11.1(b)). The subject domain is some sort of interpretive-based intervention. Interpretive-based intervention is a reaction to the obsession with finding structuralist solutions that preclude the intersubjective-debate processes necessary to define, for example, quality. Interpretivism recognises that definition of ends and means is problematic because there are

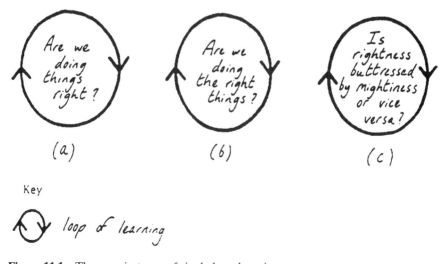

(a) Are we doing things right?

(b) Are we doing the right things?

(c) Is rightness buttressed by mightiness or vice versa?

Key

loop of learning

Figure 11.1 Three main types of single loop learning

many different viewpoints on ends and means. A new centre of learning is set that asks, *Are we doing the right thing?* This specific question in other words is, *What* should we do? Yet this is subsumed within the wider task oriented question, How can we achieve our ends and means? Ironically, new ends and means are set. Ends become accommodations or reconciliations between people. The means becomes a participative, open and free debate. Intervention is then a participative process where designs for organising processes and structuring arrangements are debated and broadened by issues introduced through interpretive thought such as cultural phenomena. The whole process, however, is dominated by an obsession with the redefined ends and means.

The third type of single loop learning reflects a concern with power–knowledge dynamics (Figure 11.1(c)). The subject domain is fair(er) practice. The reaction here is to the obsessive foci of design-based and debate-based intervention. Definition of ends and means from the How?-type obsession is considered to be problematic because it runs the risk of definition production with results that are unfair to some, if not many, people. Furthermore, the means of debate pursuing a What?-type obsession are considered to be problematic because debate is easily distorted by, say, coercive forces, meaning that it is not open and free, is not participative, and is not fair on those who are coerced. A new centre of learning is set that asks, *Is rightness buttressed by mightiness, or mightiness buttressed by rightness?* This specific question in other words is, *Why* should we do it? Yet this is subsumed within the wider task oriented question. How can we achieve our ends and means? New ends and means are set. Ends are forms of fair(er) practice. The means are ways in which fair(er) practice can be achieved including ways of education, building self-reliance and protest (Flood and Romm, 1996a: 169–206). The process is dominated by an obsession with these ends and means. Design and debate approaches consider these ends and means problematic because they are regarded as ideologically based and not scientific.[21]

Clearly, there is much conflict over what is the right centre of learning to adopt. Each loop attempts to win people over, demonstrating its superiority by attempting to solve the dilemmas it is shown to face by the other two loops. However, one attempt to overcome the conflict is a reconciliation between the first two types of single loop learning, the How?-type and the What?-type. This reconciliation is the most likely one since both centres of learning share a grave concern that intervention based on subverting forms of knowledge

---

[21] The complaint is that knowledge-generation processes provided by natural and/or social science are disregarded in the obsession with seeing knowledge–power relations. It therefore becomes impossible to judge the quality of any knowledge or learning. This is considered to be ideological by critics of Loop 3. However, might–right contenders counter-argue that ideology arises because people fail to problematise knowledge–power connections. In terms of *this* definition of ideology, both design and debate interventionists ironically become embroiled in ideology.

oppression is too ideologically based and is not scientific. The reconciliation is known as double loop learning (see Figure 11.2).

Double loop learning attempts to interplay the centres of learning embracing design and debate practices by asking, Are we doing things right and are we doing the right things? There is a bid to preserve the How? and What? centres that the two questions bring forward respectively, thus de-emphasising the task oriented nature of intervention. Intervention moves a step forward in a reflexive direction by facing up to choice between the two centres at any one time. There is a new consciousness as interventionists loop between the two centres of learning (Figure 11.2(a)). There is limited complementarism.

Double loop learners can and do slip into another less reflexive consciousness. Rather than looping between the two centres of learning, consciousness gets stuck in the middle looking out (Figure 11.2(b)). There is double vision and blurriness. Practitioners receive news from the two centres but do not try to manage it in order to act without defaulting into one of the two loops. They then clear their vision by acting according to the means and ends of a dominant loop (their preferred one) and denature the other loop either by subsuming it or by annexing some of its means. Figure 11.2(b) depicts the lack of reflexivity. It depicts an operation of consciousness, "looking out" in terms of given premises, that is, unwilling to reflect back on its premises.

Another consciousness is the eclectic one where vision remains blurred. Practitioners go ahead with any means within their immediate vicinity that they can focus on. They reach whatever ends they stumble on. The direction they blindly follow is often, however, a well-walked one that leads to a

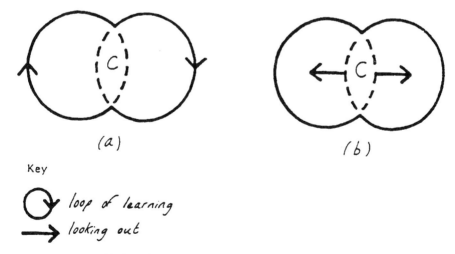

Key

loop of learning
looking out

Figure 11.2 Double loop learning

dominant end point. This too implies a failure to exercise the capacity of reflexivity.

Triple loop learning wants to establish tolerance between all three centres of learning and preserve the diversity therein. It does this by bringing together the three questions from the three loops into one overall awareness, Are we doing things right, and are we doing the right things, and is rightness buttressed by mightiness and/or mightiness buttressed by rightness? Intervention is no longer task oriented since How?, What?, and Why? centres, that the three questions bring forward respectively, come into consideration at any one time as a basis for responsible choice making. There is a new reflexive consciousness as interventionists continually loop between the three questions (Figure 11.3(a)). The looping helps people to develop a discourse for each centre of learning that enables them increasingly to become widely informed, especially as the discourse is related to (insoluble) issues that they face in their lives. Triple loop learning then manages the model and methodological diversity of the centres of learning that in turn enhances management of the diversity of (insoluble) issues to be dealt with. Triple loop learning links into a triple loop the three centres of learning. Triple loop learners loop around these three centres of learning. In this way triple loop learners operate intelligently and responsibly. Their whole consciousness becomes more than the sum of its parts, encouraging awareness of dilemmas involved when addressing issues such as those introduced above.

Triple loop learners can slip into another less reflexive consciousness just like double loop learners can. They too may slip up and get stuck in the middle looking out (Figure 11.3(b)). Looping ceases to happen or never starts.

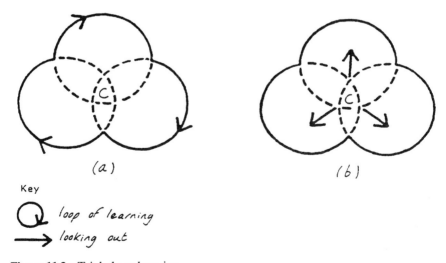

(a)

(b)

Key

loop of learning

looking out

Figure 11.3 Triple loop learning

They get triple vision and much blurriness. They either clear their vision by becoming imperialists or become stumble-in-the-dark eclectics.

We thus ascribe to the term "multimethodology" a way of dealing with (in)commensurability at the methodological level, through a process of triple looping. Triple looping encourages interventionists to keep in consciousness the purpose that they are pursuing as primary at any point in time and reminds them continuously to account for other possible commitments. This means that interventionists do not operate, wittingly or unwittingly, through a preselected loop in all situations. It means that interventionists avoid monotonous and indeed dominant calls for repeat responses in all situations.

Similarly, triple loop learning offers an option to stumble-in-the-dark eclectics where, by default, monotonous, dominant and repetitious patterns are chosen. There is a great danger that "multimethodology" may be reduced in this way to an eclectic supermarket sweety "mix and match" special offer.

Triple looping allows interventionists to engage with issues of concern in full awareness of the need to commit to some loop at decision nodes. This commitment in turn influences the way that interventionists utilise or indeed remould principles of methodologies. Triple loopers are able to consider the extent to which methodologies relate to How?-, What?- or Why?-type purposes that triple loopers have identified as core arenas for intervention. They are able to interpret methodological principles and attendant operational procedures in a way which helps them to address a chosen purpose. Thus, interventionists' choice and management of purpose is informed by their knowledge of methodological options that can be invoked.

Taking the last point to our conclusion, triple loop learning fundamentally is choice making about purposes to pursue in the circumstances. Beyond this, triple looping encourages interventionists to explore possible principles and processes for action, also in the circumstances. They become widely informed about possible different courses of action, given, for now, the chosen purpose. Methodological courses of action are hence worked out locally in time and space. Each situational engagement calls for unique "actioning" in this way. Triple loop learning therefore does not mean choice between existing methodologies (Flood, 1996b). "Multimethodology" is not really an appropriate term for it.

The contours of triple loop learning are now drawn and it remains for us to summarise the storyline of this chapter.

SUMMARY AND CONCLUSION

This chapter progresses from metatheory to so-called "multimethodology". To begin, our discussion on metatheory reviewed a number of key metatheoretical debates in the literature on knowledge production. We launched our discussion here by noting that the Enlightenment can be understood as implicated in metatheory in that it sought to impose overarching scientific methodology as a way of defining the development of scientific theories. We posed an alternative by explicating Kuhn's metatheory about the structure of scientific revolutions, which argued that understanding is inextricably theory-based. We pointed out that Kuhn provides a novel account of how scientific progress occurs, but that the contours of this are left open to (re)definition. Furthermore, he leaves open the question of how choice making can be made in the face of diversity arising from diachronic existence of multiple paradigms. This leaves "management" out of "diversity management".

Habermas's metatheory was then shown to cast new light on Kuhn's thinking, through its suggestion that knowledge is value-based. His metatheoretical solution makes provision for different human interests under the control of critical and conscious self-reflection. Habermas's metatheory is relevant to our complementarist endeavour because it recognises and differentiates between different human interests and purposes. However, there are issues that are not fully explained, such as how choices can be made between theories, and how consensus between theorists, as well as between them and the wider community, may be defined. The management in diversity management is sought through an elusive consensus. We went on to show how Foucault concentrated on the connection between power and knowledge. He highlighted the way in which knowledge becomes constituted within power relationships in social networks. We related this to Lyotard's argument that knowledge and action formulated and legitimated with reference to metanarratives is totalising thought which may become linked to social totalitarianism. We connected the concerns of Foucault and Lyotard to the postmodern project and showed how attempts at metatheoretical accounts of living with and making sense of diversity are evoked by the postmodern project. This gave us some clues towards possible ways of realising management in diversity management.

We then proceeded to discuss complementarity theory as it appears in different disciplines. We pointed to its most famous exposition in Bohr's "wavicle theory of light" in the field of physics. Similar lines of thought have been advanced in other domains such as biology. We noted, however, that the arguments are normally couched in terms which imply that criteria for scientific progress can be established and that it is feasible to know when better theories are created. We indicated why we believe that complementarism at root requires a different consciousness, able to tolerate radical diversity.

A review of the literature from a number of quarters in the social sciences surfaced a recurring theme: the existence and validity of rival modes of research practice. It also surfaced the suggestion (though seldom espoused in the mainstream of a field of study) that reflexivity may provide a way to retain a necessary tension between rival practices. We spent some time indicating the substance of these various calls to reflexivity. But we also noted that other than these calls, there has been little work done on isolating ways of managing the resulting diversity. Triple loop learning was proposed as squaring up to this challenge.

Triple loop learning is supported by a conception of diversity management which is about managing the increasing diversity of models, methodologies and theories, that continue to come to the fore, thus improving management of the increasing diversity of issues confronted. We emphasised that it is crucial that triple loop learning is operated via a consciousness which understands well that no argument is free of dilemmas, and furthermore which recognises that "castles made of sand slip into the sea, eventually" (Jimi Hendrix Experience, *Axis Bold As Love*, 1969). Pointing out the importance of bearing this in mind, we outlined our view of triple loop learning by contrasting it with single and double loop learning.

We located three types of single loop learning each with a different centre of learning. There are specific questions asked respectively for each centre. Are we doing things right? Are we doing the right things? Is rightness buttressed by mightiness and/or mightiness buttressed by rightness? But each question is fixed on the task oriented quest to do its own things right. The centres of learning are not reflexive. Or, put differently, attention becomes fixed on a single loop with over-confidence in its way of learning.

Double loop learning was defined as differing from single loop learning in that it has two centres of learning, asking, Are we doing things right and are we doing the right things? There is partial reflexivity. There is limited complementarism. There is a danger of slipping into isolationism or stumble-in-the-dark pragmatism.

Triple loop learning was then discussed as a way of increasing the fullness and deepness of learning about issues and dilemmas faced and ways of managing them. We proposed a conception of triple loop learning that wants to establish tolerance between all three centres of learning and preserve the diversity therein. We suggested that this can be done by bringing together the three questions from the three loops into one overall awareness, Are we doing things right, and are we doing the right things, and is rightness buttressed by mightiness and/or mightiness buttressed by rightness? Triple loop learning links into a triple loop the three centres of learning. Triple loop learners loop between these three questions. In this way triple loop learners operate intelligently and responsibly. Their whole consciousness becomes more than the sum of its parts. This is our brand of complementarist "multimethodology".

Finally, we pointed out that triple loop learning does not necessarily mean choice between existing methodologies and that "multimethodology" is not really an appropriate term for how we conceive triple loop learning.

REFERENCES

Ackroyd, S. (1992). Paradigms lost: paradise regained? In M. Reed and M. Hughes (eds) *Rethinking Organisation*. Sage, London.

Adorno, T.W. et al (1969). *The Positivist Dispute in German Sociology*. Herman Luchterhand Verlag. English translation, 1976, Heinemann, London.

Altieri, M. (1987). *Agroecology: The Scientific Basis of Alternative Agriculture*. Westview Press, Boulder, CO.

Ashley, D. and Orenstein, D.M. (1985). *Sociological Theory: Classical Statements*. Allyn and Bacon, Boston, MA.

Bealer, R.C. (1975). Theory and rural sociology. *Rural Sociology*, **34**, 229–233.

Benton, T. (1977). *Philosophical Foundations of the Three Sociologies*. Routledge and Kegan Paul, London.

Bleicher, J. (1982). *The Hermeneutic Imagination*. Routledge and Kegan Paul, London.

Bohr, N. (1932). Atomtheorie und Naturteschreibung. *Atomphysik u. menschliche Erkenntnis*, **I**, 10.

Bourdieu, P. (1975). The specificity of the scientific field and the social conditions of the progress of reason. *Social Science Information*, **14**, 19–47.

Brand, A. (1990). *The Force of Reason*. Allen & Unwin, London.

Brown, R.H. (1977). *A Poetic for Sociology*. Cambridge University Press, Cambridge.

Burrell, G. and Morgan, G. (1979). *Sociological Paradigms and Organisational Analysis*. Heinemann, London.

Dreyfus, H.L. and Rabinow, P. (1982). *Michel Foucault: Beyond Structuralism and Hermeneutics*. Harvester Press, Hemel Hempstead.

Driggers, P.F. (1977). Theoretical blockage: a strategy for the development of organisational theory. In J.K. Benson (ed.) *Organisational Analysis: Critique and Innovation*. Sage, Beverly Hills, CA.

Feyerabend, P. (1975). *Against Method. Outline of an Anarchistic Theory of Knowledge*. New Left Books, London.

Flood, R.L. (1995). *Solving Problem Solving*. Wiley, Chichester.

Flood, R.L. (1996a). Total Systems Intervention: Local Systemic Intervention. In R.L. Flood and N.R.A. Romm (eds) *Critical Systems Thinking: Current Research and Practice*. Plenum, New York. Published previously in 1996 as *Research Memorandum 13*, Centre for Systems Studies, University of Hull, UK.

Flood, R.L. (1996b). An essay on holism and the social action "problem solving". *Research Memorandum 12*, Centre for Systems Studies, University of Hull, UK.

Flood, R.L. and Jackson, M.C. (1991a). *Creative Problem Solving: Total Systems Intervention*. Wiley, Chichester.

Flood, R.L. and Jackson, M.C. (eds) (1991b). *Critical Systems Thinking: Directed Readings*. Wiley, Chichester.

Flood, R.L. and Romm, N.R.A. (eds) (1996a). *Critical Systems Thinking: Current Research and Practice*. Plenum, New York.

Flood, R.L. and Romm, N.R.A. (1996b). *Diversity Management: Triple Loop Learning*. Wiley, Chichester.

Foucault, M. (1984). Interviews. In P. Rabinow (ed.) *The Foucault Reader*. Random House, New York.

Freundlieb, D. (1989). Rationalism v. irrationalism? Habermas's response to Foucault. *Inquiry*, **3**, 171–192.

Gergen, K.J. (1992). Organisation theory in the postmodern era. In M. Reed and M. Hughes (eds) *Rethinking Organisation*. Sage, London.

Gouldner, A.W. (1973). *The Coming Crisis of Western Sociology*. Heinemann, London.

Habermas, J. (1971). *Knowledge and Human Interests*. Beacon Press, Boston, MA.
Habermas, J. (1981). Modernity versus postmodernity. *New German Critique*, **22**, 3–14.
Habermas, J. (1984). *The Theory of Communicative Action*, vol. 1. *Reason and the Rationalisation of Society*. Beacon Press, Boston, MA.
Habermas, J. (1987). *The Theory of Communicative Action*, vol. 2. *Lifeworld and System: A Critique of Functionalist Reason*. Beacon Press, Boston.
Habermas, J. (1993). *Justification and Application: Remarks on Discourse Ethics*. Polity, Cambridge.
Hassard, J. (1993). *Sociology and Organisation Theory: Positivism, Paradigms and Postmodernity*. Cambridge University Press, Cambridge.
Huyssen, A. (1990). Mapping the postmodern. In L.J. Nicholson (ed.) *Feminism/postmodernism*. Routledge, London.
Jackson, N. and Carter, P. (1991). In defence of paradigm incommensurability. *Organization Studies*, **12**, 109–127.
Keat, R. and Urry, J. (1982). *Social Theory as Science*. Routledge and Kegan Paul, London.
Kuhn, T. (1970). *The Structure of Scientific Revolutions*. University of Chicago Press, Chicago, IL (2nd edition, enlarged).
Leroke, W. (1994). Transcending sociology: the emergence of post-modern social theory. In N.R.A. Romm and M. Sarakinsky (eds) *Social Theory*. Heinemann, Johannesburg, pp. 369–399.
Lyotard, J.F. (1984). *The Postmodern Condition: A Report on Knowledge*. Manchester University Press, Manchester.
Lyotard, J.F. (1990). The postmodern condition. In J.C. Alexander and S. Seidman (eds) *Culture and Society: Contemporary Debates*. Cambridge University Press, Cambridge.
Manier, E. (1969). The experimental method in biology. T.H. Morgan and the theory of the gene. *Synthese*, **20**, 185–205.
Morgan, G. (1980). Paradigms, metaphors, and puzzle solving in organisation theory. *Administration Science Quarterly*, **25**, 605–621.
Morgan, G. (1984). Opportunities arising from paradigm diversity. *Administration and Society*, **16**, 306–327.
Morgan, G. (1989). *Creative Organisation Theory*. Sage, London.
Norgaard, R.B. (1989). The case for methodological pluralism. *Ecological Economics*, **1**, 37–57.
Nurse, L. (1988). Theoretical pluralism in organisational analysis. *Administration and Society*, **20**, 92–108.
Picou, J.S., Wells, R.H. and Nyberg, K.L. (1978). Paradigms, theories, and methods in contemporary rural sociology. *Rural Sociology*, **43**, 559–583.
Quine, W.V. (1964). *From a Logical Point of View*. Harvard University Press, Cambridge, MA.
Quine, W.V. and Ullian, J.S. (1978). *The Web of Belief*. Random House, New York, 2nd edition.
Radnitsky, G. (1974). Preconceptions in research: a study. *The Human Context*, **6**, 1–63.
Readings, B. (1991). *Introducing Lyotard*. Routledge and Kegan Paul, London.
Reed, M. (1985). *Redirections in Organisational Analysis*. Tavistock, London.
Romm, N.R.A. (1991). *The Methodologies of Positivism and Marxism*. Macmillan, London.
Simons, H.W. and Billig, M. (eds) (1994). *After Postmodernism: Reconstructing Ideology Critique*. Sage, London.
Spaul, M. (1993). Critical Systems Thinking: post-modernism and the philosophy of Richard Rorty. In F.A. Stowell, D. West and J. Howell (eds) *Systems Science: Addressing Global Issues*. Plenum, New York.

Swieringa, J. and Wierdsma, A. (1992). *Becoming a Learning Organisation: Beyond the Learning Curve.* Addison-Wesley, Cambridge, MA.

Taket, A. and White, L. (1993). The death of the expert. *Journal of the Operational Research Society*, **45**, 733–748.

Wexler, P. (1987). *Social Analysis of Education.* Routledge and Kegan Paul, London.

Chapter 12

Multimethodology and Critical Theory: an Intersection of Interests?

MARTIN SPAUL

INTRODUCTION

Choosing between, or amalgamating features of, systems methodologies has appeared in different contexts of discussion within the systems movement. In information systems, where debate has been led by Avison and Wood-Harper (1990), the focus has been primarily pragmatic; concentrating on practical schemes for the deployment of elements from different methodologies without dwelling on the philosophical niceties of what is being proposed. In the literature concerned with systems approaches to management, however, a different form of debate has been initiated. In this debate, methodology choice has become a reason for surfacing a wide range of issues: the forms of rationality inherent in different forms of social and organisational enquiry; the issues of emancipation, workplace participation and an attention to "human well-being" in the labour process; the utopian, socially transformative ambitions which have characterised the systems tradition; and the emergence of a "critical systems thinking" intended to bring order and practical application to these ideas.

A key moment in the development of this wider perspective was Flood and Jackson's (1991a) use of elements of Frankfurt School critical theory to

Multimethodology: The Theory and Practice of Combining Management Science Methodologies.
Edited by John Mingers and Anthony Gill.
© 1997 John Wiley & Sons Ltd.

provide a theoretical grounding for their TSI methodology choice and problem-solving framework. Their use of critical theory was a startling intellectual move since, although Marxist or critical perspectives were already established as a means of questioning the ethos or social/political orientation of systems thinking (see, e.g., Mingers, 1980; Thomas and Lockett, 1991), the use of a specific critical–philosophical doctrine to help solve the problem of methodology choice was novel. Their use of the theory of knowledge-constitutive interests (Habermas, 1978) brought with it a sense that operating within the TSI framework was intrinsically linked to an emancipatory orientation. The tenets of the version of "critical systems thinking" exemplified by TSI placed "theoretical and practical complementarism" (a methodology choice framework licensed by Habermasian theory) alongside commitments to historical and social awareness, and emancipation.

This novel stance has been difficult to evaluate in the conventional terms of management–scientific enquiry. For hostile commentators (see, e.g., Tsoukas, 1992, 1993) the importation of critical theory into management is an incoherent move occasioned by *hubris*; for more sympathetic commentators (see, e.g., Cummins, 1994) the specific formulation of TSI constitutes an aberration best quietly forgotten. In the face of this criticism, TSI appears to have undergone substantial modification (Flood, 1995; Flood and Romm, 1996), with critical theory given a less specific role in justifying its mechanisms. The time thus seems appropriate for a retrospective examination of some of the disciplinary expectations and pressures which led to Flood and Jackson's original construction of the TSI framework and its surrounding intellectual support; and to examine the subtle relationship between these and the themes of Frankfurt School critical theory.

This retrospective examination is an attempt to establish several changes in perspective on critical projects in management science. In the first section, it is suggested that Flood and Jackson's portrayal of TSI as a complete managerial problem-solving framework, licensed by well-established principles of critical theory, is substantially at variance with the overall intention and specific historical development of the work of the Frankfurt School. However, this variance should not be taken to mean that critical theory has no role in informed debate within the management sciences. Rather, it means that critical theory is best regarded not as an "instrument" which may simply be "applied" to a more or less predetermined management science project, but as a means of reflecting upon and modifying that project. The next section sketches the argument that if contemporary critical theory (Habermas's later *Theory of Communicative Action*, Habermas, 1984, 1987a) is traced through, respecting both its intention and historical circumstance, then much of the discussion surrounding competing methodologies and rationalities surfaces in a new guise. This new guise exchanges an exclusively professional managerial perspective (with its emphasis on effective problem solving in a bounded situation) for a more holistic consideration of working practice in the context of a general architecture of modern societies. This architecture provides a means of supplying both a social context for, and a theoretical representation of, each of the competing demands which shape the organisation of production and patterns of work.

MULTIPLE METHODOLOGIES, MULTIPLE RATIONALITIES AND INTERDISCIPLINARY RESEARCH

This section examines some of the major themes which arise when divergent rationalities and scientific disciplines converge on the same project. These themes are examined from two starting points: Flood and Jackson's TSI project, and the interdisciplinary research programme of the early Frankfurt School. This is an attempt to explore subtle overlaps and differences, working by piecemeal comparison. The rationale for this procedure is that in matters of intellectual history—with patterns of partial influence and affinity—the attempt to set up a clear, but rigid, comparative framework is a self-defeating enterprise.

The Primacy of Epistemology

Flood and Jackson's construction of the problem of multimethodology, and its putative solution by TSI, is strongly influenced by a particular reading of the development of systems thinking, and its fissuring into different traditions of enquiry. There are many perspectives which might be generated on the history of the formalisation and deployment of systems methodologies; but the principal one employed by Flood and Jackson (see, e.g., Flood and Ulrich, 1991; Jackson, 1991a) is that of epistemology. From this perspective, the key facet of any systems approach is its epistemological commitment: the view which it has of the process of enquiry, and the means by which it tries to secure complete and reliable knowledge as the basis of action. The history of systems thought, seen through this filter and with the help of Kuhn's analysis of scientific revolutions (Kuhn, 1970), is one of epistemological "breaks" which mark three phases of development. In the first phase, systems thinking worked with a positivist conception of enquiry and intervention; a realist epistemology in which systems science investigated a world of systemic facts with well-tried scientific methods)—an approach typified by RAND systems analysis and Jenkins' Systems Engineering. This phase is seen to come to a close with an epistemological break—apparent in the work of Ackoff (1978), Churchman (1979) and Checkland (1981)—which challenged the philosophical basis on which positivist methodologies had been constructed. The second phase, ushered in by this break, was entered with the construction of processes of enquiry and intervention founded on a hermeneutic or interpretivist epistemology, which abandons the scientific assumption of a privileged, single vantage point from which knowledge—especially in the social sphere—may be gained. Such an abandonment is exemplified by the multiple perspectives pursued during interventions undertaken using methodologies such as SAST (Mason and Mitroff, 1981) or SSM (Checkland, 1981). Flood and Jackson's account culminates in a second epistemological break, contemporary and less marked, to which they see themselves as contributing. This break separates an interpretivist epistemology from a "critical" one, marked by an attention to power relations in the definition of knowledge (Jackson, 1991b: 131).

The history of systems thought is, from this perspective, the evolution of three distinct Kuhnian scientific paradigms locked into their own assumptions and specialised discourses. All of these paradigms are still "live"; they are the basis of continuing theoretical development and professional practice, without a single approach able to gain hegemony. Each paradigm, from the distanced viewpoint adopted in Flood and Jackson's surveys, has some valid claim to competence in dealing with systems problems. This situation is seen as a paradigmatic bind; a problem situation from which escape should be sought. The reasons for seeking this escape are rooted in the popular conception that progressive sciences should tend towards unity (a conception which has been contested, see Giddens, 1994: 87–88). Jackson (1991a: 264–269, 1995) contrasts scientific, systems approaches towards management with the fads purveyed by "popular management gurus". Management fads are transparently ephemeral, offering fashionable advice which is likely to be rescinded in the next wave of fashion; a process which has gone on sufficiently long for the withdrawal of trust from management gurus to be a serious issue. Jackson is concerned to avoid such a fate for systems and OR methodologies; hence their apparent incompatibility must be shown to be only apparent, masking a deep complementarity and a demonstrable growth in knowledge.

Jackson (1991a: 253–270) surveys each possible avenue of escape from a fractured management science: an isolationist refusal to work outside the assumptions of an entrenched paradigm; an imperialist reduction of every paradigm to a favoured candidate; and a pragmatic view of systems methodologies as "mere tools", and hence a collapse of paradigmatic difference. Each of these routes is blocked by the inherent logic of scientific paradigms, marked as they are by the distinct belief systems and social practices which characterise Western science; for which each of these escape routes is reflectively inadequate. Isolationism appears to be a deliberate blindness in the face of divergent forms of enquiry which negates the essential openness of the scientific mindset—as Kuhn (1970: 167–168) made clear, a scientific community is one which has institutionalised the kind of impartial enquiry which can lead to a progressive growth in knowledge. Imperialism fails because no general translation scheme (such as that once envisaged by the "unified science movement", see Coffa, 1991, Part II) is available for the reduction of any arbitrary scientific discourse. Pragmatism appears as a form of philistinism which disavows any explanation for action other than the most direct terms of the problem in hand; a stance which denies the reflective, theoretical component of the belief system crucial to the scientist. For Flood and Jackson, for whom epistemology is a defining feature of each systems paradigm, this creates a desperate situation. Epistemologies are, historically, the outcome of a search for ultimate grounds, a final source of authority for knowledge (Tiles and Tiles, 1993)—the search for some deeper grounds, a "super epistemology", is not a well-established theme.

Flood and Jackson's "history from the standpoint of epistemology" follows an established pattern for the portrayal of the development of the social sciences (for a retrospective history see Dallmayr and McCarthy, 1977, and for an internal perspective on one of sociology's epistemological breaks see Gouldner, 1971). More proximately it was modelled on Burrell and Morgan's (1979) analysis of the development of organisation theory in terms of Kuhnian paradigms defined by epistemology. Such portrayals have a long philosophical pedigree—epistemology has been at the heart of debates about enquiry since the time of Descartes—but they do not provide a cost-free framework for discussion. As many, loosely "postmodern", writers (e.g. Rorty, 1980) have pointed out, the epistemological tradition has created a fixation with establishing "secure foundations" for knowledge at the expense of seemingly mundane, but concrete and historically aware discourse.

Portraying the development of systems thinking as, primarily, an intellectual history—a pattern of development driven by philosophical considerations and marked by shifting philosophical bases—has several effects. In particular, it serves to suppress other ways of approaching the impasse experienced by a field with several incompatible, competing forms of expertise. One alternative perspective would be to focus on the institutional frameworks which enable scientific paradigms or professional traditions to function. Thus, to work within the positivist systems paradigm is not simply to hold a belief in objectivity, a correspondence theory of truth and an ontology of precise facts; it is also a disposition to seek quantifiable variables in a practical situation, to reach for modelling tools, to seek work where such traits find a congenial home, and to communicate with others who do the same.

These dispositions were part of the institutional ideology of, for example, the RAND Corporation and the US military. Correspondingly, Checkland's descriptions of the development of SSM focus, with good reason, on the contingent factors which permitted SSM to take shape: the existence of the Lancaster group and ISCOL, the kind of students they were able to attract, companies willing to countenance the use of SSM, dissemination via a "house" journal, etc. (Checkland, 1981: 149–161). The relationship of SSM, as a concrete development within this institutional framework, to interpretivist social theory or hermeneutic philosophy is not straightforward, with many connections made on *post hoc* reflection (Checkland, 1981: 264–277). Recasting the paradigmatic bind of systems thinking in "institutional" terms does not make the bind go away—it reappears as a deep-rooted problem with existing patterns of education, allegiance and employment—but it does serve to make clear that the problem has been socially created.

Recounting the development of a discipline in epistemological terms serves a synoptic function: it enables the suppression of practical details (histories of the work of individuals, their motivations and beliefs, the institutions which they formed, etc.) in favour of a central philosophical theme which, it is hoped, captures the essence of a movement. Such an abstraction is a convenience, and practically indispensable for a perspicuous survey; but it carries the danger that philosophy is seen as a "master key" for history. A further consequence which derives from this is that clashes of epistemology or the intellectual paradoxes within a tradition take on a mythic, spell-binding status—problems which have to be solved by recourse to a realm which bursts the bounds of the "first-order" discourse in which they arise. A discipline which is not fixated by epistemology and "firm foundations" can exhibit a higher tolerance for paradox and deep intellectual divisions. Giddens (1994) suggests that the scientists of late modernity, caught up in a spiral of endlessly refined expertise, will have to institutionalise such tolerance.

Critical Theory as a Unifying Discourse

Problems of mythic proportions require solutions with the same status. In constructing the need for a "complementarist" framework in which divergent epistemologies could be accommodated, Flood and Jackson made the case that a specialised professional group—systems scientists—should reach for the alien discourse of critical theory to resolve its theoretical difficulties. At a high level of abstraction, critical theory provides a congenial model for anyone with a specific disciplinary project of bringing together diverse theoretical spheres into a coherent body of thought. Critical theory is, in conformity with the Marxist tradition, an attempt to respond to Hegel's diagnosis that modern societies have ceased to be "ethical totalities" (Habermas, 1987b: 62)—they have a structure which precludes universal understanding and consensus on the significant features of society. Specialised roles and discourses have undermined our ability to achieve a comprehension of our social circumstances. In tackling Hegel's diagnosis of modernity head on, critical theory was forced to create a mode of theorising which attempted to reach across specialised discourses. However, it is one thing to postulate such a programme, it is quite another to make it coherent and practical—and yet another to interpret the discourse of critical theory in terms which make sense from the standpoint of a specific professional group. Flood and Jackson's appropriation of critical theory as the basis of TSI has, as noted, been restricted to that of Habermas's theory of knowledge-constitutive interests. At the centre of this interpretation is the idea that "methodological complementarism", the integration of different strands of systems thought in a unified, practical choice framework, could be underpinned by Habermas's reworking of the tradition of historical materialism in which the Frankfurt School stands. Such a project requires two principal criteria to be fulfilled before it can be counted as successful: first, the critical theory on which it relies has to carry out its own task of epistemological integration successfully, and provide a practical basis for social analysis at the level proper to its own aspirations; and, second, there has to be some scheme of interpretation by which this discourse can be made meaningful within the professional sphere within which TSI intends to operate. It is not straightforwardly obvious that either of these conditions obtains.

Habermas's work is written against a dense background of German political philosophy; a background which, as McCarthy (1984: ix) remarks, is not always explicitly elaborated in his work. Thus the assumptions brought to Habermas's texts will, more emphatically than for most authors, condition what will be found within them. *Knowledge and Human Interests (KHI)* can be interpreted on several levels. First, as a self-standing work which proposes a philosophical anthropology which grounds scientific practices, diagnoses the one-sidedness of modern scientific development, and gives a glimpse of a practice which more completely serves human needs. Second, it may be read as a specialised contribution to the debate over positivism in the social sciences (it was written in a period of epistemological crisis in sociology). Third, it may be read against the background of the earlier work of the Frankfurt School—in which much of the above may be taken for granted—as an attempt to remedy some of the philosophical and methodological defects which dogged its pre-war research programme. All readings are, in their own senses, valid; but it is the last which offers the most direct route to a practical interpretation of *KHI* as a means of mediating between different rationalities in social research.

In their presentation of *KHI*, Flood and Jackson customarily adopt the first (and, to a lesser extent, the second) of the perspectives above (see, e.g., Flood and Jackson, 1991a: 49; Jackson, 1991a: 12–17) since their assumed readership is in a discipline with few previous connections with critical theory. Their interpretative task is facilitated by strong similarities between one of the central images of the tradition of historical materialism in which *KHI* stands—that of human societies struggling to survive and develop in a hostile natural environment—and that of the organic metaphors which are central to the vocabulary of systems. Thus, the universal anthropology at the centre of *KHI*—the necessary conditions under which societies develop—apparently has a direct import for the analysis of social systems viewed from the perspective of "systems thinking". Added to this connection is the intuitive appeal of Habermas's exposition: the connection of the technical interest in the domination of nature with the modern social institutions and practices of science, technology and industry; that of the practical interest with the experience of community and personal interaction; and that of the emancipatory interest with the democratic impulse underlying Western political culture, *KHI* has an undeniable resonance for the systems discipline; a discipline which has relatively recently shaken off a positivist self-understanding and requires reorientation.

The broad connections above do, however, mask difficulties for detailed practical development which only become apparent when the more specific role of *KHI*—as a reconstruction of early critical theory—is considered. Two specific difficulties arise: first, in the basic conception of interdisciplinary social research guided by historical materialism; second, in the way in which *KHI*'s abstract and programmatic guidelines are to be transformed into concrete analyses of current social formations.

The original programme of interdisciplinary research which Horkheimer set out for the Frankfurt School (Horkheimer, 1976, 1989a, b) constituted a heavily modified form of Marxism. The early critical theorists accepted as background the form of historical materialism developed by Marx during his early work (McLellan, 1995: 3–77)—the "idealist" form reconstructed by Lukacs (1971). Central to this thought was the conception that the activity of labour, suitably freed, carried a world-transforming potential; that if alienated labour and commodity exchange was superseded by a "self-fulfilling praxis" and free exchange among equals, then a rational and harmonious society would spontaneously emerge. In such a society a state of "human emancipation" (a state more radical than the limited "political emancipation" of liberal societies) would be enjoyed, in which people could work in accordance with their "species-being". These ideas are a key part of the lineage of the participatory ("emancipatory") methodologies, forming an oblique link with Frankfurt School thought. However, although the Marxist tradition focused on economic activity and the workplace, the Frankfurt School attempted to move beyond this restriction. In mainstream Marxism, it is held that the economic "base" determines the form of the social and political "superstructure". The Frankfurt School recognised a more reciprocal relationship between base and superstructure; it thus required analytic tools beyond those of political economy, since it had to comprehend the workings of the "superstructure" as an independent entity. This wider ambition complicates any attempt to set up a direct commerce between critical theory and a discipline, such as management science, with a restricted focus on productive activity.

Horkheimer realised that the only analytical tools which he could use to supplement the discourse of historical materialism would have to come from "traditional theory"—the sciences of bourgeois society. Although he regarded these sciences as historically bound, lacking the "absolute" status which a Cartesian conception of science accorded them, he had an immense respect for the standards of rationality built into their practices. His proposal was that critical theory adopt whichever sciences could be called upon to illuminate the social whole: the research agenda would be set, and the results interpreted by, historical materialism. A heavy burden was thus placed on materialist philosophy. The Lukacsian materialism of the Frankfurt School was "weak" in the sense that it did not provide immediate insights into, or interpretations of, the kind of concrete social phenomena with which "traditional" theories dealt. The difficulty was whether such a "weak" discourse could influence or assimilate work in established disciplines with their own form of practical research and standards of rationality.

The ambitions of critical theory were thoroughly holistic; Horkheimer set up broad goals such as an "account of the present" or a "comprehensive existential judgement" on the contemporary condition of Western societies. Such a theory could not afford particular disciplinary attachments; it had to show that it could genuinely absorb the work of any and every discipline (McCarthy, 1993). The key facets of the Frankfurt School research programme which were to discharge this commitment were Horkheimer's principles of "induction" and "integration". The inductive principle saved the programme from having, *per impossibile*, to encompass the whole of society; it stated that, since societies formed a densely interlocked whole, the detailed examination of a single part—an institution, a group, an idea—would reveal the features of the whole. The principle of integration stated that a feature of society could not be exhaustively understood from a single viewpoint, or even a bounded set of viewpoints; rather, comprehensive social enquiry had to utilise whichever disciplines and sciences were thrown up by history and combine their results "without being impeded by their boundaries". These principles, and their inherent weaknesses, were apparent in the studies on authority and the family carried out by the Frankfurt School in the 1930s (Wiggershaus, 1994: 149–156). In a set of disparate and loosely controlled studies of the change in authority relationships and attitudes in families under economic stress, the difficulty of achieving the kind of integration Horkheimer had envisaged became apparent. As Honneth's (1991: 5–31, 1993) analyses have subsequently shown, the interdisciplinary programme was blinded by historical materialism's bias towards the critique of political economy; it skewed the disciplines which were to be combined into a loose hierarchy ordered by the proximity of the discipline to the materialist basis. At the top of the hierarchy came economics, which was assumed to be the basic motor of history; followed by psychology, which could examine the relationship between basic human motivations and economic activity; and finally by cultural study, a weak discipline which served to analyse the integration of economic imperatives into social life. Despite the professed principle of the mutual conditioning of base and superstructure, when practical research was undertaken in earnest the discipline of sociology and the domain of social action had been screened from serious consideration.

The ambitions and defects of the early Frankfurt School programme show tantalising analogies with the problems which Flood and Jackson had diagnosed as facing systems thinking. In the one case the need to integrate sciences which had developed autonomously, with their own aims and intellectual agenda; in the other a need to produce an integrated intervention instrument from a set of autonomous instruments. In both cases there is the recognition that sciences and instruments must be respected and be used practically on their own terms, or incoherence and indiscipline are risked. There are also, of course, substantial differences: a holistic sociology of Western societies, conducted with critical intent, is hardly the same as a synoptic management problem-solving instrument (see below). There are sufficient affinities, however, for Habermas's attempt to reconstruct the Frankfurt School programme to have attracted the attention of Flood and Jackson. Whether either project is "rescued" by *KHI* is a more complex question.

Habermas began the studies which were to become *KHI* (his inaugural address at Frankfurt, Habermas 1978: 301–317) with a new departure from the point at which Horkheimer began: distinguishing critical from traditional theory, but this time on a more fully developed epistemic base. Habermas revisited the foundation of historical materialism set out in the early work of Marx and expanded the vision of human social development which it contained. Habermas proceeded from an enlarged set of anthropological universals to the necessary forms of science which all human societies must develop in the course of their evolution: the three knowledge-constitutive interests. This epistemological base has been the subject of much criticism (for an accessible overview see Honneth, 1991: 203–239), and Habermas has subsequently recast his work in other terms (see the third section below); but the feature which has the principal bearing on the interpretation of Flood and Jackson's use of *KHI* will be examined here.

KHI is offered by Habermas in support of a large-scale thesis on the development of Western societies: that they have developed the technical interest at the expense of the practical and emancipatory interests. The concrete interpretation of this claim has to be in terms of the particular properties of these societies, a judgement upon industry and science, finance and administration, etc.—and a judgement on forms of institutionalised education, research and development. *KHI*, however, goes only a short way to supplying the specifics of this interpretation. What is offered are programmatic philosophies for three abstractly conceived sciences which answer to each of the interests; concrete analyses of particular sciences and research programmes which would connect them with this base are not carried out. Habermas's abstract sciences have only an oblique relationship with even "pure" forms of research considered as a concrete practice; for example, the technical interest is not represented by concrete scientific research as it is currently practised (see Honneth, 1991: 248–250). The relationship between basic human interests and patterns of industrialisation, the development of technology, the systematic provision of health and social care, etc., is left entirely as a matter for speculation. This interpretative gap is traced by McCarthy (1984: 94–110) to a deeper ambiguity over the role of critical theory which marked Habermas's work at the time of writing *KHI*. The heritage of critical theory intertwines two notions of critique which have only become clarified in the latter stages of its development. At one level there is the reflection embodied in the analysis of the general conditions of knowledge and action. This form of reflection aims at the production of normative bases which can guide empirically grounded analysis, and it is possible to see *KHI* as pitched at this level. This general orientation can provide a guide, but not specific techniques, for a level of reflection which investigates the formative history of a particular group or practice. This specific form of enquiry can only proceed by an examination of the motives and interests (understood now as patterns of concrete social advantage) which guide the group or practice, or by unfolding the process by which they came into being. A situationally engaged critique of this sort aims at the practical change of established conditions and an insight into specific structures of power and ideology. This distinction is a refracted form of Horkheimer's original determination to pursue both philosophy and empirical research—a form also refracted through our present knowledge of how such "unmaskings" may be carried out (see Dreyfus and Rabinow, 1982).

Critical Theory and Managerial Practice?

The gap between the two forms of critique implicit in the traditions of critical theory presents a severe problem for the attempt to underpin TSI's practical choice framework with *KHI*. Flood and Jackson use *KHI* at the level of a *motif*; they outline the broad intentions of the theory of knowledge-constitutive interests but provide no detailed linkage between its themes and practical management interventions. The interpretative gulf between an orientating philosophical framework for critical theory and the discourse of a specific professional group has to be closed by some sort of detailed analysis which anchors the latter in the former. The problem for anyone wishing to use *KHI* to interpret a practical project in detail is that Habermas abandoned the development of this work before practical research programmes could be derived from it—it is worth noting, however, that if the research programme of the early Frankfurt School, or those derived from Habermas's later theory (Ray, 1993; Dryzek, 1995), are any guide then research in management problem solving would hardly have figured prominently.

This difficulty is an instance of a more general feature of the intellectual orientation and intention of critical theory. The application of critical theory to any social group or profession is problematic if the existence of the group or profession is taken at face value under current social conditions. At the heart of critical theory is an attempt to achieve a distance from current forms of discourse, and a determination not to accept concepts and social roles in their given form (see, e.g., Horkheimer, 1976: 216–221). Thus, insofar as critical theory may be used to further the ends of a professional group, it can only do so in a manner consistent with the self-understanding of critical theory if the status, historical provenance, motives, etc., of that group are placed in radical question.

This process of critical distancing and alignment with critical theory's external perspective on contemporary society and its actors is not obviously present in the formulation of TSI. A social theory, or a systematic approach to social intervention, presupposes some object with which it is principally concerned; the social reality which it attempts to reflect or transform. Some such objects are concrete and relatively easy to delineate: a particular nation-state, the community of a bounded region, a specific formal organisation, etc. Other social objects are more vaguely delineated but no less the legitimate object of theory or action: Western society, oppressed groups, turbulent organisations, etc. In such cases theory and the understanding of the social object evolve together. Critical theory has, historically, been cavalier about making its social objects clear (Held, 1980: 353–400, who also reconstructs critical theory's object as the "ideal-type" Western nation-state). However, setting up some correspondence between this vague conception and the social object presupposed by TSI is a necessary step in clarifying the philosophical basis of TSI.

In the primary text describing TSI (Flood and Jackson, 1991a) the identification of its intended object is made in a series of refinements, beginning with the target group at which the text is aimed ("practising managers") and ending with a typology of assumptions about problem contexts (the "system of systems methodologies"). TSI is presented as directly relevant to the concerns of practising managers, and constitutes a tool for a "manager facing major organisational issues" and looking for an approach to alleviate difficulties (Flood and Jackson, 1991a: 31–32). This is not simply a matter of attempting to "sell" a theoretically rooted problem-solving approach to management practitioners; the theoretical vocabulary of TSI has its origins in a managerial perception of the world as a domain in which purposeful control has to be exercised. The central concern of TSI is the diagnosis of the characteristics of "problem situations", and ensuring that "appropriate systems methodologies" are deployed to "resolve" or "improve" the difficulties which inhere in those situations. This perception of the world as an arena for effective action based on transferable professional skills can only be comprehended against the background of the commodification of expertise (Beck, 1994: 47), and only fully explained with reference to the particular commodified expertise constructed in the development of the traditions of management and systems science. For example, Checkland's (1981: 161–162, 237–240) influential formulations of the ideas of "methodology" and "problem situation" is dependent on a lengthy induction into refinements of an instrumental view of the world. Instrumentalism surfaces in guises other than crude, positivist goal seeking; the term may be applied to any disengaged or manipulative view of the world. (Taylor, 1989: 321–340). An enthusiastic embracing of instrumentalism, at any level, causes a problematic rift with the Frankfurt School.

The fact that the basic vocabulary of TSI is rooted in the traditions and culture of professional management—a historically specific group with its own interests and perceptions—in no way serves to invalidate it. A demonstration of origins only serves to set up a context of interpretation; one in which its claims are relativised to the traditions of management science. This relativisation has several important outcomes. It serves to give a *de facto* definition of TSI's social object which, broadly, is restricted to "social systems" (to use Jackson's (1991a) terminology) for which the characterisations of "problem situation" and "methodological intervention" make sense and are commonly used (which excludes, for example, an unhappy marriage at one end of the spectrum of possible candidates, and national malaise at the other). The range of such problem situations is somewhat narrower than the whole of society— an important realisation for the systems discipline with its history of completely general claims. Awareness of the traditions and perceptions of professional management should also ensure that when a social theory—developed by a group with its own traditions and outlook—is being appropriated by systems thinking, that theory is reinterpreted and distinguished from its original form. For example, to elide interpretative research in systems thinking with the kind of interpretative social research found in, say, Clifford (1988) (a set of experimental writings in ethnography) is to lose a whole realm of significant intellectual differences. Frankfurt School critical theory has its own agenda and mood—reaching towards an undescribable future "rational society", a sense of dissatisfaction with the present bordering on disgust— markedly different from that of professional management.

A specific instance of the need for this careful interpretation is provided by the general "political" ambiance of TSI's choice framework being used to license a connection with critical theory. In categorising problem situations to guide methodology choice, Flood and Jackson (1991a: 32–41) turn to a political vocabulary to provide the principal axis of their typological grid. In this task they are helped by Morgan's (1986: 141–198) elaboration of the metaphor of an organisation as a "mini-state". In developing his metaphor, Morgan is at pains to point out that there are *parallels* between phenomena within organisations and those which typify the more obvious realm of politics at the level of the nation-state. The characteristics which prove illuminating are those pitched at an abstract level: general forms of rule and basic relationships of interest or power between political participants. At a more concrete level, being on the payroll of even a large organisation is quite unlike being a citizen of a nation-state, with the major features which shape political life (the aggregation of interests into parties which compete for government, the enactment and enforcement of law, the state possession of the means of violence, etc.) having only limited analogy with organisational phenomena. Following Morgan (1986: 188–189) Flood and Jackson use the abstract political idea of interest relationships between participants to motivate their typology; but this does not provide a clear connection with other levels of political discourse, nor ensure that a tool for organisational intervention becomes, simultaneously, a general political weapon. Neither does it ensure that it shares a common conceptual background with critical theory. Critical theory has largely been concerned with macro-political phenomena—the rise of Nazism, the mass media, militarism and industrialisation, social protest, etc. (Kellner, 1989)—and the explicit linkage between its concerns and those which arise in managerial organisational interventions has to be worked for, rather than assumed.

LATE CRITICAL THEORY AND THE MANAGEMENT SCIENCES

The previous section explored the differences and affinities between praxis-philosophical critical theory and the management sciences. It was suggested that considerable difficulties stood in the way of developing closer affinities; it was also noted that critical theory is something of a "moving target", with its contemporary form having diverged from a critical theory based on historical materialism. Current Habermasian theory is marked by a concern with features of the modern state and a (relatively) practical programme for the transformation of Western democratic institutions (see especially Habermas, 1996). The old Frankfurt School ambition of a "comprehensive account of the present" has been partially realised in an interpretative schema for the broad architecture of late-modern societies and a normative model for their democratic enhancement. This model provides an (under-explored) framework for the discussion of the shape and legitimacy of different working practices, and of the nature and role of professional management expertise. This section sketches the outlines of this framework and suggests that it may provide a means for clarifying the multimethodology/critical systems thinking debate in an enriched picture of its social context.

Habermas's later work, expressed in *The Theory of Communicative Action* (Habermas, 1984, 1987a) and the subsequent development of its ethical implications (Habermas, 1990, 1993), has been the source of considerable discussion in the management and systems sphere. This work usually makes an appearance in fragmentary form: as a social action typology (Lyytinen, Klein and Hirschheim, 1991), as a universal pragmatics of communication (Midgley, 1992), or as a principle of discourse ethics (Ulrich, 1994). Such applications are instances of applying elements of critical theory to preconceived projects with a different intellectual history; a procedure which is not necessarily invalid, but which requires independent justification. Habermas's later work is constructed using a methodology which makes fragmentation and "borrowing" of this sort problematic: it is an attempt to make selected intellectual currents "cohere" in fallibilistic and universal claims about the characteristics of modern societies (Habermas, 1990: 1–20). In the manner of Horkheimer, elements from different disciplines are arranged in relations of mutual support to form a holistic picture. The selective borrowing and application of a fragment of Habermasian theory, without reference to the whole, cannot be accounted a "critical" project without further justification.

This account of Habermas's later system is an attempt to give a brief tour of the holistic picture formulated in *The Theory of Communicative Action (TCA)* (for more full introductions see White 1988 and Rasmussen, 1990). In setting out each of its well-known elements—the action framework, communicative action culled from linguistic theory, discourse ethics, the reformulation of sociological traditions into a two-tier theory of society, the critical valorisation of social movements and the public sphere—a space will be found for the re-examination of the concerns of management science. The re-examination makes the case that a critical management science should approach the professional expertise with which it deals primarily from an *external* perspective, that of the concerned citizen rather than the involved practitioner.

The Communication–Theoretic Reformulation of Critical Theory

Habermas conceived *TCA* as the construction of an account of broad, but specific, features of modern societies. In an interview (cited in Giddens, 1985: 98) he outlined his "real motive" as showing how a critique of Weber's rationalisation thesis could be reformulated as an explanation for the decline of the "welfare-state compromise" and an account of the democratic potential of new social movements. Such an intention is consonant with the traditions of the Frankfurt School (*TCA* concludes with a reconsideration of Horkheimer's original project (Habermas, 1987a: 374–403)) in giving a comprehensive account of the present—particular social groups have to look deep within the theory to find the niche which their concerns occupy. In particular, the theory has to be followed through from its abstract starting points to its development of concrete consequences before specific conclusions about social practices are drawn.

The development of *TCA* begins abstractly, at the level of philosophical principle. The critique of Weber's rationalisation thesis (Habermas, 1984:

143–272) is an attempt to get beyond the dead end at which praxis philosophy and first-generation critical theory had arrived. Weber's portrayal of Western societies was one in which purposive or instrumental rationality, embodied institutionally in capitalism, progressively triumphs. Habermas is concerned to refute this claim not just as a faulty reading of Western history (he had already given a historical account of a dimension of reason missed by Weber's analysis in *The Structural Transformation of the Public Sphere*—Habermas, 1989), but as a derivation from a faulty philosophy. The philosophy of consciousness (centred on the knowing or labouring subject, the subject to be "emancipated" in the Marxist tradition) reduces reason to, at root, subject–object relations—a view which stresses the representational, fact-cataloguing dimensions of knowledge and language. Habermas establishes the "lost dimension", which he had earlier identified historically, by a reformulated philosophy of language centred on its role in mediating intersubjective agreement among socialised individuals (Habermas, 1984: 273–337). The core of critical theory is thus read out of a "rational reconstruction"; a coherent reading of trends in the philosophy of language which produces a hypothesis about the competence of the speaking, reasoning individual. The oft-quoted action framework is developed from trends in the philosophy of language; an amalgam of speech–act theory, a de-transcendentalised version of Apel's ideal communication, and Chomskyan models of linguistic competence. The categorisation of action into instrumental, strategic and communicative comes with a priority attached: communicative action is the "original" mode of language use, and is morally privileged.

At this level of analysis action types are conceived in an abstract way, and the moral privileging of communicative action provides a principle yet to be interpreted in concrete situations—the derivation of a practical critical programme requires a detailed mapping onto real social practices and institutions. Habermas begins this mapping in a similarly abstract way, via a reflection on two of the major sociological traditions which have developed during this century (Habermas, 1987a: 117–229). Habermas traces the development of the functionalism of Parsons and Luhmann—expressed in its most sophisticated form as social systems theory (Luhmann, 1995)—and the hermeneutic tradition of Schutz and Gadamer, with its focus on the lifeworld experienced by social actors. For Habermas, the opposition between these approaches to social theory has a kind of completeness: the viewpoint of systems theory is that of the observer, the third person; the viewpoint of the hermeneutic tradition is that of the participant, the first person. In keeping with the integrative ambitions of critical theory Habermas views both approaches as necessary components of as complete a theory of society as we are able, currently, to achieve. This theoretical opposition thus becomes a "two-tier" model of society, with each strand being linked with the social institutions and contexts for which it provides the most appropriate mode of analysis. It is at this level that Habermas begins to approach the empirical concerns of mainstream sociology, and programmes of "critical" social research can emerge (see Dryzek, 1995).

The "two-tier" model of system and lifeworld enabled Habermas to return to another theme which had appeared in *The Structural Transformation of the Public Sphere*, that of the basic architecture and institutions of modern societies. In Hegel's model (Taylor, 1975: 428–461) societies are divided into state, civil society and family; with civil society encompassing both the economy and free civil associations among citizens. Habermas redraws this map, taking the economy—with the state—as systemic contexts, and regarding voluntary civil association and the intimate sphere as lifeworld contexts. This redrawn map may be programmatically associated with his action framework. The systemic spheres are integrated by strategic action via the steering media of money and power; the actions of self-interested agents serve—in largely unintended and uncomprehended ways—the functioning of the economic and political systems (thus Weber's linkage between purposive rationality and institutionalised capitalism is retained). Lifeworld contexts are integrated by the remnants of tradition (eroded by the rationalisation processes of modernity—see Giddens, 1991) and, insofar as appropriate forums for debate develop, by the rational consensus constructed through communicative action.

A Model of Critical Practice

With his theoretical framework established, Habermas is able to discharge his self-imposed obligations with respect to the crisis in the welfare-state compromise and the emancipatory potential of new social movements. For the former, he is able to elaborate the thesis of the "internal colonisation of the lifeworld", outlined initially in *Legitimation Crisis* (Habermas, 1988), since he is able to point to the "invasive" tendencies of the steering media of the economy and state. In a revised form of Lukacs' critique of reification, Habermas presents an analysis in which the political and economic systems progressively demand (in the interests of efficient functioning) the conformity of all areas of life to their standards: politicians "buy" loyalty with stylised monetary inducements, state administration imposes regimented forms of behaviour in exchange for welfare payments, the "flexible labour market" demands the surrender of freedoms in the personal sphere, and even personal relationships become mediatised with the burgeoning professional "therapies" of contemporary life. This colonisation process is experienced as a pathological deformation of the lifeworld (Habermas, 1987a: 142–143)—this social pathology gives rise to a crisis of confidence in government and a sense of anomie and dissatisfaction in working and personal life.

New social movements are regarded as both a symptom of the colonisation of the lifeworld, and a potentially emancipatory response. In Habermas's scheme they are the embodiment of the only (potentially) legitimate counterbalance to the systems of economy and state—since they arise in a sphere in which communicative action, and the development of legitimate norms, *may* be at work. This leads to his fragile and defensive formulation of the potential for a critical politics in our current historical situation:

> The goal is no longer to supersede an economic system having a capitalist life of its own and a system of domination having a bureaucratic life of its own but to erect a democratic dam against the encroachment of systems imperatives on areas of the lifeworld. Therewith we have bid a farewell to the notion of alienation and appropriation of objectified essentialist powers, whose place is in a philosophy of praxis. A radical–democratic change in the process of legitimation aims at a new balance between the forces of social integration so that the social-integrative power of solidarity . . . can prevail over the other two control resources, i.e., money and administrative power, and therewith successfully assert the practically oriented demands of the lifeworld. (Habermas, 1992: 444)

With this change, the focus of critical theory shifts decisively from traditional Marxist analyses of labour, capital and the conflicts between them. Critical politics now centres on possible mechanisms for the formation of validated norms within the lifeworld, on the recreation—in very different material circumstances—of the "public spheres" of the Enlightenment, and on the means by which these spheres exert political influence. Hence the battlegrounds of critical theory shift from those associated with the heyday of Marxism (the workplace and systems of production) to the principal sites of political conflict in the 1980s and 1990s: the media and the law courts. The bureaucratic state and the capitalist economy are no longer seen as illegitimate or as social formations to be transcended; they are systems on whose different forms of productivity we depend (Habermas appears to be greatly influenced by what he characterised as the "abysmal collapse" of state socialism in the Eastern *bloc*). They are, however, to be democratically limited and controlled, and their "steering media" to be kept, as far as possible, from civil life.

Habermas's original model of system/lifeworld conflict (Habermas, 1987a: 391–396) was structurally simple: pathological deformations of the lifeworld by the system would be experienced in the lifeworld as problematic, these experiences would—under ideal circumstances—be thematised in public spheres, rational discussion would result in the consensual formation of desired norms, and this authoritative public opinion could be mobilised to exert political or economic pressure on the system. The system then had to find a response, in its own terms, which accommodated public opinion. Similarly, the division between the action types characteristic of either side of the system/lifeworld boundary seemed particularly stark; the simple picture of political and economic systems integrated by strategic action, and a lifeworld integrated by tradition and communicative action seemed a fiction designed to keep alive the radical politics of the Enlightenment identified in *Structural Transformation* (Honneth, 1991: 278–303). Also, the division between system and lifeworld which keeps this politics alive seems to surrender too much; since the manner in which the system functions—the mechanisms of the workplace or government bureaucracy—seems no longer to be a legitimate concern of the citizen (McCarthy, 1991: 152–180).

The clarifications and developments of Habermas's position set out by Cohen and Arato (1992), and subsequently adopted by Habermas (1996: 370–373), provide a model of system function and system/lifeworld conflict which permits a relatively clear mapping of the agenda of critical systems thinking to be made. Cohen and Arato establish (1992: 700–701) that the system and lifeworld divide is not to be read as a denial of the importance of informal mechanisms of understanding and accommodation within formal organisations. Although formal organisations function by the integration of strategic actions (steered by money or the exercise of power), those actions must make some sense to the actors concerned. Actors "negotiate" (in the sense established by the interpretative tradition) the meanings of rules, orders and duties against the background supposition of the operation of power and money; the meaningful actions which they perform need not, however, have a systemic function accessible to them. Habermas's systemic spheres thus include both impersonal, objective elements accessible to functionalist systemic analysis, and elements of "negotiated order" accessible to ethnomethodological analysis (McCarthy, 1991: 158). However, questions of legitimacy cannot usefully be posed from a perspective *internal* to system functioning.

Cohen and Arato adapt Habermas's basic model of the function of social movements as a reaction to, and democratic brake on, the system. The basic model does not completely correspond to the experience of social movements and their conflicts. What is missing is the fact that many elements of system functioning can be thematised within the lifeworld and made the subject of specific protests and demands. In adopting Luhmann's dark rhetoric of the self-referentiality of systems—the idea that they have an inner logic which unfolds inexorably "behind the backs" of human actors—Habermas diverted attention from the empirical fact that economic and political systems have always been the subject of "risky" interventions based on incomplete analysis and optimism. Market speculations and political gambles are based on the "bet" that enough of system functioning has been understood to secure a favourable outcome for the actor concerned. There is no particular reason why social movements should not also base their protests and demands on similar analyses. Thus, for example, environmental groups do not simply protest against the perceived effects of a polluting system; they also propose alternative models of system functioning based on limited analysis (blueprints for "green economies" abound—the economic, social and environmental effects of their adoption are the subject of speculation). Social movements are thus shown by Cohen and Arato (1992: 492–563) to have a dual face. They act as a focus for debate and consensual norm formation in the lifeworld; thematising both system functioning and its unacceptable effects. This role must be anchored in accessible institutions for public debate. In addition, social movements must look into the system and apply focused pressure for the specific changes legitimated in public debate. This role must be anchored in mechanisms of lobbying, protest and "legal persuasion" (including the popular instruments of directed investment and consumer boycott). The ultimate form of pressure exerted on the system has to be in terms with which it can deal; similarly, the alternative forms of functioning adopted in the wake of such clashes must make systemic sense, and be integrated into its logic. System and lifeworld are not, under this model, totally mutually incomprehensible; they are joined by channels which translate between their dominant integrative action types.

Reinterpreting Critical Approaches to Management

The expanded role for social movements developed by Cohen and Arato also serves to establish a model for a critical management science, and a form of discourse in which competing rationalities and intentions can be resolved. It is not possible to point to a "social movement" concerned with the functioning of the workplace; at least, not one exhibiting the development of, say, the environmental movement. (One might speculate that trade unions still attached to an outdated model of labour politics divert much of the impetus from such a development.) However, there has been sufficient public concern over the lifeworld distortions which have come in the wake of downsizing, delayering, globalisation and general "lean competitiveness" to speak of an embryonic social movement concerned with management and working practices. The long hours, psychological and physical pressures, and the disruption of domestic life which the world of modern work entails are issues which television companies in the UK have subjected to detailed scrutiny (BBC, 1995, 1996). The voice lacking in this growing public debate is that analogous to the one heard in the environmental movement from the environmental scientist or economist unattached to corporate interests—a voice capable of analysing the quality of arguments, the effect of the vested interests which they serve, and distortions due to the professional ethos of those formulating those arguments.

A critical management or critical systems discipline would, on this version of critical politics, have to encompass the knowledge of the "methodological complementarist" and more. In addition to understanding the provenance and use of the range of management approaches (in the narrow sense covered in the disciplinary literature), it would have to achieve a critical distance from the world of commodified expertise in which these approaches are purveyed. It would have to contribute this understanding to a debate in the public sphere, in which its voice would be one among many. When questions about management and working practices are posed from the perspective of the lifeworld (rather than the specialised understanding of a professional group) then they are posed in a broad context which includes not just their role in a productive system, but also their effects on civil and intimate life. What is being sought is not simply a vision of "emancipated work", but rather the vision of a rounded life in which the experience of work is a part. This new context has been described by Stehr as characteristic of late-modern societies:

> The primary role in terms of which social struggles take place no longer involves workers as workers and the owners of the means of production as capitalists. The locus of the conflicts shifts to the individual as a configuration of roles . . . One of the principal axes of conflicts pits the consumer against production regimes of all sorts. The generalisation of issues contested in societal conflicts deprives knowledge societies of a central locus and arena in which these struggles take place. (Stehr, 1994: 150)

This reorientation dispels the idea that there is an equation to be made between the terms "critical", "emancipatory", and "participatory" as qualities of working or management *practice*. Being "critical" involves being able to make a holistic judgement on the probity of such practices; a judgement which considers consumers and shareholders, and the wider social fabric to which the work in question contributes. For Habermas, such judgements can only be made by a society in conversation with itself, not by any limited group.

Attempting to envisage a debate in which Stehr's "configuration of roles" is effectively considered is to return to the motivating problem with which the Frankfurt School began: how to achieve a comprehensive judgement on the present in the face of a mutually incomprehensible babble of specialised discourses? The late Habermasian answer is minimal, long term, and bound up with a projected process of social evolution. It is the hope that "philosophy", an interpretation of specialised discourses made available and comprehensible to all, might be able to set in motion the interplay between specialised discourses "that has come to a standstill today like a tangled mobile" (Habermas, 1990: 19). As an agenda for publicly concerned disciplines of critical management or systems thinking, it invites the trading of neat, scientific frameworks for the deployment of expertise for a public process of reflection, interpretation and education.

REFERENCES

Ackoff, R. (1978). *The Art of Problem Solving*. Wiley, New York.
Avison, D. and Wood-Harper, T. (1990). *Multiview*. Blackwell, Oxford.
BBC (1995). *Working All Hours*. BBC TV.

BBC (1996). *The Hollow State.* BBC TV.

Beck, U. (1994). The reinvention of politics. In U. Beck, A. Giddens and S. Lash (eds) *Reflexive Modernization.* Polity, Cambridge.

Burrell, G. and Morgan, G. (1979). *Sociological Paradigms and Organisational Analysis.* Gower, Aldershot.

Checkland, P.B. (1981). *Systems Thinking, Systems Practice.* Wiley, Chichester.

Churchman, W. (1979). *The Systems Approach and Its Enemies.* Basic Books, New York.

Clifford, J. (1988). *The Predicament of Culture.* Harvard University Press, Harvard, Cambridge, MA.

Coffa, J.A. (1991). *The Semantic Tradition from Kant to Carnap.* Cambridge University Press, Cambridge.

Cohen, J. and Arato, A. (1992). *Civil Society and Political Theory.* MIT Press, Cambridge, MA.

Cummins, S. (1994). An open letter to Total Systems Intervention (TSI) and friends. *Systems Practice,* **7**, 575–583.

Dallmayr, F.R. and McCarthy, T.A. (1977). *Understanding and Social Enquiry.* University of Notre Dame Press, Notre Dame.

Dreyfus, H. and Rabinow, D. (1982). *Michel Foucault: Beyond Structuralism and Hermeneutics.* Harvester Press, Hemel Hempstead.

Dryzek, J. (1995). Critical theory as a research programme. In S.K. White (ed.) *The Cambridge Companion to Habermas.* Cambridge University Press, Cambridge, pp. 97–119.

Flood, R.L. (1995). *Solving Problem Solving.* Wiley, Chichester.

Flood, R.L. and Romm, N.R. (1996). *Diversity Management: Triple-Loop Learning.* Wiley, Chichester.

Flood, R.L. and Jackson, M.C. (1991). *Creative Problem Solving: Total Systems Intervention.* Wiley, Chichester.

Flood, R.L. and Ulrich, W. (1991). A testament to conversations between two critical systems thinkers. In R.L. Flood and M.C. Jackson (eds) *Critical Systems Thinking: Directed Readings.* Wiley, Chichester.

Giddens, A. (1985). Reason without revolution? In R.J. Bernstein (ed.) *Habermas and Modernity.* Polity, Cambridge, pp. 95–124.

Giddens, A. (1991). *Modernity and Self-Identity.* Polity, Cambridge.

Giddens, A. (1994). Living in a post-traditional society. In U. Beck, A. Giddens and S. Lash (eds) *Reflexive Modernization.* Polity, Cambridge.

Gouldner, A.W. (1971). *The Coming Crisis of Western Sociology.* Heinemann, London.

Habermas, J. (1978). *Knowledge and Human Interests.* Heinemann, London.

Habermas, J. (1984). *The Theory of Communicative Action Vol. 1.* Heinemann, London.

Habermas, J. (1987a). *The Theory of Communicative Action Vol. 2.* Polity, Cambridge.

Habermas, J. (1987b). *The Philosophical Discourse of Modernity.* Polity, Cambridge.

Habermas, J. (1988). *Legitimation Crisis.* Polity, Cambridge.

Habermas, J. (1989). *The Structural Transformation of the Public Sphere.* Polity, Cambridge.

Habermas, J. (1990). *Moral Consciousness and Communicative Action.* Polity, Cambridge.

Habermas, J. (1992). Further reflections on the public sphere. In C. Calhoun (ed.) *Habermas and the Public Sphere.* MIT Press, Cambridge, MA.

Habermas, J. (1993). *Justification and Application.* Polity, Cambridge.

Habermas, J. (1996). *Between Facts and Norms.* Polity, Cambridge.

Held, D. (1980). *Critical Theory.* Polity, Cambridge.

Honneth, A. (1991). *The Critique of Power.* MIT Press, Cambridge, MA.

Honneth, A. (1993). Max Horkheimer and the sociological deficit of critical theory. In S. Benhabib, W. Bonss and J. McCole (eds) *On Max Horkheimer: New Perspectives.* MIT Press, Cambridge, MA.

Horkheimer, M. (1976). Traditional and critical theory. In P. Connerton (ed.) *Critical Sociology.* Penguin, London.

Horkheimer, M. (1989a). The state of contemporary social philosophy and the tasks of an institute for social research. In S. Bronner and D. Kellner (eds) *Critical Theory and Society: A Reader.* Routledge, London.

Horkheimer, M. (1989b). Notes on institute activities. In S. Bronner and D. Kellner (eds) *Critical Theory and Society: A Reader.* Routledge, London.

Jackson, M.C. (1991a). *Systems Methodology for the Management Sciences.* Plenum, New York.

Jackson, M.C. (1991b). Social systems theory and practice. In R. Flood and M.C. Jackson (eds) *Critical Systems Thinking: Directed Readings.* Wiley, Chichester.

Jackson, M.C. (1995). Beyond the fads: systems thinking for managers. *Systems Research,* **12**(1), 25–42.

Kellner, D. (1989). *Critical Theory, Marxism and Modernity.* Polity, Cambridge.

Kuhn, T. (1970). *The Structure of Scientific Revolutions.* University of Chicago Press, Chicago, IL.

Luhmann, N. (1995). *Social Systems.* Stanford University Press, Stanford, CA.

Lukacs, G. (1971). *History and Class Consciousness.* Merlin Press, London.

Lyytinen, K., Klein, H. and Hirschheim, R. (1991). The effectiveness of office information systems: a social action perspective. *Journal of Information Systems,* **1**, 41–60.

Mason, I. and Mitroff, R. (1981). *Challenging Strategic Planning Assumptions.* Wiley, New York.

McCarthy, T.M. (1984). *The Critical Theory of Jürgen Habermas.* Polity, Cambridge.

McCarthy, T.M. (1991). *Ideals and Illusions.* MIT Press, Cambridge, MA.

McCarthy, T.M. (1993). The idea of a critical theory and its relation to philosophy. In S. Benhabib, W. Bonss and J. McCole (eds) *On Max Horkheimer: New Perspectives.* MIT Press, Cambridge, MA.

McLellan, D. (1995). *The Thought of Karl Marx.* Macmillan, London.

Midgley, G. (1992). Pluralism and the legitimation of systems science. *Systems Practice,* **5**, 147–167.

Mingers, J. (1980). Towards an appropriate methodology for applied systems thinking. *Journal of Applied Systems Analysis,* **7**, 41–49.

Morgan, G. (1986). *Images of Organisation.* Sage, London.

Rasmussen, D. (1990). *Reading Habermas.* Blackwell, Oxford.

Ray, L. (1993). *Rethinking Critical Theory.* Sage, London.

Rorty, R. (1980). *Philosophy and the Mirror of Nature.* Blackwell, Oxford.

Stehr, N. (1994). *Knowledge Societies.* Sage, London.

Taylor, C. (1975). *Hegel.* Cambridge University Press, Cambridge.

Taylor, C. (1989). *Sources of the Self.* Cambridge University Press, Cambridge.

Thomas, A. and Lockett, M. (1991). Marxism and social systems research: values and practical action. In R. Flood and M.C. Jackson (eds) *Critical Systems Thinking: Directed Readings.* Wiley, Chichester.

Tiles, M. and Tiles, J. (1993). *An Introduction to Historical Epistemology.* Blackwell, Oxford.

Tsoukas, H. (1992). Panoptic reason and the search for totality. *Human Relations*, **45**, 637–657.

Tsoukas, H. (1993). The road to emancipation is through organisational development. *Systems Practice*, **6**, 53–70.

Ulrich, W. (1994). *Critical Heuristics of Social Planning*. Wiley, Chichester.

Wiggershaus, R. (1994). *The Frankfurt School*. Polity, Cambridge.

White, S. (1988). *The Recent Work of Jürgen Habermas*. Cambridge University Press, Cambridge.

Chapter 13

Pluralism in Systems Thinking and Practice

MIKE C. JACKSON

INTRODUCTION

Pluralism, interpreted in the broadest sense of the use of different methodologies, methods and/or techniques in combination, is a topic of considerable interest in the systems community these days. Beyond the systems field, a number of other applied disciplines are also demonstrating a concern with the possibilities offered by pluralism. Among these would be numbered organisation theory, information systems, operational research, evaluation research and management consultancy. It is timely, therefore, to undertake a review of pluralism in systems thinking and practice. This is even more the case because (as I shall suggest later) the debates in the systems field are for various reasons the most crucial, for the future of pluralism, of all those going on at present.

A review of pluralism in systems thinking and practice will need to give some account of its rise to prominence; look at it in terms of other related developments in the field, such as critical systems thinking; consider its relationship with pluralistic tendencies observed in other applied disciplines; clarify its nature and differentiate it from non-pluralist research; and discuss its strengths and weaknesses and future prospects. In this chapter, I begin by giving a personal account of my growing interest in the possibilities of basing

Multimethodology: The Theory and Practice of Combining Management Science Methodologies.
Edited by John Mingers and Anthony Gill.
© 1997 John Wiley & Sons Ltd.

systems thinking upon pluralism and in the benefits of a systems practice guided by pluralism. This involves some consideration of the "system of systems methodologies" which sought to demonstrate that the various systems methodologies could be regarded as a complementary set because they each rested upon different assumptions about the nature of some "ideal-type" problem contexts. This is followed by a review of an early attempt to theorise about the nature of "pluralism" as an approach to the development of systems thinking in opposition to "isolationism", "imperialism" and "pragmatism". The nature of "total systems intervention" (TSI) as a pluralist meta-methodology is then discussed. The next section views pluralism as one of the elements significant to the growth in critical systems thinking. According to this perspective, the establishment of a pluralist approach requires that the other "commitments" of critical systems thinking be observed; these being "critical awareness", "social awareness" and what might be described as an "ethical alertness". Pluralism only makes sense in the light of the critical systems orientation.

Having contextualised pluralism as a development in the systems field, it is worthwhile to push the boundaries of our concern a little wider and to look at pluralism in other applied disciplines. Quite a number of these areas of work have been touched by pluralist arguments, and a brief demonstration of this permits us to progress to suggest why the general intellectual climate currently seems to favour pluralist endeavour. This general review completed, it becomes possible to begin to develop the argument with sections on "the nature of pluralism" and "the future of pluralism". There is a need for further clarification of just what is meant by pluralism, and just what is useful about pluralism, if the academic debate is to progress and if practitioners are to achieve the greatest benefit from adopting pluralism. It is also necessary to try to chart our way through the intellectual minefield which surrounds whether pluralism represents a "meta-paradigm", a new paradigm in its own right, or is better conceptualised as a trend in postmodern thinking. The implications of my proposed route through this minefield are, I believe, far reaching. I try to be completely explicit about the risks involved in framing pluralism and using pluralist thinking in the manner suggested.

PLURALISM IN THE SYSTEMS FIELD

Prior to 1984 most of those who addressed the issue of combining methods or methodologies, in the systems field, did so on the basis of the "imperialist" rationale which we shall explore below. Checkland (1983), for example, divides the area of the systems movement relevant to management science into two parts—hard systems thinking and soft systems thinking—but regards the hard approach simply as a special case of the soft. In 1984, however, Linstone published a book, *Multiple Perspectives for Decision Making*, and Jackson and Keys an article, "Towards a system of systems methodologies", which, independently, put pluralism firmly on the agenda.

Early Developments

Linstone's form of multiperspective research was aimed at gaining a richer appreciation of the nature of problem situations. The traditional technical (T) perspective, dependent upon data and model-based analysis, was to be augmented by an organisational (O) or societal perspective and a personal (P) or individual perspective. The T, O and P perspectives acted as filters through which systems were viewed and each yielded insights that were not attainable with the others. Linstone argued, in an original way, that the different perspectives were most powerfully employed when they were clearly differentiated from one another in terms of the emphasis they brought to the analysis but were used together to interrogate the same complex problem. Nor, he thought, should one expect consistency in the findings; two perspectives may reinforce one another but may equally cancel each other out. A weakness of the approach is that the three perspectives are all employed within the logic of the functionalist paradigm to "provide a three-dimensional view of the real-world system" (Linstone, 1989). Other paradigms are ignored. Another limitation is that while the manner of employing pluralism to analyse complex problems is explicated, the way in which methods and methodologies might be combined to change problem situations is not thought through. Linstone is continuing to develop his pluralist vision as part of "unbounded systems thinking" (Mitroff and Linstone, 1993).

Jackson and Keys were motivated, in contrast to Linstone, to explore the relationship between the different problem-solving methodologies that had arisen as guides to intervening in problem situations and to understand the strengths and weaknesses of these different methodologies. I shall present a simplified version of this "system of systems methodologies" while trying not to go beyond the formulations of the original article. The framework has been developed since (Jackson, 1987a, 1990).

The key idea of the "system of systems methodologies" was that it is possible to construct an ideal-type grid of problem contexts that can be used to classify systems methodologies according to their assumptions about problem situations. The grid is made up of two dimensions: one defining the nature of the systems in which the problems of concern are located and the other the nature of the relationship between the participants who have an interest in the problem situation and its improvement. Systems were classified on a continuum from "simple" to "complex" and participants as to whether they could be said to be in a "unitary", "pluralist" or "coercive" relationship to one another. Combining these classifications yielded a six-celled matrix of problem contexts housing the following categories: simple-unitary, complex-unitary, simple-pluralist, complex-pluralist, simple-coercive and complex-coercive.

Given this grid of problem contexts, the next step in building the system of systems methodologies was to relate existing systems-based, problem-solving methodologies to the categories defined by the grid. Hard systems thinking (classical OR, systems analysis, systems engineering) was said to assume that problems are set in simple-unitary contexts because it takes as given that it is easy to establish objectives for the system of concern and that it is possible to model it mathematically. Sociotechnical, contingency and cybernetic approaches were related to complex-unitary contexts; various soft systems approaches to simple-pluralist and complex-pluralist contexts; and no systems methodologies were available based on coercive assumptions. A number of benefits were claimed to follow from the establishment of this system of systems methodologies. It offered a way forward from the operational research or systems in crisis debates, which saw different problem-solving methodologies as in competition, because it presented the different methodologies as being appropriate for different types of problem context. This should encourage mutual respect in management science between those proponents of different approaches who had previously seen themselves at war with one another. It should also lead analysts to ask, on each occasion they are confronted by a problem, which methodology is appropriate to this problem context. Finally, it aids understanding of exactly what goes wrong when an inappropriate problem-solving approach is employed in a particular problem context.

The breakthrough made by the system of systems methodologies (as recognised by Mingers and Brocklesby, 1996) was that it suggested that pluralism could be achieved based on methodologies (hard systems, cybernetic, soft systems, etc.) which were developed from *more than one paradigm*. In retrospect one weakness is that the pluralism is, implicitly, seen to relate to different interventions. The use of different methodologies in the same intervention is not considered. Another is that a lack of distinction is maintained between "methodology" (relating to the overall theory of method use) and "methods" or "techniques". As a result, methods and techniques were not seen as separable from the methodology with which they were commonly associated; if you chose Checkland's soft systems methodology you inevitably got rich pictures, CATWOE, etc., as well. It is also true that insufficient attention was given to the issue to which Linstone was devoting his efforts—different ways of looking at problem contexts. I should, however, quote one passage which both suggests the need to go beyond what Linstone was attempting and anticipates the later development of "total systems intervention":

> The problem solver needs to stand back and examine problem contexts in the light of different "Ws" [weltanschauungen]. Perhaps he can then decide which

"W" seems to capture the essence of the particular problem context he is faced with. This whole process needs formalising if it is to be carried out successfully. The problem solver needs to be aware of different paradigms in the social sciences, and he must be prepared to view the problem context through each of these paradigms. (Jackson and Keys, 1984: 484)

Theorising About Pluralism

My personal interest in pluralism continued with an effort to view it in the light of "Present positions and future prospects in management science" (Jackson, 1987b). This was the first explicit attempt to distinguish the nature of pluralism in the systems field and to argue that embracing pluralism was the best way forward for systems thinking. The paper looked at the breakdown in confidence in traditional management science and the growth of the soft systems, organisational cybernetic and critical systems alternatives to this orthodoxy. It suggested that each of the alternatives had a significant contribution to make to the discipline and asked how the relationship between traditional management science and the new alternatives could best be theorised and employed so that management science could make the most beneficial contribution to organisations and society. Borrowing a way of thinking and modifying some terms used in Reed's (1985) account of possible "redirections in organizational analysis", four developmental strategies for management science were put under the microscope—isolationism, imperialism, pragmatism and pluralism—and these now deserve our attention.

Isolationists see their own approach to management science as being essentially self-sufficient. They believe that there is nothing to learn from other perspectives which appear to them not to be useful or, perhaps, even sensible. Isolationists were identified as being strong in traditional management science and organisational cybernetics. The isolationist strategy would lead to the different strands of management science continuing to go their own ways, developing independently on the basis of their own presuppositions and with minimal contact between the strands. Paradigm incommensurability could be adduced in support of the isolationist strategy but, I argued, isolationism should be dismissed because it divided the discipline, forestalled the possibility of "reflective conversation" between the different strands, and discredited the profession in the eyes of clients who did not believe that one method could solve all problems.

Imperialism represents a fundamental commitment to one epistemological position but a willingness to incorporate other strands of management science if they seem to be useful and to add strength in terms of the favoured position. Insights from other tendencies will be integrated into the edifice of the favoured approach as long as they do not threaten its central tenets. Imperialists believe that they can explain the existence of alternative approaches, and analyse the limited sphere of application of these alternatives, in terms of the approach to which they grant hegemony. Strong imperialist aspirations were identified in soft systems thinking (remember Checkland's view of hard systems thinking), organisational cybernetics and critical systems thinking. This strategy for the development of management science was dismissed, however, because methodologies and methods developed in the service of one paradigm would be "denatured" if used under the auspices of another and so the full potential available to management science, if it capitalised on all the paradigms, would not be realised. It was argued, however, that the imperialist scenario might come to pass "if extra-disciplinary, broader, societal influences favoured one approach at the expense of the alternatives, squeezing the opportunities available to these alternatives" (Jackson, 1987b: 464). I shall argue, in a later section, that something very close to this has, in fact, occurred.

The pragmatist strategy is to develop management science by bringing together the best elements of what may appear to be opposing strands on the criterion of what "works" in practice. Pragmatists do not worry about "artificial" theoretical distinctions. They concentrate on building up a "toolkit" of methods and techniques, drawn from the different strands of management science, and are prepared to use them together in the course of problem solving if the situation warrants it. The choice of techniques and the whole procedure is justified to the extent that it seems to bring results in practice. The attractiveness of the pragmatist option was recognised and its support among traditional management scientists and a few soft systems thinkers detailed. It was dismissed, however, because it could not support the development of management science as a discipline. Theory, which the pragmatist strategy eschews, is necessary if we are to understand why particular methods work and others do not, so that we can learn from experience and so we can pass our knowledge on to future generations. Furthermore, pragmatism is dangerous in the social domain—it can lead to costly mistakes which theoretical understanding might have helped us avoid and it can lead to acquiescence in the use of methods which appear to "work", but do so not because they are the most suitable for the situation in which they are employed but because they reinforce the position of the powerful and implementation is therefore ensured.

In contrast to the other three options available to management science, the pluralist strategy was seen as offering excellent opportunities for successful, future development. Pluralism would seek to respect the different strengths of the various trends in management science, encouraging their theoretical development and suggesting ways in which they can be appropriately fitted to the variety of management problems that arise. It was argued that a *meta-methodology* would develop which could guide theoretical endeavour and advise analysts, confronted with different problem situations, which approach is most useful. In these circumstances the diversity of theory and methods in management science could be seen to herald not a crisis but increased competence and effectiveness in a variety of different problem situations. Jackson and Keys' "system of systems methodologies" was identified as the most formal statement of this pluralist position. Pluralism was defended against the advocates of paradigm incommensurability on the basis that the different strands of management science are necessary as supports for the anthropologically based cognitive interests of the human species, as identified by Habermas—hard and cybernetic approaches supporting the technical interest; soft approaches the practical interest; and critical approaches the emancipatory interest. Pluralism, it was stated, "offers the best hope of re-establishing management science as a cohesive discipline and profession—*and* on firmer foundations than those which supported the traditional version" (Jackson, 1987b: 456).

Total Systems Intervention

The meta-methodology that had been predicted in my 1987(b) paper emerged some years later in the shape of "total systems intervention" or TSI (Flood and Jackson, 1991). The philosophy underpinning TSI was stated to be critical systems thinking and this itself was said to rest on "complementarism", "sociological awareness" and the "promotion of human well-being and emancipation". The relationship between pluralism and the other tenets of critical systems thinking will be explored in the next section. For the moment our concern is with the "complementarism" embedded in TSI. The word complementarism was taken to be synonymous with pluralism and was, therefore, defined by distinguishing it from isolationism, imperialism and pragmatism, and grounded on Habermas's three fundamental human interests. Complementarism was chosen in preference to pluralism purely to avoid confusion with the use of the latter word to describe one setting of the participants' dimension in the system of systems methodologies. This I now see as a mistake as it suggested something of a "happy compatibility" between epistemologies and methodologies that was not intended and which pluralism does not imply. I have reverted to pluralism in this chapter.

The pluralism underlying TSI was operationalised in each of the three phases of the meta-methodology—creativity, choice and implementation. In the creativity stage managers are assisted to think about their organisations creatively using various systems metaphors. These metaphors (derived primarily from Morgan's (1986) work) were to be used as different "lenses" each highlighting certain aspects of the organisation and its problems. The "machine", "organism", "brain", "culture", "team", "coalition" and "coercive system" metaphors were recommended and detailed. The introduction of pluralism as a means of gaining a richer appreciation of problem situations echoed Linstone's earlier work but poor research meant that this was not recognised. The metaphors extended beyond Linstone's TOP perspectives, however, to embrace views from alternative paradigms. The use of metaphors also redeemed the pledge made in Jackson and Keys (1984) to formalise the process whereby the problem solver stands back to "examine problem contexts in the light of different 'Ws' ". The outcome of the creativity phase was said to be a focus on the main issues and problems for the organisation at that point in time. This then became the basis for a choice of appropriate intervention methodology or methodologies.

In the choice stage the system of systems methodologies is used (along with metaphor analysis) to reveal the strengths and weaknesses of possible candidate methodologies. An appropriate intervention methodology, or methodologies, is chosen on the basis that its strengths make it suitable to address the main issues and problems identified during "creativity". The most probable outcome of the choice phase is likely to be that there is "a 'dominant' methodology chosen, to be tempered in use by the imperatives highlighted by 'dependent' methodologies". During "implementation" the chosen methodology or methodologies are employed to tackle the current problem situation. It is stressed, however, that the meta-methodology should be used in an iterative manner. Participants' views of what are the main problem areas will change and the intervention itself will move the problem situation on. The only way to attend to these matters is to continually cycle around creativity, choice and implementation changing, as appropriate, which methodologies are "dominant" and "dependent". The dynamic aspect of TSI is captured in this quotation from the preface to the book:

> The essence of TSI is to encourage highly creative thinking about the nature of any problem situation before a decision is taken about the character of the main difficulties to be addressed. Once that decision has been taken, TSI will steer the manager or analyst towards the type of systems methodology most appropriate for dealing with the kind of difficulties identified as being most significant. As the intervention proceeds, using TSI, so the nature of the problem situation will be continually reviewed, as will the choice of appropriate systems methodology. In highly complex problem situations it is advisable to address at the same time different aspects revealed by taking different perspectives on it. This involves employing a number of systems methodologies in combination. In these circumstances it is necessary to nominate one methodology as "dominant" and others as "supportive", although these relationships may change as the study progresses. (Flood and Jackson, 1991).

The breakthrough achieved by TSI (also noticed by Mingers and Brocklesby, 1996) is to postulate a meta-methodology for using methodologies adhering to different paradigms in *the same intervention on the same problem situation*. As a meta-methodology TSI seeks to ensure that pluralism extends beyond the use of different methods and techniques guided by one methodology premised on one set of epistemological assumptions. It seeks to find a way of managing, in a coherent way, very different methodologies premised upon alternative epistemological assumptions. It would be nice to use such different methodologies alongside one another in highly complex problem situations but if this proves to be *practically* impossible, TSI suggests, then the best way to handle methodological pluralism is to clearly state that one methodology is being taken as "dominant" (and others "dependent") for some period of time, being always willing to alter the relationship between dominant and dependent methodologies as the situation changes. One methodology, encapsulating the presuppositions of a particular paradigm, is granted "imperialistic" status—but only temporarily; its dominance is kept under continual review. The other strength of TSI, as we have already suggested, was to bring together pluralism in the creativity phase (looking at the problem situation through different Ws) with pluralism in terms of the management of different methodologies in combination (in the choice and implementation phases).

If TSI's great strength was operating at the meta-methodological level, to ensure that methodologies embodying different paradigmatic assumptions were used in combination, operating at this level also led to what, it now seems to me, was one of its weaknesses. As Mingers and Brocklesby (1996) note, TSI (like the system of systems methodologies) requires the use of "whole" methodologies. Once an interpretive rationale is chosen as dominant, for example, it seems that you must employ the particular methods and techniques exactly in the manner set out in Checkland's "soft systems methodology" or Ackoff's "interactive planning". There is an unnecessary lack of flexibility here which needs addressing. There is nothing theoretically wrong with using a selection of methods and techniques, as long as they are employed according to the interpretive logic (in this case), and this allows a much greater responsiveness to the peculiarities of each problem situation as it evolves during an intervention.

Tsoukas's (1993a, b) critique brings to the fore another problem which TSI leaves unresolved. TSI seems to suggest that it can, on the basis of Habermas's three "human interests", stand "above the paradigms", picking out appropriate methodologies according to the particular human interest to be served. As Tsoukas (1993b: 313) notes, however:

> Different paradigms constitute different realities, and as such, they provide answers, either explicitly or implicitly, to *all* three human interests. Positivist problem-solving, for example, is not simply useful for achieving technical mastery over social processes. In attempting to do so, it also provides answers to the inextricably interwoven questions of interaction and power.

If TSI claims to stand "above the paradigms", how can this claim be grounded? If it has to abandon this claim does it mean that TSI, or more properly the critical systems thinking on which it is based, constitutes a new paradigm in its own right? If this is the case, what has happened to pluralism? Other possible criticisms of TSI centre on the lack of specification as to how it is to be employed, for example whether the analysis in the three stages is to be expert driven or participant driven. We shall leave TSI now, however, to consider briefly some later developments in pluralistic thinking in the systems field.

Later Developments

Since TSI (Flood and Jackson, 1991), interest in pluralism in the systems field has continued to grow. Flood (1995) has sought to "formalise" the various phases of TSI. In the process he has made the approach unusable in practice and, as Tsagdis (1996) has pointed out, has abandoned the greatest strength of TSI—its ability to operationalise a process whereby different rationalities are brought to bear on a problem situation and continually kept under review. Replacing this is an ontological commitment to "organisations as whole systems" consisting of interacting parts and with needs in the "four key dimensions" of organisational processes, design, culture and politics. Different systems methodologies can be related to these needs. "Organisations as systems" functionalism is reborn. A later contribution (Flood and Romm, 1996) seeks to take into account the postmodern challenge to critical systems thinking but is too muddled to permit detailed comment. Elsewhere, Espejo (Espejo et al, 1996) has been developing his "cybernetic methodology" as a kind of combination between Checkland's soft systems methodology and Beer's VSM, and Hoebeke (1994) has tried to integrate the systems approaches of Beer, Checkland and Jaques. In neither case, in my opinion, are the significant issues confronting pluralism in methodology use confronted. Espejo seems happy to live with an uneasy tension between the logics of soft systems methodology and cybernetics (see Jackson, 1992), while in Hoebeke a cybernetic imperialism prevails. More usefully, from the point of view of advancing pluralism, Mingers and Brocklesby (1996) have tried to develop a framework for mixing methodologies. This contribution to "multimethodology" contains a table outlining different possibilities for combining methodologies which I have made use of already in this chapter to highlight the various "breakthroughs" as pluralism in the systems field developed. It also draws particular attention to the possibility of "decomposing" methodologies into their constituent parts (methods, techniques and tools) which can then be recombined according to the requirements of particular interventions. The essence of multimethodology, for Mingers and Brocklesby (1996), "is linking together parts of methodologies, possibly from different paradigms". Whether the framework deployed to guide "multimethodology" contains sufficient safeguards to prevent relapse from pluralism, I will discuss later. It remains, in this section, only to draw attention to Brocklesby's (1995) work on the "cultural" constraints preventing easy adoption of pluralism by the systems community and by individual analysts.

PLURALISM AND CRITICAL SYSTEMS THINKING

The development of pluralism in systems thinking and practice is inseparable from the rise of critical systems thinking. If, therefore, we are to clarify the nature of pluralism and why it is a useful approach, we must ensure that at this point we understand the relationship between pluralism and the other "commitments" of critical systems thinking.

There are in existence two different types of critical systems thinking that have never learned to live very happily together. The first emanates from the work of Churchman and has been fully developed by Ulrich (1983) as "critical systems heuristics". Its concern is to realise the critical potential in the concept, crucial to systems thinking, of "boundary". Any proposal for a systems design will rest upon certain "boundary judgements" about who the client of the system should be, who the decision taker should be, what groups of those affected we should concern ourselves with, etc. If these boundary judgements can be revealed then it will become clear that they depend upon certain choices that have been made (implicitly or explicitly) and that they can be challenged. Alternative proposals for the design can be formulated based on different boundary judgements and these will have to be accepted as equally deserving of attention. The second type of critical systems thinking is a UK development which can trace its origins to the critique of soft systems thinking (Mingers, 1980; Jackson, 1982). It is this second line of critical systems thinking which has emphasised and has itself been conditioned by pluralist thinking.

By about 1991 critical systems thinking UK style (hereafter simply critical systems thinking) had stabilised sufficiently for a number of systems thinkers to try their hand at describing its important characteristics. Schecter (1991), for example, saw it as defined by three commitments: to critique, to emancipation and to pluralism. Jackson (1991), offering the most detailed account of its commitments, argued that critical systems thinking was built upon the five pillars of critical awareness, social awareness, complementarism at the methodological level, complementarism at the theoretical level, and dedication to human emancipation. Flood and Jackson (1991a), in developing TSI on the philosophy of critical systems thinking, saw this as making its stand on three positions. These were complementarism, sociological awareness and the promotion of human well-being and emancipation. Finally Flood and Jackson (1991b), in the introduction to a set of readings on critical systems thinking, recognised the critical systems endeavour as possessing three interrelated intentions—complementarism, emancipation and critical reflection. Pluralism (or complementarism) occurs in all these lists and we need to understand why.

If I had to restate the "commitments" of critical systems thinking today, on the basis of a composite of the 1991 discussions and some later thinking, I would list critical awareness, social awareness, pluralism and "ethical alertness". Critical systems thinking began with critical awareness of the limitations of all particular methodologies. Ackoff, Checkland and Churchman had, during the 1970s, criticised the limited domain of applicability of hard systems thinking but had done so primarily to create a space for and to argue the superiority of their own soft systems thinking. A self-conscious critical approach did not start to be elaborated until Mingers (1980) began to ask questions about the social theory on which soft systems thinking was based, and Jackson (1982) argued that the assumptions made by Churchman, Ackoff and Checkland about the nature of systems thinking and social systems constrained the ability of their methodologies to intervene, in the manner intended, in many problem situations. Soft systems thinking, too, had a limited domain of applicability. In particular, the kind of open, participative debate that is essential for the success of the soft systems approach, and can be the only justification for the recommendations that emerge, is impossible to obtain in problem situations where there is fundamental conflict between interest groups that have access to unequal power resources. Soft systems thinkers either have to walk away from these problem situations or fly in the face of their own philosophical principles and acquiesce in proposed changes emerging from limited debates characterised by distorted communication.

It was now clear that all systems methodologies had certain strengths and weaknesses and that the critically aware practitioner needed to understand these and use each methodology in the particular circumstances most appropriate for it. Jackson's 1991 book summarised the results of a decade's research into the strengths and weaknesses of the "organisations as systems", "hard", "cybernetic", "soft systems" and "emancipatory systems" approaches. Another obvious conclusion that followed, once critical awareness had been established as a principle, was that, in complex problem situations, systems methodologies would have to be used in combination in order to address the multifaceted characteristics exhibited by the "real world". Pluralism was necessary. The next step on the journey to critical systems thinking had to be the creation of a classification of systems methodologies that would allow for their complementary and informed use. This insight led directly to the system of systems methodologies, the theorising about pluralism and eventually to TSI, as detailed in the last section. At this point the debates surrounding pluralism and critical systems thinking begin to merge and the justifications provided for pluralism in the last section, based upon Habermas's conception of fundamental human interests, were those adduced by critical systems thinking itself in defence of the direction it was taking.

The other two commitments I now see as central to critical systems thinking in many ways arise as props to or attempts to promote pluralism. The commitment to social awareness involves considering the organisational and societal climate that determines the popularity, or otherwise, of particular systems approaches at particular times. For example, it was inconceivable that soft systems thinking could ever flourish in the old Eastern European countries dominated by the bureaucratic dictates of the one-party system. No matter how theoretically well informed systems practitioners might become about the capabilities of systems methodologies, they still needed to take into account the limits on pluralism imposed by political, economic, cultural and other pressures. Rational choice of methodology because it was most suited to the purposes of the analyst, or of the most directly concerned stakeholders, could not be guaranteed. Flood (1990) in his programme for "liberating systems theory" implicated, following Foucault's logic, the micro-politics at play in society as a key factor leading to the rise to prominence of some systems approaches and the subjugation of others, thus inhibiting pluralism. The project of liberating systems theory had to include, therefore, the emancipation of suppressed knowledges in systems theory itself. Overall, however, the commitment to social awareness has not received as much attention in critical systems thinking as it might, and Brocklesby (1995) is right to chastise critical systems thinkers for not paying sufficient attention to the "cultural constraints" which can damage the future prospects of complementarism.

Critical systems thinking's commitment to emancipation, so loudly trumpeted in the 1991 declarations, can similarly be identified with the need to buttress pluralism. Jackson and Keys' (1984) grid of ideal-type problem contexts recognised the possibility of simple-coercive and complex-coercive contexts but no systems-based problem-solving methodology appropriate to such contexts. It was in these circumstances that Jackson (1985) identified the need for "a critical approach" in social systems theory and practice. Soft systems thinkers, it was argued, had extended the range of problem situations with which systems approaches could cope. There are, however, many social systems for which even the soft systems approaches are inappropriate. A critical approach was necessary more suitable "to social systems where there are great disparities in power and in resources and which seem to 'escape' the control and understanding of the individuals who create and sustain them". For a time (for example, in TSI) Ulrich's (1983) "critical systems heuristics" was asked to stand in as a systems approach apparently capable of enhancing the pluralist response of critical systems thinkers by addressing coercive contexts. In reality this "gap" in the armoury of critical systems thinkers has never been adequately filled.

These days, following the attack on the "grand narratives" of personal and societal liberation conducted by postmodern thinkers such as Lyotard (1984), critical systems thinkers seem more circumspect about talking in terms of human emancipation. Local improvement seems more in keeping with the spirit of the times (see Jackson, 1995). Nevertheless it can be argued, on the basis of postmodern arguments, that now more than ever pluralism needs the support of "ethical alertness' if it is to be able to justify the recommendations for improvement it delivers. No rationality on its own carries conviction; in this regard pluralism concurs with postmodern thinking. But different rationalities employed together in the form of different systems methodologies, as recommended by systemic pluralism, will often, surely, lead to contradictory possibilities for change. A decision between these possibilities, it seems, can only be made on ethical grounds.

This section has been concerned to contextualise pluralism in terms of wider developments in the systems movement. Pluralism stands or falls with critical systems thinking. We need to understand the intimacy of these relationships if we are, later, to grasp the nature of pluralism and to properly frame it so that it can be successfully operationalised.

PLURALISM IN OTHER APPLIED DISCIPLINES

As was mentioned in the introduction to this chapter, other applied disciplines apart from systems thinking have shown an interest in the possibilities offered by pluralism. We shall briefly consider, in this section, the progress made in pursuing pluralism in organisation theory, information systems, operational research, evaluation research and management consultancy. If we are to chart the way forward for pluralism in systems thinking and practice, it is necessary to discover if anything can be learned from experiences with developing pluralism in these other applied disciplines.

Organisation Theory

In organisation theory we have already referred to Reed's account of possible "redirections" in which he argues for his form of pluralism against alternatives such as pragmatism. Gregory (1996) documents another discussion of developments in the discipline couched in pluralist terms. According to Bruscaglioni, she relates, there have been three stages to the development of organisational analysis: "isolation of approaches", "mechanical complementarism" and "integration of the various approaches". In the final stage we find the generation of a variety of competing general theories, based on different models of the nature of organisation and providing different explanations of organisational phenomena. Finally, we might mention Martin's (1990) dismissal of simple monomethod and complex monomethod approaches to the study of organisations in favour of a more complex alternative—the methodological chameleon. The simple monomethod approach corresponds to isolationism and its advocates argue that their method is always better than all others. This approach is said to impede the sharing of knowledge about organisational phenomena. The complex monomethod approach corresponds, after a fashion, to the position implicit in the system of systems methodologies. It argues that, for a particular theoretical issue, one method can be identified as more suitable for use than the others. Martin suggests that this approach, too, is misguided as different methods (say quantitative and qualitative) can bring something to the study of the *same* theoretical issue. Indeed, when this is done the weaknesses of one method can be compensated for by the strengths of another and vice versa. Martin believes, therefore, that multimethod approaches, such as "triangulation", are eminently sensible. Researchers should become methodological chameleons; tolerant of different methods and appreciative of the divergent conclusions that stem from employing different methods. There are, however, problems which may prevent the multimethod option being taken. Research decision making is not always governed by rational choice; method choices may instead be determined by the availability of resources, the preferences of the researcher, or the desire for particular outcomes. Further, the skills and attitudes required of methodological chameleons are daunting. Most researchers are well trained in only one or two methods. To require them to be adept at several, diverse methods may be asking too much.

From this review of some pluralist thinking in organisation theory it is possible to make the point that the concern is almost solely with the use of different methods in combination to enhance understanding of organisational phenomena. No doubt organisation theorists have much to offer systems thinkers in this regard. Virtually no consideration is given, however, to the use of intervention approaches in combination to change and improve organisations. Organisation theory, while masquerading as an applied discipline, gives little assistance, in the matter of pluralism as in many other areas, to those who would like to know how its conclusions can be put to work. Beyond this it is interesting to note similar distinctions made in systems and in organisational theory between pluralistic and non-pluralistic research, and between types of pluralism, and to witness attention being given to similar cultural constraints on the acceptance of pluralism.

Information Systems

There has been considerable clamour for complementarism in methodology use in the information systems field (e.g. Hirschheim, 1985; Klein and Lyytinen, 1985; Walsham, 1991). The attempt to provide guidelines for actually combining methods in practice has, however, been fraught with difficulties. Considerable debate has centred on the benefits of joining Checkland's SSM and various "functionalist" information systems methodologies but no agreement has been reached about whether this is possible or desirable, let alone about how it should be done. Mingers (1992) discusses efforts to "front end" SSM onto structured design methods (an approach Wood (1992) labels as pragmatist) and to embed information systems methods within SSM, with SSM guiding the whole project (an approach we would have to see as "imperialist"). There are many objections to both strategies. Mingers fears that we will end up with the worst of both worlds—losing something from both SSM and from what the structured design methods might offer. Doyle and Wood (1991) point to the problems that arise from integration because of the different and conflicting epistemologies embodied in SSM and information systems methodologies. Fitzgerald (1992) accepts the paradigmatic differences and, on this basis, argues against any formal link between SSM and IS approaches. The main danger is that the lessons and richness of SSM would get lost in the IS phase. There is nothing however, he feels, to stop SSM and structured approaches being used separately in the same intervention, with SSM being performed first and the richness of the analysis thus provided being left to influence "the second in whatever way the actors allow".

The Multiview framework and methodology, devised by Avison and Wood-Harper (1990), represents the longest running attempt to bring together soft and hard approaches to information systems development. Already, in 1985, Wood-Harper was proclaiming this approach as a realisation of information systems as a multi-perspective discipline using a pluralism of research methods. Commendable though this pluralist endeavour is, I have argued that we must be careful before accepting Wood-Harper's conclusion. Multiview fuses the work of Checkland and Mumford with ideas from harder methodologies. We need to ask, however, on the basis of what rationality this fusion of apparently contradictory approaches takes place. The first answer, provided in Wood-Harper (1985), was that Multiview had to be understood as conditioned primarily by hermeneutic philosophy. This was supported by his contention that the "ideal" use of the methodology is in the sequence prescribed—essentially moving from softer to harder approaches. Leaving aside the technical difficulties in this (for Mingers (1992) the soft analysis is simply left "up in the air"), it is easy to see, at the theoretical level, that either the "soft" rationalities must be distorted by the expectation that they will lead to a more structured intervention or the "hard" rationalities will suffer because they are operating in a hermeneutic climate and are front-ended by a soft logic. A more recent answer (Wood-Harper and Avison, 1992; Watson and Wood-Harper, 1995) is that the Multiview approach is simply a "metaphor" for the process of defining an information system. Every context in which it is used will be complex and unique and Multiview has to be adapted in each case—"people close the theory in action" (Wood-Harper and Avison, 1992). Multiview is, therefore, non-prescriptive; it provides a framework which analysts can refer to in choosing those tools and techniques appropriate for the circumstances they face. This manoeuvre increases Multiview's flexibility and ability to adapt to the specifics of particular interventions (an advantage) but risks leaving the approach prey to pragmatism and the problems associated with that. There is no easy escape from the need to handle a plurality of rationalities at the theoretical level.

The debates on pluralism in information systems have reached a high level of sophistication and we find information systems researchers grappling with the same problems as systems thinkers. They have not, however, overtaken the debates in systems thinking. In particular, we find the same uncertainty at the theoretical level. Walsham and Han (1991) put forward Giddens' "structuration theory" as a meta-theory within which other theories and methodologies can be contained. Symons and Walsham (1987) recommended using different perspectives "in parallel". While Habermas's work on knowledge-constitutive interests appeals to Lyytinen and Klein (1985) as the basis for a "multi-paradigm" research community in information systems.

Operational Research

In contrast to systems thinkers and information systems researchers, almost all those who have shown an interest in "pluralism" in operational research have decided to keep things easy for themselves. Methods, tools and techniques have been combined but under the hegemony of an implicit or explicit methodology embodying the philosophical assumptions of one paradigm. This, of course, was the typical case in classical operational research, when "hard" OR methodology was employed to steer various models and techniques according to a functionalist logic. Recently there have been projects carried out using different "soft" OR methods in combination. Ormerod (1995) describes Bennett's experiments involving hypergame analysis, cognitive maps and strategic choice; Matthews and Bennett's case study employing both cognitive mapping and strategic choice; and Bryant's thoughts on mixing cognitive mapping with hypergame analysis. Ormerod goes on to describe a project of his own in which various soft OR methods were used in the development of a new information systems strategy for Sainsbury's supermarkets. This project employed cognitive mapping, soft systems methodology and strategic choice, in its various phases, in the context of an overall orientation provided by Ackoff's interactive planning. The sorts of combinations of soft OR methods noted by Ormerod, and constructed by Ormerod himself, are managed under the "imperialism" of the interpretive paradigm. Ormerod describes Bennett's views on the similarities the methods he combines together share: ". . . he suggests that all the methods are designed to help small, relatively autonomous groups of people make non-routine choices . . . second . . . all the methods . . . are designed primarily for a style of working in which consultants work *with* clients, rather than producing analysis *for* them". The creation of such "single paradigm multimethodologies" (Mingers and Brocklesby, 1996) can of course be extremely productive and provide great flexibility in an intervention. It represents, however, a "restricted" form of pluralism (really imperialism) in which only one paradigm of analysis is employed in the intervention. The development of pluralism in operational research offers a possible case study for those, such as Brocklesby (1995), concerned with the "cultural constraints' on fully fledged pluralism.

Evaluation Research

Gregory (1996), tracing the evolution of evaluation research, argues that it shows a similar pattern of development to that described by Bruscaglioni in organisation theory. She identifies four paradigms in evaluation theory—goal-based, system-resource-based, multi-actor-based and culture-based—and suggests that for much of their history they have remained in "isolation", warring with one another. On the basis of the system of systems methodologies and TSI, however, it is possible to see how they might be used in a complementary way, with the selection of the most appropriate evaluation methodology according to the nature of the context. This is labelled mechanical-complementarism (which, incidentally, misrepresents TSI). According to Gregory, following Bruscaglioni, progress from the mechanical complementarist stage requires "integration" of the various approaches, and she discusses the recommendations made by Bruscaglioni and Francescato as to how this might be achieved. Gregory, however, is sceptical: "It is difficult to comprehend how a theoretical integration of the different methodologies can be achieved, given the conflicting assumptions on which they are based" (Gregory, 1986: 303). She prefers "multidimensional evaluation" where methodologies are used together but in parallel, in order to protect the different contributions they can offer according to their distinctive theoretical underpinnings.

Criticising some of Gregory's earlier work, when she herself was a mechanical-complementarist, Taket and White (1995) argue that the degree of complexity and heterogeneity encountered in most evaluation situations prevents the adoption of the kind of contingency logic underpinning mechanical-complementarism. They also advocate a pluralist strategy for evaluation but based on a more eclectic approach. This approach must recognise the heterogeneity within the group concerned with an evaluation and recognise evaluation as a social process. It can be thought of as a kind of "pragmatic pluralism" in which parts of different OR/systems methods are combined, ". . . in a process that might be labelled 'judicious mix and match' . . .", according to the requirements of the situation and the changing responses of the evaluation party. Taket and White allow that their strategy lays them open to the charge of combining methods based on incompatible theoretical assumptions, but make little progress in resolving this problem. We are back to the issues that have plagued the development of pluralism in systems thinking and practice.

Management Consultancy

Mingers and Brocklesby (1996) cite the fact that practitioners are increasingly combining different methods and methodologies as one justification for the need to examine the use of "multimethodology". It certainly seems to be the case that management consultants have not allowed the theoretical niceties we have been discussing to get in the way of "pluralistic practice" if this has seemed appropriate—as it increasingly has. To provide just one example, Tata Consultancy Services in India have been working for some time with a "Multi-Modelling" methodology, apparently successfully, without giving much consideration to the overall paradigm governing the approach or the particular paradigms from which the elements comprising the approach have been excised. Only recently has Ramakrishnan (1995), from Tata Consultancy Services, given some attention to this matter and sought, in an imperialist manner, to impose an interpretive rationale—the paradigm of languaging in organisations—upon the approach. Ormerod (1992, 1995) has provided accounts of his own "pluralistic practice" as a consultant, before entering academia, and has been honest enough (Ormerod, 1994) to reflect on the results. He had hoped that a stream of quality publications would ensue from his earlier consultancy experiences: "In practice, the experiences were strong but the publications weak . . . Weak in the sense of lacking theoretical underpinning." Without an explicit theoretical underpinning to their work neither consultants, nor academics and their students, can learn from "pluralistic practice".

Some Thoughts

There seems to be an eagerness to embrace pluralism, broadly defined, in the applied disciplines—and I have given examples only from those areas with which I have some familiarity. The climate is right. One reason for this seems to be the critique that has taken place, in many of these disciplines, of traditional approaches to analysis. In systems thinking, organisation theory, information systems and operational research, for example, old ways have been challenged and new perspectives for advancing each of these disciplines have been opened up. A second reason lies in the failure of the traditional methodologies and methods to deliver what was promised in practice. The failure of hard systems approaches in the context of strategic problems in social systems has been well documented (see, for example, Hoos, 1972). There is no longer the confidence that information systems designed according to traditional structured systems design methods will serve their users and bring competitive advantage to organisations. Practitioners and academics have wondered whether the success rate with traditional approaches could be improved if they were buttressed with some of the newer thinking. Another pointer as to why interest in pluralism is so widespread is the prevailing fashion for "relativism", preceding postmodern thinking but now usually associated with it. The spirit of the times is against "totalising" discourses which claim to know *the truth* about things. To be in tune with the times we must, according to Lyotard (1984), embrace postmodern knowledge which "refines our sensitivity to differences and reinforces our ability to tolerate the incommensurable. Its principle is not the expert's homology, but the inventor's paralogy."

As well as about the generality of the urge to pluralism, we have also learned from our tour of the other applied disciplines how similar the debates taking place are to those going on in systems research. It is indeed arguable that the discussion concerning pluralism in systems thinking and practice encompasses and goes beyond those in the other disciplines. The reasons for this are many and I have enumerated them fully elsewhere (Jackson, 1996). For our purposes it is enough to note, first, that systems thinking was one of the first applied disciplines to go through a period of crisis when different conceptualisations of the field fought one another for hegemony and, perhaps, the earliest to begin to emerge from this crisis. Second, that systems thinking, of all the applied disciplines, has demonstrated the greatest potential for linking theory and practice. It has used contributions from the social sciences to gain an appreciation of the diversity of viewpoints that exist on the nature of the "systems" it seeks to understand and intervene in, and it has been able, through its leadership in the construction of methodologies to guide intervention, to test in practice the usefulness of the distinctions social scientists make (see Jackson, 1991, 1993). Systems research is, therefore, in advance of organisation theory in working out the implications of pluralism for those who wish to actually intervene in problem situations. It is ahead of information systems, operational research, evaluation research and management consultancy in its ability to think through the implications of pluralism at the theoretical level and improve pluralist practice as a result. For these applied disciplines it can supply the theoretical basis which they lack (see Jackson, 1996).

Convinced, therefore, that the debates in the systems field are the most crucial for the future of pluralism we must now return to those debates and seek to develop them further. In the process, of course, we shall take advantage of what has been discovered about the relationship between pluralism and critical systems thinking, and of the discussions around pluralism that have been taking place in other applied disciplines.

THE NATURE OF PLURALISM

We are now able to begin an argument (which we will have to fully develop elsewhere) about the essence of pluralism in systems thinking and practice. In this section I will consider what pluralism can reasonably aspire to and what it needs to avoid. In the final section I will address the question of how it should be formulated and operationalised in order to realise its full potential.

Our discussions to date have given us much food for thought about what we should ask of pluralism in systems thinking and practice. I shall try to organise my own thoughts around four conclusions, although it must be recognised that these are highly interrelated. My four conclusions are that pluralism must be employable in the most complex of problem situations; that it must accept and manage a degree of incompatibility between paradigms at the theoretical level; that it should encourage diversity in the use of methodologies embodying different paradigms; and that it should encourage the maximum diversity of use of different methods, tools and techniques without lapsing into "pragmatism".

The first point concerns usability in the most complex of contexts. Because of the complexity and heterogeneity of the problem situations systems practitioners confront, the kind of pluralism they require must enable them to act with different methodologies and methods as part of the same intervention in the same problem situation. The mechanical complexity of allocating an appropriate methodology to a particular problem context, which the system of systems methodologies encouraged, is not good enough. Further, the pluralism systems practitioners embrace must permit an analysis of problem situations from multiple perspectives *and* facilitate the use of different change methodologies in combination. Linstone's work in the systems tradition, and pluralist contributions in organisation theory generally, do not enhance the second of these essentials of pluralism.

The sort of pluralism systems thinkers need must acknowledge that the problem of paradigm incommensurability continues to exist at the theoretical level and cannot be easily dismissed. It is no longer tenable, in the manner of TSI or Lyytinen and Klein (1985), to believe that it can be resolved by reference to some meta-theory such as Habermas's account of different anthropologically based human interests (or, for that matter, by reference to Habermas's later work on the three "worlds", as Mingers and Brocklesby (1996) start to suggest). Nor can paradigm incommensurability be simply ignored in the way that pragmatists essentially do. We have witnessed the difficulties that continue to dog information systems researchers at the methodological level when problems of this nature at the theoretical level are not addressed. Pluralists must learn to live with and manage a degree of paradigm incompatibility.

Indeed, systems thinkers and practitioners require our third conclusion, the sort of pluralism that encourages the use, together, of different methodologies based upon alternative paradigms. We have no way of dismissing the claims of any paradigm. It follows that we should seek to benefit from what each has to offer. Pluralism can provide its greatest benefits only in the context of paradigm diversity. This is not to decry the usefulness of sometimes employing just one methodology, embodying a particular paradigm, to guide the use of a variety of methods, tools and techniques. Such an approach needs to be followed self-consciously, however, and to permit changes of paradigmatic orientation. If it occurs without due consideration, as tends to be the case in operational research, it degenerates into imperialism. Under the imperialism of one paradigm, as we noted, even if methodologies normally associated with other paradigms are employed, they become denatured. In one way or another pluralism is deprived of the vitality it gains from being able to deploy a variety of methodologies to their true potential and, probably, of the flexibility it could gain from using the variety of methods and tools normally associated with each methodology.

In order to ensure paradigm diversity, and here we draw upon the inextricable link we discovered between pluralism and critical systems thinking, pluralism needs to provide a critical awareness of the links between different methodologies and the paradigms they represent. This requires an understanding of the theoretical underpinnings of systems methodologies. With pragmatism (as, for example, in management consultancy) such theoretical understanding is neglected and proper paradigm diversity cannot be guaranteed. Methodologies owing their allegiance to the same paradigm could be employed together in the mistaken belief that pluralism, in the manner defined here, was being observed. From critical systems thinking, too, we learn that in order to protect paradigm diversity we need to be socially aware. Political, cultural and cognitive (see Mingers and Brocklesby, 1996) constraints can delimit the range of methodologies it is possible to use and so reduce the potency of pluralism. We must also ensure, critical systems thinking tells us, that pluralism maintains a radical edge to it. Because systems practitioners often work for powerful clients there will be a tendency to slip into employing, most frequently, methodologies that support the status quo. Paradigm diversity demands that pluralism be buttressed against this tendency by requiring pluralism to give proper attention to the development and employment of alternative methodologies based on radical paradigms—for example, the "radical humanist" and "radical structuralist" paradigms as defined by Burrell and Morgan (1979).

Another point, related to paradigm diversity, requires that pluralism be applied at all stages of an intervention. It was one of the strengths of TSI that it insisted that pluralism be observed in each of the three phases of intervention it recognised—creativity, choice and implementation. It is tempting to allocate different methodologies, embodying different paradigms, to the various stages of an intervention because they seem "most suited" to particular stages. We have seen information systems researchers flirt with the idea of "front-ending" structured design approaches with SSM, in the belief that SSM gives a richer appreciation of the context while structured methodologies provide explicit guidelines for the implementation of information systems. Multiview, at least as originally described, followed the same logic. Even Mingers and Brocklesby (1996) are tempted by the devil in this respect and relapse from pluralism. They try to map the characteristics of different methodologies according to their perceived ability to assist "appreciation", "analysis", "explanation" and "action". There is no justification for such a procedure. To functionalists, for example, the "appreciation" stage of an intervention carried out according to interpretative logic is not "richer", it is simply misguided. Paradigm diversity requires that pluralism be observed at each and every stage of an intervention.

Finally, on paradigm diversity, using methodologies resting upon alternative paradigms inevitably means that, on many occasions, contradictory understandings of a problem situation will be obtained and contradictory recommendations for change will emerge. Systems thinkers and practitioners need a pluralism that can cope in these circumstances.

Our fourth argument is that the pluralism required must encourage flexibility in use of the widest variety of methods, tools and techniques in any intervention. This point, made variously by Wood-Harper and Avison (1992) in relation to Multiview, Taket and White (1995) in relation to evaluation research, and Mingers and Brocklesby (1996) in relation to multi-methodology, is well taken—particularly as it tells powerfully against TSI. Systems practitioners must be allowed the greatest freedom possible, within pluralism, to tailor their use of methods, tools and techniques (just as with methodologies) to the complexities of the problem situation they are seeking to intervene in and the exigencies of that situation as it changes during the intervention. The pluralism needed, therefore, is one that recognises, as Mingers and Brocklesby (1996) do, that the link between methodology (and the paradigm on which it is based), and the methods, tools and techniques usually associated with it, need not necessarily be a close one. They provide the example of a system dynamics model, which would usually be associated with a "hard" methodology, being used as a detailed cognitive map. The matter has to be tested, however, and this requires epistemological control at the methodological level. Only by being clear about which paradigm we are seeking to serve, with the methods and models, can we test their effectiveness. In order to learn we have to resist the lure of pragmatism. We cannot afford to allow the theoretically uncontrolled employment of diverse methods, tools and techniques that appears to occur in management consultancy.

Taking the main elements from our four conclusions we can be bold (and, probably, foolhardy) and provide a definition of the kind of pluralism our research demonstrates that systems thinking and practice require. Pluralism must be: *An approach to managing complex problems which employs a meta-methodology to take maximum advantage of the benefits to be gained from using methodologies premised upon alternative paradigms together, and also encourages the combined use of diverse methods, models, tools and techniques, in a theoretically informed way, to ensure maximum flexibility in an intervention.*

THE FUTURE OF PLURALISM

Various proposals have been made, as we have witnessed, as to how pluralism should be formulated and operationalised. We are now in a position to judge some of the main options in the light of the requirements placed upon pluralism according to the previous section. The proposals we shall consider are "pluralism as a meta-paradigm (TSI)", "pluralism as a new paradigm", "pluralism as a postmodernist approach", and "pluralism as critical systems practice". These will be looked at in turn in terms of the conclusions reached about the nature of pluralism; the aim being to evaluate the degree to which each proposal enables pluralism to realise its full potential.

TSI sought to establish pluralism as a meta-paradigm, an approach operating "above the paradigms" on the basis of Habermas's theory of the anthropologically based cognitive interests of the human species. Different paradigms and their associated methodologies, methods, techniques, etc., could be put to use according to whether they served the "technical", the "practical" or the "emancipatory" interest. The great advantage of this, according to our previous discussion, was that it guaranteed paradigm diversity. Another strength of TSI is that it promotes pluralism during each of its phases—creativity, choice and implementation. A significant weakness of TSI, the weakness that makes it untenable, is its complacency about being able to operate "above the paradigms". As Tsoukas (1993b: 313) has it: "Reality-shaping paradigms . . . are not a la carte menus; you don't just pick whatever suits you at any time." Another problem is that TSI assumes an inextricable link between paradigm-based methodologies and the methods, models, etc., with which they are associated. This inevitably makes TSI inflexible in use; unable to respond to the exigencies of particular problem situations. In fact the relationship between methodologies and their component parts is much more contingent than TSI allows.

Recognising the difficulty of justifying the complementary use of methodologies with contradictory paradigmatic roots, a number of thinkers have been tempted to declare pluralism a part of a new paradigm. Midgley (1995), for example, wants to defend a version of methodological pluralism consistent with his view of critical systems thinking as a paradigm in its own right. He objects to Flood and Jackson's claim that critical systems thinking is meta-paradigmatic: "I have argued that this cannot be the case given that Flood and Jackson make assumptions about human knowledge that are alien to, and incommensurable with, assumptions made by the proponents of other systems paradigms. Far from being meta-paradigmatic, CST is trying to establish the foundations for a *new* paradigm." In similar vein, Walsham and Han (1991) suggest Giddens' "structuration theory" might be a useful meta-theory within which other theories and methodologies can be contained. And Mingers and Brocklesby (1996) turn to Giddens and Bhaskar to provide a framework to ground multimethodology because "... both ... dispute the claim that we must choose between the competing realities offered by realist or nominalist thinking". This does not, however, mean that multimethodology is meta-paradigmatic, rather multimethodology research belongs to a new paradigm. For Walsham and Han, Mingers and Brocklesby, pluralism can be accommodated within some sophisticated and wide-ranging theory such as Giddens'.

The strength of the "pluralism as a new paradigm" approach is that it resolves the difficulty of having to combine methodologies based upon divergent philosophical and sociological assumptions. A new paradigm is proposed apparently capable of housing pluralism. The obvious weakness is that unless we accept the new paradigm as capable of containing divergent methodologies, then the power of paradigm diversity is constrained. There are many who could make convincing arguments, from alternative paradigms, against Midgley's version of critical systems thinking and Giddens' structuration theory. It follows that, in order to protect paradigm diversity, pluralism cannot sell itself to any one paradigm. One-paradigm pluralism is simply not pluralism. Another possible disadvantage of the new paradigm version of pluralism is that, dependent on the new paradigm embraced, pluralism could lose its radical edge. If the paradigm favoured to house pluralism did not give sufficient attention to emancipatory practice, then this possibility would be lost. This is ironic because I suspect the motives of those who argue for the new paradigm approach are often to do with ensuring that pluralism does maintain its radical edge. If it can be associated with a radical paradigm then, necessarily, it will be able to sustain this emphasis. I have every sympathy with those who wish to maintain the emancipatory option by privileging radical paradigms, but this is not the role of pluralism or, in my view, of critical systems thinking. It is an advantage of meta-paradigmatic pluralism that it ensures protection of the emancipatory option without committing us to emancipatory practice (defined according to the predispositions of the radical paradigms) in every case.

A third proposal, more implicit than explicit, is to align pluralism with postmodernism. This is an attractive option because postmodernism is opposed to the totalising endeavours of the "grand narratives" and committed to promoting "difference" in a world which, it is claimed, we can no longer represent with the certainty provided by the old paradigms and in which we can no longer guide action on the basis of the old moralities. It is an essentially postmodern perspective that underpins the notion of the Multiview approach as metaphor (Watson and Wood-Harper, 1995) and Taket and White's (1995) pluralist strategy for evaluation. Taket and White's experience in evaluation (to use their work as an example)

> ... has been that we need to find ways of working in situations which have a high degree of variety and in which acceptance and respect for difference is

important. Such situations display a high degree of heterogeneity . . . The pluralist strategy described is based on the acknowledgement and respect of difference, rather than its rationalisation. (Taket and White, 1995: 517)

As we have seen, this demands "judicious mix and match" of parts of different OR/systems methods in order to fit the requirements of each particular
situation as it continually changes. Taket and White use a quote from Haraway to explain the purpose of their paper: it is ". . . an argument for pleasure
in the confusion of boundaries and for responsibility in their construction".

The great merit of the "pluralism as postmodernism" argument is that it allows
the systems practitioner the flexibility of method use so that s/he can cleave
closely to what is appropriate in the problem situation confronted and to the
twists and turns required in the intervention. The weaknesses, however, far outweigh this strength and are all those associated with pragmatism. Taket and
White refer to their approach as "pragmatic pluralism", but it is not really pluralism at all in our terms. The use of methods, tools and techniques, without reference to the methodology and paradigm supporting their use, means that we
cannot learn about the effectiveness of these in supporting interventions conducted under the governance of a particular paradigm. The eclectic use of different methods, again without reference to methodology or paradigm, means that
we cannot ensure paradigm diversity. All the methods and models employed may
be used according to *one* implicit paradigm. We cannot therefore gain the benefit
of the strengths of the different paradigms. Nor can we guarantee attention is
given to the possibility of emancipatory practice. Under pragmatism, unless the
circumstances dictate, pluralism loses its radical potential. There is no real difference between Taket and White's pragmatic pluralism and management consultancy as previously described. It is hardly surprising then that Ormerod (1994)
believes that it is ". . . at least possible that postmodernism offers an underlying
philosophical stance that could support consulting practice". He cites Foucault's
concept of sources of power as multiple and diffuse, Baudrillard's ideas on the
collapse of boundaries, and Lyotard's emphasis on plurality and the pragmatic
construction of local rules and prescriptives, as postmodern notions that consultants might find easy to accept. It is interesting that he believes consultants are
unlikely to feel at ease with the theories of the critical school—especially because
radical change might be put on the agenda.

I am going to put forward a fourth proposal which I believe more clearly
allows pluralism to deliver the benefits outlined in the previous section. This is
really a development of TSI, but I would prefer to call it "critical systems
practice". In critical systems practice a meta-methodology is required which
protects paradigm diversity and handles the relationships between the divergent paradigms. The meta-methodology accepts that paradigms are based
upon incompatible philosophical assumptions and that they cannot, therefore,
be integrated without something being lost. It seeks to manage the paradigms

not by aspiring to meta-paradigmatic status and allocating them to their respective tasks, but by mediating between the paradigms. Paradigms are allowed to confront one another on the basis of "reflective conversation" (Morgan, 1983). Critique is therefore managed *between* the paradigms and not controlled from above the paradigms. No paradigm is allowed to escape unquestioned because it is continually confronted by the alternative rationales offered by other paradigms.

Under "critical systems practice" the paradigms are closely related to methodologies which are expected to deliver the benefits inherent in each paradigmatic standpoint. Attention will need to be given to specifying the essence of methodologies representing functionalist, interpretive and radical paradigms (something like Checkland and Scholes' (1990) constitutive rules for the use of SSM). The various methodologies, embodying different paradigms, can then employ a wide variety of methods, models, tools and techniques according to their own rationales. The effectiveness of these component parts of methodologies for servicing particular rationales can be tested over time. It may be that a system dynamics model does not function well to support interpretive intervention but this will not be ruled out in advance. Methods, models, etc., normally associated with methodologies based on particular paradigms can be tried out in the service of methodologies based on other paradigms. This loosening of the link between methodology and method overcomes a significant weakness of TSI and should provide the necessary flexibility in intervention without losing the ability to learn and without endangering paradigm diversity. Given the clear theoretical link back to paradigms, and the assurance of paradigm diversity, the radical option is also always going to be on the agenda.

Pluralism as critical systems practice, at the same time as avoiding the weaknesses of TSI, will also seek to protect its strengths. These, as we know, are the encouragement of paradigm diversity, to address the complexity and heterogeneity of problem situations, in all its stages.

Although critical systems practice is still in a preliminary form and currently being experimented with (a book by Jackson, Gregory and Ragsdell will appear in 1998), it is necessary to say something about the guidelines that might be offered for detailed operationalisation of the approach. Here I would like to draw attention to a somewhat neglected aspect of TSI—the explicit choice of a "dominant" methodology to run an intervention with "dependent" methodologies, reflecting alternative paradigms, in the background. The relationship between dominant and dependent methodologies must be allowed to change as the intervention proceeds to maintain flexibility at the methodology level to set alongside the flexibility we are looking for at the level of methods and tools.

There is one change I would make, however, to the rather formalistic statement of this process in TSI. This involves what I might grandly call a "historic compromise" with interpretive systems thinking. Experience tends to suggest that interventions carried out using interpretive systems thinking, for example SSM, proceed more smoothly than those governed by functionalist or emancipatory rationales. The involvement of participants in the process of change gives them a feeling of ownership of solutions. The participative emphasis of interpretive approaches tends therefore to ensure implementation in a wider range of cases than expert-driven approaches resting on functionalism. Further, since those likely to be involved, in many systems interventions, will be senior managers, emancipatory concerns are often difficult to introduce. The conclusion is that an interpretive systems methodology, such as SSM, should always be chosen initially as the dominant methodology.

Considering this in terms of the phases of TSI, creativity will be conducted on the basis of open discussion employing such techniques as "rich pictures". If models are introduced at the choice phase they will be acting as "hermeneutic enablers" (Harnden, 1989), to help structure debate about particular issues, rather than being taken as representations of the real world. If ethical issues arise during implementation they will be for discussing among those involved, not insisted upon as moral imperatives that cannot be flouted. Of course there will be occasions when the models introduced seem to "capture" so well the logic of the situation and its problems that a shift to the functionalist position will seem justifiable; the models will be taken as representations of reality, and a shift made which establishes a functionalist systems methodology as dominant. Similarly, if paradigm diversity is worth a candle, there will be occasions when the ethics of the analyst, or relevant stakeholders, will be so offended that the shift to an emancipatory rationale becomes clearly necessary. It is the language of moral imperatives that is then talked, not the "business ethics" of making managers more aware.

There are dangers in suggesting this "historic compromise" with interpretive systems thinking. Embracing an interpretive rather than functionalist logic, as initially dominant, is not so hard to take. Even insects riding on elephants, the analogy has it, like to believe they are in control because it makes the journey more interesting. Interpretive thinking is attractive because it suggests we have the freedom to design our own futures. If the elephant is occasionally recalcitrant we can learn about these constraints on our journey. Embracing an interpretive rather than an emancipatory logic, as initially dominant, is more difficult to stomach—what if we believe the elephant is heading in a direction which we regard as repugnant, if it seems about to crush everything we hold dear? There will be a temptation not to continue whispering sweet nothings in its ear, to rapidly dismount, and to set a trap for the thing or even (remember this is an analogy!) shoot it. If a historic compromise is necessary with interpretive systems thinking, if we are to grant it something close to imperialistic status, it is because the times in which we live (at least in developed economies in the North) appear to leave us very little option. Postmodern thinking has weakened faith in our ability to actually know anything for certain about how to design organisations and society (and quite right too, given the disastrous experiments carried out in the name of certainty). The collapse of communism (and postmodern assaults on the grand narrative of personal liberation) have left us uncertain about the viability of any alternatives to the status quo. New Labour wishes to try to steer the elephant. It behoves us, as critical systems thinkers, to be socially aware and to understand why the historic compromise is being made. It is also necessary for us to be clear that it is conditional. Enough horrors occur in organisations, in our own society, and at the world level, to give us pause. The emancipatory option must remain on the agenda.

CONCLUSION

We have traced the development of pluralism in systems thinking and prac-tice, acknowledged its links with critical systems thinking, and observed similarities between debates about pluralism in systems thinking and other applied disciplines. On the basis of this research it was possible to suggest what pluralism needed to be like to bring the greatest benefits to systems thinking and practice. A final section examined four ways in which pluralism might develop in terms of whether these would permit pluralism to deliver its full potential. I argued for pluralism as an essential part of "critical systems practice". As suggested earlier in the chapter, the outcome of the debates in systems thinking is, for various reasons, crucial for the other applied disci-plines. I hope this chapter helps us to get it right.

REFERENCES

Avison, D. and Wood-Harper, A. (1990). *Multiview: An Exploration into Information Systems Development.* Blackwell Science, Oxford.

Brocklesby, J. (1995). Intervening in the cultural constitution of systems— methodological complementarism and other visions for systems research. *Journal of the Operational Research Society*, **46**, 1285–1298.

Burrell, G. and Morgan, G. (1979). *Sociological Paradigms and Organizational Anal-ysis.* Heinemann, London.

Checkland, P.B. (1983). OR and the systems movement: mappings and conflict. *Jour-nal of the Operational Research Society*, **34**, 661–675.

Checkland, P.B. and Scholes, J. (1990). *Soft Systems Methodology in Action.* Wiley, Chichester.

Doyle, K. and Wood, R. (1991). Systems thinking, systems practice: dangerous liaisons. *Systemist*, **13**, 28–30.

Espejo, R., Schuman, W., Schwaninninger, M. and Bilello, U. (1996). *Organizational Transformation and Learning.* Wiley, Chichester.

Fitzgerald, G. (1992). On linking soft systems methods and information systems methods. *Systemist*, **14**, 126–127.

Flood, R.L. (1990). *Liberating Systems Theory*. Wiley, Chichester.

Flood, R.L. (1995). *Solving Problem Solving*. Wiley, Chichester.

Flood, R.L. and Jackson, M.C. (1991a). *Creative Problem Solving: Total Systems Intervention*. Wiley, Chichester.

Flood, R.L. and Jackson, M.C. (eds) (1991b). *Critical Systems Thinking: Directed Readings*. Wiley, Chichester.

Flood, R.L. and Romm, N. (1996). *Diversity Management*. Wiley, Chichester.

Gregory, A. (1996). The road to integration: reflections on the development of Organizational Evaluation Theory and Practice. *Omega*, **24**, 295–307.

Harnden, R. (1989). Outside and then: an interpretive approach to the VSM. In R. Espejo and R. Harnden (eds) *The Viable System Model*. Wiley, Chichester, pp. 441–460.

Hirschheim, R. (1985). Information systems epistemology: an historical perspective. In E. Mumford et al (eds) *Research Methods in Information Systems*. Elsevier, Amsterdam, pp. 13–35.

Hoebeke, L. (1994). *Making Work Systems Better*. Wiley, Chichester.

Hoos, I. (1972). *Systems Analysis in Public Policy: A Critique*. University of California Press, Berkeley, CA.

Jackson, M.C. (1982). The nature of soft systems thinking: the work of Churchman, Ackoff and Checkland. *Journal of Applied Systems Analysis*, **9**, 17–28.

Jackson, M.C. (1985). Social systems theory and practice: The need for a critical approach. *International Journal of General Systems*, **10**, 135–151.

Jackson, M.C. (1987a). New directions in management science. In M.C. Jackson and P. Keys (eds) *New Directions in Management Science*. Gower, Aldershot, pp. 131–162.

Jackson, M.C. (1987b). Present positions and future prospects in management science. *Omega*, **15**, 455–466.

Jackson, M.C. (1990). Beyond a system of systems methodologies. *Journal of the Operational Research Society*, **41**, 657–668.

Jackson, M.C. (1991). *Systems Methodology for the Management Sciences*. Plenum, New York.

Jackson, M.C. (1992). The soul of the viable system model. *Systems Practice*, **5**, 561–564.

Jackson, M.C. (1993). Social theory and Operational Research practice. *Journal of the Operational Research Society*, **44**, 563–577.

Jackson, M.C. (1995). Beyond the fads: systems thinking for managers. *Systems Research*, **12**, 25–42.

Jackson, M.C. (1996). Critical systems thinking and information systems research. In F. Stowell and J. Mingers (eds) *Information Systems: An Emerging Discipline?* McGraw-Hill, London, pp. 201–238.

Jackson, M.C., Gregory, A. and Ragsdell, G. (1997). *Beyond the Fads: Systems Thinking for Managers*. Wiley, Chichester, forthcoming.

Jackson, M.C. and Keys, P. (1984). Towards a system of systems methodologies. *Journal of the Operational Research Society*, **35**, 473–486.

Klein, H.K. and Lyytinen, K.J. (1985). The poverty of scientism in information systems. In E. Mumford et al (eds) *Research Methods in Information Systems*. Elsevier, Amsterdam, pp. 131–161.

Linstone, H.A. (1984). *Multiple Perspectives for Decision Making*. North-Holland, New York.

Linstone, H.A. (1989). Multiple perspectives: concept, applications and user guidelines. *Systems Practice*, **2**, 307–331.

Lyotard, J-F. (1984). *The Postmodern Condition: A Report on Knowledge*. Manchester University Press, Manchester.

Lyytinen, K.J. and Klein, H.K. (1985). The critical theory of Jürgen Habermas as a basis for a theory of information systems. In E. Mumford et al (eds) *Research Methods In Information Systems*. Elsevier, Amsterdam, pp. 219–236.

Midgley, G. (1995). What is this thing called critical systems thinking? In K. Ellis et al (eds) *Critical Issues in Systems Theory and Practice*. Plenum, New York, pp. 61–71.

Martin, J. (1990). Breaking up the mono-method monopolies in organizational analysis. In J. Hassard and D. Pym (eds) *The Theory and Philosophy of Organizations*. Routledge, London, pp. 30–43.

Mingers, J. (1980). Towards an appropriate social theory for applied systems thinking: critical theory and soft systems methodology. *Journal of Applied Systems Analysis*, **7**, 41–49.

Mingers, J. (1992). SSM and information systems: an overview. *Systemist*, **14**, 82–88.

Mingers, J. and Brocklesby, J. (1996). Multimethodology: towards a framework for critical pluralism. *Systemist*, **18**(3), 101–132.

Mitroff, I. and Linstone, H.A. (1993). *The Unbounded Mind*. Oxford, New York.

Morgan, G. (ed.) (1983). *Beyond Method*. Sage, Beverley Hills, CA.

Morgan, G. (1986). *Images of Organization*. Sage, London.

Ormerod, R.J. (1992). Combining hard and soft systems practice. *Systemist*, **14**, 160–165.

Ormerod, R.J. (1994). Combining management consultancy and research. *Systemist*, **14**, 41–53.

Ormerod, R.J. (1995). Putting soft OR methods to work: information systems strategy development at Sainbury's. *Journal of the Operational Research Society*, **46**, 277–293.

Ramakrishnan, R. (1995). Multi modeling: intervention as languaging. *Working Paper*, 1, Centre for Systems and Information Sciences, University of Humberside.

Reed, M. (1985). *Redirections in Organizational Analysis*. Tavistock, London.

Schecter, D. (1991). Critical systems thinking in the 1980s: a connective summary. In R.L. Flood and M.C. Jackson (eds) *Critical Systems Thinking: Directed Readings*. Wiley, Chichester, pp. 213–226.

Symons, V. and Walsham, G. (1987). Evaluation of information systems: a social perspective. *Research Paper*, 1/87, Management Studies Group, Cambridge University.

Taket, A. and White, L. (1995). Working with heterogeneity: a pluralist strategy for evaluation. In K. Ellis et al (eds) *Critical Issues in Systems Theory and Practice*. Plenum, New York, pp. 517–522.

Tsagdis, D. (1996). Systems methodologies, reference systems and science. In R. Trappl (ed.) *Cybernetics and Systems '96*, Austrian Society for Cybernetics, pp. 784–788.

Tsoukas, H. (1983a). The road to emancipation is through organizational development: a critical evaluation of total systems intervention. *Systems Practice*, **6**, 53–70.

Tsoukas, H. (1983b). "By their fruits ye shall know them": a reply to Jackson, Green and Midgley. *Systems Practice*, **6**, 311–317.

Ulrich, W. (1983). *Critical Heuristics of Social Planning*. Haupt, Berne.

Walsham, G. (1991). Organizational metaphors and information systems research. *European Journal of Information Systems*, **1**, 83–94.

Walsham, G. and Han, C-K. (1991). Structuration theory and information systems research. *Journal of Applied Systems Analysis*, **18**, 77–85.

Watson, H. and Wood-Harper, T. (1995). Methodology as metaphor: the practical basis for multiview methodology (a reply to M.C. Jackson). *Information Systems Journal*, **5**, 3.

Wood, J.R. (1992). Linking soft systems methodology and information systems. *Systemist*, **14**, 133–135.

Wood-Harper, A. (1985). Research methods in information systems: using action research. In E. Mumford et al (eds) *Research Methods in Information Systems*. Elsevier, Amsterdam, pp. 169–191.

Wood-Harper, A. and Avison, D. (1992). Reflections from the experience of using Multiview: through the lens of soft systems methodology. *Systemist*, **14**, 136–144.

Chapter 14

Critiquing Multimethodology as Metamethodology: Working Towards Pragmatic Pluralism

LEROY WHITE AND ANN TAKET

INTRODUCTION

> What we do is never understood but always merely praised and blamed. (Nietzsche, 1974: 264).

The chapter is in three parts, the first of which will explore the theory/practice divide, as a necessary preliminary to later discussions. The second part will present our position of pragmatic pluralism, which is then illustrated with examples from community OR practice in part three.

Theory and practice have often been conceptualised as a dichotomy. We find it necessary to deconstruct this divide in order to explore notions in multimethodology. We then move on to offer a critique of the "will to methodology", which we find traditionally as the central organising principle of management sciences/operational research. The first part concludes by discussing contested interpretations of multimethodology:

- multimethodology as metamethodology, which we find to be another version of the "will to methodology"

Multimethodology: The Theory and Practice of Combining Management Science Methodologies.
Edited by John Mingers and Anthony Gill.

- a strategy of mix and match, adopting a flexible and adaptive stance, and operationalising "doing what feels good"

The second part of the chapter expounds our position of pragmatic pluralism. This includes a discussion of the following features:

- the use of triangulation (in terms of data sources, methods, analysis team)
- combining parts of different methods
- being flexible and adaptive
- critical reflection
- a reconceptualisation of the notion of praxis

We conclude by illustrating the above pragmatic pluralism in action by discussing aspects of a number of case studies in our community OR practice. These examples demonstrate the unhelpfulness of trying to follow a metamethodological route and the opportunities opened up by pragmatic pluralism.

PART 1—EXPLORING THE THEORY/PRACTICE DIVIDE

Our Perspectivism

As a way in to exploring the theory/practice divide, we would like to start by examining Nietzsche's notion of the "will to power" and its connections to notions of truth, and hence to what counts as theory.

> What is good?—All that heightens the feeling of power, the will to power, power itself in man.
> What is bad?—All that proceeds from weakness.
> What is happiness?—The feeling that power increases—that resistance is overcome. (Nietzsche, 1969: 2)

To begin with, it is important to note that our interpretation of Nietzsche's "will to power" draws on Deleuze's writings on Nietzsche (Deleuze, 1983). When Nietzsche talks of a "will to power" he is speaking of a so-called drive for knowledge, an impulse towards the formation of truths. In our reading, this is because Nietzsche sees no single reality beyond anyone's interpretations. We are unable to escape the constraints of interpretation, since we can only interpret in and through the use of language (Taket and White, 1993), where language is understood to encompass all the various different systems of representation, including visual and verbal. Thus we adopt Nietzsche's "perspectivism", i.e. the view that the external world is to be interpreted through different alternative systems of concepts and beliefs and that there is no authoritative independent criterion for determining that one such system is more valid than another. This necessarily involves the problem of reflexivity. If we are, say, trapped within language, and we want to express our trappedness, we are unable to do so other than with the very concepts which trap us. Further this leads to the argument that nothing is true, so all possibilities must be considered (but we wish to note that this is not the same as saying anything goes—which we do not hold, see later and also our discussions in White and Taket (1993)). In our reading of Nietzsche the term "will" is used, not to refer to a transcendental will, but a will which provides many possibilities of different truths. Also, and again borrowing from Nietzsche, we view all reasonings as rationalisation and all reasonings offer different perspectives of truth.

However, as postmodernists we are mindful of the "will to truth" as the "will to power", particularly in the way in which some ways of knowing and some knowledges comes to be thought of as providing the singular truth. The works of Foucault have demonstrated this in a number of different domains, such as medicine, psychiatry, criminology (Foucault 1967, 1973, 1977). This work has been expanded by other Foucauldians to include other systems of thought. What postmodernists, drawing on Nietzsche and Foucault, have demonstrated is that, in any system of thought, a "will to power" operates to "make the world up" within a regime of truth. We have insufficient space to explore this complex body of work in more detail; further discussions, particularly relevant for OR/systems audiences, can be found in Poster (1984), Hopwood and Miller (1994), and Power (1994). In the context of this chapter, we need to be mindful of traditional OR's will to power, which appeals to a singular reasoning based on scientific rationality and seeks to privilege methodology based on such scientific rationality.

The will to methodology

> ... physics too is only interpretation ... and not an explanation of the world. (Nietzsche, 1973: 14)

It is now largely accepted that the OR that adopts a scientific rationality does not produce an absolute truth. OR methods do not provide us with value-free facts and truths about the world. OR does not produce answers, no more than anything else does, no more than the other systems of thought used by clients, practitioners, accountants and so on. These perspectives on the world are shaped through experiences just as is the case for all systems of thought. The knower cannot be separated from the OR process and cannot be separated from that which becomes known. The process of generating evidence about practice and its effects is imbued with values, but it often fails to make these values explicit. It is often an approach that masks values which are integral to the process and therefore makes them not amenable to scrutiny, accountability and possible change.

Recently, many methods have proliferated that claim not to ignore values, but to take account of them, e.g. soft systems methodology, cognitive mapping and so on. The need for a vantage point from which to act, or the will to act, was the driving force for this proliferation of methods. This opened up a space for the generation of ways to account for the methods, i.e. ways to embrace the pluralism. But as we will see, most attempts by OR/systems thinking to deal with pluralism still involve a will to a singular truth, a will to a singular metamethodology, so as to tame, control or master pluralism rather than embrace it. This will is such that it cannot, will not, admit nihilism or relativism. It will not, cannot, accept that it produces truth on its own terms.

The problem with the accounts or the metanarratives is their failure to generate moralities which reflect partial, marginal or different views. Metanarratives seek explanation and to make recourse to metanarrative is to produce explanation. The will to methodology is a moral obligation to acquire "reliable" knowledge and act to achieve practical ends in some defensible manner, the will to methodology thus implies a will to act. This can only be achieved by fixing or limiting off parameters, or homogenising that which is diverse, usually to maximise "validity" and to exclude "bias". This normalising tendency has a particular affinity for distributions with one central measure, around which all else is clustered in an orderly fashion, privileging two measures—the mean and standard deviation.

What if we reject the will to act or the will to methodology in the above sense, and court relativism, and offer instead a will to methodologies? To us, the will to methodologies is seen, drawing on our reading of Nietzsche, as a joyful, playful becoming: a Dionysean creativity which is exercised with no fixed or preconceived notion of where the will will lead us. Thus, in what follows, when we refer to our will, this should be understood as in the plural, as generating plural possibilities. The emphasis is on creativity and reflexivity working in tandem with each other. This is something we have developed in the context of our own practice (Taket and White, 1993; White and Taket, 1993).

Within much OR, the situation is seen as demanding a "will to methodology" which is rational and reasonable, as a "will to act". In contrast to this, the "truth" for us is how to create an opening within which the Nietzschean/ Dionysean will described above can flourish, we call this will pragmatic pluralism. The opening allows us a moment for reflection before acting.

Theory and practice

We now move on to look at what OR/systems thinkers have to say about theory and practice in a selection of their writings. Before we do this it will be helpful to summarise the characteristics of the scientific rationality that we are able to identify in them (other sciences have drawn/draw on rather different versions of scientific rationality, for example the work of Bhaskar (1978), but these different versions are not as present in the writings of OR/systems thinkers as the version we discuss). A summary of its characteristics is shown in Table 14.1, and we note that the Foucauldian/Nietzschean critique outlined above causes us, from a postmodern position, to doubt each of these assumptions.

As operational researchers, are we bound by its history and the definitions this has produced? Its history relates to pragmatic scientists using a version of the scientific method on pressing problems and the dominant definition of OR speaks of a singular way to act, this action being imbued with "the spirit of the scientific method". This dominant definition is, however, being increasingly contested (for example, Ackoff, 1979; Checkland, 1981; Jackson, 1987; Mingers, 1992; Rosenhead, 1992; Taket and White, 1993; Keys, 1994; White and Taket, 1994a), in particular by a view which focuses on process, but does not identify it with the scientific method. Often, however, process is conceptualised in singular terms, different writers identify different (singular) processes through the adoption of a particular theoretical position. For us this poses a number of problems, in particular, around the assumptions made

Table 14.1   The characteristics of the scientific rationality (drawing on Flax 1987)

1. Existence of stable, coherent self, capable of a "reason" which offers privileged insight into its own processes and "laws of nature"
2. Reason and its "science"—philosophy—can provide an objective, reliable and universal foundation for knowledge
3. Knowledge acquired from correct use of reason will be "true" in the sense of describing something real and unchanging about our minds and the structure of the natural world
4. Reason has transcendental and universal qualities, it is independent of the self's contingent existence
5. All claims to truth and rightful authority are to be submitted to the tribunal of reason. Freedom consists of obedience to laws that conform to the necessary results of the correct/right use of reason
6. By grounding claims to authority in reason, conflicts between truth, knowledge and power can be overcome. Truth can serve power without distortion; in turn, by utilising knowledge in the service of power, both freedom and progress will be assured. Knowledge can be both neutral (e.g. grounded in universal reason, not particular interests) and also socially beneficial
7. Science, as the exemplar of the right use of reason, is also the paradigm for all true knowledge
8. Language is in some sense transparent and can provide the medium through which the real can be represented. Objects are not linguistically (or socially) constructed; they are merely made present to consciousness by naming and the right use of language

about the separability of ontology and epistemology; we do not have space to explore this here, it is discussed elsewhere (Taket and White, 1996a). The proliferation of processes has led to a number of writers being concerned with how to make sense of this lack of singularity, e.g. Jackson and Keys (1984) and Rosenhead (1989), both of which (Jackson and Keys explicitly, Rosenhead implicitly) find a resolution in proposing some kind of metamethod, which imposes singularity not at the level of process, but at a meta-level. This seems to us problematic for a number of reasons. First, it excludes heterogeneity by (artificially) imposing singularity at a meta-level. A second problem is the lack of focus on the interventionist(s) and the consideration (implicit) of the interventionist as a singular homogeneous entity. Third, there is the treatment of "rationality" as an unproblematic "given". We move on to expand on some of these points below.

In the existing reflections on the above issues (for example, Mingers, 1980; Rosenhead, 1989; Flood and Jackson, 1991; Checkland, 1992; Eden, 1993) what is expressed are various different versions of the "will to methodology". The first example we consider is Flood and Jackson's TSI:

> We need to retain rigorous and formalised thinking, while admitting the need for a range of "problem-solving" methodologies, and accepting the challenge which that brings. The future prospects of management science will be much enhanced if (a) the diversity of the "messes" confronting managers is accepted, (b) work on developing a rich variety of methodologies is undertaken, and (c) we continually ask the question: "what kind of problem situation can be managed with which sort of methodology?" (Flood and Jackson, 1991: xi)

In the above quote, we can see elements of the will to methodology discussed earlier, in that a particular vantage point (rigorous and formalised thinking—a version of the scientific method) is sought in order to deal with diversity, bias, mess. There is, however, a tension between this and the admission of a plurality of methodologies, and an appeal to a meta-methodology (matching contexts to methodologies) is required to resolve this tension. Without such a move to metamethodology, the requirements of "rigorous formalised thinking" make the alternatives (methodological imperialism, relativism or nihilism) unacceptably unpalatable. Or as Jackson phrases it elsewhere:

> . . . instead of seeing different strands of OR as competing for exactly the same area of concern, alternative approaches can be presented as being appropriate to the different types of situation in which management scientists are required to act. Each approach will be useful in certain defined areas and should be used in circumstances where it works best. (Jackson, 1993: 575)

The same kind of appeal to scientific rationality and "will to methodology" can be found in Checkland:

... the most significant issue in any field of intellectual endeavour ... making clear the relation between the epistemology of the subject area and the ontology of the perceived world with which it is concerned ... clarity demands that we be very careful about the difference between ontological statements of the form: the perceived world is something or other and epistemological statements which are not about the perceived world but about knowing the perceived world. (Checkland, 1992: 1026–1027)

From the point of view of the Foucauldian/Nietzschean critique we have outlined above, this aim becomes distinctly problematic.

Not only in terms of methodologies, but also in terms of intervention, we can see this "will to methodology" displayed:

[In intervention] the process of merging wisdom, playing with it, experimenting with alternative solutions, and doing so within the structure, but not preciseness, of science builds on the power of the role equivocality plays in mediation and international conciliation ... Interactive models act as a vehicle to make the fight productive and negotiative within, what members of the group take to be, a rational procedure. (Eden, 1993: 152)

More recently we come to the works of Flood and Romm (Flood and Romm, 1995) which are particularly interesting to us because of their claims to deal with diversity and to "[find] a balance between modernism and postmodernism" (page 473). This work is represented in another chapter in this book, so will not be discussed at length here. We would wish to note, however, that although we can find many points of similarity between their approach and ours, there are also many differences, not least in their reliance on Habermas's theories of communicative competence and the possibilities of dialogue guaranteeing the achievement of unforced consensus.

Most thinkers see the need to respond to pluralism; however, they do this by taming and controlling it, seeking to master it through some version of "rigorous" or "formalised" or "intellectually disciplined" rationality, which reduces to some version of the highly problematic scientific rationality. Their will to truth is an appeal to a metamethodological vantage point.

Finally, before we move on to pragmatic pluralism, we would like to say a few words on "critical reflection". It will seem quite obvious to the reader by now that our reflections draw on our interpretation of Nietzsche (or even interpretation of interpretation) and that found in Foucault's work. Thus, it is a scepticism towards essentialism and about freeing oneself from our constructedness and to begin to reinvent oneself and seeing this as endless. Our critical perspective is a scepticism towards all concepts and incredulity to all meta-theorising. But we do not wish the reader to think of this as negative doubting of all things but, and we have termed this so elsewhere, as "positive scepticism". What we take from Foucault is a critical decentring of ourselves as expert and to encourage others to employ their own reason and to indulge in theorising for themselves alongside action. To adopt an often quoted extract from Foucault "the [expert] no longer has to play the role of the advisor. The projects, tactics, goals to be adopted are a matter for those who do the fighting. What the [expert] can do is provide the instrument of analysis" (Gordon, 1980: 62). We have explored this position in more depth elsewhere (White and Taket, 1994a). We are critical of critical thinking as being ideological, not only when it assumes it can speak for those to be emancipated, but also when it masks this position by a succession of abstractions and constructions.

PART 2—PRAGMATIC PLURALISM

What we do is never understood but always merely praised and blamed. (Nietzsche, 1974: 264)

We can contrast two interpretations of multimethodology:

- Multimethodology as metamethodology, which we find to be another version of the "will to methodology", and which we find in many other OR/ systems writings, as noted above.
- A strategy of mix and match, adopting a flexible and adaptive stance, and operationalising "doing what feels good".

This second interpretation is one we feel more comfortable with, both on theoretical grounds (as fitting with our poststructuralist proclivities) and on practical grounds (that it describes aspects of what we see—in critical reflection—as the successful features of our practice). Once again in making these two points, they are not seen by us as in opposition—but rather as intertwined and interacting. Our aim in the rest of this chapter is to present a framework we use for intervening which we call "pragmatic pluralism", which we find in keeping with this second interpretation of multimethodology, and to illustrate this in use by considering aspects from two case studies drawn from our practice. It is also important to state that this is *not* an attempt at prescription (although there are some things in the course of our description that are proscribed). Since we espouse a postmodern or poststructuralist position in all of this, we do not provide a "justification" of what is presented in the "normal" terms. To do so would be somewhat self-contradictory since we believe in the metanarrative that there is no Archimedean vantage point from which what we describe can be seen to be absolutely right (or absolutely wrong for that matter!). Putting it another way, in the words of Rorty (1989: 48–49):

> To accept the claim that there is no standpoint outside the particular histori-
> cally conditioned and temporary vocabulary we are presently using from which
> to judge this vocabulary is to give up on the idea that there can be reasons for

using languages as well as reasons within languages for believing statements. This amounts to giving up the idea that intellectual or political progress is rational, in any sense of "rational" which is neutral between vocabularies. But because it seems pointless to say that all the great moral and intellectual advances of European history—Christianity, Galilean science, the Enlightenment, Romanticism, and so on—were fortunate falls into temporary irrationality, the moral to be drawn is that the rational–irrational distinction is less useful than it once appeared. Once we realise that progress, for the community as for the individual, is a matter of using new words as well as of arguing from premises phrases in old words, we realise that a critical vocabulary which revolves around notions like "rational", "criteria", "argument" and "foundation" and "absolute" is badly suited to describe the relation between the old and the new.

Instead of seeking a prescription we will seek guidelines, examples, stories, metaphors for use in planning an interaction, in carrying out the interaction, and in reflecting on it afterwards. In moving away from prescription, we seek to maintain an open and flexible stance, capable of responding creatively to the characteristics of a particular moment, continually disrupting the comfort of identification with a fixed theory or view, and seeking instead to mix different perspectives. In an earlier paper (Taket and White, 1993), we talked about the move to action, arguing that:

> . . . we can move away from theory to theatre (acknowledging in passing that they have the same Greek root). The call for action is the call for theatre, not for theory. The world is not just a stage provided by an invisible stage-hand. It is an ever changing scene. We need to act to change our scenes which then, in turn, change the way we act. We cannot unravel ourselves from the scene: we must aim to de-centre ourselves. There is no one theory providing the ideal plot, but many to choose from, like different soundtracks for different occasions. (Taket and White, 1993: 879)

The language that we have used already in this chapter should also have alerted the reader to the "fact" that we are not utilising the traditionally valued scientific route (or even root) here, wishing to avoid the problem identified by Rorty (1989: 8), that is the problem that: "arguments against the use of a familiar and time-honoured vocabulary . . . tend to be phrased in that very vocabulary". Instead we would like to adapt/adopt his "new" approach, i.e. to move away from the sorts of approach that work piece by piece, analysing concept after concept, or testing thesis after thesis, and to work instead holistically and *pragmatically*. This approach encourages us to say things like "try thinking of it this way"—or more specifically "try to ignore the apparently futile traditional questions by substituting the following new and possibly interesting questions".

So, within this chapter, drawing on Rorty, we will delete (as unhelpful) the "old" questions, which might be phrased as:

- what is the *best* way to act?
- what is the *best* thing to do now/next?

and replace them with the following "new" questions:

- how does this feel?
- is this fun?
- does this do what we want?
- is h better than f? (in dialogue: do we prefer f to h; in action: select one, do it, change it if we don't like what we see)

The focus with which the chapter is concerned is the process or task of intervention, and more specifically the exploration of three (overlapping and interacting) questions pertinent to those who would intervene:

- what is to be done?
- how shall we decide what to do?
- what can guide our actions?

The sections that follow illustrate how pluralism in a number of aspects of intervention contributes to the achievement of our practice. In terms of what we will describe as pragmatic pluralism (our response to the questions identified earlier), we intend this to be read in several different ways and on several different levels. We will talk about pluralism in each of the following features:

- in the use of specific methods/techniques
- in the role(s) of the interventionists
- in the modes of representation employed
- in the "nature" of the client

Below we discuss each of these in turn, illustrating with reference to a number of case studies drawn from our work. We also discuss elsewhere (Taket and White, 1996a) pluralism in the use of different rationalities and pluralism in possible outcomes from an intervention.

Our Pluralism

Pluralism, to use an illustrative simile drawn from Wittgenstein (1969), is like a spun thread or rope, which gains its strength, not from a continuous strand that runs its entire length, but from the overlapping and entwining of many separate fibres. In what will be described in this chapter, we will argue for the need for pluralism in order to deal with diversity and heterogeneity. This is our reinterpretation of Ashby's "law of requisite variety", which states that one needs variety to deal with variety, and that it is quite easy to fail to find a solution to issues because the solutions on offer have too little variety. Next we summarise some of the features of the different aspects of pluralism identified above.

One pluralism: the choice of methodologies

The charge of relativism has been repeatedly made to our position, but to us this weakness is a strength, in that it frees us from the "intellectual myopia" that is common in research and critical reflection and argues against "standard write-ups" and "normal science" whose ultimate aim is a regulation of texts. Thus we embrace relativism, since as intervenors we recognise that no cultural structure can analytically encompass the language of another cultural structure, since to encompass the "other", it would have the effect of silencing the "other". This means that we aim to resist the seductive lure of the Enlightenment vision, of ethical absolutism, the desire for a firm transcendent footing for our practice and the difficulty of embracing the shifting sands of postmodernism, the uncomfortable knowledge that the only certainty is uncertainty, and that all knowledge is partial, provisional and contingent. But, as Jacques observes: "A world of multiple knowledge frameworks is not valueless; it is a world of possibility and responsibility. It is a world in which we refuse to use 'objectivity' as reason for avoiding personal involvement in our knowledge productions" (Jacques, 1989: 708). This pluralism is not without potential criticisms; one such objection is to perceive a problem with the possible use of methods based on incompatible ontological or epistemological assumptions. Our response to this is that it only represents a problem from a strongly positivist standpoint, from postmodern or poststructuralist standpoints; this is not of concern, not least because the question of how to accord precedence to any set of ontological/epistemological assumptions is regarded as unanswerable. To draw on Luhmann's discussion of the pervasiveness of intransparency (Luhmann, 1995), we find ourselves inside operationally closed autopoietic systems, with respect to the lack of possibility of checking what is known with recourse to anything that stands outside the systems. There are no mechanisms for such outside checks. We note also that such pluralism has the added advantage of imposing no requirement on participants in any intervention to negotiate a singular common set of ontological and epistemological beliefs as the first stage in the process.

However, it is extremely important to stress that this recognition of relativism does not amount to a position of "anything goes"; in Haraway's words: "the alternative to relativism is partial, locatable, critical knowledges sustaining the possibility of webs of connections called solidarity . . . Relativism is a way of being nowhere while claiming to be everywhere equally. The 'equality' of positioning is a denial of responsibility and critical inquiry" (Haraway,

1991: 191). So our pluralism is not "anything goes" (even Feyerabend argues for reflection), but "doing what feels good". However, how does this fit in with methodological choice? In practice, our re-solution to this is as follows. The first component is recognising and valuing the differences in the methodologies on which we draw and attempting to match these with variety in the local context worked within, the participants in the interaction, and the purpose of the interaction. This is not to imply the existence of any simple mappings between these factors and the methodologies. The second component is the proviso that in the interaction we work to support disempowered or marginalised groups, which are identifiable in any specific local context.

To us (referring back to the discussions on Nietzsche and Foucault), the question whether one method provides better truths than others has no meaning. What actually matters about the choice of, say, a method is not so much whether or not it provides "truth" because surely all methods provide truths in one way or another, but whether or not it is capable of giving to those entertaining it feelings of freedom and em(power)ment; but we are not the judge of this, only the interlocutors.

The implication of this postmodern critique is the view that it is dangerous to see any form of methodology as *inherently* liberatory or emancipatory. Whether it succeeds in achieving some outcomes that can be seen as liberatory or emancipatory is only ever locally decidable. We can still, however, talk about guidelines that are useful to help us choose, but these must be used without allowing us to duck the responsibility of choice. We have selectively paraphrased Foucault's introduction to the work of Deleuze and Guattari (Foucault, 1972), together with some of our own guidelines into a guide for critical action:

1. free action from unitary and totalising paranoia;
2. develop action, thought, and desires by proliferation, juxtaposition, and disjunction, and not by subdivision and pyramidal hierarchisation;
3. withdraw allegiance from the old categories of the Negative (law, limit, castration, lack, lacuna), which Western thought has so long held sacred as a form of power and an access to reality. Prefer what is positive and multiple: difference over uniformity; flows over unities; mobile arrangements over static systems. Believe that what is productive is not sedentary but nomadic;
4. do not think that one has to be sad in order to be militant, even though the thing one is fighting is abominable. It is the connection of desire to reality (and not its retreat into forms of representation) that possesses revolutionary force;
5. the group must not be the organic bond uniting hierarchised individuals, but a dynamic collection of multiplication, displacement, and diverse combinations;

6. it is important to recognise the co-responsible (Heldke, 1988) nature of the encounter, with the co-participation of the different parties involved;
7. aim to achieve "skill" transfer (both ways), and empowerment of all involved;
8. recognise difference and work with it (difference as generator of multiple possibilities, acting to increase choice rather than constraining it) but work non-hierarchically;
9. aim to break down stereotypes of the "expert", the "professional" and reduce the perceived distance between practitioner and client;
10. work for consent (dynamic and contingent, not fixed and absolute) not consensus;
11. aim for flexibility, be ready to adapt and work in different ways at different times, willing to depart from plans and from detailed methodologies.

The first five of these deserve some expansion. The first is a restatement of the need to resist the seductive lure of grand narrative, replacing this by an attitude of positive scepticism. The second is the use of a form of deconstructive practice to replace the prescriptive application of a set methodology. The third summarises the need to move away from the binary thinking that dominates Western thought, and in particular from the negative–positive and normal–pathological couplets (see the discussions in Taket and White, 1993). The fourth begins by calling for resistance to the interpretation of postmodern stances as despairing, nihilistic and miserabeiist, arguing that despite the actuality of oppression in many different violent forms, or as Shange puts it: "Yes we still have to have romance in the face of adversity, this is a fact" (Shange, 1992: 19). In discussing representation (through systems models, for example), this should not be enacted to reinscribe the disciplinary relations of power, but to identify and work with points of resistance to such relations. The aim of representation is not then to accurately reproduce what existed at a particular point in time, but as a device to enable change. The fifth point identifies the need to recognise and embrace plurality, multiplicity and diversity rather than homogenising (and sterilising) the diversity into a set of unitary distinct categories and according an unacknowledged privileged position to only one of these: the average rational economically active heterosexual able-bodied middle-class white male.

Pluralism in the role(s) of the interventionists

As already noted in the above discussion, careful attention is required to the role of the interventionist(s). Pluralism is required in terms of the adoption of different roles or guises (White and Taket, 1995a) at different times in the course of an intervention, and of different roles in relation to different individuals/groups involved in the intervention (at the same time). Another way of putting this is to argue that in practice we can mix and match different guises in the course of an intervention, assuming in this way the role of the "shaman" or "shapeshifter". Our practice here is to be understood in distinction from any notion of a metamethod for selecting guises (for example relying on any type of contingency table approach which would attempt to match guise to characteristics of intervention context), and which we find too rigid, formulaic and unhelpful to deal with the complexities of any intervention. We would like to say a few words about how the guises we use are to be understood, and to point to some future directions for exploration. The guises are discussed in detail elsewhere (White and Taket, 1995a; Taket and White, 1996b). The guises are not sharply separable, and in fact they can be interwoven in the course of a single intervention. This brings us to the notion of the "bathaguise": we have coined this word to allude to the process of immersing ourselves within guises in the course of an intervention. We will develop this further elsewhere (Taket and White, forthcoming).

Pluralism in the modes of representation employed

One of the many issues we are conscious of in our interventions is the role we play in constructing that which we later claim to discover. To draw on the metaphor of the constellation used by many to express this problem, we can ask whether the constellation has existed as long as the stars it comprises, or did it come into being only when chosen and designated. We would claim that the latter is what happens. We make constellations by selecting and demarcating particular stars rather than others, so we make the world up by drawing boundaries around some rather than others. Thus as "experts" we are usually in a privileged position to ascribe meaning through selecting and putting together some aspects of what we see rather than others. This position we have criticised elsewhere (White and Taket, 1994a). In that paper we conveyed the inescapable and active participation we "experts" undertake when we intervene and represent (i.e. produce models). We are generally uncritical of the process of making up the world we are observing, and instead we need to reflect continuously on this.

Thus where do we go from here? The work by Freire is informative in this process. In his writings on education (Freire, 1972), he claims that education needs to be based upon genuine dialogue and it requires the sensitive use of linguistic codes in problematising interactions between different participants. Similarly, the OR and systems processes need to involve sensitive use of representations/models which are transparent and relevant to the participants (examples of these types of representations are given in Taket and White (1996b) and White and Taket (1997). We need to develop modes of representations in OR and systems that are transparent, mutually produced with the participants, are owned by the participants and can be interrogated by the participants. The representations are produced from shared analysis and results in shared meaning between all parties.

Seeking after transparency and shared meaning, however, cannot be accorded the status of an unproblematic, universally applicable goal. This calls for a process of critical reflection on the processes used in the intervention, and the facilitator(s) must necessarily assume the responsibility for deciding what is most appropriate and suitable to each particular moment in the intervention.

Within our practice we are also experimenting with the use of other modes of representation. First, there are the set of action methods, including sculpting (building a physical representation to explore an issue or situation using people and objects), and sociometric diagrams (using spatial distributions to depict aspects of relationships between actors or things). Second, there is the use of scripts, storytelling, narrative analysis, and so on. From within operational research and systems, we also make use of such modes as cognitive mapping, influence diagrams, decision trees and rich pictures. We will explore the use of all of these at length elsewhere (Taket and White, 1996b; Taket and White, 1997).

Pluralism in the nature of the client

From our experience as interventionists, we have found that organisations/groups are increasingly exposed internally to the challenges of heterogeneity and diversity, while at the same time experiencing external pressure to reconstruct their collective identities along pluralistic lines. Individuals within organisations/groups, as well as organisations/groups within the wider setting, are increasingly subject to identity crises. As interventionists, in adopting a pluralist strategy for intervention, we seek to respect and acknowledge the views of a wide range of stakeholders, i.e. the heterogeneity within the group/organisation. The danger with this perspective, however, is its tendency towards relativism, and our attitude to this with respect to methods has been discussed earlier.

In working with groups therefore, in some situations it may be necessary to work with more than one rationality. For example, in the course of evaluating a health service project, some of the parties to the evaluation may operate under what might be referred to as an "economic rationality"—seeking evidence in the form of cost–benefit ratios, where all relevant costs and benefits are assumed quantifiable. A second rationality may be present in the situation in terms of parties who wish to see evaluation in terms of the achievement of equal access to services for different groups in the population, where quantifiable measures of these are assumed *not* to exist. It will not necessarily be possible or desirable to seek to achieve consensus on a dominant rationality in this situation, and instead work can be carried out with both. By way of a further example, however, when views are reinforced by boundaries socially and linguistically constituted which act to oppress particular groups, for example those of race or ethnicity, then the interventionists need to separate these out in the course of the intervention and explicitly challenge any introduction of them into the process to reinforce the oppression. Our practice is to provide a space where participants can acknowledge the differences of others, and which may also allow them to articulate what before remained private and personal and perhaps even unsymbolised. In terms of an intervention, for example, where racist statements are offered as "evidence", they would not be taken into account, and would be challenged vigorously in dialogue. During an intervention, we also need to contest as "facts" any mythic stories which function oppressively to maintain or reinforce inequality or discrimination. Many such examples were found in the case studies discussed here. Again the "problem" of relativism rears its head (see also the discussions earlier in this chapter); here we have found like many others that in the local situation, one useful tactic can be the deployment of "strategic essentialism" (Butler, 1990; Hooks, 1990).

Our notion of pragmatic pluralism also involves a particular notion of the relationship between theory and practice—utilising the notion of praxis— where theory in itself is downplayed and instead the emphasis is on collective theorising for action and intervention, and theorising as a means of critical reflection on practice. So, in adopting a position of pragmatic pluralism, we argue for the need to move beyond conceptualising theory and practice as a dichotomy, following instead a strategy of mix and match, adopting a flexible and adaptive stance, and operationalising "doing what feels good". This means arguing for an end to theory as providing an abstract yet foundational basis for practice, but *not* an end to theorising as a part of a process of critically reflective practice. This position of pragmatic pluralism incorporates the following features:

- the use of triangulation (in terms of data sources, methods, analysis team)
- combining parts of different methods
- being flexible and adaptive
- critical reflection
- a reconceptualisation of the notion of praxis

As well as the discussions in this chapter there are a number of other papers (Taket, 1993; Taket and White, 1994, 1995a, 1996a; White, 1994; White and Taket, 1993, 1994a, 1994b, 1995a, 1995b, 1995c) discussing case studies which illustrate this approach in action. In the future we will continue to develop these further, in particular focusing on the development of pluralism in modes of representation. We now move on to consider two case studies which illustrate aspects of this in practice.

PART 3—TWO CASE STUDIES

It is worth noting that both case studies are examples drawn from our experience in doing community OR; a field of practice where the issues around diversity are heightened, in particular with the common presence of conflict, and where a number of practitioners have experimented with mixing and matching techniques, processes and methodologies (e.g. Thunhurst *et al*, 1992a; Thunhurst *et al*, 1992b; Rosenhead and White, 1996).

The first case study is an extended engagement with a voluntary sector coordinating group. The group has a management committee with a wide range of expertise in research in different parts of the voluntary sector. There are also three staff members. There were three different types of heterogeneity/variety involved in the work: variety in the make-up of the management committee; variety in the pertinent issues and problems; and variety in the ideas about methods that were used in the work with the group. The work involved arose because the group was half way through their current batch of funding, which came from a single source that was considering (due to the economic climate) reprioritising their funding commitments, possibly resulting in a loss to the group. It was decided to hold a series of sessions to explore relevant issues. These sessions were also held with the perceived need to explore the roles of the management committee and staff, and the relationships between them, and to explore how to take the organisation forward. The first session was organised where three different members of the management committee would facilitate the session at different times.

We now explore the content and processes involved in the sessions to illustrate the relevance of adopting a multimethodological approach, in the sense described above. In the first session, three facilitators were used, in turn, to look at three different aspects. The first facilitator (a professional management consultant) was supposed to cover the aims of the day and explore priorities for the day. Nominal Group Technique (NGT) was used; however, no thought had been given to how the group should be divided up, this caused some problems. The question that was posed to the groups was not equally relevant to everyone, this caused further difficulties. There were two different issues that were important: a strategic view and staff–management committee relations. Not clarifying which was being dealt with led to different interpretations being placed on the question posed for the NGT work, and to confusion over priorities for the day. In this part of the session, the tensions and conflicts in the group were not surfaced or acknowledged.

After this, a second facilitator took over and jumped into a SWOT analysis, during which work was carried out in small groups. This part of the session was satisfactory to some members of the management committee because it was looking at strategy, but the staff felt unable to contribute. Because there had been a lack of attention to certain critical issues, there were tensions and uneasiness in the group. It can be seen that there was a lack of reflection on the group dynamics beforehand and during the process by the first two facilitators. There was also a lack of interaction between the different facilitators during the day.

The third facilitator, recognising the problems that this was causing, began to explore the group dynamics using a particular form of sociometrics in which people were asked to group themselves in terms of who they thought they had close links to on particular issues. This provided an opportunity for the staff who had been marginalised in the first two sessions to explore what they thought had been neglected. Following this, an agenda was agreed upon, and using elements of the strategic choice approach, the whole group focused on building a commitment package, planning what should be done at the next workshop. It was felt necessary to keep the whole group working together at this stage, rather than splitting into smaller groups, in order to get important issues surfaced and shared among the group as a whole.

At the next workshop, organised by the third facilitator, people worked in small groups, in order that work could be carried out on a number of different issues, and so that each person could work on issues that were important to them (this was based on NGT). The results of the small groups' work were shared in a plenary session, which explored different types of uncertainties and developed the commitment package further, specifically utilising the resources available and seeking to bring in new people with different skills.

In examining the case study thus far we can now contrast the approach adopted by the facilitators. The first two facilitators used different methods unreflectively, with the result that these parts of the sessions did not work satisfactorily. The third facilitator, on the other hand, let his use of different methods be guided by a process of reflection. Uppermost in his mind was the lack of attention, by the group and the other facilitators, to the anxiety being felt by the staff. Also, the group as a whole was not allowed to develop. It was clear at the time and in that locality that attention to "group issues" and group development was necessary so that the tasks at hand could be addressed. The group supported the notion that the sociodynamics of the group should be explored. The resultant analysis of the sociometric nature of the group helped to bring out into the open some of the tensions. In this way, the facilitator was able to shape the group process in order to deal with the relevant concerns of the moment and to pay attention to group dynamics. From this, the facilitator wanted to move from dealing with the structure of the group to dealing with tasks, but at the same time bearing in mind the potential tensions arising from the structure. It felt good to start to structure the issues drawn from the two previous exercises, but also to add others that reflected the needs of the staff. Full participation was needed as well as an appropriate and inclusive means of representing the issues. Parts of the strategic choice approach felt relevant to use, and the group found them easy to work with. The second session built on the first, using NGT and the strategic choice approach. These parts of the sessions were thus viewed as much more productive.

What happened in the case a little while later brings out some points of interest for the "would-be" community OR practitioner and multimethodologist. It appeared that the review sessions had brought out into the open differences in outlook between the staff and the management committee, and the commitment packages drawn up appeared to be little more than a temporary truce declaration. This reinforces in our mind that agreement and outcomes from group technologies or group decision-making processes are fragile *and* contingent to time and space.

It was clear that the management committee wanted to move the organisation forward in a direction that would make it attractive to funders. It was made up of researchers with a wide interest in voluntary sector research. Each believed they had a strategic view of the sector and research needs. The director was a long-time member of the organisation and felt threatened by the momentum building up to shift the direction of the organisation. The director was also anxious about the changes in the relationship between the staff and the management committee, even though they were changes she had wanted. The result of this was that the director left the organisation (and some of the management committee resigned). The organisation had one year's funding remaining and some quite difficult decisions needed to be made about the future of the organisation. A number of extraordinary meetings and teleconferencing sessions led to the development of a revised plan for the final year of the funding. During this time one of the authors was involved in building spreadsheet models to ask "what-if" questions. But the decisions about the future were not just contingent on the financial state of things. The organisation had to consider options taking into account a range of other issues. In one meeting it was clear to the group that it could not juggle with so many issues without "somehow" graphically representing them. An analytical approach was necessary, in which everyone present could participate. It was suggested by one of the authors that the decision areas could be drawn up and the interconnections, as well as the options available, explored. An option tree was drawn after a discussion about which options were barred and it was clear to all which were the feasible decision schemes. Each was debated and judged according to costs, funding potential and acceptability to the group. The uncertainties brought up by the analysis were discussed and a plan of action based on what the group thought was the best decision was developed. The group then divided into teams to deal with the various aspects of the plan. This, at the moment, is the present state of the organisation. It now remains to draw some conclusions from the case.

In the first instance, the role of the facilitator was different at different times. Conflict resolution was a priority and later the guise of the facilitator moved from peacemaker to analyst. Also it can be seen that the same method was used differently at different times, i.e. dealing with conflict and dealing with decision making. At different stages the choice of what methodologies to use had to be decided for that particular time and that location, and, as was shown, the commitments agreed on were fragile. This emphasises a point we made earlier on consensus. Consensus to us is hard to achieve. What happens is only ever a system of consent. We prefer to drop the notion of consensus and instead promote temporary contingent consent. In this way when consent changes and has to be renegotiated it is not seen as a failure of the process, but as allowing for flexibility and adaptation. Organisations are dynamic and some are ever-changing. Our response to what to use and how can never be guided by any overarching scheme: it is always a case of being aware of one's location.

The second case study is based on some work with a voluntary sector organisation involved in campaigning on issues of civil and human rights. In the last few years the organisation had seen an increase in the interest in its activities and its profile had correspondingly been raised. This change brought with it the need for the organisation to look at the way it organises its work and manages its staff and projects, and so one of its major innovations was to hold regular staff "away days". These are where the whole staff undergo a review of the organisation's processes and operations using an outside facilitator. The object of this is to provide a place where innovations can be discovered and commitment made to enable the group to operate more effectively. We (both authors) were involved in one such away day to explore possibilities, problems, and identify opportunities. We have described elsewhere the process aspects of the work and our evaluation of its success (White and Taket, 1993). Here we wish to focus on aspects of the work relating to the use of pragmatic pluralism.

Prior to the day, we discussed several issues in considering how to structure the day's activities. Our overall approach was to adopt a flexible programme, the agenda for the day was fixed only in terms of time slots, no details of session content were given. This enabled us to respond to the particular issues and concerns as they arose, without giving participants the opportunity to enter into concern and debate about "falling behind on the workplan"—something that we have seen used as a diversionary tactic in other settings.

Another aspect of our flexible approach was that we were *not* searching for a single method to apply throughout the day. Overall, we wanted to aim to work towards the outcome of some sort of commitment package at the end of the day. We discussed the potential usefulness of several different methods, and drew on some of these to compile a series of worksheets to be used to allow individuals to explore their own views at various points during the day preparatory to group discussion. Apart from that, we made no fixed selection of methods. Not all of the worksheets were used on the day. Within the various sessions of the day, we aimed to be creative in responding to what we saw as the needs of the moment by selecting from, adapting and mixing various methods, which resulted in some of the plans being used, others not.

The object of the encounter was to clear the ground for shared understanding of their situation, to encourage the whole group to be committed to taking action or to explore possible avenues, and to ensure everyone was sufficiently informed, so that there was as universal as possible support for any decisions made. The organisation wanted all the workers and staff to participate, hence that make-up of the group ranged from the General Secretary to the switchboard operator.

Each participant was asked to think about what things they liked in the organisation, and what they disliked as a warm-up. After this round, the first session, conducted in the group as a whole, concentrated on identifying strengths and weaknesses (problems/issues) of the organisation. Each participant individually completed a worksheet, items were then shared and recorded on flipcharts, with some discussion. The problems/issues that had surfaced were then used to identify, by means of "voting", which were most important, which were most urgent and which were of most interest in terms of wanting to work on them during the remainder of the day. For each of the three measures in turn, each person was given 10 votes which they placed according to their rating of the different problems/issues. The two issues scoring highest on the third measure were:

- internal communication, planning and coordination
- lack of management time (delegation, campaign and project management)

Following this, participants were asked to organise themselves into two groups for the subsequent session, working on building up a detailed picture of these two issues. Groups were chosen by the participants, in a way that mixed management and workers, campaign and administration in each group.

In this initial group session, one group concentrated on generating a rich/ thick description of the problems/issues, exploring links between different factors identified (simple cognitive mapping, if you like, although there was no explicit attempt to draw maps). Constraints and limitations affecting the different factors involved in the issues were identified. The emphasis was placed on generating diversity, and no attempt was made to reach consensus. At this stage, different (conflicting) views emerged and were acknowledged. The manner of work in this group could be viewed as the equivalent of the shaping phase in strategic choice, elements of stakeholder analysis were used, and some of the critical systems heuristics (CSH) boundary questions were also useful. The feedback from this group to the group as a whole involved each individual contributing, there was no use of a rapporteur; this served to maintain the diversity expressed.

In the other group, guided by some simple prompts, they were asked to describe for themselves how they saw the problem. Following this and guided by the CATWOE mnemonic, they were asked to come up with, collectively, root definitions for their situation. A debate ensued where different perceptions were aired, many bouts of conflictual comments were observed. The result was that it was possible to express the situation as a root definition. There was then an agreement that this provided a suitable basis to take forward and share with the other group. It is also worth noting that diagrams were used to map out various perceptions of the situation. This aided the debates because they were seen as quick summaries of the key points.

During the review session the findings of each group were aired and a discussion followed. Following lunch, during the afternoon session, the groups continued to work on the issues started in the morning session. For one group, the emphasis of this session was to get an impression of how or what improvements could result. Traditional OR encounters would be looking for some sort of model of the situation. What was done here was simply to guide participants to describe what would be feasible for the future. The other group concentrated on the generation of realistic, feasible opportunities for change; discussion enabled negotiations, and consensus on the feasibility of different options was reached. The opportunities for change identified were not expressed explicitly in commitment package form during the group session, owing to lack of time to fully air all the opportunities identified, this took place during the feedback to the group as a whole.

On the flexibility of the approach, perhaps the most structured element, the worksheets used for self-reflection at the beginning of each session, were useful for *most* participants to start them off thinking on their own. However, once group discussions started, it was important to move away from these, and it was then that flexibility in combining elements from different methods was particularly useful. The second thing to note was that using different methods when working separately in the two groups did not preclude bringing the whole thing together when the groups recombined. During the day we deliberately worked to permit divergence of views, as well as divergence of methods used; the plural process allowed for sufficient negotiations by the end of the day to identify a commitment package. We would like to emphasise that this did not represent a closed solution to the problems/issues worked on in any closed fashion, but rather represented a (temporary) re-solution in terms of identifying opportunities for change, which at a later stage may be revisited for revision or re-solution.

The atmosphere created during the day was productive; sufficient "safety" was created to allow the airing of difficult issues and the acknowledgement of strong feelings that needed to be dealt with. Decisions were reached on what was to be done, and these were carried out in the following week.

DISCUSSION

This chapter has presented our interpretation of multimethodology as a strategy of mix and match, adopting a flexible and adaptive stance, and operationalising "doing what feels good". This includes recognition of the importance of the following features:

- the use of triangulation (in terms of data sources, methods, analysis team)
- combining parts of different methods
- being flexible and adaptive
- being critically reflective

We would like to emphasise that our pragmatic pluralism is not an argument for "anything goes". Throughout the processes involved there is a need for continuous critical reflection on the part of the multimethodologists. For us this also involves a reconceptualisation of the notion of praxis, which within our pragmatic pluralism involves rethinking the relationship between theory and practice, so that theory itself is downplayed and instead the emphasis is on collective theorising as a means of prompting action and intervention, and theorising as a means of critical reflection on practice. Theorising is not undertaken for the purpose of producing a theory (or even theories), but for the purpose of stimulating action. So, in adopting a position of pragmatic pluralism, we argue for the need to move beyond conceptualising theory and practice as a dichotomy. This means arguing for an end to theory as providing an abstract yet foundational basis for practice, but *not* an end to theorising as a part of a process of critically reflective practice.

To us, the question whether one method provides better truths than the other has no meaning. What actually matters about the choice of, say, a method, is not so much whether or not it provides "truth", because surely all methods provide truths in one way or another, but whether or not it is capable of giving to those entertaining it feelings of freedom and em(power)ment. To recapitulate: it is dangerous to see any form of methodology as *inherently* liberatory or emancipatory. Whether it succeeds in achieving some outcomes that can be seen as liberatory or emancipatory is only ever locally decidable. We can still, however, talk about guidelines that are useful to help us choose, and we have discussed some earlier.

From the two case studies presented in part 3, there are a number of general points that arise. The first is the importance of paying attention to group dynamics, explicitly acknowledging difficult issues and allowing them to be analysed sufficiently so that work of the group could continue. A key point is the participation of everyone in this. Here the flexibility of multimethodologists is important—switching tack according to demands of the moment. This recognition is one that is rarely found in the OR or systems literatures, one notable exception is Phillips and Phillips (1993) we have discussed this more fully elsewhere (White and Taket, 1994a; White and Taket, 1995a). The case studies also demonstrate that ISMs can be split, can be combined and recombined, with their utility judged in their practice and not in their theory. Conversely, there can be nothing in the theory underlying a particular ISM which guarantees its success in practice. No particular ISM can guarantee an emancipatory or liberatory outcome, demonstrating the difficulty inherent in the "will to methodology" discussed earlier.

In terms of future avenues for development, we would like to indicate some of the work we are developing. The first of these is experimenting with the use of different modes of representation. First, there are the set of action methods, including sculpting (building a physical representation to explore an issue or situation using people and objects), and sociometric diagrams (using spatial distributions to depict aspects of relationships between actors or things). Second, there is the use of scripts, storytelling, narrative analysis, and so on. From within operational research and systems, we also make use of such modes as cognitive mapping, influence diagrams, decision trees and rich pictures. Part of the purpose of doing this is in order to widen participation in the process of analysis and to respond to the diversity of people, groups and organisations involved. One thing that needs to be explored here is achieving an appropriate balance between level of detail of representation and extent of participation. Connected to this is our notion of metamodelling (Taket and White, 1996b), understood as a process of modelling *with* the client(s), i.e. an interactive process for involving the client(s) in (1) eliciting model structures and parameters for use in a particular intervention, and (2) using some model(s) to explore a particular decision situation. This involves working with a combination of different forms of representation (for example, cognitive mapping, sculpting, influence diagrams, visualisation, systems dynamics, simulation), selected according to the context and according to the client(s)' preferences for different modes of representation.

A second avenue for development is the role of the multimethodologist(s) and the notion of different guises for use in facilitating an intervention. We have already begun work on this (White and Taket 1995a; Taket and White, 1996a). We will explore the use of all of these at length elsewhere (Taket and White, forthcoming).

REFERENCES

Ackoff, R. (1979). The future of operational research is past. *Journal of the Operational Research Society*, **30**, 93–104.

Bhaskar, R. (1978). On the possibility of social scientific knowledge and the limits of naturalism. *Journal of the Theory of Social Behaviour*, **8**(1), 1–28.

Butler, J.P. (1990). *Gender Trouble: Feminism and the Subversion of Identity*. Routledge, New York.

Checkland, P. (1981). *Systems Thinking, Systems Practice.* Wiley, Chichester.

Checkland, P. (1992). Systems and scholarship: the need to do better. *Journal of the Operational Research Society*, **43**(11), 1023–1030.

Deleuze, G. (1983). *Nietzsche and Philosophy.* University of Minneapolis Press, Minneapolis, MN.

Eden, C. (1993). From the playpen to the bombsite—the changing nature of management science. *OMEGA*, **21**(2), 139–154.

Flax, J. (1987). Postmodernism and gender relations in feminism theory. Reprinted in L.J. Nicholson (ed.) *Feminism/Postmodernism*, 1990. Routledge, New York, pp. 39–62.

Flood, R.L. and Jackson, M.C. (1991). *Creative Problem Solving: Total Systems Intervention.* Wiley, Chichester.

Flood, R. and Romm, N. (1995). Diversity Management: Theory in Action. *Systems Practice* 8, 469–482.

Foucault, M. (1967). *Madness and Civilization: a History of Insanity in the Age of Reason.* Tr. R. Howard. Tavistock, London.

Foucault, M. (1972). Preface. In G. Deleuze and F. Guattari (eds), Tr. R. Hurley, M. Steem and H.R. Lane *Anti-Oedipus: capitalism and schizophrenia.* London, Athlone, 1984, pp. xi–xiv.

Foucault, M. (1973). *The Birth of the Clinic: an Archaeology of Medical Perception.* Tr. A.M. Sheridan. Routledge, London.

Foucault, M. (1977). *Discipline and Punish.* Penguin, Harmondsworth.

Freire, P. (1972). *Pedagogy of the Oppressed.* Sheed and Ward, London.

Gordon, C. (1980). *Power/Knowledge.* Pantheon Books, New York.

Haraway, D.J. (1991). *Simians, Cyborgs and Women: the Reinvention of Nature.* Free Association Books, London.

Heldke, L. (1988). Recipes for theory making. *Hypatia*, **3**, 15–29.

Hooks, B. (1990). Postmodern blackness. *Postmodern Culture*, **1**(1).

Hopwood, A.G. and Miller, P. (1994). *Accounting as Social and Institutional Practice.* Cambridge University Press, Cambridge.

Jackson, M.C. (1993). Social theory and operational research practice. *Journal of the Operational Research Society*, **44**, 563–577.

Jackson, M.C. (1987). Present positions and future prospects in management science. *OMEGA*, **15**, 455–466.

Jackson, M.C. and Keys, P. (1984). Towards a system of systems methodologies. *Journal of the Operational Research Society*, **35**(6), 473–486.

Jacques, R. (1989). Post-industrialism, postmodernity and OR: toward a "custom and practice" of responsibility and possibility. In M.C. Jackson, P. Keys and S.A. Cropper (eds) *Operational Research and the Social Sciences.* Plenum, New York, pp. 703–708.

Keys, P. (1994). *Studies in the Process of Operational Research.* Wiley, London.

Luhmann, N. (1995). The control of intransparency. Plenary address, ISSS conference, July 1995, Amsterdam.

Mingers, J. (1980). Towards an appropriate social theory for applied systems thinking: critical theory and soft systems methodology. *Journal of Applied Systems Analysis*, **7**, 41–49.

Mingers, J. (1992). Recent developments in critical management science. *Journal of the Operational Research Society*, **43**, 1–10.

Nietzsche, F. (1969). *The Anti-Christ.* Penguin, Harmondsworth.

Nietzsche, F. (1973). *Beyond Good and Evil.* Penguin, Harmondsworth.

Nietzsche, F. (1974). *The Gay Science.* Random House, New York.

Phillips, L. and Phillips, M. (1993). Facilitated work groups: theory and practice. *Journal of the Operational Research Society* **44**, 533–549.

Poster, M. (1984). *Foucault, Marxism and History.* Polity Press, London.
Power, M. (1994). *The Audit Explosion.* Demos, London.
Rorty, R. (1989). *Contingency, irony and solidarity.* Cambridge University Press, Cambridge.
Rosenhead, J. (ed.) (1989) *Rational Analysis for a Problematic World.* Wiley, Chichester.
Rosenhead, J. (1992). Into the swamp: the analysis of social issues. *Journal of the Operational Research Society,* **43**, 293–305.
Rosenhead, J. and White, L. (1996). Nuclear fusion: some linked case studies in community operational research. *Journal of the Operational Research Society* **47**, 479–489.
Shange, N. (1992). The love space demands—an interview. *Spare Rib,* **238**, 17–19.
Taket, A.R. (1992). Review of: *Creative Problem Solving: Total Systems Intervention* by R.L. Flood and M.C. Jackson (Wiley, Chichester, 1991). In *Journal of the Operational Research Society,* **43**(10), 1013–1016.
Taket, A.R. (1993). Mixing and matching: OR and innovatory health promotion projects. *OR Insight,* **6**(4), 18–23.
Taket, A.R. and White, L.A. (1993). After OR: an agenda for postmodernism and poststructuralism in OR. *Journal of the Operational Research Society,* **44**(9), 867–881.
Taket, A.R. and White, L.A. (1994). Doing community operational research with multicultural groups. *OMEGA,* **22**(6), 579–588.
Taket, A.R. and White, L.A. (1995a). Working with heterogeneity: a pluralist strategy for evaluation. *4th International Conference of UKSS: Critical Issues in Systems Theory and Practice.* Hull, July 1995. Plenum, New York, pp. 517–522.
Taket, A.R. and White, L.A. (1995b). Visible responsibility: a guide for critical action. *ISSS Conference: Systems Thinking, Government Policy and Decision Making.* Amsterdam, July 1995, pp. 1054–1061.
Taket, A.R. and White, L.A. (1996a). Pragmatic pluralism—an explication. *Systems Practice,* **9**(6), 571–586.
Taket, A.R. and White, L.A. (1996b). Metamodelling: a case study in the health sector. Paper presented at IFORS conference, July 1996, Vancouver.
Taket, A.R. and White, L.A. (1997). Wanted: Dead OR Alive—ways of using problem structuring methods in community OR. *International Transactions in Operational Research* 4.
Taket, A.R. and White, L.A. (forthcoming). Managing in the multi-agency setting.
Thompson, J.C. (1992). Program evaluation within a health promotion framework. *Canadian Journal of Public Health,* **83**(Sup. 1), S67–S71.
White, L.A. (1994). Development options for a rural community in Belize—alternative development and operational research. *International Transactions in Operational Research,* **1**(4), 453–462.
White, L.A. (forthcoming). *What is a Model?*
White, L.A. and Taket, A.R. (1993). Community OR—doing what feels good. *OR Insight,* **6**(2), 20–23.
White, L.A. and Taket, A.R. (1994a). The death of the expert. *Journal of the Operational Research Society,* **45**(7), 733–748.
White, L.A. and Taket, A.R. (1994b). Using rapid appraisal for evaluating the voluntary sector's delivery of health care programmes. SYSTED 94. Proceedings of the Fifth International Conference on Systems Sciences in Health and Social Services for the Elderly and the Disabled, Geneva CICG 2–6 May 1994. J.C. Rey and C. Tilquin (eds). Aarau, Institut Suisse de la santé publique, pp. 812–817.
White, L.A. and Taket, A.R. (1995a). Changing faces: an investigation of guises for intervention. *ISSS Conference: Systems Thinking, Government Policy and Decision Making.* Amsterdam, July 1995, pp. 1088–1097.

White, L.A. and Taket, A.R. (1995b). Paradigm lost? June 1995. Paper for Second International Workshop on multiorganisational partnerships: Working together across organisational boundaries, Strathclyde, Scotland.

White, L.A. and Taket, A.R. (1995c). Relationships between non-governmental organisations: an analysis using autopoeisis and social networks. Paper presented at the International Social Network Conference, London, July 1995.

White, L.A. and Taket, A.R. (forthcoming). Beyond Appraisal: Participatory Appraisal of Needs and the Development of Action (PANDA). *OMEGA*.

Towards Critical Pluralism

JOHN MINGERS

It is not practicing criticism either to validate the status quo or to join up with a priestly caste of acolytes and dogmatic metaphysicians . . . [t]he realities of power and authority—as well as the resistances offered by men, women, and social movements to institutions, authorities, and orthodoxies—are the realities that . . . should be taken account of by criticism and the critical consciousness. (Said, 1983: 5)

INTRODUCTION

In the introductory chapter I introduced the general notion of multimethodology, considered its desirability and feasibility, and demonstrated that there was a range of possible approaches. In this chapter, I wish to be more partisan and put forward my own preferred version of multimethodology, or at least an early development thereof, paying particular attention to its *critical* employment.

As the theoretical part of this book has shown, most of the work so far on the general subject of managing a diversity of methodological approaches has been that carried out under the banner of critical systems thinking (CST) at Hull/Humberside, beginning with the system of systems methodologies (SOSM), and culminating with total systems intervention (TSI) in its various versions, and triple loop learning. My argument is that this development, fruitful as it has been, does not fully operationalise *multi-paradigm*

Multimethodology: The Theory and Practice of Combining Management Science Methodologies.
Edited by John Mingers and Anthony Gill.
© 1997 John Wiley & Sons Ltd.

multimethodology. It has generally been more concerned with the *selection* of methodologies than their *combination*, and with the use of complete methodologies rather than with their component parts (although case studies in books such as Flood and Jackson (1991) and Flood (1995) have often combined methodologies, there is little in the *theory* to assist the agent in doing this). It is also the case that there are various unresolved debates, issues, and questions, particularly insofar as CST is claimed to be genuinely *critical*. Perhaps of even more importance than these issues that are internal to critical systems, are the important critiques that have been raised, especially by postmodernists, about the very possibility of any *critical, rationalist* project. This brings to the fore the much debated question of what it means to be critical, or to conduct critique. This chapter presents an attempt to rethink the nature of a critical approach within a multimethodology context, given these important issues and debates. The thinking recounted here is still in its early stages and many of the details need to be filled in, but it does lay out a number of important signposts as to the way in which a *critical* employment of multimethodology must proceed.

This chapter begins by highlighting the dilemmas of the current situation. It describes three markedly different views of critique—Habermasian, communitarian, and Foucauldian—and then picks out the major debates or issues both internal and external to CST. These show that it is not sufficient to simply adjust at the edges CST as so far developed. Once the substance of these claims has been made clear it is then possible to rethink the nature of *critical intervention* in the light of three areas of difficulty—the limitations of critical systems/TSI; the move to multimethodology; and the fundamental critiques of postmodernism. The most important conclusions are: a movement away from abstract methodologies towards an emphasis on the importance of the real agent(s) who will use them; recognising that *critically oriented* methodologies cannot guarantee their critical employment—this rests with the commitments of the agent; and accepting that any emancipatory potential must be local and contextual rather than general and abstract. The later parts of the chapter present practical frameworks to assist in a critical pluralist use of multimethodology.

CURRENT DILEMMAS IN CRITICAL SYSTEMS THINKING

The Nature of Critical Engagement

To begin with, some discussion of the related themes of *critique (and critical theory)*, *enlightenment*, *emancipation*, *morality*, and *ethics* is necessary although each is steeped in its own complex history. The term *emancipation* derives from the Latin "to release" (Munro, 1997) and connotes the freeing of a person or people from some form of constraint. It has been used in connection with the ending of slavery, the attainment of women's suffrage, and by Habermas in terms of a human species interest in autonomy and freedom from distorted knowledge. This latter usage is clearly related to Kant's view of *enlightenment*, a process by which people would use their reason and knowledge to free themselves from dogma. Thus enlightenment can be seen as a particular means towards certain forms of emancipation. This process can also be seen as one of *critique*, that is, a deliberate questioning of prevailing forms of knowledge (idealist), or of particular, oppressive, social and institutional arrangements (materialist). *Critical theory* (or critical systems) is a specialised type of knowledge used within the process of critique. Finally, *morality* concerns general principles of valued human behaviour (i.e. that which is accepted, within a particular culture, as good/bad or right/wrong), and *ethics* refers either to processes of determining moral principles, or to particular sets of principles held by individuals or groups.

In terms of traditions, the pre-eminent one has been the modernist–rational tradition beginning with Kant, extending through Hegel and various forms of Marxism, to Habermasian critical theory. It is certainly this tradition upon which critical management science has drawn. The central themes have been the possibility of attaining some oppression-free, ideal social situation; the employment of reason, rationality and knowledge in achieving such a state; the constraining and distorting effects of power; and the role of the autonomous human subjects in this process. Some of the strands of diversity have been an idealistic concentration on a critique of ideas as opposed to a materialistic emphasis on action to change society. And, particularly with Habermas (1984, 1987), a switch to communication and language, and to discourse and dialogue rather than individual cognition (Young, 1990; Benhabib, 1992). Habermas's most recent work has been aimed at developing what he terms "discourse ethics" (Habermas, 1990, 1992, 1993a, b). This will be discussed later.

A second strand, particularly within the domain of ethics, is communitarianism (MacIntyre, 1985[1]; Spaul, 1995; Munro, 1997) reviving traditional Aristotelian ideas concerning the "good life". The main argument is against the Kantian notion that a universal, rational morality can be created. General morality is seen to be firmly anchored in individual personal values and these in turn can only be generated through historical interactions among a group of people within a community. Morals cannot be prescribed from the outside as appropriate for all because, in total, there is such divergence of experiences, situations, and viewpoints. There can be no universal moral viewpoint to be

---

[1] MacIntyre himself is not comfortable with the label "communitarian", but it is satisfactory for the purposes of this chapter.

aimed at. Instead we should encourage the development of localised communities within which agreements about worth and value may develop.

Recently, however, many of the assumptions of the traditional approach have been challenged from a postmodern perspective, particularly through the work of Foucault (Foucault, 1980a, b; Foucault, 1982; Taket and White, 1993; Broklesby and Cummings, 1996). This draws on another tradition, stemming from Nietzsche and Heidegger, and sharply undermines the very roots of modernism. It questions the idea that rationality and reason can be neutral tools suggesting instead that they themselves are inevitably entwined with the exercise of power; it questions the idea that power is simply a constraining imposition that can be removed, seeing it as inextricably constitutive of our everyday practices; and it emphasises the extent to which the subject can never be autonomous but is always constructed through the disciplining practices of society.

The particular position to be argued for in this chapter I have termed "critical pluralist". This emphasises an acceptance of plurality at many levels—philosophical, social, methodological—but also grounds this from a perspective that is fundamentally critical of the unequal and constraining nature of current social arrangements.

Debates within Critical Systems Thinking/TSI

This section highlights a number of issues or debates *within* CST/TSI that are particularly relevant to the issue of various versions of multimethodology and its critical usage. It is not intended to deny the importance and relevance of this work for the development of critical management science. Indeed, the comprehensiveness and explicitness of CST/TSI makes it clear as to the areas in which development must come. This section is based on the main published material up to 1995/6, but the area is continually being developed and the latest expositions of Jackson's and Flood's work are found in their chapters elsewhere in this book.[2]

Debate 1—Is TSI meta-paradigmatic?

The first issue concerns the exact nature of TSI as a whole—is it meta-paradigmatic or simply a new paradigm that subsumes the older ones (Midgley, 1989a, b)? Flood and Jackson themselves have tended to the view that it is meta-paradigmatic:

> . . . the metamethodology [*sic*] recently developed by Flood and Jackson to help realize in practical applications the benefits that can be gained from accepting

---

[2] As Flood and Jackson no longer work together, their ideas may well now be diverging.

> complementarism in theory and practice. This "total systems intervention" (TSI) approach . . . (Jackson, 1991: 208)

> Our task . . . is . . . to manufacture a meta-paradigmatic net with which we can assess the legitimacies and limitations of the various systems methodologies. (Flood and Jackson, 1991: 60)

The commitment to theoretical and methodological complementarism means that the different methodologies are seen to stem from paradigms based on competing assumptions and rationalities. These paradigms must be respected and not subsumed or absorbed.

> These alternative positions must be respected, and the different theoretical underpinnings and the methodologies to which they give rise developed in partnership. Further, the claim of any one theoretical rationality—whether functionalist, structuralist, interpretive, or emancipatory—to absorb all others must be resisted. (Jackson, 1991: 186)

Instead they are to be orchestrated by the meta-level use of the system of systems methodologies and TSI. The philosophical justification for this complementarism is based on a straightforward appeal to Habermas's theory of knowledge-constitutive interests.

There are, however, a number of problems with this position that make it particularly inappropriate for multi-paradigm multimethodology. First, it leads directly to the problem of paradigm incommensurability which will be discussed below. Second, it is somewhat contradictory to propose the notion of some high level position that accepts incompatible assumptions in lower-level paradigms and yet apparently makes no ontological or epistemological presuppositions of its own. Third, it is based on the premise that the different methodologies (and their supporting paradigms) are complementary in the sense that they are appropriate for different situations. They should be both developed and used separately. This makes the idea of mixing different methodologies together in the same intervention rather difficult. And it makes even more problematic the notion of methodological partitioning, i.e. mixing together *parts* of methodologies from different paradigms. Again this will be discussed below.

Midgley (1989a, b) argues, and I would agree, that it is more coherent to see critical systems in fact as a new paradigm of its own—one that subsumes within it the other sub-paradigms. This would allow the competing assumptions to be reconciled within some wider framework; methodologies to be partitioned and mixed; and the foundational assumptions of the new paradigm to be developed and explored. Midgley (Midgley, 1992) bases his version of pluralism on Habermas's "three worlds" (Habermas, 1984, 1987) rather than the knowledge-constitutive interests. I would combine this with other conceptualisations, especially Bhaskar's (Bhaskar, 1989) "critical realism".

Debate 2—Problems of incommensurability and feasibility

The second issue is that complementarism (Flood and Jackson's version of pluralism) does not deal adequately with the problem of paradigm incommensurability, or cultural and cognitive feasibility. As clearly recognised by Jackson and Flood, their particular complementarist position is threatened by the contradictory nature of the different paradigms.

> The main difficulty . . . is that arguments in favour of "paradigm incommensurability" are so strong . . . It would seem inconceivable . . . that different systems methodologies, based on irreconcilable theoretical assumptions, could ever be employed together in some complementarist way. There is the insurmountable difficulty of how it is possible to stand above the paradigms and work with them in this manner. (Jackson, 1991: 201)

This "insurmountable difficulty" is "resolved" simply by an appeal to Habermas's theory of human interests:

> While it is not possible to quell all doubts at this time . . . The preferred vehicle to support critical systems thinking's complementarism at the theoretical level . . . is Habermas's theory of human interests . . . different systems methodologies represented as serving . . . different human species imperatives. (Jackson, 1991: 202)

After this bald assertion little more is ever said about the matter in the main texts on TSI, although it has been taken up briefly by Flood and Romm (1995a, 1996) who now use the term "(in)commensurability" to highlight the idea that theory/methodology choice involves valuing a radical diversity of positions. This seems to give a name to a problem without resolving it. However, the problem cannot be resolved so easily. First, the theory of knowledge-constitutive interests was only an epistemological, not an ontological, device. It aimed to provide a justification for different forms of scientific knowledge but never claimed to overcome all problems of paradigm incommensurability. In particular, it cannot resolve ontological conflicts about, say, the nature of the social world. Second, the theory itself has been subjected to sustained criticism (see Habermas, 1978, Postscript; Thompson and Held, 1982; McCarthy, 1984, Ch. 2; Honneth, 1991, Ch. 7), particularly concerning the "quasi-transcendental" cognitive interests, to such an extent that few people would now accept it whole-heartedly even within its own domain, and Habermas himself no longer utilises it. However, the incommensurability thesis has, in fact, been increasingly criticised in recent years in sociology, philosophy, and organizational behaviour, and it now seems possible to construct strong arguments against it. This has been done in Mingers and Brocklesby (1996) and will be summarised later in this chapter.

Critical systems has also not considered the possible problems with the cultural and cognitive feasibility of working with several paradigms (Brocklesby, 1994). Given that paradigms make fundamental, reality-shaping, assumptions about the world, it is not likely that individuals may find it hard to switch between different paradigms, and that cultures and organisations will tend to favour certain paradigms at the expense of others? Again, these problems are addressed in Mingers and Brocklesby (1996), and in more detail in Chapter 8.

Debate 3—Selection or combination of methodologies?

The third weakness from the multimethodological viewpoint is intimately connected with the previous two. It is that the general thrust has been towards the choice of a single appropriate methodology rather than the combination of a number. This is an almost necessary concomitant of Jackson and Flood's theoretical complementarism.

> All that is required is the guidance offered by complementarism, so that each systems approach is put to work only in problem situations for which its theoretical rationality is appropriate. (Jackson, 1991: 186).

> . . . the domain of effective application of each approach will become established. A metatheory will develop that . . . can advise analysts confronted with different problem situations as to which approach is most suitable. (Jackson, 1991: 263)

> Instead of seeing different strands of OR as competing for exactly the same area of concern . . . alternative approaches can be presented as being appropriate to the different types of situation in which management scientists are required to act. Each approach will be useful in certain defined areas and should only be used in the circumstances where it works best. (Jackson, 1993: 575)

In fact, Flood and Jackson have shifted their position over time to recognise that sometimes more than one methodology may be necessary. In *Creative Problem Solving* they wrote:

> In highly complex problem situations it is advisable at the same time to address different aspects revealed by taking different perspectives on it. This involves employing a number of systems methodologies in combination. In these circumstances it is necessary to nominate one methodology as "dominant" and others as "supportive" . . . (Flood and Jackson, 1991: xiv)

While in the 1995 version of TSI, Flood states:

> *Choose actual method.* Continue by asking which method(s) . . . has/have a purpose directly relevant to the problems that must be dealt with . . . (a) method(s) is/are chosen that has/have an immediate and given purpose which tackles head-on core organisational problems. (Flood, 1995: 109)

Thus, the theoretical position seems to be that a methodology should be chosen having regard to its appropriateness in a particular problem situation, while in practice several (whole) methodologies *may be* employed to deal with the varied problems encountered. The message is the same in Flood's latest work, *Triple Loop Learning*.

> The need for choice between loops arises because the management of issues is linked up with the way issues are problematised . . . [t]he interventionists' choice of core issues is also a choice of core loop through which they commit their action. (Flood and Romm, 1996: 208)

However, the multimethodology perspective that I am advocating takes a different viewpoint. Here, the argument is that *all* problem situations are complex and multi-dimensional, involving material, social and personal aspects. An intervention should therefore be more effective if it addresses, within the limitations of time and resources, all of these features. This suggests that, wherever possible, a range of methodologies (or parts thereof), across the paradigms, should always be used. If a problem situation is approached through the perspective of a single methodology (or paradigm) then important aspects will be ignored, or will have to be dealt with in an *ad hoc* or intuitive way.

While critical systems/TSI allows the use of multiple methodologies, it does not require it, nor does it provide much practical assistance in joining together and linking different methodologies. Recently, the idea of using methodologies *obliquely*, i.e. not for their given purpose, has been suggested within TSI—see below under Debate 6.

Debate 4—Splitting/partitioning methodologies

The fourth point again follows on in that CST/TSI does not propose, at least explicitly,[3] the partitioning of methodologies into parts which can then be combined with each other within an intervention (Midgley, 1989b, 1990). Again, the position here argued is that it is precisely the combining of parts of methodologies, often from different paradigms, that will provide the greatest rewards in being able to effectively address problem situations. Yet, this is the most complex and difficult multimethodology option as it brings in philosophical problems of linking across paradigms, and practical problems of how best to link and the extent to which practitioners can work in different paradigms (see Debate 2 above).

---

[3] I say "explicitly" because implicitly it does. Several of the case studies (Flood and Jackson, 1991; Flood, 1995) do link together parts of methodologies.

Debate 5—How critical is critical systems?

It would seem that the *critical* nature of critical systems/TSI has become cloudy, to say the least, as it has evolved from an embodiment of Habermas's emancipatory praxis to a "potent force for effective management"[4] (Taket, 1992, 1994; Cummings, 1994; Midgley, 1995a, b; Probert, 1995). There are many questions that need to be addressed: is it valid to distinguish between an "emancipatory" systems approach that aims to emancipate human actors in oppressive situations, and a "critical" systems approach that hopes to assist managers, problem solvers and decision makers in general? Are only some situations "coercive" and thus in need of emancipatory methodologies? Conversely, can we expect everyone involved in a situation, including managers, to adopt a critical stance? What exactly does a "commitment" to critical awareness and emancipation actually mean? Do all users of TSI have to be committed to human emancipation? Who or what makes the commitment, and what if they do not? Is there anything to stop the use of the mechanisms of TSI to more effectively oppress people? Do the published case studies of TSI (that are presumably exemplary) generally exhibit a strong commitment to emancipation and disimprisoning or do these principles always get suppressed in practice because of questions of feasibility and client power? Can intervention, conducted for and on behalf of (and paid for by) a powerful client ever be seriously challenging to the status quo?

These questions are not meant as cheap jibes since they point to deep and complex issues in considering what could be the nature of a "critical" approach within "management" or, indeed, the "management sciences" (Alvesson and Willmott, 1992a). It is important that the work done so far within critical systems has, possibly because of its very success, made these issues very clear. I do not think that it has been quite so successful in addressing or resolving them but a start has been made. Flood and Romm (1995b) explicitly discuss several of these questions, accepting that they pose problems for TSI and emancipatory methods in general. Either practitioners press forward with an emancipatory agenda and risk the project being terminated; or they withdraw from the situation themselves; or they get results but at the expense of TSI principles. Flood and Romm suggest that one possible approach is to use methodologies *obliquely*. That is, to use them not in the way that they are intended, but to fulfil another (emancipatory) purpose; to confront the coercive situation from a less direct and challenging angle. I would certainly accept this strategy as a good example of multi-paradigm multimethodology although one does have to address the issue of whether whole methodologies can be disconnected from their paradigms or only parts of them.

---

[4] The subtitle of Flood (1995).

Debate 6—The central role of the agent using methodology

Finally, along with most other methodological work, critical systems has been conspicuous in ignoring the importance of the agent(s) or practitioner(s) who is/are actually using the methodologies in an engagement with a problem situation. Apart from half a page on "personal style" (Flood, 1995: 64) there is no real reference to the background, personality, beliefs and commitments, or relationship to the situation of the users of critical systems. Yet, for a number of reasons, this must be the starting point for any *critical, committed* use of multi-methodology. First, if a variety of methodologies are to be used, the choice will depend in part in the *particular users'* knowledge, experience, style, and abilities. Users cannot use methodologies that they are unaware of, and their own personal history will predispose them to particular methodologies. Clearly we would wish users to be familiar and competent with a range, and would hope that their competence develops over time, but we must nevertheless recognise that at any particular moment of choice the user's predilections must be considered. Second, as was argued above and will be further supported below, no methodology can *force* its users to deploy it critically, i.e. in opposition to the prevailing dispositions of power. Even an explicitly critical methodology can be (mis)used. This again focuses attention on the individual user and their own values and commitments. Ultimately it is people, not methodologies, that choose to act in ways that disturb the status quo.

Significant Challenges for Critical Systems Thinking

Given the above context of critical systems in particular and the more general critical traditions, this section will outline the main challenges that face the development of a critical pluralist philosophy and concomitant multi-methodology. Brief rebuttals, responses, or counter-arguments will be given for each challenge, but these will be fleshed out in the presentation of the overall approach in the following section. Each of these issues is highly complex and deserves a book in its own right, so the purpose of the section is simply to register them as themes conditioning the rethinking of a critical approach.

First, there is confusion within the critical dimension of TSI/critical systems. As discussed above, the distinction between *critical* systems and *emancipatory* systems raises many problems. In particular, can we really expect any problem-solving/management approach that is *critical* towards the status quo to be universally applicable? Surely some groups gain from the status quo and will resist any change? Equally, if a critical or multimethodological approach be effective is there anything to stop it being subverted and used oppressively? My response is that we have to accept that genuinely emancipatory approaches will challenge the position of particular actors and groups within a situation, and thus cannot expect to gain the universal approval or acceptance of participants in a problem situation. Critical systems or management science can only be a subset or, rather, a particular commitment within management science as a whole. As with all tools/artifacts, methodologies, even when they are designed with a particular interest in mind, can be used inappropriately. Thus we have to recognise that methodologies, or multimethodology, can and will be used to support the status quo no matter what assumptions or commitments underpin them.

Second, critical systems can no longer unthinkingly rely on Habermas's theory of knowledge-constitutive interests (KCI) as its underpinning. Criticism of KCI (as mentioned above in Debate 2) make it no longer tenable as a solid foundation for critical systems or multimethodology (see also Martin Spaul's chapter in this book for a detailed analysis of the relation between critical systems and critical theory). This means that it is no longer possible to justify a critical approach from a theoretical basis. We cannot argue that a species-wide interest in emancipation, combined with current distortions in knowledge domains, make a critical approach necessary. In accepting this point, we recognise that critical approaches become weaker. We can only claim that they are *desirable*, not that they are *necessary*. This, and the previous point, focus attention away from the abstract framework and methodologies onto the person using them, and their commitments, history, values and choices.

Third, there is Foucault's critique of rationality and power/knowledge. It can be argued that the work of Foucault, especially, undermines the whole modernist, rationalistic enterprise (Brocklesby and Cummings, 1996; Munro, 1997). It shows that *all* knowledge, and indeed rationality itself, is inevitably constituted through and intertwined with the exercise of power. There is no external standpoint from which knowledge can be used to unmask itself. My argument here is that while Foucault's work does demonstrate the historical and social contextuality of human knowledge, it does not thereby totally destroy the critical potential of knowledge. Foucault himself employed a very systematic and rigorous methodology in his study of historical discourses. As he said, not long before his death:

> What I have studied are the three traditional problems: (1) What are the relations we have to truth through scientific knowledge . . .? (2) What are the relationships we have to others through those strange strategies and power relationships? And (3) what are the relationships between truth, power, and self? . . . What could be more classic than these questions and more systematic than the evolution through questions one, two, and three and back to the first? I am just at this point. (Foucault, 1988c: 15)

He explained his own commitment to rationality (Foucault, 1988d), and his own work, I would argue, provides a very good example of the way in which the reflexivity of knowledge may be a beneficial rather than vicious circle.

Fourth, a related postmodern concern is Lyotard's (1984) critique of the "grand metanarrative"—the idea that there can be some underlying, coherent theory that can be applied to all situations (such as Habermas's critical theory). Within the management science context, this has been endorsed by Taket and White (1993, 1994; White and Taket, 1996) (see also Chapter 14) who espouse a postmodern position of "pragmatic pluralism".

> . . . we argue for the need to move beyond conceptualising theory and practice as a dichotomy, following instead a strategy of mix and match, adopting a flexible and adaptive stance, and operationalising "doing what feels good" . . . we would argue for an end to theory . . . but not an end to theorising as a part of a critically reflective practice. (White and Taket, 1996: 55)

I have much sympathy with White and Taket's position. Their pragmatic pluralism ends in a very similar practical position to critical pluralism with an emphasis on triangulation, on combining parts of methodologies, and on critical reflection. However, I would not accept their denial of theory and their support for "doing what feels good" as a guiding principle for action. Actions are always the result of choices made, consciously or unconsciously, explicitly or implicitly. But Taket and White's line seems to preclude either an evaluation of actions as being more or less effective or legitimate (e.g. violence or racism), or an explanation of particular patterns of action in terms of underlying motivations or social situations. In fact, of course, Taket and White make strong prescriptions (e.g. against racist statements, see for example Chapter 14) but it is not clear what justifies this other than their "feeling good".

The fifth issue is that traditional critical theory (i.e. that of the Kantian/Habermasian tradition) has adopted, or implicitly assumed, a particular view as to the nature of the person or subject on whose behalf it works. This view can be characterised as assuming a *universalistic, ahistorical, acultural, disembodied, (male)* subject. It is argued (Young, 1990; Benhabib, 1992) that such a view of the reasoning subject can no longer be accepted. Our world is increasingly diverse, pluralistic, transitory, and local. We can no longer expect to be able to specify norms, values, and principles that hold for all people and for all time. Critique must be grounded in the actual cultural and political contexts of real people with their individual blends of uniqueness and commonality.

In large measure, I accept these arguments and that means that critical pluralism must become embodied and embedded, a microemancipation (Alvesson and Willmott, 1992b), driven by the commitments of the agent within the constraints and possibilities of a particular, historical and contextual situation. This further emphasises the importance of the intervener or agent within critical multimethodology.

TOWARDS CRITICAL PLURALISM

The previous section has outlined the background against which a rethinking of critical systems must take place. This section seeks to address some of these issues in developing the outlines of an approach that can be characterised as "critical pluralism", particularly within the context of multimethodology.

In broad terms, the situation envisaged is as follows. An agent or agents[5] will commit themselves to taking action within a situation regarded by some participants (including possibly the agents) as problematic. They may have no previous relationship to the situation or they may have some history of inter-actions such as previous projects, ongoing consultation, or actual employment. Whatever the case, we can distinguish two types of continual activity— actual actions within the problem situation some of which may draw on particular methodologies and techniques; and critical reflection *about* the intervention determining the particular combinations of actions and methodologies that are employed. The following sections expound some theories and frameworks that can assist in this process of multimethodology construction; they do not yet constitute a comprehensive approach to methodology design.

The Multimethodology Context

The general context for the use of multimethodology is the purposeful engagement of an agent(s) with some aspect of their social or organisational world. Checkland (1981) interprets such situations in terms of two notional systems, a *problem-solving system* (PSS) and a *problem-content system* (PCS), but then, arguably, downplays the agents involved in the PSS in favour of disembodied methodological considerations. The use of multimethodology clearly lays extra emphasis on the agents, and the various methodologies and techniques available, and so a framework with three notional systems, and the relations between them, is more useful as shown in Figure 15.1.

The Intervention System (IS) is the particular agent or agents engaged with the problem situation. This could include participants from the organisation(s) involved, or the agents themselves may be members of the organisation. The Intellectual Resources System (IRS) consists of those frameworks of theories, methodologies, and techniques that could potentially be relevant to

---

[5] This chapter is written largely from the perspective of a single agent or practitioner. In practice, interventions will often involve teams of people with a variety of relationships to each other and to the problem situation. The extra complexity generated by this differentiation is not addressed here, but one approach would be to apply multimethodology at a meta-level to the working of the team. That is, to make this a problem situation in itself. The practicalities of this will be pursued in further work. Other relevant dimensions are whether the agent is expected to be an expert or a facilitator, and whether they are internal or external to the organisation.

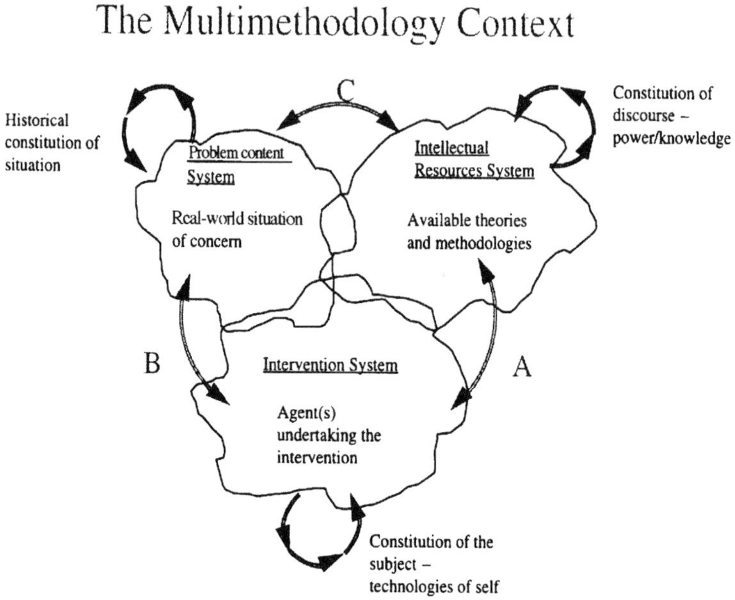

The Multimethodology Context

Figure 15.1 The multimethodology context

the problem situation, although not necessarily within the agents' current repertoire. There are self-referential relations of each system with its own past history that leads it to be the way that it is. It is one of the contentions of this chapter that, in the development of management science, too little attention has been paid to the nature and role of the agent(s) involved in interventions in terms of their relationships to both the problem situation and the intellectual frameworks available to them. In some ways this is ironic—the development of soft and then critical approaches focused attention on the human actors in the problem situation but generally remained silent about the users of methodology.[6]

More important from the point of view of multimethodology are the relationships (labelled A, B and C in Figure 15.1) *between* these notional systems—those between agents and methodologies/techniques (A), those between the agents and the situation (B), and those between methodologies/techniques and the situation (C). It is these relationships that are unique to a particular intervention and it is a consideration of these that will guide the agents in their methodology choices. Some of the important dimensions of these relations can be highlighted in a series of questions. (These questions should not be confused with Ulrich's 12 critical systems heuristics questions.

---

[6] There is virtually no mention of the analyst/agent in such classics as Checkland and Scholes (1990) or Flood and Jackson (1991), and only brief consideration in Flood (1995) (page 64).

These questions are about the *design of the intervention* whereas CSH are about the actual problematic situation.) The questions relevant to one relationship include second-level questions that refer to the other two relationships. For example, in considering relation A, what methodologies the agent might use, it is also necessary to consider (B) the agent's relationship to the situation (e.g. am I expected to be a facilitator or an expert?), and (C) the relation between methodologies and the situation (e.g. does the organisation have any experience of this particular methodology?).

(A) Relations between agent(s) and intellectual resources

- What is my level of critical awareness/understanding of potential methodologies?
- What is my experience and skill in using them?
- What is my personality/cognitive style comfortable with?
- To what extent can I work in varied paradigms?
- To what extent am I comfortable with the values implicit in particular methodologies?
- Nature of relationship (B)—IS to PCS—e.g. what might I be able to use in this situation?
- Nature of relationship (C)—PCS to IRS—e.g. what methodologies might be relevant to this situation?

(B) Relations between agent(s) and problem situations

- What has initiated this engagement?
- What, if any, is my history of interactions in regard to this situation?
- What are my commitments to various actors in the situations?
- Who do I see as clients/victims/problems owners, etc.?
- What are the expectations about my role, e.g. facilitator or expert?
- What resources are available, e.g. time, money, access, participants?
- What power sources do I have?
- Nature of relationship (A)—IS to IRS—e.g. what methodologies am I experienced in that may be useful? What might I have to learn?
- Nature of relationships (C)—PCS to IRS—e.g. what methodologies may or may not be seen as legitimate here? What methodologies have they experienced?

(C) Relations between problem situation and intellectual resources

- What is the culture of the organisation/situation with regard to methodology use?
- What is the history of past methodology use?

- What methodologies are likely to be useful in this situation, given the particular tasks or concerns initiating the intervention?
- To what extent are the values embedded in the methodologies appropriate to the situation?
- Nature of relationship (A)—IS to IRS—e.g. will the agent's experience allow the use of a particular methodology here?
- Nature of relationship (B)—IS to PCS—e.g. does the agent's history with this organisation suggest particular methodologies?

These three domains and their relations constitute the context at the point of engagement in an intervention. Consideration of these sorts of issues will determine both the initial actions taken and the planning or design of the intervention (Ormerod, 1996) as a whole. During an intervention they both condition, and change in response to, what happens. Thus they serve as continual reference points for the process of critical reflection that is necessary to structure the methodological choices made during the process.

Given this background, what space is there for critical stance and how would such a stance mould one's deployment of multimethodology? I shall aim to construct a position that is in essence Habermasian, but with necessary variants that take on board criticisms of this position. I shall structure the suggestions in terms of their contribution to the three notional systems just described.

Problem-content System: the Material, Social, and Personal Worlds

Habermas's (1984, 1987) theory of communicative action proposes that communicative utterances—that is, speech acts oriented towards understanding rather than, say, strategic action—raise validity claims concerning *comprehensibility*, *truth*, *truthfulness*, and *rightness* with respect to the domains of language, the objective world, the subjective world and the social world. These may be generalised (Mingers and Brocklesby, 1996) to suggest that human action (or inaction) in general embodies or expresses relationships to these three worlds—the material, the social, and the personal—plus a medium, language. This categorisation was introduced in Chapter 1 and Figure 1.1 and draws also on a similar trichotomy by Searle (1996) who considers the objective, subjective, and institutional worlds. Habermas's scheme, however, is based on, but different from, Popper's three worlds (see Habermas, 1984: 75–80). We must be clear that these distinctions are purely analytical, there are not three separate ontological worlds, nor are they independent of each other. But it is a fruitful way of clarifying the different dimensions of our actions (a broadly similar route has been followed by Midgley (1992)). We may analyse these relationships from many perspectives (see Table 15.1).

Table 15.1 Habermas's three worlds

	Mode of interaction	Validity claims	Form of science	Power/ knowledge technologies*	Axiology**
Linguistic	We communi-cate through	Compre-hensibility	Semio-logical	Signification/ meaning	Expressive-ness
Material	We observe and mould	Truth, possibility	Empirical/ analytical	Production/ manipulation	Effective-ness, concern
Social	We participate in and reproduce	Rightness	Socio-logical/ cultural	Power/ conduct	Morality
Personal	We experience and express	Truthful-ness	Herme-neutic/ phenom-enological	The self/ transforma-tion	Ethicality

* See Foucault (1988b).
** See Habermas (1993b).

The material world refers to aspects of problem situations that concern physical space–time, entities and objects. This world is governed by natural laws that are independent of human beings in that they would exist without us and we cannot change them. We can clearly manipulate the material world subject to these laws. This world includes the physical aspects of people, i.e. their bodies, and such matters as health and safety, although these also have personal and social aspects. Our epistemological relationship with this world is one of observation—we can only observe tables and chairs, not experience[7] or participate in them. But our observation is not neutral passive transmission but active involved construction (Maturana, 1987; Mingers, 1995a). Knowledge is generally of an analytic/empirical nature and we can often represent such aspects in mathematical and computer models. Our relationship is reciprocal in that while we can mould the material, ultimately it provides a necessary medium for our continued existence.

The second world is the social which can be characterised in terms of intersubjective practices and the duality of structure (Giddens, 1984). This world is dependent on humans in the broad sense that it would not exist

---

[7] Thus we cannot experience what it is like to be a physical object whereas we can experience being ourselves, a human being. We can in some sense experience our own body, and the embodied nature of cognition and knowledge is increasingly being acknowledged (Mingers, 1996b).

without them, but is generally independent of any particular person. It can be seen as a consensual domain of implicitly agreed rules, practices, norms, and meanings. Our epistemological relationship to it is one of participation rather than pure observation. Our actions are determined as appropriate/ inappropriate, legitimate/illegitimate, and ultimately as meaningful or not in accordance with its rules. Whereas physical laws apply equally to all, social rules and practices apply differentially, that is, they inherently privilege certain characteristics or groups over others. Knowledge, from the domains of sociology and cultural theory, is inherently normative, value-laden, and power-based. The inherent intersubjectivity of language implies a need for dialogue and discursivity rather than the monologue of the isolated ego.

Finally, the personal world, our individual experiences, feelings, desires, and beliefs, the result of our own history of choices, interactions and structural couplings. A world that, while constituted through the intersubjectivity of language, and therefore inevitably to some extent shared with others is, nevertheless, particular and peculiar to our own self. A world that only we can experience and, in some measure, express to others. Knowledge is based on hermeneutics and phenomenology.

Apart from the dimensions of mode of interaction and form of science discussed above, there are two other dimensions of particular importance for critical intervention—that of *axiology*, i.e. that which is valued or considered right, and that of *power/knowledge* or technology of reason (Foucault, 1988b).

Axiology—what is good or valued

The next dimension of importance to all three worlds is that of axiology, i.e. what we value or judge to be right or good. This ultimately provides the criteria by which we evaluate possible actions and make choices. Here, Habermas's (1990, 1992, 1993a, b) recent work on "discourse ethics" provides a useful framework. Habermas considers the question "how *should* I act". This question, after all, lies at the very heart of management science which is concerned, fundamentally, with taking effective action on the basis of knowledge and rationality. Habermas suggests that the type of answer to be given to this question differs according to different contexts—the *pragmatic*, the *ethical*, and the *moral*. Pragmatic contexts are those of purposive rational action—situations where we are concerned with the most effective choice of means (given agreed or accepted ends) or of ends (given agreed preferences)—very much the domain of traditional, hard OR/systems. Thus mending a car or getting somewhere on time are essentially pragmatic questions. Ethical questions are deeper, concerning the self-understanding of the individual (or, possibly, the group or community). They address the Aristotelian, communitarian issues of the nature of the "good life"—that which is important or good for the individual. What sort of person/group are we? What kind of activities should we engage in? Finally, moral questions concern our relations with other people (and possibly nature), our duties and responsibilities, justice, and acceptable norms and practices.

Habermas appears to see these three as alternatives, i.e. that situations or context are, or can be identified as, of one or other type. This is reminiscent of the problem contexts of the system of systems methodologies. However, from the multimethodology perspective proposed in this chapter, it is more helpful to see these as dimensions or characteristics, all of which are relevant to any particular situation. Thus, even deciding how to act in order to get somewhere on time can have moral dimensions (should I push in front of someone to get on the train?), and ethical dimensions (should I cross a picket line at a station?), as well as the pragmatic one of the most efficient method of transport.

What is Habermas's approach to these issues? First, he accepts that in our fragmented and pluralistic age it is not possible to determine universal and abstract answers to these questions (Habermas, 1994). We cannot specify what everyone must accept. Instead, we can specify procedures to enable people to determine and apply such standards in a rational way. The main principles of the procedure are: first, that it consists of a process of *actual* dialogue and debate by real people. So individuals cannot determine principles in a lone, monological way, nor can there be imagined or conceptual debates. Equally, all those who will be affected by the outcomes should be involved, or at least represented, in the discussions. Second, for standards to become generally accepted they must be such that everyone affected by them would agree that they should be obeyed by all. Third, that in participating in such debates we should make a genuine effort to put ourselves in the place of the other(s).

Clearly these principles are highly idealistic in the sense that they are unlikely to be realised in full in practice. However, they can stand as an ideal towards which we can aim and against which we should judge actual arrangements.

Power/knowledge—technologies of the self

It has generally been considered that the works of Foucault and Habermas are mutually contradictory, particularly concerning the limits of rationality and the nature of power. However, a number of commentators (McCarthy, 1991; Bernstein, 1992; Ingram, 1994; Kelly, 1995; Probert, 1996) have argued that in fact the differences are not that great and that the two are better seen as complementary. Commenting on the Frankfurt School in general rather than Habermas in particular, Foucault said:

> Now, obviously, if I had been familiar with the Frankfurt School, if I had been
> aware of it at the time, I would not have said a number of stupid things that I did

say and I would have avoided many of the detours that I made while trying to pursue my own humble path—when meanwhile, avenues had been opened up by the Frankfurt School. It is a strange case of non-penetration between two very similar types of thinking which is explained, perhaps, by that very similarity. Nothing hides the fact of a problem in common better than two similar ways of approaching it. (Foucault, 1988a: 26)

This chapter is not the place to delve into this debate, but I will provide two examples of resonances between Habermas and Foucault that illustrate the possibility of complementarity, and that are potentially useful in developing critical pluralism. Foucault's complex work can be seen as moving through three stages, as mentioned above (Foucault, 1988c). From an initial concern with the formation of science and knowledge, to a recognition of the importance of power and domination in both knowledge and our relations with others, to a study of the ways in which power and knowledge condition the formation of the self as a subject. In thus examining the nature of human experience, Foucault (1988b) categorised four techniques or technologies that apply to our understanding and action: *technologies of production* that allow us to manipulate objects, *technologies of signs* that allow us to communicate, *technologies of power* that control our conduct with respect to others, and *technologies of the self* that are used for self-transformation. These four technologies relate, in essence, to Habermas's three worlds and to language. Moreover, one of the technologies of self is the concept of "self-examination"—a scrutiny of our thoughts and conscience. Foucault (1988b: 46) categorises three types of self-examination—the relation between our thoughts and reality, the relation between our thoughts and rules of conduct, and the relation with our own hidden thoughts. These three relations bear an interesting similarity, although in a different domain, with Habermas's three validity claims—truth (the relation of speech acts to the material world), rightness (the relation to the normative social world), and truthfulness (the relation to our inner, personal world).

From the viewpoint of critical intervention, Foucault offers many useful insights into the subjugation and suppression of knowledge, the practical mechanisms of power and resistance, and the nature of the individual's constant struggle with the constraints of their own subjectivity. His work shows the necessarily bounded and local nature of critique and emancipation, and that critique should no longer be seen as the discovery of universal and necessary limits, but an exploration of the contingency and plasticity of constraints and boundaries:

The point, in brief, is to transform the critique conducted in the form of necessary limitation into a practical critique that takes the form of a possible transgression . . . critique will be genealogical in the sense that it will not deduce from the form of what we are what is impossible for us to do and to know; but it will separate out, from the contingency that has made us what we are, the possibility of no longer being, doing, or thinking what we are, do, or think. (Foucault, 1988d: 46)

This is a view of critique very different from the Kantian version of critique on which Habermas draws. It does not propose a search for some universal foundations or limitations, that apply to all people for all time, on which critique can be founded. Rather, it recognises that we come to be as we are, both individually and culturally, as a result of historical processes of disciplinary power that could, in various ways, have been otherwise. We experience this in terms of structures, both individual and social, that are preformed, in existence *always already*, before we experience or reflect on them. The question then becomes one of trying to distinguish which of these constraints and limitations are really fixed and which can be to some extent moved or altered. This can only be discovered by attempting to go beyond them, by transgressing boundaries, and not accepting custom and convention. Although this approach is markedly un-Kantian, Habermas himself is moving in this direction as will be mentioned in the next section.

The Intervention System: the Agent

Any consideration of critical action must begin (and ultimately end) with the actual, embodied, and embedded agent(s) whose choice and action it is. This is because: first, in the light of postmodernism, it is no longer tenable to maintain, with traditional critical theory, the idea of a universal, ahistorical, rational (male) subject—the critical analogue to "economic man". The Cartesian cleavage of mind from body, relentlessly pursued by Kant and Husserl, has broken down in the light of, for example: (i) the recognition of the embodied nature of cognition (Mingers, 1996b); (ii) the cultural and temporal relativity of knowledge and reason itself, as highlighted particularly by Foucault; (iii) the postmodern insistence on the importance of difference and heterogeneity (Taket and White, 1993; Taket and White, 1994); and (iv), as feminist theory has revealed, the implicit masculine bias in critical conceptions of rationality (Young, 1990). Habermas himself has to some extent accepted these points (Habermas, 1994), recognising that processes of enlightenment only ever refer to particular individual subjects (rather than an "emancipated society" he refers to "undisabled subjects"); that one cannot specify in advance the future nature of a utopia, only conditions under which it might be generated; and that reason and rationality must not wipe out separateness and difference.

    Second, with multimethodology a particular combination of methodologies is woven together anew each time by a particular agent to meet a unique set of circumstances. This, of necessity, is dependent on the characteristics of the agent—their knowledge, history, relationship to the situation, personality, values and commitments—and so inevitably brings them centre-stage. Third, I would argue that no critical theory or methodology can, *of itself*, compel its users to employ it critically. As we saw in the discussion of TSI, no matter what principles or commitments a methodology or framework has, its mechanisms and procedures can be used in antithetical ways. It is, indeed, one of the dilemmas of critical management studies in general that its own methods and knowledge could be used to further oppression rather than emancipation (Alvesson and Willmott, 1992a). Thus, any methodology or framework of ideas is ultimately subservient to its users.

Given this starting point, we must now consider the cognitive and social context of the agent, beginning with a brief historical/evolutionary perspective. The physical medium gave rise to the self-producing (autopoietic), autonomous entities (Maturana, 1981; Maturana and Varela, 1987; Mingers, 1995b) that we distinguish as living. It afforded both possibilities and constraints for the material domain of interaction. Through evolution, there developed organisms with nervous systems that could interact with abstract relations, and finally human beings with the capacity for self-consciousness and language. The advent of language brought into existence two new, intimately related, domains of interaction—the personal and the social. Language (interpreted broadly as any form of communicational interaction) provides the medium for the social and personal in the same way that physical forces do for our material world. It is significantly different, however, in that it is, ultimately, dependent on humans and their cultures in a way that physical forces are not.

Thus, the embodied agent exists in a prestructured world of language, practices, norms and values, oppressions and distortions. A social world that is of its nature moralised and value-laden. From what position can we both be constituted from this, in a Foucauldian sense, and yet stand outside it and be critical? And what, in any case, would be the motivation for this? The motivation can only ever arise from the *desire* of the individual (Young, 1990; Maturana, 1991) that things be different from how they are. From a recognition that all action (or inaction) either reinforces or struggles against the status quo, and thence a reflection on one's own response to that inevitability, there can arise the desire that currently unrealised possibilities be brought about. That either unnecessary and unwanted constraints be removed, or that absences be filled (Bhaskar, 1989, 1994). These two possibilities correspond to the dual nature of power, power as constraining and restricting, and power as enabling and productive (Foucault, 1982; Mingers, 1992).

This perspective brings in another factor that is seldom considered—the *emotions* of the agent. Most of the theory is concerned with the *rationality* of approaches to intervention, but real embodied people always act in a way that is conditioned by their emotions (Heidegger, 1962; Maturana, 1988). Indeed, it is precisely their emotional relation to a situation that motivates action in the first place, whether it be anger, sympathy, interest, or desire for gain, and sustains it through the intervention. However, traditionally emotion and rationality would have been seen as in opposition with rationality displacing emotion as a basis for choice and action. I would argue that emotion cannot be eliminated from *human* action but needs to be seen in terms of a positive synthesis with rationality.

This critical moment occurs in the *agonistic* (Foucault, 1982: 208; Tsouvalis, 1995) question faced by agents, *what should I/we do?* that continually confronts us in our praxis. We always have to make choices, to act or not to act, to move in this way or that, circumscribed by the apparent constraints and absences of the social and material worlds on the one hand, and our own personal world on the other. We push against these constraints, always testing their immutability by a continual reappraisal of our *appreciation* (understanding how the situation is), our *analysis* (explanation of why the situation is as it is), our *assessment (exploring the potential for change)*, and finally our *actions*. The process is renewed through the consequences, both intended and unintended, of our actions both for ourselves and for others.

In this ongoing process, we are continually concerned with all three worlds and the types of methodology that may help us deal with them, regulating our choices with regard to effectiveness (what works), morality (what is just) and ethicality (what is desirable, individually), in which power is an ever-present, unavoidable force that both enables and constrains. This process is a continual testing of the boundaries, both those we experience within the situation, and those we experience within ourselves formed through the disciplining practices of society.

The Intellectual Resources System: Frameworks for Integrating Methodologies

As we discussed above, agents need to reflect critically about the process and design of each unique intervention in order to construct an appropriate combination of methodologies and techniques. In this section two frameworks to assist this task are presented. The first tries to identify the particular contributions that the various methodologies can make in terms of the different dimensions of the problem situation, and the different phases of the intervention. The second is addressed to the problem of partitioning methodologies—i.e. splitting them up or decomposing them into parts that can then be used in combination with others.

Terms such as "methodology", "method", and "technique" are commonly used with a variety of meanings. Mingers and Brocklesby (1996) have made clear distinctions that will be used in this section. Briefly, a *paradigm* is a very general worldview based on a set of fundamental philosophical assumptions that define the nature of possible research and intervention. A *methodology* is a structured set of guidelines or activities to assist an individual in undertaking research or intervention. Generally, a methodology will develop, either implicitly or explicitly, within a particular paradigm and will embody the philosophical assumptions and principles of the paradigm. A *technique* is a specific activity that has a clear and well-defined purpose within the context of a methodology. Examples of techniques are: developing a discrete-event simulation model; undertaking statistical analysis; or producing root definitions and conceptual models in SSM. We can see the relation between methodology and technique as that between a *what* and a *how*. The methodology specifies what type of activities should be undertaken, and the techniques are particular ways of performing these activities. We can also see the philosophical dimensions of a paradigm as providing the *why* for the methodology, i.e. providing the grounds for the types of activity that the methodology generates. Finally, a *tool* is an artifact, often computer software, that can be used in performing a particular technique (e.g. an LP optimiser, a systems dynamics package, or COPE for cognitive mapping) or whole methodology (e.g. STRAD for strategic choice).

A framework for mapping methodologies

Chapter 1 discussed the desirability of multimethodology in terms of two important features of interventions—their multidimensionality and the different types of activity that need to be undertaken. By combining these two factors, a grid is produced (see Figure 15.2) that can be used to map the characteristics of different methodologies to help in linking them together.

	Appreciation of	Analysis of	Assessment of	Action to
Social	social practices, power relations	distortions, conflicts, interests	ways of altering existing structures	generate empowerment and enlightenment
Personal	individual beliefs, meanings, emotions	differing perceptions and personal rationality	alternative conceptualisations and constructions	generate accommodation and consensus
Material	physical circumstances	underlying causal structure	alternative physical and structural arrangements	select and implement best alternatives

Figure 15.2   Linking phases and dimensions of an intervention

The logic of this framework is that a fully comprehensive intervention needs to be concerned with the three different worlds—material, personal, and social—and the four different phases. Thus each box generates questions about particular aspects of the situation/intervention that need to be addressed. Such questions should not be interpreted objectivistically, that is, capable of answers independent of the agents involved. Rather they will involve ongoing debate, construction and reflection among the agents and actors participating in the intervention. This framework can be used in a number of ways. First, it is possible to look at particular methodologies, mapping them onto the framework to see to what extent they address these questions, and to appraise their relative strength in each box. Figure 15.3 shows a tentative mapping for a number of well-known methodologies.

For example, SSM mainly contributes to exploring the personal dimension and is particularly strong (darker shading) for analysis and appraisal, although it does have some techniques for appreciating the social dimension (analyses 1, 2 and 3). Strategic choice also covers the full range of intervention activities, and is strongest for assessment and action (its designing and choosing modes). But, we argue, it is not aimed so much at generating and exploring a diversity of individual viewpoints (i.e. the personal world), more at generating commitment to a particular viewpoint, hence its location across the personal/material line. VSM is seen as relating essentially to the material and social worlds, providing a model of viable organisational structure based on an objectivist analysis of biological organisms, and thus having power to analyse weaknesses and suggest effective alternatives. It does not, however, address the individual participants' views and beliefs. Cognitive mapping and SODA have strengths in appreciating and analysing individuals' patterns of belief, and in gaining commitment to action (through merging maps), but is weak in assessing possible alternatives.

Alternatively, we can address the boxes and ask which methodologies can be of assistance in that particular aspect of an intervention thus generating a range of possibilities to choose from. Mingers (1996a) has catalogued a variety of intervention and research approaches within the context of information systems research.

We can use such mappings to design effective multimethodologies, one example of which is shown in Figure 15.4. Here a range of complementary techniques is used in the appreciation phase—statistical analysis, SSM rich pictures and analyses 1, 2, and 3, and critical systems heuristics. In the analysis and exploration phases cognitive mapping, and root definitions and conceptual models are used, with some help from VSM. Finally, a strategic choice-type commitment package is used to facilitate agreement and implementation. Note that we are not advocating standardised multimethodologies (although some may emerge in practice), but designs specific to each intervention.

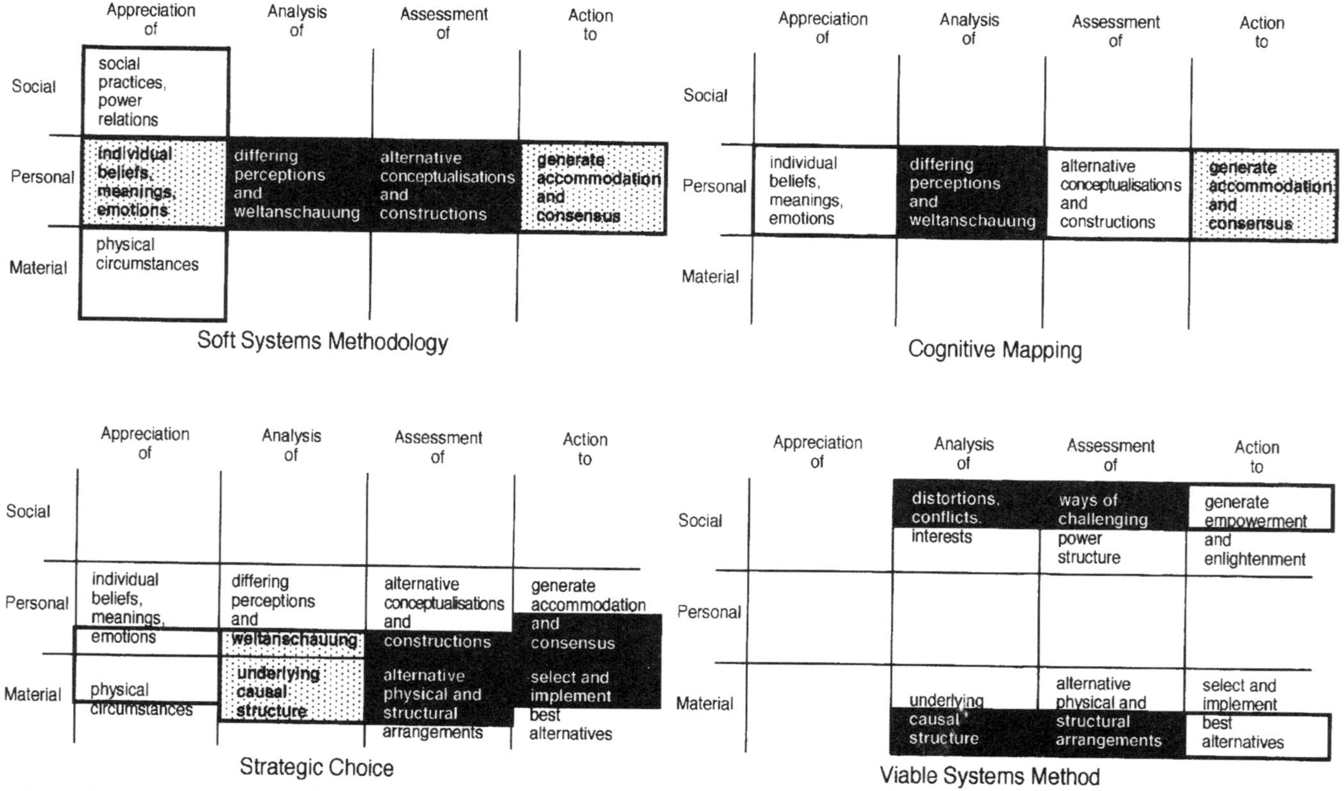

Figure 15.3 Mappings of some methodologies

	Appreciation of	Analysis of	Exploration of	Action to
Social	**CSH + SSM**	distortions. conflicts, interests	ways of challenging power structure	generate empowerment and enlightenment
Personal	**Cognitive mapping + SSM**	**SSM**	**SSM**	**Strategic choice**
Material	**Statistics**	underlying causal structure	**Viable System Method**	select and implement best alternatives

Figure 15.4 A particular multimethodology combination

Some *caveats* are in order. First, it is not intended that methodologies are slotted into particular boxes like the system of systems methodologies (Jackson and Keys, 1984). Rather they are mapped across all the different areas to which they can contribute, and some indication of the strength of the contribution is indicated. Second, clearly the precise placing of a particular methodology or technique is debatable. Some people may feel that, for example, traditional OR techniques such as simulation may be useful in assessing alternative social arrangements and would therefore wish to locate them in more areas of the framework. Obviously, there should be debate about this, and I would be happy for the scope of methodologies to be widened on the framework, subject to it still being able to discriminate between them. Third, as will be discussed in the next section, the multimethodology approach advocated in this chapter includes the possibility of taking parts of methodologies (techniques) and using them within an alternative paradigmatic perspective. For example, VSM could be used as a *conceptual* model within SSM to represent a personal viewpoint. The framework as described above only maps methodologies and techniques as they were originally developed, from within a particular paradigm. Clearly it could be used to map alternative ways of using them.

Decomposing methodologies

The essence of multimethodology is linking together parts of methodologies, possibly from different paradigms. This requires detailed study of the different methodologies to see where fruitful links can be created, but is in any case dependent on the idea that techniques can be detached from one methodology and used in another. Generally, such a transfer will conserve the original function, for example using cognitive mapping within SSM to explore actors' viewpoints. However, it is possible to transfer a methodology or technique into a setting that makes different paradigm assumptions. For example, mathematical programming models are usually seen as empirical/analytic, being putative models of *external reality*. However, they could be used as models of *concepts*, i.e. as models of how things might be from a particular viewpoint (Bryant, 1988), as part of an interpretivist debate within SSM. Equally, a systems dynamics model could be seen as a model of reality, or as a detailed and dynamic cognitive map (Eden, 1994). Moving in the opposite direction, a root definition and conceptual model that are usually assumed to refer to notional systems, could be used as the basis for the design of an actual, real-world, activity system. This approach is similar to Flood and Romm's (1995b) "oblique" use of methodology to help tackle coercive situations, although more general.

This linking process requires that methodologies be decomposed in some systematic way to identify detachable elements and their functions or purposes. It is proposed this can be done in terms of the distinctions, outlined above, between philosophical principles (*why*), methodological stages (*what*), and techniques (*how*). The primary focus of a methodology is its stages—a conceptual account of what needs to be done. These are justified by the principles, and actualised by a set of activities or techniques. The techniques may be complementary to each other in that several must occur, or they may be substitutes, any one being potentially satisfactory. It seems potentially possible to detach either at the level of techniques or at the level of methodological stages. The former is more straightforward and is particularly useful in methodological enhancement. While a technique does have a particular purpose or output, this needs to be interpreted within the context of the particular methodological stage that it realises. Thus in moving a technique from one methodology (and possibly paradigm) to another, its context and interpretation may be changed. To take one of the examples above, if a systems dynamics model is built as part of a hard methodology its context will lead to the results being interpreted as a model of reality. If it is detached and used within a soft setting it will be interpreted as a model of a notional system. The model-building process will be essentially the same, although the previous stage of generating inputs to the model will be different.

Figure 15.5 shows a decomposition of SSM and concentrates on the stages concerned with expressing the real-world situation and modelling relevant conceptual systems. Each of these stages has particular techniques that help accomplish them, for example rich pictures and analyses 1, 2 and 3 for expressing the situation. Some techniques may have tools such as CATWOE or a computerised CASE tool. It is these techniques (and their lower level tools) that can be disconnected from the methodology, as shown by the thick lines, and used in other contexts within other methodologies. The figure also shows how techniques can be imported into the methodology, for example cognitive maps (and the associated computer tool COPE) instead of, or as well as, rich pictures; Ulrich's (Ulrich, 1994) critical systems heuristics (CSH) as a complement to Analysis 3; or a Viable System Model (VSM) (Beer, 1985) to aid development of a conceptual model.

The main emphasis in Figure 15.5 is on the disconnection of techniques. The second possibility mentioned above, of detaching stages, is possible and occurs in both methodological enhancement (adding a stage to another methodology that is deficient) and multimethodology (combining various stages to construct a new, *ad hoc*, methodology). It is, however, more problematic, particularly in the multi-paradigm case since the stages are strongly related to their philosophical paradigm. More consideration needs to be given to this situation. To make the framework outlined above practically useful, decomposition diagrams such as Figure 15.5 would need to be constructed for all possible methodologies, and the various techniques and stages tabulated and cross-referenced.

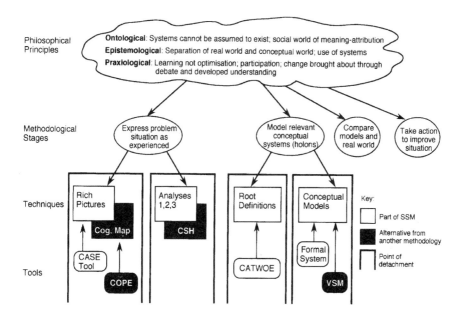

Figure 15.5 Decomposition of SSM to show possible disconnection of techniques

CONCLUSIONS: IMPLICATIONS FOR THE CRITICAL PRACTICE OF MULTIMETHODOLOGY

In this section I will highlight briefly some of the main implications of the position expressed above for the practice of critical methodology. This should not be seen as a fully worked out, practical methodology, but some guidelines that should inform such a methodology.

The starting point for a critical employment of multimethodology must be the real, situated, embodied, activities and desires of actual agents, not abstract theories, frameworks or methodologies themselves. As agents, we find ourselves in a context of an always/already constituted and moralised situation, where all our actions (or inactions) will have effects both on ourselves and on others. We can never be neutral or disinterested. The motivation for action is emotional—desire that the situation be other than it is—that unnecessary and unwanted constraints be broken, or that absences and needs be fulfilled.

Change and emancipation will be local, context-dependent, and often very limited, a challenging or transgressing of boundaries, both social and individual. This can take place through four stages of critical reflection—*appreciation* of the situation as it is, *analysis* of *why* it is as it is, *appraisal* of how the situation might be different, and *action* towards generating movement. The drawing of boundaries is central to this process, for in drawing a boundary we are separating that which we consider (at a particular moment) unchangeable from that which may be altered. The more that we accept as fixed the narrower will become the domain of possible change and development.

Our actions (linguistic and otherwise) stand in relation to three analytically separate domains—the material world, our social world, and my (the individual's) subjective world. These three worlds provide a second dimension to the concept of critical reflection. Each of the four stages mentioned above should concern itself with each of the worlds. Our actions involve both validity claims—*truth*, *rightness*, and *truthfulness*—and axiological claims—*effectiveness*, *morality* and *ethicality*—that should continually raise questions concerning the appropriateness of both the existing situation, and our actions and proposals (Gregory and Romm, 1994). Power is also integral to all three worlds, and is a facet of even our most minute and intimate action. Power has a dual nature—it is constraining and enabling—and is thus what we fight against, and what we use, in bringing about change.

Knowledge, including our methodologies and meta-methodologies, is inevitably linked to power. Knowledge is generally suppressed and distorted, constituted so as to maintain prevailing constraints and structures, yet at the same time, just as with power, it has a positive side for it is knowledge and critical reflection that can assist us in bringing about change. We must recognise that the different methodologies that we might employ are all embedded in their own paradigms, embodying particular and partial views of the world. With critical reflection, we must be aware of the underpinning paradigm in order to properly appreciate the methodology, but we do not simply accept this. We should always reinterpret the methodology or technique within a critical framework. Thus, for example, statistical analysis is generally wedded to objectivist assumptions. But statistics can still be used very effectively within a critical engagement, for example to highlight the extent of inequality, provided that we have an awareness of their contentious nature.

Interventions in situations should be made so as to provide the conditions of rationality and discourse, not the final judgements. This should aim towards maximum participation in real, open debate among all those affected by decisions; encouragement for participants genuinely to try to put themselves in the place of the other; and discourse about both general norms and agreements as well as their application in particular situations.

The actual *process* of critical multimethodology will be a continual cycle of reflection, judgement, and action. It will bring in and knit together methodologies and techniques as seems appropriate to assist action. Such choices depend on both the stage of the intervention and the particular domain of interest at the time as well as the wider context of relationships discussed above.

We must not expect change to come about easily. The social world is constituted and structured through the micro-operation of power, and individually our structural coupling within varied domains is strongly conservative and resistant to change (Brocklesby, Chapter 8).

REFERENCES

Alvesson, M. and Willmott, H. (eds.) (1992a). *Critical Management Studies.* Sage, London.

Alvesson, M. and Willmott, H. (1992b). On the idea of emancipation in management and organization studies. *Academy of Management Review*, **17**(3), 432–464.

Beer, S. (1985). *Diagnosing the System for Organizations.* Wiley, Chichester.

Benhabib, S. (1992). *Situating the Self: Gender, Community and Postmodernism in Contemporary Ethics.* Polity Press, Cambridge.

Bernstein, R. (1992). Foucault: critique as philosophical ethos. In A. Honneth et al (eds) *Philosophical Interventions in the Unfinished Project of Enlightenment.* MIT Press, Cambridge, MA, pp. 280–310.

Bhaskar, R. (1989). *Reclaiming Reality.* Verso, London.

Bhaskar, R. (1994). *Plato Etc.* Verso, London.

Brocklesby, J. (1994). Let the jury decide: assessing the cultural feasibility of Total Systems Intervention. *Systems Practice*, **7**(1), 75–86.

Brocklesby, J. and Cummings, S. (1996). Foucault plays Habermas: an alternative philosophical underpinning for critical systems thinking. *Journal of the Operational Research Society*, **47**(6), 741–754.

Bryant, J. (1988). Frameworks of inquiry: OR practice across the hard–soft divide. *Journal of the Operational Research Society*, **39**(5), 423–435.

Checkland, P. (1981). *Systems Thinking, Systems Practice.* Wiley, Chichester.
Checkland, P. and Scholes, J. (1990). *Soft Systems Methodology in Action.* Wiley, Chichester.
Cummings, S. (1994). An open letter to total systems intervention (TSI) and friends: a postmodern remedy to make everybody feel better. *Systems Practice,* **7**(5), 575–587.
Eden, C. (1994). *Cognitive mapping and problem structuring for systems dynamics model building.* Dept. of Management Science, Strathclyde University.
Flood, F. (1995). *Solving Problem Solving.* Wiley, Chichester.
Flood, R. and Jackson, M. (1991). *Creative Problem Solving.* Wiley, London.
Flood, R. and Romm, N. (1995a). Diversity management: theory in action. *Systems Practice,* **8**(4), 469–482.
Flood, R. and Romm, N. (1995b). Enhancing the process of methodology choice in total systems intervention (TSI) and improving chances of tackling coercion. *Systems Practice,* **8**(4), 377–408.
Flood, R. and Romm, N. (1996). *Diversity Management: Triple Loop Learning.* Wiley, Chichester.
Foucault, M. (1980a). *The History of Sexuality—an Introduction.* Random House, New York.
Foucault, M. (1980b). *Power/Knowledge.* Harvester Press, Brighton.
Foucault, M. (1982). Afterword: the subject and power. In H. Dreyfus and P. Rabinow (eds) *Foucault: Beyond Structuralism and Hermeneutics.* University of Chicago Press, Chicago, IL, pp. 208–226.
Foucault, M. (1988a). *Politics, Philosophy, Culture.* Routledge, London.
Foucault, M. (1988b). Technologies of the self. In L. Martin, H. Gutman and P. Hutton (eds) *Technologies of the Self: An Interview with Michel Foucault.* University of Massachusetts Press, Amherst, MA, pp. 16–49.
Foucault, M. (1988c). Truth, power, self: an interview with Michel Foucault. In L. Martin, H. Gutman and P. Hutton (eds) *Technologies of the Self: An Interview with Michel Foucault.* University of Massachusetts Press, Amherst, MA, pp. 9–15.
Foucault, M. (1988d). What is Enlightenment? In P. Rabinow (ed.) *The Foucault Reader.* Penguin, London, pp. 32–50.
Giddens, A. (1984). *The Constitution of Society.* Polity Press, Cambridge.
Gregory, W. and Romm, N. (1994). *Developing multi-agency dialogue: the role(s) of facilitation.* Centre for Systems Studies, University of Hull.
Habermas, J. (1978). *Knowledge and Human Interests.* Heinemann, London.
Habermas, J. (1984). *The Theory of Communicative Action Vol. 1: Reason and the Rationalization of Society.* Heinemann, London.
Habermas, J. (1987). *The Theory of Communicative Action Vol. 2: Lifeworld and System: a Critique of Functionalist Reason.* Polity Press, Oxford.
Habermas, J. (1990). Jürgen Habermas: morality, society and ethics. *Acta Sociologica,* **33**(2), 93–114.
Habermas, J. (1992). Discourse ethics: notes on a programme of philosophical justification. In J. Habermas (ed.) *Moral Consciousness and Communicative Action.* Polity Press, Cambridge, pp. 43–115.
Habermas, J. (1993a). *Justification and Application.* Polity Press, Cambridge.
Habermas, J. (1993b). On the pragmatic, the ethical, and the moral employments of practical reason. In J. Habermas (ed.) *Justification and Application.* Polity Press, Cambridge, pp. 1–17.
Habermas, J. (1994). What theories can accomplish—and what they can't. In M. Haller (ed.) *The Past as Future: Jürgen Habermas Interviewed by Michael Haller.* Polity Press, Cambridge, pp. 99–120.
Heidegger, M. (1962). *Being and Time.* Blackwell, Oxford.

Honneth, A. (1991). *The Critique of Power: Reflective Stages in a Critical Social Theory.* MIT Press, Cambridge.

Ingram, D. (1994). Foucault and Habermas on the subject of reason. In G. Gutting (ed.) *Cambridge Companion to Foucault.* Cambridge University Press, Cambridge, pp. 215–261.

Jackson, M. (1991). *Systems Methodology for the Management Sciences.* Plenum Press, New York.

Jackson, M. (1993). Social theory and operational research practice. *Journal of the Operational Research Society,* **44**(6), 563–577.

Jackson, M. and Keys, P. (1984). Towards a system of system methodologies. *Journal of the Operational Research Society,* **35**, 473–486.

Kelly, M. (1994). Foucault, Habermas, and the self-referentiality of critique. In M. Kelly (ed.) *Critique and Power: Recasting the Foucault/Habermas Debate.* MIT Press, Massachusetts, MA, pp. 365–400.

Lyotard, J-F. (1984). *The Postmodern Condition—a Report on Knowledge.* Manchester University Press, Manchester.

MacIntyre, A. (1985). *After Virtue.* Duckworth, London.

Maturana, H. (1981). Autopoiesis. In M. Zeleny (ed.) *Autopoiesis: A Theory of Living Organization.* Elsevier-North Holland, New York, pp. 21–33.

Maturana, H. (1987). The biological foundations of self-consciousness and the physical domain of existence. In E. Caianiello (ed.) *Physics of Cognitive Processes.* World Scientific, Singapore, pp. 324–379.

Maturana, H. (1988). Reality: the search for objectivity or the quest for a compelling argument. *Irish Journal of Psychology,* **9**, 25–82.

Maturana, H. (1991). Response to Berman's critique of "The Tree of Knowledge". *Journal of Human Psychology,* **31**(2), 88–97.

Maturana, H. and Varela, F. (1987). *The Tree of Knowledge.* Shambhala, Boston.

McCarthy, T. (1984). *The Critical Theory of Jürgen Habermas.* Polity Press, Cambridge.

McCarthy, T. (1991). The critique of impure reason: Foucault and the Frankfurt School. In T. McCarthy (ed.) *Ideals and Illusions: On Reconstruction and Deconstruction in Contemporary Critical Theory.* MIT Press, Massachusetts, MA, 43–75.

Midgley, G. (1989a). Critical systems and the problem of pluralism. *Cybernetics and Systems,* **20**, 219–231.

Midgley, G. (1989b). *Critical systems: the theory and practice of partitioning methodologies.* 33rd Annual Meeting of the ISSS, Edinburgh, Scotland.

Midgley, G. (1990). Creative methodology design. *Systemist,* **12**, 108–113.

Midgley, G. (1992). Pluralism and the legitimation of systems science. *Systems Practice,* **5**(2), 147–172.

Midgley, G. (1995a). Systemic intervention: a critical systems perspective. In G. Midgley and J. Wilby (eds) *Systems Methodology: Possibilities for Cross-Cultural Learning and Integration.* Centre for Systems Studies, Hull, pp. 57–64.

Midgley, G. (1995b). What is this thing called Critical Systems Thinking? In K. Ellis et al (eds) *Critical Issues in Systems Theory and Practice.* Plenum Press, New York.

Mingers, J. (1992). Recent developments in Critical Management Science. *Journal of the Operational Research Society,* **43**(1), 1–10.

Mingers, J. (1995a). Information and meaning: foundations for an intersubjective account. *Information Systems Journal,* **5**, 285–306.

Mingers, J. (1995b). *Self-Producing Systems: Implications and Applications of Autopoiesis.* Plenum Press, New York.

Mingers, J. (1996a). Combining research methods in information systems: multi-paradigm methodology. Warwick Business School Research Papers 239, Warwick University, Coventry.

Mingers, J. (1996b). Embodying Information Systems. In M. Jones et al (eds) *Information Technology and Changes in Organizational Work*. Chapman Hall, London, pp. 272–292.

Mingers, J. and Brocklesby, J. (1996). Multimethodology: towards a framework for critical pluralism. *Systemist*, **18**(3), 101–132.

Munro, I. (1997). An exploration of three emancipatory themes within OR and systems thinking. *Journal of the Operational Research Society*, **48**(6), 576–584.

Ormerod, R. (1996). On the nature of OR—entering the fray. *Journal of the Operational Research Society*, **47**(1), 1–17.

Probert, S. (1995). The cynicism of systems thinking. In K. Ellis et al (eds) *Critical Issues in Systems Theory and Practice*. Plenum Press, New York, pp. 499–502.

Probert, S. (1996). Is Total Systems Intervention compelling? *40th Annual Meeting of ISSS, International Society for the Systems Sciences*.

Said, E. (1983). *The World, the Text, and the Critic*. Harvard University Press, Cambridge, MA.

Searle, J. (1996). *The Construction of Social Reality*. Penguin, London.

Spaul, M. (1995). An ethical basis for critical systems thinking: communicative or communitarian? In K. Ellis (ed.) *Critical Issues in Systems Theory and Practice*. Plenum Press, New York, pp. 511–516.

Taket, A. (1992). A review of "Creative problem solving: total systems intervention". *Journal of the Operational Research Society*, **43**(10), 1013–1018.

Taket, A. (1994). A review of "Beyond TQM". *Journal of the Operational Research Society*, **45**(6), 723–728.

Taket, A. and White, L. (1993). After OR: an agenda for postmodernism and poststructuralism in OR. *Journal of the Operational Research Society*, **44**, 9.

Taket, A. and White, L. (1994). Postmodernism—why bother? *Systemist*, **16**(3), 175–186.

Thompson, J. and Held, D. (eds) (1982). *Habermas: Critical Debates*. Macmillan, London.

Tsouvalis, C. (1995). *Agonistic thinking in problem solving: the case of soft systems methodology*. Department of Management Science, Lancaster University, Lancaster.

Ulrich, W. (1994). *Critical Heuristics of Social Planning*. Wiley, Chichester.

White, L. and Taket, A. (1996). The end of theory? *OMEGA*, **24**(1), 47–56.

Young, I. (1990). *Justice and the Politics of Difference*. Princeton University Press, Princeton, NJ.

Index

Action research   128
Agent(s)   189–216, 416, 427–429
Ashby's Law of Requisite Variety   137, 193, 388

Cognitive mapping   1, 8, 12, 24, 25, 44, 45, 47, 48, 49, 60, 61, 68, 81, 82, 193, 207, 219, 265, 363, 382, 393, 399,402, 430,431,434, 435
Complementarism   9, 189, 244, 258, 315, 318, 319, 324, 353, 360–1, 364, 411, 412, 413
Conflict analysis   25, 60, 61, 82
COPE   63, 74–79, 81, 219, 223, 430, 435
Critical path method   26, 49, 53, 106, 115, 116, 125
Critical systems thinking (CST)   2, 4–6, 16, 129, 192, 243, 244, 246, 247, 249–51, 255, 257, 266, 276, 280, 284, 341, 347, 352, 353, 356, 357, 358, 366, 368, 370, 371, 407, 410–12, 414, 416
    Critical appreciation/awareness/ reflection   267–8, 270, 272, 274, 333, 336, 340, 343, 348, 385, 386, 393, 396, 401, 407–8, 409, 445, 416, 418, 420, 422, 431, 436
Critical Theory   323–348, 409, 415–418, 422
Cybernetics   26, 106, 109, 110, 112, 114, 116, 119, 124, 127–37, 139, 141, 149, 158, 181, 193, 256, 258, 265, 272, 310, 350, 352, 353, 356, 358

Decision analysis   38, 53, 82
Decision support modelling   43, 61, 62, 146

Decision support systems (DSS)   39, 81, 233
Deployment flowcharting   27, 158, 161–62, 166–68
Discourse ethics   409
Discrete-event simulation   74, 78, 430
Diversity management   292, 308, 310–11, 318

Emancipatory systems thinking   5, 204, 252, 254, 256, 259, 267, 273, 323–4, 330, 353, 357, 358, 359, 390, 401, 407–9, 411, 415, 416, 436
Entity relationship model   41
Evaluation theory   364

Functional decomposition model   41, 43

Game theory 64
    Hypergame analysis   64, 67, 363

Incommensurability of methodologies/ paradigms   2–4, 13–14, 46, 148, 189, 243, 245–47, 256–57, 266, 275–76, 280, 294–95, 296, 297, 311, 317, 351, 353, 366, 367, 411, 412
Imperfect objectivity   30, 31, 34, 36
INTERACT negotiation modelling software   69–70
Interactive planning   44, 363
Interpretavism   3, 313–4, 326, 328, 380, 411, 434
Interpretive systems thinking   374

Intervention competence   15, 25, 31, 32,
    35, 37, 44, 47, 49, 51, 55, 56, 85, 187,
    188, 208, 361, 416
Intervention transformation   31, 32, 35,
    45, 50, 52, 56, 103

Kelly's Repertory Grid   26, 53, 106,
    110–12, 125, 265
Knowledge management   188, 218, 225,
    228–30, 235, 237–39

Linear programming   37, 38, 47

Mental modelling   90, 101, 221
Multiview methodology   362, 368, 369,
    371

Negotiation modelling/analysis   64–74
Nominal Group Technique   172, 395

Observation   10, 194–5, 199, 201–202,
    207, 278, 279, 423

Paradigm alignment   192, 197, 200, 201,
    202, 257
Paradigm diversity   367–74
Pluralism   2, 3, 4, 5, 8, 9, 243–45, 247,
    249–52, 255, 256, 262, 263, 264, 265,
    267, 268, 269, 274, 275, 276, 280,
    Chapter 13, Chapter 14, Chapter 15
Positivism   3, 10, 14, 15, 129, 141, 148,
    149, 294, 299–300, 325, 327, 329, 355
Power/knowledge   425–427
Problem-structuring   35, 50, 60, 64, 70,
    80, 82, 83, 84, 172, 173, 180

Queuing theory   8, 34, 47

Reflective conversation   373
Reflexivity   307, 315–16, 318, 319, 381,
    417
Rich pictures   52, 167, 181–82, 192, 207,
    219, 350, 374, 393, 402, 431, 434, 435

Root definitions   8, 13, 48, 51, 52, 92,
    207, 400, 430, 431, 434

Scenario planning   26, 38, 53, 90
Structuration theory   14, 363, 370–71
SODA methodology   1, 4, 8, 62, 64, 82,
    86, 431
Soft systems methodology (SSM)   1, 4,
    6, 8, 11, 26, 44, 45, 47, 48, 49, 50, 51,
    52, 53, 90, 91, 92, 101, 102, 129, 140,
    145, 167, 192, 207, 219, 254, 259, 262,
    272, 326, 327, 350, 355, 361, 363, 364,
    368, 373, 374, 382, 430, 431, 433, 434
Statistical modelling   37, 47, 430, 431
Statistical process control   90, 93, 101,
    160
Statistical regression   38
Strategic choice approach   44, 45, 47, 49,
    50, 53, 82, 86, 363, 396, 431
Structural determinism   195, 201, 212
Structuration theory   14, 363, 370–71
System dynamics   1, 8, 25, 26, 27, 60, 74,
    77, 90, 92, 93, 139, 145, 146, 192, 224,
    230, 258, 262, 369, 373, 402, 430, 434
System of systems methodologies
    (SOSM)   2, 5, 8, 56, 252, 254–57,
    258, 259, 260, 261, 262, 263, 267, 271,
    276, 334, 348–50, 353, 358, 367, 407,
    433

Tacit knowledge   187, 188, 220–25, 230,
    238, 239
Total Systems Intervention (TSI)   2, 4,
    5, 6, 8, 243, 245, 258, 270, 276, 324,
    325, 329, 334, 335, 348, 350, 353, 354,
    358, 364, 367, 368, 369, 370, 373, 374,
    407, 410, 411, 413, 414, 415
Triangulation   4, 34, 361, 380, 394, 401,
    418
Triple loop learning   245, 246, 292, 303,
    307, 308, 312, 316, 317, 319, 407,
    414

Variance analysis   38
Viable System Model (VSM)   1, 26, 27,
    51, 106, 118–19, 125, 133, 134, 137,
    153, 154, 155, 161, 162, 168, 193, 227,
    356, 430, 433, 435